Birnbaum's 94

Eastern Europe

A BIRNBAUM TRAVEL GUIDE

Alexandra Mayes Birnbaum
EDITORIAL CONSULTANT

Lois Spritzer
Executive Editor

Laura L. Brengelman
Managing Editor

Mary Callahan
Senior Editor

Patricia Canole
Gene Gold
Jill Kadetsky
Susan McClung
Beth Schlau
Associate Editors

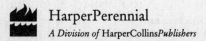 HarperPerennial
A Division of HarperCollinsPublishers

For Yetta Kreisel.

FIRST EDITION

ISSN 0749-2561 (Birnbaum Travel Guides)
ISSN 1056-439X (Eastern Europe)
ISBN 0-06-278124-3 (pbk.)

94 95 96 CC/CW 10 9 8 7 6 5 4 3 2 1

Cover design © Drenttel Doyle Partners
Cover photograph © D. & J. Heaton/First Light

BIRNBAUM TRAVEL GUIDES

Bahamas, and
 Turks & Caicos
Berlin
Bermuda
Boston
Canada
Cancun, Cozumel &
 Isla Mujeres
Caribbean
Chicago
Disneyland
Eastern Europe
Europe
Europe for Business
 Travelers

France
Germany
Great Britain
Hawaii
Ireland
Italy
London
Los Angeles
Mexico
Miami &
 Ft. Lauderdale
Montreal &
 Quebec City
New Orleans
New York

Paris
Portugal
Rome
San Francisco
Santa Fe & Taos
South America
Spain
United States
USA for Business
 Travelers
Walt Disney World
Walt Disney World
 for Kids, By Kids
Washington, DC

Contributing Editors

Duncan Anderson
Carmen Anthony
David Appel
Kathy Arnold
Melvin Benarde
Virginia Blackert
Mark Brayne
John Buskin
Ann Campbell-Lord
Linda Carreaga
Rik Cate
Paul Century
Stacey Chanin
Vinod Chhabra
Count Jacob
 Coudenhove-kalergi
Charles Cupic
Roman Czajkowsky
Clare Devener
Daniela Drazanova
Brad Durham
Thomas S. Dyman
William Echikson
Bonnie Edwards
Donna Evieth
Jackie Fierman
Ted Folke
Reuven Frank
Lisa Gabor
Fradley Garner
Norman Gelb

Jerry Gerber
Andrew Gillman
Agnes Gottlieb
Don Graff
Patricia Graves
Petar Hadji-Ristic
Jessica Harris
Jack Herbert
Ritva Hildebrandt
Elva Horvath
David Howley
Julian Isherwood
Bruce Johnston
Virginia Kelley
Alexander Kushnir
Carole Landry
Suzanne Lavenas
André Leduc
Richard Lee
Theodora Lurie
Sirrka Makelainen
Jan McGirk
Erica Meltzer
Diane Melville
Drusilla Menaker
Anne Millman
Tamara K. Mitchell
Jack Monet
Cara Morris
Michael Moynihan
Carol Offen

Pat Patricof
Sy Pearlman
Dan Petreanu
Fred Poe
Alemka Porobic
Allen Rokach
Margery Safir
Jerrold L. Schecter
Patrick Schultz
George Semmler
Leslie Shepherd
Natasha Singer
Tracy Smith
Janet Steinberg
Janet Stobbart
Phyllis Stoller
Donald Stroetzel
Nancy Patton Van Zant
Betty Vaughn
Florence Vidal
Richard Walbleigh
Dennis Weber
David Wickers
Mark Williams
Sandy Wolofsky
Jennifer Wright
Derrick Young
Eleni Zlogas
Sonya Zalubowski
Emilia Zino

Maps

Folio Graphics Co. Inc.
B. Andrew Mudryk

Contents

Getting Ready to Go

Practical information for planning your trip.

Facts in Brief

*A compilation of pertinent tourist information such
as entry requirements and customs, language,
currency, clothing requirements, and more for 11
Eastern European countries.*

The Cities

Thorough, qualitative guides to each of the 14 cities most visited by vacationers and businesspeople. Each section offers a comprehensive report on the city's most compelling attractions and amenities — highlighting our top choices in every category.

Diversions

A selective guide to active and/or cerebral vacation themes, pinpointing the best places in which to pursue them.

Exceptional Experiences for the Mind and Body

Directions

Eastern Europe's most spectacular routes and roads, most arresting natural wonders, most magnificent châteaux and castles, all organized into over 20 specific driving tours.

Foreword

There is absolutely nothing about a trip to Eastern Europe that has anything at all to do with any conventional definitions of a holiday or vacation. A trip to the Baltic States or Bulgaria is likely to be difficult, tiring, and notable by the absence of the kinds of creature comforts that are routinely present in the West. Having said that, even the most arduous experience of this kind is likely to be fascinating.

But fascinating has little to do with fun, and while there are inevitable moments of pure pleasure to savor, often your time in Eastern Europe will provide insight rather than amusement. There is, however, no denying the very exciting feeling of being right in the middle of history in the making. There have been few moments in modern times when more dramatic happenings were taking place almost daily, and there is an authentic thrill to being witness to such cataclysmic changes.

I should also add that these rapid changes continue to cause everyone who works on this guide to consume several cartons of Maalox. For example, life in much of today's Russia is hardly a happy meal of borscht and bialys. And the tragedies taking place in what was Yugoslavia have led us to the conclusion that, due to safety concerns, this year we would exclude that cluster of countries from this guide. It is our fervent hope that by next year, we will feel that our readers will not be at risk traveling to this corner of the Continent. It's not even a question of what's hot and what's not, but what still *is* and what is *not*. Even on-the-spot stringers and researchers have had a hard time trying to keep up with the heroics (and in some instances bloodshed) that seem to result in altered street and building names. Street numbers — and sometimes the streets themselves — suddenly cease to exist, making directions a thornier-than-usual dilemma. We've done the best we can, but we hope you'll understand a level of imprecision that we usually are able to avoid.

The nature of Eastern European travel — and even of the travelers who now routinely make the trip — has changed dramatically of late. That's why any 1994 Eastern European guidebook worth its price must keep pace with and reflect the real needs of today's travelers. That's also why we've tried to create a guide that's specifically organized, written, and edited for the more demanding modern traveler who needs to know how social and political changes have altered local moods, and for whom qualitative information is infinitely more desirable than mere quantities of unappraised data.

For years, dating back as far as Herr Baedeker, travel guides have tended to be encyclopedic, much more concerned with demonstrating expertise in geography and history than with a real analysis of the sorts of things that actually concern a typical modern tourist. I think you'll notice a different, more contemporary tone to the text, as well as an organization and focus that are distinctive and more functional. Early on, we realized that giving up the encyclopedic approach precluded our listing every single route and restaurant, a realization that helped define our overall editorial focus. Similarly, when we discussed the possibility of presenting certain information in other than strict geographic order, we found that the new format enabled us to arrange data in a way we feel best answers the questions travelers typically ask.

Travel guides are, understandably, reflections of personal taste, and putting one's name on a title page obviously puts one's preferences on the line. But I think I ought to amplify just what "personal" means. I don't believe in the sort of personal guidebook that's a palpable misrepresentation on its face. It is, for example, hardly possible for any single travel writer to visit thousands of restaurants (and nearly as many hotels) in any given year and provide accurate appraisals of each. And even if it *were* physically possible for one human being to survive such an itinerary, it would of necessity have to be done at a dead sprint, and the perceptions derived therefrom would probably be less valid than those of any other intelligent individual visiting the same establishments. It is, therefore, impossible (especially in a large, annually revised and updated guidebook *series* such as we offer) to have only one person provide all the data on the entire world.

I also happen to think that such individual orientation is of substantially less value to readers. Visiting a single hotel for just one night or eating one hasty meal in a random restaurant hardly equips anyone to provide appraisals that are of more than passing interest. No amount of doggedly alliterative or oppressively onomatopoeic text can camouflage a technique that is essentially specious. We have, therefore, chosen what I like to describe as the "thee and me" approach to restaurant and hotel evaluation and, to a somewhat more limited degree, to the sites and sights we have included in our text. What this really reflects is personal sampling tempered by intelligent counsel from informed local sources, and these additional friends-of-the-editor are almost always residents of the city and/or area about which they are consulted.

In addition, very precise editing and tailoring keep our text fiercely subjective. So what follows is the gospel according to Birnbaum, and it represents as much of our own taste and instincts as we can manage. It is probable, therefore, that if you like your cities genteel and your mountainsides uncrowded, prefer small hotels with personality to huge high-rise anonymities, and recognize chocolate as the real reason for remaining alive, we're likely to have a long and meaningful relationship.

I also should point out something about the person to whom this guidebook is directed. Above all, he or she is a "visitor." This means that such elements as restaurants have been specifically picked to provide the visitor with a representative, enlightening, stimulating, and above all, pleasant experience. Since so many extraneous considerations can affect the reception and service accorded a regular restaurant patron, our choices can in no way be construed as an exhaustive guide to resident dining. We think we've listed all the best places, in various price ranges, but they were chosen with a visitor's enjoyment in mind.

Other evidence of how we've tried to tailor our text to reflect modern travel habits is most apparent in the section we call DIVERSIONS. Where once it was common for travelers to spend an Eastern European visit imprisoned by a rigid government-dictated itinerary, the emphasis today is more on pursuing some special interest while seeing the surrounding countryside. Therefore, we have collected these exceptional experiences so that it is no longer necessary to wade through a pound or two of superfluous prose in order to find unexpected pleasures and treasures.

Finally, I also should point out that every good travel guide is a living enterprise; that is, no part of this text is carved in stone. In our annual revisions, we refine, expand, and further hone all our material to serve your travel needs better. To this end, no contribution is of greater value to us than your personal reaction to what we have written, as well as information reflecting your own experiences while using the book. Please write to us at 10 E. 53rd St., New York, NY 10022.

We sincerely hope to hear from you.

Alexandra Mayes Birnbaum

ALEXANDRA MAYES BIRNBAUM, editorial consultant to the *Birnbaum Travel Guides,* worked with her late husband Stephen Birnbaum as co-editor of the series. She has been a world traveler since childhood and is known for her lively travel reports on radio on what's hot and what's not.

Eastern
Europe

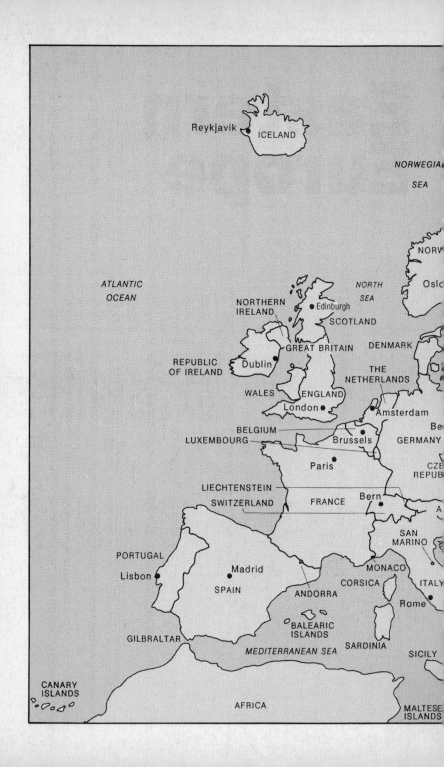

How to Use This Guide

A great deal of care has gone into the special organization of this guide-book, and we believe it represents a real breakthrough in the presentation of travel material. Our aim is to create a new, more modern generation of travel books and to make this guide the most useful and practical travel tool available today.

Our text is divided into five basic sections, in order to present information in the best way on every possible aspect of a visit to Eastern Europe. Our aim is to highlight what's where and to provide basic information — how, when, where, how much, and what's best — to assist you in making the most intelligent choices possible.

Here is a brief summary of the five basic sections. We believe that you will find both your travel planning and en route enjoyment enhanced by having this book at your side.

GETTING READY TO GO

This mini-encyclopedia of practical travel facts offers all the precise data necessary to create a successful trip to Eastern Europe. Here you will find how to get where you're going, plus selected resources — including pertinent publications, and companies and organizations specializing in discount and special-interest travel — providing a wealth of information and assistance useful both before and during your trip.

FACTS IN BRIEF

Here is a compilation of vital tourist information, such as entry and customs requirements, languages, currencies, and clothing and climate data on 11 Eastern European countries. This section provides easy and immediate access to crucial information to be used at the planning stage as well as on the road.

THE CITIES

Individual reports on the 14 Eastern European cities most visited by travelers and businesspeople offer short-stay guides, including an essay introducing the city as a historic entity and a contemporary place to visit; *At-a-Glance* material is actually a site-by-site survey of the most important, interesting, and sometimes most eclectic sights to see and things to do; *Sources and Resources* is a concise listing of pertinent tourism information, such as the address of the local tourist office, which sightseeing tours to take, where to find the best nightspot or hail a taxi, which shops have the finest merchandise and/or most irresistible bargains, and where the best museums and theaters are to be found. *Best in Town* lists our collection of cost-and-quality choices of the best places to eat and sleep on a variety of budgets.

DIVERSIONS

This section is designed to help travelers find the best places in which to engage in a variety of exceptional — and unexpected — experiences, without having to wade through endless pages of unrelated text. In each case, our particular suggestions are intended to guide you to that special place where the quality of experience is likely to be highest.

DIRECTIONS

Here is a series of more than 20 Eastern European itineraries, from the forested Danube Bend of Hungary to the subtropical climes of Russia's Black Sea resorts. These itineraries follow Eastern Europe's most interesting routes and roads, past its most spectacular natural wonders, through its most historic cities and most scenic countryside. DIRECTIONS is the only section of this book that is organized geographically, and its itineraries cover the touring highlights of 11 countries in short, independent journeys of 3 to 5 days' duration. Itineraries can be connected for longer trips, or used individually for short, intensive explorations.

To use this book to full advantage, take a few minutes to read the table of contents and random entries in each section to get a firsthand feel for how it all fits together. You will find that the sections of this book are building blocks designed to help you put together the best possible trip. Use them selectively as a tool, a source of ideas, a reference work for accurate facts, and a guidebook to the best buys, the most exciting sights, the most pleasant accommodations, the tastiest food — *the best travel experience* that you can possibly have.

Getting
Ready to Go

When to Go

The climate varies considerably from one region of Eastern Europe to another. In Moscow, winters can be fiercely cold and snowy, while along the Black Sea in Ukraine, winter weather is comparatively mild. Late spring through early autumn is pleasant throughout much of the region. For specific information on climate and suggested clothing for various Eastern European countries, see FACTS IN BRIEF.

Mid-May to mid-September has long been — and remains — the peak travel period, traditionally the most popular vacation time. Travel during the off-season (roughly November to *Easter*) and shoulder seasons (the months immediately before and after the peak months) also offers relatively fair weather and smaller crowds. During these periods, travel also usually is less expensive. Exceptions include ski areas such as the High Tatras in Slovakia, where winter is the peak travel season.

The *Weather Channel* (2600 Cumberland Pkwy., Atlanta, GA 30339; phone: 404-434-6800) provides current weather forecasts. Call 900-WEATHER from any touch-tone phone in the US; the 95¢ per minute charge will appear on your phone bill.

Traveling by Plane

SCHEDULED FLIGHTS

Leading airlines offering flights between the US and Eastern Europe include *Aeroflot, Air France, Alitalia, American Airlines, Austrian Airlines, British Airways, Continental, Czechoslovak Airlines (CSA), Delta, Finnair, KLM Royal Dutch Airlines, LOT Polish Airlines, Lufthansa, MALEV, Olympic, Sabena, SAS, SwissAir, Tarom Romanian Air Transport, TWA,* and *United.*

FARES The great variety of airfares can be reduced to the following basic categories: first class, business class, coach (also called economy or tourist class), excursion or discount, and standby, as well as various promotional fares. For information on applicable fares and restrictions, contact the airlines listed above or ask your travel agent. Most airfares are offered for a limited time period. Once you've found the lowest fare for which you can qualify, purchase your ticket as soon as possible.

RESERVATIONS Reconfirmation is strongly recommended for all international flights. It is essential that you confirm your round-trip reservations — *especially the return leg* — as well as any flights within Eastern Europe.

SEATING Airline seats usually are assigned on a first-come, first-served basis at check-in, although you may be able to reserve a seat when purchasing your ticket. Seating charts often are available from airlines and are included in the *Airline Seating Guide* (Carlson Publishing Co., PO Box 888, Los Alamitos, CA 90720; phone: 310-493-4877).

SMOKING US law prohibits smoking on flights scheduled for 6 hours or less within the US and its territories on both domestic and international carriers. These rules do not apply to nonstop flights between the US and international destinations. A free wallet-size guide that describes the rights of nonsmokers is available from *ASH* (*Action on Smoking and Health;* DOT Card, 2013 H St. NW, Washington, DC 20006; phone: 202-659-4310).

SPECIAL MEALS When making your reservation, you can request one of the airline's alternate menu choices for no additional charge. Call to reconfirm your request 24 hours before departure.

BAGGAGE On a major international airline, passengers usually are allowed to carry on board one bag that will fit under a seat or in an overhead bin. Passengers also can check two bags in the cargo hold, measuring 62 inches and 55 inches in combined dimensions (length, width, and depth) with a per-bag weight limit of 70 pounds. There may be charges for additional, oversize, or overweight luggage, and for special equipment or sporting gear. Note that baggage allowances may vary for children (depending on the percentage of full adult fare paid) and on intra-European and domestic routes abroad. Check that the tags the airline attaches are correctly coded for your destination.

CHARTER FLIGHTS

By booking a block of seats on a specially arranged flight, charter operators frequently offer travelers bargain airfares. If you do fly on a charter, however, read the contract's fine print carefully. Charter operators can cancel a flight or assess surcharges of 10% of the airfare up to 10 days before departure. You usually must book in advance (no changes are permitted, so invest in trip cancellation insurance); also make your check out to the company's escrow account. For further information, consult the publication *Jax Fax* (397 Post Rd., Darien, CT 06820; phone: 203-655-8746).

DISCOUNTS ON SCHEDULED FLIGHTS

COURIER TRAVEL In return for arranging to accompany some kind of freight, a traveler may pay only a portion of the total airfare and a small registration fee. One agency that matches up would-be couriers with courier companies is *Now Voyager* (74 Varick St., Suite 307, New York, NY 10013; phone: 212-431-1616).

Courier Companies
Courier Travel Service (530 Central Ave., Cedarhurst, NY 11516; phone: 516-763-6898).

Discount Travel International (169 W. 81st St., New York, NY 10024; phone: 212-362-3636; and 940 10th St., Suite 2, Miami Beach, FL 33139; phone: 305-538-1616).

Excaliber International Courier (c/o *Way to Go Travel,* 6679 Sunset Blvd., Hollywood, CA 90028; phone: 213-466-1126).

F.B. On Board Courier Services (10225 Ryan Ave., Suite 103, Dorval, Quebec H9P 1A2, Canada; phone: 514-633-0740).

Halbart Express (147-05 176th St., Jamaica, NY 11434; phone: 718-656-8279).

International Adventures (60 E. 42nd St., New York, NY 10165; phone: 212-599-0577).

Midnight Express (925 W. High Park Blvd., Inglewood, CA 90302; phone: 310-672-1100).

Publications

Insider's Guide to Air Courier Bargains, by Kelly Monaghan (The Intrepid Traveler, PO Box 438, New York, NY 10034; phone: 212-304-2207).

Travel Secrets (PO Box 2325, New York, NY 10108; phone: 212-245-8703).

Travel Unlimited (PO Box 1058, Allston, MA 02134-1058; no phone).

World Courier News (PO Box 77471, San Francisco, CA 94107; no phone).

CONSOLIDATORS AND BUCKET SHOPS These companies buy blocks of tickets from airlines and sell them at a discount to travel agents or to consumers. Since many bucket shops operate on a thin margin, before parting with any money check the company's record with the Better Business Bureau.

Bargain Air (655 Deep Valley Dr., Suite 355, Rolling Hills, CA 90274; phone: 800-347-2345).

Council Charter (205 E. 42nd St., New York, NY 10017; phone: 800-800-8222 or 212-661-0311).

International Adventures (60 E. 42nd St., New York, NY 10165; phone: 212-599-0577).

Travac Tours and Charters (989 Ave. of the Americas, New York, NY 10018; phone: 800-872-8800 or 212-563-3303).

Unitravel (1177 N. Warson Rd., St. Louis, MO 63132; phone: 800-325-2222 or 314-569-0900).

LAST-MINUTE TRAVEL CLUBS For an annual fee, members receive information on imminent trips and other bargain travel opportunities. Despite the names of these clubs, you don't have to wait until literally the last minute to make travel plans.

Discount Travel International (114 Forest Ave., Suite 203, Narberth, PA 19072; phone: 215-668-7184).

Last Minute Travel (1249 Boylston St., Boston, MA 02215; phone: 800-LAST-MIN or 617-267-9800).

Moment's Notice (425 Madison Ave., New York, NY 10017; phone: 212-486-0500, -0501, -0502, or -0503).

Spur-of-the-Moment Cruises (411 N. Harbor Blvd., Suite 302, San Pedro, CA 90731; phone: 800-4-CRUISES in California; 800-343-1991 elsewhere in the US; or 310-521-1070).

Traveler's Advantage (3033 S. Parker Rd., Suite 900, Aurora, CO 80014; phone: 800-548-1116 or 800-835-8747).

Vacations to Go (1502 Augusta, Suite 415, Houston, TX 77057; phone: 713-974-2121 in Texas; 800-338-4962 elsewhere in the US).

Worldwide Discount Travel Club (1674 Meridian Ave., Miami Beach, FL 33139; phone: 305-534-2082).

GENERIC AIR TRAVEL These organizations operate much like an ordinary airline standby service, except that they offer seats on not one but several scheduled and charter airlines. One pioneer of generic flights is *Airhitch* (2790 Broadway, Suite 100, New York, NY 10025; phone: 212-864-2000).

BARTERED TRAVEL SOURCES Barter is a common means of exchange between travel suppliers. Bartered travel clubs such as *Travel World Leisure Club* (225 W. 34th St., Suite 909, New York, NY 10122; phone: 800-444-TWLC or 212-239-4855) offer discounts to members for an annual fee.

CONSUMER PROTECTION

Passengers with complaints who are not satisfied with the airline's response can contact the US Department of Transportation (DOT; Consumer Affairs Division, 400 7th St. SW, Room 10405, Washington, DC 20590; phone: 202-366-2220). If you have a complaint against a local travel service, contact the tourist authorities of the country in which the airline is based. Also see *Fly Rights* (Publication #050-000-00513-5; US Government Printing Office, PO Box 371954, Pittsburgh, PA 15250-7954; phone: 202-783-3238).

Traveling by Ship

Your cruise fare usually includes all meals, recreational activities, and entertainment. Shore excursions are available at extra cost, and can be booked in advance or once you're on board. An important factor in the price of a cruise is the location and size of your cabin; for information on ships' layouts and facilities, consult the charts issued by the *Cruise Lines International Association* (*CLIA;* 500 Fifth Ave., Suite 1407, New York, NY 10110; phone: 212-921-0066).

Most cruise ships have a doctor on board, plus medical facilities. The US Public Health Service (PHS) also inspects all passenger vessels calling at US ports; for the most recent summary or a particular inspection report, write to Chief, Vessel Sanitation Program, National Center for Environmental Health (1015 N. America Way, Room 107, Miami, FL 33132; phone: 305-536-4307). For further information, consult *Ocean and Cruise News* (PO Box 92, Stamford, CT 06904; phone: 203-329-2787). And for a free listing of travel agencies specializing in cruises, contact the *National Association of Cruise Only Agencies* (*NACOA;* PO Box 7209, Freeport, NY 11520; phone: 516-378-8006).

A potentially less expensive alternative to cruise ships is travel by freighter — cargo ships that also transport a limited number of passengers. For information, consult the *Freighter Travel Club of America* (3524 Harts Lake Rd., Roy, WA 98580; no phone), *Freighter World Cruises* (180 S. Lake Ave., Suite 335, Pasadena, CA 91101; phone: 818-449-3106), *Pearl's Travel Tips* (9903 Oaks La., Seminole, FL 34642; phone: 813-393-2919), and *TravLtips Cruise and Freighter Travel Association* (PO Box 218, Flushing, NY 11358; phone: 800-872-8584 or 718-939-2400 throughout the US; 800-548-7823 from Canada). In addition, a number of companies offer cruises along Eastern Europe's inland waterways.

International Cruise Lines

Chandris Celebrity and Chandris Fantasy Cruises (5200 Blue Lagoon Dr., Miami, FL 33126; phone: 800-437-3111).

Classical Cruises (132 E. 70th St., New York, NY 10021; phone: 800-252-7745 in the US; 800-252-7746 in Canada; or 212-794-3200).

Crystal Cruises (2121 Ave. of the Stars, Los Angeles, CA 90067; phone: 800-446-6645).

Cunard (555 Fifth Ave., New York, NY 10017; phone: 800-5-CUNARD or 800-221-4770).

Epirotiki Lines (551 Fifth Ave., New York, NY 10176; phone: 212-599-1750 in New York State; 800-221-2470 elsewhere in the US).

EuroCruises (303 W. 13th St., New York, NY 10014; phone: 800-688-EURO or 212-691-2099).

Holland America Line (300 Elliot Ave. W., Seattle, WA 98119; phone: 800-426-0327).

Odessa America Cruise Company (170 Old Country Rd., Mineola, NY 11501; phone: 800-221-3254 or 516-747-8880).

Pearl Cruises (6301 NW 5th Way, Suite 4000, Ft. Lauderdale, FL 33309; phone: 800-556-8850).

Princess Cruises (10100 Santa Monica Blvd., Los Angeles, CA 90067; phone: 800-421-0522).

Regency Cruises (260 Madison Ave., New York, NY 10016; phone: 212-972-4774 in New York State; 800-388-5500 elsewhere in the US).

Renaissance Cruises (1800 Eller Dr., Suite 300, Ft. Lauderdale, FL 33335-0307; phone: 800-525-2450).

Royal Viking Line (95 Merrick Way, Coral Gables, FL 33134; phone: 800-422-8000).

Seabourn Cruise Line (55 Francisco St., Suite 710, San Francisco, CA 94133; phone: 800-929-9595).

Special Expeditions (720 Fifth Ave., New York, NY 10019; phone: 800-762-0003 or 212-765-7740).

Sun Line (1 Rockefeller Plaza, Suite 315, New York, NY 10020; phone: 800-468-6400 or 212-397-6400).

Swan Hellenic Cruises (c/o *Esplanade Tours,* 581 Boylston St., Boston, MA 02116; phone: 800-426-5492 or 617-266-7465).

Inland Waterway Cruise Companies

Abercrombie & Kent/Continental Waterways (1520 Kensington Rd., Suite 212, Oak Brook, IL 60521; phone: 708-954-2944 in Illinois; 800-323-7308 elsewhere in the US).

Adriatic Tours and Travel (691 W. 10th St., San Pedro, CA 90731; phone: 800-262-1718 or 310-548-1446).

Elegant Cruises and Tours (31 Central Dr., Port Washington, NY 11050; phone: 800-683-6767 or 516-767-9302).

EuroCruises, (303 W. 13th St., New York, NY 10013; phone: 800-688-3876 or 212-691-2099).

European Cruises (241 E. Commercial Blvd., Ft. Lauderdale, FL 33334; phone: 800-327-8223).

Russian Cruise Lines, a division of *French Cruise Lines* (*FCL;* 701 Lee St., Des Plaines, IL 60016; phone: 800-222-8664 or 312-694-9330).

Tourpak International (106 Calvert St., Harrison, NY 10528-3199; phone: 800-234-4000).

Traveling by Train

In most Eastern European countries, train service is provided by government-owned and -operated rail lines. Although the newer *Euro City (EC)* and *Intercity (IC)* trains found elsewhere on the continent operate on only two routes in Eastern Europe — Vienna to Prague and Vienna to Budapest — express and local service is provided in most countries.

Most trains have both first and second class cars. Meal service ranges from traditional dining cars to vendors dispensing sandwiches and beverages from a cart. Some trains also provide sleeping accommodations — usually first and second class *couchettes* (coach seats of a compartment converted to sleeping berths). Baggage often can be checked through to your destination, but it is best to make arrangements a day in advance. You also may be able to check your luggage overnight at major train stations. Travel as light as possible — porters and self-service carts often are scarce.

Tickets can be purchased at train stations and, in some cases, from separate sales offices of national railway or tourist companies. For a number of Eastern European countries, you can buy your rail tickets before leaving the US either from travel agents or from Rail Europe (226-230 Westchester Ave., White Plains, NY 10604; phone: 800-438-7245), which is the North American representative for national rail systems of these countries. *Rail Europe* can make reservations for train trips of 3 hours or more in duration, including overnight excursions. Reservations — which are advisable during the summer and other peak travel periods — can be made up to 2 months prior to the date of travel. Various rail passes also are available. Although the most familiar of these — the Eurailpass — covers travel in only one Eastern European country (Hungary), the European East Pass is good in the Czech and Slovak Republics, Hungary, and Poland. Some of the national rail companies also issue their own passes. Note that most rail passes must be purchased before you leave the US.

Some Eastern European rail lines offer sightseeing excursions for tourists. Information and reservations can be obtained from railway offices once you arrive in Eastern Europe. *Accent on Travel* (112 N. 5th St., Klamath Falls, OR 97601; phone: 503-885-7330 in Oregon; 800-347-0645 elsewhere in the US), which specializes in train tours, can make advance arrangements for rail packages in Eastern Europe.

FURTHER INFORMATION

Rail Europe (address above) offers a *Travel Guide,* as well as brochures on the Eurailpass and train travel in Europe. The *Thomas Cook European Timetable,* a compendium of information about European rail services, is available in bookstores and from the *Forsyth Travel Library* (PO Box 2975, Shawnee Mission, KS 66201-1375; phone: 800-367-7984 or 913-384-3440). Other useful resources include the *Eurail Guide,* by Kathryn Turpin and Marvin Saltzman (Eurail Guide Annuals, 27540 Pacific Coast Hwy., Malibu, CA 90265) and *Europe by Eurail,* by George Wright Ferguson (Globe Pequot Press, PO Box 833, Old Saybrook, CT 06475; phone: 203-395-0440).

Traveling by Car

Driving is the most flexible way to explore many of the countries of Eastern Europe. To drive in Eastern Europe, a US citizen needs a US driver's license. An International Driving Permit (IDP) also is required in a number of countries, including Hungary, Russia, and Ukraine. Bulgaria requires that a US license be accompanied by a translation (and the IDP is the best form for this), and *strongly* recommends that American drivers obtain an IDP. International Driver's Permits can be obtained from US branches of the *American Automobile Association (AAA).*

Proof of liability insurance also is required and is a standard part of any car rental contract. (To be sure of having the appropriate coverage, let the rental staff know in advance about the national borders you plan to cross.)

If buying a car and using it abroad, you must carry an International Insurance Certificate, known as a Green Card, which can be obtained from your insurance agent or through the *AAA*. Note that some countries may require you to obtain a specific policy available only *upon arrival*. For instance, in Russia, Ukraine, and other former Soviet republics, Green Cards are not recognized and drivers still are required to purchase insurance from local insurance companies. Your insurance carrier or the country's national tourism office can provide information on such special requirements and application procedures.

Driving in Eastern Europe is on the right side of the road. Unless otherwise indicated, cars coming from the right have the right of way — even if coming from a minor side street or entering a traffic circle from an approach road — but streetcars usually have priority over all other vehicles. Pictorial direction signs are standardized under the International Roadsign System, and their meanings are indicated by their shapes: Triangular signs indicate danger, circular signs give instructions, and rectangular signs provide information.

Distances are measured in kilometers (1 mile equals 1.6 kilometers; 1 kilometer equals .62 mile) and speeds are registered as kilometers per hour (kph) on speedometers. In many European countries, the use of seat belts is compulsory for the driver and front-seat passenger. In some cities and towns, honking is forbidden; at night, flash your headlights instead. Pay attention to parking signs in large cities. If you park in a restricted zone, you may return to find a wheel "clamped," which renders the car inoperable and involves a tedious–and costly — process to get it freed. *Be forewarned:* Particularly in Eastern Europe, speed limits and other driving regulations are strictly enforced and violators are subject to hefty fines and — in some cases — even jail sentences. For more information, consult *Euroad: The Complete Guide to Motoring in Europe* (VLE Ltd., PO Box 444, Ft. Lee, NJ 07024; phone: 201-585-5080).

MAPS

Road maps are sold at gas stations throughout Europe. Stateside, some free maps can be obtained from the individual countries' national tourist offices (see *For Further Information,* in this section, for addresses).

Freytag & Berndt maps cover most major destinations throughout Eastern Europe, and can be ordered from *Map Link* (25 E. Mason St., Suite 201, Santa Barbara, CA 93101; phone: 805-965-4402). The atlases, maps, and guides published by Rand McNally (8255 N. Central Park Ave., Skokie, IL 60076; phone: 800-627-2897 or 708-329-8100) also are good sources of information on Eastern European roads and routes. Regional and country maps of all of Eastern Europe are available from HarperCollins-Bartholomew (77-85 Fulham Palace Rd., Hammersmith, London W6 8JB, England; phone: 44-81-741-7070), which is represented in the US by

Hammond (515 Valley St., Maplewood, NJ 07040; phone: 201-763-6000). Michelin Guides and Maps (PO Box 3305, Spartanburg, SC 29304-3305; phone: 803-599-0850 in South Carolina; 800-423-0485 elsewhere in the US) publishes Europe-wide maps (although, at press time, they did not publish any maps of individual Eastern European countries), as well as a *Motoring Atlas of Europe* and a *Road Atlas of Europe,* both of which cover Eastern Europe.

AUTOMOBILE CLUBS AND BREAKDOWNS

To protect yourself in case of breakdowns while driving through Eastern Europe, and for travel information and other benefits, consider joining a reputable automobile club. The largest of these is the *American Automobile Association (AAA;* 1000 AAA Dr., Heathrow, FL 32746-5063; phone: 407-444-7000); among its useful publications are an overall Europe planning map, the *Travel Guide to Europe,* and *Motoring in Europe.* Before joining this or any other automobile club, check whether it has reciprocity with Eastern European clubs in the countries you plan to visit. (At press time, the *AAA* had reciprocal agreements with local automobile clubs in such Eastern European countries as Bulgaria, the Czech Republic, Estonia, Hungary, Latvia, Lithuania, Poland, Romania, Russia, and Ukraine.)

GASOLINE

Gasoline is sold in liters (about 3.7 liters to 1 gallon). Leaded and diesel fuel are generally available; unleaded fuel may be hard to find — or more expensive — in some countries. Some Eastern European countries experience periodic fuel shortages. Check with tourist authorities and/or the US State Department before planning an extended driving tour.

RENTING A CAR

You can rent a car through a travel agent or international rental firm before you leave, through one of the national Eastern European tour companies, or from a regional or local company once you arrive in Eastern Europe. Reserve in advance.

Most car rental companies require a credit card, although some will accept a substantial cash deposit. The minimum age to rent a car is set by the company; some also may impose special conditions on drivers above a certain age. Electing to pay for collision damage waiver (CDW) protection will add to the cost of renting a car, but releases you from financial liability for the vehicle. Additional costs include drop-off charges or one-way service fees. One way to keep down the cost of car rentals is to deal with a car rental consolidator, such as *Connex International* (phone: 800-333-3949 or 914-739-0066).

Note that government and rental car company policies regarding driving a rental car across national borders in Eastern Europe vary widely and are in a constant state of flux. Always inquire about the conditions of the rental before booking and read the fine print carefully before signing. Although rental car contracts differ very little from one another in the US (except, perhaps, for limits on liability), the situation in Eastern Europe is so changeable that there are almost no standard contracts.

International Car Rental Companies

Auto Europe (phone: 800-223-5555).

Avis (phone: 800-331-1084).

Budget (phone: 800-472-3325).

Dollar Rent A Car (known in Europe as *Eurodollar Rent A Car;* phone: 800-800-4000).

European Car Reservations (phone: 800-535-3303).

Hertz (phone: 800-654-3001).

Kemwel Group (phone: 800-678-0678).

National (known in Europe as *Europcar;* phone: 800-CAR-EUROPE).

Package Tours

A package is a collection of travel services that can be purchased in a single transaction. Its principal advantages are convenience and economy — the cost usually is lower than that of the same services bought separately. Tour programs generally can be divided into two categories: escorted or locally hosted (with a set itinerary) and independent (usually more flexible).

When considering a package tour, read the brochure *carefully* to determine what is included and other conditions. Check the company's record with the Better Business Bureau. The *United States Tour Operators Association* (*USTOA;* 211 E. 51st St., Suite 12B, New York, NY 10022; phone: 212-944-5727) also can be helpful in determining a package tour operator's reliability. As with charter flights, always make your check out to the company's escrow account.

Note that travelers to Eastern Europe — particularly first-time visitors — are strongly advised to buy package arrangements. A la carte travel arrangements have a tendency to come unglued in countries that for many years worked only through central planning. In addition, the shortage of hotel rooms, rental transportation, restaurants, and other tourist necessities make highly necessary an intermediary who thoroughly knows the ropes. Information and referrals for tour operators specializing in Eastern Europe are available from the *American Tourism Society* (419 Park Ave. S., New York, NY 10016; phone: 212-532-8845).

Many tour operators offer packages focused on special interests such as the arts, nature study, sports, and other recreations. *All Adventure Travel* (PO Box 4307, Boulder, CO 80306; phone: 800-537-4025 or 303-499-1981) represents such specialized packagers; some also are listed in the *Specialty*

Travel Index (305 San Anselmo Ave., Suite 313, San Anselmo, CA 94960; phone: 415-459-4900 in California; 800-442-4922 elsewhere in the US).

Package Tour Operators

Abercrombie & Kent (1520 Kensington Rd., Oak Brook, IL 60521; phone: 708-954-2944 in Illinois; 800-323-7308 elsewhere in the US).

Above the Clouds Trekking (PO Box 398, Worcester, MA 01602; phone: 800-233-4499 or 508-799-4499).

Academic Travel Abroad (3210 Grace St. NW, Washington, DC 20007-3600; phone: 202-333-3355).

Adriatic Tours and Travel (691 W. 10th St., San Pedro, CA 90731; phone: 800-262-1718 or 310-548-1446).

Adventure Center (1311 63rd St., Suite 200, Emeryville, CA 94608; phone: 510-654-1879 in northern California; 800-227-8747 elsewhere in the US).

Alaska Airlines Vacations (phone: 800-468-2248).

Albania Tours and Travel (438 E. 75th St., New York, NY 10021; phone: 212-535-1700).

All Adventure Travel (Box 4307, Boulder, CO 80306; phone: 800-537-4025 or 303-440-7924).

American Airlines FlyAAway Vacations (phone: 800-832-8383).

American Express Vacations (offices throughout the US; phone: 800-241-1700 or 404-368-5100).

American Jewish Congress (15 E. 84th St., New York, NY 10028; phone: 212-879-4588 in New York State; 800-221-4694 elsewhere in the US).

American Media Tours (16 W. 32nd St., Suite PH, New York, NY 10001; phone: 800-969-6344 or 212-465-1630).

American Museum of Natural History Discovery Tours (Central Park West at 79th St., New York, NY 10024; phone; 212-769-5700).

American Travel Abroad (250 W. 57th St., New York, NY 10107; phone: 212-586-5230 in New York State; 800-228-0877 elsewhere in the US).

Angling Travel and Tours (1445 SW 84th Ave., Portland, OR; phone: 800-288-0886 or 503-297-2468).

Atlas Ambassador (60 E. 42nd St., New York, NY 10165; phone: 212-697-6767).

AutoVenture (425 Pike St., Suite 502, Seattle, WA 98101; phone: 800-426-7502 or 206-624-6033).

Balkan Holidays USA (41 E. 42nd St., Suite 508, New York, NY 10017; phone: 800-852-0944 or 212-573-5530).

Baltic Tours (77 Oak St., Suite 4, Newton, MA 02164; phone: 617-965-8080).

Biological Journeys (1696 Ocean Dr., McKinleyville, CA 95521; phone: 800-548-7555 or 707-839-0178).

Bombard Society (6727 Curran St., McLean, VA 22101; phone: 800-862-8537 or 703-448-9407)

Brendan Tours (15137 Califa St., Van Nuys, CA 91411; phone: 800-421-8446 or 818-785-9696).

Butterfield & Robinson (70 Bond St., Suite 300, Toronto, Ontario M5B 1X3, Canada; phone: 800-387-1147 or 416-864-1354).

Caravan Tours (401 N. Michigan Ave., Chicago, IL 60611; phone: 800-CARAVAN or 312-321-9800).

Carpati International (152 Madison Ave., Suite 1103, New York, NY 10016; phone: 800-447-8742 or 212-447-1534).

Catholic Travel (4925 St. Elmo Ave., Bethesda, MD 20814; phone: 800-284-4681 or 301-654-4681).

Cedok (10 E. 40th St., Suite 3604, New York, NY 10016; phone: 800-800-8891 or 212-689-9720).

Chieftain Tours (c/o *European Travel Management,* address below).

Club Med (phone: 800-CLUB-MED).

Collette Tours (162 Middle St., Pawtucket, RI 02860; phone: 800-752-2655 in New England, New York, and New Jersey; 800-832-4656 elsewhere in the US).

Contiki Holidays (300 Plaza Alicante, Suite 900, Garden Grove, CA 92640; phone: 800-466-0610 or 714-740-0808).

Creative World Rallies and Caravans (4005 Toulouse St., New Orleans, LA 70119; phone: 800-732-8337 or 504-486-7259).

Dailey-Thorp (330 W. 58th St., New York, NY 10019-1817; phone: 212-307-1555).

Delta's Dream Vacations (phone: 800-872-7786).

Earthwatch (680 Mt. Auburn St., PO Box 403, Watertown, MA 02272; phone: 800-776-0188).

Equitour (PO Box 807, Dubois, WY 82513; phone: 307-455-3363 in Wyoming; 800-545-0019 elsewhere in the US).

European Travel Management (237 Post Rd. W., Westport, CT 06880; phone: 203-454-0090 in Connecticut; 800-992-7700 elsewhere in the US).

Exodus (9 Weir Rd., London SW2 OLT, England; phone: 44-81-675-5550; in the US, contact *Safari Center,* 3201 N. Sepulveda Blvd., Manhattan Beach, CA 90266; phone: 800-624-5342, 800-223-6046, or 310-546-4411).

FinnWay (354 Eisenhower Pkwy., Livingston, NJ 07039; phone: 201-535-1610 in New Jersey; 800-526-4927 elsewhere in the continental US).

Fishing International (PO Box 2132, Santa Rosa, CA 95405; phone: 800-950-4242 or 707-539-3366).

FITS Equestrian (685 Lateen Rd., Solvang, CA 93463; phone: 805-688-9494).

Five Star Touring (60 E. 42nd St., New York, NY 10165; phone: 800-792-7827 or 212-818-9140).

Forum Travel International (91 Gregory La., Suite 21, Pleasant Hill, CA 94523; phone: 510-671-2900).

Frontiers International (PO Box 959, 100 Logan Rd., Wexford, PA 15090; phone: 412-935-1577 in Pennsylvania; 800-245-1950 elsewhere in the US).

Gadabout Tours (700 E. Tahquitz Canyon Way, Palm Springs, CA 92262-6767; phone: 800-952-5068 or 619-325-5556).

General Tours (139 Main St., Cambridge, MA 02142; phone: 800-221-2216 or 617-621-9911).

Globus and Cosmos (5301 S. Federal Circle, Littleton, CO 80123; phone: 800-221-0090 or 800-556-5454).

Hungarian Hotels Sales Office (6033 W. Century Blvd., Suite 670, Los Angeles, CA 90045; phone: 310-649-5960).

IBUSZ (One Parker Plaza, Suite 1104, Fort Lee, NJ 07024; phone: 201-592-8585 in New Jersey; 800-367-7878 elsewhere in the US).

Insight International Tours (745 Atlantic Ave., Suite 720, Boston, MA 02111; phone: 800-582-8380 or 617-426-6666).

Intourist USA (630 Fifth Ave., Suite 868, New York, NY 10111; phone: 800-932-8416 or 212-757-3885).

Isram Travel (630 Third Ave., New York, NY 10017; phone: 800-223-7460 or 212-661-1193).

ITS Tours and Travel (1055 Texas Ave., Suite 104, College Station, TX 77840; phone: 800-533-8688 or 409-764-9400).

Jet Vacations (1775 Broadway, New York, NY 10019; phone: 800-JET-0999 or 212-247-0999).

Kobasniuk Travel (157 Second Ave., New York, NY 10003; phone: 800-535-5587 or 212-254-8779).

Kompas International (2826 E. Commercial Blvd., Ft. Lauderdale, FL 33308; phone: 800-233-6422 or 305-772-9200).

Kutrubes Travel (328 Tremont St., Boston, MA 02116; phone: 800-878-8566 or 617-426-5668).

Legend Tours (3990 Old Town Ave., Suite 100C, San Diego, CA 92110; phone: 800-333-6114 or 619-293-7040).

Liberty Travel (contact the central office for the nearest location: 69 Spring St., Ramsey, NJ 07446; phone: 201-445-4771).

Love Holidays/Uniworld (16000 Ventura Blvd., Suite 200, Encino, CA 91436; phone: 800-733-7820 or 818-382-7820).

Marathon Tours (108 Main St., Charlestown, MA 02129; phone: 800-783-0024 or 617-242-7845).

Maupintour (PO Box 807, Lawrence, KS 66044; phone: 800-255-4266 or 913-843-1211).

Meier's International (6033 W. Century Blvd., Suite 1080, Los Angeles, CA 90045; phone: 800-937-0700 or 310-215-1980).

Mill-Run Tours (424 Madison Ave., 12th Floor, New York, NY 10017; phone: 212-486-9840 in New York State, 800-MILL-RUN elsewhere in the US).

Mountain Travel-Sobek (6420 Fairmount Ave., El Cerrito, CA 94530; phone: 510-527-8100 in California; 800-227-2384 elsewhere in the US).

New England Vacation Tours (PO Box 560, W. Dover, VT 05356; phone: 800-742-7669 or 802-464-2076).

Northwest World Vacations (phone: 800-727-1400).

Olson Travelworld (970 W. 190th St., Suite 425, Torrance, CA 90502; phone: 800-421-2255 or 310-354-2600).

Orbis Polish Travel Bureau (342 Madison Ave., Suite 1512, New York, NY 10173; phone: 212-867-5011).

Paul Laifer Tours (106 Parsippany Rd., Parsippany, NJ 07054; phone: 800-346-6314 or 201-887-1188).

Professional Adventures Kleinburger (800 S. Michigan St., Seattle, WA 98108-2651; phone: 800-232-3708 or 206-763-4009).

Prospect Music and Art Tours (454-458 Chiswick High Rd., London W4 5TT, England; phone: 44-81-995-2151 or 44-81-995-2163).

Putnik Travel (39 Beechwood Ave., Manhasset, NY 11030; phone: 800-669-0757 or 516-627-2636).

Quasar Tours (1523 W. Hillsborough, Tampa, FL 33603; phone: 800-444-1770 or 813-237-4990).

Rahim Tours (12 S. Dixie Hwy., Suite 203, Lake Worth, FL 33460; phone: 800-556-5305 or 407-585-5305).

Russian Travel Bureau (225 E. 44th St., New York, NY 10017; phone: 800-847-1800 or 212-986-1500).

Steve Currey Expeditions (PO Box 1574, Provo, UT 84603; phone: 800-937-7238 or 801-224-6797).

Sunny Land Expeditions (166 Main St., Hackensack, NJ 07601; phone: 201-487-2150 and 800-783-7839).

Take-A-Guide (11 Uxbridge St., London W8 7TQ, England; phone: 800-825-4946 in the US).

Tauck Tours (PO Box 5027, Westport, CT 06881; phone: 800-468-2825 or 203-226-6911).

Thomas Cook (Headquarters: 45 Berkeley St., Piccadilly, London W1A 1EB, England; phone: 44-71-408-4191; main US office: 2 Penn Plaza, 18th Floor, New York, NY 10121; phone: 800-846-6272 or 212-967-4390).

Trafalgar Tours (11 E. 26th St., Suite 1300, New York, NY 10010-1402; phone: 800-854-0103 or 212-689-8977).

Travcoa (PO Box 2630, Newport Beach, CA 92658; phone: 800-992-2004 in California; 800-992-2003 elsewhere in the US; or 714-476-2800).

Travel Bound (599 Broadway, Penthouse, New York, NY 10012; phone: 212-334-1350 in New York State; 800-456-8656 elsewhere in the US).

TWA Getaway Vacations (phone: 800-GETAWAY).

Uniontours (79 Madison Ave., Suite 1104, New York, NY 10016; phone: 800-451-9511 or 212-683-9500).

University Educational Travel (*UET;* 8619 Reseda Blvd., Suite 103, Northridge, CA 91324; phone: 800-525-0525 or 818-886-0633).

U.S. & International Travel & Tours (117 S. Main St., Mishawaka, IN 46544; phone: 800-759-7373 or 219-255-7272).

Value Holidays (10224 N. Port Washington Rd., Mequon, WI 53092; phone: 800-558-6850).

Value World Tours (14126 Sherman Way, Suite 303, Van Nuys, CA 91405; phone: 800-795-1633 or 818-787-1633).

Vega International Travel Services (201 N. Wells St., Chicago, IL 60606; phone: 800-359-3437 or 312-332-7211).

Victor Emanuel Nature Tours (PO Box 33008, Austin, TX 78764; phone: 800-328-VENT or 512-328-5221).

Volare (1560 Broadway, Suite 808, New York, NY 10036; phone: 212-768-1313).

World Tracks Limited (12 Abingdon Rd., London W8 6AF, England; phone: 44-71-937-3028; represented in the US by *Himalayan Travel,* 112 Prospect St., Stamford, CT 06901; phone: 800-225-2380).

Worldwide Nordic (PO Box 1129, Maplewood, NJ 07040; phone: 201-378-9170).

Insurance

The first person with whom you should discuss travel insurance is your own insurance broker. You may discover that the insurance you already carry protects you adequately while traveling and that you need little additional coverage. If you charge travel services, the credit card company also may provide some insurance coverage (and other safeguards).

Types of Travel Insurance

Baggage and personal effects insurance: Protects your bags and their contents in case of damage or theft anytime during your travels.

Personal accident and sickness insurance: Covers cases of illness, injury, or death in an accident while traveling.

Trip cancellation and interruption insurance: Guarantees a refund if you must cancel a trip; may reimburse you for the extra travel costs incurred in catching up with a tour or traveling home early.

Default and/or bankruptcy insurance: Provides coverage in the event of default and/or bankruptcy on the part of the tour operator, airline, or other travel supplier.

Flight insurance: Covers accidental injury or death while flying.

Automobile insurance: Provides collision, theft, property damage, and personal liability protection while driving your own or a rented car.

(Some Eastern European countries have special automobile insurance requirements; see above.)
Combination policies: Include any or all of the above.

Disabled Travelers

Make travel arrangements well in advance. Specify to all services involved the nature of your disability to determine if there are accommodations and facilities that meet your needs. Hotel and restaurant guides, such as those published by Michelin (Michelin Guides and Maps, PO Box 3305, Spartanburg, SC 29304-3305; phone: 803-599-0850 in South Carolina; 800-423-0485 elsewhere in the US), use a symbol of access (person in a wheelchair) to point out accommodations suitable for wheelchair-bound guests.

Note that in much of Eastern Europe, access for the disabled is still somewhat limited, as most countries are concentrating on their basic tourism infrastructure. Only the newest hotels are likely to be accessible. And unless you are on a tour, you will need to rely mostly on taxis for transportation.

Organizations

ACCENT on Living (PO Box 700, Bloomington, IL 61702; phone: 309-378-2961).

Access: The Foundation for Accessibility by the Disabled (PO Box 356, Malverne, NY 11565; phone: 516-887-5798).

American Foundation for the Blind (15 W. 16th St., New York, NY 10011; phone: 800-232-5463 or 212-620-2147).

Holiday Care Service (2 Old Bank Chambers, Station Rd., Horley, Surrey RH6 9HW, England; phone: 44-293-774535).

Information Center for Individuals with Disabilities (Ft. Point Pl., 1st Floor, 27-43 Wormwood St., Boston, MA 02210; phone: 800-462-5015 in Massachusetts; 617-727-5540 or 617-727-5541 elsewhere in the US; TDD: 617-345-9743).

Mobility International USA (*MIUSA;* PO Box 3551, Eugene, OR 97403; phone: 503-343-1284, both voice and TDD; main office: 228 Borough High St., London SE1 1JX, England; phone: 44-71-403-5688).

National Rehabilitation Information Center (8455 Colesville Rd., Suite 935, Silver Spring, MD 20910; phone: 301-588-9284).

Paralyzed Veterans of America (*PVA;* PVA/ATTS Program, 801 18th St. NW, Washington, DC 20006; phone: 202-872-1300 in Washington, DC; 800-424-8200 elsewhere in the US).

Royal Association for Disability and Rehabilitation (*RADAR;* 25 Mortimer St., London W1N 8AB, England; phone: 44-71-637-5400).

Society for the Advancement of Travel for the Handicapped (*SATH;* 347 Fifth Ave., Suite 610, New York, NY 10016; phone: 212-447-7284).

Travel Information Service (MossRehab Hospital, 1200 W. Tabor Rd.,

Philadelphia, PA 19141-3099; phone: 215-456-9600; TDD: 215-456-9602).

Tripscope (The Courtyard, Evelyn Rd., London W4 5JL, England; phone: 44-81-994-9294).

Publications

Access Travel: A Guide to the Accessibility of Airport Terminals (Consumer Information Center, Dept. 578Z, Pueblo, CO 81009; phone: 719-948-3334).

Air Transportation of Handicapped Persons (Publication #AC-120-32; US Department of Transportation, Distribution Unit, Publications Section, M-443-2, 400 7th St. SW, Washington, DC 20590).

The Diabetic Traveler (PO Box 8223 RW, Stamford, CT 06905; phone: 203-327-5832).

Directory of Travel Agencies for the Disabled and ***Travel for the Disabled,*** both by Helen Hecker (Twin Peaks Press, PO Box 129, Vancouver, WA 98666; phone: 800-637-CALM or 206-694-2462).

Guide to Traveling with Arthritis (Upjohn Company, PO Box 989, Dearborn, MI 48121).

The Handicapped Driver's Mobility Guide (*American Automobile Association,* 1000 AAA Dr., Heathrow, FL 32746; phone: 407-444-7000).

Handicapped Travel Newsletter (PO Box 269, Athens, TX 75751; phone: 903-677-1260).

Handi-Travel: A Resource Book for Disabled and Elderly Travellers, by Cinnie Noble (*Canadian Rehabilitation Council for the Disabled,* 45 Sheppard Ave. E., Suite 801, Toronto, Ontario M2N 5W9, Canada; phone: 416-250-7490, both voice and TDD).

Incapacitated Passengers Air Travel Guide (*International Air Transport Association,* Publications Sales Department, 2000 Peel St., Montreal, Quebec H3A 2R4, Canada; phone: 514-844-6311).

Ticket to Safe Travel (*American Diabetes Association,* 1660 Duke St., Alexandria, VA 22314; phone: 800-232-3472 or 703-549-1500).

Travel for the Patient with Chronic Obstructive Pulmonary Disease (Dr. Harold Silver, 1601 18th St. NW, Washington, DC 20009; phone: 202-667-0134).

Travel Tips for Hearing-Impaired People (*American Academy of Otolaryngology,* 1 Prince St., Alexandria, VA 22314; phone: 703-836-4444).

Travel Tips for People with Arthritis (*Arthritis Foundation,* 1314 Spring St. NW, Atlanta, GA 30309; phone: 800-283-7800 or 404-872-7100).

Traveling Like Everybody Else: A Practical Guide for Disabled Travelers, by Jacqueline Freedman and Susan Gersten (Modan Publishing, PO Box 1202, Bellmore, NY 11710; phone: 516-679-1380).

Package Tour Operators

Accessible Journeys (35 W. Sellers Ave., Ridley Park, PA 19078; phone: 215-521-0339).

Accessible Tours/Directions Unlimited (Lois Bonnani, 720 N. Bedford

Rd., Bedford Hills, NY 10507; phone: 800-533-5343 or 914-241-1700).

Beehive Business and Leisure Travel (1130 W. Center St., N. Salt Lake, UT 84054; phone: 800-777-5727 or 801-292-4445).

Classic Travel Service (8 W. 40th St., New York, NY 10018; phone: 212-869-2560 in New York State; 800-247-0909 elsewhere in the US).

Dialysis at Sea Cruises (611 Barry Pl., Indian Rocks Beach, FL 34635; phone: 800-775-1333 or 813-596-4614).

Evergreen Travel Service (4114 198th St. SW, Suite 13, Lynnwood, WA 98036-6742; phone: 800-435-2288 or 206-776-1184).

Flying Wheels Travel (143 W. Bridge St., PO Box 382, Owatonna, MN 55060; phone: 800-535-6790 or 507-451-5005).

Good Neighbor Travel Service (124 S. Main St.; Viroqua, WI 54665; phone: 608-637-2128).

The Guided Tour (7900 Old York Rd., Suite 114B, Elkins Park, PA 19117-2339; phone: 800-783-5841 or 215-782-1370).

Hinsdale Travel (201 E. Ogden Ave., Hinsdale, IL 60521; phone: 708-325-1335 or 708-469-7349).

MedEscort International (ABE International Airport, PO Box 8766, Allentown, PA 18105; phone: 800-255-7182 or 215-791-3111).

Prestige World Travel (5710-X High Point Rd., Greensboro, NC 27407; phone: 800-476-7737 or 919-292-6690).

Sprout (893 Amsterdam Ave., New York, NY 10025; phone: 212-222-9575).

Weston Travel Agency (134 N. Cass Ave., PO Box 1050, Westmont, IL 60559; phone: 708-968-2513 in Illinois; 800-633-3725 elsewhere in the US).

Single Travelers

The travel industry is not very fair to people who vacation by themselves — they often end up paying more than those traveling in pairs. Services catering to singles match travel companions, offer travel arrangements with shared accommodations, and provide useful information and discounts. Also consult publications such as *Going Solo* (Doerfer Communications, PO Box 123, Apalachicola, FL 32329; phone: 904-653-8848) and *Traveling on Your Own,* by Eleanor Berman (Random House, Order Dept., 400 Hahn Rd., Westminster, MD 21157; phone: 800-733-3000).

Organizations and Companies

Club Europa (802 W. Oregon St., Urbana, IL 61801; phone: 800-331-1882 or 217-344-5863).

Contiki Holidays (300 Plaza Alicante, Suite 900, Garden Grove, CA 92640; phone: 800-466-0610 or 714-740-0808).

Gallivanting (515 E. 79th St., Suite 20F, New York, NY 10021; phone: 800-933-9699 or 212-988-0617).

Globus and *Cosmos* (5301 S. Federal Circle, Littleton, CO 80123; phone: 800-221-0090 or 800-556-5454).

Insight International Tours (745 Atlantic Ave., Boston, MA 02111; phone: 800-582-8380 or 617-482-2000).

Jane's International and *Sophisticated Women Travelers* (2603 Bath Ave., Brooklyn, NY 11214; phone: 718-266-2045).

Marion Smith Singles (611 Prescott Pl., N. Woodmere, NY 11581; phone: 516-791-4852, 516-791-4865, or 212-944-2112).

Partners-in-Travel (11660 Chenault St., Suite 119, Los Angeles, CA 90049; phone: 310-476-4869).

Singles in Motion (545 W. 236th St., Riverdale, NY 10463; phone: 718-884-4464).

Singleworld (401 Theodore Fremd Ave., Rye, NY 10580; phone: 800-223-6490 or 914-967-3334).

Solo Flights (63 High Noon Rd., Weston, CT 06883; phone: 203-226-9993).

Suddenly Singles Tours (161 Dreiser Loop, Bronx, NY 10475; phone: 718-379-8800 in New York City; 800-859-8396 elsewhere in the US).

Travel Companion Exchange (PO Box 833, Amityville, NY 11701; phone: 516-454-0880).

Travel Companions (Atrium Financial Center, 1515 N. Federal Hwy., Suite 300, Boca Raton, FL 33432; phone: 800-383-7211 or 407-393-6448).

Travel in Two's (239 N. Broadway, Suite 3, N. Tarrytown, NY 10591; phone: 914-631-8301 in New York State; 800-692-5252 elsewhere in the US).

Umbrella Singles (PO Box 157, Woodbourne, NY 12788; phone: 800-537-2797 or 914-434-6871).

Older Travelers

Special discounts and more free time are just two factors that have given older travelers a chance to see the world at affordable prices. Many travel suppliers offer senior discounts — sometimes only to members of certain senior citizen organizations, which provide other benefits. Prepare your itinerary with one eye on your own physical condition and the other on a topographical map, and remember that it's easy to overdo when traveling.

Publications

Going Abroad: 101 Tips for Mature Travelers (*Grand Circle Travel*, 347 Congress St., Boston, MA 02210; phone: 800-221-2610 or 617-350-7500).

The Mature Traveler (GEM Publishing Group, PO Box 50820, Reno, NV 89513-0820; phone: 702-786-7419).

Take a Camel to Lunch and Other Adventures for Mature Travelers, by

Nancy O'Connell (Bristol Publishing Enterprises, PO Box 1737, San Leandro, CA 94577; phone: 510-895-4461 in California; 800-346-4889 elsewhere in the US).

Travel Tips for Older Americans (Publication #044-000-02270-2; Superintendent of Documents, US Government Printing Office, PO Box 371954, Pittsburgh, PA 15250-7954; phone: 202-783-3238).

Unbelievably Good Deals & Great Adventures That You Absolutely Can't Get Unless You're Over 50, by Joan Rattner Heilman (Contemporary Books, 180 N. Michigan Ave., Chicago, IL 60601; phone: 312-782-9181).

Organizations

American Association of Retired Persons (*AARP;* 601 E St. NW, Washington, DC 20049; phone: 202-434-2277).

Golden Companions (PO Box 754, Pullman, WA 99163-0754; phone: 208-858-2183).

Mature Outlook (Customer Service Center, 6001 N. Clark St., Chicago, IL 60660; phone: 800-336-6330).

National Council of Senior Citizens (1331 F St. NW, Washington, DC 20004; phone: 202-347-8800).

Package Tour Operators

Elderhostel (PO Box 1959, Wakefield, MA 01880-5959; phone: 617-426-7788).

Evergreen Travel Service (4114 198th St. SW, Suite 13, Lynnwood, WA 98036-6742; phone: 800-435-2288 or 206-776-1184).

Gadabout Tours (700 E. Tahquitz Canyon Way, Palm Springs, CA 92262; phone: 800-952-5068 or 619-325-5556).

Grand Circle Travel (347 Congress St., Boston, MA 02210; phone: 800-221-2610 or 617-350-7500).

Grandtravel (6900 Wisconsin Ave., Suite 706, Chevy Chase, MD 20815; phone: 800-247-7651 or 301-986-0790).

Insight International Tours (745 Atlantic Ave., Suite 720, Boston, MA 02111; phone: 800-582-8380 or 617-482-2000).

Interhostel (UNH Division of Continuing Education, 6 Garrison Ave., Durham, NH 03824; phone: 800-733-9753 or 603-862-1147).

Ridgebrook Travel (104 Wilmont Rd., Deerfield, IL 60015; phone: 800-962-0060 or 708-374-0088).

Saga International Holidays (222 Berkeley St., Boston, MA 02116; phone: 800-343-0273 or 617-262-2262).

Money Matters

The best sources of information for Eastern Europe generally are the tourist boards of the individual countries you plan to visit. Exchange rates for some Eastern European currencies also are posted in international newspapers such as the *International Herald Tribune*. Foreign currency information and currency-related services are provided by banks and companies such as *Thomas Cook Foreign Exchange* (for the nearest location, call 800-621-0666 or 312-236-0042); *Harold Reuter and Company* (200 Park Ave., Suite 332E, New York, NY 10166; phone: 212-661-0826); and *Ruesch International* (for the nearest location, call 800-424-2923 or 202-408-1200).

Note that most Eastern European currencies still are not "convertible." This means that these currencies are not freely traded on the open market — they cannot be bought or sold in the US and exchange rates are set by the government. Although a number of countries have announced plans to allow their currencies to be freely traded, timetables for this conversion are uncertain.

In Eastern Europe, you usually will find the official rate of exchange posted in banks, money exchange houses — which have begun to appear in a number of countries — airports, hotels, and some shops. Since you will get more for your US dollar at banks and money exchanges, don't change more than $10 for foreign currency at other commercial establishments. Ask how much commission you're being charged and the exchange rate, and don't buy money on the black market (it may be counterfeit). Estimate your needs carefully; if you overbuy, you lose twice — buying and selling back.

Although travelers to *Western* Europe generally are advised to convert their travel funds into the local legal tender immediately to avoid a loss in buying power, this advice does not apply to most Eastern European countries. Governments and individuals often are eager to get their hands on "hard currency" and frequently (and cheerfully) accept US dollars for small purchases and services. Governments also operate hard currency stores where the most desirable merchandise is available only to those who are able to pay with Western currency.

This does not mean that you can *always* pay for goods and services in US dollars, however; for some transactions, you will have to convert to the local currency. The legality of US currency transactions varies from country to country. For example, some of the former Soviet republics — such as Latvia and Lithuania — are introducing their own currencies and may require that only these are used. Some countries also may require that a minimum amount in dollars be exchanged for local currency for a given length of stay. For further information on specific Eastern European currencies, see FACTS IN BRIEF.

TRAVELER'S CHECKS AND CREDIT CARDS

It's wise to carry traveler's checks while on the road, since they are replaceable if stolen or lost. You can buy traveler's checks at banks and some are available by mail or phone. Traveler's checks are accepted in many hotels and restaurants in Eastern Europe — though with great reluctance in

Russia and the Baltic states (cash or credit cards are preferred). However, except in the "hard currency" stores mentioned above, traveler's checks often cannot be used in small stores and other retail establishments; you must have them converted to the local currency first. For additional information, contact the embassy or consulates of the countries you plan to visit.

Although most major credit cards enjoy wide domestic and international acceptance, not every hotel, restaurant, or shop in Eastern Europe accepts all (or in some cases any) credit cards. When making purchases with a credit card, note that the rate of exchange depends on when the charge is processed; most credit card companies charge a 1% fee for converting foreign currency charges. Keep a separate list of all traveler's checks (noting those that you have cashed) and the names and numbers of your credit cards. Both traveler's check and credit card companies have international numbers to call for information or in the event of loss or theft.

CASH MACHINES

Automated teller machines (ATMs) are increasingly common worldwide. Most banks participate in one of the international ATM networks; cardholders can withdraw cash from any machine in the same network using either a "bank" card or, in some cases, a credit card. Most ATMs belong to the *CIRRUS* or *PLUS* network. Note that at the time of this writing only *CIRRUS* had machines in Eastern Europe — in the Czech and Slovak Republics. For further information, ask at your bank branch.

SENDING MONEY ABROAD

Should the need arise, it is possible to have money sent to you via the following services:

American Express (*MoneyGram;* phone: 800-926-9400 or 800-666-3997 for information; 800-866-8800 for money transfers). Available in the Czech Republic, Latvia, and Poland.

Western Union Financial Services (phone: 800-325-4176). Available in Bulgaria, Hungary, Romania, and Russia.

If you are down to your last cent and have no other way to obtain cash, the nearest US Consulate will let you call home to set these matters in motion.

Accommodations

Eastern Europe boasts a wide range of accommodations — from centuries-old castle hotels to modern high-rises, as well as inexpensive inns and the beginnings of a bed and breakfast industry. However, room shortages are still a problem, and — particularly in smaller towns and rural areas —

the quality of facilities and services may not be as high as in Western Europe.

Before you go, consult the brochures and booklets available free from Eastern European tourist offices in the US. Most of these offices also have lists or guides that rate hotels by the types of facilities they offer. For specific information on hotels and other selected accommodations, see *Best in Town* in THE CITIES and *Best en Route* in DIRECTIONS.

BED AND BREAKFAST ESTABLISHMENTS

Bed and breakfast properties (commonly known as B&Bs) are a staple of the lodging scene in many parts of Europe, and range from humble country cottages to small inns, guesthouses, and apartments. Although not yet really common in Eastern Europe, they are growing in number — in cities as well as in rural areas. Eastern European tourist offices sometimes can provide information on such establishments, and most tourist information centers abroad also have information on B&Bs in their areas.

Among the bed and breakfast reservations services representing establishments in Eastern Europe are the following:

Anglo-American Reisebüro (*AAR;* 2 Vidumstr., Westerkappeln 49492, Germany; phone: 49-5404-96080).

Hometours International (1170 Broadway, Suite 614, New York, NY 10001; phone: 800-367-4668 or 212-689-0851).

ITS Tours and Travel (1055 Texas Ave., Suite 104, College Station, TX 77840; phone: 800-533-8688 or 409-764-9400).

RENTAL OPTIONS

An attractive accommodations alternative for the visitor content to stay in one spot is to rent a property in Eastern Europe. For a family or group, the per-person cost can be reasonable. To have your pick of the properties available, make inquiries at least 6 months in advance. The *Worldwide Home Rental Guide* (369 Montezuma, Suite 297, Santa Fe, NM 87501; phone: 505-984-7080) lists rental properties and managing agencies.

Rental Property Agents

Creative Leisure (951 Transport Way, Petaluma, CA 94954; phone: 800-4-CONDOS or 707-778-1800).

Hometours International (address above).

Interhome (124 Little Falls Rd., Fairfield, NJ 07004; phone: 201-882-6864).

Rent a Home International (7200 34th Ave. NW, Seattle, WA 98117; phone: 206-789-9377).

HOME STAYS

The *United States Servas Committee* (11 John St., Room 407, New York, NY 10038; phone: 212-267-0252) maintains a list of hosts throughout the world willing to accommodate visitors free of charge. The aim of this nonprofit cultural program is to promote international understanding and peace, and *Servas* emphasizes that member travelers should be interested mainly in their hosts, not in sightseeing, during their stays. Another organization that arranges home stays in Eastern Europe is *American-International Homestays* (PO Box 7178, Boulder, CO 80306-7178; phone: 800-876-2048 or 303-938-8257).

Time Zones

The countries of Eastern Europe fall into the following time zones:

Greenwich Plus 1: The time is 6 hours later than in East Coast US cities in the Czech and Slovak Republics, Hungary, and Poland. Also called Central European Time.

Greenwich Plus 2: The time is 7 hours later than in East Coast US cities in Bulgaria, Estonia, Latvia, Lithuania, Romania, and Ukraine.

Greenwich Plus 3: The time is 8 hours later than in East Coast US cities in western Russia (including the cities of Moscow and St. Petersburg).

Greenwich Plus 4: The time is 9 hours later than in East Coast US cities in Russia's west-central region (which includes the cities of Gorky and Kirov).

Greenwich Plus 5: The time is 10 hours later than in East Coast US cities in that part of Russia roughly bisected by the Urals (traditionally considered the dividing line between the European and Asian regions of Russia).

Most European nations move their clocks ahead an hour in the spring and back an hour in the fall, corresponding to the daylight saving time in the US, although the exact dates of the changes are different from those observed in the US. Note that European timetables use a 24-hour clock to denote arrival and departure times, which means that hours are expressed sequentially from 1 AM.

Business Hours

Most Eastern European businesses open on weekdays between 8 and 9 AM and close between 4 and 7 PM. In some of the southern countries of Eastern Europe, businesses follow a more Mediterranean schedule, opening and closing later, with a mid-afternoon break of about 2 hours. The trend, however, is toward shorter, 1-hour breaks starting at 12:30 or 1 PM.

As a rule, banks open at about the same time as other businesses on weekdays, but close an hour or two earlier. In some countries, selected branches also may be open for a half or full day on Saturdays. For additional information about business hours, as well as public holidays, in various Eastern European countries, see FACTS IN BRIEF.

Mail

Eastern European post offices usually are open weekdays during the same hours as most businesses, and frequently offer Saturday morning hours as well. In a few of the larger cities, there may be a branch or two open 24 hours a day. Stamps are sold at post offices, newsstands, and kiosks in most countries. Letters can be mailed from private and public mailboxes; however, it always is advisable to send packages directly from post offices.

Mail delivery to and from Eastern Europe can be slow. If your correspondence is especially important, you may want to send it via one of the international courier services, such as *Federal Express* or *DHL Worldwide Express,* both of which serve much of Eastern Europe.

You can have mail sent to you care of your hotel (marked "Guest Mail, Hold for Arrival") or to a post office (c/o the local equivalent of "General Delivery"). *American Express* offices also will hold mail for customers ("c/o Client Letter Service"); information is provided in their pamphlet *Travelers' Companion.* US Embassies and Consulates abroad will hold mail for US citizens *only* in emergency situations.

Telephone

Although Eastern European telephone systems have long been known for their unreliability, this situation has begun to change. Direct dialing — within a country, between nations, and overseas — which was impractical, if not impossible, in most countries just a few years ago, is now available in major cities throughout Eastern Europe. In the Czech Republic, Hungary, and Poland, direct dialing is possible nationwide. Public telephones are widely available in metropolitan areas and, in some countries, there also are telephone offices from which long-distance calls can be made. Pay phones in most Eastern European countries take coins only; however, phones that take special calling cards (increasingly common elsewhere in Europe) have been introduced in some cities in the Czech Republic and Hungary.

The number of digits in phone numbers varies throughout Eastern Europe. Where possible, the procedure for calling a number in Eastern Europe direct from the US — and for calling from one Eastern European country to another — generally is to dial the international access code (011 in the US) + the country code + the city code + the local number. To call the US from Eastern Europe, dial the international access code (which varies from country to country) + 1 (the US country code) + the area code + the local number. To call from one city to another within a given country, dial an access code (usually 0 or 1) + the city code + the local number. To call a number within the same city code coverage area, just dial the local number. The procedure for making operator-assisted calls varies from country to country in Eastern Europe.

Long-distance telephone services that help you avoid the surcharges that hotels routinely add to phone bills are provided by *American Telephone and Telegraph* (*AT&T Communications,* International Information Service, 635 Grant St., Pittsburgh, PA 15219; phone: 800-874-4000), *MCI* (323 3rd St. SE, Cedar Rapids, IA 52401; phone: 800-444-3333), *Metromedia Communications Corp.* (1 International Center, 100 NE Loop 410, San Antonio, TX 78216; phone: 800-275-0200), and *Sprint* (offices throughout the US; phone: 800-877-4000). Some hotels still may charge a fee for line usage.

AT&T's Language Line Service (phone: 800-752-6096) provides interpretive services for telephone communications in over 140 languages and dialects, including most major Eastern European languages. Also useful are the *AT&T 800 Travel Directory* (available at *AT&T Phone Centers* or by calling 800-426-8686), the *Toll-Free Travel & Vacation Information Directory* (Pilot Books, 103 Cooper St., Babylon, NY 11702; phone: 516-422-2225), and *The Phone Booklet* (*Scott American Corporation,* PO Box 88, W. Redding, CT 06896; phone: 203-938-2955).

EMERGENCY NUMBERS

Bulgaria: Dial 150 for an ambulance or 166 for the police.
Czech Republic: Dial 155 for an ambulance or 158 for the police.
Estonia: Dial 03 for an ambulance or 02 for the police.
Hungary: Dial 04 for an ambulance or 07 for the police.
Latvia: Dial 03 for an ambulance or 02 for the police.
Lithuania: Dial 03 for an ambulance or 02 for the police.
Poland: Dial 999 for an ambulance or 997 for the police.
Romania: In Bucharest, dial 961 for an ambulance or 955 for the police; elsewhere in Romania, dial 091 for an operator who will connect you to the police or other emergency services.
Russia: Dial 03 for an ambulance or 02 for the police.
Slovakia: Dial 155 for an ambulance or 158 for the police.
Ukraine: Dial 03 for an ambulance or 02 for the police.

Electricity

Most of Eastern Europe uses a 220-volt, 50-cycle, alternating current (AC) system. Travelers from the US will need electrical converters to operate the appliances they use at home, or dual-voltage appliances, which can be switched from one voltage standard to another. (Some large tourist hotels may offer 110-volt current or may have converters available.) You also will need a plug adapter set to deal with the different plug configurations found in Eastern Europe. For specific information on electrical standards, see *Electricity* in the individual country entries in FACTS IN BRIEF.

Staying Healthy

It is difficult to generalize about a region as diverse and changeable as Eastern Europe. Although, *in general,* it probably is safe to say that risks to travelers' health are not especially serious in the countries covered in this guide, caution is always advisable, and travelers should inquire about the specific destinations they intend to visit. For example, at press time, an increase in cases of diphtheria and typhoid had been reported in both Russia and Ukraine. For information on current health conditions in Eastern Europe, call the Centers for Disease Control's *International Health Requirements and Recommendations Information Hotline:* 404-332-4559.

Tap water generally is clean and potable in metropolitan areas, although the water supply may not be throughly purified in rural areas. If you're at all unsure, bottled water may be available in stores — though only in the so-called "hard currency" stores in Russia (see above). Do not drink water from freshwater streams, rivers, or pools, as it may be contaminated. Dairy products usually are safe to eat — although milk may not be pasteurized in more remote areas. Fruit, vegetables, meat, poultry, and fish are all safe to eat. (Because of pollution, however, all seafood should be eaten cooked, and make sure it is *fresh,* particularly in the heat of summer, when inadequate refrigeration is an additional concern.)

Eastern Europe has some fine beaches, but it's important to remember that the sea can be treacherous. When you are swimming, be careful of the undertow (a current running back down the beach after a wave has washed ashore), which can knock you down, and riptides (currents running against the tide), which can pull you out to sea. If you see a shark, swim away quietly and smoothly. Also beware of eels and Portuguese man-of-war (and other jellyfish).

Most Eastern European cities and towns usually have either a public hospital or medical clinic nearby. Some hospitals also have walk-in clinics to serve people who do not really need emergency service, but who have no place to go for immediate medical attention. In more remote areas, however — particularly in some of the newly independent republics — the availability and the sophistication of medical treatment may be limited, and overall, medical care may fall short of Western standards. A number of Eastern European countries that used to have socialized medicine are privatizing their health care systems. Even where health care systems still are government-run or -subsidized, however, foreign travelers do not receive free medical care.

Ask at your hotel for the house physician or for help in reaching a doctor, or contact the US Consulate. There should be no problem finding a 24-hour pharmacy in most major Eastern European cities. Pharmacists who are closed may provide the addresses of the nearest all-night drugstores in the window; in some areas, night duty may rotate among pharmacies.

In an emergency: Go directly to the emergency room of the nearest hospital, dial one of the emergency numbers given above, or call an operator for assistance.

Additional Resources

International Association of Medical Assistance to Travelers (*IAMAT*; 417 Center St., Lewiston, NY 14092; phone: 716-754-4883).

International Health Care Service (440 E. 69th St., New York, NY 10021; phone: 212-746-1601).

International SOS Assistance (PO Box 11568, Philadelphia, PA 19116; phone: 800-523-8930 or 215-244-1500).

Medic Alert Foundation (2323 Colorado Ave., Turlock, CA 95380; phone: 800-ID-ALERT or 209-668-3333).

TravMed (PO Box 10623, Baltimore, MD 21285-0623; phone: 800-732-5309 or 410-296-5225).

Consular Services

The American Services section of the US Consulate is a vital source of assistance and advice for US citizens abroad. If you are injured or become seriously ill, the consulate can direct you to sources of medical attention and notify your relatives. If you become involved in a dispute that could lead to legal action, the consulate is the place to turn. In cases of natural disasters or civil unrest, consulates handle the evacuation of US citizens if necessary.

US Embassies and Consulates in Eastern Europe

Bulgaria: 1 A. Stambolijski Blvd., Sofia (phone: 2-884801, 2-884802, or 2-884803).

Czech Republic: 15-125 Třžistě, Prague 11716 (phone: 2-536641 through 2-536649).

Estonia: 20 Kentmanni, Tallinn EE 0001 (phone: 2-312021).

Hungary: V, 12 Szabadság Tér, Budapest (phone: 1-112-6450).

Latvia: 7 Raina Blvd., Riga LV 1050 (phone: 2-227045).

Lithuania: 6 Akmenu G., Vilnius 2000 (phone: 2-223032).

Poland: 29-31 Aleje Ujazdowskie, Warsaw (phone: 2-628-3041 through 49); 9 Ul. Stolarska, Cracow (phone: 12-227793).

Romania: 7-9 Tudor Arghezi, Bucharest, Sector 1 (phone: 1-312-4042).

Russia: 19-21-23 Ulitsa Chaykovskogo, Moscow (phone: 95-252-2450 through 95-252-2459); 15 Ulitsa Petra Lavrova, St. Petersburg (phone: 812-274-8235).

Slovakia: 4 Hviezdoslavovo Nam., Bratislava (phone: 33-0861, 33-3338, or 33-5083).

Ukraine: 10 Y. Kotsubinsky, Kiev (phone: 044-244-7349).

The US State Department operates a 24-hour *Citizens' Emergency Center* travel advisory hotline (phone: 202-647-5225). **In an emergency, call 202-647-4000 and ask for the duty officer.**

Entry Requirements and Customs Regulations

ENTERING EASTERN EUROPE

For information on visa requirements, see the individual country listings in FACTS IN BRIEF. Where visas are not required, the only document a US citizen needs to enter a given Eastern European country, or to re-enter the US, is a valid US passport. Immigration officers at the airport also *may* want to see that you have sufficient funds for your trip and a return or ongoing ticket. Depending on the country, a US passport entitles the bearer to remain in Eastern Europe for anywhere from 30 to 90 days as a tourist. (Resident aliens of the US may need different documents.) A visa usually is required for study, residency, work, or stays of more than this 30- to 90-day period, and US citizens should contact the applicable embassy or consulate well in advance of a proposed trip. Proof of means of independent financial support during the stay is pertinent to the acceptance of any long-term–stay application.

Eastern European countries have strict regulations regarding the amounts of specific types of goods that may be imported duty-free, and the duties required on quantities above these limits. Restrictions generally apply to items such as alcoholic beverages; cigarettes, cigars, and loose tobacco; coffee and tea; cologne and perfume; and gifts valued over a specified amount. When planning a trip to Eastern Europe, contact the embassy or consulate of each country you plan to visit (for offices in the US, see *For Further Information,* following) for information on procedures, the type and quantity of goods regulated, and duties imposed.

RETURNING TO THE US

You must declare to the US Customs official at the point of entry everything you have acquired in Eastern Europe. The standard duty-free allowance for US citizens is $400; if your trip is shorter than 48 continuous hours, or you have been out of the US within 30 days, it is cut to $25. Families traveling together may make a joint declaration. Antiques (at least 100 years old) and paintings or drawings done entirely by hand are duty-free (note, however, that some Eastern European countries restrict the export of antiques; see below).

A flat 10% duty is assessed on the next $1,000 worth of merchandise; additional items are taxed at a variety of rates (see *Tariff Schedules of the United States* in a library or any US Customs Service office). With the exception of gifts valued at $50 or less sent directly to the recipient, items shipped home are dutiable. Some articles are duty-free only up to certain limits. The $400 allowance includes 1 carton of (200) cigarettes, 100 cigars (not Cuban), and 1 liter of liquor or wine (for those over 21); the $25 allowance includes 10 cigars, 50 cigarettes, and 4 ounces of perfume. To avoid paying duty unnecessarily, before your trip, register the serial numbers of any expensive equipment you are bringing along with US Customs.

Forbidden imports include articles made of the furs or hides of animals on the endangered species list. In addition, some Eastern European countries will not allow articles over 50 years old to be exported. Those interested in taking antiques, archeological finds, or other original artifacts out of a given Eastern European country must obtain a special permit; for information, check with the customs agency of the country of origin.

For further information, consult *Know Before You Go; International Mail Imports; Travelers' Tips on Bringing Food, Plant, and Animal Products into the United States; Importing a Car; GSP and the Traveler; Pocket Hints; Currency Reporting;* and *Pets, Wildlife, US Customs;* all available from the US Customs Service (PO Box 7407, Washington, DC 20044). For tape-recorded information on travel-related topics, call 202-927-2095 from any touch-tone phone.

| **DUTY-FREE SHOPS AND VALUE ADDED TAX** | Located in international airports, |

these provide bargains on the purchase of foreign goods. But beware: Not all foreign goods are automatically less expensive. You *can* get a good deal on some items, but know what they cost elsewhere.

Value Added Tax (VAT) is a tax added to the purchase price of most goods and services. Although common in Western Europe, such taxes have only recently been introduced in some Eastern European countries, including the Czech Republic, Hungary, Poland, and Romania, and at press time, refund policies for tourists remained unresolved. Contact the embassy or consulates of the countries you plan to visit for current information.

For Further Information

TOURIST INFORMATION OFFICES

Eastern European government tourist offices in the US are the best sources of travel information. Offices generally are open on weekdays, during normal business hours.

Bulgaria
Balkan Holidays/USA/Ltd.: 41 E. 42nd St., Suite 508, New York, NY 10017 (phone: 212-573-5530).

Czech Republic

Cedok, Czechoslovak Travel Bureau: 10 E. 40th St., Suite 3604, New York, NY 10016 (phone: 800-800-8891 or 212-689-9720).

Information also is available from the *Embassy of the Czech Republic* (address below).

Estonia

At press time, *Estonian Holidays,* the official Estonian tourist authority, had no offices in the US. Limited tourist information was available from the *Estonian Embassy* or the *Estonian Consulate General* (addresses below).

Hungary

IBUSZ Hungarian Travel Company: One Parker Plaza, Suite 1104, Ft. Lee, NJ 07024 (phone: 201-592-8585 in New Jersey; 800-367-7878 elsewhere in the US).

Latvia

At press time, Latvia had no official tourist bureau. For visa and other basic tourist information, contact the *Embassy of Latvia* (address below). For additional tourist information, the Embassy recommends that prospective travelers contact the following two agencies:

- *ChipsTravel* (15330 E. Bagley Rd., Middleburg Heights, OH 44130; phone: 800-822-3533).
- *Union Tours* (79 Madison Ave., Suite 1104, New York, NY 10016; phone: 800-451-9511).

Lithuania

At press time, the *Lithuanian Travel Agency* had no offices in the US. For visa and other basic information, contact the *Lithuanian Embassy* or one of its *Consulates General* (addresses below).

Poland

Orbis Polish Travel Bureau: 342 Madison Ave., Suite 1512, New York, NY 10173 (phone: 800-223-6037 or 212-867-5011).

Polish National Tourist Office: 333 N. Michigan Ave., Suite 224, Chicago, IL 60601 (phone: 312-236-9013).

Romania

Romanian National Tourist Office: 342 Madison Ave., Suite 210, New York, NY 10173 (phone: 212-697-6971).

Russia

Intourist USA: 630 Fifth Ave., Suite 868, New York, NY 10111 (phone: 800-982-8416, 212-757-3884, or 212-757-3885).

Slovakia

Cedok, Czechoslovak Travel Bureau: 10 E. 40th St., Suite 3604, New York, NY 10016 (phone: 800-800-8891 or 212-689-9720).

Information also is available from the *Embassy of the Slovak Republic* (address below).

Ukraine

At press time, Ukraine had no official tourist bureau. For basic tourist information, contact the the *Embassy of Ukraine* or either of the country's *Consulates* (addresses below).

EMBASSIES AND CONSULATES

For information on visa and other entry requirements, contact the Eastern European embassies and consulates in the US.

Bulgaria

Embassy and Consulate: 1621 22nd St. NW, Washington, DC 20008 (phone: 202-387-7969 for the Embassy; 202-483-5885 for the Consulate).

Czech Republic

Embassy: 3900 Spring of Freedom St. NW, Washington, DC 20008 (phone: 202-363-6315).

Estonia

Embassy: 1030 15th St. NW, Suite 1000, Washington, DC 20005 (phone: 202-789-0320).

Estonian Consulate General: 630 Fifth Ave., Suite 2415, New York, NY 10111 (phone: 212-247-1450).

Hungary

Embassy: 3910 Shoemaker St. NW, Washington, DC 20008 (phone: 202-362-6737).

Consulates General:
- 223 E. 52nd St., New York, NY 10022 (phone: 212-879-4127).
- 11766 Wilshire Blvd., Suite 410, Los Angeles, CA (phone: 310-473-9346).

Latvia

Embassy: 4325 17th St. NW, Washington, DC 20011 (phone: 202-726-8213).

Lithuania

Embassy: 2622 16th St. NW, Washington, DC 20009 (phone: 202-234-5860).

Consulates General:
- 6500 S. Pulaski Rd., Chicago, IL 60629 (phone: 312-582-5478).
- 3236 N. Sawtooth Ct., Westlake Village, CA 91362 (phone: 805-496-5324).

Poland

Embassy: 2640 16th St. NW, Washington, DC 20009 (phone: 202-234-3800).

Consulates General:
- 1530 N. Lake Shore Dr., Chicago, IL 60610 (phone: 312-337-8166).
- 3460 Wilshire Blvd., Suite 1200, Los Angeles, CA 90010 (phone: 213-365-7900).
- 233 Madison Ave., New York, NY 10016 (phone: 212-889-8360).

Romania

Embassy and Consulate: 1607 23rd St. NW, Washington, DC 20008 (phone: 202-232-4747 for Embassy; 202-387-6902 for Consulate).

Consulate: 573-577 3rd Ave., New York, NY 10016 (phone: 212-682-9120 or 212-682-9123).

Russia

Embassy: 1125 16th St. NW, Washington, DC 20036 (phone: 202-628-7551 or 202-628-7554).

Consulates:
- 9 E. 91st St., New York, NY 10128 (phone: 212-348-0926).
- 2790 Green St., San Francisco, CA 94123 (phone: 415-202-9800).
- 1825 S. Phelps Pl. NW, Washington, DC 20008 (phone: 202-939-8907 or 202-939-8918).

Slovakia

Embassy of the Slovak Republic: 2201 Wisconsin Ave. NW, Washington, DC 20007 (phone: 202-965-5160).

Ukraine

Embassy and Consulate of Ukraine: 3350 M St. NW, Washington, DC 20007 (phone: 202-333-7507 for Embassy; 202-333-0606 for Consulate).

Consulates:
- 2247 W. Chicago Ave., Chicago, IL 60622 (phone: 312-384-6632).
- 240 E. 49th St., New York, NY 10017 (phone: 212-371-5690).

Facts in Brief

Facts in Brief

The tourist authority addresses listed below are for information within each country. For US addresses of national tourist authorities and the embassies and consulates of the countries below, see GETTING READY TO GO. We also feel obliged to say that much of Eastern Europe remained in the midst of very significant change as we went to press. That means that matters of visa/entry requirements, currency exchange, and even national holidays are quite likely to change during the 12-month life of this book. The dates noted here were correct at press time, but the vagaries of Eastern Europe make double-checking especially prudent during 1994. Note: Since all countries now celebrate *Easter* and *Christmas*, these dates have been omitted from the list of holidays.

The Baltic States

ESTONIA

TOURIST INFORMATION General tourist information can be found at the Estonian Tourist Board (2-4 Kiriku, Tallinn; phone: 6-450486). For local information, visit the Tallinn Tourist Office (8 Raekoja Plats, Tallinn; phone: 6-666959 or 6-448886) Many new private travel agencies have opened in Estonia; for a complete list of travel agencies, contact the *Estonian Association of Travel Agents* (*Eesti Turismifirmade Liit*; 71 Pikk Jalg, Tallinn; phone and fax: 6-601705).

ENTRY REQUIREMENTS US citizens need only a current passport for visits up to 90 days.

TELEPHONE The country code for Estonia is 372.

GETTING THERE/GETTING AROUND

Airlines From New York to Tallinn, *Finnair* has service with a stop in Helsinki; *SAS* connects through Copenhagen or Stockholm; and *Lufthansa* flies via Frankfurt. *Estonian Airlines* connects Tallinn with Amsterdam, Copenhagen, Frankfurt, Hamburg, Helsinki, Moscow, Stockholm, and Vilnius.

Cars A variety of rental cars, including Volvos, Ladas, and Toyota Corollas, are available through agencies in Tallinn. The laws against driving after drinking are strictly enforced in Estonia and penalties for violations are stiff.

Ferries *Saimaa Lines* (14 Fabianinkatu, Helsinki; phone: 90-658733) offers daily service between Tallinn and Helsinki from late March through early December. Travel time is about 2 hours from Tallinn to Helsinki; the return trip is a half-hour shorter. *Kristina Cruises* (45 Korkeavuorenkatu, Helsinki; phone: 90-629968) also has a ferry line connecting Estonia and Finland. *Estline* provides overnight travel from Stockholm to Tallinn. In Tallinn, the booking office is located at 5A Aia (phone: 6-666579).

Trains *Eesti Raudtee* is the national rail service. There are trains daily to St. Petersburg (a change of train is necessary to continue to Moscow), Kiev, and Riga. Service is available with connections to major European cities. The city train station is located at 39 Paldiski Maantee (phone: 6-446756). The Baltic Rail Pass is available for 8- and 15-day excursions throughout Estonia, Latvia, and Lithuania.

CLIMATE AND CLOTHES During the summer, the average temperature is about 55F (13C), the warmest weather is in July (when the average temperature is a balmy 61F/16C). February is the coldest month, with an average temperature of 23F (−5C). Warm clothes are advised for any season, since summer evenings can become rather chilly. With approximately 107 days per year of overcast weather, expect rain except in the coldest winter months, when snow gear is a must. Casual dress is acceptable in the capital city of Tallinn, except in the fanciest restaurants and nightclubs. The theater also requires more formal attire — a jacket and tie for men and a dress or skirt for women is the norm.

LANGUAGE Estonian is the official language; it is one of the Finno-Ugrian languages, bearing similarities to Finnish and Hungarian. The majority (60%) of the population speaks Estonian, along with some Finnish and Russian; many Estonians also understand English. About 30% of the population is Russian. Other languages often spoken are English and German.

ELECTRICITY 220 volts, AC.

MONEY The Estonian kroon is the official currency. One kroon equals 100 sents.

TIPPING It is not considered mandatory to tip at restaurants and hotels, but a small amount (the equivalent of a dollar or two) for good service always is appreciated.

BANKING/BUSINESS HOURS Offices generally are open weekdays, either from 9 AM to 5 PM or from 10 AM to 6 PM; banks are open from 9 AM to 3 PM.

HOLIDAYS *New Year's Day* (January 1), *Independence Day* (February 24), *Good Friday* (April 1), *May Day* (May 1), *Victory Day* (June 23), *Midsummer Day* (June 24), and *Boxing Day* (December 26).

LATVIA

TOURIST INFORMATION The official government tourist information office is the Tourism Division, Traffic Ministry (4 Pils Laukums, 2nd Floor, Riga; phone: 2-229945). Another agency recommended by the embassy is *Latvia Tours* (22-24 Grecinieku Iela, Riga; phone: 2-213652 or 2-220047). An

American Express Travel Service office now operates in Riga from *Latvia Tours* offices offering travel-related services, credit card replacement, travelers' check cashing, and currency exchange.

ENTRY REQUIREMENTS US citizens need a valid passport and a visa for entry into Latvia. Visas also are available upon arrival at the Riga airport, ferry terminal, and train station.

TELEPHONE The country code for Latvia is 371.

GETTING THERE/GETTING AROUND

Airlines *Lufthansa* has service between Frankfurt and Riga; *FinnAir* flies between Helsinki and Riga; and *SAS* flies from Riga to Copenhagen and Stockholm. Flights from New York's JFK Airport to Riga are provided by *Aeroflot* (via Moscow) and *Lufthansa* (via Frankfurt). The only direct flight from the US to Latvia is offered by *American Trans Air*. This twice-weekly service from New York's JFK Airport to Riga departs Wednesdays and Saturdays and returns Thursdays and Sundays, with a stopover either in Belfast or Shannon, Ireland.

Cars Automobile travel is becoming an increasingly popular mode of transportation since nearly 95% of Latvia is now open to foreign travelers. Cars can be rented with or without drivers through car rental companies in Riga. Long delays at the border make it preferable to rent cars within Latvia. When traveling outside of Riga, it is best to inquire about locations and hours of gas stations.

Trains There are daily trains from Riga to Berlin, and frequent service to Moscow, Tallinn, and Vilnius, with connections to the major European cities. The Baltic Rail Pass is a popular way to see the Baltic States (see *Estonia, above*).

CLIMATE AND CLOTHES Winters are cold, with average temperatures of 15 to 20F (−9 to −6C); warm clothes are strongly recommended. In summer, the temperature averages a moderate 64F (18C), but the weather can be extremely changeable, so layered clothing is suggested.

LANGUAGE The official language is Latvian, which is similar only to Lithuanian. Most people also speak Russian, and German is widely understood. With the country's increasing contact with the West, more and more Latvians also are learning English.

ELECTRICITY 220 volts, AC.

MONEY Latvia is gradually converting from the Latvian rublis to the lat.

TIPPING It is not considered mandatory to tip at restaurants and hotels, but a small amount (the equivalent of a dollar or two) in appreciation of good service always is accepted.

BANKING/BUSINESS HOURS Offices and banks generally are open weekdays, either from 9 AM to 5 PM or from 10 AM to 6 PM.

HOLIDAYS *New Year's Day* (January 1), *Good Friday* (April 1), *St. John's Day* (June 23–25), *National Day* (November 18), and *Boxing Day* (December 26).

LITHUANIA

TOURIST INFORMATION The former *Intourist* office, now known as the *Lithuanian Travel Agency,* is on the ground floor of the *Lietuva* hotel in Vilnius (20 Ukmerges Gatve; phone: 2-642612). A number of other agencies have opened since the demise of *Intourist.* An *American Express Travel Service* office now operates in Vilnius (2-30 Vilnius Gatve; phone: 615975; fax: 211716) offering travel-related services, credit card replacement, travelers' check cashing, and currency exchange.

ENTRY REQUIREMENTS US citizens need a valid passport and a visa to enter Lithuania.

TELEPHONE The country code for Lithuania is 370.

GETTING THERE/GETTING AROUND

Airlines *Lithuanian Airlines,* which inherited its fleet from *Aeroflot,* flies between Vilnius and Berlin, Copenhagen, Frankfurt, Kiev, London, Moscow, St. Petersburg, and Warsaw. Other airlines flying into Vilnius are *LOT, SAS, Lufthansa, Malev, Swissair, Estonian Air, and Austrian Airlines.* Flights from New York's JFK Airport to Vilnius are provided by *Aeroflot* (via Moscow) and *Lufthansa* (via Frankfurt).

Cars Automobile travel is becoming an increasingly popular mode of transportation in Lithuania. In the capital, cars can be rented either with or without a chauffeur at a number of private agencies. Typical fuel shortages mean long lines at the gasoline pumps.

Trains There is regular rail service to Moscow, most Baltic cities, and many other European destinations from Vilnius. (For information on the Baltic Rail Pass, see *Estonia,* above.)

CLIMATE AND CLOTHES Winters are cold, with average temperatures around 15 to 20F (−9 to −6C); drops down to −20F (−29C) are not uncommon. Sensible, heavy winter clothing is essential, including a warm coat, gloves, hat, scarf, and sturdy boots. Summers are moderately warm, with temperatures up to 70F (21C); still, a light sweater is suggested, and bring along an umbrella and rain gear. During the spring and fall, temperatures are erratic.

LANGUAGE Lithuanian is the official language. It is the most ancient Eastern European language, with roots in Sanskrit, and is similar to Latvian. Most

Lithuanians also speak Russian, and Polish and English are understood by some.

ELECTRICITY 220 volts, AC.

MONEY A transitional currency called talonas (coupon) was introduced in October 1992. Lithuania is striving to produce a more stable currency for the near future.

TIPPING The practice is accepted everywhere; a US dollar or two should be sufficient.

BANKING/BUSINESS HOURS Offices and banks generally are open weekdays, either from 9 AM to 5 PM or from 10 AM to 6 PM..

HOLIDAYS *New Year's Day* (January 1), *Lithuania Independence Day* (February 16), *Mothers' Day* (May 8), *All Saints' Day* (November 1), and *Boxing Day* (December 26).

Bulgaria

TOURIST INFORMATION *Balkan Holidays International,* the country's largest travel company, is currently being privatized. Its headquarters is in Sofia, the capital (5 Triaditsa Ulitsa; phone: 2-831211; fax: 2-883739), and there are branch offices in all the main hotels throughout the country. The Tourist Information and Reservations (*TIR*) agency in Sofia (22 Lovele Ulitsa; phone: 2-880139; fax: 2-803201) also provides travel information and arrangements, and makes hotel reservations. Local tourist information offices throughout the country provide maps and other materials and assistance.

ENTRY REQUIREMENTS US citizens need a current passport to enter the country; no visa is required for stays of up to 30 days. Visas may be obtained in Bulgaria at the Consular Office of the Ministry of Foreign Affairs in Sofia (2 Zhendov Ulitsa; phone: 2-71441 or 2-71431).

TELEPHONE The country code for Bulgaria is 359.

GETTING THERE/GETTING AROUND

Airlines *Jes Air,* a Bulgarian airline, operates two weekly flights (Wednesdays and Sundays) between Sofia and New York City's JFK Airport. *Balkanair* flies between major cities in Bulgaria and connects Sofia to all European capitals. *Aeroflot* has flights to Sofia from Kiev, Moscow, and St. Petersburg.

Buses The state-owned bus line, *Autotransport,* has service throughout the country. However, tours run by *Balkan Holidays International* (see above) are suggested for sightseeing; they are accompanied by multilingual guides, thus alleviating language problems.

Cars Probably the best bet for the tourist. Cars can be rented in Bulgaria's major cities through a number of agencies. Free emergency assistance is provided by road service cars that patrol the highways or can be called (phone: 146). When entering the country by car, it is necessary to have a vehicle registration card, a valid driver's license, and an insurance liability policy (known as a "Green Card"), which is available at the border. The laws against driving after drinking are strictly enforced in Bulgaria.

Trains The *BDG* (*Bulgarian State Railway*) service between Sofia and Varna on the Black Sea is frequent and efficient, but most other trains are locals and crowded. There also is service between Sofia and other major European capitals, such as Athens, Berlin, Bucharest, Budapest, Istanbul, and Moscow.

CLIMATE AND CLOTHES The Balkan Mountains (the highest range is the Rila Dagh, at more than 9,000 feet) crisscross the country and reach straight to the edge of the Black Sea and its golden beaches. Summers are dry but not oppressively hot (80s F, high 20s C); winters are cold, dry, and relatively windless with temperatures in the 30s F (around 0 degrees C). Informality is the keynote in summer dress. Jackets and ties (and warm coats) are best for fall and winter in Sofia.

LANGUAGE Bulgarian, a south-Slavic tongue, is similar to Russian and uses the Cyrillic alphabet. You can navigate the tourist circuit with English (Russian is the second language), but should consider using English-speaking guides if you wish to communicate in the countryside. German is also understood.

ELECTRICITY 220 volts, AC.

MONEY The lev (plural, leva) equals 100 stotinki. It is illegal to import or export Bulgarian currency.

TIPPING About 10% of a restaurant bill is sufficient.

BANKING/BUSINESS HOURS Generally weekdays from 9 AM to 5 PM.

HOLIDAYS *New Year's Day* (January 1), *National Liberation Day* (March 3), *Greek Orthodox Easter* (April 10), and *Cyrillic Alphabet Holiday* (May 24).

The Czech Republic and Slovakia

TOURIST INFORMATION Although no national tourist board existed at press time, travel information is easily obtained at any newsstand. Also, the now privatized *Cedok*'s blue sign with the white bird in flight signifies general travel services at some 150 locations throughout the country. The main office of this agency is in Prague (18 Na příkopě; phone: 2-212-7111). Travel services are also provided by the Prague Information Service (20 Na příkopě, Prague; phone: 2-544444), and *American Express Czech Republic*

(56 Václavské náměstí, Prague; phone: 2-229487). For general tourist information in Bratislava, contact the Ministry of Economy of the Slovak Republic (19 Mierová; phone: 7-82715; fax: 230122).

ENTRY REQUIREMENTS US citizens need only a current passport for visits of up to 30 days in either republic.

TELEPHONE The country code for both the Czech Republic and Slovakia is 42.

GETTING THERE/GETTING AROUND

Airlines *Czechoslovakia Airline (CSA)* flies the New York–Prague route nonstop in summer and from Montreal year-round. *Delta* flies from New York to Prague via Frankfurt or Vienna, and *KLM* flies from Los Angeles to Prague through Amsterdam. Prague is the hub from which domestic flights on *CSA* radiate to 13 airports in the Czech and Slovak Republics, including Brno, Bratislava, Košice, Ostrava, Piešťany (for spas), and Poprad in the Tatras (for skiing and mountaineering). *Aeroflot* flies from Prague to Kiev, Moscow, and St. Petersburg.

Buses Next to flying, express buses to Germany, Austria, Poland, Yugoslavia, and Hungary, as well as domestic service aboard *Ceskoslovenské Státní Dráhy (CSD)* coaches, are probably the fastest ways of traveling to and from the rest of Europe and throughout the Czech and Slovak Republics.

Cars Rentals are available from *Pragocar,* with outlets in the major cities. The Yellow Angels in four-wheel-drive vehicles of the *Ustredni Automotoklub* provide emergency service for motorists. Gas coupons are sold at frontier crossings and at the automobile club office in Prague (29 Opletalova; phone: 2-223544).

Trains There's frequent service aboard *CSD* trains, and various European express trains stop at Prague, Bratislava, and Brno.

CLIMATE AND CLOTHES The Czech and Slovak Republics are really three contiguous areas — Bohemia, Moravia, and Slovakia — snaking across Central Europe, and the climate is about the same in all three. Temperatures average around 70F (21C) in summer and the low 20s F (a little below 0 degrees C) in winter, although mountains are chillier in both seasons. Prague has cold, damp winters (average temperature is 30F/−1C) and pleasantly warm summers (70F/21C). Dress is casual but conservative. Evenings at luxury resorts such as *Karlovy Vary* (*Carlsbad*) and *Mariánské Lázně* (*Marienbad*) call for reasonably dressy clothes.

LANGUAGE Czech is spoken by those living in the Czech Republic (a combination of the Bohemian and Moravian regions), who make up about two-thirds of the population; Slovak is the native language of the Slovak Republic. Both languages are Slavic and very similar. Those engaged in tourism speak English, and Russian is widely understood.

ELECTRICITY 220 volts, AC.

MONEY The Czech and Slovak Republics each has its own currency, both called koruna (kčs); it is necessary to use the appropriate currency for each republic.

TIPPING Restaurant bills don't include service charges, and at least 10% should be added; taxi drivers also expect 10% tips; 5 to 10 korunas should be given to porters and doormen.

BANKING/BUSINESS HOURS Banks generally are open weekdays from 8 AM to 4 PM; some are open until 6 PM twice a week and until noon once a week. Most other businesses are open weekdays from 8 AM to 4 PM.

HOLIDAYS *New Year's Day* (January 1), *Easter Monday* (April 4), *Labor Day* (May 1, Slovak Republic only), *Anniversary of WW II Liberation* (May 8), *National Holiday* (July 5–6, Czech Republic; July 5, Slovak Republic), *Day of National Uprising of World War II* (August 29, Slovak Republic only), *Proclamation of Czechoslovak Republic* (October 28), and *Boxing Day* (December 26).

Hungary

TOURIST INFORMATION Branches of *IBUSZ,* the country's now privatized travel company, are found in all major cities. The central office is in Budapest (V, 10 Ferenciektére, Budapest; phone: 1-142-3140). The government-run Budapest Tourist Office (V, 5 Roosevelt tér; phone: 1-117-3555) provides information about Budapest and the rest of the country. *IBUSZ* also has a 24-hour accommodations service in Budapest (3 Petőfi tér; phone: 1-118-5707). Tourist offices in smaller cities and towns are called *Idegenforgalmi Hivatal.* Travel services also are available through *American Express Hungary* (10 Deak Ferenc ut, Budapest; phone: 1-266-8680).

ENTRY REQUIREMENTS No visa is necessary for US citizens holding a valid passport for stays of up to 90 days. For extensions beyond 90 days, it is necessary to apply to a local police station in Hungary.

TELEPHONE The country code for Hungary is 36.

GETTING THERE/GETTING AROUND

Airlines *MALÉV,* the Hungarian national airline, flies nonstop from New York to Budapest. Other flights to Budapest are offered from New York by *KLM,* via Amsterdam; *Lufthansa,* via Munich and Düsseldorf; *SAS,* via Copenhagen; *British Airways,* via London; *Air France,* via Paris (with a change of airport); and *Finnair,* via Helsinki. *MALÉV* has service between Ferihegy Airport, Budapest, and 40 major cities in Europe and the Middle East.

Cars International firms and *IBUSZ* rent European models. Some words of caution: The law against driving while drinking is strictly enforced; stiff penalties and fines are incurred if you are found driving with *any* alcohol in your blood.

Trains Budapest is a transfer point for some 25 international expresses, including the *Nord Orient Express* and the *Wiener Walzer*. Nationally, the *MAV* (*Magyar Allamvasutak*) diesel or electric express trains run often and are comfortable. Hungary is a member of the *Eurail* network. From the US, *Eurail* information for Hungary can be obtained through *French Rail* or *German Rail*.

CLIMATE AND CLOTHES Hungary is a small — 35,919 square-mile — nation bisected by the Danube River. Lake Balaton to the west is Europe's second-largest lake and a good place to cool off during the typically hot summers, with temperatures averaging 86F (30C). Winters are cold (about 30F, −1C) and dry. In Budapest, the wooded Buda Hills protect the city against extremes of heat and cold, but summers can be hot and humid. In summer, the temperatures can be extremely variable, but average about 72F (22C); in winter it is about 34F (1C). Dress in Hungary tends to be more informal than in the US. Men usually wear open-neck shirts, except in theaters and fine restaurants, where ties and dark suits are the norm.

LANGUAGE Hungarian, a Finno-Ugrian tongue, is the native language of 95% of the population. German is the second language (a heritage of the Austro-Hungarian Empire) but English is becoming increasingly common.

ELECTRICITY 220 volts, AC.

MONEY The forint (ft) equals 100 fillér.

TIPPING Add 15% to restaurant bills, taxi fares, and hotel service; 200 forints is the usual tip for strolling musicians in restaurants if you request them to play.

BANKING/BUSINESS HOURS Banks and many offices are open weekdays from 8 or 9 AM to 2 or 4 PM. Currency exchange facilities outside the banks are numerous.

HOLIDAYS *New Year's Day* (January 1), *Anniversary of the 1848 Revolution* (March 15), *Easter Monday* (April 4), *Labor Day* (May 1), *St. Stephen's Day* (August 20), *1956 Revolution Day* (October 23), and *Boxing Day* (December 26).

Poland

TOURIST INFORMATION *Informacja Turystyczna (IT)* centers are everywhere: in hotels; at the frontier; along highways; and at airports, railway stations, and seaports. The main *IT* center is in Warsaw (1-13 Plac Zamkowy;

phone: 22-310464). *Orbis Travel* in Warsaw (142 Ulica Marszalkowska; phone: 22-278031) offers a variety of travel services, as does *American Express Travel Service* (11 Ulica Krakowskie Przedmieście; phone: 2-635-2002). The main *IT* center in Cracow is at 8 Wsystkich Swietych (phone: 12-227127). Another major source of information in Cracow is the *Wawel Travel Agency* (9 Rynek Podgorski; phone: 12-562012).

ENTRY REQUIREMENTS A valid passport is required for US citizens; no visa is necessary for stays of up to 90 days.

TELEPHONE The country code for Poland is 48.

GETTING THERE/GETTING AROUND

Airlines *LOT,* the Polish national airline, flies nonstop from Chicago and New York to Warsaw. *LOT* also offers charter flights to Poland from Los Angeles. *Delta* offers nonstop service from New York to Warsaw and direct flights via Frankfurt. Within Europe, *LOT* connects with most countries; within Poland, *LOT*'s reasonably priced flights connect Warsaw with 10 cities and has flights from Cracow and Katowice to Gdańsk, Poznań, and Szczecin.

Cars Both self-drive and chauffeured Fiats and Fords are available for rent from *Orbis* (24 Ulica Nowogrodzka, Warsaw; phone: 22-210271). *PZM* (Polish Automobile and Motorcycle Association; 63 Aleje Jerozolimskie, Warsaw 00697; phone: 2-628-6251) is the organization to contact for reservations, emergency assistance, maps, guidebooks, and information on auto routes in Poland.

Ferries *Polish Baltic Lines* (*PZB*) provides year-round connections to Denmark, Sweden, and Finland, and summer service to and from Germany.

Trains Polish train fares are relatively inexpensive by most Western European standards. The *Polskie Koleje Panstwowe* or *PKP*'s PolRailPass for 8, 15, 21, or 30 days of unlimited rail travel is a bargain. The modern expresses, which provide frequent intercity service, are the best-equipped trains.

CLIMATE AND CLOTHES Autumn, normally crisp and sunny, is a long, lovely season, especially in the forests and hills that cover about a third of the country. Snow covers the Carpathian Mountains by mid-December and lasts until April. Winter temperatures average around 26F (-3C) with lows about -4F (-20C); summers are warm and dry, with an average temperature of 68F (20C). Rainwear is essential during most of the year, especially in Warsaw. Blue jeans are okay for daytime touring and shopping, but evenings at the theater and fine restaurants call for dresses and jackets and ties.

LANGUAGE Polish, Slavic in origin, is the official language, but German and some English also are spoken; Russian and Ukrainian are widely understood.

ELECTRICITY 220 volts, AC.

MONEY The złoty (zl) is made up of 100 groszy. When entering and leaving Poland, you must declare how much currency (of any country) you have with you; no import or export of Polish currency is allowed. Unused złotys must be left at the border — there are exchange counters at most transportation centers.

TIPPING The usual tip is 10% of hotel, restaurant, hairdresser, and taxi bills. Service charges are not included in most bills.

BANKING/BUSINESS HOURS Banks generally are open weekdays from 8 AM to 4 PM. Most other businesses keep the same hours.

HOLIDAYS *New Year's Day* (January 1), *Easter Monday* (April 4), *May Day* (May 1), *Constitution Day* (May 3), *Corpus Christi* (June 2), *Feast of the Assumption* (August 15), *All Souls' Day* (November 1), *Independence Day* (November 11).

Romania

TOURIST INFORMATION *Carpaţi,* the national tourist office, is currently being privatized. It covers all phases of travel and is headquartered in Bucharest (7 Calea General Magheru; phone: 1-614-5160). In towns where there is no *Carpaţi* office, the Oficiul Judetean de Turism (County Tourist Office) provide travel assistance. In addition, numerous private travel agencies have opened in Romania during the past 2 years. An *American Express Travel Service* office operates from the *Carpaţi-Bucureşti* tourist office (phone: 1-612-2596), offering travel-related services, credit card replacement, travelers' check cashing, and currency exchange.

ENTRY REQUIREMENTS US citizens need a valid passport and a visa to enter Romania. Tourist visas, good for a single-entry visit of up to 6 months, are available at any Romanian diplomatic office. They also can be obtained upon arrival at any border entry point or at Otoponi Airport in Bucharest.

TELEPHONE The country code for Romania is 40.

GETTING THERE/GETTING AROUND

Airlines *Tarom, Romanian Air Transport,* has direct flights from New York and Chicago to Bucharest via Vienna and Luxembourg (note, however, that this airline is not recommended due to poor service). Several major airlines have connecting flights from other European cities. *Tarom* also offers one or more flights a day between Bucharest and 14 Romanian destinations.

Cars *Carpaţi* offices in the major cities offer car rentals (currently limited to the nationally produced Dacia 1300 and 2000 and the Oltcit-Club), accommodations, itineraries, and road assistance.

Cruises The Danube (Dunărea) River enters the Black Sea from southern Romania, forming a natural boundary between Romania and Yugoslavia (Serbia) and Bulgaria. River cruises from Vienna to the Black Sea and the Danube Delta, and shorter trips between Romanian towns, are run by *NAVROM* (contact local tourist offices in Romania for information).

Trains *Căile Ferate Române* (*CFR;* the *Romanian Railway Company*), with diesel and electrically equipped trains, accepts *Interail,* but not *Eurail,* passes. International express trains connect Romania with both Eastern and Western European countries.

CLIMATE AND CLOTHES The mode of dress reflects the atmosphere here: It's relaxed and casual. Black Sea bathing resorts are informal, in keeping with the summer heat (daytime temperatures average around 82F/28C in July and August). Carpathian ski resorts, usually blanketed in 3 feet of snow during the high season (December to March), have temperatures in the mid- to upper 30s F (around 0 degrees C). Overall, the four seasons are clearly defined and the climate is similar to New York City's.

LANGUAGE Romanian, a Romance language derived directly from Latin, shows some Slavic influences. French, the second language until after World War II, is not spoken much now but still is understood because of similarities to Romanian; English is becoming more common.

ELECTRICITY 220 volts, AC.

MONEY The leu (plural lei) equals 100 bani. It still is illegal to enter or leave the country with Romanian currency.

TIPPING Though not expected, small tips (the equivalent of a dollar or two) are accepted for special services.

BANKING/BUSINESS HOURS Banks are open weekdays from 8:30 or 9 AM to 4:30 or 5 PM. Most other businesses are open weekdays from 8 AM to 4:30 PM.

HOLIDAYS *New Year's* (January 1 and 2), Greek Orthodox *Easter* (April 18), and *National Day* (December 1).

Russia

TOURIST INFORMATION Former *Intourist* offices now operate under new names — in Moscow it is known as *Intourservice* (4 Belinskovo Ulitsa; phone: 095-202-9975 or 095-203-8943; fax: 095-200-1243). In St. Petersburg, contact the *St. Petersburg Tourist Company* (11 Isaakievskaya Ploshchad; phone: 812-315-5129 for information; 812-272-7887 for guides; fax: 812-312-0996). Travel assistance (including financial services and sightseeing tours and information) also is available at the *American Express Travel Service* offices (21A Sadovaya-Kudrinskaya Ulitsa, Moscow; phone: 095-

254-4495) and (*Grand Hotel Europe,* 1-7 Mikhailovskaya Ulitsa, St. Petersburg; phone: 812-315-7487).

ENTRY REQUIREMENTS US citizens need a valid passport and a visa to enter Russia. At present there are three kinds of visas: tourist, ordinary (for business or family visits), and transit. Visa applications can be filed through a travel agent or directly with a consular office in the US; allow a minimum of 14 days before your departure. An itinerary that describes the time and duration of all stops within the country, travel arrangements, and hotel reservations must be submitted along with a $20 fee (there is an additional $10 fee for processing within a week; the cost is $50 for a 24-hour turnaround); processing fees vary between consular offices.

TELEPHONE The country code for Russia is 7.

GETTING THERE/GETTING AROUND Travel has become a bit more flexible in recent years with many restrictions lifted within Russia. Still, visitors are expected to stick to predetermined itineraries.

Airlines *Aeroflot* flies direct (with no change of plane) between Moscow and Anchorage, Chicago, Montreal, New York, San Francisco and Washington, DC; direct flights to St. Petersburg fly from New York and San Francisco. Nonstop flights from most major cities in Europe to Moscow and St. Petersburg are also available. *Finnair* flies to Moscow and St. Petersburg from New York via Helsinki. In addition, many major foreign carriers (*Air Canada, Air France, Austrian Airlines, KLM, Sabena, Swissair, SAS*) offer connecting flights to Russia.

Cars Russia is becoming more receptive to tourism by car. Today's travelers can drive on more than 12,000 miles of main and secondary roads, and in major cities such as Moscow, cars can be rented through *Avis, Auto Europe, Hertz,* or *Intourservice* (in Moscow). You also can drive a rental car or your own automobile into Russia at certain border points. Driving routes still must be pre-arranged, and a specific itinerary submitted with your visa application. *Intourservice* can provide the necessary papers for car touring and insurance. One word to the wise motorist: Obey Russian rules of the road — they're strictly enforced.

Trains Russian trains connect points across the country and across Europe. Overall, the trains aren't terribly fast, but most are comfortable. Passage is arranged through *Intourservice* (in Moscow), the *St. Petersburg Tourist Company* (in St. Petersburg), or through US agents handling Russian travel. Buy your ticket in advance in order to avoid the inevitable difficulties at the station. Two classes of train travel are available: soft class, which consists of fully upholstered seats; and the more rugged hard class, which provides firm leather or plastic seating. Certain daytime express trains are only hard class. On most trains, tea is served by the conductors.

CLIMATE AND CLOTHES The European portion of Russia is warm in summer and very, very cold in winter. In Moscow, summers rarely get above the 70s F (20s C). Moscow winters are dry, crisp, and often sunny; the average winter temperature is 20F (−7C), but it's often colder. St. Petersburg averages 16 to 19F (−9 to −7C) during January and in the mid-60s F (16 to 18C) during July, with about 6 to 13 days of precipitation per month. Boots, warm socks, heavy coats, and lined gloves are essential in winter. In warmer weather, a raincoat with a removable lining or a sweater and raincoat will suffice. You are expected to check your coat when entering any public building or restaurant. All garments are hung on hooks, so it is a good idea to sew a chain or heavy loop into your coat collar to prevent damage — and dark looks from the cloakroom attendant. Visitors need not dress up in Moscow or St. Petersburg, but on the other hand, shorts are in poor taste and blue jeans are inappropriate for evenings out. If you're part of a tour group, bring something festive to wear to the (inevitable) farewell gala.

LANGUAGE Russian, an East Slavic language, is the official language. Tourism industry personnel and workers in the hotel and restaurant industries speak English.

ELECTRICITY 220 volts, AC.

MONEY One ruble (R or Rub) is made up of 100 kopecks.

TIPPING Tipping is not officially sanctioned, though tips are not refused.

BANKING/BUSINESS HOURS There are banking branches for currency exchange at major hotels, open weekdays from 9 AM to 5 PM. In Moscow, there's a foreign exchange bank on Tverskaya Ulitsa (formerly Gorky Ulitsa); it is open from 8:45 AM to noon, and from 12:50 to 7:50 PM. Most other businesses are open weekdays from 9 AM to 5 or 6 PM.

HOLIDAYS *New Year's Day* (January 1), Russian Orthodox *Christmas* (January 7), *Soviet Army Day* (February 23), *International Women's Day* (March 8), *Easter, Day of Spring and Labor* (May 1), *Victory Day* (May 9), and *Independence Day* (June 12), *Anniversary of the 1917 Bolshevik Revolution* (November 7).

Ukraine

TOURIST INFORMATION The now privatized *Intourist* in Kiev (12 Hospitalna Vulytsia; phone: 044-225-3051; fax: 044-224-8987) handles virtually all aspects of travel. Another travel office in Kiev is *Ukar-tour* (36 Yaroslaviv Val; phone: 044-212-5570; fax 044-212-4524). Travelers needing information in Odessa should contact *Londonskaya* travel office (Primorskiy Bulvar; phone: 0482-228468).

ENTRY REQUIREMENTS US citizens need a valid passport and a visa to enter Ukraine. A 1-month single-entry visa costs $30; for $60 it can be prepared within 1 week; same-day processing costs $100. Hotel confirmation is required for visa processing, as is a letter from a travel agency booking the reservations.

TELEPHONE The country code for Ukraine is 7.

GETTING THERE/GETTING AROUND

Airlines *Air Ukraine* flies to Kiev from New York's JFK Airport three times weekly, twice weekly from Chicago, and once a week from Washington, DC. Nonstop service is also available to most major European cities, as well as throughout Ukraine.

Cars Cars may be rented through *Intourist,* in advance through a travel agent that does business in Ukraine, or through local car rental firms in Kiev and Odessa.

Trains There is frequent train service from Kiev to Moscow, Odessa, Karkov, Lvov, and Rostov-on-Don, as well as Athens, Bratislava, Bucharest, Budapest, Istanbul, Rome, Sofia, Vienna, and Zagreb.

CLIMATE AND CLOTHES Winters in Ukraine are relatively windless, but snowy and very cold, with average temperatures ranging from $-15F$ to 0 degrees F (-26 to $-17C$); while summers are warm, with temperatures reaching 80F to 85F (26 to 29C). A warm coat for winter is suggested; summer dress is informal.

LANGUAGE Ukrainian is the official language; it uses a Cyrillic alphabet and is similar to Polish and Russian. Russian is more often spoken in Odessa, and is commonly spoken elsewhere as well. People associated with tourism speak some English.

ELECTRICITY 220 volts, AC.

MONEY The former Soviet Union's common currency, the ruble, is no longer considered legal tender in Ukraine and has been temporarily replaced by the Ukrainian "kupon" (coupon). At press time, Ukraine was planning to introduce its own national currency called the "hryvnia," to replace the kupon.

TIPPING Tipping is not customary, but a small amount (a dollar or two) will be not be refused.

BANKING/BUSINESS HOURS Banks are open weekdays from 10 AM to 6 PM.

HOLIDAYS *New Year's Day* (January 1), Ukrainian Orthodox *Christmas* (January 7), *Liberation Day* (May 9), and *Kiev City Day* (July 1).

The Cities

Bratislava

On January 1, 1993, throngs of citizens gathered in the main square of Bratislava, the newly designated capital of the Slovak Republic, to celebrate the birth of their new nation. It was for the most part a joyous moment for a people who have long felt politically disenfranchised and economically repressed by what they saw as a Prago-centric government. This long-standing dissatisfaction prompted Slovak citizens, in part, to give 40% of their vote to Vladimír Mečiar's Movement for a Democratic Slovakia in the June 1992 federal elections. A dynamic and forceful figure, Mečiar promised to put the brakes on the economic reforms which threatened the very existence of the large, inefficiently run industrial plants that employ the bulk of Slovakia's working population.

Declaring independence may seem extreme, but consider that Slovakia has had little or no control over its own destiny for close to a millennium. Magyars invaded in the 10th century, and Slovakia remained under Hungary's thumb until May 1918, when the Pittsburgh Declaration created the Czechoslovak Republic. Twenty years later, Slovakia was granted a false autonomy by the Munich Pact, which reorganized the republic into two independent states, but somehow allowed Prague to remove Father Jozef Tiso as Slovakian premier a year later. In a shortsighted attempt to stay in power, Tiso joined forces with Germany during World War II. Though many Slovaks resisted, they found it impossible to remove Tiso while German troops remained on their soil. When the smoke cleared, Slovakia was returned to its pre–Munich Pact provincial status.

The 45 years of Communist policy that followed the end of World War II were less than kind to Slovakia, as Prague continually punished the Slovak territory for its Catholic — and anti-Communist — sympathies. It wasn't until after the Soviet invasion in 1968 that Slovakia was granted even regional autonomy, an empty victory considering the 2 decades of economic and intellectual oppression that followed.

The "velvet revolution," the relatively peaceful toppling of the Communist leadership in November 1989, brought new hope to a republic that felt itself the inferior partner in a 71-year marriage. The Hyphen War, in which the Slovaks lobbied hard for the introduction of a hyphen into the national moniker (Czecho-Slovakia), was representative of the Slovaks' struggle for autonomy.

Yet though independence has brought Slovak music, art, and dance to the cultural forefront, the population of 440,000 is more preoccupied with rising prices, high insurance premiums, social security taxes, and the still rampant unemployment. Today's grim realities seem to make Bratislavans nostalgic for the more distant past, when things weren't all *that* bad. Between 1541 and 1784, Bratislava — then called Pozsony — served as

BRATISLAVA

Points of Interest

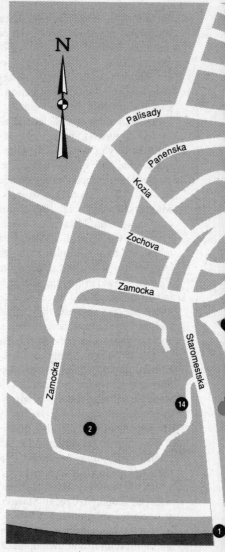

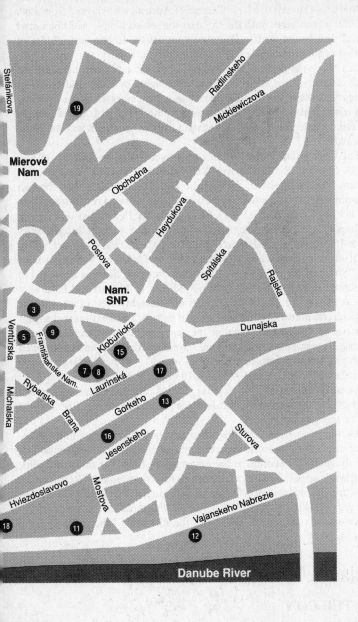

Stefánikova

Radlinskeho

Mickiewiczova

19

Mierové
Nam

Obchodna

Heydukova

Postova

Spitálska

Rajska

Nam.
SNP

3

Dunajska

Venturska

5

9

Klobučnicka

15

Františkanske Nam.

7 8

17

Rybarska

Laurinská

Michalska

Brana

Gorkeho

13

16

Jesenskeho

Sturova

Hviezdoslavovo

Mostova

Vajanskeho Nabrezie

18

11

12

Danube River

Hungary's capital, and 11 Hungarian kings and 7 queens were crowned in St. Martin's Cathedral. Maria Theresa of Austria, who reigned from 1740 to 1780, was so taken with the city that she settled here — and convinced several well-heeled Austro-Hungarian nobles to do the same. Most of Bratislava's baroque palaces date from this era.

In 1991 — the 2,000th anniversary of the first settlement here and the 700th anniversary of the granting of town rights by King Andrew III of Hungary — the city's illustrious past was commemorated by the opening, with much fanfare, of the "Coronation Route." The path traces roughly the same route traveled by Hungarian royalty on their way to being crowned.

The Coronation Route — and nearly every other gem in this city — can be found in the Old Town. While greater Bratislava features drab, Eastern-bloc architecture, the historic Old Town houses 9th- through 19th-century structures such as the 10th-century Bratislava Castle, where in 1968 the Constitutional Act of Czechoslovak Federation was signed; Michael's Gate, the sole remainder of the four gates that protected the city in the 15th century; the Palace of the Hungarian Royal Chamber, where the Hungarian Parliament met from 1802 to 1848; and Ventúrska ulica (the "Street of Music"), where Bratislava's musical heritage is evoked in the Renaissance palaces that once played host to Mozart and Liszt.

It is in the Old Town that visitors are brought face-to-face with the multicultural influences that have made it easy for Bratislavans to discount their ties to Prague. Throughout the centuries, Hungarians (Magyars), Saxons, Romanians, and Ukrainians have all settled here and contributed something to the richness of the city. Hungary — by far the largest single influence on Slovak culture — is only 10 miles (16 km) due south, and the people of Bratislava claim to have far more in common with the Viennese, 40 miles (64 km) to the west, than with the people of Prague, 250 miles (400 km) to the northwest.

Bratislava does not have the urban elegance of Prague, with its abundance of beautiful palaces, churches, and 16th-century street scenes. Despite the modern buildings in the newer parts of the city and its suburbs, Bratislava's appeal is more rural. With its lovely examples of Renaissance, baroque, Gothic, and neo-Gothic architecture, its charming tile-roofed cottages, well-kept garden plots, and lush vineyards that slope down the banks of the river, it can still claim the nickname "the Beauty of the Danube."

Bratislava At-a-Glance

SEEING THE CITY

Head for the Danube and begin with coffee and pastries in the futuristic *Bystriča* restaurant (1 Dunaj; phone: 51345), which towers above the modern Most SNP (Bridge of the Slovak National Uprising). The vista will unfold and reveal the layout of Bratislava, which is built into a countryside dotted with small houses and family garden plots.

For a more regal perspective, the tower of Bratislava Castle on the opposite side of the Danube affords a spectacular view across the river and into Austria and Hungary.

SPECIAL PLACES

Probably the best tool for traversing the city is a good, updated map, available at the airport and the city's main train station, bus terminal, and bookstores. In addition, *Cedok* offers a 4-hour bus tour, and a 2-hour walking tour of the city (see *Sources and Resources*). A few Slovak words that may help with your navigations: "námestie" and "nábrežie" are the words for square or place; "ulica" means street; and "trieda" is the word for avenue.

STARÉ MESTO (THE OLD TOWN)

If you have the chance for only one close encounter with Bratislava, make it in the Old Town. Most of the sights of interest in the city can be found in this area on the banks of the Danube. Flanked by Bratislava Castle on the west, the Old Town stretches roughly to the south and east.

BRATISLAVSKÝ HRAD (BRATISLAVA CASTLE) Actually situated on a hill above the Old Town, this towering fortress on the southernmost spur of the Little Carpathian Range is the most visible and most frequented tourist attraction in the city. Though the museum inside is of marginal interest (unless you're a Slovak nationalist), the view from the castle's tower is astounding. Remains of the Moravian civilization from the 9th century, and of 10th- to 12th-century buildings are preserved near the castle's eastern wall. The castle served as the seat of Hungarian royalty until it was gutted by fire in 1811. It has been reconstructed several times (most recently in 1968). The *Hradná Vináren* (Castle Wine Cellar) is a pleasant place for lunch (see *Eating Out*). The best way to enter the castle is through the reconstructed Gothic Sigmund's Gate. Open 9 AM to 5 PM Tuesdays through Sundays. Admission charge. Just west of the city center (phone: 311444 or 314508).

MICHALSKÁ BRÁNA (MICHAEL'S GATE) Enter the Old Town through this portal, the only remaining gate of the four that once protected the city. The view from its 15th-century tower is wonderful, and a collection of antique weaponry is housed inside. The tower and gate are the best-preserved portion of the Old Bratislava fortifications. On top of the tower's onion dome is a statue of Michael the Dragonslayer. Extending out from Michael's Gate is Michalská ulica (Michael's Street), where some of Bratislava's most beautiful buildings can be found.

PRIMACIANSKÝ PALÁC (PALACE OF THE HUNGARIAN ROYAL CHAMBER) Built in 1756, this palace was the meeting place of the Hungarian Parliament from

1802 to 1848. It currently serves as the university library. Serfdom in Hungary was officially abolished here in 1848. Open 9 AM to 5 PM Tuesdays through Sundays. Admission charge. 1 Michalská ulica.

MIRBACHOV PALÁC (MIRBACH PALACE) This renovated historical palace houses a branch of the *Galéria Mesta Bratislavy* (Bratislava Gallery). There are works of 17th- to 19th-century European art and 20th-century Slovak art on the second floor and, occasionally, international exhibits on the ground floor. Of special interest is the original stucco decoration of the palace ceilings, the richly decorated main staircases, and the original 18th-century decor in the first-floor exhibition rooms. The palace's gallery is the site of concerts held every Sunday at 10:30 AM. Open Tuesdays through Fridays 10 AM to 6 PM, Saturdays and Sundays until 5 PM. Admission charge. 11 Františkánské námestie (phone: 331556).

KLARISKÁ KAPLE (CHAPEL OF THE SISTERS OF ST. CLAIR) Built in the 14th century for the nuns of the Clarissine Order, this church is one of the oldest Gothic buildings in Bratislava. It features a single, elegant spire and a pentagonal tower supported by buttresses. Klariská ulica.

VENTÚRSKA ULICA Known as the "Street of Music," this avenue, lined with Renaissance buildings, is one of Bratislava's most picturesque. In the 18th century the palaces here were alive with the music of Liszt, Mozart, and many others.

MESTSKÉ MÚZEUM Set in the Old Town Hall, this museum contains exhibits (unfortunately none identified in English) dating from 5,000 years ago through the 20th century. All traces of the Soviet period have been purged from the collection. The real gem on display is the midget-size piano of the child prodigy Mozart. Unfortunately, the keyboard is kept covered, so the instrument looks like a small table. Perhaps the most beautiful of the exhibits is the 18th-century furniture and glassware collection from the reign of the Hungarian Hapsburg dynasty. Don't ignore the building itself, a striking bit of period architecture with arched arcades and courtyards teeming with flowers and statues. Apony Palace, home of the *Expozícia Vinohradnícko-Vinárska* (Slovakian Museum of Wine Production) is in the courtyard. Open 10 AM to 5 PM; closed Mondays. Admission charge. 1 Primaciálné námestie (phone: 333-40116).

PRIMACIONÁLNÍ PALÁC (PRIMATIAL PALACE) Just outside the Old Town Hall courtyard (go out through the east gate) is Primaciálné námestie, site of this palace and its famous Hall of Mirrors. Napoleon and the Austrian Emperor Franz I signed the Peace of Pressbourg here after the Battle of Austerlitz in 1805. There is a gallery on the second floor, adorned with rare English tapestries from the 17th century and other examples of 17th-, 18th-, and 19th-century European art. Try to visit on Saturday, when the palace is crowded with couples exchanging wedding vows — visitors are welcome to join the party. Primaciálné námestie.

FRANTIŠKÁNSKÉ KOSTOL (FRANCISCAN CHURCH) This Gothic Franciscan church, built at the end of the 13th century, is one of Bratislava's most historic buildings. The Franciscans played a prominent role in the coronation of royalty in Bratislava from the 16th to 19th centuries; they were responsible for raising certain noblemen to the Order of Knights of the Golden Spur. The church has a 2-story chapel and a crypt. Open Saturdays only. Františkánské námestie.

DOM SV. MARTINA (ST. MARTIN'S CATHEDRAL) This Gothic structure, built in the 14th and 15th centuries, was the coronation church of Hungarian kings, symbolized by the crown that tops the 1,280-foot (384-meter) church tower. The cathedral was erected on the site of the Romanesque Savior's Church and consists of three naves, a presbytery (housing members of the clergy), three Gothic chapels, a late Gothic entrance hall, and the baroque Chapel of St. John the Almoner. Arguably the most beautiful of Bratislava's churches, it features a poignant, 18th-century sculpture of St. Martin on horseback, tearing his coat in half to share it with a beggar. Dobšinského námestie.

CORONATION ROUTE At just over a mile long, this pedestrian zone in Bratislava's historical district is a reminder that, from 1536 until early in this century, this city was Hungary's capital. The regal road was opened in 1991 during the celebration of two important events — the 700th anniversary of the granting of town rights to Bratislava by King Andrew III of Hungary, and the second millennium of uninterrupted occupation of the land on which the city is built.

THE DANUBE SHORE

A cruise on the not-so-blue Danube is one of the most relaxing and interesting ways to see Bratislava. Ferries depart several times a day during warm weather from the Danubis port in the city center. Hydrofoil trips to Budapest, Komárno, and Vienna are also available during the spring and summer. Since space is limited, book in advance through *Blue Danube Travel* (2 Fajnorovo nábrežie; phone: 59501; fax: 333905). The following are the noteworthy sites along the river's shore.

SLOVENSKÁ NARODNÁ GALÉRIA (SLOVAK NATIONAL GALLERY) Located near the waterfront, this is Bratislava's major art collection. It includes an excellent Gothic section and is housed in an ultramodern building that incorporates an 18th-century palace into its design. Open 10 AM to 5 PM; closed Mondays. 2 Rázusovo nábrežie (phone: 332081/2).

DEVÍN HRAD (DEVIN CASTLE) This strategic border fortification of the Moravian Empire stands high on a promontory where the Moravia River meets the Danube, just across from the Austrian border. There has been a settlement here since Neolithic times. The Celts used the site as a military stronghold, and the Romans later established a military post here. In 1809, Napoleon's troops reduced the castle to ruins; they are now open to the public daily.

Some parts of the castle have been reconstructed. About 6 miles (10 km) west of the city.

SLOVENSKÁ NARODNÁ MÚZEUM (SLOVAK NATIONAL MUSEUM) Built in 1928, the museum houses exhibits of anthropology, archaeology, natural history, and Slovakian geology. Located across from the hydrofoil and ferry terminal on the Danube at 2 Vajanského nábrežie (phone: 336511).

> | **EXTRA SPECIAL** | Year-round, the Sunday *Philharmonic* concerts held at the concert hall in Bratislava
>
> Castle are a melodious way to wind up the weekend. Since these musical events are very popular, book with *BIS* (*Bratislavská Informačňa Služba*, or Bratislava Information Service) or *Cedok* (see below for information on both) before you arrive, or with your hotel's information desk as soon as you check in.

Sources and Resources

TOURIST INFORMATION

For general information, maps, brochures, and details about group tours and bookings, contact the now privatized *Cedok* travel agency (5-9 Jesenského ulica; phone: 499142; fax: 499591), open weekdays 8 AM to 4 PM, Saturdays 8 AM to 1 PM. The staff here can be either surly, or cheerful and eminently helpful. Information is also available at *Cedok*'s New York office, 10 E. 40th St., New York, NY 10016 (phone: 212-689-9720).

General information about Bratislava is the domain of *BIS* (Bratislava Information Service; 18 Pánská; phone: 333715 or 334370), which also will arrange accommodations in hotels, pensions, and private homes as well as provide guides and translation services. The service desk at your hotel also may be helpful in booking tours, obtaining theater tickets, and making restaurant reservations.

Most hotels have currency exchanges. Branches of Všeobecná Uverová Banka at 15 SNP námestie will exchange Czech for Slovak crowns. Bank hours are weekdays from 7:30 to 11:30 AM and noon to 5:30 PM. For emergencies there is a 24-hour electronic exchange machine at the north end of Michalská ulica.

TELEPHONE The country code for the Slovak Republic is 42; the city code for Bratislava is 7.

GETTING AROUND

AIRPORT Most major Czech, Slovak, and Eastern European cities are served from Bratislava's Ivanka Airport, about 5 miles (8 km) northeast of the city (phone: 220036). The airport is small and quaint — after disembarking, passengers must negotiate a long staircase before reaching passport control. There is an airport shuttle operated by *CSA,* originating from its offices on Sturová ulica; service is every 2 hours. Bus No. 24 connects Ivanka Airport with the rail station.

BUS/TROLLEY Tickets are available throughout the city in vending machines, at stations, and at most newspaper kiosks. There is a 24-hour tourist pass available at the DPHMB Transportation Office (Hodžovo námestie).

CAR RENTAL American and Czech automobiles may be rented through *Hertz* at the *Forum* hotel (phone: 348155). *Hertz* also has an office at the airport (phone: 291482), as does *Europcar* (phone: 220285). Prices are high: A *Hertz* economy-size car (Opel or Renault Clio) rents for roughly $400 per week with unlimited mileage; a mid-size car (Opel Vectra) rents for about $515 per week with unlimited mileage. Renting through *Pragocar* is generally less expensive (14 Hviezdoslavovo námestie; phone: 333233).

TAXI Cabs are not hard to find in Bratislava, and can be hailed in the street or booked by your hotel service desk. Officially, payment is in korun, but dollars are also welcome. The fares are reasonable.

TRAIN The main railroad station is Hlavná Stanica (1 Dimitrovo námestie; phone: 46945 for information, 46701 for tickets).

LOCAL SERVICES

The desks at most large hotels are the best places to inquire about special services. The *Forum* and the *Danube* hotels provide dry cleaning and some business services (see *Checking In*). Hotel concierges can prove useful as translators.

MEDICAL EMERGENCY The number to call for an ambulance is 155; the police emergency number is 158. English is not always spoken; it's best to ask the service desk at any major hotel to make the call for you. Emergency medical aid is provided at the clinics at 6 Pionierska ulica (phone: 44444), 5 Mýtna ulica (phone: 46580), 3 Bebravská ulica (phone: 242461), and 1 Robniaková ulica (phone: 825043).

PHARMACY There are 24-hour pharmacies at 3 Spitálska ulica (phone: 51447), 9 Mýtná ulica (phone: 46580), and 12 Ružinovská ulica (phone: 231143).

POST OFFICE Located at 35 SNP námestie (phone: 278111).

SPECIAL EVENTS

Bratislava is a city steeped in music and enriched by a long history of visits from the greats — Mozart, Haydn, Beethoven, and Liszt, to name just a few. The city honors its musical tradition by staging several music festivals throughout the spring, summer, and fall. For rock 'n' roll fans (many Czechs, including President Václav Havel, are among them) the *Bratislava*

Lyre features a series of rock concerts in late May and early June. *Bratislava Jazz Days* are held in September, and in October the city hosts an *International Music Festival,* during which the beautiful *Reduta Theater* (2 Paleckeho; phone: 333351) features classical performances almost every night.

MUSEUMS

In addition to those mentioned in *Special Places,* there are other interesting Bratislava museums you may wish to visit. All those listed charge a nominal admission.

HUDOBNA EXPOZÍCIA RUDNÝ DOM J.M. HUMMELA (HUMMEL MUSIC MUSEUM) The birthplace and onetime home of Johann Hummel, the early-19th-century composer. Concerts are held outside the house on summer weekends. Open 1 to 5 PM; closed Mondays. 2 Klobučnícká ulica.

MÚZEUM HODIN (EXHIBITION OF HISTORICAL CLOCKS) For the timepiece buff. Open 10 AM to 5 PM; closed Tuesdays. 1 Zidovska ulica.

MÚZEUM ROMANSKEJ KULTURY (MUSEUM OF ROMAN CULTURE) A relatively new exhibit that features treasures from the excavations of the Roman settlement of Gerulata. Located in Ruscovce, across the Danube and several miles south of Bratislava. Ask *BIS* for directions.

PÁLFFYHO PALÁC (PALFFY PALACE) This 19th-century palace houses a branch of the *Municipal Gallery of Bratislava,* featuring a collection of European art from the 16th through 19th centuries, as well as 19th- and 20th-century Slovak art. Originally the home of the powerful Palffy family, the palace has been entirely restored and maintains portions of its original Celtic, Moravian, and Gothic details. The *Liszt Pavilion* and the *Mozart Hall* are the settings for chamber music concerts. Open Tuesdays through Fridays 10 AM to 5 PM, Saturdays and Sundays 10 AM to 5 PM. 12-21 Pánská ulica.

SHOPPING

Souvenirs from Slovakia include lovely crystal and lavish gold-rimmed china, particularly tea sets. *Dom Odievania* (on SNP námestie) is the city's main department store, carrying crystal and other souvenir items. Keep an eye out for the blue- and yellow-painted ceramics known as majolica, as well as hand-painted *Easter* eggs and gingerbread ornaments. Fine handicraft items can be found at *Ustredie Ludovej Umeleckej Výroby* (The Center for Folkcrafts; 7 SNP námestie; phone: 53802 or 4 Michalská; phone: 332288). Boutique items and exquisite examples of Slovak ceramics, glass, and paintings are offered at the *Dielo Centram* (12 SNP námestie; phone: 490648). Try *Folkfolk* (2 Rybarska Brána; phone: 17317703) for crystal and Swiss army knives. A good buy is classical music on cassette tape and compact disk (about $7 and $15, respectively), and don't overlook the high-quality vinyl pressings from the Opus label. A small selection of books in English is available at *Mestská Knižnica* (2 Obchodná ulica; no phone) and at *S. Kniha* (1 Rybarská ulica; no phone).

SPORTS AND FITNESS

The *Forum* hotel, a visitor's premier recreation venue, features a swimming pool, a fitness center, and massage and sauna facilities. The new *Danube* hotel also has a pool, fitness center, and sauna. Several outdoor swimming pools open to the public include *Rosnička* (Dolné Krčace trieda), *Tehelné Pole* (Odbojárov ulica), *Matador* (Petržalka), and *Delfin* (18 Ružová Dolina). The three major indoor pools open to the public are *Pasienky* (4 Junacka), *Central* (2 Miletičova ulica), and *Grossling* (3 Kupelna).

THEATER

"Sold out" in Bratislavan theater parlance doesn't necessarily mean that seats to the performance in question are unavailable. Simply go to the theater and ask to speak with an usher or a theater employee; you will be told to return half an hour before the performance, whereupon seats will magically be found for you.

For non-Slovak speakers, one of Bratislava's best theater experiences is the *Divadelný Súbor Stoka* (Gutter Theater; 1 Pribinová ulica; phone: 201-3161 or 68016). Other innovative, non-traditional theater can be seen at the *Nová Scéna* (New Stage; 20 Kollarová námestie; phone: 55741), *Studio Novej Scény* (Studio of the New Stage; 17 Suche mýto; phone: 338840); and *Studio's* (51 Maja námestie; phone: 499552). The *Statné Bábkové Divadlo* (State Puppet Theater; 36 Dunajska; phone: 53668) is charming and a wonderful venue regardless of the language barrier.

The *Slovenské Národné Divadlo* (Slovak National Theater; 1 Hviezdoslava námestie; phone: 51146 or 333890) presents plays and ballets. Tickets are available at the corner of Jesenskéno ulica and Komeského námestie. They have a second site for drama at the *P.O. Hviezdoslav Theater* (21 Laurinská ulica; phone: 333083) and the *Malá Scéna* (Small Stage; 7 Dostojevskeho; phone: 53775), which offers more innovative productions.

MUSIC

The chamber music concerts held every Sunday at 10:30 AM at Mirbachov Palác (Františkánské námestie; phone: 331556) are local favorites. The *Slovak Philharmonic* is one of the finest orchestras in Eastern Europe. Its performances of the works of Smetana, Dvořák, and other native composers are immensely popular, so book in advance. Concerts are given at two locations in the city: the *Koncertná Sien Slovenskej Filharmónie Reduta* (Reduta Theater; 2 Palachého; phone: 333351) and the *Slovenskej Filharmónie Moyzesová Sien* (Slovak Philharmonic Concert Hall; 12 Vajanského nábrežie; phone: 50130). Other concert venues are the *Divadlo Hudby*

(Music Auditorium; 14 Nedbalov; phone: 53337), the concert hall at Bratislava Castle (phone: 313020), and the *Slovenského Rozhlasové Kultúrne Centrum* (Slovak Radio Concert Hall; 1 Mýtna; phone: 44462).

NIGHTCLUBS AND NIGHTLIFE

The after-dark entertainment in Bratislava has much improved in the past year with more clubs featuring a variety of entertaining options. The *Forum* and *Devín* hotels (see *Checking In*) offer floor shows nightly. Aficionados of blues, jazz, and country music should try *Mefisto* (24 Paneska; no phone). Live bands are featured at the *Rock, Pop, and Jazz Klub* (12 Jakubovo námestie; no phone). And for hip rock music, concerts, and cultural events, try the smoky cavern of the *New Model* (2 Obschodna; no phone). By far the best place to quaff a Budvar, sample Slovak pub food, and listen to the region's *dechovaka* (polka), country, and jazz music is *Stará Sladovna;* known locally as "Mamut," it's billed as Eastern Europe's largest beer hall (Laurinská; no phone).

Best in Town

CHECKING IN

Hotel reservations may be made through *Cedok* or through your own travel agent. Happily, the image of the dreary Eastern-bloc hotel does not apply to many properties in Bratislava. Some are surprisingly modern, well-appointed, and offer many Western amenities. For a double room, expect to pay $70 or more at an expensive hotel; $40 to $70 at a moderately priced hotel; and about $30 at an inexpensive place. Be aware that at press time, the Slovak government had imposed a 23% sales tax on hotel rooms, so check in advance to see whether or not that has been included in the price you are quoted. Most of Bratislava's major hotels have complete facilities for the business traveler. Those hotels listed below as having "business services" usually offer such conveniences as English-speaking concierge, meeting rooms, photocopiers, computers, translation services, and express checkout, among others. Call the hotel for additional information. All telephone numbers are in the 7 city code unless otherwise indicated.

For an unforgettable experience, we begin with our favorites in Bratislava, followed by our cost and quality choices of hotels, listed by price category.

SPECIAL HAVENS

Danube This French-built luxury property, which opened in 1993, is located directly on the banks of the Danube. There are 280 rooms, 36 suites, and 4 deluxe apartments, all decorated in pastel hues. Guests also enjoy the *Pressbourg* restaurant, a café, a bar overlooking Bratislava Castle, a nightclub, and a fitness center with pool and sauna. Business services. 1 Rybniché námestie (phone: 340000 or 340833; fax: 314311).

Forum Inter-Continental Bratislava One of the newer hotels in the country, it's also one of the best-staffed properties in Eastern Europe — they'll arrange everything from restaurant reservations to theater tickets, and offer advice on interesting sights and places to shop. The entrance and lobby are large and attractively decorated in glass and chrome. The 230 rooms and 10 suites are comfortable and all have mini-bars and color TV sets. There's also a fitness center with a pool, gym, and solarium; plus 3 bars; a nightclub; and 2 restaurants, one French and one Slovak. The latter, the first-rate *Slovakia*, offers regional fare and cheery Slovak music (see *Eating Out*). Business services. 2 Hodžovo námestie (phone: 348115; fax: 334308).

EXPENSIVE

Devín In the center of the Old Town right on the Danube, this modern hotel has 98 rooms, 5 suites, and 3 restaurants — the *Azia* is best (see *Eating Out*) — plus a café, wine bar, and terrace. 4 Riečná (phone: 330854; fax: 330682).

MODERATE

Bratislava This is the largest hotel in the Bratislava vicinity, but it is about 3 miles (5 km) outside of town. Its modern facilities include 344 rooms, a restaurant, and a nightclub. Business services. 9 Urxova ulica (phone: 293524; fax: 236420).

Gracia Anchored on the river near the *Slovak National Gallery,* this 29-room, 3-story floating "botel" boasts a modern blue and black decor, surprising large and comfortable cabins, all equipped with telephones, color TV sets, and mini-bars. There is a restaurant featuring continental dishes, and a summer terrace for dining and dancing. Razušovo nábrežie (phone: 332132 or 332430; fax: 332131).

Zachová Chata Located 22 miles (35 km) from the city, this typical wood and stone *chata* (mountain cottage) has 15 small, comfortable rooms. It is best known for its wood-adorned *Koliba* restaurant, featuring an open-pit barbecue for spit-roasted meats and live folk and gypsy music. There's access to a nearby swimming pool, tennis courts, and ski facilities. 900-01 Modrá-Piesok, Modra (phone: 704-923919; fax: 704-92291).

INEXPENSIVE

Zlaté Piesky (Golden Sands) Chalets Located about 5 miles (8 km) northeast of Bratislava, on a gorgeous lake suitable for swimming and other water sports, this campground rents bungalows and, during the summer months, campsites. The motel, with 33 rooms, is open year-round. 12 Senecka cesta. Take trams No. 2, 4, or 10 to the end of the line, then bus No. 32 or 35 direct to Zlaté Piesky (phone: 65170 or 60578).

EATING OUT

Heavy peasant food is standard fare throughout the Slovak Republic. Great stews, goulash (a thick, spicy soup here), the filling Slovak-style *kapustovsfá polieuka* (cabbage soup), goose liver, breaded cutlets, cabbage, and sauerkraut are in abundance. Many meals are accompanied by a *knedliky,* a large dumpling. A particular Slovak specialty is *Halušky z brynzo,* a small dumpling filled with cheese made from sheep's milk. Pastries are lavish, occasionally fruit- or cream-filled, and scrumptious. Note that fried potato pancakes are sold at outdoor stands throughout the city and, though they may not appear appetizing at first blush — they're served in grease-soaked napkins — they are delicious; restaurants frequently serve them with applesauce and sour cream. On the lighter side, Slovakian streams contain some excellent trout. In addition, look for *morčdicia prsa,* lightly sautéed turkey breast, which is very popular on most menus. Some restaurants, particularly those in the better hotels, offer something resembling continental cuisine, but they generally are not as colorful nor as authentic as the local spots.

Bratislava is ideally located in the middle of the country's best wine region. It is, therefore, no coincidence that the city's wine cellars are the best places to eat and drink. Though many feature Slovak music and costumes and have become tourist haunts, Bratislavans continue to frequent them because of the good food, grog, and warm atmosphere they offer.

Slovaks brew their own beer, the well-known Sariš, but Czech brands — Budvar, Pazdroj, and Pilsner Urquell — are widely available as well. Your Slovak hosts may ask you to drink a toast of *slivovice* (plum brandy) before dinner, or you may opt for *borovička.* Made from juniper berries, it is as fragrant as a freshly cut *Christmas* tree.

Cafés and coffeehouses are also plentiful, a legacy of the Turks, who introduced thick, sludgy coffee to Vienna and Bratislava during the heyday of the Ottoman Empire.

For dinner for two, including wine, expect to pay $40 or more at a very expensive restaurant; $30 to $40 at an expensive restaurant; $15 to $30 at a moderately priced place; and less than $15 at an inexpensive one. Note that many restaurants do *not* accept credit cards. All restaurants are in the 7 city code unless otherwise indicated.

VERY EXPENSIVE

Casablanca If you crave good seafood, this is the only place in town. Choose from a wide variety — lobster, salmon, crayfish, swordfish, and oysters — all shipped daily from the Moroccan city of the same name. Open daily for lunch and dinner. Reservations necessary. Major credit cards accepted. 53 Jeseniová ulica (phone: 371767).

Slovakia The *Forum* hotel's finest restaurant features Slovak specialties. Polite and congenial waiters wear colorful folk costumes and recommend dishes they often have trouble describing. At lunch there's a salad bar selection (rare in this country). Slovak music enhances the cheery, informal atmosphere that prevails here. Open daily 11 AM to 10 PM. Reservations necessary. Major credit cards accepted. 2 Hodžovo námestie (phone: 348111).

EXPENSIVE

Arkádia This first class dining spot perched on the side of a hill below Bratislava's castle offers fine Slavic fare in formal surroundings. Open daily from 11 AM to 10 PM. Proper attire and reservations necessary. No credit cards accepted. Zamocké ulica (phone: 335650).

Azia The best of the three dining rooms in the Old Town's *Devín* hotel has an international and eclectic menu, including Chinese dumplings and some good stir-fry–type dishes. Though the Chinese food is tasty, it's far from authentic. Open for lunch and dinner 11:30 AM to 10 PM; closed Sundays. Major credit cards accepted. 4 Riečná (phone: 333640).

MODERATE

Hradná Vináren (Castle Wine Cellar) This delightful eatery in Bratislava Castle serves both light and robust meals. Particularly crowded during the summer months. Closed Sundays. Reservations advised. No credit cards accepted. In the Old Town (phone: 311682).

Korzo A combination café-restaurant located across from the *Danube* hotel. A pianist accompanies the first-rate fare and fine service in the spacious, candlelit dining room. Try the traditional *tatranský pochutka na zemiakovej placke* (pork loin with potato pancakes). Open daily from 9 AM to midnight. Reservations advised. No credit cards accepted. 11 Hviezdoslavovo námestie (phone: 334974).

Slovenská If a full day of trotting about has left you famished, this is an ideal spot for a traditional Slovakian feast. The kitchen is run by an award-winning chef, and the wine list features a good regional selection. Open for lunch and dinner from 11 AM to 10 PM. Reservations advised. No credit cards accepted. 15 Sturova ulica (phone: 52881).

Slovenská Restauracia pod Machnačom From the exterior it's just another cement bunker. The charming interior, however, is designed as a Slovak peasant cottage. Costumed waitresses serve generous portions of traditional Slovak fare including *česnaková* (garlic) soup. Folk music performed nightly. A beer hall with oak tables is located downstairs. Open daily from 11 AM to 11 PM. Reservations advised. No credit cards accepted. 42 L. Svobody nábrežie (phone: 314580 or 314219).

INEXPENSIVE

Klastorna Vináren (Monastery Wine Cellar) One of the very best cafés in the city. Located in the picturesque vaulted cellars of a former monastery in the Old

Town, its walls are adorned with ancient manuscripts and other "brotherly" paraphernalia. The regional specialties are excellent, as is the selection of Slovak and Moravian wines and world-renowned Czech beer. Open for lunch and dinner from 11:30 AM to 10 PM; closed Sundays. Reservations unnecessary. No credit cards accepted. 2 Františkánské námestie (phone: 338282).

Restauracia pod Baštou (Restaurant Under the Tower) This cheerful wine cellar with brick vaulted ceilings and oak benches joins others lining the small street to the left of Michael's Gate. Well-cooked meals, modest prices, and a good selection of wines make this a favorite of Bratislava natives. Try the *misa bašta* for two (pork, beef, and chicken with bacon and mushrooms). Open from 11 AM to midnight. Reservations unnecessary. No credit cards accepted. Bašta ulica (phone: 331765).

Bucharest

A full 5 years after the world's first live televised people's revolution in December 1989, pre-revolutionary graffiti still remains on façades; and government buildings, their windows broken and surfaces riddled with bullet holes, are cordoned off and secured by police. But the tricolor Romanian flag — *sans* its Communist symbol, sometimes with a jagged hole in its place — flies proudly over this city of 2.2 million people. In almost every sense, the scene is bizarre, a combination of *Alice in Wonderland* and some surrealistic horror show.

In addition to being the capital of Romania since 1862, Bucharest is the capital (since 1659) of the southern Romanian region of Walachia, which spans the foothills of the Carpathian Mountains across the southern Danube plain to the lush, white beaches of the Black Sea. The other two major regions of the country are Transylvania, bounded by the Carpathians in the west, and Moldavia, bordering Ukraine and the republic of Moldova, in the east. Though Transylvania has a large ethnic Hungarian minority (whose ancestors were imported as colonists in the 13th century by the Hungarian monarchy, which had great influence in the area), the language and culture of Romania as a whole have their origins in the Roman conquest of the area's Thracian tribes during the 1st century. This is why Romanians, unique among Eastern Europeans, speak a Romance language — related to French, Italian, and Spanish — that evolved from Latin between the 7th and 10th centuries.

From the 3rd through the 12th centuries, the territories of what was later to become Romania were repeatedly swept by Germanic and Slavic invaders; they then came under the domination of the Hungarians. According to folklore, the city of Bucharest was founded in the 11th or 12th century when a shepherd named Buchur settled at a bend in the Dîmbovița River and built a Christian church. The Eastern Orthodox form of Christianity had been introduced in the area by invading Bulgars in the 9th century, and ever since Romania's history has been closely aligned with that of Eastern Orthodoxy, whose local epicenter became Bucharest's Cathedral of the Patriarch.

The first historical records of Bucharest — then called Dîmbovița Citadel because it was astride the Dîmbovița River — date from 1368. The city's name was changed in the 15th century when it became a residence of the Walachian princes. The earliest official reference to the name Bucharest is a 1459 document signed by Prince Vlad Tepeș. The son of Prince Vlad Dracul (Vlad the Devil), Vlad Tepeș became known as Vlad the Impaler (because of a propensity to impale his enemies) and Dracula (Son of the Devil). Legends surrounding this historical figure inspired the Bram Stoker novel *Dracula*.

Points of Interest

1. Cathedral of the Patriarch; Romanian National Parliament
2. Palace Square
3. US Embassy; Inter-Continental Hotel
4. University Square; Ambassador Hotel
5. Carpati Travel Agency
6. Gradina Cismigiu (Cismigiu Gardens)
7. Amzei Piață
8. Stavropoleos Church
9. Curtea Veche Church
10. Opera Romana
11. Hanul Manuc
12. Romanian Treasury and History Museum
13. National Art Museum
14. National Theater
15. Princely Court Museum; Dimbovita Citadel
16. Romanian Athenum
17. National Unity Square; "House of the People"; Unirea Department Store
18. Triumphal Arch; Village Museum; Herastrau Park; Free Press Square

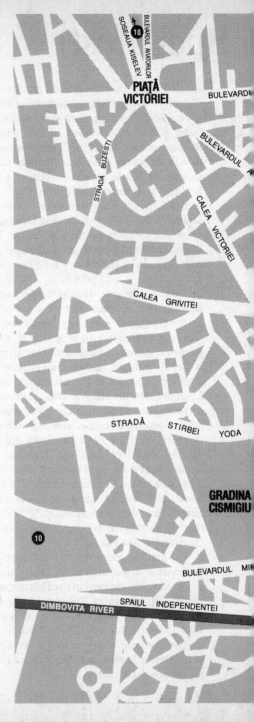

BUCHAREST

N

CALEA DE HUNEDOARA

CALEA DOROBANTILOR

STRADĂ MIHAIL EMINESCU

PIAȚĂ ROMĂNA

BULEVARDUL DACIA

STR. BISERICA

BULEVARDUL GENERAL MAGHERU

⑦

AMZEI PIAȚĂ

⑤

⑯

STRADĂ C. A. ROSETTI

PIAȚĂ PALATULUI

⑬ ②

BULEVARDUL N. BALCESCU

③

CALEA VICTORIEI

DA BREZOIANU

⑭

BULEVARDUL REPUBLICII

LNICEANU

④ PIAȚĂ UNIVERSITATII

RADĂ LIPSCANI

STRADĂ LIPSCANI

⑫ ⑧

IULIU MANTIU

PIAȚĂ ȚIUNILE UNITE

⑰

⑮ ① ⑨ ⑪

After the 15th century, Walachia, Moldavia, and Transylvania were under constant attacks from the Turks, who managed to control substantial chunks of territory well into the 19th century. In fact, it was the Turks who, working with local rulers, established Bucharest as Walachia's capital, and played a great part in the Romanian principalities' history and politics. These rulers, sometimes heroic figures such as Constantin Brâncoveanu, Prince Michael the Brave, and Stefan cel Mare ("the Great"), had to deal with not only the Turks but also the Hungarians, the kingdom of Poland, and Czarist Russia (which had occupied Walachia and Moldavia during the late 18th and early 19th centuries). It was not until 1859, with the consent of Russia, that Walachia and Moldavia were able to unite permanently. The country was officially declared an independent nation with the signing of the Treaty of Berlin, ending the 2-year Russo-Turkish War. The 1881 coronation of King Carol I ushered in a golden age for Bucharest, though not for the rest of the country. Outside the capital city, the country was fraught with financial difficulties and popular — particularly peasant — unrest.

Nineteenth-century Bucharest was an exotic and stylish city that enticed businessmen with its commercial possibilities, and travelers came from around the world to enjoy its pleasant climate, its relatively accessible language, its folklore, and its tradition of princes and kings. As in much of Europe at the time, the French held the monopoly on style here, and Bucharest affected a Parisian air, with wide, spacious boulevards, fashionable restaurants and cafés, an avenue called the Stradă Paris (Paris Street), and eventually even an Arc de Triomphe, built to commemorate the World War I Allied victory, in which Romania participated during the war's final days.

After World War I, Romania struggled to recover from its wartime occupation by Germany and Austria-Hungary (Bucharest had been occupied from December 1916 to November 1918). New political parties sprang up, and in 1921 a limited land reform was put into effect, which produced some benefits for the country's peasantry (then 80% of the population). That same year, the Romanian Communist Party was formed, but it remained primarily an underground movement until 1948. Though progress in the political and economic spheres was fitful at times, a reasonably free election was held for the first time in 1927, and controls on the economy were eased, allowing for greater decentralization and the introduction of foreign capital. During this same period, Crown Prince Carol, the son of King Ferdinand and his English-born wife, Queen Marie, renounced his rights to the throne. When Ferdinand died in 1927, Carol's 6-year-old son Michael became regent.

Economic crises returned with the worldwide depression in the 1930s, and in this atmosphere a fascist group called the Iron Guard arose to feed on popular discontent (as well as widespread anti-Semitism). In 1930, Carol reclaimed the throne, becoming King Carol II. Of a somewhat dictatorial bent, Carol II started cooperating with the Iron Guard and sought rapprochement with its sponsor, Nazi Germany. This backfired in 1940, when Hitler pressured Romania into ceding parts of Transylvania and other areas to his allies, Hungary and Bulgaria. Because of this humiliation, Carol was forced to abdicate, and power was given by his son, King Michael, to Marshal Ion Antonescu, who turned the country into a fascist state in alliance with the Axis powers.

Though the fascists had been initially abetted by King Michael, as the war turned against the Axis and Soviet troops closed in around Romania, he helped engineer a coup that deposed the Antonescu regime in August 1944. Michael himself was forced to abdicate in 1947 as the Soviet-sponsored Communists (under Gheorghe Gheorghiu-Dej) consolidated their hold over the country. The aristocracy of Bucharest was displaced, private enterprise and tourism were all but obliterated, and the elegant establishments, "liberated for the people," quickly fell into neglect and decay. The city's famed hotel and restaurant trade fell away, too, a victim of the general apathy produced by lack of competition. Once a city of princes, the Paris of the Balkans gradually deteriorated into just another fading monument to doctrinaire Communism, patrolled by the Securitate, the regime's feared secret police.

In 1965, Nicolae Ceauşescu took over the leadership of the Romanian Communist party, beginning a 24-year reign that saw a gradual leaning toward association with some Western countries, particularly West Germany. Bucharest was ostensibly given a face-lift; dozens of dilapidated old buildings that housed the city's increasingly deprived masses were destroyed in order to build grandiose government palaces and monuments to socialism. Many of these are still unfinished, except for their impressive façades.

The Romanian people (today a nation of 23 million) paid the price for Ceauşescu's extravagances. Profits from the textile and poultry industries were used to pay for Ceauşescu's shrines to himself, while food shortages were commonplace. There was a psychological price to be paid as well. Censorship was the norm; even ownership of a typewriter was illegal. The 1989 overthrow of the Ceauşescu regime helped bring about fundamental reforms: Food appeared on store shelves again, birth control was permitted — and typewriters allowed. The first free elections in Romania since World War II were held in May 1990. Ion Iliescu was elected president, and as leader of the National Salvation Front, Petre Roman became Prime Minister of the Parliament. Roman launched a program of market-oriented economic changes, but the resulting economic hardships led to his fall from power in 1991. However, his successor, Teodor Stolojan, has resisted pressure to return the country to a centralized economy and has pledged to carry out Roman's program of economic reform while finding ways to make the transition to a market economy more tolerable.

Bucharest still retains a faded fin de siècle air, though a number of buildings are still under scaffolding or bear scars from the December 1989 upheavals. The Ceauşescus didn't quite raze all of gracious Old Bucharest, and now many of the beautiful mansions, palaces, villas, parks, vineyards, and marinas that had been reserved for the Ceauşescu family's exclusive use are open to the public.

Although Bucharest long ago had to forgo its claim as the Paris of the Balkans, visitors will find that some of the city's old *je ne c'est quoi* remains.

Bucharest At-a-Glance

SEEING THE CITY

There is really no one spot from which to behold all of Bucharest, but the courtyard of the Cathedral of the Patriarch — perched on a quiet hillside overlooking the city just south of the *Palatul Voyavodal* (Princely Court) — does offer a nice view of the Old Quarter. Perhaps the best panoramic view of the city as a whole is from the *Balada* restaurant on the 22nd floor of the *Inter-Continental* hotel (see *Checking In*).

SPECIAL PLACES

The vivid mood of post-revolutionary Bucharest is one of the most exciting aspects of the city. Right now the streets still pulsate with an intensity that will soon fade into everyday life. A visit to Bucharest affords an opportunity to witness a piece of history — though visitors must be willing to expend some energy, and endure considerable discomfort. Getting a sense of the recent changes in the city is not all that difficult, however, as you will find many people eager to share their experiences with you. Hire an English-speaking guide and/or driver and car through *Carpaţi*, the state-run Romanian travel agency, and ask to be taken on a tour of the sites of the 1989 revolution. With a little luck, your guide/driver will have taken part in the December uprising. He or she can be your key to insights into the heart of Bucharest, which the official tours, heavy on ancient history, don't reveal. Note: "Stradă" is the Romanian word for street, "alçea" means alley, "piaţă" means square, and "calea" means avenue.

OLD BUCHAREST

The core of this district is the *Palatul Voyavodal* (Princely Court), the central part of the original Dîmboviţa Citadel and now a museum. Portions of the ruins of the medieval citadel and its surrounding streets are being reconstructed; parts of the area are open for viewing. Other attractions of the Old City are the Lipscani trading area and several old houses of worship.

PALATUL VOYAVODAL (PRINCELY COURT) Once the home of the kings and princes of Walachia, it is now a historical museum, located almost entirely underground, showing the progressive building of the citadel from the 15th to the 18th century. The outlines of the original citadel are preserved in stone; later additions are brick. From the outside, only chimneys and archways are visible, but inside are artifacts and portions of the original citadel. The open-air museum is open daily from 10 AM to 5 PM; closed Mondays. Admission charge. 31 Stradă Iuliu Maniu.

CURTEA VECHE (OLD COURT CHURCH) Orthodox masses are held daily in this 16th-century church located across from the *Princely Court*.

BASILICA PATRIARHIEI (CATHEDRAL OF THE PATRIARCH) This, the seat of the Patriarch of the Romanian Orthodox church, was built in 1658 and was later enlarged when the patriarchate was transferred from the province of Moldavia to Walachia. Inside, groups of old women dressed in black can be seen sitting on the floor sharing a lunch of bread, cheese, and melon; later they clean and decorate the cathedral with flowers. Though never closed by the Communist regime, like many houses of worship in the area it was slated for demolition and saved only by the 1989 revolution. The courtyard and cemetery, erected during the mid-19th century in memory of bishops and monks already dead for 3 centuries, are filled with headstones and crosses inscribed in ornate Old Slavonic. The cathedral is open for daily services at 10 AM and sometimes in the evening. 21 Alęea Patriarhiei (phone: 163455).

PARLAMENTUL NATIONAL (ROMANIAN NATIONAL PARLIAMENT) Situated across from the cathedral, this long, gray, neo-classical structure was built in 1907, and was formerly the seat of the rubber-stamp Grand National Assembly under the Communist regime. The building is open to the public when Parliament is in session (from September through July); parliamentary sessions themselves also are open to the public. The entrances are guarded by friendly Romanian soldiers dressed in sharp new khakis that replaced the old Soviet-style green uniforms. Alęea Parliamentului.

BISERICĂ STRAVROPOLEOS (STAVROPOLEOS CHURCH) This 18th-century structure is a fine example of Brâncovenesc architecture, a uniquely Romanian style named after the illustrious 18th-century Walachian Prince Constantin Brâncoveanu. The curvy style, executed in both wood and stone, is a fusion of late Renaissance, Byzantine, and Romanian folk-art designs. Services are held here regularly. 6 Stradă Postei.

STRADĂ LIPSCANI (LIPSCANI STREET) Just 2 blocks from the *Princely Court* is the most historical part of Bucharest, the principal trading street of the Old City. A wonderful place to walk for its myriad small shops and outdoor stands, and also because the narrow lane so teems with people, pushcarts, bicycles, and even horses, sheep, and fowl that it is next to impassable for cars. Merchants and farmers from all over the Balkans used to bring their wares to trade in the district, which dates from the 18th century.

BURSE ROMÂBEASCĂ (ROMANIAN STOCK EXCHANGE) One of the most ornate pieces of architecture in Bucharest, the Burse was built in 1880 and restored by the Ceauşescu government 100 years later. It's no longer used for its original purpose, as a new stock exchange opened in 1991 at another location. The style reflects Byzantine and Romanesque features: Magnificent marble columns are topped with dosserets (a sort of secondary capital) of hammered copper, the floor is of patterned stone, the octagonal ceiling is a mosaic of leaded glass stained in vibrant shades of blue. Iron gates, cherubs, and other finely carved statuary preside over the variety of shoe and cosmetics stores now housed here. 18 Stradă Lipscani.

PIAȚĂ UNIVERSITATII (UNIVERSITY SQUARE) North of Lipscani, at the intersection of Nicolae Bălcescu and Republicii boulevards, this plaza, the seat of Bucharest's university, was the site of much of the fighting of the December 1989 Revolution. Demonstrators, unhappy with the presence of former Communists in the new government, continued to gather here after the elections until they were forcibly and brutally removed by government-sponsored miners brought to the city for the purpose.

GRĂDINA CIŞMIGIU (CIŞMIGIU GARDENS) This grand 19th-century park is a picturesque place to escape the urban bustle. There's a small zoo, a lake, and numerous gardens on the 34 acres. Off Bulevardul Republicii, west of Piață Universitatii.

PIAȚĂ PALATULUI (PALACE SQUARE) Just northwest of University Square, this plaza, part of Piață Revolutiei (Revolutionary Square), and formerly called Piață Gheorghe Gheorghiu-Dej, was named for the former royal palace, which became a government building and half of which now houses the *Museum of National Art*. Across from the palace is the monumental Civic Center, the old Communist Party headquarters, from whose roof the Ceauşescus temporarily escaped by helicopter during the 1989 uprising. In front of the building (which is cordoned off and protected by armed guards) are shrines to the victims of the revolution. One of these is a massive cross brought by an Orthodox priest and his followers from Timişoara, the city where the revolution began. Citizens decorate the shrine daily with fresh flowers and votive candles.

CENTRAL CIVIC (CIVIC CENTER) Ceauşescu razed thousands of old buildings just south of the Lipscani area to make way for this huge neo-classical Socialist complex, intended to house the Communist Party elite. Its main artery, connecting Piață Unirii (Unity Square) to the gargantuan House of the Republic was to be named the Boulevard of the Victory of Socialism. Although widely condemned as an architectural atrocity, Bulevardul Unirii, as it is now called, has ironically become a center of the emerging capitalist class, with luxury car dealerships, bars, and galleries, all lit at night by the neon glare of signs advertising Japanese electronics. The House of the Republic is worth a visit: Dubbed the House of the People, it cost more than $1 billion over a 6-year period of construction. This 5,000-room marble monstrosity, intended as Ceauşescu's personal head-quarters, is said to be the second-largest edifice in the world, second only to the Pentagon. The building is only intermittently opened to the public; access to the inner rooms usually requires pre-arranging a tour through city officials.

PIAŢĂ VICTORIEI (VICTORY SQUARE) This is the point from which most of Bucha-rest's main streets emanate. Across the plaza is Soseaua Kiseleff, bordered on either side by parkland and leading through the Arcul de Triumf (Triumphal Arch) past Free Press Square into Herăstrău Park, Bucharest's largest nature preserve.

ARCUL DE TRIUMF (TRIUMPHAL ARCH) Modeled on Paris's Arc de Triomphe, this structure was erected in 1922 to celebrate the Allied victory in World War I and to honor Romania's war dead. (Unfortunately, you can't go up to the top.) Soseaua Kiseleff, north of Piaţă Victoriei.

PIAŢĂ PRESEI LIBERE (FREE PRESS SQUARE) This plaza used to be named for *Scinteiei*, the Communist Party journal which was published here for 40 years, until the 1989 revolution (now it is the site of a non-Communist paper's offices). It took two cranes 4 days to remove the 7,000-pound bronze statue of Lenin that stood here. Soseaua Kiseleff.

FOREST PARKS Bucharest is blessed with extensive greenery and spacious parks, including several nature preserves and recreation areas. Perhaps the best known is Herăstrău Park, whose 1 1/2-square-mile expanse is home to a large lake, more than a half-dozen pleasant restaurants, the outdoor *Muzeul Satului* (Village Museum), a collection of houses, churches, and other structures from throughout Romania (see *Museums*). The pastoral settings provide a pleasant respite from urban Bucharest, and the museum displays a good cross section of the very different architectural styles found in the various regions of the country. For those who want to take photographs, the 2-lei (less than 5¢) admission charge is raised to 5 or 6 lei (depending on whether you enter for the whole day or just an afternoon). Open daily.

Băneasa Forest, located within the city limits to the north of Herăstrău, has areas for picnicking and such outdoor games as volleyball and bad-minton, as well as the *Băneasa Forest* restaurant, which offers outdoor dining and Romanian folk shows.

ENVIRONS

LACUL SI MINASTRIEA SNAGOV (SNAGOV LAKE AND MONASTERY) A lovely recre-ation area located 20 miles (34 km) north of Bucharest, Snagov is very popular with the residents of the capital for family outings (as well as with the Romanian national sculling team for training). It's about a 30- to 40-minute drive from downtown, depending on how many Gypsy carts, herds of sheep, or gaggles of geese make you yield the right of way.

Snagov Island is in the middle of the lake and was formerly closed to the public because Ceauşescu had built a villa on its western shore; the island now is open to all and can be reached via an 85-person ferry (see below). Also on the small island is the 15th-century church and monastery founded by Vlad Tepeş (better known as Vlad the Impaler or Dracula), who is buried in the crypt here. In the portrait of him that rests before the altar, the prince is long-lashed, wide-eyed, and somewhat demented looking. (Though certainly fierce and ruthless, even by the standards of 5 centuries past, Vlad is revered throughout Romania as one of the country's greatest rulers, and was not literally a bloodsucker; Count Dracula was a 19th-century fictional exaggeration dreamed up by Irish author Bram Stoker. Vlad did, however, earn the sobriquet "The Impaler," due to his fondness for skewering the bodies of invading Turks — nearly 20,000 of them — on their own swords.)

The original church, with its monastery, dates from the 6th century. In 1383 it was christened the Church of Princes and was fortified, serving until 1418 as a fortress to defend Walachia. In 1456 Vlad Tepeş built the current Snagov Monastery and fortifications (including an underground escape tunnel to the shore, which is now in disrepair and unusable). The church's altar table is from the original 6th-century structure and has never been moved, as is customary in the Orthodox faith. On display in the church are a number of ancient ecclesiastical documents, including copies of the first Romanian Bible, printed at Snagov toward the end of the 17th century (the original is in Bucharest's Romanian Academy). The Snagov Printing Press was brought here in 1695. The monastery is still home to four monks, and Sunday and holiday services are held at 9 AM (Sunday mass is open to the public).

Also along the lakeshore are a number of small cafés, outdoor food stands selling barbecued meat and *mititei* (lamb sausage), and a restaurant at the Snagov Lake recreation area. Rowboats can be rented for 20 lei (about $1) per hour (don't try to row all the way out to the island, though, since there's no place to dock). A number of small villas on the island offer interesting tourist accommodations, which can be booked through *Carpaţi* (phone: 145160).

A note on the ferry: It operates during the summer on no particular schedule — just whenever the captain feels there are enough passengers for a run to the island, generally once every hour. These "scheduled" rides cost $5 a head. The ferry also can be chartered, for around $45 per hour. *Carpaţi* will tell you it's impossible to visit the island during the winter, but you can arrange private passage with one of the weekly supply boats (again, on no particular schedule; you simply have to show up at the dock and ask around, or ask your guide to find out what day the boat leaves).

MOGOŞOAIA PALACE A visit to the elegant 18th-century estate of Prince Constantin Brâncoveanu, 9 miles (13 km) through the parks and forests to the northwest of the city, is one of Bucharest's finest day trips. Now a museum of medieval art and artifacts, the palace itself overshadows its contents. A formal structure, it was built on the scale of a Venetian palazzo, with ornately arched colonnades, a stately, close-cropped garden, and a quiet reflecting pond. Open daily. Admission charge. 1 Valea Parcului (phone: 685560).

EXTRA SPECIAL The most exotic and typical example of traditional Romanian life is found just outside the capital. Only a few miles from the center of Bucharest are villages where peasants still live off the land; where Gypsies roam the countryside in tarpaulin-covered wagons pulled by horses or oxen; and public wells are sheltered by brilliantly painted shrines.

Worthwhile excursions include the 2-hour ride through rural Walachia to the lovely medieval monastery at Curtea de Argeş, once the seat of Walachia's rulers; and the trip to the red-roofed medieval Transylvanian town of Braşov, some 115 miles (184 km) north of Bucharest.

Stays in some of Moldavia's beautiful working monasteries and convents are available on a very limited basis. All prospective visitors must be screened well in advance for a stay of 2 to 3 days. Quarters are modest and clean, and the environment is one of complete peace and serenity. Apply through *Carpaţi* (and be persistent).

Sources and Resources

TOURIST INFORMATION

In Bucharest, the main branch of the *Carpaţi-Bucureşti* National Tourist Office is located at 7 Calea General Magheru (phone: 614-5160). In the United States, information is available from the Romanian National Tourist Board (152 Madison Ave., New York, NY 10016; phone: 212-447-1537). Hours and days of operation can be somewhat erratic, so be sure to call ahead. The tourist offices also will make hotel and other reservations for you, but your own travel agent may be more efficient and reliable.

LOCAL COVERAGE The most prominent daily is *Evenimentul Zilei* (The Daily Event), followed by the *Romania Libera* (Free Romania). English-language publications such as the *International Herald Tribune* and *Time* magazine are available at the *Inter-Continental* and other major hotels, where some French and German language publications are also available.

TELEPHONE The country code for Romania is 40; the city code for Bucharest is 1. The public phones generally work, and are easily operable with 10-lei coins. Overseas calls must be made from private or hotel phones.

GETTING AROUND

Bucharest's roughly 43 square miles are easy to navigate, and are best covered on foot or in a rental or chauffeured car (parking spaces generally are available). Taxis are a good option, too; they're inexpensive, and drivers will often wait while you eat or sightsee. The most difficult area to navigate is Lipscani, where it's generally best to go on foot.

AIRPORT Buses leave Otoponi International Airport and Bǎnseasa (domestic) Airport for Bucharest about every hour from 5 AM to 10 PM and cost the equivalent of 25¢. To get out to the airport, catch the buses that depart from the *Tarom* airlines office in downtown Bucharest (10 Stradǎ Brezoianu) about 12 times a day (7 times on Sunday). The taxi fare to or from Bǎnseasa is about 100 lei (about $5) or more, and slightly higher to Otoponi (both are just under a half hour from the city center). For flight information and reservations contact *Tarom* (6 Stradǎ Domnit Anastasia; phone: 615-0499; or 14 Stradǎ Mendeleev; phone: 659-4185). The airport telephone number for information on international flights is 633-3137, for information on domestic flights, 633-0030.

BUS/TROLLEY/STREETCAR They crisscross the city and are relatively inexpensive, but crowded and dirty. Buses are the least reliable form of transportation; often you will see crowds of people waiting for buses that never arrive.

CAR RENTAL Automobiles, with or without drivers, are available through *Carpaţi*. Though costs are reasonable, you may be able to get an even better bargain by hiring a *Carpaţi* driver independently to take you around the city for a day. *Hertz* and *Avis* have outlets at major hotels, and *VIP Tours,* a private rental agency, is behind the *Athénée Palace* hotel. Payment is in hard currency or by credit card only. Many private travel agencies in Bucharest also rent cars — a complete list can be found at the *Carpaţi-Bucureşti* National Tourist Office (see *Tourist Information,* above).

METRO Three interconnected lines serve Bucharest: The first travels around the city in a circle, the second traverses the city, and the third serves the outlying industrial areas. The system, called *metroul,* is clean, efficient, inexpensive, and crowded, and runs all night (which is more than can be said for subways in such advanced Western European capitals as Paris and London). No maps are available, though there are some diagrams affixed to the walls in the stations (along with some intriguing graffiti left over from the revolution).

TAXI State taxis, distinguishable by their yellow license plates, will take you anywhere in the city for about $3; they can be ordered by phone from anywhere in Bucharest by dialing 953. Private, state-licensed taxis have white plates and signs in the window reading "P Taxi" or "Taxi Particular." They generally charge three to four times more than the state taxis, but they're also more readily available. Unlicensed cabs with no signs also will stop to pick up passengers — particularly handy at night, when there's a scarcity of regular taxis. Insist that drivers in state-run cabs run the newer digital meters. If the meters are "broken," agree on a price *before* getting in or be prepared to be taken for a ride you hadn't bargained for. The best way to hail any taxi is still by palming a package of Kent cigarettes (Bucharest's brand of choice). Though the fare is generally in lei, drivers won't turn down dollars or other hard currency.

TRAIN The main railway station, through which 90% of the rail traffic passes, is the Garǎ de Nord, which occupies an entire city block on Calea Griviţei. There are a handful of lesser stations that provide service only to a few small towns around Bucharest. It's best to book train reservations and pay in advance with *Carpaţi* before leaving the US if you want to be assured of private, first class accommodations (if you really want to meet the Romanian people, consider traveling what is known as regular class). The local trains make a lot of stops, they don't take reservations, and are generally quite crowded, but eventually you'll find a seat. For Garǎ de Nord train schedule information dial 952 in Bucharest.

LOCAL SERVICES

Most hotels will try to arrange for any special services a business traveler might require.

DENTIST (ENGLISH-SPEAKING) Most hospitals have dental services, and many of their dentists speak some English. Inquire at your hotel for more information.

DRY CLEANER In addition to the hotels, there is a chain called *Nufarul,* with branches throughout the city; most dry cleaning will take 2 or 3 days.

FAX/TELEX Most hotels and the main post office have fax and telex facilities.

LIMOUSINE SERVICE Available through *Carpaţi* (see *Tourist Information,* above).

MEDICAL EMERGENCY The telephone number is 961. The *Spidalul de Urgenta* (Hospital of Urgency; Bulevardul Stefan cel Mare) handles all emergencies in Bucharest.

MESSENGER SERVICE Available from any of the large hotels. The service is free if it is a matter of 5 or 10 minutes, but they charge for longer deliveries.

NATIONAL/INTERNATIONAL COURIER *DHL Worldwide Express* is offered through *International Romexpresx Service* (47 Stradǎ Eminescu; phone: 312-2661). "Overnight" services usually take 2 days.

OFFICE EQUIPMENT RENTAL Available from the larger hotels.

PHARMACY To find the all-night pharmacy closest to your hotel, call the 24-hour pharmacy hotline 951. Most pharmacies have someone who speaks some English.

PHOTOCOPIES At the *Inter-Continental* hotel (4-6 Bulevardul Nicolae Bălcescu; phone: 613-7040 or 614-0400); some storefront services also are opening up — inquire at your hotel.

POST OFFICE The main post office is at 37 Calea Victoriei. All post offices throughout the city are open weekdays from 8 AM to 7 PM; Saturdays from 8 AM to 2 PM; closed Sundays.

SECRETARY/STENOGRAPHER (ENGLISH-SPEAKING) Contact the Chamber of Commerce at 22 Bulevardul Nicolae Bălcescu (phone: 615-4706/7).

TAILOR Inquire at your hotel for the closest one.

TRANSLATOR Through *Carpaţi* or the Chamber of Commerce (address and phone above).

SPECIAL EVENTS

A music festival featuring the works of Romanian composer Georges Enesco is held at the *Ateneul Român* (Romanian Athenaeum; 1 Stradă Franklin; phone: 615-6875) in September. An international trade show primarily geared for businesses takes place twice a year, in May and October (1 Piaţă Presei Libere; phone: 617-6010; in the US call the Romanian Trade Mission: 212-682-9120). International festivals are held several times a year at the *Village Museum*. On the *Feast of Saint Dimitru* (in June — the date changes each year; ask at *Carpaţi*), the saint's coffin is taken from the Cathedral of the Patriarch and carried through the streets so that the faithful can see and touch it. But the most colorful and unusual events generally take place in the provincial villages, not in Bucharest. The *Feast of the Goat* is a masked winter carnival held in many villages from *Christmas Eve* through the *Feast of the Epiphany* (January 6).

MUSEUMS

Besides the museum of the *Palatul Voyavodal* (Princely Court) listed in *Special Places,* other museums of interest include the following.

MUZEUL NATIONAL DE ARTA (NATIONAL MUSEUM OF ART) The museum's superb collection of Romanian and European paintings and sculpture showcases the talent of such local artists as the 19th-century painter Grigorescu as well as European giants including Rubens and van Gogh. Sculpture also is represented, including works of the world-renowned Romanian-born sculptor Constantin Brancusi (1876–1957). Open from 9 AM to 5 PM; closed Mondays. Admission charge. Piaţă Revolutiei; entrance is at 4-3 Stradă Stirbei Voda (phone: 614-9774).

MUZEUL NATIONAL DE ISTORIE SI TREZORIE (ROMANIAN TREASURY AND HISTORY MUSEUM) The worthwhile part of this museum is on the ground floor (upstairs is mostly empty); to get in you will have to relinquish all cameras, notebooks, and anything else the soldiers standing guard think you might use to compromise Romania's national treasures. There is an exquisite collection of gold and jewelry dating as far back as the 5th century BC: headdresses, icons, goblets, coins, and military and religious ornaments from the Dacian and Roman eras through the 19th century. Displays are marked in Romanian and English. Open from 10 AM to 6 PM; closed Mondays. Admission charge. 12 Calea Victoriei (phone: 650-3415).

MUZEUL SATULUI (VILLAGE MUSEUM) Just outside the city limits on the grounds of Herăstrău Park is this beautifully arranged "community" of 300 houses, churches, wells, kiosks, and other structures brought here from every section of the nation's three provinces. The spacious park is the perfect setting in which to learn about peasant life — particularly the different types of wooden houses that peasants live in throughout the country. Also quite charming are the Transylvanian houses, which feature peak-roofed side porches and outdoor kiosks that sell bread and water to passersby. In summer, the "museum" hosts crafts demonstrations, including weaving, carving, wool spinning, and making *nai* (wooden wind instruments). The park is also home to a large lake and several restaurants, making a trip here a pleasant respite from urban Bucharest. Open daily. Admission charge. 28-30 Soseaua Kiseleff, Herăstrău Park (phone: 617-5920).

SHOPPING

The city now boasts private shops selling virtually any Western-made good, but your best bet for a wide selection is *Coleus,* a new citywide chain, whose main store is on 100 Bulevardul Dacia (phone: 611-5301). Open 9 AM to 9 PM. No credit cards.

A wide selection of Romanian products — such as gorgeous leaded crystal, handmade lace, woodcarvings, embroidery, pottery (including the beautiful shiny black Margina pottery), wool sweaters, hats, and blankets — are available at *Comturist* shops located in major hotels throughout Bucharest and the rest of the country. These shops offer some decent bargains, especially on crystal. Payment is in hard currency *only* — cash or credit card. Most of what you'll probably want to take home from Romania will be bulky or breakable, so plan to leave some extra room in your luggage.

Stores where Romanians shop (and pay in lei) also can offer some interesting finds. Store hours are generally open daily from 8 AM to 4 PM, though some open from 8 AM to noon, close until 4 PM, then reopen from 4 to 8 PM. Food and department store hours are from 6 AM to 9 PM.

AMZEI MARKET This huge indoor/outdoor market is open year-round, and in late summer and fall sells the fresh fruit and vegetables so noticeably absent at most restaurants. There also are booths for crafts, including hand-knit wool sweaters, blankets, and throws, as well as the bright red and black embroidered table runners that decorate homes and restaurant walls. Stradă Amzei Biserică (behind the *Bucureşti* hotel).

APOLLO A gallery of fine paintings, sculpture, and Romania's famous glassware. Also on display are some examples of contemporary art done during the Soviet regime. Open 11 AM to 7 PM; closed Saturdays and Sundays. 2 Bulevardul Bălcescu (phone: 613-1516).

BIBLIOTECĂ The name simply means "library." Both Romanian and foreign-language books are sold here, the latter mostly in German and Russian (including some beautifully illustrated 20th-century texts). 54 Stradă Iuliu Maniu (no phone).

BRUITERE A jewelry shop with a good selection of ivory pins and inexpensive costume jewelry, as well as outdated Eastern-bloc camera equipment. 122 Calea Victoriei (no phone).

COGSIGNATIA Any one of several consignment stores among the wonderful little shops along Stradă Lipscani. They sell everything from antiques to Western goods imported from Turkey and Greece. As you enter the street from the east, an alleyway on the left leads into a cobblestone courtyard with iron-shuttered windows, part of the original 15th-century marketplace. The shops are about eight doors down on the left-hand side of the courtyard. Stradă Lipscani.

GALERIE DE ARTA VECHE SI MODERNA (OLD AND MODERN ART GALLERY) Romanian artifacts — from religious icons to dusty thousand-year-old volumes on history and art — many of which were confiscated by the Communists from the Romanian bourgeoisie. Open daily from 9 AM to 7 PM. 1 Bulevardul Unirii (phone: 631-2271).

OFICIU POŞTAL (POST OFFICE BUILDING) Not only are stamps sold here, but also picture postcards and decorative envelopes. There are often long lines. Open Mondays through Saturdays from 7 AM to 8 PM. 150 Calea Dorobanţilor (no phone).

PHOTO MUZICĂ Wonderful woodcarvings and ceramics at absurdly low prices. Also record albums and cassette tapes. Corner of Stradă Scoală Floreasco and Calea Dorobanţilor (no phone).

UNIREA The city's central department store, with a good souvenir department. Sometimes you'll find handmade wool rugs, scarves, and national costumes and blouses. 1 Piaţă Natiunile Unite, just south of Stradă Lipscani (no phone).

UNIUNEA ARTISTILOR PLASTICI (UNION OF PLASTIC ARTISTS) Look for this sign on the doors of a series of small art galleries located in the courtyard off

Stradă Lipscani. They sell cards and small prints, oil lamps, ceramics, jewelry, glassware, and paintings. Be sure to get a receipt from the shop-keeper that will allow you to take original art out of the country.

SPORTS & FITNESS

Physical fitness and sports activities are considered a fundamental activity for all Romanians — at school, in the factories, and in the villages. International recognition has come to a few Romanians — who can forget the darling of the *1976 Summer Olympics* in Montreal, Nadia Comăneci? In the tennis world, players Ion Tiriac and Ilie "Nasty" Nastase have had their share of aces. As elsewhere in Europe, soccer is the national game here, and matches are played during summer and fall at several stadiums in Bucharest, including the *Dinamo* (2 Stefan cel Mare; phone: 619-2426). Fitness centers and swimming pools can be found at the *Bucureşti, Flora, Inter-Continental,* and *Parc* hotels. About 3 miles north of downtown in Herăstrău Park, 4 clay tennis courts are available daily from 7 AM to 4 PM. Call for reservations (phone: 679-5948).

THEATER

Tickets to shows and musical events are generally quite inexpensive and can be obtained at box offices, through most hotels, *Carpaţi,* or at ticket agencies around town (*Casă Aria* is at 68-70 Calea Victoriei, near the *National Art Museum*). The *Ateneul Român* (Romanian Athenaeum; 1 Stradă Franklin; phone: 615-6875) is the home of the *Bucharest Philhar-monic Orchestra and Madrigal,* which performs here during the winter. The *Caragiale National Theater* (2 Bulevardul N. Nicolae Bălcescu; phone: 614-7171) stages Romanian classics, Shakespeare, and other plays. Native son Eugène Ionescu's works are popular in Bucharest, and have been frequently presented at the *Theater of Comedy* (2 Stradă Mandinesti; phone: 166460). Opera and ballet fans should check the September-through-May schedule at the *Opera Romana* (70 Bulevardul Kogal-niceanua; phone: 614-6980). The only theaters open during the summer season (mid-June through mid-September) are puppet and comedy thea-ters; they offer satire, very popular with Romanians.

MUSIC

The *Rapsodia Romana Artistic Ensemble Hall* (53 Stradă Lipscani; phone: 613-0228) offers folkloric song and dance from Walachia, Moldavia, and Transylvania. Those with more contemporary tastes can take in pop and jazz concerts at the *Hall of the Radio and Television Building* (191 Calea Dorobanţilor). The *Bucharest Radio-Television Orchestra* also gives classi-cal performances here featuring many guest artists. Watch especially for Alexandru Andrias, a favorite balladeer since his underground days before the 1989 revolution.

NIGHTCLUBS AND NIGHTLIFE

The last 3 years have seen a surge in the nightlife scene, which was generally oriented toward cabarets and floor shows at the larger hotels. Popular among locals, especially the under-30 crowd, is the *Salion Spaniol* (120 Calea Victoriei; phone: 312-3999), with offerings ranging from amateur entertainment to special guest stars. For a blend of cabaret, vaudeville, and satire that can be entertaining even if you don't speak Romanian, try *Tanasr* (174 Calea Victoriei) and the *Savoy Theater* (Stradă Academie). The *Bar Melody* (Stradă Pitcor Perona; phone: 611-8099) has floor shows. The *Vox Maris* (2 Bulevardul Kogolniceanu; phone: 615-5030) is a new, plush disco ensconced in quarters on the first floor of the exquisite army general staff building. Open Tuesdays through Saturdays from 8 PM to the wee hours of the morning. The *Carioca Club* (97 Dacia; phone: 611-3126 or 611-9012) is an elegant, minimally furnished new bar that features live jazz Thursdays through Sundays; rock music on Mondays through Wednesdays. Reservations necessary. Although the *Insomnia Bar* (18 Bibescu Voda; phone: 614-8351) is in Ceauşescu's overwhelming Civic Center, it is basically an unpretentious American-style bar that attracts a mix of Romanians and foreigners — an ideal place for a late-night cheeseburger and beer; there's dancing to live music most nights. Although some might characterize *Sarpele Rosu* (The Red Snake; 133 Galati St.; phone: 610-7825) as a dive, it is also one of the most fascinating places to spend an evening in Bucharest, featuring rousing jam sessions of live Gypsy music. The mostly local crowd often includes some unsavory types, but fear not: They are kept in check by the owner who presides over his establishment from a corner table. *Caru Cu Bere* (5 Stavopolous St.; phone: 613-7560) is a splendid German-style beer hall. The beer tends to be watered down and the place closes much too early (10 PM), but it's definitely worth a visit if only for a glimpse of its spectacular interior.

Best in Town

CHECKING IN

Although some effort is being made to renovate or upgrade accommodations for the first time in more than 4 decades, Romania's economic difficulties still dog the country's hotel industry, with tourists sometimes turned away due to shortages of such basics as lightbulbs. Without exception, hotels in Bucharest and Romania's other major cities are the most inexpensive in Eastern Europe, and their quality is adequate to good, though hardly comparable to their "deluxe" counterparts in Western Europe. Expect to pay $155 or more for a double room listed as very expensive; between $95 to $155 per night in a hotel listed as expensive; moderate accommodations run about $56 to $80. Reservations are particularly important during the summer months. Most of Bucharest's major hotels have complete facilities for the business traveler. Those hotels listed below as having "business services" usually offer such conveniences as English-speaking concierge, meeting rooms, photocopiers, computers, translation services, and express checkout, among others. Call the hotel for additional information. All telephone numbers are in the 1 city code unless otherwise indicated.

For an unforgettable experience, we begin with our favorite Bucharest hostelry, followed by our cost and quality choices of hotels, listed by price category.

A SPECIAL HAVEN

Hanul Manuc Built as an inn 300 years ago around a courtyard forming part of the city's old Princely Court, this historic 2-story wooden structure was first renovated in the 19th century. Located near the old market district, it has 32 guestrooms (try to get one that overlooks the courtyard). The on-site *Cramma* restaurant serves Romanian and continental fare, as well as a wide variety of Romanian vintages (*manuc* means "wine cellar"). The rooms have TV sets and telephones, and there's even a hair salon on the premises. Business services. 62 Stradă Iuliu Maniu (phone: 613-1415).

VERY EXPENSIVE

Inter-Continental Bucharest's most modern property boasts 417 rooms at a great downtown location, but it has none of the Old World charm of the *Bucureşti* (see below). Many of the amenities are similar, though, including a pool and fitness center, 3 good restaurants serving Romanian and international food, 2 bars, a casino, and a nightclub complete with a floor show (admission is free to guests; non-guests pay $20). Business services. 4-6 Bulevardul Nicolae Bălcescu (phone: 613-7040 or 614-0400; fax: 613-6470).

EXPENSIVE

Ambassador Built in 1937, this is a typical example of the Stalinesque cement-block style. The 13-story hostelry is eminently serviceable, as well as conveniently located near Piaţă Universitatii and *Carpaţi's* main office. There is a good restaurant and a wonderful pastry shop. Rooms are adequate, with bulky phones and TV sets. As for room service, it exists but be patient. There's also foreign currency exchange. 10 Bulevardul General Magheru (phone: 615-9080).

Athénée Palace Once grand, and now merely atmospheric. Many of its rooms were damaged during the December 1989 revolution, but most have been restored to their original elegance. There are 2 restaurants (one featuring musical entertainment and the other offering Chinese food), a good take-out pastry shop in the lobby, and a good nightclub in the basement. Business services. 1-3 Episcopiei St. (phone: 614-0899).

Bucureşti An Old World–style, yet modern 448-room establishment located on one of Bucharest's main thoroughfares and convenient to most sites in the city center. Its rooms and suites are small but comfortable. There's a good restaurant (see *Eating Out*) with a nightly Romanian music show, a brasserie, snack bar, and hard-currency beer bar. Other amenities include indoor and outdoor swimming pools, saunas, a hairdresser, one of the only Western-style fitness centers in Romania, and even a dental clinic. Business services. 63-81 Calea Victoriei (phone: 615-5850; fax: 143105).

Capitol The location more than makes up for the somewhat simple accommodations. All 80 rooms have telephones and TV sets, and there is a good restaurant serving Romanian fare along with a coffee shop on the premises. Just off the Piaţă Universitatii, 29 Calea Victoriei (phone: 615-8030; fax: 613-9440).

Flora-Cure A pleasant 4-story hotel with a lovely setting in pastoral Herăstrău Park on the outskirts of Bucharest. In addition to a restaurant, brasserie, cafeteria, and bar, facilities include a swimming pool and sauna. For jet-lagged travelers, skin-care and anti-aging treatments are available for an additional fee. Business services. 1 Calea Poligrafiei (phone: 618-4640 or 611-4438).

MODERATE

Griviţa Thanks to reasonable prices and a convenient location near the Gară de Nord train station, all 62 rooms here are often full. Amenities are minimal, but there is a passable restaurant. 130 Calea Griviţei (phone: 312-9632).

Lebăda A 127-room hotel on the site of a recently razed monastery on an island in Lake Pantelimon. There's a restaurant and bar, tennis courts, and a bowling alley. Business services. 3 Bulevardul Biruinţei, near the eastern edge of the city (phone: 624-3010; fax: 312-8041).

Opera An old-style establishment where guests sometimes have small sinks in their rooms but must share bathrooms; rooms do have phones and TV sets. Even though there is no restaurant on the premises, the hotel is close to some of Bucharest's best eating establishments and to the theater district. 37 Stradă Brezoianu (phone: 614-1075; fax: 312-5291).

Palas A pleasant 173-room hostelry also located within walking distance of Bucharest's theater district, it has a decent restaurant and cafeteria. 18 Stradă C. Mille (phone: 613-6735).

Parc Located in Herăstrău Park, next door to the *Flora-Cure,* this 257-room property is not quite as exclusive, but comfortable nonetheless, with modern amenities including a pool and a sauna, a restaurant, a cafeteria, a brasserie, and a bar with nightly entertainment. Skin treatments can be had here, too. Business services. 3 Calea Poligrafiei (phone: 618-0950; fax: 312-8419).

Triumf Away from the downtown area in a quiet rose and statue garden surrounded by a wrought-iron fence is this privately run 3-story red stone and brick hostelry. Originally built in 1938 to house the mistress of King Carol II, its 125 rooms are furnished in 19th-century style; suites boast Oriental carpets and antiques. Formerly called *Le President,* this is a favorite among members of the foreign diplomatic corps, particularly for its lovely restaurant (see *Eating Out*). 12 Soseaua Kiseleff (phone: 618-4110; fax: 312-8411).

HOPE FOR HOTELS	Scheduled to open next year is Radisson's *Grand Hotel* featuring 339 rooms,

restaurants, a casino, nightclubs, and theaters. Located in the city's Civic Center, which was razed and targeted for redevelopment by the Ceauşescu regime, the new hotel will also include an office complex.

EATING OUT

Though Bucharest was once a gastronomic capital rivaling Paris, the city is struggling to regain even a soupçon of its former reputation. Happily, things are slowly improving, and there are a handful of restaurants that are a cut above the rest.

Authentic Romanian food is usually simple but varied, due to multifarious cultural influences — Slavic, Germanic, and French among them. Fish dishes abound. The favorite appetizer is *mititei,* a small skinless lamb or pork sausage spiced with garlic and herbs and grilled. *Ciorbă* is a hearty soup that comes in many varieties, among them *ciorbă de perişoare* (a milky broth with meatballs and vegetables) and *ciorbă de burta* (a creamed soup with veal tripe, rice, and vegetables, highly seasoned with vinegar and garlic). Perhaps the primary national staple is *mămăligă,* a creamy corn porridge that accompanies the entrée at lunch or is eaten by itself as a light supper, served with fresh unsalted cheese and sour cream. Perhaps the best Romanian dishes are the desserts, like cream-filled chocolate pastries, mocha- or fruit-filled strudel, and rich Austrian-style tortes and honey-nut pies. Wash all this down with a selection of quite good red and white wines from Transylvania, Moldavia, and the Black Sea area. Murfatlar wines (mostly white) have won medals in worldwide competitions, and *cotnari,* a northern Moldavian white, was a favorite of the 15th-century Moldavian Prince Stefan cel Mare (the Great). Another national drink is *ţuică,* an aromatic (and very potent) plum eau-de-vie.

The major meal of the day in Romania is generally taken at noon, though many restaurants, including those listed here, serve a full menu at both lunch and dinner. Lunch usually is served from noon to 3 PM, and dinner from 7 to 10 PM. For the widest menu selection, have dinner as early as possible in Bucharest. Even in good restaurants, the best dishes are rarely available in abundance and are likely to run out later in the evening.

Restaurant meals in Romania are a bargain by European — and even Eastern European — standards. Most restaurants charge only about $15 for even the most lavish, three-course extravaganza for two. At more moderately priced establishments, expect to pay between $6 and $8. Payment is in lei unless otherwise noted. All telephone numbers are in the 1 city code unless otherwise indicated.

For an unforgettable dining experience, we begin with our culinary favorite, followed by our cost and quality choices, listed by price category.

DELIGHTFUL DINING

Capşa Founded in 1852 by a Parisian restaurateur, this became the city's premier culinary institution, as well as an artistic and literary salon and magnet for Bucharest's aristocratic elite. Red velvet banquettes, gold-framed beveled mirrors, crystal chandeliers, and pink marble columns suggest some of the grandeur of a lost age, a time when the capital lived up to its sobriquet, the Paris of the Balkans. The food is continental, with a variety of Romanian specialties, and the kitchen makes as much use as possible of fresh local produce. There's also an elegant tearoom. Open daily. Reservations necessary (but only can be made in person or in advance through *Carpaţi* or your hotel service bureau). Major credit cards accepted by advance arrangement through *Carpaţi*. The side entrance at 16 Stradă Edgar Quintet is used for the restaurant, while the front entrance at 36 Calea Victoriei mostly is used for the tearoom (phone: 613-4482).

EXPENSIVE

Bucureşti In the hotel of the same name, meals here are well prepared, with fresh, if not particularly imaginative, fare such as beef Stroganoff, roast pork, and lamb chops. A wonderful tradition left over from 19th-century Bucharest is the "show table," which allows diners to peruse the specials of the day before ordering (a boon for non-Romanian speakers). Desserts are creamy and irresistible. Entertainment includes a Romanian pop-rock band and folkloric song and dance. Open daily for lunch and dinner. Reservations advised. Major credit cards and hard currency accepted. At the *Bucureşti Hotel*, 63-11 Calea Victoriei (phone: 615-5850).

Oriental Popular with the growing Middle Eastern community, this eatery serves fine hummus and tabbouleh, delicious *shawarma*, shish kebab, and other exotic specialties. The fast service actually scares away many Romanians who are inclined to view dinner as an evening's entertainment. Open daily until 2 AM. No reservations. Major credit cards accepted. 118 Bulevardul Libertatii (phone: 623-3209).

La Premiera This gathering place for diplomats, foreigners, as well as assorted members of Romanian bohemia, serves consistently high-quality continental and Romanian fare in a modern, pleasant atmosphere, located in the back of the National Theater Building. During the summer, the terrace is the most "in" place for dinner or late-night drinks or snacks. Be sure to try the excellent quail and schnitzel, as well as a selection from the good wine list. Owner Theo Oltean is always on hand to provide personal service. Open daily. Reservations necessary. Major credit cards accepted. Alexadru Sahia (phone: 312-4397).

Select A mixture of good Romanian and international dishes are featured at this dining spot. Open daily for lunch and dinner. Reservations necessary. Major credit cards accepted. 18 Alęea Alexandru (phone: 679-4120).

Triumf One of the establishments that is trying hard to restore some luster to the culinary arts in Bucharest — and it's succeeding. Romanian dishes mix with continental specialties, including superb chateaubriand, pâté, fresh fruit, and cakes and pastries that taste as heavenly as they look. Open daily. Reservations necessary. Major credit cards or hard currency only. At the *Triumf Hotel,* 12 Şoseaua Kiseleff (phone: 618-4110).

Velvet This elegant dining room, decorated with plush pink chairs and white wooden tables, is an excellent place for a business dinner, offering French-inspired food that is probably the best in Bucharest. Try the chateaubriand, which is excellent, or the seafood salad. There is also an upstairs café. Open daily for lunch and dinner. Reservations necessary. No credit cards accepted. 2 Stirboi Voda St. (phone: 625-9241)

MODERATE

Casă Lido Originally built in 1890, neo-classical touches were added later to this dining spot, whose decorative focal point is a grand spiral staircase. The Romanian food is adequate rather than inspired, but the service is quite elegant, and there is a good selection of wines and cognacs (but no *ţuică*). Open daily. Reservations necessary. Major credit cards accepted by advance arrangement through *Carpaţi.* 13 Stradă C.A. Rosetti; entrance through a courtyard at 3 Bulevardul Magheru (phone: 615-5085).

Casă Romana Romanian specialties, plus pizza and other Italian dishes, as well as steaks. Occasionally a shipment of Italian wine or German beer livens up the menu. Open daily from 11 AM to midnight. No reservations. Major credit cards accepted. 2 Calea Victoriei (phone: 614-6808).

Dong Hai The best of the dozen or so Chinese restaurants that have sprung up throughout the city. Try the spicy pork. Open daily from 11 AM to midnight. Reservations necessary. No credit cards accepted. 14 Str. Blanari (phone: 615-6494).

Elite A former aircraft factory canteen located near the Băneasa Airport, it now is a fine restaurant serving Romanian specialties, plus excellent pork filet, roast beef, and several French-inspired dishes. Open daily for lunch and dinner. Reservations advised. No credit cards accepted. Complexul Aviatiei Băneasa (phone: 312-9973).

Padurea Băneasa A popular indoor/outdoor place in a park setting, with a good menu. Recommended Romanian specialties include cold stuffed vegetable appetizers. Entertainment is provided by a five-piece band and there's a folkloric show. A bit touristy, but you might spot a few Romanians here, too. Open daily for lunch and dinner. Reservations advised and should be made in person. Major credit cards accepted. In Băneasa Forest (phone: 679-5203).

Pescăruş A large, 2-story dining spot (whose name means "seagull"), situated on a lovely lake in Herăstrău Park. It's well-suited for large groups, and evening folkloric shows can be arranged. The fare is a combination of international and Romanian dishes. Open for lunch and dinner; closed Mondays. Reservations necessary. Major credit cards accepted. Calea Aviatorilor (phone: 679-4640).

Podul Magosoare No music and not much atmosphere, but the Romanian specialties are as close to homemade as you're likely to find anywhere. A favorite dinner spot for locals. Open daily for lunch and dinner. No reservations. No credit cards accepted. Corner of Calea Victoriei and Stradă Lemnea (no phone).

Warshowia A Polish place, it specializes in the fare of the capital, as its name implies. Good bets are stuffed Warsaw duck (with apples, raisins, and bread stuffing), steaks, and pork with mushrooms and sour cream. There's a good wine list, including some Polish vintages. Breakfast also is served. Open daily. Reservations advised. No credit cards accepted. 98 Calea Dorobanţilor (phone: 679-5180).

Budapest

The Danube, central Europe's great river — which flows for 1,770 miles from the Black Forest to the Black Sea, through Ulm, Regensburg, Linz, and Vienna — is particularly wide and beautiful when it reaches Budapest. Visitors arriving from Vienna on the hydrofoil — a 4½-hour trip around the Danube Bend — see Budapest at its most splendid. Buda and Pest, two of the city's three parts (along with smaller Obuda), both face that mighty river, which forms the physical and spiritual center of the Hungarian capital.

Sprawling over the rolling hills of Buda and the almost endless plain of Pest, the two halves of the city form strophe and antistrophe around the Danube. Buda rises and falls along its hills in a swelling reprise of medieval cobblestone streets and ancient buildings, crowned by the neo-Gothic tower of Matthias Church. The streets of Pest — the governmental and commercial center of the city — run in rings and radials around grand squares of monumental buildings and dramatic statues and memorials. The hilly parts of Buda have much cleaner air than busy Pest, which is quite noisy and polluted. From the river, an observer clearly sees the two buildings that best characterize Budapest's two halves: Matthias Church in Buda, where generations of Hungarian kings were crowned; and Pest's neo-Gothic Parliament, towering like a huge wedding cake on the banks of the river. It is as if both parts of the city relate to the Danube more comfortably than to each other.

So beautiful is this city of 2 million people — one-fifth of the country's population — that visitors might not suspect that Budapest, like other European cities, has a history of recurrent invasion, destruction, and reconstruction that only intensified in this century. Heavy bombing in World War II demolished 33,000 buildings and all the city's bridges. Both before that time and since, Hungary, located at the crossroads between East and West, has been no stranger to social and political turmoil.

Although it may have been settled as early as the Neolithic period, the first-known settlement in the region that is now Budapest was a community called Ak-In, established by the Celts in the 3rd century BC. In the 1st century AD it became a Roman town of considerable size called Aquincum, Latin for "Ample Water." The Hungarian nation, however, was not founded until the 9th century, when Arpad, a semi-legendary chief of the Magyars, brought his people here from the Urals. The Magyar cities of Buda and Pest grew as trade and craft centers, thriving especially under Hungary's first king, St. Stephen (who reigned from 997 to 1038). But a bloody invasion by the Mongols in 1241 destroyed both Buda and Pest. The cities were rebuilt, however, and became even more splendid. In the 13th century, King Béla IV had a fortified castle built, and in the 14th

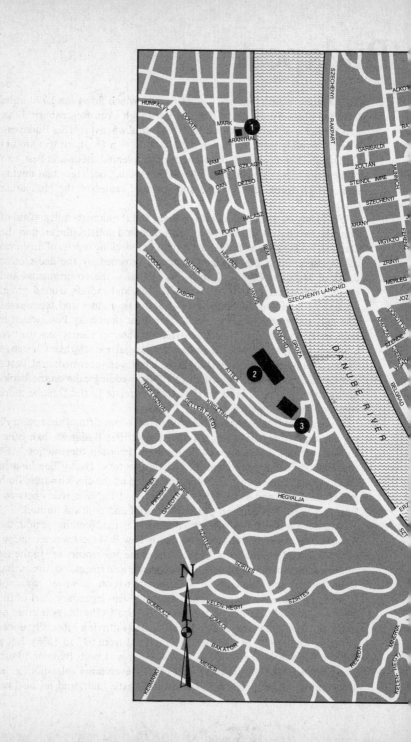

BUDAPEST

Points of Interest

1. Matthias Church
2. National Gallery
3. Historical Museum of Budapest
4. St. Stephen's Basilica
5. Aquincum Museum
6. National Museum
7. Museum of Applied Arts

century, Emperor Sigismund erected a palace for the Hungarian rulers here. Buda became the capital of Hungary in 1361.

The Ottoman Turks arrived in the 16th century, bringing 150 years of decay, poverty, and captivity. When they fell to the Hapsburg Empire in 1686, both Buda and Pest were in ruins, but they were resettled, Buda with Germans and Pest with Serbs and Hungarians. A century and a half later, in 1848, when a liberal uprising started in Pest, czarist troops brutally suppressed the revolt at Vienna's request. In 1867 the Austro-Hungarian Empire was established, granting the cities greater home rule, but the Hapsburg Empire maintained control over the country until the end of World War I.

During the early days of Hapsburg rule, Pest was a commercial center inhabited by Germans, while Buda developed as an imperial garrison. After the two cities were united in 1873, Budapest grew rapidly as one of the capitals of the Austro-Hungarian Empire. From the time of the 1848 uprising to 1918, the combined population of Buda and Pest increased from 100,000 to 1 million. Industries developed, and with thousands of peasants flocking to the city to work in its factories, by the end of the century Budapest became almost totally populated by Magyars. Other groups, lured by Budapest's economic success, also migrated here. The Serbs, who basically ran the Danube's shipping industry, and the Greeks and other Balkan peoples became merchants. A large number of Jews also came from the eastern provinces, where they had been prohibited from owning land; in Budapest they became merchants and bankers. By 1900 there were almost 200,000 Jews in Budapest, where they prospered until World War II, when the Nazi occupation destroyed their community — and their lives.

Under the bitterly resented Trianon Peace Treaty (1920), Hungary lost a third of its territory to the new states of Czechoslovakia, Romania, and Yugoslavia. Then Miklós Horthy, a former admiral in the imperial navy, set up an oppressive right-wing regime that later allied itself with Nazi Germany. Germany occupied Hungary from 1944 until the country's liberation by the Soviet army in April 1945. Another oppressive regime — this one Communist — came into power soon after.

In May 1989, Hungary gained the attention of the world when it opened its border with Austria and allowed tens of thousands of East Germans, who had filled refugee camps in Hungary, to leave the country freely. The following October, Hungary's Communist Party changed its structure and its name to the Socialist Party, making Hungary the first Eastern European country to formally abandon communism. On the 33rd anniversary of its 1956 anti-Communist uprising — quashed almost immediately by Soviet tanks — Hungary once again declared itself an independent republic, but this time without military retribution. Hungary's first free elections since 1947 were held in March 1990, and in August of the same year, the country's first post-Communist Parliament elected Arpád Göncz president for a 5-year term. The full effects of the country's fledgling social democracy and free market economy remain to be seen. With a 23% inflation rate and unemployment at 11% and rising, Hungarians are no longer quite so euphoric about capitalism. Just putting food on the table has become a struggle. It is this change in the economic situation that has given rise to a grass roots nationalism, the likes of which haven't been seen here since World War II.

In the absence of an aristocratic elite, Hungary venerates its artists, writers, and musicians, and, increasingly, its new class of millionaires enriched by private ventures. Budapest's rich and diverse cultural life embraces 29 theaters, 2 opera houses, an operetta theater, 3 concert halls, a puppet theater, and more than 20 museums. These venues are so popular that natives often have to vie with visitors for theater tickets or a quiet space in a museum.

Budapest is also a capital of sculpture; there were once more than 500 life-size sculptures — from political leaders to poets — throughout the city. (Last spring, a sculpture park was created in Nagytétény — a small town only 30 minutes away from the city center — to house those "politically incorrect" effigies of the former Soviet regime.)

The city is also filled with bookstores, now stocked with titles of once forbidden authors, and cafés where artists and intellectuals gather to discuss the latest news. Happily, the Gypsy violinists who have plied their trade on street corners for centuries can still be heard.

Today's Budapest is a city that loves good living. Rock 'n' roll, jeans, provocative T-shirts in various languages, a tradition of satire, Western magazines, fads, and foods have long been evident on the city's streets. With the influx of foreign capital, international boutiques — from *Estée Lauder* and *Christian Dior* to *Benetton* and *Stefanel* — now add a new Western-style glamour to the city's main shopping street, Váci utca. Nagymezö utca, once known as "Hungarian Broadway," is lined with many of the city's best theaters, including *Arizona, Thalia, Radnóti,* and *Operett*. Plans are underway to transform this area into a cultural district called Kis (Little) Broadway. Likewise, Falk Miksa utca, a street near the Parliament building crowded with antique shops, is the "antiques row" of Budapest.

Hungarian cuisine has absorbed Turkish, French, Italian, Slavic, and other influences into a deliciously unique blend. The wines of Hungary, particularly the whites from Balaton, the reds from Eger, and the world-famous dessert wine tokay, are very good. Hungarian pastries rank among the best in the world. There is a popular saying in Budapest that goes something like, "If only we could afford to live as well as we do — how well we would live." Budapest's slightly irreverent humor is characteristic of a city where, despite a history of strife, it has always been considered both a duty and a pleasure to live life to its fullest.

Budapest At-a-Glance

SEEING THE CITY

The best view of Budapest is from the top of Gellérthegy (Gellért Hill) on the Buda side, which can be climbed from Gellért tér (Gellért Square). From the balustrades of a stone fort built in 1850 you will enjoy a panorama of the Danube with its bridges — Margit híd (Margaret Bridge) to Margitsziget (Margaret Island) in the middle of the Danube, the recreational center of the city; the historic Lánc híd (Chain Bridge) to Castle Hill on the Buda side, the oldest part of town; and the Erzsébet híd (Elizabeth Bridge) that connects Buda with the Inner City on the Pest side, the busy downtown commercial and shopping center.

In front of the fort, or Citadella, is the gigantic Liberation Monument, a statue of a woman holding an olive branch, which is sometimes called Budapest's Statue of Liberty; it commemorates the Soviet liberation of Budapest from Nazi occupation in 1945.

Since Buda is built on seven hills, there are several views of the city. One of the best is from the Halászbástya (Fishermen's Bastion) in the Castle Hill district, from which the Danube, Margaret Island, and the flat Pest side of the river, including the spectacular façade of the Hungarian Parliament, are all clearly visible.

Budapest is divided into numerous districts designated by a Roman numeral before the street address. Streets have been renamed, and on many corners visitors will find both the new and old signs; the older one usually bearing the name of a Communist hero has a red "X" drawn through it. "Utca," "út," and "útja" mean "street" in Hungarian; "tér" means "square"; "körút" refers to the ring-shaped avenues that form concentric circles radiating from the Danube in Pest; and "rakpart" is the name given to the quays that run parallel to the Danube.

SPECIAL PLACES

Budapest, once actually three cities — Buda, Obuda, and Pest — sprawls along both banks of the Danube River and is difficult to explore on foot because of the distances involved. To make matters worse, the streets of Pest can be polluted, and Buda's streets are hilly and often cobbled. A detailed map, recently printed, is strongly advised (see *Sources and Resources*). Public transportation is good, and fares are low.

BUDA

VÁRHEGY (CASTLE HILL) Topped by monuments, this hill is the heart of medieval Budapest, with cobbled streets, narrow alleys, and lovely squares. Homes are painted in pastel colors, each marking the trade of its owner. Its baroque and classical public buildings, also painted in lovely pastel shades, now house famous restaurants, writers' studios, a student quarter, and many landmarks of old Budapest. Unfortunately, few Hungarians live in this area anymore, since the charming medieval district has become a visitor's paradise in which almost everyone speaks a foreign language. Much of the area was badly damaged during World War II, and restorations include a 19th-century funicular railway (Budavári Sikló) that climbs up the hill from the Danube. The funicular leaves from Clark Ádám tér, and runs daily from 7:30 AM to 10 PM; round-trip tickets cost about $1.50; the trip takes 50 seconds each way.

HALÁSZBÁSTYA (FISHERMEN'S BASTION) Named for the fishermen of the city who protected this northern side of the Royal Castle from siege in medieval times, the bastion is a turn-of-the-century *Disneyland*-type version of Romanesque ramparts and turrets. Originally built as a showpiece for the *1896 World's Fair,* today the structure affords good views of the Danube and the city. I, Hunyadi János út.

MÁTYÁS TEMPLOM (MATTHIAS CHURCH) This neo-Gothic edifice atop Castle Hill, where King Matthias was married twice, dates from the 13th century, although it has been rebuilt many times, most recently after World War II. Its proper name is the Church of Our Lady. With its Gothic spires and colored tile roof, this coronation church of Hungarian kings has one of Europe's most memorable silhouettes. Inside, the splendor of the baroque gilt nave is especially noteworthy, as are the original chalices and vestments in the treasury. During the Turkish occupation of Hungary in the 16th and 17th centuries, the church served as a mosque. Sunday morning mass is celebrated with music, and there are frequent organ recitals. I, 2 Szentháromság tér.

BUDAVÁRI PALOTA (ROYAL PALACE) Reduced to rubble by bombs in 1944–45, the palace has carefully been rebuilt to incorporate all the styles of its historic past. Prior to the bombing, it existed primarily as an 18th-century building with some baroque touches; before that it had been destroyed and rebuilt several times and in several architectural styles since it was first constructed as a castle in the 13th century. It now houses the *Historical Museum of Budapest*, the *National Gallery,* the *National Library,* and the *Museum of Contemporary Times* (formerly the *Museum of the Worker's Movement*). On Várhegy, I, 2 Szent György tér (phone: 175-7533).

BUDAPESTI TÖRTÉNETI MÚZEUM (HISTORICAL MUSEUM OF BUDAPEST) In Wing E (the southern wing) of the Royal Palace, the museum contains archaeological remains of the ancient town and exhibits on the history of the palace's construction. Also on display are splendid furniture, sculpture, ceramics, glass, and china; the halls, dating from the 15th century, have Renaissance door frames carved in red marble. To appreciate the richness of this collection, one must remember that Hungary's King Matthias had a greater income at the end of the 15th century than either the English or the French king. Open from 10 AM to 6 PM; closed Mondays. Admission charge. I, 2 Szent György tér (phone: 175-7533).

NEMZETI GALÉRIA (NATIONAL GALLERY) Housed in the Royal Palace, this museum displays the works of the greatest Hungarian artists of the 19th and 20th centuries. English-language guides are available. Open Tuesdays through Sundays from 10 AM to 6 PM. Admission charge. I, 17 Dísz tér, Wings B, C, and D (phone: 175-7533).

PEST

BELVÁROSI TEMPLOM (INNER CITY PARISH CHURCH) This is the oldest building in Pest, begun in the 12th century. It shows evidence of many styles of construction, including a Romanesque arch, a Gothic chancel, a Moslem prayer niche, and a Roman wall. V, 2 15 Március (March 15) tér (phone: 118-3108).

SZENT ISTVÁN BAZILIKA (ST. STEPHEN'S BASILICA) The largest church in the city, with its huge dome and two tall spires, the basilica (officially known as St. Stephen's Parish Church) dominates the flat landscape of Pest. Built in the 19th century, its murals and altarpieces are by leading Hungarian painters and sculptors. V, Bajcsy-Zsilinszky út.

MAGYAR NEMZETI MÚZEUM (HUNGARIAN NATIONAL MUSEUM) This oldest and most important museum in Budapest houses the greatest historical and archaeological collections in the country. The first collections were bequeathed to the museum in 1802, and the buildings were erected between 1837 and 1847. One of the prehistoric exhibitions displays the most ancient remnant of European man, the skull from Vértesszölös. There are also Roman ceramics, Avar gold and silver work, and the famous Hungarian Crown of St. Stephen and other historic crown jewels. Among the gold objects are a chiseled Byzantine crown (called the Crown of Monomachos) and the gold baton of Franz Liszt. There also is an exhibition of minerals. Open from 10 AM to 5:30 PM; closed Mondays. Admission charge. VIII, 14-16 Múzeum körút (phone: 138-2122).

IPARMŰVÉSZETI MÚZEUM (MUSEUM OF APPLIED ARTS) Another of the great museums of Budapest, its most important collections are European and Hungarian ceramics, the work of goldsmiths and silversmiths from the 15th to 17th century, Italian Renaissance textiles, Turkish carpets, and Flemish tapestries from the 17th century. The museum's artifacts were a gift of Odön Lechner (architect of the museum) in 1896. Open Tuesdays through Sundays from 10 AM to 6 PM. Admission charge. IX, 33-37 Ullői út (phone: 117-5222).

ORSZÁGHÁZ (PARLIAMENT) Mirrored in the Danube, these impressive buildings on the Pest side are reminiscent of London's Houses of Parliament. Finished in 1902, they were built over a period of 17 years. A maze of 10 courtyards, 29 staircases, and 88 statues, Parliament is a favorite haunt for lovers after dark. In 1950, the Communist Party placed a giant red star atop the Parliament building. During the 1989 revolt, it took workers 2 months to remove it. Along Széchenyi rakpart and backed by Kossuth Lajos tér.

ANDRÁSSY UT (ANDRÁS STREET) Named after 19th-century statesman Gyula Andrássy and also known as Embassy Row, this noble avenue, which runs from the inner city of Pest and crosses two concentric rings toward Városliget (City Park), has had many names throughout Budapest's stormy past — among them, Sugár (Radial) in the 19th century, Andrássy in the early 20th century, Stalin Avenue and Avenue of Hungarian Youth in 1956, Népköztársaság (People's Republic) in 1957, and Andrássy again in 1990. The avenue is lined with palaces on both sides, many of which were designed by the architect Miklós Ybl in the 1870s and 1880s; among these buildings are the neo-Renaissance *State Opera House* at No. 22 and the building that once housed the Gestapo and the Communist secret police at No. 60.

HŐSÖK TÉR (HEROES' SQUARE) At the end of Andrássy is a large square marked with the Millennial Monument, which was begun in 1896 to celebrate Hungary's 1,000-year anniversary. A semicircular colonnade displays a pantheon of Hungarian historical figures; on top of the 119-foot pillar in the middle of the square is a statue of the Angel Gabriel who, according to legend, offered a royal crown to King Stephen I, founder of the kingdom. On this square are the *Museum of Fine Arts* (phone: 142-9759) and the *Art Gallery* (phone: 122-7405).

SZÉPMŰVÉSZETI MÚZEUM (MUSEUM OF FINE ARTS) Here is the greatest collection of its kind in the country. The building is at the entrance of Városliget (City Park), on the left as you face the Millennial Monument. More than 100,000 works of art are housed in this neo-classical structure. Among the masterpieces are seven paintings by El Greco and five by Goya. The Italian and Dutch sections have many world-famous paintings, including the *Madonna Esterházy* by Raphael and the *Sermon of St. John the Baptist* by Pieter Breughel the Elder. The museum also has permanent exhibitions of Egyptian antiquities, Greco-Roman antiquities, and modern European painting and sculpture. Open Tuesdays through Sundays from 10 AM to 5:30 PM. Admission charge. XIV, Hősök tér (phone: 142-9759).

VÁROSLIGET (CITY PARK) This large park just behind Heroes' Square contains an artificial lake; the Széchenyi Baths (a public spa); a zoo; a botanical garden; an amusement park; and Vajdahunyad Castle (built for the *1896 World's Fair*), which encompasses a conglomeration of Hungarian architectural styles. In winter there's an ice skating rink, too.

GALLERY 56 Opened in 1992 by Yoko Ono and Samuel Havadtoy, it showcases works of acclaimed contemporary artists from around the world. The gallery's minimalist interior and provocative exhibits make it a unique cultural spot in Budapest. V, 7 Falk Miksa utca (no phone).

MERLIN CULTURAL CENTER What was once a private club of the Budapest City Council is now a hip cultural center that houses a restaurant, a late-night jazz club, and, during the summer, a theater presenting plays in English and German. 4 Gerlóczy utca (phone: 117-9338).

NYUGATI PÁLYAUDVAR (WESTERN STATION) This glass-and-iron railroad station was designed by Gustave Eiffel (of Eiffel Tower fame) in 1874 and is well worth a visit, even if you're not taking a train. VI, 57 Teréz Körút.

OBUDA

FÖ TÉR (MAIN SQUARE) Located along the northwestern bank of the Danube River is Obuda, the city's most recently developed residential area, with its charming old houses and taverns intermingled with towering apartment complexes. Obuda's cobblestoned main square boasts a life-size sculpture called "Strollers in the Rain," by contemporary artist Varga. Encompassing the square are numerous art galleries, cafés, and restaurants including the Zichy Mansion (No. 1 Fö tér), but restaurants, such as *Sipos Halászkert* (see *Eating Out*), are an even bigger attraction. Some have outdoor seating in the warm weather months.

ELSEWHERE IN THE CITY

MARGITSZIGET (MARGARET ISLAND) This resort and recreation island lies right in the middle of the Danube, accessible from both banks by the Margit híd (Margaret Bridge). Cars and trains enter from Arpad Bridge to the north; on summer weekends, a bus runs between the southern end of the island and the hotels near Arpad Bridge. The whole island is a park, with a sports stadium, a large municipal swimming pool, a rose garden, a fountain, and several hotels, restaurants, and spas. During the summer months, when theaters close, the performances move to outdoor quarters here; you can see plays, concerts, films, and sports events. For specific programs, inquire at the tourist office, *IBUSZ* (see *Sources and Resources*).

KEREPESI TEMETÖ (KEREPESI CEMETERY) Once you've tired of walking from monument to church to museum, visit the Kerepesi Cemetery, an oasis in the heart of the city. Wealthy Hungarians spent fortunes building mausoleums adorned with sculptures and decorations, and the century-old trees here offer pleasant shade. At one side of the cemetery are monuments to people who died during the 1919 revolution and the 1956 uprising. Off Kerepesi út.

AQUINCUM One of the most significant excavations of a Roman urban area outside Italy, Aquincum (meaning Ample Water) in its heyday had almost

100,000 inhabitants. Its streets, houses, temple, and amphitheater have been unearthed 4 miles upstream of the city center on the western bank of the Danube. The museum on the site has mosaics depicting public baths, jewelry, glass, and inscribed stones. Open from mid-April through October.

EXTRA SPECIAL A boat trip on the beautiful (if not blue) Danube is an experience you will not soon forget. From May to September, *IBUSZ* offers several day tours to the Danube Bend area, about 31 miles north of Budapest, where the Danube makes a hairpin turn, changing its course from west-east to north-south. The area is rich in scenery, with limestone hills and volcanic mountains, and in history, with river communities that date from Roman times. Tours depart Wednesdays and Saturdays at 8:30 AM from the Vigadó tér landing dock; cost is $35 (phone: 118-1223 or 129-5844; or call *IBUSZ;* phone: 142-3140). From the middle of April through October, there are daily hydrofoil trips between Budapest and Vienna, but it's necessary to reserve a spot 2 or 3 months in advance. The trip costs $69 one way and $104 round trip. Contact *European Cruises* (241 E. Commercial Blvd., Fort Lauderdale, FL 33334; phone: 800-5-DANUBE). For information in Budapest, call *MAHART* (V, Belgrád rakpart; phone: 118-1953 or 118-1706). For more details, see *Classic Cruises and Wonderful Waterways* in DIVERSIONS.

Sources and Resources

TOURIST INFORMATION

For general information, brochures, and maps, contact the now-privatized *IBUSZ* — Hungary's largest travel agency (V, 10 Ferenciektére; phone: 142-3140; or 3 Petőfi tér; phone: 118-5707), open 24 hours; or the Budapest Tourist Office (V, 5 Roosevelt tér; phone: 117-3555). You may also contact *Tourinform* (V, 2 Sütő utca; phone: 117-9800), open from 8 AM to 8 PM. Of the many local travel agencies offering sightseeing tours of the country, *IPV Tourisme* offers particularly imaginative packages with an accent on Hungarian culture and history (22 Angol utca; phone: 163-3406). English-language guidebooks to Budapest and elsewhere in Hungary may be purchased at the city's hotels and bookstores. City maps, booklets on Budapest attractions, and other information are available from the US offices of *IBUSZ* (1 Parker Plaza, Suite 1104, Ft. Lee, NJ 07024; phone: 201-592-8585 or 800-367-7878) or *IBUSZ* in Chicago (233 N. Michigan Ave., Suite 1308, Chicago, Ill 60601; phone: 312-319-3150).

LOCAL COVERAGE *Programme in Hungary* (in English and German) and *Budapest Panorama* (in English, German, and Italian) are comprehensive monthly bulletins that list concerts, theater events, literary evenings, museum exhibits, sporting events, horse races, restaurants, and casinos. The *Budapest Panorama* also lists information regarding transportation, airlines, credit cards, and rental cars. Both are available free at hotel desks. For a complete listing of all restaurants in Budapest, look for *Foglaljon Helyet!* (Have a Seat!), available in bookstores.

Budapest now has three English language newspapers: the *Budapest Week*, the *Budapest Post*, and the *Daily News*, available at newsstands and hotels. Major international papers, such as the European edition of the *Wall Street Journal* and the *International Herald Tribune*, are available at most newspaper stores in the city center.

TELEPHONE The country code for Hungary is 36; the city code for Budapest is 1.

GETTING AROUND

AIRPORT Ferihegy Airport handles all international flights. A second terminal handles *MALÉV* (the Hungarian national carrier) flights (phone: 118-4333). The drive from the airport to downtown Budapest takes about a half hour, and a taxi ride should cost approximately 1,300 forints (about $20). Waiting taxi drivers are likely to overcharge you. Hail an incoming cab or go upstairs to the domestic cab pickup area. Avoid gypsy cabs, which often have "less than accurate" meters and substantially overcharge. The recently revamped *Airport Minibus* (phone: 157-8555 or 157-8993) is a much less expensive alternative. Reservations can be made in advance either by phone or at hotel desks (about $5 one way).

BUS/TRAM/SUBWAY Public transportation is efficient and cheap. Tickets are sold at tobacco shops, kiosks, and ticket offices only (not on the vehicles). Each ticket, valid for one trip, must be punched in the machines inside the vehicles. Yellow tickets are good on the metro (subway), trams, and trolleybuses; blue tickets are good for bus transportation only.

BUS TOURS You might wish to get acquainted with Budapest by taking the 3-hour tour (about $20) of the city offered daily by *IBUSZ* (see *Tourist Information*, above); contact the branch offices listed above or the Budapest Tourist Office. A 4-hour *IBUSZ* tour, conducted Thursdays at 10 AM from Erzsébet tér, offers a look at the city's cultural life, with art studio and museum visits and concerts ($15).

CAR RENTAL Automobiles may be rented with or without drivers from *IBUSZ-Avis* (V, 8 Martinelli tér; phone: 118-4240 or 118-4158); *Hertz* (VII, 24-28 Kertész utca; phone: 111-6116; or V, 4-8 Aranykéz utca; phone: 117-7533); *Coupcar* (43 Ferenc körút; phone: 113-1466); and *Europcar* (V, 5 Kecskeméti utca; phone: 117-4713). All companies have branches at the airport.

TAXI Taxi stands can be found throughout the city; rates vary widely by company as there is no fare regulation. Budapest's best cab companies include *Főtaxi* (phone: 122-2222) and *Volántaxi* (phone: 166-6666); both companies offer drivers for guided tours of the city. Also serving Budapest are *Tele5* (phone: 155-5555), *City Taxi* (phone: 122-8855), and *Budataxi* (phone: 129-4000).

TRAIN The main office of the *Magyar Allamvasutak (MAV; Hungarian State Railways;* VI, 35 Andrássy út; phone: 122-8049) handles tickets, reservations, and general train information. Major stations are the Eastern (Keleti; Baross tér; phone: 113-6835), for eastbound and most international trains; and the Western (Nyugati tér; phone: 149-0115), for trains headed west. A fast, dependable, and air conditioned *EuroCity (EC)* train — the *Lehár* — runs between Budapest and Vienna in under 3 hours. For international schedule and fare information, call 122-4052.

LOCAL SERVICES

For services in Budapest, the larger hotels are the best bet for businesspeople who would like lots of services under one roof. Most of these hotels provide dry cleaning and tailoring, photocopying, and more, along with a concierge who will help find anything the hotel can't supply.

DENTIST (ENGLISH-SPEAKING) Once there were only a few, but now there are many dental clinics in Budapest where English is spoken. For a recommendation, ask your hotel concierge or *Superdent KFT XIII* (65 Dózsa György utca; phone: 129-0200), which is open Mondays, Wednesdays, and Fridays from 8 AM to 2 PM, Tuesdays and Thursdays from 2 to 8 PM; or the *Dental-Coop* (XII, 60 Zugligeti út; phone: 176-0243), which is open weekdays from 10 AM to 6 PM, but call the switchboard in case of an emergency.

DRY CLEANER/TAILOR Recommended are *Cooperative Dry Cleaning* (6-9 Flórián tér, *Flórián Shopping Center*) and the *Patyolat* dry-cleaning chain (look for the swan logo), which is found all over the city. Major hotels also offer dry-cleaning services.

LIMOUSINE SERVICE Budapest has no "limousine" rental companies, but you can rent a car with a driver from *IBUSZ-Avis* (phone: 118-4240 or 118-4158) or *Főtaxi* (phone: 122-2222).

MEDICAL EMERGENCY Emergency cases are handled by hospitals on a rotating basis. Dial 04 for the ambulance, and it will take you to the facility on duty.

MESSENGER SERVICE Ask your hotel concierge.

NATIONAL/INTERNATIONAL COURIER *DHL Worldwide Express,* 4 Peter Bod Lejtö (phone: 186-1776).

OFFICE EQUIPMENT RENTAL Check with the main hotels that offer conference rooms and other business services.

PHARMACY There is 24-hour service at five pharmacies (*gyógyszertár*) located at VI, 41 Teréz körút; VIII, 86 Rákóczi utca; II, 22 Frankel Leó utca; IX, 3 Borános tér; and XII, 1-6 Alkotás.

PHOTOCOPIES At all major hotels.

POST OFFICE Post office No. 62 (VI, 51 Teréz körút, near the Western Railway Station) and post office No. 70 (VII, 1 Verseny utca, at the Eastern Railway Station); both have 24-hour service.

SECRETARY/STENOGRAPHER (ENGLISH-SPEAKING) Ask your hotel concierge.

TRANSLATOR *IBUSZ* (phone: 142-3140) or inquire at your hotel.

SPECIAL EVENTS

The *Budapest Spring Festival,* 10 days in March, is the highlight of the cultural season and features concerts, folk dance, and other performances. In 1986, Hungary became the host country for the annual *Formula 1 Grand Prix* on the *Hungaroring* at Mogyoród, about a half-hour's drive from Budapest. This international auto race takes place every year in August. Tickets are available at the *Autoclub* (phone: 115-8469). *Budapest Music Weeks,* in early fall, include international competitions for various types of musicians and many concerts. For information about this and other special events, contact *IBUSZ* (see above), which also has a counter in most hotels. Late November marks *Kierkegaard Week,* which honors the life of Danish philosopher Soren Kierkegaard. Festivities include lectures, seminars, and concerts held throughout the city. For more information contact the *Budapest Chamber Theater* (phone: 202-7587).

In addition to official celebrations, peaceful marches and demonstrations organized by opposition groups are the order of the day (motorists take note). Budapest also has announced that it will host the *1996 World's Fair.*

MUSEUMS

Several museums provide an introduction to Hungary's rich religious heritage: *Collections of Ecclesiastical Treasures* at the Matthias Church (I, Szentháromság tér) and at St. Stephen's Basilica (V, Szent István tér); the *National Evangelical Museum* (V, 4 Deák tér); and the *Bible Museum* (IX, 28 Ráday utca). In addition to these museums and those listed in *Special Places,* the following are worth a visit. All museums are open daily from 9 AM to 4 PM; closed Mondays. Unless otherwise indicated, all have a nominal admission charge.

BARTÓK EMLÉKHÁZ (BÉLA BARTÓK MEMORIAL HOUSE) Concerts are presented here on occasion. II, 29 Csalán utca (phone: 176-2100).

BÉLYEGMÚZEUM (MUSEUM OF POSTAGE STAMPS) An extensive collection that includes some very rare stamps. VII, 47 Hársfa utca (phone: 142-0960).

LISZT FERENC MÚZEUM (FRANZ LISZT MUSEUM) A collection of the composer's personal possessions displayed in his apartment in the old Academy of Music. Piano recitals are occasionally held here. VI, 35 Vörösmarty utca (phone: 122-9804).

MAGYAR KERESKEDELMI ÉS VENDÉGLÁTÓIPARI MÚZEUM (MUSEUM OF HUNGARIAN COMMERCE AND CATERING) A delightful small museum on Castle Hill featuring a replica of a turn-of-the-century confectioner's shop and odd artifacts — advertising signs, appliances, and other consumer goods — from Budapest's capitalist past. I, 4 Fortuna utca (phone: 175-6242).

NÉPRAJZI MÚZEUM (ETHNOGRAPHIC MUSEUM) A glimpse into the country's past. Concerts are held here on Sundays. V, 12 Kossuth tér (phone: 132-6349).

SEMMELWEIS ORVOSTÖRTÉNETI MÚZEUM (SEMMELWEIS MUSEUM OF THE HISTORY OF MEDICINE) A fascinating look at the development of European and Hungarian medicine from Roman times to the present. Dr. Ignác Semmelweis, the man responsible for the cure for childbed fever, was born in the building that now houses the museum. I, 1-3 Apràd utca (phone: 175-3533).

VARGA IMRE GYÜJTEMÉNY (IMRE VARGA COLLECTION) Monuments by the internationally famous sculptor are scattered throughout his native Hungary. Samples of his work are on permanent exhibition here, and sometimes the artist himself is on hand. III, 7 Laktanya utca (phone: 180-3274).

ZENETÖRTÉNETI MÚZEUM (MUSICAL HISTORY MUSEUM) An exhibition called "Béla Bartók's Workshop" traces the composer's creative process. In addition, a collection of historical musical instruments is on display. A concert series also is presented here. I, 7 Táncsics Mihály utca (phone: 175-9011 or 175-9487).

ZSIDÓ MÚZEUM (JEWISH MUSEUM) The history of Hungarian Jewry is shown through liturgical objects and documents. On the outside wall is a plaque honoring Theodor Herzl, founder of Budapest's Zionist movement, whose house once stood on this site. VII, 8 Dohány utca (phone: 142-8949).

SHOPPING

The change from state-owned to private business is most apparent in the city's shops. Once stocked with limited amounts of goods, they are now brimming with every imaginable consumer item. Along Váci utca, the Hungarian equivalent of Fifth Avenue, clothing stores that once sold few styles in even fewer colors now have racks of the latest fashions — some with well-known designer labels. But the best goods and gifts are those that are uniquely Hungarian. The many boutiques that line the streets of the

Castle Hill district are also where you'll find traditional folk-inspired garments — from embroidered peasant shirts and shawls to assorted leather goods and embroidered sheepskin jackets. Other local crafts include dolls in regional costumes and woodcarvings made by herdsmen. Pottery and porcelain are also plentiful in Budapest's tourist shops. Especially prized are Herend (produced by the world-famous factory), Zsolnay, and Arföldi porcelain. The best selections can be found at *Folk Art Centers* located throughout the city (V, 14 Váci utca; V, 12 Régiposta utca; V, 2 Kossuth Lajos utca; and XIII, 26 Szent István körút).

At any grocery store you can buy an authentic, inexpensive, and very portable souvenir — a packet of Hungarian paprika, the real stuff, not the red dust generally sprinkled on as a decorative touch in the US. The towns of Kalocsa and Szeged are famous for growing this fragrant red pepper, available in both spicy and sweet varieties. Best for gifts are the small cloth bags of paprika decorated with a folkloric motif. Hungarian wine is also another good buy. Various gift items can be found at one of the many *Intertourist* shops scattered throughout the city. For information about locations, call 122-7217.

Falk Miksa utca, near the Parliament building, is the antiques district of Budapest. The street is lined with small shops filled to overflowing with furniture, paintings, carpets, and objets d'art from all over Eastern Europe. Most shops are open daily from 10 AM to 8 PM. Below are some other shops of interest:

AMFORA CRYSTAL A wide selection of crystal, porcelain, and other decorative items. V, 24 Károly körút (no phone).

ANTIKVÁRIUM A secondhand bookstore in the center of the city, it offers 16th- and 17th-century tomes in Latin, as well as old maps, prints, and photographs. V, 281 Váci utca (phone: 118-5673).

ANTIQUITAT Art Nouveau–inspired porcelain, glass, and furniture. V, 3 Vitkovics M. utca (no phone).

ARTZ MODELL A popular boutique offering unique and trendy clothing, designed by the young Hungarian designer. V, 2 Semmelweiss utca (no phone).

BIANCA Fashionable Hungarian- and Italian-made clothing for men and women. V, 2 Sütő utca (no phone).

EQUUS High-quality riding clothing and accessories at affordable prices. I, 2 Országház utca (phone: 156-0517).

FOLKART CENTRUM A large selection of traditional craft items. V, 14 Váci utca (phone: 118-5840).

HABITUS Elegant women's wear by up-and-coming local designers. V, 2 Semmelweiss utca (no phone).

HELIA D STUDIO A wide selection of natural Hungarian-made beauty products. V, 19-21 Váci utca (phone: 138-2015).

HEREND Outlet for the distinctive porcelain, many with designs based on traditional folkloric motifs. V, 11 József Nádor tér (no phone).

LIBRI KÖNYVESBOLT Centrally located, this bookstore has a wide array of English- and foreign-language books, maps, and magazines. V, 32 Váci utca (phone: 118-2718).

LUCA FOLKLOR SHOP A tiny treasure trove of gift items. Open daily. V, 7-9 Régiposta utca (no phone).

LUXUS The foremost department store in the city, carrying designer labels. V, 3 Vörösmarty tér (phone: 118-2277).

MUSEUM SOUVENIR ANTIQUES AND MUSEUM COPIES Beautiful and unique museum reproductions. I, 7 Szentháromság utca (phone: 155-8165).

NATIONAL CENTER OF MUSEUMS SHOP Reproductions of museum objects. V, 7 József Nádor tér (no phone).

RÓZSAVÖLGYI Hungarian classical and folk music. V, 5 Martinelli tér (no phone).

ZSUZSA LÖRINCZ Genuine folk costumes and pottery, mostly from Transylvania. V, 14 Régiposta utca (no phone).

SPORTS AND FITNESS

BOATING By arrangement with *IBUSZ* (see *Tourist Information*), you can rent a sailboat, sailing dinghy, motorboat, small hydrofoil, and even water skis by the hour or by the day. It is the very best way to enjoy the Danube.

FISHING Licenses are issued by the *National Federation of Hungarian Anglers* (*MOHOSZ;* V, 6 Október utca; phone: 132-5315); and at the fishing information bureau (II, 1 Bem József utca; no phone).

FITNESS CENTERS The facilities at both the *Forum* and the *Atrium Hyatt* hotels (see *Checking In*) are open to non-guests for a charge.

GOLF The *Budapest Golf Park and Country Club*, operated by the *Hilton* hotel, has a 9-hole island course set amid oak and acacia trees on Szentendresziget in the Danube, just north of the city limits (Kisoroszi, Szentendrei Island; phone: 117-6025). An all-day pass costs 2,600 florints (about $3) Mondays through Thursdays, and 3,000 florints (about $3.50) on Fridays and Saturdays. It is advisable to make advance reservations, as the club is open to the public.

GREYHOUND RACING On the Danube embankment, just outside Budapest, there are races from May to September. Inquire at *IBUSZ* for details (see *Tourist Information*).

HORSE RACING There are trotting races at the track at *Ugetópálya* (VIII, 9 Kerepesi utca), and flat racing at the *Kincsem Park* track (X, 9 Albertirsai utca).

HORSEBACK RIDING A very popular pastime in this land of horsemen. There are schools and stables in and around Budapest, including the *Petneházy Riding School* (II, 5 Feketefej utca; phone: 176-5992). Information on riding tours is provided by *IBUSZ* or *Pegazus Tours* (V, 5 Károlyi Mihály utca; phone: 117-1644).

JOGGING Margitsziget (Margaret Island), in the center of the city in the Danube River, is the best place to run. The island is roughly 2 miles long and half a mile wide, and most of it is given over to sports facilities. Either take a cab to the island's *Thermál* hotel and choose a path from there, or jog over on the pedestrians-only Margit híd (Margaret Bridge). Running is also pleasant along the foothills near the *Budapest* hotel (II, 47-49 Szilágyi Erzsébet fasor). For information on jogging, call the *Futapest Club* (62-64 Váci utca; phone: 118-1638).

SKATING There is a large outdoor ice skating rink in City Park, near Vajdahunyad Castle (XIV, Stefánia út). Skating competitions and other athletic events take place at the *Budapest Sports Hall* (XIV, 1-3 Istvánmezei utca; phone: 163-6430).

SKIING The Buda Hills, accessible by bus and funicular, have several slopes, the most popular of which is the Szabadsághegy.

SOCCER As in many European countries, soccer (called football) is the most popular spectator sport. The largest city stadium is the *Népstadion* (People's Stadium) near the Városliget (City Park) in Pest, seating 96,000 spectators (XIV, 1-3 Istvánmezei utca; phone: 251-1222). Information on games and other sports events is available from the ticket bureau (at VI, 6 Andrássy út; phone: 112-4234).

SPAS Visitors from all over the world come to Budapest hoping that the waters will help ailments ranging from asthma to arthritis. Treatments include drinking cures (mineral waters), baths in lukewarm or very hot mineral pools, mud packs, and massages, all directed by specialists under the supervision of doctors.

TAKING THE WATERS

Aquincum Although the waters here have been known for centuries, the hotel and spa facilities are relatively new and very luxurious. An attentive staff offers a wide variety of spa treatments. 94 Arpad Fejedelem útja (phone: 188-6360; fax: 168-8872).

Gellért The springs beneath Budapest's oldest spa-hotel (it was built in 1918) have been known for almost 2,000 years. Today, in addition to the thermally heated mineral water baths, there are also treatments, an outdoor pool that ripples with mechanically produced waves, and a sun terrace. XI, 4 Kelenhegyi út (phone: 185-2200).

Király This bath house, arguably the most exotic in Budapest, was built during the 16-century Turkish occupation. With its cupola, domes, and elaborate Moorish design, this is one of Budapest's most interesting architectural gems — well worth taking the time for a dip and a good look at its fabulous (if steamy) interior. I, 84 Fö utca (phone: 115-3000).

Rác Originally built in the 15th century, this spa was later reconstructed according to the classical designs of famed architect Miklós Ybl in the late 19th century. Today, it houses thermal baths as well as treatment and fitness rooms. 8-10 Hadnagy utca (phone: 156-1322).

Rudas Construction of this spa began during Turkish rule in the 16th century. Located near the Gellért Hill and Elizabeth Bridge, Rudas remains a tranquil spot in the center of a busy city. 9 Döbrentei tér (phone: 175-4449).

Széchenyi Housed in a large, impressive building dating from 1913, this facility offers both indoor and outdoor spas and pools. The outdoor spa pools are filled with thermally heated waters in which men and women bathe and play chess on floating, cork chessboards — even if there's snow covering the ground. XIV, 11 Allatkerti út (phone: 121-0310).

Thermál Margitsziget This spa facility on Margaret Island is shared by both the *Thermál* and *Ramada Grand* hotels. A variety of treatments, as well as state-of-the-art fitness rooms are available. Margitsziget (phone: 132-1100).

SWIMMING Budapest has many indoor and outdoor pools. People swim in the Danube, but it is not too clean and sometimes has strong currents. The largest public facility — both indoor and outdoor — is the *National Swimming Pool* on Margaret Island. In addition, many hotels have pools, both ordinary and thermal. The stately *Gellért,* for example, has an outdoor pool with artificial waves, in a park setting. In the Városliget (City Park), the turn-of-the-century *Széchenyi Baths* (see *Spas,* above) include 3 large outdoor pools, also open in winter (XIV, 11 Allatkerti körút).

TENNIS There are tennis courts near *Dózsa Stadium* on Margaret Island; at *FTC Sporttelep* (Sports Grounds; 129 Ullöi utca); and on Szabadság Hill, near the *Olympia* hotel (40 Eötvös utca). Both the *Flamenco* and *Novotel* hotels (see *Checking In*) provide indoor courts for guests.

THEATER

In Budapest everyone goes to the numerous theaters, which are subsidized by the state and are very inexpensive. Most performances are in Hungarian, but you might enjoy seeing a Shakespearean or some other familiar play in Hungarian. If not, the *Municipal Operetta Theater* (VI, 17 Nagymező utca in Pest; phone: 142-8687) offers performances of Kálmán, Lehár, Romberg, and other great operetta composers whose works need no translation. The *Állami Bábszínház* (Main Puppet Theater; VI, 69 Andrássy út; phone: 143-8976) presents everything from the *Three Little Pigs* to *The Miraculous Mandarin* for children and revues and satires for adults. The *Fövárosi Nagy Cirkusz* (Municipal Grand Circus), open weekdays, is in the Városliget (City Park; XIV, 7 Allatkerti körút; phone: 142-8300). Hungarian plays are performed in English from May through October at the *Merlin Cultural Center* (4 Gerlóczy utca; phone: 117-9338); the center also houses a jazz club, a restaurant, and an art gallery.

For tickets and more details see the current *Programme in Hungary,* contact *IBUSZ* (see *Tourist Information*), or call the *Central Booking Agency for Theaters* (VI, 18 Andrássy út; phone: 112-0000).

MUSIC

Budapest has a rich musical life; this city of Bartók and Kodály has two opera houses, several symphony orchestras, and a great many chamber groups.

HIGH NOTES

Hungarian State Opera House Built from 1844 to 1875, the opera house is part of the legacy of Franz Liszt and of Ferenc Erkel, composer of the Hungarian opera *Bank Ban.* The theater retains its original splendor and looks rather like the *Bolshoi* in Moscow, with domed ceilings, chandeliers, and ornate frescoes. Operas are performed in Hungarian. VI, 22 Andrássy út (phone: 153-0170).

In addition, the *Erkel Theater* (VIII, 30 Köztársaság tér; phone: 133-0540) offers operas and ballets. Concerts are given at the *Academy of Music* (VI, 8 Liszt Ferenc tér; phone: 142-0179) and at the *Pest Concert Hall* (V, 1 Vigadó tér; phone: 118-9167 or 118-9909), facing the Danube. The Matthias Church also has concerts; tickets may be purchased at the *Concert Ticket Office* (V, 1 Vörösmarty tér; phone: 117-6222). On Sundays at 11 AM concerts are held at the *Néprajzi Múzeum* (Ethnographic Museum; V, 12 Kossuth tér; no phone), sometimes featuring children's folk dancing.

In the summer, the music moves outdoors to Margaret Island. For tickets and information about performances at the above-mentioned musical venues, contact *IBUSZ* or the *Central Booking Agency* (see *Theater*).

NIGHTCLUBS AND NIGHTLIFE

Once virtually nonexistent, Budapest's nightlife is now flourishing. On any given night, there are a host of venues — from traditional cabarets in hotels such as the *Bellevue* in the *Duna Inter-Continental* and the *Buda-Penta*'s hip *Horoszkóp* to after-dark activity at the *Maxim Varieté* (VII, 3 Alkácfa utca; phone: 122-7858). All stay open until at least 4 AM, most until 5 AM. Other popular night spots on a rapidly changing scene include *Biliárd Fél 10* (VII, 48 Maria utca; no phone), where you can hear great jazz and hang out with the "in" crowd. *Café Pierrot* (14 Fortuna utca; phone: 175-6971), a charming and romantic piano bar located in the Castle Hill district, is an ideal spot to stop for a nightcap. The *Fondue Bar* (II, 25 Keleti Karoly utca; no phone), a small tavern with a lot of energy, is a great spot to hang out with some real local characters. *Fekete Lyuk* (VIII, 3 Golgota utca; phone: 113-0607), which literally means "Black Hole," is a hip music club. For rock, there's *Hold* (XIII, 7 Hegedüs Gyula utca; no phone), which in Hungarian means "moon," and does indeed have an "otherworldly" atmosphere. A newcomer on the late-night scene, the *Jazz Café* (V, 25 Balassi Bálassi Bálint utca; phone: 132-4377) is a funky place that's a popular hangout for the under-25 set who come here to shoot pool and listen to rock 'n' roll. The *Made Inn* (V, 112 Andrássy út; phone: 132-2959) is another favorite late-night watering hole for the young set. Arguably the oldest nightclub in Budapest, the *Miniatur* (II, 1 Rózsahegy utca; no phone) is the most enduringly cool. This piano bar, where Hungarian interpretations of Cole Porter hits are de rigueur, is best after midnight. The piano bar and nightclub *Piaf* (VI, 20 Nagymezö utca; phone: 112-3823) is one of the most exciting after-dark spots in the city. Located in City Park, the *Petöfi Csarnok* (XIV, 14 Zichy Mihaly utca; phone: 142-4327) attracts a younger crowd and is more a concert hall than a club, featuring rock bands from all over the world. The *Merlin Jazz Club* (4 Gerlóczy utca; phone: 117-9338) is part of the *Merlin Theater Complex* and a good place to hear jazz played into the wee hours. Though *Tilos Az A* (VIII, 2 Mikszáth tér; phone: 118-0684) literally means "Winnie the Pooh," this is no place for kids. The alternative rock club attracts interesting bands from all over Central Europe.

Folk dancing sessions known as "dance houses," which feature traditional songs and dance steps, are held in Budapest a few times a week from mid-September to mid-June. They're an interesting way to experience a bit of Hungarian culture, and some of the chain and round dances are simple enough even for rank beginners. Dance houses take place in community centers across the city, including *Almássy Téri Szabadidö Központ* (Almassy Square Free Time Center; VII, 6 Almássy tér; no phone); the *Belvárosi Ifjusági Ház* (Downtown Youth House; V, 9 Molnar út; no phone); the *XII Kerület Polgármesteri Hivatal* (Twelfth District Municipal Building; XII, 23-25 Böszörményi út; phone 153-6567); and the *Szakszervezetek Fövárosi Müuvelödési Ház* (Union Culture House; XI, 47 Fehérvári út). A comprehensive schedule of dance house sessions appears in the English-language monthly *Budapest Program*.

Gamblers are in luck, as every new year sees at least one or two more casinos open their doors. In addition to the *Hilton*'s elegant *Casino Budapest,* the *Atrium Hyatt* has opened the *Las Vegas Casino,* and the *Béke Radisson* is now home to the *Orfeum Casino* (see *Checking In*). Other casinos where gamblers can try their luck include *Casino Budapest Gresham* (V, 5 Roosevelt tér; phone: 117-2407), *Casino Budapest Schönbrunn* (1-3 Hess András tér; phone: 138-2016), *Casino Citadella* (XI, 4 Citadella Sétány; phone: 166-7686), and *Casino Vigadó* (V, 2 Vigadó utca; phone: 117-0869).

Best in Town

CHECKING IN

September is the peak season in Budapest, so it is advisable to make reservations well in advance, either through your own travel agent or through *IBUSZ* (see *Sources and Resources*).

Hotel prices in Budapest, however, are quite reasonable compared with those of other European capitals. Hotels described below as expensive charge from $100 to $200 or more a night for a double room; places in the moderate category charge $50 to $100; and inexpensive places charge under $50. Note that *IBUSZ* rents rooms in private homes (usually with shared baths) from $18 per day. Also, *American-International Homestays* (1515 W. Penn St., Iowa City, IA 52240; phone: 319-626-2125) arranges for stays with Hungarian families in Budapest and several other Eastern European cities. Most of Budapest's major hotels have complete facilities for the business traveler. Those hotels listed below as having "business services" usually offer such conveniences as English-speaking concierge, meeting rooms, photocopiers, computers, translation services, and express checkout, among others. Call the hotel for additional information. All telephone numbers are in the 1 city code unless otherwise indicated.

For an unforgettable experience, we begin with our favorites, followed by our cost and quality choices of hotels, listed by price category.

SPECIAL HAVENS

Budapest Hilton International This elegant establishment occupies one of the most historic sites in Buda, high on Castle Hill, overlooking the Danube. The 323 rooms are modern and comfortable, though not particularly lavish; the views from the picture windows are priceless. The construction of the building took 10 years, primarily because, as excavation proceeded, archaeologists kept uncovering ruins and artifacts dating from the 13th century, which the hotel incorporated into the new structure. As a result, its modern stone-and-glass façade includes the walls and tower of a 13th-century Dominican church and a Jesuit monastery. Reflected in a rosy glass wall of the 6-story hotel is the famous Fishermen's Bastion, a neo-Romanesque series of arches and towers overlooking the Danube. Its

Miklós Tower (on the street side), once a church tower, has been converted into an elegant casino (hard currency only). Inside another tower of the Fishermen's Bastion is *Halászbástya* (see *Eating Out*), a restaurant that features Hungarian food, Gypsy music, and a fabulous view of the Parliament building and the town. There's also the *Troubador,* which offers cabaret performances; a wine cellar dubbed *Dr. Faust;* a coffee shop with rustic decor; a 2-level espresso bar with an outdoor terrace; the colorful *Kalocsa* restaurant; and the *Codex Bar,* which occupies the site of the country's first printing workshop, opened in the 15th century. Business services. I, 1-3 Hess András tér (phone: 175-1000; fax: 156-0285).

Gellért On the Buda side of the Danube near Liberation Memorial Park, this 240-room Old World hotel at the foot of Gellért Hill makes up in history what it lacks in decor. Built in 1918 in the ornate Art Nouveau style, the hotel was recently renovated, although the new, modern decor is not up to the original fairy-tale standards. What makes the *Gellért* special, however, is its old-fashioned spa (see *Sports and Fitness*). The restaurant is famous for Hungarian food served to the sounds of soulful Gypsy music. There also is an espresso bar, a beer hall, and a nightclub. Business services. XI, 1 Szt. Gellért tér (phone: 185-2200).

EXPENSIVE

Aquincum Built over one of the city's ancient sources of medicinal thermal waters, this spa-hotel on the Buda side of the Danube near the Arpad Bridge is elegant, luxurious, and absolutely modern. All of the 312 rooms have balconies and all have views of Margaret Island and the Danube. The restaurants located here, the *Ambrosia* and the *Apicius*, both serve consistently good Hungarian fare; and there are drinks and snacks available at *Café Iris* and the *Calix Bar*. The spa includes diagnostic and therapeutic facilities. Business services. 94 Arpad Fejedelem útja (phone: 188-6360; fax: 168-8872).

Atrium Hyatt A central courtyard lined with hanging greenery is the focus of this 357-room luxury establishment. It has a top-floor VIP Regency Club, a swimming pool, a health club, and 24-hour room service. Its *Old Timer* restaurant serves international cuisine, the *Tokaj* has Hungarian fare and Gypsy music, the *Atrium Terrace* is a coffee shop, and the rustic *Clark Brasserie* is very popular for snacks accompanied by draft beer. Business services. V, 2 Roosevelt tér (phone: 138-3000; fax: 118-8271).

Béke Radisson A reconstructed old hotel with 246 rooms and a turn-of-the-century ambience, evident particularly in its beautiful *Zsolnay Café*. There's also a swimming pool and 24-hour room service. Business services. VI, 43 Teréz körút (phone: 132-3300; fax: 153-3380).

Duna Inter-Continental This deluxe 350-room hotel is on Pest's riverside Corso, a traditional promenade between the Chain and Elizabeth bridges. All rooms have balconies and views of Buda Castle on the opposite bank. Amenities include a pool with a view of the Danube, a fitness center, a squash court, a solarium, a sauna, and 24-hour room service. Among the restaurants: the peasant-inn–style *Csárda,* the *Rendezvous,* and the *Bellevue,* in addition to the *Intermezzo* terrace café, a wine cellar, and a nightclub. Business services. V, 4 Apáczai Csere János utca (phone: 117-5122; fax: 118-4973).

Dunapart Budapest's only floating hotel, this onetime merchant ship, permanently anchored on the Buda side of the Danube, offers spectacular views of the Parliament building, 32 rooms, a restaurant, and a bar. I, Szilágyi Dezsö tér (phone: 155-9001; fax: 155-3770).

Flamenco Popular with the business set, this Spanish-style hotel features 336 comfortable rooms. There's a small lake on the pleasant grounds as well as indoor tennis, a pool, a fitness center, 2 restaurants, and 24-hour room service. Business services. Tas Vezer utca (phone: 161-2250; fax: 165-8007).

Forum A first class, 408-room property next to the *Hyatt,* featuring river views and an efficient staff. It's the hotel of choice for businesspeople; at night the lobby fills with wheeler-dealers. It boasts a swimming pool and a health club with a bar. For dining, choose between the elegant *Silhouette* restaurant and the informal *Forum Grill* (open from 6 AM to 2 AM). For pastries and coffee, stop by the *Viennese Café* or take advantage of the 24-hour room service. Business services. V, 12-14 Apáczai Csere János utca (phone: 117-8088; fax: 117-9808).

Grand Hotel Corvinus Kempinski Located within walking distance of Budapest's shopping, business, and cultural districts, this gray granite 368-room hotel, offers an array of amenities. All rooms are furnished with cable TV and telephones, and personal computer outlets are available upon request. The health club with a swimming pool, sauna, solarium, and exercise equipment is a particularly welcome feature for those who have overindulged at the hotel's dining room (there's also a pub, a coffee shop, and 2 bars). Business services. V, 7-8 Erzsébet tér (phone: 226-1000; fax: 226-2000).

Helia This 8-story, 256-room property is set on the Pest side of the Danube embankment, just opposite Margaret Island (a bridge leads from the hotel to the island). It has 2 restaurants — the *Jupiter,* a buffet-style eatery, and the *Saturnus,* with an à la carte menu. Recreational pluses include a pool, tennis courts, a sauna, and a solarium. Business services. 62-64 Kárpát utca (phone: 129-8650; fax: 120-1429).

Korona Best Western runs this modern luxury property, which is situated in the main shopping and business area opposite the *Hungarian National Museum.* The two wings of the hotel are connected by a bridge, and the 8-story building has 440 rooms, a swimming pool, solarium, and sauna, as well as several restaurants. Air conditioned rooms are more expensive. Business services. 12-14 Kecskeméti utca (phone: 117-4111; fax: 118-3867).

Nemzeti Another Old World (1880s) establishment, it was restored a few years ago but could use additional touching up. This 76-room place has an elegant restaurant with Gypsy music and a beer hall. Take heed: The location is noisy. Cable television news is available. V, 4 József körút (phone: 133-9160; fax: 114-0019).

Petneházy Country Club Located in the Buda Hills in a country-like setting 8 miles (13 km) from the center of the city, this sports-oriented resort offers individual Scandinavian-style luxury cabins equipped with private kitchens, terraces, and saunas. Tennis, bicycling, horseback riding, hunting, and swimming in an indoor pool are some of the options available here. The *Petneházy* restaurant serves international cuisine. A private minibus service transports guests to and from the city. II, 2-4 Feketefej utca (phone: 176-5992; fax: 176-5738).

Ramada Grand Hotel Margitsziget On Margaret Island, this renovated spa dating from the 19th century is now a resort hotel; it's connected to its sister hotel, the *Thermál,* by an underground passage. In former days, the hotel reportedly housed famous spies-in-hiding, among them the infamous terrorist known simply as Carlos. Business services. XIII, Margitsziget (phone: 111-1000; fax: 153-3029).

Thermál Hotel Margitsziget This 340-room luxury spa-hotel has health facilities with diagnostic and treatment centers and equipment for hydrotherapy and physiotherapy. Business services. XIII, Margitsziget (phone: 132-1100; fax: 153-3029).

MODERATE

Astoria This small, 128-room renovated hostelry (it was built in 1912) is the best of the moderately priced hotels. There's a marvelous Art Deco café and restaurant. Business services. V, 19 Kossuth Lajos utca (phone: 117-3411; fax: 118-6798).

Buda-Penta Near the Southern Railway Station and Underground Terminal in Buda, it has 392 rooms plus 7 suites, all with air conditioning, plus a swimming pool and health club, a restaurant, coffee shop, beer hall, and nightclub. Business services. I, 41-43 Krisztina körút (phone: 156-6333; fax: 155-6964).

Erzsébet An attractive modern property with 123 rooms on the site of a much older one. The hotel's *János Beer Cellar* has, in fact, kept the furnishings of its popular predecessor. Business services. V, 11-15 Károlyi Mihály utca (phone: 138-2111; fax: 118-9237).

Grand Hotel Hungária This bustling establishment opposite the Eastern Railway Station is the biggest hotel in the country, with 529 rooms (beware, the walls are paper thin), a restaurant, beer hall, wine cellar, *Jugendstil* (Art Nouveau) café, and nightclub. Business services. VII, 90 Rákóczi utca (phone: 122-9050; fax: 122-8029).

Liget A simple establishment opposite the zoo side of the Városliget (City Park). The 140 rooms are clean and pleasant, though some are noisy. There's also a good restaurant, a gym, and a sauna. 106 Dózsa György út (phone: 111-7050).

Normafa Set in an oak forest on the highest point in the Buda Hills 15 minutes from downtown Budapest, this hotel offers 71 rooms, all with balconies. The *C'est la Vie* restaurant serves international cuisine, and the *Mormafa Grill and Garden* prepares traditional Hungarian fare. The hotel has a fitness center, garden swimming pool, and tennis courts. Business services. VI, 52-54 Eötvös út (phone: 156-3444; fax: 175-9583).

Novotel Budapest A quick drive from the city center, it has 324 rooms, a small pool, tennis courts, and several restaurants and bars. The *Budapest Convention Center* is next door. Business services. XII, 63-67 Alkotás utca (phone: 186-9588; fax: 166-5636).

Olympia Located on the outskirts of town in the residential Buda Hills, this pleasant property has 172 rooms (most with private baths), a swimming pool, health club, tennis court, and restaurants. There's also a nightclub. Business services. XII, 40 Eötvös utca (phone: 156-8720; fax: 156-8720).

Taverna The main pedestrian shopping street in Pest boasts a well-designed, post-modern hotel with 224 rooms, a restaurant, beer hall, pastry shop, fast-food eatery, and a champagne bar. Business services. V, 20 Váci utca (phone: 138-4999; fax: 118-7188).

Victoria Centrally located, with striking views of the Danube, Parliament, and Chain Bridge, this 27-room hotel offers comfortable accommodations, a restaurant, and 24-hour room service. Business services. I, 11 Bem rakpart (phone: 201-8644; fax: 201-5816).

INEXPENSIVE

Kulturinnov Housed in a once-grand university building, this simply furnished, reasonably priced 18-room hostelry is ideally located in the center of the Castle Hill district (only 4 rooms have private baths). Attracting scholarly types, it offers 2 lecture rooms, each accommodating 140 people; and 2 smaller lecture halls, each seating 50 people. There are also 9 rooms which can be used for seminars, a library, a reading room, and a cafeteria. I, 6 Szentháromság tér (phone: 155-0122; fax: 175-1886).

EATING OUT

The justly celebrated cuisine of Hungary dates from ancient times. The most famous ingredient is paprika, the red pepper that comes in different strengths and is used copiously, most notably in *paprikás csirke* (paprika chicken) and in sauces. (Don't worry about paprika dishes being too hot; any restaurant will be glad to spice to your taste.) Another culinary distinction is the use of pork drippings, which — in concert with the ubiquitous sour cream — make meals here conspicuously caloric. Various Hungarian dishes have become world famous, particularly *gulyás* (goulash), which will not be what you expect if you have eaten it outside Hungary. Here, it is a very thick soup with meat (usually beef or pork), onions, carrots, sour cream, and a lot of paprika. If you like fish, try *halászlé,* Hungary's famous fish soup, made with *fogas* (a unique pike-perch caught only in Lake Balaton) or bream, and seasoned with onions and many spices including paprika. Another traditional dish, *kolozsvári rakott káposzta* (layered cabbage), includes eggs and sausage, heaps of sour cream, and crisp pork chops.

Hungarian rye bread is superb, and *pogácsa,* a flaky biscuit strewn with bits of crackling pork, is delicious. Hungarian pastries are absolutely fabulous; whether filled with *barack lekvár* (apricot preserves), *aszalt szilva lekvár* (prune preserves), walnuts, hazelnuts, crushed poppy seeds, or chocolate, they are all sinfully delectable. You might start with *rétes* (strudel) or *dobos torta,* the famous multilayered cake — but the sky is the limit. Budapest is the place to let that diet go.

Hungarian wines are wonderful, especially tokay, which is often sweet; *tokaji szamorodni* and *tokaji aszú* are famous dessert wines made from hand-picked, shriveled, "noble rot" grapes. A popular choice with meals is *egri bikavér* (bull's blood), a heavy red wine. *Leányka* is a delicious white wine.

Hungarians love to linger over small cups of strong coffee, called *eszpresszó,* or over *dupla kavé,* which is strong double mocha brew. These are available everywhere — in pastry shops, cafés, and the *Mackó* shops, whose symbol is a bear cub.

Budapest has over 2,000 restaurants, cafés, pastry shops, wine and beer cellars, and taverns. A few of the highlights are listed below. There is an important distinction to be made among eating establishments in Budapest: whether the restaurant is privately owned or still state-run. The food at private establishments is generally of a higher quality, the service is better, and the price is sure to reflect it. The native word for "restaurant" is *étterem;* a *vendéglö* is a more informal establishment. For a dinner for two with wine, expect to pay $80 to $100 in restaurants listed as expensive; $35 to $80 in those categorized as moderate; and $20 to $35 in places described as inexpensive. Reservations are essential in Budapest; most restaurants won't seat you without them even if the place is empty. All telephone numbers are in the 1 city code unless otherwise indicated.

For an unforgettable dining experience, we begin with our culinary favorites, followed by our cost and quality choices, listed by price category.

DELIGHTFUL DINING

Gundel Not only is this the cradle of Hungarian cooking, it's the place where this country's rich culinary traditions are kept alive. The restaurant, founded by Károly Gundel, perhaps the most highly esteemed chef in Budapest's history, is now owned by a Hungarian-born American, restaurateur/entrepreneur George Lang (owner of New York City's *Café des Artistes*), and Ronald Lauder, the former US Ambassador to Austria. After a long hiatus, it reopened in 1992 with all the beauty and culinary excellence that has made it a legend since 1894. The turn-of-the-century building (including a main dining room, a rococo ballroom, and 6 private dining rooms) has been fully refurbished and the park-like garden (with seating for 450) restored. The decor celebrates Hungarian culture with native paintings and antiques. Among chef Kálmán Kalla's featured dishes are *fogas*, Hungarian goose and goose liver from the restaurant's own farm, and game and game birds in season. There are also fresh fruits and vegetables, traditional breads, pastries, and desserts — including Károly Gundel's legendary *palacsinta* (crêpes filled with hazelnuts and cream and smothered with a bittersweet chocolate sauce) — and tokay wines from the restaurant's own vineyards. Live entertainment, from a Gypsy orchestra to Hungarian operettas, completes the illusion that you've somehow stepped back into Budapest's golden age. Ties required. Open daily. Reservations necessary. Major credit cards accepted. XIV, 2 Allatkerti út, in the Városliget (phone: 122-1002).

New York/Hungária A landmark since 1894, when it opened as the *Café New York,* this most famous of the city's restaurants is worth seeing, even if the food does not live up to the decor. So grand is the interior, with its gilt columns, frosted glass globes, chandeliers, and glittering mirrors, that you'll almost feel as if you're dining in an opera house, or even a palace. Among the specialties are *kengurufarokleves* (kangaroo tail soup), *crêpes à la Hortobagy* (crêpes stuffed with meat and served with a paprika sauce), and a dessert called omelette surprise (parfait in sponge cake baked in a froth of egg white). As an alternative to an expensive but undistinguished meal, consider a snack or coffee in the café, where you still get the full benefit of the elaborate decor. There's also a nightclub. Be prepared, however, to see only a roomful of tourists. Open daily. Reservations necessary. Major credit cards accepted. VII, 9-11 Erzsébet körút (phone: 122-3849).

EXPENSIVE

Alabárdos In one of the most beautiful Gothic buildings in the Castle Hill district, and probably the best restaurant on the hill. Try the house specialty, flambéed meat served with great ceremony on a sword. Closed Sundays. Reservations necessary. American Express and Visa accepted. I, 2 Országház utca (phone: 156-0851).

Les Amis The perfect little bistro, it serves consistently good Hungarian staples such as goulash plus a selection of French-inspired dishes. Open daily until

4 AM. No reservations. Major credit cards accepted. II, 12 Rómer Flóris utca (phone: 135-2792).

Apostolok This old brasserie decorated with carved wood and paintings by local artists is centrally located, and very popular, especially for lunch. It's also a good place to have a few beers. Open daily. Reservations advised on weekends. No credit cards accepted. V, 4-6 Kígyó utca (phone: 118-3704).

Barokk This delightful dining spot, where the waitresses wear baroque garb against a backdrop of taped Mozart music, authentic 18th-century furniture, and gilded plaster wainscoting, serves what may be the best food in Budapest. Dishes are based on 17th- and 18th-century recipes. Try the sublime fish crêpes in remoulade sauce or the filet of beef with goose liver. The vegetables, desserts, and other extras are all unusually good and innovative as well. Open daily. Reservations necessary. Major credit cards accepted. 12 Mozsar utca (phone: 131-8942).

Halászbástya This dining spot is located next to the *Hilton,* inside one of the towers of the Fishermen's Bastion (see *Special Places*). The fare is unexceptional, but the view of the Parliament building and the town is fabulous. Hungarian food and Gypsy music are featured. Open daily. Reservations necessary. Major credit cards accepted. I, Fishermen's Bastion (phone: 156-1446).

Kacsa (Duck) This charming establishment features a large menu with excellent game including wild duck (hence the name) with pears and apples, a superb goulash, and grilled carp. There's also a good wine list. Open daily. Reservations necessary. Major credit cards accepted. I, 75 Fö utca (phone: 135-3357).

Kis Lugas Located in a former mansion in Buda, this new venture by pioneer restaurateur Béla Hegedus is the most Western establishment in Budapest. Service is exceptional, and the food — Italian specialties and seafood — is not only good, but healthful. Try the lobster and zucchini ravioli or the salmon. There is also an excellent salad bar. In summer, dine alfresco in the garden. Open daily. Reservations necessary. Major credit cards accepted. II, 77 Szilágyi Erzsébet Fasor (phone: 156-4765).

Krónikás Étteremben Budapest natives love this small, club-like restaurant which serves traditional Hungarian fare as well as some non-Hungarian dishes (shrimp and lobster). Open daily. Reservations necessary. Major credit cards accepted. XIII, 2 Szent István körút; phone: 131-6278).

Légrádi Testvérek (Légrádi Brothers) Make reservations at least a week in advance for this fine private dining place favored by businesspeople. A good selection of hors d'oeuvres and traditional Hungarian specialties is prepared at the table. Dinner only, weekdays. Reservations necessary. No credit cards accepted. V, 23 Magyar utca (phone: 118-6804).

Ménes Csárda This small, cozy establishment with an equestrian decor became an instant hit after it opened in 1982. It serves unusual Hungarian specialties — often prepared at your table — in attractive ceramic dishes made for the restaurant by a local artist. Try the stuffed filet of pork and the cherry or cottage cheese *túrós* (strudel). Good, light wines are available. While you dine, a Gypsy *cimbalom* player performs. Open daily. Reservations necessary. Major credit cards accepted. V, 15 Apáczai Csere János utca (phone: 117-0803).

Robinson Located in the Városliget (City Park) adjacent to a swan-populated, artificial lake, this private dining spot is currently all the rage. Lace curtains and airy colors provide the background for classic Hungarian specialties. Open daily. Reservations necessary. Major credit cards accepted. Városliget (phone: 142-0955).

Vadrózsa In a private villa with a shady garden, it features charcoal-broiled specialties such as goose liver and pike-perch, plus other tempting dishes. This place is frequented by diplomats and, perhaps diplomatically, no longer lists prices on the menu. Very friendly service. Closed Mondays. Reservations necessary. Major credit cards accepted. II, 12 Pentelei Molnár utca (phone: 115-0044).

Vasmacska Popular with out-of-towners, the interior of this restaurant evokes the atmosphere of an officers' wardroom on a ship. The house specialty is a hearty bean dish with different kinds of smoked meat. Downstairs is a less expensive beer hall. Open daily. Reservations advised. No credit cards accepted. III, 3-5 Laktanya utca (phone: 188-7123).

Vén Buda (Old Buda) Serving traditional Hungarian dishes, this elegant, private dining place is a favorite among locals and visitors alike. Closed weekends. Reservations necessary. Major credit cards accepted. II, 22 Erőd utca (phone: 201-2928).

MODERATE

Aranybárány Borozó (Golden Lamb Wine Bar) Lamb dishes, naturally, are the specialty at this cellar eatery with a shepherd motif. Open daily. Reservations advised on weekends. No credit cards accepted. V, 4 Harmincad utca (phone: 117-2703).

Aranymókus Kertvendéglő (Golden Squirrel Garden) Traditional game dishes (but no squirrel) are served at this spot, a short taxi ride from the city center. Pleasant garden dining in the summer. Closed Mondays. Reservations advised on weekends. No credit cards accepted. XII, 25 Istenhegy utca (phone: 155-6728 or 155-9594).

Borkóstoló (Gresham Wine Bar) Near the Houses of Parliament, here you can taste fine Hungarian wines such as tokay, which is often sweet; *egri bikavér* (bull's blood), the famous dry red wine believed to have medicinal value; and *leányka,* a good white wine. Closed Sundays. Reservations advised on weekends. No credit cards accepted. V, Mérleg utca (phone: 117-4445).

Chicago Popular with American expatriates, this restaurant is famous for its spectacular chicken wings, hamburgers, and beer. Open daily. No reservations. No credit cards accepted. VII, 2 Erzsébet körút (phone: 122-9230).

Dunakorzó Situated near the riverside, this place offers an undistinguished decor but a great location and heaping portions of solid Hungarian fare. Open daily. Reservations advised on weekends. No credit cards accepted. V, 3 Vigadó tér (phone: 118-6362).

Kisbuda Gyöngne Don't look for anything formal or fancy here — this is an authentic Hungarian bistro. For starters, try the crêpes filled with caviar and cheese. Among the excellent entrées is wild pheasant with cherries; the savory strudel is the dessert of choice. Open daily. Reservations advised on weekends. No credit cards accepted. III, 34 Kenyeres utca (phone: 115-2244).

Kiskakukk An extensive year-round menu of game dishes is the draw here. The decor, however, is plain, and the restaurant can get noisy. Closed Sundays during the summer. Reservations advised. Major credit cards accepted. XIII, 12 Pozsonyi utca (phone: 132-1732).

Kis Pipa A brasserie atmosphere — bright lights, red tablecloths, and friendly chatter by diners who all seem to know each other — prevails at this private eatery. It features an extensive menu of Hungarian specialties and almost anything else you might wish to eat. It's a 5-minute taxi ride from the major hotels in Pest. Closed Sundays. Reservations necessary. Major credit cards accepted. 38 Akácfa utca (phone: 142-2587).

Mátyás Pince Tourists fill this ornately romantic beer cellar in central Pest, where the real attractions are copious quantities of wine and even richer servings of Gypsy music and old Budapest spirit. If you actually get hungry, its fish dishes are well known around the city. Open daily. Reservations advised on weekends. No credit cards accepted. V, 7 Március 15 tér (phone: 118-1650).

Náncsi Néni A must on any list of Budapest's eateries, this homey little restaurant has a devoted following. Dishes have unusual names — such as "Kammermeyer's (Budapest's first mayor) Happiness" — and all are unquestionably *finon* (delicious). The restaurant is about 20 minutes from the city center but well worth the trip. Open daily. Reservations necessary. Major credit cards accepted. III, 34 Kenyeres utca (phone: 115-2244).

Pest-Buda A good, informal dining option, this cozy eatery has occupied the same vaulted quarters in the Castle Hill district since 1880. Try the Wiener schnitzel. Open daily. Reservations advised on weekends. No credit cards accepted. I, 3 Fortuna utca (phone: 156-9849).

Pilvax An old café-restaurant in the heart of the Inner City of Pest, it is noted for its chicken broth, pastries, and cakes. Gypsy music accompanies the meal. Open daily. Reservations advised on weekends. No credit cards accepted. V, 1-3 Pilvax köz (phone: 117-5902).

Régi Országház This old inn on the north side of the castle in Buda offers many dining rooms with different decors, traditional fare, a wine cellar, Gypsy music, and jazz. Open daily. Reservations advised on weekends. No credit cards accepted. I, 17 Országház utca (phone: 175-0650).

Seoul House The food at this authentic Korean dining spot is exceptionally good, if not typically spicy. Delectable meat is flambéed at the table. The decor is simple and attractive. The owner, chef, and staff are all Korean-born. Open daily. Reservations advised. Major credit cards accepted. I, 8 Fő utca (phone: 201-9607).

Sipos Halászkert Known as the *New Sipos* — to distinguish it from the original *Régi Sipos Halászkert* (Old Sipos; 46 Lajos utca; phone: 686480) — this branch serves first-rate fish dishes. There is music and a garden. Open daily. Reservations advised on weekends. Major credit cards accepted. Fő tér in the Obuda district (phone: 188-7745).

Vegetárium Étterem Until recently, vegetarians have had a tough time in Budapest, but things are looking up. The selection of vegetables here is generally good, the decor clean and functional, and the preparation is at times quite interesting. Open daily. Reservations advised. Major credit cards accepted. IV, Cukor utca (phone: 138-3710).

INEXPENSIVE

Alföldi This is where Hungarians come for Sunday lunch; it's noisy and offers simple, traditional fare. Open daily. No reservations. No credit cards accepted. V, 4 Kecskeméti utca (phone: 117-4404).

Fészek Popular with the art crowd, this eatery offers tempting cold fruit soup, chicken paprika, veal stew, and *palascinta* (Hungarian crêpes). During the summer there is alfresco dining in the pretty, trellis-lined garden. Open daily for lunch and dinner. Reservations advised. No credit cards accepted. VII, 36 Kertész utca (phone: 122-6043).

Kádár At this very special lunch-only restaurant, you'll find an eclectic mix of students, workers, and artists, who come here for the large portions of good Kosher dairy food. There is no English menu, the place is small, and you might have to share a table with locals. Open Tuesdays through Saturdays from 11:30 AM to 3:30 PM. No reservations. No credit cards accepted. VII, 9 Klauzál tér (no phone).

Marxim For the eat-and-run set, here's Budapest's best pizza — thick crust and all. Open Mondays through Saturdays from noon to 2 AM; Sundays from 6 PM to 1 AM. No reservations. No credits cards accepted. III, 23 Kisrokus utca (no phone).

CAFÉ SOCIETY

Just as they were at the turn of the century, Budapest's coffeehouses are places where people meet to discuss the day's events. They are also wonderful venues for visitors to experience a slice of life while sampling a slice of delicious cake and sipping an espresso. Below are some worth visiting. All cafés listed are open daily, do not require reservations, and are categorized as inexpensive.

KAFFEKLATSCH

Café Gerbeaud In the heart of Pest, facing a beautifully restored square bustling with tourists and street entertainers, this is no mere pastry shop; it is an institution. Its decadent pastries and leisure atmosphere are reminiscent of days gone by. V, 7 Vörösmarty tér (phone: 118-6823).

Café Ruszwurm Just down the block from Matthias Church is this fabulous 1827 pastry shop, still serving the best baked goods in Central Europe. With displays of old utensils once used by pastry chefs, 19th-century signs, and Biedermeier cherrywood furniture, it has been designated a historic monument. Try *rétes,* or strudel; vanilla slices; or Ruszwurm cake, a chocolate cake filled with chocolate cream and seasoned with orange peel and rum. I, 7 Szentháromság tér (phone: 175-5284).

Korona Another pastry shop, convenient for strollers on Castle Hill, this is also a gathering place for literary types and tourists, featuring poetry readings and other bookish events, often in foreign languages. I, 16 Dísz tér (phone: 175-6139).

The *Angelika* (I, 7 Batthyány tér; phone: 201-4847), on the Buda side of the Danube, boasts an authentic Old World atmosphere; the popular bookstore café, *Littea* (I, 4 Hess András tér; no phone), offers books and classical music disks along with a pot of tea; the *New York* (VII, 9-11 Erzsébet körút; phone: 122-3849), once *the* meeting place for the literary glitterati in Budapest, is now a favorite of tourists drawn here by the dramatic Art Nouveau–inspired decor; *Café l'Orient-Express* (I, 17 Fö utca; phone: 202-1133), a new café located on the second floor of the new sleek French Institute, is a favorite of the city's young set; *Wiener Kaffehaus* (V, Apáczai Csere János utca; phone: 117-8088), located in the *Forum* hotel, is popular with locals and visitors alike who come for the sinfully delicious pastries and confections.

Cracow

This is the legend of the trumpeter of Cracow: Many centuries ago, from his perch atop St. Mary's Church, a sentry spotted an invading Tatar army. He blew his trumpet to arouse the town's militia, but an arrow pierced his throat before he could complete the call to arms. To this day, every hour, a trumpeter sounds from the church tower — only to be cut off just at the moment the arrow is said to have struck the original sentry.

Cracow loves its legends. Little wonder, for the city is steeped in a history of almost mythic proportions. Here Polish kings first ruled; here the Roman Catholic church first sank its roots into Polish soil; and here the Cracow Academy was founded, the second-oldest university in all of Europe.

Not surprisingly, Cracow's genesis is also a matter of legend. It is said that at one time a dragon lived in a cave at the foot of Wawel Hill, eating every man and beast that passed his way. A clever boy named Krak stuffed a lamb with sulfur and threw it on the bank of the Vistula River near the mouth of the cave. The dragon soon came upon the carcass and ate it, and when the sulfur began to gnaw at his stomach, he stumbled to the riverbank and drank until he burst into a thousand pieces. Overjoyed, Krak founded a town (hence the name Cracow, Kraków in Polish) on the spot.

Today, a modern sculpture of the dragon stands at the foot of Wawel Hill. Historians revere the spot as well, but for different reasons. Because the hill overlooked a bend in the Vistula River, it provided the inhabitants of the area with a natural defensive advantage over potential attackers. This is one reason the limestone plateau and its environs have been settled for millennia (the oldest artifacts unearthed here date back 50,000 years).

There was plenty of activity to survey from Wawel Hill. Nearby, the Vistula flows through a narrow gap between the Carpathian Mountains and the Jura Krakowska. Medieval travelers passed through the gap on their way from the Black Sea and Kiev to Prague and Western Europe. Traders journeying from the Carpathians to the Hungarian plains also passed this way. Cracow was born where the routes converged. The first written reference to Cracow appears in an entry dated AD 965 in the journals of Ibrahim ibn-Yaqub, a Jewish merchant from Spain, who described it as a "bustling market town."

Though merchants founded Cracow, clerics and kings soon followed. By the year 1000, the Christian mission on Wawel Hill had been recognized by the church of Rome, and within a half century it became the main seat of Polish rulers. A Tatar invasion — the one heralded by the church trumpeter — destroyed the city in 1241. The Main Market Square, laid out in 1257, was among the largest in medieval Europe; it maintains its colossal proportions today. Early in the 14th century, King Wladyslaw I united the country and made Cracow its capital. A Gothic cathedral, completed in 1364, was built atop the hill, and King Sigismund the Old built a Renaissance palace near the cathedral in the 16th century. Four centuries later, Cracow's see was served by Karol Cardinal Wojtyła of Cracow before he became Pope John Paul II.

Even after Warsaw became the capital in 1596, Polish kings came to Wawel Hill to be crowned. During the years from 1795 to 1918, when Cracow fell under Austrian rule, Wawel Hill came to symbolize an independent Poland. Inspired, Cracow's citizens managed to keep the Polish language and culture alive while awaiting the day when they would be free again.

But the Cracovians' work was nearly undone when Poland fell prey to the Nazi war machine. By 1945, Hitler was set to dynamite the castle and the cathedral on Wawel Hill — as well as other important monuments — when a surprise attack by the Russian army drove his forces out of the area. As a result, Cracow alone escaped the physical devastation wreaked on other Polish cities during World War II. Much of the town is still the same symphony of Gothic and Renaissance spires and cobbled squares that it was before the war. The city did not, however, escape human devastation: There were about 60,000 Jews in Cracow before World War II; today there are perhaps 200. Only one of the city's eight surviving synagogues is open for worship.

Not all of Cracow is still charming. After the war, the USSR-controlled Communist government built a steel mill — the largest in Europe — just 9 miles (14 km) from Wawel Hill. The act was a subtle form of revenge against Cracow's deeply Catholic (and anti-Communist) aristocracy. About 300,000 people lived in Cracow before World War II, and the city had some 250 churches, a powerful clergy, and a wealthy merchant class. The Communists resolved to give Cracow a proletariat as well.

They soon succeeded. The mill, with smokestacks so tall they can be seen from Wawel Castle on a clear day (which is rare because of pollution), originally employed 33,000. Within a few years, Cracow's population had swelled to 700,000. Today, nearly 250,000 workers live in the rows of dreary Soviet-style apartment buildings near the plant in the suburb known as Nowa Huta (New Mill).

Rather than crushing the spirit of those who lived there, Nowa Huta became a symbol of popular rebellion against Communist rule. When the Solidarity movement was founded in 1980 in the northern city of Gdańsk, the steelworkers of Nowa Huta took up its banner, demonstrating against the government and knocking the huge statue of Vladimir Lenin in the Main Market Square off its pedestal. Government troops were called in to guard the mill after martial law was declared in December 1981. In 1988, the steelworkers launched a 2-week strike, setting off a chain of events that led, a year later, to the restoration of Solidarity's legal status and the toppling of the Communist regime.

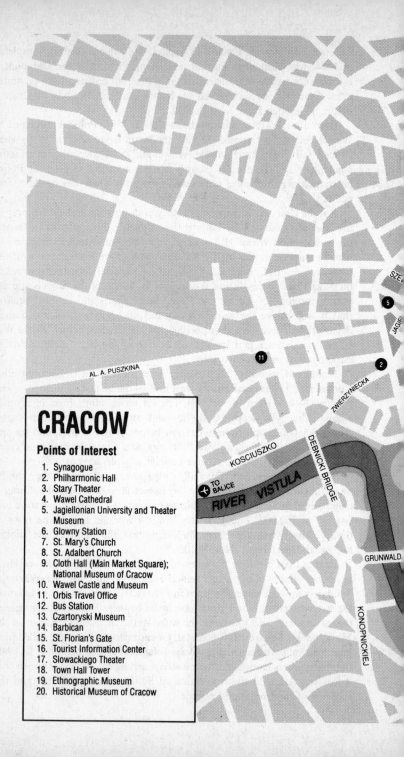

CRACOW

Points of Interest

1. Synagogue
2. Philharmonic Hall
3. Stary Theater
4. Wawel Cathedral
5. Jagiellonian University and Theater Museum
6. Glowny Station
7. St. Mary's Church
8. St. Adalbert Church
9. Cloth Hall (Main Market Square); National Museum of Cracow
10. Wawel Castle and Museum
11. Orbis Travel Office
12. Bus Station
13. Czartoryski Museum
14. Barbican
15. St. Florian's Gate
16. Tourist Information Center
17. Slowackiego Theater
18. Town Hall Tower
19. Ethnographic Museum
20. Historical Museum of Cracow

Though Nowa Huta's grim apartment blocks are hardly of interest, the Church of the Queen of Poland is worth seeing. The modern ark-shaped cathedral is no aesthetic wonder, but it has a fascinating history. The architects who drew up the plans for Nowa Huta made no provision for a church — a decision that didn't sit well with the town's devoutly Catholic citizens. After years of petitioning the local authorities, workers won the right to build the church — with their own materials and on their own time — in a pasture several kilometers from Nowa Huta. The project took over 7 years to complete, and native son Pope John Paul II consecrated the building in 1978. Today, some 68,000 parishioners worship here. Masses are held from morning to night on Sundays, and even during the most bitter winter months a crowd gathers outside to listen to the service over a loudspeaker.

The steel plant has done more than transform Cracow's demography — it has threatened the city's very existence. Soot from the towering smokestacks has defaced entire blocks of 500-year-old buildings. As soon as the structures are cleaned, they turn black again. The bodies of cars parked on Cracow's streets are eaten through by acid rain, and residents regularly complain of burning eyes and shortness of breath.

Parts of the Nowa Huta steelworks have been closed by the new democratic city government or have fallen victim to economic hard times, but the environmental cleanup process will take years. Now the population faces an additional menace: unemployment. Though the Communists promised everyone a job, as Poland proceeds with its market reforms, the unemployment lines are growing, especially in one-factory towns like Nowa Huta. To make matters worse, apartment shortages prevent residents from moving to more economically vibrant areas.

In the face of difficult conditions, Cracow residents always have found refuge in biting humor. But in the city's many cozy cabarets, actors who once improvised sketches that deftly criticized even the secret police without raising the hackles of government censors are finding the going somewhat rougher now. "Cabaret has lost a little of its punch," claims Regina Putlik, the Cracow official in charge of culture. "There is now so much open criticism that artists have difficulty coming up with the daring things that make people laugh."

Censors or no, Cracow has always had a rich cultural life. There are over a dozen theaters in the city, and Tadeusz Kantor, Poland's most famous director, lived here until his death in 1990. The *Kraków Philharmonic* is affiliated with conductor Krzysztof Penderecki, Poland's best-known living composer.

If Warsaw is the political center of Poland, Cracow is its intellectual capital. More than 50,000 students from across Poland come to study at the prestigious Jagiellonian University (formerly the Cracow Academy). Nearby are the offices of the liberal Catholic weekly *Tygodnik Powszechny* and the monthly *ZNAK*, two publications that dared to confront the government during the years of Communist rule. In 1990, several of *Tygodnik Powszechny*'s editors were tapped as ministers in Poland's new democratic government, and *ZNAK*'s editor-in-chief, Jacek Wosniakowski, was elected Mayor of Cracow.

Free enterprise is making noticeable headway in Cracow. Entrepreneurs are lovingly restoring centuries-old buildings for use as swank boutiques and elegant restaurants; for their part, civic leaders are ensuring that the redevelopment enhances, rather than overpowers, this historic city. The former Communist headquarters have been taken over by a branch of the Bank of America. Poland's first independent manufacturing association was founded here well before Solidarity assumed power. In true Cracovian style, the association began as a dining club. Intellectuals and businessmen gathered for a meal at a private home. Fortified by several rounds of vodka, the intellectuals would expound upon the theoretical aspects of free enterprise while the businessmen countered with practical advice. The proceedings were written up in an underground journal called *13*. Now legitimate, the association is plotting leveraged buyouts of several local industries.

No amount of soot, poverty, and economic upheaval could completely begrime Cracow. Down in the Old Town, Renaissance mansions still crowd the cobbled streets. Dozens of narrow passageways still open onto tiny courtyards lined with workshops and balconied houses. And Main Market Square, dominated by the magnificent 14th-century Cloth Hall, is just as imposing and stately as it was after World War I.

Cracow At-a-Glance

SEEING THE CITY

For a spectacular view of the Old Town, climb to the top of St. Mary's Church in Main Market Square. Visitors must ask for permission from area firemen before climbing. The best time to visit is at noon, when the trumpeters — they're actually firemen — put on their show, which is broadcast daily on Polish radio.

Wawel Hill is another fine vantage point, especially on the days when the air is not completely clogged with smog (a rarity). For the best view, climb the bell tower in the Wawel Cathedral. The cathedral is open all day, and no permission is needed to ascend the tower.

SPECIAL PLACES

Cracow is a good place for walking. The Old Town is small and compact, and most of the streets are reserved for pedestrians. Only a few cars are allowed in the city center, and most of these are unlicensed cabs. Scores of new private agencies offer guided tours, and in the summer, *PTTK* offers a bus tour of the city; hotel receptionists can make recommendations.

As you make your way through the city, it's helpful to remember that "ulica" is the Polish word for street, "aleja" is the word for avenue, and "plac" means square. Also, many Communist-era street names have been changed, but updated maps are available at kiosks, bookstores, and hotels.

RYNEK GŁÓWNY (MAIN MARKET SQUARE)

For centuries, Main Market Square, filled with 14th- to 16th-century buildings, has been the city's heart and soul. Locals and tourists alike come here to shop or relax in the pleasant open-air cafés. Flower vendors and flocks of pigeons congregate on the square, and horse-drawn cabs stand in front of the graceful arcades of Cloth Hall, the huge covered market that dominates the center of the square. A statue of Adam Mickiewicz, Poland's most famous poet, stands at the southwest end.

SUKIENNICE (CLOTH HALL) Perhaps the city's most beautiful building. When Cracow received its town charter in 1257, there was already a row of market stalls here. In the mid-14th century, Kazimierz the Great ordered the construction of a Gothic brick marketplace on the spot. Fire gutted the building in 1555, and Italian architects created a neo-Renaissance masterpiece. The parapets are decorated with carvings of grimacing creatures intended to ward off evil spirits. Another neo-Gothic reconstruction was completed in the 1870s.

The upper level of the market houses a gallery specializing in 18th- and 19th-century Polish painting. The colonnaded arcades on the ground floor are occupied by traders, craftsmen, and souvenir vendors selling everything from wooden toys to woolens. Wall hangings, amber jewelry, pine boxes, decorative wooden plates and eggs, dolls, candlesticks, and woodcarvings are also available. Shoppers patient enough to sift through the kitsch may find some real gems here. There are also two street cafés open during the summer months.

KOŚCIÓŁ SW. MARIACKI (ST. MARY'S CHURCH) Built in 1221 and remodeled a century later, St. Mary's, opposite Cloth Hall, is one of Cracow's most impressive structures. The nave and chapels were added in the 15th century. The taller of the two spires — the Gothic spire — is where the trumpeters blow their horns every hour on the hour.

The church's chief treasure is its massive altar, carved by the artist Wit Stwosz. At 43 feet high and 36 feet wide, it is one of the masterpieces of 15th-century Gothic art. When closed, the altar's wings render the life of the Holy Family in 12 panels. When opened, the wings form a triptych with the altar's interior to depict the Annunciation, the Nativity, the Adoration of the Magi, the Resurrection, the Ascension, and the Pentecost. The figures in the scenes were probably modeled after real Cracow citizens. The altar is opened with great ceremony every day except Sunday at noon.

RATUSZ (TOWN HALL TOWER) Completed in 1383, the tower stands near the southwest corner of Cloth Hall. A fire destroyed the original Gothic spire, and the baroque structure that now tops the tower was added in 1680. The tower is all that remains of the old Town Hall, which was dismantled in 1820. It now houses a branch of the *Cracow History Museum,* and there is a cheerful café in the cellar.

KOŚCIÓŁ SW. ADELBERT (ST. ADALBERT'S CHURCH) The oldest building in Main Market Square, this 12th-century church is a curious blend of pre-Romanesque, Gothic, Renaissance, and baroque architecture. Legend holds that St. Adalbert, a 10th-century bishop from Prague, preached on this spot before setting out to convert the heathens in northern Prussia. The elliptical dome above the church is sheathed in copper.

WZGÓRZE WAWELSKIE (WAWEL HILL)

The hill on which Cracow was founded is crowded with an impressive array of Gothic and Renaissance buildings. Together they comprise a virtual museum of Polish history, for each generation of Polish rulers over the course of the last millennium has left its mark here. Splendid old mansions of noblemen and merchants are clustered on the streets at the bottom of the hill; here, too, are narrow passageways between shops that open onto tiny courtyards with artisans' workshops and balconied houses.

KATEDRA WAWELSKA (WAWEL CATHEDRAL) Polish kings were crowned and buried here until the 18th century, and Karol Cardinal Wojtyła preached from its pulpit before he was elected to the papacy. Its foundations were laid in the 14th century, on the site of two older Romanesque churches. The elaborate tomb of St. Stanislaw, Poland's patron saint, stands in the nave. Of the cathedral's 18 chapels, two are particularly noteworthy. The first is the Chapel of the Holy Cross, which was begun in 1447 for Kazimierz IV and his wife, and is a classic example of the Cracow Gothic style. The second is the Bartolomeo Berrecci–designed King Sigismund's Chapel, in which the red marble tombs of the king and his family stand out strikingly against the white marble walls. Also in the cathedral is an 11th-century crypt, salvaged from one of the Romanesque churches that originally stood on this site. It contains the remains of kings, queens, bishops, and Polish national heroes, including Tadeusz Kościuszko, the Polish general who fought with the colonials in the American Revolution before returning to Poland to fight for his own country's freedom, and Marshal Józef Piłsudski, leader of newly independent Poland after World War I.

ZAMEK KRÓLEWSKI (ROYAL CASTLE) Entered through an arcaded courtyard, this castle is one of Europe's best surviving examples of Renaissance architecture. Among the treasures here are a fine collection of rare 16th- and 17th-century Flemish tapestries and a 16th-century coffered ceiling decorated with painted heads of members of the royal court in relief. The castle's 71 spacious rooms are all richly appointed; several are covered entirely in embossed and hand-painted Spanish leather. Open daily from 10 AM to 3 PM; some exhibits are closed on Mondays. Admission charge. Wawel Hill (phone: 225747).

OTHER SIGHTS

UNIWERSYTET JAGIELLOŃSKA (JAGIELLONIAN UNIVERSITY) Founded in 1364 by King Kazimierz the Great, this is the second-oldest university in Europe. It was formerly called Cracow Academy. During World War II, the Nazis purged the university of its teaching staff. Today, some 50,000 students are enrolled here. The Collegium Maius, the university seat, is a red brick Gothic building with a beautiful arcaded courtyard; it has been converted into a museum. On display is the globe that is said to have convinced Copernicus of the existence of America. The museum is open on weekdays from 11 AM to 2:30 PM. Admission charge. 15 Ulica Jagiellońska (phone: 220549).

PLANTY (GREEN BELT) In the Middle Ages, walls and moats surrounded the Old City. They were demolished in the 19th century under Austrian rule and replaced by an attractive 2-mile swath of gardens and tree-lined walks called the Planty, or Green Belt. Two parts of the old wall remain — the Barbican and St. Florian's Gate. Built around 1498, the Barbican was supposedly modeled after fortresses common in the Middle East. Its turrets and tiled roofs give it an Oriental flair. St. Florian's Gate was built around 1300, and the baroque spire was added 350 years later. The south face of the tower is decorated with a bas-relief of St. Florian.

> | **EXTRA SPECIAL** | Before World War II, about 60,000 Jews lived in Kazimierz, the Jewish quarter in the
>
> southern part of Cracow; now there are only a few hundred in the city. Created as a separate fortified town by King Kazimierz the Great in 1335, it became the Jewish quarter during the late 15th century when the Jews of Cracow were driven out of the city proper. The king had encouraged Jews to settle in Poland; and despite periods of persecution, they prospered in Kazimierz until the Swedish invasion in 1655. The district remained largely Jewish until the Nazi occupation, when a walled ghetto was created across the Vistula River and the extermination of Jews began. Today, only the Remu'h Synagogue (40 Ulica Szeroka) remains open for worship. In the adjoining cemetery, used from the 1530s to the 1800s, fragments of desecrated tombstones have been cemented together to create a single wall monument. The *Old Synagogue* (24 Ulica Szeroka; phone: 220962) is among the oldest surviving in Europe. Begun in the late 15th century, it was rebuilt in the Renaissance style after a 1557 fire. For centuries it was an administra-

tive as well as a religious center, and during World War II it was used as a stable by the Nazis. Restored, it is now a museum chronicling the history and culture of Polish Jews. Open Wednesdays to Sundays.

ENVIRONS

NOWA HUTA (NEW MILL) To see the antithesis of the graceful monuments of Old Cracow, visit this massive industrial suburb. Built in the early 1950s, the town center is grim, with bleak gray housing blocks extending from the center in every direction. The steel plant for which this suburb was built is closed to the public, but visitors should stop to see the Kościói Sw. Mariacki (St. Mary's Church), which was built by the steelworkers on their own time and with their own money. Those without a car can reach Nowa Huta by tram; the best lines are Nos. 1, 4, 5, and 15. Buses A, B, and 139 also stop in the suburb, which is 9 miles (14 km) from downtown Cracow.

KOPIEC KOŚCIUSZKI (KOŚCIUSZKO MOUND) The people of Cracow have a long tradition of creating earthen monuments. The most famous is the Kościuszko Mound (you can't miss it), which was built in 1820 by the townspeople in honor of Tadeusz Kościuszko, the Polish freedom fighter. Skiers glide down the hill in winter, and every toddler in Cracow comes here to play when the weather's warm. On a clear day (hard to come by), you can see the Tatra Mountains from the top of the mound. At the western end of Ulica Kościuszki.

KOPALNIA SOLI W WIELICZE (WIELICZKA SALT MINE) About 8 miles (13 km) southeast of Cracow is one of the largest and oldest working salt mines in Europe. People have mined salt here for more than 5,000 years. In the Middle Ages, Wieliczka was one of the major crossroads along the European salt routes. Today, visitors can descend 394 wooden steps leading to the first level of the mine, a 180-foot (54-meter) chapel carved out of rock salt and lit with salt-crystal chandeliers. There are many other chambers with salt carvings, an underground museum, tennis and volleyball courts for current miners, and a clinic for the treatment of respiratory diseases. Open daily from 10 AM to 4 PM, although flooding has caused periodic closings. Check with *Orbis,* the Polish tourist agency (see *Sources and Resources*).

OŚWIĘCIM (AUSCHWITZ) The infamous Nazi concentration camp is located in the town of Oświęcim (Auschwitz is the German name), 34 miles (54 km) west of Cracow. Nearly 4 million people perished here. Auschwitz is really two camps — the Auschwitz work camp and Birkenau, the site of the extermination center. The entrance to Auschwitz bears the chilling slogan *"Arbeit Macht Frei"* — Work Makes One Free. The camp has been turned into a heartbreaking museum. The displays of objects taken from the inmates — thousands of pairs of spectacles, heaps of brushes, worn-out boots, artificial limbs, and suitcases inscribed with the names of their late owners — offer mute testimony to the horrors committed here.

About 2 miles (3 km) away is Birkenau (Brzezinka in Polish), where most of the prisoners perished. Birkenau has been left untouched, and the barren setting is befitting of the most appalling atrocity of the modern age. Visitors are free to tour the site on their own or to participate in a guided tour. This is not an experience for the fainthearted, but it should be a required pilgrimage. Both camps are open daily from 8 AM to 3 PM (phone: 381-32022). For more information, see *Quintessential Eastern Europe* in DIVERSIONS, and *Poland* in DIRECTIONS.

Sources and Resources

TOURIST INFORMATION

The main tourist center is the Central Tourist Information Office near the train station (8 Ulica Pawia; phone: 226091). The national tourist agency, *Orbis,* has offices in the *Orbis-Cracovia* hotel (1 Aleje Focha; phone: 224632). In addition, there are scores of new private travel agencies, some operating in conjunction with hotels. Maps are sold at kiosks, bookstores, and hotels, as are good, updated English-language local guides, including several by Jan K. Ostrowski.

LOCAL COVERAGE The monthly English-language guides *When, Where, and What* and *Welcome to Cracow* are available at hotels and tourist offices. The *International Herald Tribune* and other English-language newspapers and magazines are also available.

TELEPHONE The country code for Poland is 48. The city code for Cracow is 12. The country's telephone system has improved in recent years, and it's now much easier to make overseas calls. *AT&T* has a "USA Direct" number (phone: 010-480-0111) for Poland-to-US calls.

GETTING AROUND

Old Cracow is easily seen on foot, and several nice hotels are within its confines. For the larger hotels in the modern city or on the outskirts, public transportation or cabs are the best bet.

AIRPORT Cracow's Balice Airport (phone: 227078) is almost an hour from the city center and offers only limited service to Warsaw and a few European cities. *Air Tours Poland* runs bus service between the airport, hotels, and the *LOT* (Polish Airlines) office at 15 Ulica Basztowa (phone: 219491). The fare is about $3.

CAR RENTAL Renting a car is expensive in Poland — count on at least $300 to $400 a week — but better prices can sometimes be obtained by making arrangements in advance. The major car rental companies represented are

Hertz (1 Aleje Focha; phone: 371120) and *PZM* (Polish Automobile and Motorcycle Association; phone: 664730). It makes sense to check with the privately owned local travel agencies: They often rent cars for the lowest prices in town; ask at your hotel reception desk.

TAXI It used to be almost impossible to find a cab in Cracow. Economic reform has changed all that, and visitors will be delighted to see taxis lined up at stands all over the city. Settle on a price before setting out, though. (The fare from the airport to the city center is about $25.) Cabs also can be ordered by calling *Radio Taxi* (phone: 365919).

TRAIN Cracow is less than a 3-hour ride from Warsaw on the express train, which is relatively comfortable and clean. Główny, the central train station (Plac Kolejowy; phone: 223933), is located just outside the Green Belt. Some trains arrive at the suburban Plaszow Station (phone: 227022). The express usually runs in the early morning and early evening. Be aware, however, that incidents of muggings and pocket picking have become commonplace at the Warsaw end of the line.

SPECIAL EVENTS

The best time to visit Cracow is in June, when the city holds its *Days of Cracow* festival to celebrate both the Cracovian folk tradition and the artistic accomplishments of the past year. The *Polish and International Short Film Festival* also takes place in June, and the *International Biennial of Graphic Arts* is held in August (in even-numbered years) at 4 Ulica Szczepański.

In September, the city hosts the *Folk Art Fair.* Artisans from all over Poland converge on Cracow with everything from straw baskets and brightly colored embroidery to decorated pottery and paintings on glass. During the fair, peasants in traditional garb set up booths throughout Main Market Square. Each specializes in a certain regional product, such as tablecloths from the Tatras or dresses from Kasubia. Folk music and dance ensembles perform on a stage in the middle of the square.

Christmas is a particularly lovely time in Poland. Cracow celebrates with a *Christmas Crèche Competition,* in which residents compete to make the finest ornately decorated crib. The cribs are displayed in Main Market Square.

MUSEUMS

In addition to those described in *Special Places,* Cracow has several other interesting museums. Most are free or charge a minimal fee, but they are often closed on Mondays. Generally, museums are open from 9 AM to 4 PM. Hours may also vary according to season.

DOM MATEJKI (MATEJKO MUSEUM) The onetime home of 19th-century Polish painter Jan Matejko, this charming museum preserves the artist's studio and much of his memorabilia. Included are his collection of historical costumes, research tools, and several sketches and smaller paintings. In the Old Town at 41 Ulica Florianska (phone: 225926).

MUZEUM ARCHEOLOGICZNE (ARCHAEOLOGICAL MUSEUM) The most famous of its kind in the country, exhibits here cover the history of human civilization in the area that is now Poland from 150,000 BC to the early Middle Ages. Of special interest is the stone statue of the god Swiatowid. 3 Ulica Senacka (phone: 227560 or 227761).

MUZEUM CZARTORYSKIUM (CZARTORYSKI MUSEUM) This museum houses a collection of 550 13th- through 18th-century European paintings — including a Rembrandt and a Da Vinci — once owned by the noble Czartoryski family. There are also objects from ancient Rome, Flemish tapestries, and several Persian carpets. 19 Ulica Sw. Jana (phone: 225566).

MUZEUM ETNOGRAFICZNE (ETHNOGRAPHIC MUSEUM) Poland's oldest and largest collection of folk art and crafts. 1 Plac Wolnica (phone: 662963 or 663975).

MUZEUM HISTORYCZNE MIASTA KRAKOWA (HISTORICAL MUSEUM OF CRACOW) Exhibitions illustrating the city's history are featured here. Located in the Krzysztofory Palace, a beautiful 17th-century townhouse created by Crown Marshal Adam Kazanowski. 35 Rynek Główny (phone: 229922).

MUZEUM NARODOWE W KRAKOWIE (NATIONAL MUSEUM OF CRACOW) Located on the upper level of the Cloth Hall, this museum is best known for its three paintings by Polish painter Jan Matejko. The most moving is probably *Kościuszko at the Battle of Raclawice,* portraying the victory of a largely Polish peasant army over czarist troops during the 1794 insurrection. Rynek Główny (phone: 221166).

MUZEUM STANISŁAWA WYSPIAŃSKIEGO (STANISLAWA WYSPIANSKI MUSEUM) Works by the turn-of-the-century Polish poet and painter are featured here. 9 Ulica Kanonicza (phone: 228337).

MUZEUM TEATRALNE (THEATER MUSEUM) A tribute to Cracow's long and rich thespian tradition. Located at Jagiellonian University. 1 Ulica Jagiellońska (phone: 228566).

SHOPPING

Stores come and go with incredible speed these days in Poland, but the overall trend is unmistakable — the quality and quantity of many goods are fast approaching Western standards. It's difficult to recommend specific shops in Cracow, as the boutique we recommend one day may very well be out of business the next. So take your time and explore the shops of the Old Town. For folk arts and crafts, try the *Cepelia* shops in the Cloth Hall (12 Ulica Mikołajska; phone: 225337) or *Milenium* (17 Rynek

Główny; phone: 219305). *Desa* specializes in antiques (8-17 Ulica Stolarska; phone: 227041). For glassware try the well-known outlet shop of the *Krosno* factory in southern Cracow (15 Ulica Floriańska; phone: 229018). Silver and amber jewelry are among the best Polish offerings; shops featuring these treasures include *Ofir* (12 Ulica Florisańska; phone: 219885), *Skarbiec* (35 Ulica Grodzka; no phone), and *Black Gallery* (24 Ulica Mikołajska; phone: 211853). Among the many art galleries are *Inny Swiat* (37 Ulica Floriańska; phone: 217764) and *Hadar* (20 Ulica Poselska; phone: 210208), which specializes in art and crafts by Jews.

SPORTS AND FITNESS

In addition to the manmade mounds near the city, which locals have converted into ski runs, Cracow has quite a few sports facilities.

ICE SKATING There is an indoor rink (7 Ulica Siedleckiego; phone: 211317). Open weekdays from 5 to 6:30 PM; Saturdays and Sundays from 10 AM to noon, 2 to 4 PM, and 5 to 6:30 PM.

SWIMMING There are pools at the *Forum Inter-Continental* and *Holiday Inn* hotels. There's also a good facility at the sports center at 8 Ulica Krowoderska (phone: 229111).

TENNIS The city has 3 sets of courts (at 7 Ulica Siedleckiego; phone: 211069; 20 Ulica Koletek; phone: 222122; 1 Ulica Blonie; phone: 220414). In addition, the *Holiday Inn* and *Forum Inter-Continental* hotels have courts for guests.

THEATER

Cracow boasts a long and rich theater tradition. The city's repertory theaters are well known for the quality of their productions. Famous theaters include the *Teatr im J. Slowackiego* (1 Plac Sw. Ducha; phone: 224022) and the *Stary Teatr im Helena Modrzejewska* (1 Ulica Jagiellońska; phone: 224040). Director Andrzej Wajda often stages productions at the latter, and almost every premiere at its branch, the *Scena Kameralny Teatr,* is of interest. The *Cricot 2 Teatr* (5 Ulica Kanonicza; phone: 228332) was the late director Tadeusz Kantor's favorite venue. Also recommended are the *Groteska* (Ulica Skarbowa; phone: 333762, 334822, or 339604), which specializes in avant-garde productions using masks; the *Bagatela* (6 Ulica Karmelicka; phone: 224544), which stages classics; and the *Teatr Stu* (16 Aleja Krasińskiego; phone: 222263), which also features the avant-garde. Theater tickets are available at the box office, or ask at your hotel reception desk.

MUSIC

The *Kraków Philharmonic* offers concerts at 1 Ulica Zwierzyniecka (phone: 220958 or 229477). Performances generally are given on Fridays and Saturdays. Tickets are available at the box office or from the reception desk of major hotels.

NIGHTCLUBS AND NIGHTLIFE

Cracow is famous for its cabaret. The two most popular spots are *Kabaret Jama Michalikowa* (45 Ulica Floriańska; phone: 221561), a cozy place where you can enjoy a leisurely drink before or after the performance; and the more idiosyncratic *Piwnica pod Baranami* (27 Rynek Główny; phone: 223265). Directed by satirist Piotr Skrzynecki, the latter's specialty is improvisation, and performances take place only on evenings when sufficient numbers of actors feel inclined to take the stage. Student clubs, which feature music and cabaret performances, can be enjoyed by travelers of all ages. Some of the best in the city are the *Pod Jaszczurami* (7 Rynek Główny; phone: 220922), the *Rotunda* (1 Ulica Oleandry; phone: 333538 or 336160), and the *Piast* (27 Piastowska; phone: 374933).

Best in Town

CHECKING IN

Lodging remains a bit of a problem in Cracow. There are only a handful of decent hotels and reservations can be hard to come by during the tourist season, so visitors are advised to book well in advance. Moreover, the hotels in the Old Town, where most of the interesting sights are found, are small, while the larger hotels are well away from the city center.

The shift to private enterprise has allowed some Polish families to venture into the lodging trade, and bed and breakfast establishments are beginning to appear. The local tourist office can make reservations, or ask at the *Central Tourist Information Office* (see *Sources and Resources,* above). Another option is *American-International Homestays* (1515 W. Penn St., Iowa City, IA 52240; phone: 319-626-2125), which arranges for stays with Polish families in Cracow and several other Eastern European cities.

Prices are somewhat unstable, because many hotels have recently changed hands (or may soon), and managements seem to change tariffs arbitrarily, almost from night to night. For a double, expect to pay $85 to $150 at an expensive hotel; $70 to $85 at a moderately priced hotel; and under $70 at an inexpensive one. Most of Cracow's major hotels have complete facilities for the business traveler. Those hotels listed below as having "business services" usually offer such conveniences as English-speaking concierge, meeting rooms, photocopiers, computers, translation services, and express checkout, among others. Call the hotel for additional information. All telephone numbers are in the 12 city code unless otherwise indicated.

EXPENSIVE

Forum Inter-Continental The most complete facilities in town, though decor is not its strong suit. But it has 284 air conditioned rooms, each with a private bath, mini-bar, and color TV set. Half of the rooms overlook the Vistula River and Wawel Castle. There is also a restaurant (really a coffee shop), a nightclub, 3 bars, a casino, a rooftop café, tennis courts, a swimming pool, and a sauna. Business services. 28 Ulica Marii Konopnickiej (phone: 669500; fax: 665827).

Holiday Inn Although this place leans more toward functionalism than luxury, its 293 comfortable rooms and 4 suites are all air conditioned. There is also a swimming pool, a sauna, and a restaurant. The drawback is the location: the hotel is 2 miles (3 km) from downtown, a 10-minute bus ride or a 5-minute drive to Main Market Square. Business services. 11 Aleje Armii Krajowej (phone: 375044; fax: 375938).

Orbis-Cracovia A leviathan of a hotel, it is within walking distance of the Old Town, with 335 austere rooms, a restaurant, a café, and several shops. 1 Aleje Focha (phone: 228666; fax: 219586).

MODERATE

Grand Conveniently located in the Old Town, this lovely hotel has 51 modern rooms, a pool, a restaurant (see *Eating Out*), and a coffee shop. 5-7 Ulica Sławkowska (phone: 217255).

Orbis-Francuski Built just after the turn of the century, this centrally situated property has 57 good rooms. Recently renovated, it is one of the most charming of the city's hotels. The *Francuski* restaurant is quite good (see *Eating Out*). 13 Ulica Pijarska (phone: 225122; fax: 225270).

Pod Różą The oldest hostelry in the city, it boasts such former guests as Czar Alexander I and Franz Liszt. Centrally located and renovated (though still a bit faded), it's a convenient place to stay. There are 35 rooms, a restaurant (see *Eating Out*), and a café. 14 Ulica Floriańska (phone: 229399).

Royal Newly renovated, this hotel features 70 comfortably furnished rooms, a restaurant, and a café. Conveniently situated at the base of Wawel Hill on the edge of the Old Town. 26 Ulica Sw. Gertrudy (phone: 213500).

Wanda Eighty spare and simple rooms are offered at this place, located right next to the *Holiday Inn,* 15 Aleje Armii Krajowej (phone: 371677).

INEXPENSIVE

Krak The best camping site and motel just outside of Cracow. 99 Ulica Radzikowskiego (phone: 372122).

Pollera After 40 years, this beautiful 150-year-old hotel has returned to local family ownership. All 40 rooms are comfortable and quiet with an ideal Old Town location. A good restaurant provides a tasty menu and courteous service. 30 Ulica Szpitalna (phone: 221044 or 221128).

Polonia Recent renovations have improved this once-drab hotel, now boasting sparkling chandeliers and a faux-marble reception area. The 148 rooms, however, remain basic — although many have French doors facing the Planty gardens. There's a good restaurant, too. 38 Ulica Narutowicza (phone: 331896).

Polski Pod Białym Orłem Small and private, this 43-room property is conveniently situated in the Old Town. No restaurant. 17 Ulica Pijarska (phone: 221144 or 221529).

EATING OUT

Although it's no culinary hot spot, Cracow has seen enough new restaurants open to offer reasonable fare in pleasant-enough settings. Among the particular pleasures of Cracow are the plentiful cafés that line its narrow streets.

For dinner for two, expect to pay about $30 or more at an expensive restaurant; $20 at a moderately priced one; and as little as $10 at an inexpensive place. Prices do not include wine or drinks. In general, the ambience is casual at Cracow restaurants. All restaurants are in the 12 city code unless otherwise indicated.

For an unforgettable dining experience, we begin with our culinary favorite, followed by our cost and quality choices, listed by price category.

DELIGHTFUL DINING

Wierzynek Long the most elegant and best-known dining place in Cracow, it was here that the King of Poland wined and dined the Holy Roman Emperor Charles IV in 1364. More recently, Polish President Wojciech Jaruzelski entertained Mikhail Gorbachev here during the then–Soviet leader's ground-breaking 1989 trip to Poland. Presided over by imperious waiters when it was an oasis of relative quality in Communist Poland, *Wierzynek* must now compete with dozens of newer eateries. The attempt at haute cuisine is not always successful, but the setting — a centuries-old house with a magnificent location on Main Market Square — makes up for the occasional culinary deficiency. Try the wild game and enjoy the Old World atmosphere. Open daily 9 AM to 11 PM. Reservations advised. Major credit cards accepted. 15 Rynek Główny (phone: 221035).

EXPENSIVE

Francuski This charming hotel dining room serves good traditional fare. Open daily. Reservations advised. Major credit cards accepted. *Orbis-Francuski Hotel,* 13 Ulica Pijarska (phone: 225122 or 225270).

Grand Traditional Polish fare is served in a nicely restored Old World setting. Try the *flaki* (tripe stew with vegetables) and the ever-present *kotlet schabowy* (pork cutlet) with garden-fresh vegetables. Open daily. Reservations advised. Major credit cards accepted. In the *Grand Hotel,* 5-7 Ulica Sławkowska (phone: 217255).

Da Pietro A wide variety of Italian dishes served in a cellar setting on the Main Market Square. Open daily for lunch and dinner. Reservations advised. Major credit cards accepted. 17 Rynek Główny (phone: 223279).

Pod Kopcem Housed in a 19th-century Austrian fortress, this hotel restaurant is perched on top of a hill with a great view. Open daily for lunch and dinner. Reservations advised. No credit cards accepted. Ulica Waszyngtona (phone: 220355; telex: 221035).

Pod Różą International fare à la Polonaise is featured at this hotel dining room. Open daily for lunch and dinner. Reservations advised. Major credit cards accepted. 14 Ulica Floriańska (phone: 229399).

MODERATE

Balaton Hungarian-style food and music at a convenient Old Town location. Open daily 9 AM to 10 PM. Reservations advised. No credit cards accepted. 37 Ulica Grodzka (phone: 220469).

Królewska Good Polish specialties, including traditional sausages and *naleśniki* (dessert pancakes) smothered with fresh fruit. Open for lunch and dinner. Reservations necessary. No credit cards accepted. 59 Ulica Grodszka (phone: 229694).

Staropolska Considered one of the city's best eateries. Polish dishes here include several types of wild game. Service sometimes is slow; order and then relax. Open daily for lunch and dinner. Reservations advised on weekends. No credit cards accepted. 4 Ulica Sienna (phone: 225821).

INEXPENSIVE

Almajer Cracow's first Chinese restaurant serves zesty fare — from steamed dumplings to Peking duck. Open daily from 2 PM to midnight. Reservations advised. No credit cards accepted. 30 Rynek Główny (phone: 223224).

Cechowa Near the university, this eatery offers *zrazy* (beef roll with groats) and other homemade Polish dishes. Open daily for lunch and dinner. No reservations. No credit cards accepted. 11 Ulica Jagiellońska (phone: 210936).

Grace A lively student quarter spot serving good crusty pizza. Open daily for lunch and dinner. No reservations. No credit cards accepted. 7 Ulica Sw. Anny (no phone).

U Pani Staśi Although it's really more a cafeteria than a restaurant, this self-service eatery always has a line of folks waiting to feast on the truly home-style Polish fare. The *pirogi* are particularly good. Open daily for lunch. No reservations. No credit cards accepted. 16 Ulica Mikołajska (no phone).

Kiev

One of the oldest cities in Eastern Europe, the ancient, gold-domed capital of Ukraine predates Moscow by several centuries and St. Petersburg by nearly 1,000 years. The third-largest city in the erstwhile Soviet Union, magnificent Kiev (Kyiv in Ukrainian) was also the cradle of East Slavic culture. Though battered by wars, revolutions, and assorted upheavals over the course of its rich history, a good part of its fabled beauty has remained. Its broad boulevards and leafy parks, medieval monasteries perched majestically on high bluffs above the Dneiper (Dnipro in Ukrainian) River, and splendid rococo, baroque, and even Art Deco and Art Nouveau architecture give Kiev a decidedly Western European flair and help explain the locals' fierce pride in their city.

There were settlements in Kiev as early as the 1st century AD, and it was a commercial center by the 5th century. The earliest history of the city is steeped in legend. According to folklore, Kiev got its name from Kyi, a leader of a prominent East Slav tribe called the Polyani, who founded the city with his sister and two brothers.

The origins of Kievan Rus, the political, commercial, and cultural entity of which Kiev became the capital and which became one of the great European powers of its era, remain murky. What is known is that the early rulers were Varangians (Scandinavians), who probably were first attracted to the area because of its location along an important trade route to Constantinople, Christendom's richest city. In fact, some historians hold that the word "Rus" derives from the Finnish word for Swedes, although others associate it with the names of rivers in central Ukraine.

Because Kievan Rus came to encompass all the territories inhabited by the East Slavs, including much of Ukraine's contemporary region, Ukrainians and Russians both lay claim to Kievan Rus as part of their national histories, and each group feels that it is the only rightful heir to the old Kievan legacy. Making the issue more complex are such questions as direct ethnic lineage and the evolution of modern statehood. The issue continues to be one of bitter dispute. After centuries of being ruled from Moscow, Ukrainians especially are sensitive to what they perceive as an "imperialist Russian" attempt to usurp their history.

Because of its hilly terrain, Kiev developed into three separate settlements which still retain some of their independent character. There is the regal Verkhny Horod (Upper Town); the Podil (Low) district, which was a trading center next to the navigable Dnieper River; and Pechersk, the site of a series of natural caves that became home to hermits and many of the town's ecclesiastics. These settlements traded heavily with the countries of Western Europe, the Baltics, Byzantium, and Asia Minor; together they made early Kiev the trading center of Eastern Europe.

Kiev's golden era began in AD 980, with the rule of Great Prince Volodymyr (Vladimir), whose crowning achievement was the Christianization of East Slavdom. An enlightened ruler and a shrewd politician, Volodymyr set out to supplant pagan worship with a new religion, believing that his realm had reached a higher plateau in its development. The choice was essentially between Christianity and Islam, representing the worlds to which Kievan Rus looked and with which it had forged the closest ties. An early Rus chronicle offers a fanciful account — discounted by historians — of how Volodymyr set out to make his choice. He first, it is said, looked at Judaism, which he thought admirable, but was discouraged when he concluded that Jews were scattered around the world as a result of their sins. He then considered Islam, but was put off by its prohibition of alcohol. Rome's Christianity was rejected because the prince did not want to answer to Rome. The Byzantine version of Christianity was chosen after several of Volodymyr's envoys to Byzantium returned with tales of the splendor of the cathedrals there. "We only know that God dwells there among men, and their service is fairer than the ceremonies of other nations. We can never forget that beauty," the envoys are said to have reported. In any case, by AD 988 Volodymyr had converted, married (in return for helping Constantinople put down a rebellion) Princess Anna, sister of one of the Byzantine co-emperors, and ordered his entire country to be baptized into the Byzantine faith.

This was the beginning of the Orthodox church that was to play such an important role throughout so much of the East Slavs' history. Byzantine architecture, the style most closely identified with Ukraine and Russia, was introduced in Kiev by the progeny of Prince Volodymyr, who commissioned churches in the designs of the colorful cathedrals of Constantinople. (Kiev borrowed heavily from Byzantine culture, and adopted its autocratic tradition of government as well.) Probably Kiev's greatest architectural legacy is the Cathedral of St. Sophia, built by Volodymyr's son, Yaroslav the Wise. This church, which blends Byzantine with early Kievan Rus design, is one of Ukraine's finest.

The golden age of Kiev ended soon after the reign of Yaroslav the Wise, when Kiev began a steady decline, and eventually the city of Vladimir took its place as the disintegrating state's principal municipality (at the time, Moscow was still a one-troika town). In this vulnerable state, Kiev was plundered by the Tatars (Mongols) in 1240 after a long and bloody siege. The Tatars held the city in its yoke well into the following century. It was then subjugated in turn by the neighboring Lithuanians (who controlled the region from 1320 to 1455) and then the Poles. Oddly enough, in Kiev today there remains hardly a trace of over 4 centuries of Tatar, Lithuanian, and Polish occupation.

In the 17th century, after a long and costly struggle to free Kiev and Ukraine from the Poles, the Ukrainian cossack leader Bohdan Khmelnytsky turned to Moscow for protection. (The Russian Empire, with Mos-

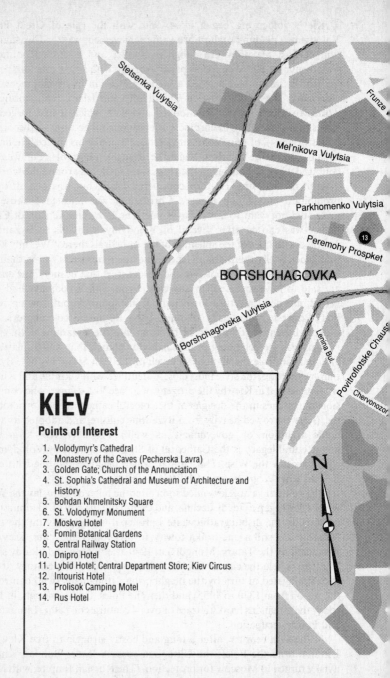

KIEV

Points of Interest

1. Volodymyr's Cathedral
2. Monastery of the Caves (Pecherska Lavra)
3. Golden Gate; Church of the Annunciation
4. St. Sophia's Cathedral and Museum of Architecture and History
5. Bohdan Khmelnitsky Square
6. St. Volodymyr Monument
7. Moskva Hotel
8. Fomin Botanical Gardens
9. Central Railway Station
10. Dnipro Hotel
11. Lybid Hotel; Central Department Store; Kiev Circus
12. Intourist Hotel
13. Prolisok Camping Motel
14. Rus Hotel

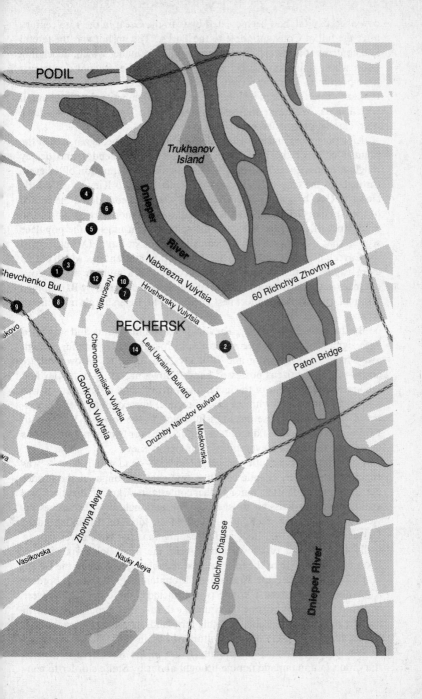

PODIL

Trukhanov
Island

Dnieper

River

4

6

5

3

1

12

Kreschatik

10

7

Naberezna Vulytsia

Hrushevsky Vulytsia

60 Richchya Zhovtnya

Shevchenko Bul.

8

9

skovo

PECHERSK

14

Lesi Ukrainki Bulvard

2

Paton Bridge

Chervonoarmiiska Vulytsia

Gorkogo Vulytsia

Druzhby Narodov Bulvard

Moskovska

Zhovtnya Aleya

Nauky Aleya

Vasilkovska

Stolichne Chausse

Dnieper River

va

cow as its capital, had been created by Ivan the Great in the 15th century after the fall of Constantinople to the Turks.) The upshot was the fateful and controversial Pereiaslav Agreement of 1654, under which, depending upon who's doing the historical interpretation (the original documents have been lost), Ukraine merely agreed to a form of vassalage — without the czar's interference in its internal affairs — or submitted to total union with Russia. Whatever the case, Ukraine's and Russia's histories have been closely intertwined ever since.

Kiev prospered under Russian dominion and became, again, one of the premier cities of the land. With its architectural splendor and deeply religious ethos, it was long the primary pilgrimage destination of believers throughout the empire. Czars and noblemen came to Kiev to get a little closer to God by getting a little closer to what was considered the source of the Russian Orthodox church. With its ancient monasteries, icons, and abundance of churches, Kiev met the spiritual yearnings of the populace so well that its religious centerpiece, the Pecherska Lavra (Monastery of the Caves), became enormously wealthy by the 18th century. Much of this extra capital in turn funded the construction of a number of gorgeous churches in the baroque style, some of which were designed by Bartolomeo Rastrelli, the Italian architect best known for St. Petersburg's magnificent palaces.

By the early 19th century, Kiev had 30,000 inhabitants and was filled with significant architecture and the spirit of growth. It was far enough away from St. Petersburg and Moscow to hold on to its own culture and — since its citizens possessed handed-down memories of a Kiev and a Ukraine independent of the increasingly heavy hand of Russia — it was frequently out of step with the czarist regime. For example, the "Decembrists," noblemen whose unsuccessful revolt in the town of Vasilkov in 1825 opened a wound of discontent that festered for two more generations before the Bolshevik Revolution, often met in Kiev.

Following the Revolution of 1917, Ukraine — and with it Kiev — was engulfed in a bitter, chaotic civil war that raged throughout the former czarist empire and pitted, among other contestants, Ukrainian nationalists against invading Russian Bolsheviks. The nationalists — themselves divided into sparring factions — managed to declare an independent Ukraine, but amid the chaos and spreading anarchy, were never able to really take control of the country. After the final Bolshevik victory, Ukraine became one of the four original republics that formed the USSR in 1922. Later, after the Carpathian Mountain region (which borders Romania) and Western Ukraine (which includes the city of Lviv) were added to Ukraine, it became the country's third-largest republic, and with its seemingly endless stretch of fertile farmland, its primary breadbasket. Ironically, despite Ukraine's agricultural riches, in 1932-33 an estimated 5 to 7 million Ukrainians — including many in the Kiev area — died of starvation in a manmade famine brought about by Stalin's order to confiscate food and grain from the countryside. Stalin's aim was to force collectivization on a recalcitrant and nationally conscious peasantry and to finance rapid industrialization.

Kiev suffered considerably during World War II. Many irreplaceable architectural and cultural treasures were destroyed, and Khreshchatyk, the city's main boulevard, was blown up by retreating Soviet partisans. But the greater tragedy was the toll the war took on the populace. More than 195,000 Kievans lost their lives, including those killed in the mass executions that took place on the Babyn Yar (Babi Yar in Russian) killing fields. In all, according to official records, at least 7 million Ukrainians perished in the war.

Following World War II, Kiev once again became a busy crossroads and grew at a rapid rate. The city is divided into 12 districts, many of which were built to accommodate a burgeoning population.

Ukraine's movement toward democracy gained momentum in the mid-1980s. Rukh, the republic's grassroots movement for independence and democracy (and now a political party), was one of the old USSR's strongest and most committed, instrumental in organizing miners' strikes, support for progressive parliamentary legislation, and calls for secession and Ukrainian independence. Their fervor was not in vain. In the weeks immediately following the tumultuous events in Moscow in the summer of 1991, Ukraine declared its independence subject to a referendum, which passed by an overwhelming majority on December 1, 1991.

Yet despite independence, progress toward political and economic reform has been slow and painful since those heady days when jubilant Kievans danced through their city's streets carrying long-suppressed nationalist symbols, including the blue and yellow flag that is now Ukraine's official banner. At press time, Parliament and much of the economic sector continued to be dominated by former Communists loath to see their old power and privileges erode. For his part, President Leonid Kravchuk, himself a former Communist but self-described convert to market economics, has introduced tough new measures to enforce reform, among them liberalization of prices and a sweeping privatization program. Tensions remain strong between Ukraine and Russia: Heavily dependent on oil from Russia and trade with the other former Soviet republics, Ukraine used to count on the Soviet Union for 80% of its trade and over a third of its industrial output.

Modern Kiev is an airy city with acres of parkland, timeworn cathedrals, and wide, attractive boulevards. Unlike most ancient cities of the former Soviet Union, there are no remains of a kremlin or fortified citadel (it was destroyed long ago), though ancient architecture mixes with modern (spelled Soviet dull) buildings throughout the city. Monuments are everywhere — honoring ordinary, as well as extraordinary, Ukrainian and Russian figures. (Elderly female pensioners, known as *babushkas,* who supplement their income by cultivating the city's parks and gardens, think nothing of "shooing" away visitors who have the nerve to sit at the base of — or even near — statues or monuments, an act that is considered a sign of disrespect.) The city cherishes its culture, and many monuments and statues commemorate writers, including Taras Shevchenko, the 19th-century Ukrainian nationalist whose poetry helped rally the dissent against czarist rule; Ivan Franko, a political radical and prolific writer; and Lesya Ukrainka, a late-19th-century poet and playwright. In addition, Kiev's museums are richly endowed; and there is theater, opera, ballet, and other cultural events. Today the city's many charms — not to mention its distinctive native fare (it's the home of chicken Kiev and borscht) — have attracted scores of foreign visitors. While the pace of tourist traffic was for several years held down due to Kiev's proximity to the destroyed reactor at the nuclear generating plant at Chernobyl, by now the health risks to short-term visitors at least are minimal. (The plant's three remaining reactors are scheduled to be permanently shut down later this year.) Those travelers who have time to visit just a few places in the vast patchwork that was the Soviet Union should not miss the ancient city of Kiev.

NOTE At press time, prompted by the increase in reported cases of diphtheria in Russia and Ukraine, travelers are advised to update their immunizations before entering these regions. For further information call the US State Department's *Citizen's Emergency Center* at 202-647-5225.

Kiev At-a-Glance

SEEING THE CITY

Begin with a walk up Andriyivska Hirka (Andrew's Hill), the highest spot in Kiev. Around the spectacular turquoise, white, and gold St. Andrew's Church is a wall built during the early 18th century and a path with views of the older sections of Kiev, the Podil district, the Dnieper River, and the Ukrainian plain that stretches out east of the city. A funicular railway runs from the Podil up Volodymyrska Hirka (Vladimir's Hill), which affords a partial view of the city from on high. The funicular runs year-round and is very inexpensive. Another wonderful spot to see the city is from the 318-foot Great Belfry, located on the north side of the Monastery of the Caves.

A cruise along the Dnieper River, offering a lovely view of the parkland at the water's edge, is another excellent way to see the city. Comfortable ships with 4 decks, accommodating up to 360 passengers, set sail during the summer months. Cruises go as far as central and southern Ukraine, stopping at numerous ports of call along the way. For further information, contact the *Rich Kovy Vokzariver* (River Passenger Transport Agency; phone: 416-1268).

SPECIAL PLACES

There are several areas of the city of particular interest to visitors. The Verkhny Horod (Upper Town), the oldest section of the city, is steeped in Kiev history. Khreshchatyk is Kiev's bustling main thoroughfare. Shevchenko Bulvar is another important street, site of Shevchenko University, the *Shevchenko Museum,* and St. Volodymyr's Cathedral. Much of Kiev's lush parkland lies in the Pechersk district, along the Dnieper River to the southeast of Khreshchatyk. The name of this area is derived from the Pecherska Lavra (Monastery of the Caves), a fascinating, intricate complex of stone structures that dates back to the 11th century. To the west of the Podil district, which lies at the foot of Vladimir's Hill, is the site of the moving Babyn Yar memorial to Kievans and others killed during World War II. Across the Dnieper, beyond an area of industrial blight, are sandy beaches and tree-lined parks frequented by Kievans and visitors alike.

NOTE The following information was accurate as we went to press, but it is more than possible that, given the current state of politics and economics, even more statues have been toppled, streets and squares renamed, and that hotels and restaurants have changed hands. Although some signs are still in Russian in Kiev, Ukrainian is rapidly becoming the everyday language. Ukrainian translations, therefore, appear throughout this chapter. "Vulytsia" means "street," "ploshcha" means "square," and "bulvar" means boulevard.

VERKHNY HOROD (UPPER TOWN)

ZOLOTI VOROTA (GOLDEN GATE) Though Kiev lacks the walled fortifications typical of so many other ancient European cities, two parallel walls still remain of the Golden Gate, an arch built by Yaroslav the Wise (son of Prince Volodymyr) in 1037. The gate, at the corner of Volodymyrska Vulytsia and Yaroslaviv Val, was a monumental structure, about 25 feet wide, with a passage 40 feet high and 80 feet long. Probably inspired by the Golden Gate in Constantinople, it was built to be ornamental as well as functional. Damaged in 1240 during an invasion of Mongol Tatars, the Golden Gate continued to serve as the entrance to the city until the 17th century, at which time it fell into disuse and eventually was buried under layers of earth and rubble. Rediscovered by an archaeologist in 1832, the gate subsequently was reinforced to prevent further destruction. Supposedly once partly covered with hammered gold (hence, its name), the gate also served as a defensive fortification to the capital's citadel and as the entrance to the tiny Church of the Annunciation. The church was restored for the city's 1,500th birthday celebration in 1982. The Golden

Gate represents the center of the city and is the starting point for many tours of Kiev.

SOFIYSKY SOBOR (ST. SOPHIA'S CATHEDRAL AND MUSEUM OF ARCHITECTURE AND HISTORY) This 11th-century structure was built by Yaroslav the Wise in a customary gesture of gratitude for a victory over an invading tribe from the east. The cathedral was clearly inspired by Byzantine architecture, and was reputedly based on the same design as St. Sophia's in Constantinople (Istanbul), though it reflects early Ukrainian woodworking styles as well. Kiev's St. Sophia's has been a work in progress since its inception. A tower and tomb (built for a son of Yaroslav) were added in the 11th century, the stone walls were covered with plaster in the 12th and 13th centuries, a belfry was built in the 17th century, and in the 18th century, six golden domes were added to the original 19, and a refectory was built. The cathedral was the center of social and cultural life in Kievan Rus — here princes were crowned, couples were wed, public festivals were held, and political issues were heatedly debated. Peter the Great celebrated the decisive Russian victory over the Swedes and rebellious Ukrainian cossacks at St. Sophia's in 1709, and ordered the entire complex restored. Wall frescoes that depict hunting, games, and dancing are the only surviving paintings of everyday life in Kievan Rus. The cathedral is now a museum featuring exhibits on the architecture of the Kievan Rus and Ukraine. An English-language guided tour is offered; check with *Intourist* (see *Sources and Resources,* below) or your hotel for details. Open 10 AM to 5 PM; closed Thursdays. Behind Khmelnytsky Ploscha.

BOHDANA KHMELNYTSKOHO PLOSHCHA (KHMELNYTSKY SQUARE) The statue of Khmelnytsky, the cossack leader who freed the Ukraine region from Polish land barons, points north to Moscow, in commemoration of the Kievans' controversial pledge of loyalty to the czar in 1654. Opposite St. Sophia's Cathedral.

ANDRIYIVSKY SOBOR (ST. ANDREW'S CHURCH) This turquoise, white, and gold church stands atop Andriyivska Hirka. Designed by Bartolomeo Rastrelli, and completed in 1753, St. Andrew's is to many Kievans the city's most familiar and cherished landmark. The church was built by Peter the Great's daughter Elizaveta and stands on a site said to have been chosen for the placement of a cross by St. Andrew himself, who first preached the gospel in these lands. Inside, the painting *Prince Vladimir Selects a Faith* tells the story of the conversion of Kievan Rus to Christianity. The terrace surrounding the church provides an excellent view of the river and the Podil district. Leading down from the terrace is Andriyivsky Uzviz, a steep, narrow, cobblestone path usually crowded with artists who paint and display their completed canvases. Although at press time the church was closed for renovations, there are small cafés, snack bars, and shops to explore along the hill. Of special note is the museum (13 Uzuiz) devoted to popular Russian writer Mikhail Bulgakov, author of such novels as *Master and Margarita* and *The White Guard.* Andriyivska Hirka.

ST. VOLODYMYR MONUMENT In the park on Volodymyrska Hirka (Vladimir's Hill) stands a statue of Prince Volodymyr the Great, dressed as an ancient Rus warrior holding a cross and gazing into the waters of the Dnieper (where he once held mass baptisms). The monument celebrates the pious side of the ruler, who in AD 988 ordered that his entire country convert to Christianity. The bronze likeness was created in 1802 by Klodt, a sculptor revered for the winged horses on the Anichkov Bridge in St. Petersburg. Also in this park is a monument titled "Return to Kiev of the Magdeburg Code of Law," a tall, white column that, ironically, commemorates the various rights and freedoms — including self-government — that returned to Kiev in 1798 after the reign of Czar Paul I and the emancipation of the serfs. The park itself is the northernmost in a chain of green lands stretching south as far as the Monastery of the Caves. On Volodymyrska Hirka, at the northeastern end of Khreshchatyk.

KHRESHCHATYK

This is Kiev's main thoroughfare and, unquestionably, its busiest. Dating back to the early days of the city's development, it was the site of a deep valley crossed by ravines, which was called Khreshchata (meaning "crossed"). The street runs southwest to northeast. Many fashionable restaurants, shops, banks, and homes were located here at the beginning of the 20th century, only to be blown up during World War II by retreating Soviet partisans. Three hundred and fifty buildings were destroyed along the street's mile-and-a-half length. Though there are a few older buildings still standing (today, most house a variety of shops), the majority of the structures that line Khreshchatyk are relatively new. After the war, the width of the street was doubled and the steep (odd-numbered) side was turned into parkland with trees, flower beds, and benches. The buildings on this side are, for the most part, residences; rather grandiose Soviet-style administrative and office buildings line the other side. Along Khreshchatyk is the *Moskva* hotel, on Maidan Nezalezhnosty (Independence Square); the elaborate main post office; the city's main metro station (Khreshchatyk); and several large stores, including *Tsentralny* (Central Department Store).

BESSARABSKIY RYNOK (BESSARABIAN MARKET) No visit to a Ukrainian city is complete without a visit to a farmer's market, and this is Kiev's finest. The present indoor-outdoor market buildings were built in the early 1900s, although the site has been a marketplace since Bessarabian (Moldavian) merchants came to the fast-growing city to sell their wares nearly 1,000 years earlier. Today, well-heeled Kievans flock to the *rynok* (market), where individual stalls are run by independent merchants and farmers, who sell a bountiful selection of their own produce at fluctuating market prices. While prices are high by local standards, these markets usually offer goods that are quite a bargain for foreigners. The best time to visit is at the height of the harvest, in late summer or early fall. If your timing is right you may find pomegranates, dried apricots, almonds, figs, or some fruit you've never seen before. Open daily. Bessarabska Ploshcha, at the west end of Khreshchatyk.

SHEVCHENKO BULVAR

TARAS SHEVCHENKO UNIVERSITY Founded in 1834, this is Ukraine's most prestigious university. The main building, which is fronted by eight huge columns, has worn its red color since its construction. Just across from the university is a statue of the great Ukrainian poet Taras Shevchenko where, incidentally, a statue of Czar Nicholas I once stood. At the head of Shevchenko Bulvar at the intersection of Volodymyrska Vulytsia.

BOTANICHNY SAD IMENI FOMINA (FOMIN BOTANICAL GARDENS) Just opposite the main entrance of Shevchenko University are 56 acres of carefully arranged and painstakingly maintained tree-lined paths and garden plots. First laid out in 1841, the gardens are named after a famed botanist who fought to preserve them after the Bolshevik Revolution. Approximately 2,000 plant species grow here. There's a sampling of flora native to Ukraine, Georgia, and Siberia; numerous species of tropical and subtropical plants, including what is reportedly the world's largest collection of cacti under one roof; rare species such as the ginkgo, the Indian ficus, and the cinchona tree; and over 40 species of palm tree. The plants are labeled (handy only for those who understand botanical Ukrainian or Latin), and there are plenty of paths for strolling and benches for sitting to enjoy the lush foliage. Shevchenko Bulvar.

SHEVCHENKO STATE MUSEUM It is apparent from the collection at this intriguing museum that Ukraine's greatest poet, like the Russian poet Vladimir Mayakovsky, could also hold his own with a paint brush. Displayed in the museum's 24 rooms are over 800 works of art by Taras Shevchenko, who was originally trained as a drawing instructor at the St. Petersburg Academy of Arts. Incredibly, Shevchenko was a serf and, despite his artistic talents, still had to be bought from his owner in order to attend the academy. His plans to become a teacher were thwarted by his arrest along with the other members of the Cyril and Methodius Society, an organization whose aim was to abolish serfdom. Volumes of his literary works and some of his personal possessions are also on display. Open 10 AM to 5 PM; closed Mondays. Admission charge. 12 Shevchenko Bulvar (phone: 244-2556).

PECHERSK

Most of Kiev's lovely parkland is situated in the Pechersk district of the city along the Dnieper River. This is the most historical area of the city and derives its name from the Pecherska Lavra (Monastery of the Caves), a massive complex of stone structures that date back to the 11th century. A number of government buildings, including Ukraine's Parliament, are located in the Pechersk area.

PARKLAND An ancient buffer zone between Kiev and the Dnieper, this green area is the pride and joy of Kiev. Stretching from St. Andrew's Church above Podil as far south as the Academy of Sciences Botanical Garden, this lovely sash of greenery is the ideal place for an evening stroll, a midday walk, or a concert. The parkland is the focal point of community activity, and many Kievians can be found here on sunny days at week's end. There are many monuments, restaurants, as well as a large amphitheater (capacity 1,500) with a wall formed from the remains of the 19th-century Kiev fortress. Be sure to walk along Dniprovskiy Uzuiz, a sloping road that meanders along the riverside parks. In one of the parks is a rotunda where, according to legend, Prince Askold of Kiev was buried in 882. This area is perhaps the most beautiful in the city. Not far from here stands an obelisk and an eternal flame marking the grave of an unknown soldier from World War II.

MARIINSKY PALATZ (MARIINSKY PALACE) This turquoise building, with its set of imposing white columns and blue and white wrought-iron fence, is patterned after a design by Italian architect Bartolomeo Rastrelli. Built in 1752, it was originally the palace of the Empress Elizaveta, daughter of Peter the Great, and was thereafter used as the local residence of the czar. In 1819 it was damaged by fire, and was later rebuilt for the arrival of Alexander II and his wife, Maria, after whom the palace was named. After being battered during World War II, it was later restored to its original baroque design. Today, the palace is used for official receptions for visiting heads of state and other dignitaries. Guided tours (in Ukrainian and Russian) are offered Wednesdays and Saturdays and must be arranged through the *Museum of the History of Kiev* (8 Plylypa Orlyka Vulytsia; phone: 293-4909). Admission charge. In Pershotravenevy Park along the Dnieper River.

PECHERSKA LAVRA (MONASTERY OF THE CAVES) The most famous historical site in Kiev (*pechera* means "cave" in Ukrainian and *lavra* is the term used by the Christian Orthodox church for monastery), this complex of churches was built in natural caves in 1051 by two monks, Anthony and Theodosius. The two monastics apparently chose these silent underground refuges to avoid the persistent attacks of pagan invaders. Additional churches, both subterranean and aboveground, have been added over the centuries. Forty of the 100 original stone structures still remain and are treasured examples of 11th-, 12th-, 17th-, and 18th-century art and architecture. The site — also called the "Kiev Crypt" — was a favorite pilgrimage destination for the czars and members of the Russian royal family, and the monastery became exceedingly wealthy as a result. In the early 17th century, a printing press was established at the monastery, and it soon became the center for printing and engraving in Ukraine. The first Ukrainian-language dictionary, containing about 7,000 words, was compiled and printed here in 1627. Early volumes and exhibits tracing the origins of the Slavic written language are on display at the *Museum of Books & Book Printing* in the building that originally housed the monastery press. Spread over 66 acres, encompassing two hills and the valley between them, the monastery became so large and lucrative that, by the 18th century, it comprised 189 villages, 56,000 serfs, 13 monasteries, 7 settlements, and 3 glassworks.

Among the other noteworthy structures in the complex is Trinity Church, which serves as the main entryway. It was built in 1108 but contains wooden icons and frescoes painted in the 18th century. The building is a good specimen of the Ukrainian baroque style. Murals on the exterior and interior walls were painted in the early 18th century by masters of the monastery's own school of icon painting. The *Istorychny Muzey Koshtovnostey* (Historical Treasures of Ukraine Museum), located in the monastery's bakery building, has a collection of items from the 6th to the 19th centuries, including jewelry, coins from the Kievan Rus and ancient Scythian settlements on the Black Sea, and artifacts and tools of Greek and Roman origin excavated in the area.

The Tserkva Spas na Berestovi (Church of the Redeemer in the Birchwood, also called the Church of Our Saviour) features the cross dome and six pillars characteristic of late-11th- and early-12th-century architecture, but the structure was in fact built in two parts. While the older sections of the church date from the 12th century, the newer section was completed in 1644 and is decorated with frescoes. The interior of the church is considered to be one of the latest examples of true Byzantine art. The gray marble tomb of Yuri Dolgoruki, the son of a Kievan prince, is located in the older section of the church. Dolgoruki founded the city of Moscow in 1147 and was buried here a decade later (an equestrian statue of Dolgoruki stands across from the Moscow City Council in the Russian capital).

Perhaps the most recognizable building in the complex is the Church of St. Nicholas, a 17th-century Ukrainian baroque-style structure that probably appears on more postcards than any other Kievan landmark. Distinguished by its bright blue dome covered with gold stars, All Saints' Church is another 17th-century Ukrainian baroque building topped with five golden domes. It got its start as a watchtower on the wall surrounding the monastery complex. On the north side of the Monastery of the Caves is the 318-foot (95-meter) Great Belfry, which affords spectacular views of the Lavra and the city.

There are two sets of caves within the Pecherska Lavra complex. The Near Caves, sometimes called St. Anthony's Caves, contain 73 tombs of monks who lived underground (some monks probably never saw the light of day), and 3 underground churches. The frescoes and decorations of the nearly half-mile-long viewing area are among the richest and most interesting in the entire enclave. There are also inscriptions in Old Slavonic, Armenian, and Polish; fragments of 18th-century frescoes; and religious artifacts, icons, and crosses. Because of the chemical composition of the soil and the cool air, many of the bodies of those buried here (including monks, high clergy, and princes) are preserved and can be seen and identified by their name tags through the small windows on their tombs. These mysteriously preserved bodies added to the aura of holiness here, and probably were the reason that the caves became the destination of countless pilgrimages.

The Far Caves, or St. Theodosius's Caves, consist of 3 underground caves and 47 tombs. The most famous tomb is that of the chronicler Nestor, who died in 1115. A bell tower, the Belfry of the Farther Caves, was built in the 18th century in an unusual design; its upper tier is decorated with graceful Gothic columns crowned by four sword-like spires. On the way down to the caves don't miss the graves of the cossack leaders Kochubei and Iskra, executed in 1708 by Ukrainian cossack leader Ivan Mazepa for telling Peter the Great of a secret plan to throw off Russia's rule that the Ukrainian cossacks were cooking up with King Charles XII of Sweden. Also located in the Far Caves is St. George's Cathedral, which boasts five golden domes and a spire-topped bell tower with 3 tiers and a cupola in the Ukrainian baroque style. Services are held daily in the cathedral. The Far Caves are open from noon to 5 PM; closed Tuesdays. The Pecherska Lavra complex is open from 9:30 AM to 6 PM; closed Tuesdays. Admission charge. The best entrance is at 21 Sichnevoho Povstannya Vulytsia, between the Metro Bridge and Paton Bridge in the parkland along the Dnieper, about 2½ miles (4 km) from the center of Kiev. Check with *Intourist* or your hotel for information on guided tours.

PODIL

Once a lively suburb of the Upper Town, and the home of tradesmen and artisans, this district — whose name means "Plain Below a Hill" — begins at the foot of Vladimir's Hill.

KONTRAKTOVA PLOSHCHA (CONTRACT SQUARE) Called Krasnaya Ploshchad (Red Square) during the Soviet years, this square now has reverted to its earlier name, which derives from its dominant landmark, the Kontraktova Dim (House of Contracts). Built in 1817, it was the headquarters for negotiations and the signing of agreements between Ukrainian merchants and landowners, and is a good example of 19th-century Russian classic style. In the northwest corner of the square are the remains of the Bratsky Monastery, where, in 1706, Peter the Great prepared for his attack on

King Charles XII of Sweden and his Nordic troops, who were within 25 miles (40 km) of Kiev. Off Pokrovska (formerly Zelinsky) Vulytsia.

BABYN YAR Just west of Podil is the memorial to Kievans slaughtered by the Nazis during World War II. The occupation of Kiev lasted 779 days, and during the fall of 1941 Nazi forces rounded up thousands of Kiev men, women, and children — mostly Jews, but also some members of the Soviet underground, partisans, and Ukrainian nationalists — and murdered and buried them in a pit at Babyn Yar (known as Babi Yar during the Communist era). Later, Soviet soldiers and officers taken prisoner by the Nazis were shot here as well. All told, some 200,000 perished here. The monument to their memory consists of 11 dramatic bronze figures — including an officer, a sailor, a young boy who refused to bow his head before the Nazis, and a member of the Communist resistance — frozen in mid-motion and standing on a platform above a ravine. The site is reached by a long path through a tranquil park lined with roses and birch trees. The memorial has long been controversial because it does not specifically acknowledge the preponderance of Jewish victims and because of its location, some distance away from the actual killing and burial sites. More recently, a memorial in the shape of a menorah, a gift from Israel, was dedicated at a site overlooking the burial ravine.

ENVIRONS

Beauty and the beast are found just across the Dnieper River. The Darnitsa district, its landscape pockmarked with a cluster of manufacturing and chemical plants, is known for its urban blight. The jungles of apartment houses here are no less bleak. Farther north along the river, however, are sandy beaches and tree-lined parks that afford relaxation for Kievans during the warm-weather months.

TRUKHANOV ISLAND Kiev's most-frequented bathing beach and recreational area on the Dnieper River. There are tennis courts, volleyball nets, and ample swimming facilities. Sports-minded Kievans make their way to Trukhanov in the winter for cross-country skiing, skating, and ice fishing.

MUZEY NARODNOYI ARKHITEKTURY TA POBUTU UKRAINY (MUSEUM OF FOLK ARCHITECTURE AND LIFE OF UKRAINE) This outdoor cultural park encompasses over 200 acres just south of the city in the village of Pyrohiv. Authentic Ukrainian houses, mills, churches, and other buildings, over 400 years old, have been assembled here to form a traditional Ukrainian village. There are numerous exhibits that depict rural Ukrainian life since the 16th century as well as demonstrations of pottery making, embroidery, wooden spoon making, *pysanky* (elaborately decorated *Easter* eggs), painting, and other folk arts. The museum is surprisingly interesting and a nice place to stroll on a balmy Ukrainian afternoon (phone: 266-2416).

EXTRA SPECIAL It's been said that in order to truly know Kievans you must meet them at the *bani* (baths), when they strip to the buff, swill vodka as though it were tap water, whack themselves unmercifully on the backs with bound birch branches (it's supposed to open the pores, or at least discipline them), and indulge in some serious gossiping and sweating.

The convivial atmosphere of the *bani* is comparable to that of an American ballpark where everybody, by virtue of their love of the game, is your friend. Though the concept of the *bani* probably has its roots in the Finnish sauna, the local version originated in Kievan Rus, where each house had a log hut that was used by the whole family for bathing. Though many houses in the countryside still have these private baths, most Kievans visit the public *bani*.

Many of the public *bani* have a pool that is kept so cold it seems like runoff from a glacier. It's part of the tradition to take a bracing plunge after a steambath. There's usually a buffet in the changing room, where snacks or beverages may be purchased (alcohol is not officially condoned; the locals simply bring their own).

The *bani*'s shabbiness contributes to their earthy charm, but since the standards of cleanliness here are nowhere near that of the typically sanitized American health clubs, you may want to bring along a pair of flip-flops and your own towel. Check with your hotel for the closest public *bani* in the area. There's usually no need to make a reservation — just show up, pay the small fee, and try to conceal your "Americanness" by being as lethargic as your *bani* brethren. Two of the best *bani* can be found at 3 Malozhytomyrska Vulytsia (phone: 228-0378) and 26 Ivana Kudri St. (phone: 269-0234). Also see *Quintessential Eastern Europe* in DIVERSIONS.

Sources and Resources

TOURIST INFORMATION

While *Intourist* is still the largest travel organization in Ukraine, it has undergone major changes since the Soviet Union's breakup. Now independent of its Russian counterpart, Ukraine's *Intourist* is often run much like an independent travel agency.

American travelers should also note that the Ukraine's *Intourist* no longer has representation at the (now Russian) *Intourist* information bureau in New York City. Ukraine's *Intourist*-affiliated hotels and restaurants no longer accept credit cards; under the old system of payment, Moscow kept most of the money from credit card transactions. Moreover, while still a quasi-governmental agency, Ukraine's *Intourist* may be privatized and broken up even more in the near future. A name change is likely. Contact *Intourist* Kiev at their offices at 12 Hospitalna Vulytsia, right behind the *Intourist* hotel (phone: 225-3051; fax: 224-8987).

A number of cooperative and independent travel and tourism agencies have emerged recently to challenge *Intourist's* preeminence. A good source of local guides is the *Slvutych* travel agency (phone: 290-8680). General housing services, including short- and long-term apartment rentals for businesspeople are also available from the Ukrainian Services Corporation, Ltd., a joint US–Ukrainian venture (125A Horkoho Vulytsia; phone: 269-8565).

Economic turmoil, including frequent and steep price increases on many goods and services, makes it impossible to provide accurate information on prices, including the cost of basic services such as public transportation and the telephone. The former Soviet Union's common currency, the ruble, is no longer legal tender in Ukraine and has been temporarily replaced by the Ukrainian "kupon" (coupon). In addition, at press time Ukraine was planning to introduce its own national currency, the "hryvnia," to replace the kupon.

LOCAL COVERAGE For more general background information about recent events in Ukraine, contact the Ukrainian Congress Committee in New York City (phone: 212-228-6840). Another good source of information is the US–based *Ukrainian Weekly,* which also devotes a significant portion of its editorial content to news and events in Ukraine. Just write or call to order an issue or two (30 Montgomery St., Jersey City, NJ 07032; phone: 201-434-0237). Other sources of information include the Ukrainian National Information Service in Washington, DC (phone: 202-547-0018), and the Washington Office of the Ukrainian National Association (phone: 202-347-8629).

TELEPHONE The country code for Ukraine is 7. The city code for Kiev is 044.

Because of the shortage of coins, local calls from public pay phones were free at press time. Long-distance calls from Kiev are best handled through your hotel's service bureau; be sure to ask if you will be expected to pay in local currency or dollars. For Kiev directory assistance, dial 09; to place a long-distance call from a private residence, dial 8.

GETTING AROUND

AIRPORT Borispil International Airport is on Kharkov Highway, approximately 18 miles (29 km) southeast of the center of Kiev (phone: 295-6701 or

295-2252). To get into the city, take a taxi — there's an ample fleet at the airport. It's best to arrange for a pickup before your arrival. The Ukrainian Services Corporation (phone: 269-8565) offers a shuttle service to city hotels for about $15.

BOAT Local boats serve Kiev and the smaller Ukrainian cities. Cruises that stop at any number of cities along the Dnieper River set sail during the summer months. Excursion boats also leave from the Prihgorodna landing (3 Naberezhna Vulytsia) during the summer months. The *River Passenger Transport Agency* (Rich Kovy Vokzar; phone: 416-1268) sets the schedules and should be contacted for further information. Trams No. 21, 28, 31, and 32 stop at the landing.

BUS, TRAM, AND SUBWAY Kiev is built on hills, and the relatively efficient bus and trolley system is an exciting way to see some parts of the city (avoid public transportation during rush hours). Buses and trolleys operate on the honor system. You are expected to buy a ticket that is validated in a machine on the bus or tram. If you are spotted by an inspector *sans* ticket, expect a rather dishonorable fine. Tickets can be purchased either from the bus or trolley driver or at kiosks near the stops (to save time, buy a whole string of them if your plans call for public transportation only). The central bus station is at 3 Moskovska Ploshcha (phone: 265-0430). Take trams No. 9 or 10 or trolleys 1, 11, or 12 to get there.

The metro (subway) system, which costs less than a nickel, consists of six lines that serve a good percentage of the city. The main transfer point is the Khreshchatyk station on Khreshchatyk.

CAR RENTAL At press time, cars in Kiev could only be rented with drivers. Try your hotel or *Intourist* (phone: 225-3051). The prices will vary, but expect to pay at least $50 per day. Also, the *Ukrainian Services Corp.* (phone: 269-8565) rents cars with drivers for $30 an hour (there's an 8-hour day minimum).

TAXI Don't take it personally if first one, then another, and finally a whole stream of taxi drivers pull over, size you up, shake their heads vigorously as you recite your destination, and speed off without you. Taxi drivers in Ukraine seem to have much loftier things to do than to take passengers where they want to go. As a general rule, landing one in three is a good rate. A pack of Marlboros in the hand signaling the cab or a dollar bill peeking out of the breast pocket of a jacket has been known to work wonders. For a more conventional approach, try calling the *Central Taxi Bureau* (phone: 058).

TRAIN There are rail connections to all major European cities from Kiev's train station on Vokzalna Ploshcha. Purchase tickets through your hotel or *Intourist*. The metro and trolleys No. 2, 8, and 17 go to the train station.

LOCAL SERVICES

DENTIST (ENGLISH-SPEAKING) At *Polyclinic #1,* 5 Verkhna Vulytsia (phone: 293-8221).

DRY CLEANER/TAILOR *Stolichny* in the Budynok Pobutu complex (28 Kominterna Vulytsia; phone: 224-3577); also at most hotels.

FAX/TELEX Public machines are located at the main post office (22 Khreshchatyk; phone: 228-2613), where no English is spoken; at the *Intourist* office (12 Hospitalna Vulytsia; phone: 225-3051), which is open 24 hours a day; and at most major hotels.

MEDICAL EMERGENCY *Zhovtneva Likarnia* (Zhovtneva Hospital; 39 Libknekhta; phone: 227-9111). To reach the city's 24-hour medical emergency telephone line, dial 03. (The fire emergency telephone number is 01; for police dial 02). Also try the American Embassy (phone: 244-7349) or the *Ukrainian Services Corp.* (phone: 269-8565) for information on medical services and English-speaking medical personnel.

NATIONAL/INTERNATIONAL COURIER *DHL Worldwide Express* and *Federal Express* services are offered through major hotels.

OFFICE EQUIPMENT RENTAL *Rank Xerox* (phone: 228-6423).

PHARMACY Ask at your hotel service bureau for the closest pharmacy.

PHOTOCOPIERS Available at most major hotels.

POST OFFICE The main post office is at 22 Khreshchatyk (phone: 228-2613).

TRANSLATOR Contact your hotel service bureau.

SPECIAL EVENTS

Kiev Spring, an annual arts festival featuring the best of theater, music, and dance companies from throughout the republic, is held May 18 to 30. Folk holidays are celebrated each month from April or May through November at the *Muzey Narodnoyi Arkhitektury ta Pobutu Ukrainy* (Museum of Folk Architecture and Rural Life of Ukraine) near the village of Pyrohiv. Closed Wednesdays (phone: 266-2416). For more details, see *Special Places.*

MUSEUMS

There are many fascinating museums documenting the city's history. In fact, because the Communists converted most formerly active churches into museums (many have now been changed back into houses of worship, and with the outlawing of the party, more probably will follow suit), Kiev has an excess of museums. In addition to those listed in *Special Places,* other museums worth a visit include the following:

DERZAVNY MUZEY UKRAINSKOHO OBRAZOTVORCHOHO MYSTETSTVA (STATE MU-SEUM OF UKRAINIAN FINE ARTS) Built at the turn of the century in the style of a Greek temple, this museum houses Ukrainian art from the 15th to 19th centuries. Sculpted lions grace the granite stairs that lead to the main entrance. Open 10 AM to 5 PM; closed Fridays. Admission charge. 6 Hrushevskoho (formerly Kirov) Vulytsia (phone: 228-6482).

MUZEY ROSIYSKOHO MYSTETSTVA (MUSEUM OF RUSSIAN ART) Russian art from the 12th to 17th centuries, including icons, considered the finest in the country, of the Moscow, Stroganov, and Novgorod schools. The 18th- to 19th-century collection features the works of Ilya Yefimovich Repin, the foremost 19th-century Ukrainian realist painter, and other period painters. There's also a section devoted to Soviet art. The house once belonged to the wealthy Tereshchenko family. Open 10 AM to 6 PM; closed Thursdays. Admission charge. 9 Repina Vulytsia (phone: 224-6218).

MUZEY ZAKHIDNOHO TA SKHIDNOHO MYSTETSTVA (MUSEUM OF ORIENTAL AND WESTERN ART) This broad collection includes Byzantine paintings of the 6th to 8th centuries; Italian Renaissance art, including works of Bellini, Guardi, and Tiepolo; and 15th- to 18th-century Flemish and Dutch paintings, including works by Hals and Rubens, among others. Other periods and styles represented are 18th-century French art, the golden age of Spanish art, and traditional Chinese scroll paintings and carvings. Open 10 AM to 6 PM; closed Wednesdays. Admission charge. 15 Repina Vulytsia (phone: 224-6162).

SHEVCHENKO MEMORYALNY MUZEY (SHEVCHENKO MEMORIAL MUSEUM) Set in a cramped seven-room house, this museum is devoted to the great Ukrainian poet's life and works during his Kiev years. His landscape paintings are displayed, and some of his personal belongings may be seen in the attic, where he lived in 1846. Open 1 to 5:30 PM; closed Mondays. Admission charge. 81 Shevchenko Vulytsia (phone: 224-2556).

CHURCHES

The Christian Orthodox church, which celebrated its 1,000th anniversary in Ukraine in 1988, is as near and dear to the Ukrainian soul as sugar beets or *varenyky,* the filled dumpling that is the national dish. Kiev's history, its greatness, its architecture, and the faith of its people can all be found behind the doors of the city's magnificent churches, many of which are being opened for services for the first time in 75 years. (Sadly, many of Kiev's most magnificent churches, some dating back many centuries, were mercilessly razed by an atheistic Communist regime that viewed religion as one of the last bulwarks of Ukrainian nationalism.) Nowhere else in the former Soviet Union are the churches more splendid and the power of religion over the people more marked than in Kiev, where Christianity was first introduced to the East Slavs. In addition to those churches mentioned in *Special Places,* the following houses of worship are worth a look.

VOLODYMYSKY SOBOR (ST. VLADIMIR'S CATHEDRAL) The choir at St. Vladimir's is one of the loveliest in the land; masses are held daily and the choir sings on Sundays. It was built in the mid-1800s by a group of architects and artisans to celebrate the 900th anniversary of Christianity in Kiev. Located opposite the Fomin Botanical Gardens. 20 Shevchenko Bulvar.

VOZNESENSKA TSERKVA (CHURCH OF THE ASCENSION) The church and bell tower were built between 1740 and 1821. A 17th-century refectory stands opposite. This is once again functioning as a house of worship; services are held regularly. Podil district.

VYDUBYTSKI MONASTYR (VYDUBYTSKY MONASTERY) An ensemble of churches and monastery buildings, some dating from the 11th century and located on a picturesque hill on the wooded right bank of the Dnieper River. The monastery acquired its present look, including the splendid, five-cupola St. George's Cathedral and pretty blue-and-gold-domed belfry, during the 17th and 18th centuries. Closest to the river is St. Michael's Church, founded by the son of Yaroslav the Wise. Compact and tranquil, the Vydubytsky Monastery grounds are a little oasis that can transport a visitor back to the times of ancient Kiev. Services are held at St. Michael's at 10 AM on Sundays and feast days.

SHOPPING

Economic reforms have brought changes to Kiev's shopping scene. For example, a shop you've read about may be history by the time you arrive. Meanwhile, some shops, especially those catering to tourists, accept only hard currency. Most stores close for an hour in the afternoon and all day Sunday. The hard currency–hungry *Beriozka* (Birch Tree) shops, once ubiquitous throughout the old Soviet Union, are known as *Kashtan* (Chestnut Tree) shops in Ukraine, though their future is very much in doubt as Ukraine moves toward a capitalist-style economy. The *Kashtan* shop in Kiev (Lesya Ukrainka Ploshcha) features a wide selection of furs, *palekh* (lacquer boxes), food and beverages (including Russian champagne and caviar). There's also a selection of woodcarvings and other Ukrainian arts and crafts.

To rub elbows with the locals at an old-fashioned farmer's market, head for the *Bessarabskiy Rynok* (Bessarabian Market) at Bessarabska Ploshcha (see *Special Places*). For sheer sprawl (though many of the shelves are empty), the *Ukraina* department store (Peremohy Ploshcha, next to the *Lybid* hotel) features 4 floors of clothing, fur hats, glassware, scarves, Ukrainian woven goods, and woodenware — cutting boards, spoons, and figures. Browse through *Ukrainsky Souvenir* (23 Chervonoarmiyska Vulytsia) for embroidered blouses and tablecloths, dolls, woodenware, and other souvenir items; *Slavutycha* (32 Khreshchatyk) is a great place for last-minute gift items such as Russian *matryoshka* dolls, *palekh* boxes, Ukrainian woodenware, and amber jewelry. Souvenir hunters will also find a wide selection of arts and crafts at *Vyroby Maistriv Ukrainy* (15 Khreshchatyk). For ceramics, including the coveted black pottery from western Ukraine, visit the *Honchari Art Gallery* (10A Andriyivsky Uzviz); and *Khudozny Salon* (27-1 Bohdana Khmelnytskoho Vulytsia) boasts an array of locally made jewelry, and a fine selection of artwork. The *Mystetstvo* bookshop (26 Khreshchatyk) carries current and out-of-print art and photography books in Ukrainian, English, and other languages, plus a good assortment of art and antiques. *Nika* (2 Shevchenko Bulvar) is a Western-style supermarket selling a huge assortment of imported foods and liquor (hard currency only).

SPORTS AND FITNESS

HOCKEY The *Palatz Sportu* (Sports Palace; Sportyvna Ploshcha) hosts national and international ice hockey and basketball matches.

SAUNA The operative word here is *bani* (baths). For a detailed account of this Kievan tradition, see "Extra Special" in *Special Places.*

SOCCER Kiev is the home of *Dynamo,* a soccer (they call it *futbol*) juggernaut that has won the national championship many times. If there's a home game, by all means try to get a ticket (*billet*) through *Intourist* or your hotel. Matches are held during spring, summer, and fall at the *Republican Stadium* (55 Chervonoarmiyska Vulytsia).

Even if you don't find a ticket, there are over 160 municipal soccer fields in Kiev at which *you* can play. With some perseverance, you're bound to find a pick-up game at or near your speed.

SWIMMING There's an indoor public swimming pool, as well as handball and tennis courts, at the *Dynamo Stadium* (3 Hrushevskoho Vulytsia).

THEATER

Ukrainians are passionate and dramatic, and this vitality is reflected in Kiev's lively cultural scene. Probably Ukraine's most noteworthy cultural institution is the *Teatr Opery ta Baletu imeni T. Schevchenka* (Shevchenko Opera and Ballet Theater; 50 Volodymyrska Vulytsia; phone: 229-1169), which stages ballet and opera in Ukrainian, Russian, and other languages. Founded in 1868 as the *Russian Opera Theater,* it's the oldest theater of its kind in Ukraine. Another Ukrainian theatrical tradition is musical comedy. The *Teatr Operety* (Operetta Theater; 53-3 Chervonoarmiyska Vulytsia) and the *Teatr Dramy ta Komedii* (Theater of Drama and Comedy; 25 Zhovtnia Prospekt) are both renowned. The latter features performances primarily in Ukrainian. The *Ivan Franko Ukrainian Drama Theater* (3 Ivan Franko Ploshcha; phone: 229-5991) stages Ukrainian plays only. The works of great Russian masters such as Pushkin, Gorky, and Ostrovsky may be experienced firsthand at the *Rosiyski Dramatychny Teatr imeni Lesi Ukrainky* (Lesya Ukrainia Russian Drama Theater; 5 Bohdana Khmelnytskoho; phone: 224-4223), the home of the city's oldest drama company. Between the *Ivan Franko* and the *Lesya Ukrainka* theaters, there is a performance staged nearly every night.

Finally, try to attend the *Kiev Circus* on Peremohy Ploshcha (Victory Square); it offers performances year-round. Contact your hotel or *Intourist* for ticket and schedule information for any of the above-mentioned theaters.

Best in Town

CHECKING IN

Hotel accommodations in Kiev can be booked through Kiev *Intourist*, or through your travel agent.

In years past, virtually all hotel reservations for foreign guests were booked through *Intourist*, and only to *Intourist*-associated hotels. Attempts at market reform and decentralization, however, have struck the government-owned travel agency a mighty blow. Today, *Intourist* is a loosely controlled group of travel agencies, authorized to book travelers into *all* hotels. It is likely that most if not all *Intourist*-built hotels will be privatized, and *Intourist* itself will go the way of the hammer and sickle. In addition, fledgling private firms and joint ventures are now authorized to put up foreigners in hotels and private homes, and are starting to pose some stiff competition. *East-West Ventures* (PO Box 14391, Tucson, AZ 85732; phone: 602-795-5414), run by Soviet émigré Sergei Lysenko and his American wife, Diane, arranges accommodations in private homes or apartments with Kiev families (you can even request a family that speaks English) or in a private apartment with a maid (the refrigerator is stocked with staples and you do the cooking). They also can arrange for lodging in virtually any city in the former Soviet Union. Prices for a stay with a family in Kiev range from $42 for single accommodations to $60 per night for a double room for a minimum of 7 days, all meals included. The cost of a private apartment with food services is $60 for a single room and $75 for a double room per night. It is a refreshing and interesting alternative to staying in hotels. Also, Kiev-based *Adis* (phone: 229-7471; fax: 224-8250) offers budget-minded travelers rooms at the *Zona Vidpochynku* (9-13 Yunkerova Vulytsia), a complex of spas featuring saunas, a swimming pool, and therapeutic baths, just a short 45 minutes from Kiev. Although the accommodations are Soviet-style (read: spartan), the $15 per night for a double room includes a hearty breakfast. Another option is *American-International Homestays* (1515 W. Penn St., Iowa City, IA 52240; phone: 319-626-2125), which arranges for stays with Ukrainian families in Kiev and several other Eastern European cities.

The country's dramatically fluctuating economy makes it difficult to provide accurate rates for hotels, most of which accept payment in hard currency only. At press time, Ukraine was using an interim currency called the "kupon" but was planning eventually to introduce its own currency, the "hryvnia." We suggest you check costs — and the operative exchange rate — immediately prior to your departure. Most of Kiev's major hotels have complete facilities for the business traveler. Those hotels listed below as having "business services" usually offer such conveniences as English-speaking concierge, meeting rooms, photocopiers, computers, translation services, and express checkout, among others. Call the hotel for additional information. All telephone numbers are in the 044 city code unless otherwise indicated.

Bratislava Like most hotels in the area, this 13-story, 363-room place is devoid of character. The restaurant serves excellent Ukrainian dishes, such as stuffed dumplings and smoked fish, and a lively folk band plays nightly. Business services. It's away from the center of town on the left bank of the Dnieper River, but near the subway. 1 Malyshka Vulytsia (phone: 551-7646; fax: 558-2454).

Dnipro This circa-1964 property with 180 rooms has an ideal location on Kiev's central thoroughfare. Most city tours begin here or nearby. There is an excellent view of the river. The restaurant is one of the better hotel dining rooms. Business services. 1-2 Khreshchatyk (phone: 229-8387).

Intourist Opened in 1991, this 370-room property is the best that *Intourist* ever built. Centrally situated near the *Rus* hotel (the two properties are under joint management), it offers restaurants, a casino featuring roulette and blackjack, a bar, a pool, a sauna, and several shops. Business services. 12 Hospitalna Vulytsia (phone: 220-4144; fax: 220-4568).

Kiev Efficiency is what makes this modern, 120-room high-rise hotel so popular with government officials (Parliament is just across the street) and foreign embassy personnel. Rooms on the upper floors offer a wonderful view of the city and river; and there's a restaurant offering good Russian-Ukraine fare. Business services. Well-located at the edge of the Pechersk district. 26-1 Hrushevskoho Vulytsia (phone: 293-0155 or 293-0042).

Moskva An imposing, 16-story, 200-room hotel, right across from the city's liveliest square. There's a restaurant and bar. Business services. 4 Zhovt-nevoyi Revolutsi Vulytsia (phone: 228-2804; fax: 229-1353).

Natsionalny The former *Zhovtnevyj,* this 200-room modern property was once an exclusive Communist Party hotel. Among the best features: the deep bath-tubs. There's also a good restaurant. Business services. Expensive — but well worth it! 3 Lypska Vulytsia, down the street from the *Kiev* hotel (phone: 291-8877 or 291-8277; fax: 291-5468).

Prolisok Camping Motel Open during the warm-weather months, this is the ideal place to indulge in the great national pastime, camping, at a very reasonable price. There are campsites as well as simple accommodations, and a good regional restaurant, in a small, 3-story (105-room) motel. Located in a lovely pastoral setting in the village of Svyatoshino, just 8 miles (13 km) from the center of Kiev. 139 Peremohy Prospekt, Svyatoskino (phone: 444-0093 or 444-1293).

Rus In the city center, this modern 22-story, 477-room property features several restaurants and bars, a bowling alley, a hard currency souvenir shop, a post and telegraph office, and a pharmacy. It's jointly managed with the *Intourist* hotel (above). Business services. 4 Hospitalna Vulytsia (phone: 220-4255 or 220-5122; fax: 220-4568).

Salut An elegant 105-room hotel, even by Western standards, with a reputable restaurant on the premises (see *Eating Out*). Business services. Located in what is considered a very chic district, near the Arsenal metro station. 11A Sichnevoho Poustannia (phone: 290-6130; fax: 290-7270).

Slavutych A 17-story, 500-room property on the east bank of the river (about a 15-minute metro ride to the city center). Despite its somewhat out-of-the-way location, it's popular with travel agents booking larger tours. There's a restaurant, a café, a bar, a sauna, and shops. 1 Entuziastiv Vulytsia (phone: 555-0911).

Ukraina Once the *Palace* hotel, this 6-story property still retains its former grandeur. Popular with seasoned travelers, it's within walking distance of the *Bessarabskiy Rynok,* Khreshchatyk Prospekt, and the opera. All 328 rooms are large and high-ceilinged (some offer terraces). There's also a good restaurant (see *Eating Out*), which features a Ukrainian menu. Business services. 5 Shevchenka Bulvar (phone: 229-4303).

EATING OUT

Although Kiev is no culinary capital, Ukrainians enjoy eating out. Hotel restaurants — long the principal dining venues for hungry travelers — traditionally have dished out mediocre food (though well-prepared Ukrainian fare is quite delicious) and dismal service (indifferent restaurant staff and ear-splitting noise from live bands as early as 7 PM). Happily, Ukraine's drive toward a capitalist-style economy is bringing change — even in the kitchen.

A number of privately run eating establishments offering innovative menus have sprung up. Typically, they're also smaller, more elegant, and quieter than their state-run counterparts; a growing number of them are quite expensive and accept only hard currency. But given the chronic shortages here, the menu is dependent upon the type of food available on a given day (most menus are printed in Ukrainian and Russian).

The best-known Ukrainian dish is chicken Kiev, the fried white meat of a hen rolled and stuffed with garlic and butter. *Varenyky,* an old Ukrainian favorite, is a dumpling filled with any number of ingredients (try it with fruit) and topped with sour cream. Many people don't know it but borscht, that quintessentially "Russian" soup, is actually Ukrainian. Beef Stroganoff is a staple entrée, as are many kinds of meat with sour cream sauce and mushrooms. Ukrainian pastries are beautifully decorated and generally are not too sweet. Many Kievan restaurants offer wine from Odessa or the Crimea as well as cognac (Armenian is the best), and champagne. Some cooperative restaurants are not allowed to serve alcohol.

There are a number of cafés in the Upper Town that serve desserts and ice cream and light meals. Street vendors do a brisk business pushing *pirozhky,* delicious fried or steamed turnovers filled with meat, cabbage, cheese, or cherries. It is customary for Kievans to make a night out of dinner, stopping for a dance, a round of toasts, and a cigarette between each course. As a result, there is little turnover of tables, and reservations are required at many restaurants. Although *Intourist* or your hotel may at times be prevailed upon to make reservations, it's often just as easy to do it yourself. You can call, but because of the language barrier, the best approach is to stop in at the restaurant early on the day you wish to dine there.

The dramatically fluctuating economy makes it difficult to provide accurate prices for restaurants; we suggest that you check costs — and the operative exchange rate — immediately prior to your departure. If you go to the cafés or restaurants on your own, rather than having your hotel or *Intourist* make arrangements, you pay in local currency. At press time, credit cards were not widely accepted. All telephone numbers are in the 044 city code unless otherwise indicated.

For an unforgettable dining experience, we begin with our culinary favorite, followed by our cost and quality choices.

DELIGHTFUL DINING

Salut A longtime favorite of government officials who often dine here with visiting dignitaries. Located in the *Salut* hotel, this restaurant's 30 tables are graced with crystal, linen, and fresh flowers; quiet piano and violin music add to the air of elegance. Caviar and caviar dishes are among the house specialties, along with tender chicken Kiev, steaks, and veal cutlets. Open daily. Reservations necessary. Local currency only. Near the Arsenal metro station (phone: 290-6130).

Apolon (Apollo) Swiss-owned, this was the first Western-style restaurant in Kiev when it opened several years ago. The menu has a German influence with such distinctive dishes as Wiener schnitzel and pork cutlets, as well as various pasta entrées. Decor is elegant; there's a bar adjacent to the dining room. Open daily. Reservations advised. Hard currency only; major credit cards accepted. 15 Khreshchatyk (phone: 229-0437).

Eldorado All white marble, black leather, and mirrors, this intimate 70-seat dining room typifies a new breed of Kiev restaurants. The German chef produces a small and eclectic menu of German, Italian, and Ukrainian dishes including *kalbsbraten* (stuffed leg of veal), *tagliatelle al pesto,* and borscht. There's also a good selection of desserts. Open Sundays for dinner only. Reservations necessary. Hard currency only. 13 Chervonoarmiyska Vulytsia (phone: 225-5007).

Hostynny Dvir (Hospitable Court) Here, traditional Ukrainian fare is served in a friendly and welcoming setting, complete with waiters in traditional folk dress. The vaulted dining room is bright and airy, and there's an outdoor court for warm-weather dining. Specialties include *sashlik,* pork cutlets, *varenyky* (stuffed dumplings — try the sweet variety filled with cheese), and fish. Dinner begins with a complimentary serving of *tartynky* (small puff pastry breads). Open Tuesdays through Sundays. Reservations advised. Payment for lunch in local currency; hard currency accepted for dinner. 4 Kontraktova Ploshcha (phone: 416-2271).

Italia Beyond the threshold of this clean and airy restaurant, you'll find exceptional homemade pasta, carpaccio, pizza, and salads. Menu selections include roasted red peppers, mozzarella marinara, and lemon-flavored angel hair pasta in cream sauce. The wine list is brief but good. A floor show is provided for guests nightly. Open daily for dinner. Reservations necessary. Hard currency only. 8 Prorizna Vulytsia (phone: 224-2054).

Kiev Despite its location in a glass and steel Soviet-style hotel, the food here is more than adequate (an opinion shared by the many state officials who bring guests here). The music begins at 8 PM, and can be loud and raucous. There are banquet areas away from the band and, occasionally, a waiter can be persuaded to open a private room for diners interested in a more peaceful meal. Light lunches are served in the less expensive café on the first floor. Open daily. Reservations necessary. Major credit cards accepted. In the *Kiev Hotel,* 26-1 Hrushevskoho Vulytsia (phone: 293-0310).

Maxim Kiev's oldest cooperative restaurant, the menu features a number of Ukrainian favorites. Open daily. Reservations advised. Local currency only. 21 Khmelaytskoho Vulytsia (phone: 224-7021).

Mlyn Ukrainian food is served in this converted mill on an island in the Dnieper River. Open during summer only. Make reservations through *Intourist.* Near the Hidropark metro station (phone: 225-3051).

Skhody (Stairs) A block off Kiev's main square, this intimate place serves some of the city's best Ukrainian, Russian, and Jewish food. Order a table-full of *zakusky* (appetizers), which include everything from caviar to fish pâtés. Live violin and piano music. Closed Mondays. Reservations necessary. Local currency only. 7 Borysa Grynchenka Vulytsia (phone: 229-8629).

Spadschyna (Heritage) Popular with locals, this place offers a variety of delicious Ukrainian and Russian dishes. Start off with the assorted cold fish platter, featuring red caviar on a dollop of butter, smoked sturgeon and sardines. An exceptional entrée is *cotelette spadschyna* (chopped veal with egg, mushrooms, and onions) or opt for *kurcha tabaka* (baked chicken with garlic and spices). Live dinner music starts at 8 PM. Attentive service in a pleasant booth-style setting. Open daily for dinner. Reservations necessary. Local currency only. 8 Vulytsia Spaska (phone: 417-0358).

Ukraina In the basement of the *Ukraina* hotel, it's a good place for a quick snack or more leisurely dinner of traditional Ukrainian dishes. Excellent soups such as borscht and *kapusniask* (cabbage soup) top the menu. Open daily. Reservations for dinner only. Local currency only. 5 Shevchenka Bulvar (phone: 229-7183).

NATIONAL RESTAURANTS For the full Ukrainian experience, spend an evening at one of the restaurants that feature waiters and waitresses bedecked in Ukrainian costumes, folk music programs, dancing, and authentic Ukrainian cuisine. Reservations are required — first try to contact the restaurants directly since you might then arrange to pay in local currency (if you book through *Intourist* or your hotel you'll pay in dollars). Some of the better Ukrainian folk restaurants are *Khata Karasya* (*Prolisok Camping Motel;* Svyatoskino; phone: 444-8632); *Natalka Poltavka* (18 Kharkivske Shose; phone: 556-1539); *Dubky* (1 Stetsenka Vulytsia; phone: 440-5188); *Vitriak* (The Windmill; 11 Akademika Prospekt; phone: 266-7138); and *Kureni* (19 Parkova Doroho; phone: 293-4062).

Moscow

The 1990s have been a turbulent time for Russia and its capital city, Moscow. It began with Mikhail Gorbachev as president of the Soviet Union, firmly in control of the Kremlin, the hammer-and-sickle flag snapping in the wind overhead. By the end of 1991, after a failed coup, his job, his Communist party, and his country, were gone, replaced by 15 independent countries. Russia, led by Boris Yeltsin, its first freely elected (in June 1991) president, inherited the bulk of this disjointed empire. The Russian tricolor flag now flies from rooftops and government buildings, and has replaced Lenin's unsmiling face on the ruble. Statues of Communist leaders have been toppled, consigned to the dustbins of history.

The transition has not been a painless one. The majority of Russians have been thrown into poverty by the changeover to capitalism. Many buildings and roads have deteriorated from years of neglect. Yet, it seems that no matter how much hardship Russians have had to endure, Yeltsin remains a popular leader. He and his ever-changing government have shouldered much of the blame for moving forward too quickly; his ambitious privatization program has allowed prices on most goods to fluctuate freely, leading to skyrocketing inflation. The Russian ruble, still worthless outside the country, plummeted in value after the government stopped artificially setting its exchange rate in 1992. Today, the ruble's rate is determined by currency auctions, which more accurately reflect supply and demand.

In recent years, frustrated hard-liners, elected before the collapse of the Soviet Union, have opposed Yeltsin's policies. In turn, the Russian president dissolved parliament in September 1993, calling for new elections later in the year. The opposition, led by ousted vice president Aleksandr Rutskoi, retaliated with a violent 13-day stand-off. Although peace has been restored to the streets of Moscow, the future of democracy in Russia remains uncertain at press time as events continue to unfold.

The effort to change and renew the moribund Russian economy and adjust to a democratic way of life will be a Herculean task for the Russian people. Last July, a surprise move by the Central Bank to control inflation sent shockwaves through the country: The Finance Ministry, which oversees the banking industry in Russia, declared all pre-1993 ruble notes worthless. But though the bureaucratic complexity of dealing with everyday life continues to dampen Muscovites' enthusiasm during working hours, when it's time to play, Russian spirits revive rapidly.

In fact, never has Russia, its people, and its historic capital been so open and accessible to foreigners. No longer is Moscow a cold, dreary place where all foreigners are under suspicion, watched by their *Intourist* guides and KGB "observers."

Formerly stoic and uncommunicative, Muscovites long to talk to Westerners these days. Eavesdrop on a wedding reception in your hotel, visit the circus or racetrack, or dine at one of the local restaurants — you will witness the zest and exuberance with which Russians celebrate life.

And through it all, Moscow retains its historic mystique — part Asian, part European, part devoutly Orthodox, part atheist. With its huge onion domes, St. Basil's Cathedral in Red Square remains one of the most impressive sights in the world. Across the square, Lenin lies in his mausoleum and Stalin is buried in the Kremlin walls. Directly opposite, the massive *GUM* department store has been transformed from a dreary testimonial to socialist inefficiency into a thriving emporium.

Moscow always has been on the periphery of Europe. Situated on the Moskva River deep in the northwestern region of Russia, it was impervious to outside cultural and economic influences for centuries. The original Moscow architecture, for example, developed in the 15th century when imported Byzantine traditions were forced into conformity with the native arts of northwestern Russia. The bulbous domes that are a characteristic feature of Russian churches are apparently a native Russian form.

A bit of history helps to explain the city. There is archaeological evidence that people occupied this area along the Moskva as early as the Neolithic period, but the first mention of the tiny village of Moscow is found in Russian chronicles of 1147. Yuri Dolgoruki, a Prince of Suzdal, had established a small wooden fortress on a hill overlooking the river, in the same vicinity as the present Kremlin. (The word *kremlin* is derived from *kreml,* the old Russian word for fortress.) At first merely a stop on the river trade route between the Baltic Sea and the Black Sea, Moscow became the capital of the principality in the 13th century and was the center of power in the northern area when Mongol Tatars overran the Russian lands.

The present brick walls of the Kremlin were firmly in place by the late 15th century, but they could not prevent the town that was growing up outside the fortress from being destroyed by the Crimean Tatars in 1571 — and again by the Poles in the 17th century. Following these troubled times, Moscow began to expand and establish itself as a powerful city under a long line of Romanov czars. The most famous Romanov was Peter I, called Peter the Great, who was much enamored of Holland and Western Europe. In 1714, he moved the capital from Moscow to a new city he was building on the Gulf of Finland to reflect the taste and culture of the West.

Although the capital was moved to St. Petersburg, Moscow remained an important center of the Russian Orthodox church, and, as they had done since the reign of Ivan the Terrible, Russian czars continued to return to the Uspenskiy Sobor (Assumption Cathedral) in the Kremlin for their coronations. During the 18th and 19th centuries, Moscow established its university and its major theaters and continued to expand its boundaries. As the city spread out from the Kremlin complex, the ring of fortress

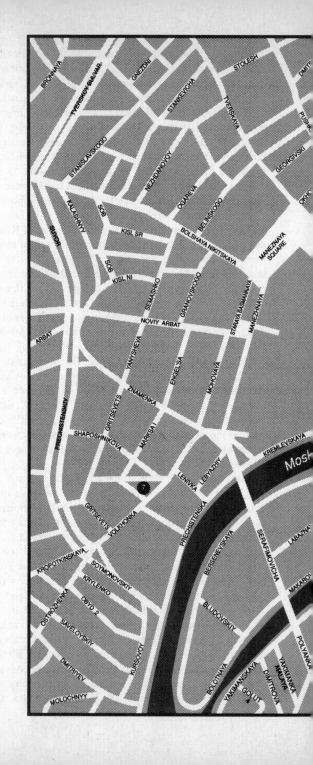

MOSCOW

Points of Interest

1. Bolshoi Theater
2. Central V. I. Lenin Museum
3. GUM
4. V.I. Lenin Mausoleum
5. St. Basil's Cathedral
6. Kremlin
7. Pushkin Museum of Fine Arts
8. Tretyakov Gallery

monasteries and convents that had served as Moscow's protective perimeter became an integral part of the city itself. A contemporary city map reflects this gradual expansion in ever-widening rings from the Kremlin–Red Square center.

In his zeal to ensure that his new capital would have no rival, Peter the Great decreed that no stone buildings be erected anywhere in Russia except in St. Petersburg. So even though Napoleon's armies failed to conquer Moscow in 1812, nearly three-quarters of the city was destroyed in the fires set in the wake of the French occupation. A special commission was set up by Alexander I to reconstruct Moscow in 1825, and several magnificent buildings were constructed in the imperial style, including the renowned *Bolshoi Theater*.

After the 1917 Revolution, the new Bolshevik government returned the capital to Moscow, and the Kremlin once again became the seat of power. Since then, Moscow has undergone a series of transformations. Between 1926 and 1939, the population doubled; today it exceeds 8.5 million. New office buildings, and later skyscrapers, created the city's contemporary skyline. Streets were widened and old areas of the city were razed to make way for modern hotels and offices. In 1935, the first part of Moscow's extensive metro (subway) system was completed. During World War II, 75 Nazi divisions massed against the city, but they were unable to conquer it, and Moscow handed the German armies one of their first major defeats.

Moscow today is about three-quarters the size of Los Angeles. A circular bypass highway, about 16 miles (26 km) from the city's center, marks its present boundaries. Beyond the bypass are miles of slender white birch trees and, occasionally, one of the quaint wooden houses with intricately carved façades once typical of this area. The generally flat country surrounding Moscow has facilitated the construction and maintenance of a railway network that makes Moscow a manufacturing and industrial hub as well as the seat of government. It is, indeed, the center of today's Russia, its most powerful and important city. In addition, while the Soviet Union is no more, the ethnic diversity it brought to Moscow's streets remains. Ukrainians, Armenians, Caucasians, Georgians, central Asians — they all come here, as visitors, to shop or to bring their goods to sell at farmers' markets throughout the city.

Since foreign business and news organizations have been feverishly establishing outposts here since the advent of *perestroika,* Moscow's foreign community of around 40,000 people has become a veritable city within a city. They have their own newspaper (the English-language *Moscow Times*), their own supermarkets, clothing stores, restaurants (*Pizza Hut* and a steakhouse are among the many new establishments that have recently opened), nightclubs, and a host of other amenities that they have brought with them. By tapping into this Western-style economy, visitors can experience Moscow while being able to enjoy at least some of the comforts of home.

Moscow's character has taken on new color, and its appearance may change with new construction, but to the Western eye, it may always be more imposing than beautiful. It is, nonetheless, a city that exudes energy and a new sense of power, leaving the visitor feeling that he or she has gained new insight into the new (and old) Russian psyche.

NOTE At press time, prompted by the increase in reported cases of diphtheria in Russia and Ukraine, travelers are advised to update their immunizations before entering these regions. For further information call the US State Department's *Citizen's Emergency Center* at 202-647-5225.

Moscow At-a-Glance

SEEING THE CITY

The lookout point in front of Moscow State University in Lenin Hills affords the best panorama of the city. Below is the Moskva River and the *Luzhniki* sports complex, while in the distance are the gold and silver domes of Novodevichiy Monastyr (New Maiden Convent) and the Kremlin complex (see *Special Places*), and the seven look-alike skyscrapers built by Stalin as monuments to himself. The university is near the Leninskiy Gory metro stop. There's a fine view of Red Square and the Kremlin from the *Rossiya* restaurant on the top floor of the 21-story tower wing of the *Rossiya* hotel (phone: 298-1562 or 298-5400).

Russian is an almost completely phonetic language, so when you sound out the letter on signs, you will recognize many English and French cognates. Here are a few Russian words to help you in your travels: "Ulitsa" is the Russian word for street; "prospekt" means avenue; "bulvar" means boulevard; "naberezhnaya" is embankment; "proyezd" is passage; "shosse" means highway; and "ploshchad" is the word for square.

The following information on Moscow was accurate as we went to press, but it is more than possible that streets and squares will be renamed, and hotels and restaurants will have changed hands. Many of those newly deposed statues are now resting in an impromptu park behind the *Tretyakov Gallery,* across from Gorky Park. Also note that after years of neglect under a Communist regime, Russia's cultural institutions and cathedrals are now undergoing much needed repair. Many already have been closed for several years, with no scheduled dates for reopening. Check with hotel service bureaus for up-to-date schedules of museums and cathedrals.

SPECIAL PLACES

Moscow grew up in concentric rings around the Kremlin, and much of what is of interest to the visitor is within the area bounded by the Bulvar Koltso (Boulevard Ring). However, there is also much to explore in the area between the Boulevard Ring and the outlying Sadovoye Koltso (Garden Ring), which roughly follows the line of an old earthen wall that was demolished early in the last century. Gorky Ulitsa, part of which has been renamed Tverskaya Ulitsa, runs from Voskresenskaya Ploshchad (Square of the Resurrection) northwest to Tverskaya Zastava and the railway terminal for trains from Western Europe, and is considered Moscow's main street.

INSIDE THE KREMLIN

KREMLIN COMPLEX Kremlins, or fortresses, can be found in a number of old Russian towns. None, however, is as well known as the Moscow Kremlin, which occupies 69 acres overlooking the Moskva River. For most of the 20th century the seat of the central Soviet government, it is once again the stronghold of the Russian government. The entire complex is surrounded by a red fortress wall studded with towers. Atop five of these towers are gigantic ruby-red stars that are lighted at night. Buried in the Kremlin walls are the ashes of various Russian heroes and two Americans — John Reed, whose book *Ten Days That Shook the World* is an eyewitness account of the Russian Revolution of 1917, and William ("Big Bill") Haywood, founder of the International Workers of the World (IWW), forerunner of the American Communist Party. There are guided tours of the Kremlin complex, or you can walk through the grounds on your own. Open from 10 AM to 7 PM; closed Thursdays. Admission charge.

KAFEDRAINAYA PLOSHCHAD (CATHEDRAL SQUARE) The central square in the Kremlin takes its name from the three principal cathedrals situated here. The largest one, Uspenskiy Sobor (Assumption Cathedral), with its white limestone walls and five gilded domes, was built around 1475. This was the private cathedral of the czars, many of whom were crowned here, but when Napoleon occupied Moscow, his men used it for a stable and burned some of its icons for firewood. Blagoveshchenskiy Sobor (Annunciation Cathedral) had three cupolas when it was built in early-Moscow style between 1484 and 1489. But when six new domes were added during reconstruction after a fire in the 16th century, it became known as the "golden-domed" cathedral. The five domes of Arkhangelskiy Sobor (Archangel Michael Cathedral), built between 1505 and 1509, are painted silver. All the pre-Romanov czars, with the exception of Boris Godunov, are buried here (the Romanovs are buried in St. Petersburg). Also on the square are the Granovitaya Palata (Granovitaya Palace), the oldest public building in Moscow, dating from 1473 to 1491; the bell tower of Ivan the Great; and several other early cathedrals. Tickets for admission to all cathedrals may be purchased at a kiosk in the square.

BOLSHOI KREMLEVSKIY DVORETS (GRAND KREMLIN PALACE) Once the residence of the imperial family in Moscow, the palace is now a government building. The Supreme Soviet of the USSR and of the Russian Federation met here until the abortive coup of August 1991. From the outside, the yellow-and-white–walled palace (built from 1838 to 1849) appears to have 3 floors; actually, there are only 2 — the second floor has 2 tiers of windows. Not open to the general public except by special tour (phone: 929-7990).

ORUZHENAYA PALATA (STATE ARMORY) The luxury of court life during czarist times comes alive in the halls of this museum next to the Grand Kremlin Palace. Lovers of *War and Peace,* and those intrigued by the checkered history of Russian royalty — from Ivan the Terrible to the ill-fated Roma-novs — will be fascinated by the splendid collection of royal regalia: arms and armor; clocks and carriages; jewel-encrusted robes of priceless silk, velvet, and brocade; thrones, including Ivan the Terrible's ivory seat and the throne of Czar Alexei, emblazoned with over 2,000 precious and semi-precious stones; royal crowns; and the many gifts presented to and by the czars, including the beautiful bejeweled eggs created by Fabergé. If you are lucky, you may be able to join one of the very small tour groups admitted to the Almazniy Fond (Diamond Fund). This section of the armory holds Catherine II's diamond-encrusted crown, her scepter with its Orlov diamond, and her golden orb, as well as other precious gems. Advance arrangements for this tour (in English) may be made through your hotel service bureau or by contacting the museum directly. The Diamond Fund is open from 10 AM to 5 PM; closed Thursdays. Admission charge (phone: 229-2036). The Armory is open from 10 AM to 5 PM; closed Thursdays. Admission charge (phone: 921-4720).

OUTSIDE THE KREMLIN

KRASNAYA PLOSHCHAD (RED SQUARE) This enormous square — 2,280 feet long by 426 feet wide — is the heart of Moscow and of Russia. This recently repaired cobblestone area is bounded on the west by the Kremlin wall and the Lenin Mausoleum; on the south by St. Basil's Cathedral; on the east by the mammoth department store, *GUM;* and on the north by the *State History Museum.* Red Square — its name will not change since it derives from a word that meant "beautiful" before it meant "red" as in commu-nism — is steeped in history. Centuries ago the square was chiefly used as a marketplace. Only later did it become the venue for official proclama-tions and public events. On the southeast quadrant, between St. Basil's and *GUM,* is a circular platform known as Lobnoye Mesto (Place of the Execution). Official decrees were read here, but it was better known as the spot where high-profile executions were carried out. For over 7 decades, the chief festivals — *May Day* on May 1 and *Revolution Memorial Day* on November 7 — rumbled through here amid much flag waving and under the smug approval of the nation's rulers standing atop the Lenin Mauso-leum. (Both have since been redesignated as nonpolitical holidays.) In recent years, Red Square also has been the site of demonstrations both in favor of and against the government's program of economic reforms. For further information see, *Quintessential Eastern Europe* in DIVERSIONS.

MAUZOLEY V. I. LENIN (V. I. LENIN MAUSOLEUM) The body of V. I. Lenin, the Russian revolutionary and founder of Bolshevism, is still displayed in its glass sarcophagus; the impressive changing of the guard ceremony still takes place in front of the mausoleum every hour; and incredible numbers of people still pass through the mausoleum each week to view the body. But Lenin's days in this huge red and black stepped mausoleum in Red Square seem numbered. With the death of the Soviet Union and the Communist Party, the new regime may soon decide to remove Lenin's remains and bury them elsewhere. (In all probability, it won't be in Moscow, since Lenin specifically requested to be interred with other members of his family in St. Petersburg.) Until then, it's symbolic of the changing times in Moscow that the traditionally long line to get into the tomb has been eclipsed in length by the queue to the counter at *McDonald's*, a 10-minute walk away. No cameras are allowed, and no talking is permitted once inside. Open from 10 AM to 1 PM; closed Mondays. Krasnaya Ploshchad (phone: 224-5115).

POKROVSKIY SOBOR (ST. BASIL'S CATHEDRAL) Although this Moscow landmark houses numerous frescoes, icons, and other artifacts, the building itself is much more interesting than any of its collections. With its distinctive multicolored onion-shaped domes, St. Basil's has become *the* symbol of Moscow, gracing numerous books and providing the backdrop for countless television news reports. Located on the south side of Red Square, it was built at the bidding of Ivan the Terrible in the mid-16th century to celebrate the liberation of the Russian state from the Tatar yoke. According to legend, Ivan had the architects blinded when it was finished, so they could never build a finer church.

The cathedral actually encompasses nine churches — a central building that stands more than 100 feet high surrounded by eight domed chapels. First walk around the exterior of the building, noting both its complex structure and its intricately painted decorations in blue, yellow, red, green, and gold (these were added in the late 17th century — the church was originally white with gilded domes). Take time to go inside and wander through the narrow passages to the tiny but extensively frescoed chapels. Though it was used as a museum (an annex of the *Historical Museum* directly across Red Square) after the Bolshevik Revolution, St. Basil's, as well as the Kremlin cathedrals, were returned to the Russian Orthodox Church in 1992. Holiday (*Christmas, Easter*) church services are now once again being celebrated here. Open from 11 AM to 3:30 PM; closed Tuesdays. Admission charge. Krasnaya Ploshchad (phone: 298-3304).

GORKY PARK To most Muscovites, this massive park along the banks of the Moskva River is the centerpiece of their city. Year-round, it's the place parents take their children for a special day outing. In summer, there is horseback riding available, as well as carnival rides for kids of all ages. In winter, Muscovites test their skills at cross-country skiing and ice skating here. Open daily until sunset. The main gate is just off Krymskiy Val.

GUM One of the largest, best-known, and until recently most poorly stocked department stores in the world, *GUM* (pronounced *Goom*) was built in the late 19th century as an arcade for nearly 1,000 small shops. It is said that some 350,000 shoppers wander through the 3 levels of this emporium each day. The store, which celebrated its 100th anniversary in 1992, is attempting to remodel itself into Moscow's premier shopping mall: The building, with its vaulted glass ceiling, etched-glass storefronts, and wrought-iron railings has been undergoing a face-lift since privatization. It is now a collection of hard-currency shops, including *Botany 500, Samsonite, Benetton, Yves Rocher, L'Oréal, Estée Lauder, Arrow Shirts*, and *Galeries Lafayette*. Shares in the originally state-run store were sold to private investors in 1992, and the coming of capitalism to this venerable venue presages some interesting changes to come. Open 8 AM to 8 PM; closed Sundays. Krasnaya Ploshchad (phone: 921-5763 or 921-5692).

TSENTRALNIY MUSEY V. I. LENIN (CENTRAL V. I. LENIN MUSEUM) Photographs of early revolutionary leaders and documents relating to Lenin's rise to power are housed in this red brick Duma (Parliament) building on Manezh Ploshchad (formerly Revolution Square), just north of Red Square. Among the thousands of exhibits in the museum's 22 halls are many of Lenin's manuscripts, letters, and personal belongings, including a 1920 Rolls-Royce. Open Tuesdays through Thursdays from 10:30 AM to 7 PM; and Fridays through Sundays from 9:30 AM to 6 PM. No admission charge. 4 Manezh Ploshchad (phone: 925-4808).

METRO In addition to being a generally clean and efficient means of transportation, Moscow's subway system is actually one of the city's most interesting museums. Each of its more than 100 stations has its own aesthetic qualities: Stained glass windows, mosaics set with gold, crystal chandeliers, marble and stainless steel columns, and bronze statues are some of the decorative elements. Most interesting and beautiful are the Mayakovskaya, Kievskaya, and Komsomolskaya stations. The first metro line opened in 1935; the newer the station, the less ornate it is likely to be. Some of the station platforms, reached by fast escalators, are as much as 300 feet underground. For a single, very small fare, you can ride the entire system, getting off at every station for a look. Since trains arrive every 2 to 4 minutes, you can cover much of the system in a short time. The most central stop is a junction of three stations — Manezh Ploshchad, Teatralnaya Ploshchad, and Okhotniy Ryad — joined by underground passages. Open daily from 6 to 1 AM.

NOVODEVICHIY MONASTYR (NEW MAIDEN CONVENT) Recently renovated and rededicated by the Russian Orthodox church, this richly endowed convent was part of a ring of fortress-monasteries and convents that formed a protective circle around the Kremlin. Founded in 1524 to commemorate the liberation of Smolensk, it has a long and varied history. Boris Godunov was proclaimed czar from this convent; Peter I's sister, Sophia, was imprisoned here when she encouraged rebellion against her brother; and noble families sent their unmarried daughters and widowed (or unwanted) wives to live here. (When he grew tired of her, Peter the Great sent his first wife to the Lopukhin Palace, a brick building on the right near the convent entrance.) There is a functioning Russian Orthodox church here, but the convent's Smolensky Cathedral now serves as a museum of Russian applied arts from the 16th and 17th centuries. Chekhov, Gogol, Prokofiev, Stanislavsky, Khrushchev, and other famous Russians are buried in a cemetery to the south of the convent. Both the convent and cemetery are open from 10 AM to 5 PM; closed Tuesdays and the first Monday of the month. Admission charge. Near the Sportivnaya metro station. Also reached by trolley No. 11 or 15; or by bus No. 64, 132, or 808. 1 Novodevichiy Proyezd (phone: 246-8526).

MOSKOVSKIY UNIVERSITET (MOSCOW STATE UNIVERSITY) South of the convent, across the Moskva River, this monumental university towers above the city from its 415-acre site in Lenin Hills. Statistics offer the best summary of its status as the world's largest bastion of learning. The buildings put up during the late Stalinist period (between 1949 and 1953) contain 45,000 rooms connected by some 90 miles of corridors. The main building is 787 feet tall and its façade is 1,470 feet long. The university was founded in 1755 by Russian scientist Mikhail Lomonosov and officially bears his name. Near the Universitet and Leninskiy Gory metro stops. Also reached by bus and trolley. Universitetskiy Prospekt (phone: 939-1000).

GOSUDARSTVENNIY MUZEY IZOBRAZITELNIKH ISKUSSTV IMENI A. S. PUSHKINA (PUSHKIN MUSEUM OF FINE ARTS) Near the Kremlin, this museum houses an eclectic collection of 550,000 pieces of ancient Eastern, Greco-Roman, Byzantine, European, and American art (including several works by 20th-century American painter, illustrator, and former Communist sympathizer, Rockwell Kent) as well as a library of 200,000 volumes. Its most important collections are its ancient Oriental and Renaissance art and 19th- and early- 20th-century French paintings, including the work of Paul Cézanne, Claude Monet, Pierre-Auguste Renoir, and Maurice Utrillo. Open from 10 AM to 7 PM; closed Mondays. Admission charge. 12 Volkhonka Ulitsa (phone: 203-6974).

VYSTAVKA DOSTIZHENIY NARODNOVO KHOZYAYSVA SSR-VDNKH (USSR EXHIBITION OF ECONOMIC ACHIEVEMENTS) This is the *Smithsonian Institution* of the former Soviet Union, now commonly referred to by its initials, *VDNKh*. All aspects of Soviet life — agriculture, industry, culture, and science — are detailed by the exhibits at this 553-acre park and pavilion site in northwest Moscow. The park, which has a zoo (if you have any love for animals, *don't* go) and a circus, is a popular place for Muscovites to spend a free day. In winter there is skiing, skating, and *troika* (a Russian horse-drawn sleigh) riding. In summer, rowboats are available to rent for relaxing sojourns on the pond. Near the main entrance is an impressive monument to the Soviet space effort, a gleaming titanium rocket called *Conquerors of Space.* The famous sculpture *The Worker and the Collective Farm Woman,* created by Vera Mukhina for the *1937 Paris Fair,* stands at the North Gate entrance. Lately, the *VDNKh* has hosted Western exhibitions. It's also the site of Moscow's new commodities exchange. The various buildings have different hours and closing days. The *VDNKh* metro stop is just beside the main entrance. Pervaya Meshchanskaya Ulitsa (phone: 181-9162).

ENVIRONS

KOLOMENSKOYE ESTATE-MUSEUM Established as a country estate for the ruling family in the 14th century, Kolomenskoye is on a hill beside the Moskva River, about 10 miles (16 km) southeast of the Kremlin. The first stone church in the Russian "tent roof" style was erected here by Czar Ivan Kalita in 1532, and several churches and buildings from the 16th and 17th centuries also can be seen here. The museum has interesting exhibitions of door locks and keys, ceramic tiles and stones, and carved-wood architectural details. Open 11 AM to 5 PM, closed Mondays and Tuesdays. Admission charge. The buildings can be seen from the main road, but the entrance is from a dirt road off the Kashirskoye Shosse. 39 Andropova Prospekt (phone: 112-5217).

KUSKOVO ESTATE One of the best collections of 18th-century Russian art can be found in the palace of this estate that once belonged to the Sheremetiev family, among the oldest Russian noble families. The palace, built by serf craftsmen, has pine-log walls faced with painted boards. Since 1932, this also has been the site of the *State Museum of Ceramics,* with collections of Russian porcelain, glass, china, and majolica. There is also a formal 70-acre French garden. Open 10 AM to 4 PM; closed Mondays and Tuesdays. 2 Yunosti Ulitsa (phone: 370-0160). The estate is about 6 miles (10 km) from central Moscow, along the Ryazanskoye Shosse.

Sources and Resources

TOURIST INFORMATION

Once the all-powerful monopoly through which all travel arrangements had to be made, *Intourist* is now referred to as *Intourservice* (4 Belinskovo Ulitsa; phone: 202-9975 or 203-8943; fax: 200-1243). *Intourservice* provides general information, brochures, and maps, as well as English-speaking guides for general and specific sightseeing in Moscow and its environs, including tours of the Kremlin grounds and cathedrals.

Although good transportation and city maps are available at hotels in Moscow, comprehensive travel guides in English should be purchased before you leave the US. The *Blue Guide* to Moscow and St. Petersburg (W. W. Norton; $19.95) is a particularly good handbook.

The *Moscow Times* now publishes a quarterly magazine that offers suggestions on restaurants, cultural events, nightlife, and sightseeing. It's available at all hotels, and at the *Moscow Times* office (*Radisson Slavyanskaya* hotel; phone: 941-8952 or 941-8958).

The *Falkplan City Map of Moscow* (Falk-Verlag; $7.95) is a good backup to local maps and is available in bookstores throughout the US. An invaluable tool for negotiating the streets of Moscow, it highlights public transportation routes; lists of hotels, museums, and theaters; as well as a street index.

> **NOTE** Economic turmoil, including frequent and steep price increases on many goods and services, makes it impossible to provide accurate information on prices, including the costs of basic services such as public transportation and the telephone. At press time, the Russian ruble's exchange rate was determined by twice-weekly currency auctions, and its value was plummeting. The Russian government periodically announces plans to ban domestic commercial transactions in currencies other than the ruble, putting an end to the common practice of charging foreigners hard currency at shops, restaurants, and hotels.

LOCAL COVERAGE Moscow's only English-language newspaper, the *Moscow Times* (see above) features local and international news and survival tips for foreigners. The *International Herald Tribune, Time, Newsweek,* and other European and North American dailies and weeklies often can be purchased at kiosks, hotels, and hard-currency shops, although not necessarily on the day of publication. For local coverage of the economy and Western business ventures, Russia's premier publication is the English-language edition of *Commersant,* available at hotels and kiosks throughout the city. In addition, several US newspapers now publish editions in Russian, including *The New York Times.*

The *Moscow Metro Restaurant Guide* and the *Moscow Hotel Restaurant Guide* are two new brochures compiled by American John E. Felber. They can be obtained by sending $1 and a self-addressed stamped envelope to *International Intertrade,* PO Box 636, Federal Sq., Newark, NJ 07101.

TELEPHONE It is now possible to dial Moscow direct from the US. The country code for Russia is 7; the city code for Moscow is 095.

A word about telephones: The Russian telephone system is notoriously bad. There are no residential telephone directories, although there are a number of recently published English-language business directories such as *Information Moscow* and the *All Moscow Directory* that are available in most hard-currency stores. Your hotel service bureau can contact Moscow information for residential numbers. If you speak Russian, dial 09 for local information.

To use a pay phone, deposit a 1-ruble coin in the slot before picking up the receiver; dial only *after* you hear a continuous buzzing sound.

If your hotel does not have direct-dialing service, it can book a long-distance call for you, but it is advisable to arrange the call at least a half-day before you wish to make a connection. To book an international call yourself, dial 8, wait for the dial tone, then dial either 194 or 196. Keep trying until you reach an operator, rather than a recording. Few operators speak English. At press time, it was possible to call abroad yourself from 9 PM to 9 AM and all day on Sunday: Just dial 8, wait for the tone, then dial 10, the country code (the country code for the US and Canada is 1), and the area code and local number. Another certain, although more expensive, way of getting a direct international line is from any of 25 *Comstar* telephone booths around town (call 979-1692 or 210-0962 for their locations), which take American Express, Visa, or a prepaid phone credit card issued by *Comstar*. Finally, if you're determined to use rubles (quite a bargain if you have the patience), go early in the day to the Central Telephone and Telegraph office (7 Tverskaya Ulitsa). They have international lines.

If you are going to be doing business in Moscow, you can rent a cellular phone at the *Americom Business Center,* located on the second floor of the *Radisson Slavyanskaya* hotel (phone: 941-8427 or 578-2765).

GETTING AROUND

Moscow has an efficient and exceptionally inexpensive public transportation system that includes a subway (metro), buses, trams, trolleys, and even boats in summer.

AIRPORTS Sheremetevo I (phone: 155-0922 for domestic flights) and Sheremetevo II (phone: 578-7518 or 578-7816 for international flights) are about 30 minutes from downtown by taxi. Three other airports, Domodedovo, Bykovo, and Vnukovo, serve domestic flights and are from 40 minutes to 1 hour from downtown Moscow.

BOAT From late spring through early fall, low-priced boats cruise along the Moskva River, stopping to drop off and pick up passengers in different parts of the city. The view of the Kremlin and St. Basil's from the water around sundown, with the day's last flickers of light glinting off the gilded towers, is one to remember. The main dock is to the rear of the *Rossiya* hotel (see *Checking In*).

BUS/TRAM/TROLLEY These transport lines operate from 6 to 1 AM (tram) or to 1:30 AM (trolley and bus) and are inexpensive to ride. Bus tickets can be obtained from the driver in units of 10 or from a hotel newsstand. Riders punch their own tickets and retain them until the end of the ride. (There are random inspections to enforce the honor system of paying the fare.) Maps showing the routes for all lines are available at hotels and many street kiosks.

CAR RENTAL Automobiles, with or without drivers, may be rented through major hotels. A word of caution: Roads — especially in the center of Moscow — are often in need of repair. To complicate matters further, there are myriad obscure traffic rules designed to bedevil you. For instance, there are no left turns except at a handful of designated intersections, and driving with headlights on at night is prohibited (only parking lights are permitted).

Agencies for foreign-made cars include the Japanese-Russian joint venture *InNis* (32 Bolshaya Ordynka Ulitsa; phone: 155-5021); *Business Car* (18-1 Ovchinnikovskaya Naberezhnaya; phone: 233-1796), which is open 24 hours; *Hertz,* under the licensee *MTD Service* (152 Gorbunovo Ulitsa; phone: 448-8035); *Avis* (7 Vernadskovo Prospekt; phone: 578-5676); *Rozec-Car* (phone: 241-5393 or 241-7715); and *Mosrent* (79 Krasnobogatirtskaya Ulitsa; phone: 248-0251).

METRO The subway has seven interconnected lines. One runs in a circle; the others radiate out to different parts of the city. Though all else may be unraveling in this city, the metro is still generally clean, efficient, and inexpensive. Trains arrive and depart at the various stations frequently and operate from 6 to 1 AM.

TAXI Visitors will find that all taxi fares are subject to negotiation. Russians now pay as much as 25 times what the meter reads, but a metered taxi ride into Moscow is no longer an option for foreigners. A ride within the center of Moscow will probably cost about $2. Taxis are generally yellow, black, or white Volga sedans with a checkered pattern on the door. However, expect several rejections before you find one willing to take you where you want to go. Taxis also can be ordered in advance, through your hotel service bureau or, if you speak Russian, by calling 927-0000 or 927-2108. It is best to order a taxi at least an hour in advance.

| BE ALERT! | There have been an increasing number of reports of tourists being robbed by bands of young people commonly known as Russian "mafia," who lurk outside major hotels and restaurants posing as taxi drivers. The best advice is to never get into a taxi with other passengers, and walk away if anything looks or sounds suspicious. |

TRAIN Moscow supports over a dozen railroad stations. Ask your hotel service bureau for information about locations, fares, and schedules. The train stations tourist are most likely to frequent are Sankt Peterburgskiy (1 Kalanchovskaya Ploshchad; phone: 262-4281), where trains depart for and arrive from St. Petersburg, Finland, and Estonia; Byelorusskiy (Byelorusskaya Ploshchad; phone: 253-4908), with trains to and from Berlin, London, Warsaw, Paris, and Lithuania; Kievskiy (Kievskaya Ploshchad; phone: 240-7622), with arrivals from and departures for Ukraine and Central Europe; and Yaroslavskiy (Kalanchovskaya Ploshchad; phone: 266-0595), with trains to and from the Far East, including the *Trans-Siberian* line. The *Intourservice* telephone number for train information and reservations in English is 921-4513.

For those who want to explore Moscow and beyond, *Cox & Kings* provides 11-, 13-, and 14-day tours on their *Bolshoi Express* steam locomotive to the Golden Ring cities, St. Petersburg, and the Baltic States. Accommodations and meals are provided. For more information contact *Cox & Kings,* 511 Lexington Ave., New York, NY 10017 (phone: 212-935-3854).

LOCAL SERVICES

The major Western-style hotels (see *Checking In*); the British-Russian *Comstar Business Center* (10 Petrovka Ulitsa, Suite 301; phone: 924-0892 or 924-1385); and the *Retour Business Center* (6 Savelyevskiy Pereulok; phone: 202-7610 or 202-2662) offer business services (international phone lines, fax machines, conference rooms, and comprehensive bilingual secretarial services).

The new *Red Square Business Center* on the second floor of the *GUM* department store (phone: 921-0911; fax: 921-4609) offers international phone service, faxing, and photocopying.

Computer supplies (for hard currency only) can be purchased at *Future Technology* (6A-22 Festivalnaya Ulitsa; phone: 453-4204); *Computerland* (8 Kutuzovskiy Prospekt; phone: 243-3553); or *Computer Supply Services* (35 Prechistenka Ulitsa; phone: 202-0480). The only official Apple dealership in Russia is *InterMicro* (39 Nizhnaya Krasenoselskaya; phone: 267-4352 or 267-3210). Repairs on IBM-compatible computers can be made through the *Hewlett Packard Repair Center,* opposite the *Cosmos* hotel (phone: 184-8002).

CURRENCY EXCHANGE The best places to exchange dollars for rubles are hotel service bureaus or the larger souvenir shops. Cash traveler's checks for rubles or dollars (but not to convert rubles into dollars) at the Dialog Bank in the *Radisson Slavyanskaya* hotel (phone: 941-8349 or 941-8434). Bring your passport, customs declaration form, and a lot of patience. You will not be able to use traveler's checks in most restaurants and shops, so it is best to bring cash instead. Although it is no longer illegal to exchange money outside the state-owned central banks, it is very unwise to deal with just anyone who approaches you on the street or inside a store; they may shortchange you or, worse yet, give you counterfeit money instead. *Visa* installed the first ATM (automatic teller machine) in the lobby of the

Metropol hotel (see *Checking In*). In addition, there are banks in several hotels, including the *Mir* (phone: 252-9519) and the *Ukraina* (phone: 243-3030). At press time, however, these locations did not cash traveler's checks.

DENTIST (ENGLISH-SPEAKING) Dental problems should be taken to *Medical Interline* (5 Tverskaya Ulitsa, Room 2030; phone: 203-8631), a Swiss-Italian-Belgian-Hungarian-Russian joint venture with a multilingual staff, Western equipment, and reasonable prices. A new clinic, the *Adventist Health Center of Moscow* (21-60 Letiya Oktybrya Prospekt; phone: 126-3391), offers an English-speaking dentist and dental lab technicians.

DRY CLEANING Dry cleaning outlets can be found at the *Aerostar, Mezhdunarodnaya, Olympic Penta, Pullman,* and *Savoy* hotels (see *Checking In*).

MEDICAL EMERGENCY Most hotels have a doctor on call (some speak English). For serious problems go directly to the *American Medical Center* (3 Shmitovskiy Proyezd, near the *Mezhdunarodnaya* hotel; phone: 256-8212 or 256-8378). It offers Western-trained doctors and nurses, an emergency room with life-saving equipment, a laboratory, X-ray facilities, and a pharmacy. Open weekdays 8:30 AM to 6 PM; Saturdays 10 AM to 2 PM. The *European Medical Clinic* has reopened *Polyclinic No. 6* (3 Gruzinskiy Pereulok; phone: 253-0703 or 240-9999) with Russian and Western staff, all of whom speak English. The *Sana Medical Center* (65 Nizhnaya Pervomaiskaya Ulitsa; phone: 464-1254 or 464-2563) is open Mondays through Saturdays from 10 AM to 8 PM; Sundays from 10 AM to 5 PM; it caters to foreigners although there are few on staff who speak English — bring your own translator. As a last resort try the *Botkin Hospital* (2 Botkinskiy Proyezd; phone: 255-0015), formerly reserved for Western diplomats. For information on medical evacuations, contact *Delta Consulting* (12 Berezhkovskaya Naberezhnaya; phone: 434-4389).

NATIONAL/INTERNATIONAL COURIER Moscow has become crowded with couriers, including *Federal Express* (12 Krasnopresnenskaya Naberezhnaya; phone: 253-1641), *TNT* (3 Baltiyskiy Pereulok; phone: 156-5771); *DHL Worldwide Express* (two locations: the *Olympic Penta* hotel; phone: 971-6101, and the *Mezhdunarodnaya* hotel, phone: 253-1194); and *UPS* (15A Bolshaya Ochakovskaya Ulitsa; phone: 430-7069 or 430-6373).

PHARMACY There are several reputable drugstores in Moscow. Among the best are *Unipharm* (13 Skaterniy Pereulok; phone: 202-5071), the German *Seidel Medizin GmBH* (59A Beskudnikovsiy Bulvar; phone: 905-4227), the pharmacy of the *American Medical Center* (3 Shmitovskiy Proyezd, near the *Mezhdunarodnaya* hotel; phone: 256-8212 or 256-8378), and the Swiss-operated *International Pharmacy of Moscow* (4 Tchernyakhovskava Ulitsa; phone: 155-7080 or 155-8780). Also, *Eczacibasi* (2-15 Moroseika Ulitsa; phone: 928-9189), open 9 AM to 7 PM; closed Sundays. At press time, all medical supplies were sold for hard currency.

PHOTOCOPIES An American/Canadian outpost of quality printing services is *Alphagraphics* (50 Tverskaya Ulitsa; phone: 251-1208 or 251-1215). They will make photocopies, business cards, and passport pictures in a flash. Their fax services are competent but expensive. Several hotels also offer photocopying services.

TRANSLATOR The city's translation services are largely provided by *Intourservice* and most Western hotels. Also check the classified ads in the *Moscow Times*. *Inlingua* (2-1 Semyonovskaya Naberezhnaya; phone: 360-0847) and *IP Interpret* (1 Kaidashevskiy Pereulok; phone: 231-1020) are private agencies offering translators and interpreters.

SPECIAL EVENTS

Although April 22 commemorates Lenin's birthday, not surprisingly, this day — and other old Soviet holidays such as May 1, *International Labor Day* — are no longer officially observed in post-Communist Russia. The *Moscow Film Festival* is held annually in June and July. The *Russian Winter Festival,* a major arts event, runs from December 25 to January 5.

MUSEUMS

Besides those mentioned in *Special Places,* Moscow has numerous museums devoted to Russian art and folk crafts, the work of famous writers and composers who lived here, and various aspects of Russian history. Unless otherwise noted, the museums below do not have an admission charge.

FILIAL MUZEY L. N. TOLSTOVO (LEO TOLSTOY HOME) The restored home of the writer, who lived here from 1882 to 1909. The museum has 3 rooms filled with antiques, porcelains, and paintings that the author collected during his extensive travels throughout Europe. Open from 10 AM to 3:30 PM October through March; 10 AM to 5:30 PM April through September; closed Mondays and the last Friday of the month. 21 Lva Tolstovo Ulitsa (phone: 246-9444).

GOSUDARSTVENNIY MUZEY ISKUSSTV NARODOV VOSTOKA (STATE MUSEUM OF ORIENTAL ART) Crafts of the Russian Far East, plus Chinese, Indian, and Japanese art. Open from 11 AM to 8 PM; closed Mondays. 12A Suvorovskiy Bulvar (phone: 202-4953 or 202-4555).

GOSUDARSTVENNIY MUZEY ISTORII (STATE HISTORY MUSEUM) Moscow's oldest museum, which has been closed for renovations since 1986, is scheduled to reopen this year. The museum documents the history of the country and contains such relics as clothes worn by Ivan the Terrible, Peter the Great's carriage, Napoleon's saber, and decrees written by Lenin after the Revolution. It also houses the country's largest archaeological collection as well as coins, medals, and precious ornaments. 1-2 Krasnaya Ploshchad (phone: 928-8452). For further information, check with your hotel service bureau.

GOSUDARSTVENNIY TSENTRALNIY MUZEY MUSIKALNOY KULTURI IMENI M. I. GLINKI (GLINKA STATE CENTRAL MUSEUM OF MUSICAL CULTURE) Dedicated to Mikhail Ivanovich Glinka and other Russian composers of the 19th century, the collection includes 1,500 musical instruments. Open Wednesdays, Fridays, Saturdays, and Sundays from 10 AM to 6 PM; Tuesdays and Thursdays from 2 to 8 PM; closed Mondays and the last day of the month. 4 Fadeyeva Ulitsa (phone: 972-3237).

KVARTIRA MUZEY DOSTOEVSKOVO (DOSTOYEVSKY APARTMENT-MUSEUM) Memorabilia of the great author Fyodor Mikhailovich Dostoyevsky. Open Wednesdays and Fridays from 2 to 7:30 PM; Thursdays, Saturdays, and Sundays from 11 AM to 5:30 PM; closed Mondays, Tuesdays, and the last day of the month. 2 Dostoyevskaya Ulitsa (phone: 281-1085).

MUZEY ANDREYA RUBLOVA (ANDREI RUBLEV MUSEUM OF OLD RUSSIAN ART) A good collection of restored icons, housed in Moscow's oldest cathedral. The collection includes icons by students and contemporaries of Rublev, but none by the 14th-century master himself. The museum was undergoing renovation at press time; inquire at your hotel service bureau or call ahead before going. Open 10:30 AM to 5:30 PM; closed Wednesdays and the last Friday of the month. 10 Andronyevskaya Ploshchad (phone: 278-1429).

MUZEY CHEKHOVA (CHEKHOV MUSEUM) Exhibitions relating to Russia's greatest playwright, Anton Pavlovich Chekhov. Open Wednesdays and Fridays from 2 to 7 PM; Tuesdays, Thursdays, Saturdays, and Sundays from 11 AM to 5 PM. 6 Sadovaya-Kudrinskaya Ulitsa (phone: 291-6154).

MUZEY GORKOVO (MAXIM GORKY MUSEUM) The writer's life in letters, manuscripts, and pictures. Open Mondays, Tuesdays, and Thursdays from 10 AM to 5:30 PM; Wednesdays and Fridays from noon to 7 PM. 25A Povarskaya Ulitsa (phone: 290-5130).

MUZEY L. N. TOLSTOVO (LEO TOLSTOY MUSEUM) In the former Lopukhin mansion, it contains manuscripts and other memorabilia. Open 11 AM to 6 PM; closed Mondays and the last Friday of the month. 11 Prechistenka Ulitsa (phone: 202-2190).

MUZEY MAYAKOVSKOVO (MAYAKOVSKY MUSEUM) The former home of Russian poet/playwright/painter Vladimir Vladimirovich Mayakovsky is now Moscow's most innovative museum. Mayakovsky's personal effects are arranged in such a way that the building resembles an avant-garde gallery of modern art. The author of such poems as *A Cloud with Trousers* and such plays as *The Bedbug* would have approved of the disorienting effect this gallery has on the senses. Open Tuesdays, Fridays, Saturdays, and Sundays from 10 AM to 6 PM; Mondays from noon to 8 PM; Thursdays from 1 to 9 PM; closed Wednesdays and the last Friday of every month. Admission charge. 3-6 Serova Proyezd, near Lubyanaka (formerly Dzerzhinsky) Ploschad (phone: 921-9387 or 921-9560).

MUZEY NARODNOVO ISKUSSTVA (MUSEUM OF FOLK ART) Embroidery, enamel-work, and woodcarvings are displayed here. Open from 11 AM to 5:30 PM; closed Mondays. 7 Stanislavskovo Ulitsa (phone: 291-8718).

NOVAYA TRETYAKOVSKAYA GALEREYA (NEW TRETYAKOV GALLERY) Modern (post-Soviet) Russian art is the focus of this new branch of the *Tretyakov Gallery* (below). Paintings, sculpture, and documents from the 1930s are featured. Open 10 AM to 6 PM; closed weekends. 10 Krymskiy Val (phone: 231-1352).

PAVILION-MUZEY LENINSKIY PAKHORONIY POEZD (LENIN FUNERAL TRAIN PAVIL-ION-MUSEUM) The railway car that transported Lenin's coffin to his funeral, with an exhibit of Lenin memorabilia. Open from 10 AM to 6 PM; closed weekends. Located at the Paveletskiy Station, 1 Lenina Ploshchad (phone: 235-2898).

TRETYAKOVKA (TRETYAKOV GALLERY) Even though this world-renowned art gallery was slated to reopen last year after major renovations, funds have not been available to finish the work. At press time, only one small wing featuring several icons and paintings has reopened, and the museum's treasure remains locked away in climate-controlled storerooms. That treasure is one of the most extensive collections of homegrown art in the world — a veritable "who's who" in Russian art from the 10th through the 20th centuries. Open 10 AM to 7 PM; closed Mondays. 10 Lavrushinskiy Pereulok (phone: 231-1362).

TSENTRALNIY MUZEY REVOLYTSIY (CENTRAL MUSEUM OF THE REVOLUTION) Formerly the *English Club* for Russian noblemen, since 1923 this building has featured exhibits on the 1905 and 1917 revolutions, and the Great October Socialist Revolution. Though still open at press time, its future is uncertain. Open from 11 AM to 7 PM; closed Mondays. 21 Tverskaya Ulitsa (phone: 299-5217).

SHOPPING

Despite all you may have heard or read, there are many interesting and desirable items to buy in Russia: amber, furs, samovars, lacquer boxes, balalaikas, caviar, and that ultimate Russian souvenir, *matryoshka* dolls, a family of gaily painted wooden dolls hidden one inside the other (*matryoshkas* featuring Russian and Soviet leaders — from Yeltsin all the way back to Lenin — nesting inside one another are quite popular these days). And don't forget to take home some Russian vodka, which comes in several flavors, including lemon, pepper (very hot!), and a very pleasantly aromatic variety called "hunter's vodka." Russian porcelain is very popular, both the colorful hand-painted cups, saucers, and teapots, and the distinctive blue and white pottery from the nearby Gzhel region (be sure it has the distinctive Gzhel marking on the bottom). In addition to diamonds, pearls, sapphires, and semi-precious stones, scout out antiques shops and commission stores for unexpected good buys. If you're in the market for good souvenirs, don't miss the small arts and crafts shops set up inside the churches lining Varvarka Ulitsa, behind the *Rossiya* hotel.

The city has a weekend flea market at Izmailovskiy Park on the northeast edge of the city (see below). Prices are in rubles or hard currency.

Moscow has several art galleries that sell works both old and new (several are listed below). Good deals can be found, considering Russian works are now in vogue in the world's art circles. Exporting art from Russia is a little tricky, however. If you buy art from an established gallery, the paperwork will be done for you. Otherwise, before you take your purchase out of the country, it should first be appraised by the city export commission (29 Chekhova Ulitsa, open only on Tuesdays from 10 AM to 2 PM). Bring two small photos of the item with you (those planning to buy art in Moscow might consider bringing along a Polaroid camera for this purpose) and expect to pay a small fee. No items made before 1945 or books printed prior to 1977 may be taken out of the country. You should also be aware that it is illegal to take caviar purchased for rubles out of the country; only caviar accompanied by a hard-currency receipt will safely make it past customs.

Visitors from the West no longer have to travel to Moscow like packhorses, loaded down with cheese, fruit, Pepto-Bismol, and cartons of cigarettes. For groceries and other food items, the city's joint-venture supermarkets — the lifeline for Moscow's burgeoning foreign community — are recommended. Perhaps the best is *Stockmann's* (4-8 Zatsepskiy Val Ulitsa; phone: 233-2602 or 231-1924), a Finnish-Russian joint venture that is always well stocked with fresh fruit and vegetables, frozen meat, milk and other dairy supplies, household appliances, a heady selection of liquor, foreign publications, and other items ordinarily found in Western supermarkets. Open daily from 10 AM to 8 PM; credit cards only accepted, and you will have to bring your passport. Smaller but better situated is the Swiss-Russian supermarket *Sadko* (16 Bolshaya Dorogomilovskaya Ulitsa, near the *Ukraina* hotel; phone: 243-6659). It's open Mondays through Saturdays from 10 AM to 8 PM; Sundays from 10 AM to 6 PM. A second, more modern supermarket with ample parking is the *Sadko Arcade* (at the *ExpoCenter* on Krasnaya Presnya Naberezhnaya; phone: 256-2213). Open from 9 AM to 9 PM. Even more centrally located is the *Irish Store* (19 Novy Arbat Ulitsa, second floor), which has the distinct advantage of carrying goods with labels in English; it's usually crowded — especially on Saturdays. The same management has recently opened a second store, the *Garden Ring Supermarket* (1 Bolshaya Sadovaya; phone: 209-1572), open from 9 AM to 9 PM. Down the street is *Colognia*, a German-Russian venture located in the *Peking* hotel (phone: 209-6561), and stocked with cheeses from almost every region of Europe that has a cow or goat. Open weekdays from 10 AM to 8 PM; weekends 11 AM to 7 PM. In the same neighborhood is the *Lavash* bread co-op (3-6 Bolshaya Sadovaya), offering a great selection of freshly baked flat bread from the Caucasus.

Some other shops — both Western and Russian — of interest in Moscow include the following:

DETSKIY MIR (CHILDREN'S WORLD) Once the Russian version of *Toys 'R' Us,* this one-time kids' emporium has diversified and offers games for children of all ages. Open 8 AM to 8 PM. 5 Teatralniy Proyezd, near the *Bolshoi Theater* and the *Metropol* hotel (phone: 927-2007).

DOM KNIGI (HOUSE OF BOOKS) Beautiful souvenir books about Moscow and Russia and colorful political posters and postcards can be purchased here. Souvenir stamps and some English-language books are available on the second floor. Open from 10 AM to 7 PM; closed Sundays. 26 Novy Arbat Ultisa (phone: 290-4507).

GALERIE DU VIN Moscow's first specialty wine shop, located on an embankment along the Moskva River, within walking distance of the *Radisson Slavyanskaya* hotel. Open weekdays from 2 to 7:30 PM; Saturdays from 10 AM to 7:30 PM. 1-7 Kutuzovskiy Prospekt (entrance is off Tarasa Shevchenko Naberezhnaya; phone: 243-0365 or 243-7256).

GUM Moscow's huge, government-run department store (see *Special Places*). Open daily from 8 AM to 8 PM. 3 Krasnaya Ploshchad (phone: 926-3471).

IZMAILOVSKIY PARK An outdoor weekend art market, it offers a wide range of contemporary paintings by both amateurs and accomplished artists. Arts, crafts, jewelry, antiques, and such timeless favorites as *matryoshka* dolls, lacquered chess sets, boxes, and military garb also are for sale. Be prepared to bargain, beware of forgeries (there seems to be very little control), and bring loads of rubles. Barbecued kebabs and street jazz add to the lively atmosphere here. Open weekends from around 10 AM to 4 PM. 17 Narodniy Prospekt, a 5-minute walk from the Izmailovskiy Park metro station (phone: 166-7909).

MAGASIN GZHEL Hard to find (there's no sign outside) but worth it, this is the best place in Moscow to buy the traditional blue-and-white Gzhel pottery, including dishes, vases, and ornaments, for a fraction of what the hard-currency hotel shops charge. Open Tuesdays through Fridays from 10 AM to 7 PM; Saturdays from 10 AM to 6 PM; closed for lunch between 2 and 3 PM. In a mustard-colored building on the corner of Tverskaya Ulitsa (phone: 200-6478).

MELODIYA As its name suggests, this is the place to buy records of some of those catchy Russian folk songs you've been hearing since you arrived. Open from 9 AM to 9 PM; closed Sundays. 40 Novy Arbat Ulitsa (phone: 291-1421). *Melodiya*'s other branch carries compact discs. 11 Leninskiy Prospekt (phone: 237-4801).

PETROVSKIY PASSAGE Renovated to its pre-revolutionary glory with lots of marble and wrought-iron staircases, this mall near the *Bolshoi Theater* offers everything from Russian souvenirs and fur coats to Japanese cars. One shop, a salon on the ground floor named *Valentin Yudashkin* after its proprietor, has a particularly good selection of creative hats, coats, shoes, and dresses. Shops on the second floor carry a wide assortment of things Western. Open 9 AM to 8 PM; closed Sundays. 10 Petrovka Ulitsa (phone: 921-5777, 921-3117, or 923-2398).

PHILATELIST SHOP A good stop for stamp collectors, if you can get into the front door without being inundated by stamp merchants who are all trying to sell you their grandfather's collection. Open daily from 10 AM to 7 PM. 1 Tara Shevchenko Ulitsa (phone: 243-0162).

PROGRESS Books, many in English, as well as posters. Open from 10 AM to 7 PM, with a lunch break between 2 and 3 PM; closed Sundays and Mondays. 17 Zubovskiy Bulvar (phone: 246-9976).

PTICHY RYNOK (PET MARKET) Russians love animals — the bigger the better — and there is no finer place than this colorful market near Taganka Ploshchad. Locals flock here to admire the many animals — dogs, cats, rabbits, reptiles, and birds are just a few of the species — for sale. The market is open weekdays from 9 AM to 3 PM; weekends from 7 AM to 5 PM. 42A Bolshaya Kalitnikovskaya Ulitsa (no phone).

RUSSKIY SOUVENIR (RUSSIAN SOUVENIR) The best collection of Russian souvenirs under one roof in the entire city. Offered are *matryoshkas*, jewelry, painted metal trays, chess sets, wooden toys, pottery, and huge blue Uzbek platters for under $5. Open from 10 AM to 7 PM, with a lunch break between 2 and 3 PM; closed Sundays. 9 Kutuzovskiy Prospekt (phone: 243-6985).

RUSSKIY UZORY (RUSSIAN PATTERNS) Jewelry and handicrafts made in traditional Russian styles. Open from 10 AM to 7 PM; closed Sundays. 16 Petrovka Ulitsa, near Petrovskiy Passage (phone: 923-3964).

SOVMEHKASTORIA For furs and leather goods, including hats, jackets, and coats, from the lowliest sheepskin to the slinkiest sable. Open from 9 AM to 8 PM, with a lunch break from 2 to 3 PM; closed Sundays. Hard currency only. 14 Bolshaya Dorogomilovskaya Ulitsa (no phone).

TSENTRALNIY RYNOK (CENTRAL MARKET) Flowers and produce are available year-round at this market (including remarkable bargains on saffron and caviar). Farmers from the now-independent southern republics converge here to sell their goods. Open daily from 7 AM to 7 PM. 15 Tsvetnoy Bulvar (phone: 923-8687).

TSUM Another big department store, near Red Square and about a mile from *GUM*. Amid the kitsch is an occasional gem, perhaps a piece of amber or a fur hat, or a rug from Central Asia. Open 8 AM to 9 PM; closed Sundays. 2 Petrovka Ulitsa (phone: 292-7600).

YANTAR (AMBER) Wide assortment of jewelry. Open from 10 AM to 7 PM; closed Sundays. 14 Gruzinskiy Val (phone: 252-4430).

ZWEMMER BOOKS Moscow's first English-language bookstore, selling Russian art and travel books, as well as novels and thrillers for those long train rides. Open 10 AM to 7 PM; closed Sundays. Hard currency only. Kuznetskiy Most (phone: 928-2021).

SPORTS AND FITNESS

Muscovites are avid sports fans, particularly of ice hockey, soccer, and horse racing. Attending such events is a good way to see Russian citizens at leisure. Schedules and tickets are available through your hotel service bureau. The *Olimpiyskiy Sportivniy* (Olympic Sports Complex; 16 Olimpiyskiy Prospekt; phone: 288-5663), which was built for the *1980 Olympic Games,* includes the *Olimpiyskiy Stadion* (Olympic Stadium), the largest indoor stadium in Europe and the site of numerous soccer matches.

There is also a major sports facility in Luzhniki Park, across the Moskva River from Moscow State University. The *Tsentralniy Stadion Luzhniki* (Luzhniki Central Stadium; 24 Luzhnikovskaya Naberezhnaya; phone: 201-0155 or 201-0995) seats 103,000 people and is used for soccer matches and track and field meets, international competitions, and occasionally for rock concerts. Several Western hotels now have fitness clubs; the one in the *Radisson Slavyanskaya* hotel (phone: 941-8031) also sells memberships to non-guests.

After exercising, or even if you don't, there is nothing more Russian than relaxing in a *banya*, or sauna. Moscow boasts several, the best known being the *Tsentralnaya Banya* (3 Teatralnaya Proyezd), which is open from 8 AM to 8 PM; closed Mondays. Bring your own towel and toiletries.

FOOTBALL Gridiron rivalry has hit the Moscow sports scene. Already on the lineup are American-style football teams including the *Russian Czars,* the *Siberian Devils,* and the *Moscow Mustangs.* The season runs through the dead of winter, but, fortunately, games are played in an indoor sports complex. Though some of the coaches are American, all the players are Russian. This year the second annual *Kremlin Bowl* will be played in December at *Olympic Stadium.* For further information, contact the US Embassy for tickets and schedule information (phone: 252-2451), or your hotel service bureau.

GOLF The Swedish-built *Tumba Golf Club* (1 Dovzhenko Ulitsa; phone: 147-6254) is located in the Lenin Hills near *Tsentralniy Stadion Luzhniki* and Moscow State University. The 9-hole course is open to the public. The club also has a restaurant featuring continental fare. Another choice is the *Park* hotel's 18-hole Robert Trent Jones, Jr., course at Nahabino, 19½ miles (31 km) west of the Kremlin (see *Checking In*).

HORSE RACING Harness and thoroughbred racing with low-stake pari-mutuel betting takes place each Sunday at 1 PM, as well as on Wednesdays and

Fridays at 6 PM at the *Hippodrome* racecourse (22 Begovaya Ulitsa; phone: 945-4516). At the *Ramenskiy Hippodrome* (phone: 8-246-36489 or 8-246-30331; about 31 miles/50 km from Moscow on Kazanskoe Shosse), there are races on Saturdays at 1 PM. In winter, exciting *troika* races are held on the snow or ice.

ICE HOCKEY The most popular ice hockey teams in Moscow are *Spartak, Dynamo,* and *CSKA.* Ticket and schedule information is available from your hotel service bureau.

SOCCER This sport is a passion with many Muscovites. The *Dynamo Stadium* (36 Leningradskiy Prospekt; phone: 212-7092 or 212-2252) holds 60,000 people and was built for one of Moscow's powerhouse teams, but the main events are held at the *Tsentralniy Stadion Luzhniki.*

SWIMMING The water in the *Otkryty Baseyn "Moskva"* (Moscow Open-Air Swimming Pool; 37 Prechistenka Naberezhnaya; phone: 202-4725) is heated so the pool can be used all year. In winter, when the steam gathers over the pool, it may look like something from Dante's *Inferno,* but this steam layer protects the swimmers from the cold. Open from 7 AM to 9 PM. Swimming competitions take place at the *Dvoretz Vodnikh Sportov* (Palace of Water Sports; 27 Mironovskaya; phone: 369-2925). Several hotels also have swimming pools, such as the *Cosmos* hotel (150 Mira Prospekt; phone: 217-0785/6).

TENNIS Court space is available at *Druzhba Hall* (phone: 246-5515), located next to the *Luzhniki Central Stadium.*

THEATER

Your hotel service bureau can provide schedules and tickets, but don't expect to get tickets for popular events, such as the ballet, unless you book well ahead of time. Also check the *Moscow Times* for theater listings or the *IPS Theater Box Office* in the *Metropol* hotel (phone: 927-6729 or 927-6728). Open weekdays from 11 AM to 7 PM; weekends from 10 AM to 3 PM. Here are some Moscow venues that rate our applause:

CURTAIN CALLS

Bolshoi The *Bolshoi* dance tradition goes back to the mid-19th century. Highpoints of its history include the early 20th century, when it was revitalized by Alexander Gorsky; the 1930s, when Igor Moiseyev experimented with folk-dance ballets; and after World War II, the company danced to such works as Sergei Prokofiev's *Cinderella* and *The Stone Flower.* The company is based at the magnificent *Bolshoi Theater,* one of several imperial-style buildings built after Alexander I established a special commission to reconstruct Moscow in 1825. All crystal chandeliers, red plush, and ornate gold, just being here is a big part of the pleasure of a night at the ballet. Though the *Bolshoi* has lapsed into a financial crisis since the demise of the USSR, this great Russian cultural institution is now under the personal jurisdiction of Russian President Boris Yeltsin while it considers finding private sponsors. The *Bolshoi* ballet company also performs at the 6,000-seat *Palace of Congresses Theater,* inside the Kremlin complex. Book ahead as far as possible. Note: A scheduled 3-year refurbishment of the theater is set to begin in 1997. *Bolshoi Theater,* 8-2 Teatralnaya Ploshchad (phone: 292-9986); *Palaces of Congresses Theater,* The Kremlin (phone: 227-8263).

Moskovskiy Tsirk (Moscow Circus) Long renowned for its breathtaking aerial feats, nimble acrobats, special animal acts (bears on bicycles and roller skates, and the like), and spectacular finales, in recent years the circus has added more contemporary elements, including modern dance numbers and dazzling light shows. But this circus is perhaps best loved for its clowns. Central to the entire evening, the master clown is seen between each act, filling time with silly skits and riotous routines. Even the most skeptical adults can't help but be amused (and occasionally amazed) by a night at the circus. Performances start at 7 PM. 7 Vernadskovo Prospekt (phone: 930-2815). There also is a circus at 13 Tsvetnoi Bulvar (phone: 200-0668). To book tickets, call the State Foreign Tourist Office's special number (phone: 203-7581).

Moskovskiy Teatr Dramy i Komedy (Moscow Drama and Comedy Theater) Also known as *Taganka,* this is Russia's most famous experimental theater. Tickets for musical and dramatic performances are difficult to come by, so try to order in advance through your travel agent. Upstairs, the *Taganka Café* serves light suppers, champagne, and beer. 76 Zemlyanoy Ulitsa (phone: 272-6300).

On Teatralnaya Ploshchad (formerly Sverdlova Ploshchad) is the *Maly Teatr* (Small Theater; 1-6 Teatralnaya Ploshchad; phone: 923-2621), which stages Russian classics; and the *Tsentralniy Detskiy Teatr* (Central Children's Theater; 2-7 Teatralnaya Ploshchad; phone: 292-0069), which often presents such children's classics as *Pushkin Tales.*

One of the oldest and most famous theaters in Russia is the *MKAT* (pronounced *Mkhut*), an acronym for *Moscovskiy Khudozhestvenniy Academicheskiy Teatr* (Moscow Art and Academic Theater; 3 Kamergerskiy Pereulok; phone: 229-8760), which features classical and modern dramas. The *Muzykalniy Academicheskiy Teatr imeni Stanislavskovo i Nemirovitcha-Danchenko* (Stanislavsky and Nemirovich-Danchenko Academic Musical Theater; 17 Pushkinskaya Ploshchad; phone: 229-0649) is reviving the pre-revolutionary Russian appetite for satirical theater while also hosting regular musical performances and ballet. The *Tsyganskiy Teatr "Romen"* (Gypsy Roman Theater; 32-2 Leningradskiy Prospekt; phone: 250-7334) is the only one of its kind in Russia. It features plays about the lives of Gypsies and their folk music; Shakespeare also is performed here. Marionettes are featured at the *Teatr Studio Marionette*

(Theater-Studio Marionette; 37 Starokonushennaya Pereulok; phone: 202-2483) and puppets at the *Gosudarstvenniy Tsentralniy Kulolniy Teatr* (State Central Puppet Theater; 3 Sadovaya-Samotechnaya Ulitsa; phone: 299-3310). Finally, Moscow's famed pre-revolutionary cabaret theater, *Lietutchaya Mysh* (The Bat; 10 Bolshoi Gnezdikovskiy Pereulok; phone: 229-7087) — which reopened in 1990 after a 69-year hiatus — once again is delighting cabaret lovers with its irreverent, bawdy performances.

MUSIC

Ticket and schedule information is available from your hotel service bureau. The three most important concert halls in Moscow are the *Moskovskiy Gosudarstvennaya Konservatoriya* (Moscow State Conservatory; 13 Gertzenaya Ulitsa; phone: 229-7412 for information, 229-8183 for reservations); the *Konsertniy Zal imeni Tchaikovskovo* (Tchaikovsky Concert Hall; Mayakovskiy Ploshchad; phone: 299-3681); and the *Kolonniy Zal* (Hall of Columns) in the Trade Union House (1 Pushkinskaya Ulitsa; phone: 292-0178 for information, 292-0956 for reservations). Opera is performed at the *Bolshoi Theater* and the *Stanislavsky and Nemirovich-Danchenko Academic Musical Theater* (see *Theater*).

NIGHTCLUBS AND NIGHTLIFE

The city offers a rich assortment of evening entertainment: theater, opera, the circus, ballet, musical and sports events. Many Muscovites, looking for a night out, book a table at a restaurant with a risqué floor show such as the *Dehli* (23 Bolshaya Presnenskaya Ulitsa), *Skazka,* or *Tsentralniy* (see *Eating Out*).

If you want to see Moscow's well-to-do at play, drop by *Night Flight* (17 Tverskaya Ulitsa; phone: 229-4165), a Swedish-owned club with 2 floors, 3 bars with the latest hits on the sound system, and plenty of dancing. The club, which would be right at home in New York or Paris, draws the type of crowd that can afford the $15 cover charge. Open from 9 PM to 5 AM. The *Metropol*'s *Night Show* nightclub (Neglinnaya Ulitsa entrance of the hotel, across from the *Detskiy Mir* store; phone: 927-6738) is a little classier but a lot more expensive. Open 10 PM to 4 AM.

Casinos are very popular, but again you'd be better off playing at your hotel. The *Savoy* hotel opened the first casino in the Soviet Union. Its 3 tables — 2 for blackjack and 1 for roulette — are open from 8 PM to 4 AM. Gamblers at the *Casino Royale* (at the *Hippodrome* racecourse, 22 Begovaya Ulitsa; phone: 945-1410) have their choice of blackjack, roulette, poker, slot machines, and *punto banco* (Spanish baccarat). All gambling is in US dollars. The casino offers free transportation from major hotels.

Best in Town

CHECKING IN

Hotel accommodations in Moscow, which can be booked directly or through numerous travel agencies, come in two varieties — Western or

Soviet. Western hotels, while still partly owned by Russian or Moscow government agencies, are operated by the major hotel chains, such as Penta, Radisson, and Inter-Continental.

Also on the Moscow accommodations scene are several bed and breakfast establishments, which offer foreigners rooms with private baths, and opportunities to experience life with a Russian families. Contact *IBV Bed & Breakfast Systems* (13113 Ideal Dr., Silver Spring, MD; phone: 301-942-3770; fax: 301-933-1124) or *ITS Tours & Travel* (1055 Texas Ave., Suite 104, College Station, TX 77840; phone: 409-764-9400 or 800-533-8688; fax: 409-693-9673). At *ITS* properties, at least one member of the host family is English-speaking. The company also arranges for rentals of furnished apartments, for those visitors on extended stays. In addition, *American-Russian Homestays* (15115 W. Penn St., Iowa City, IA 52240; phone: 319-626-2125) arranges stays with Russian families in Moscow and in several other Russian cities. *Room With the Russians* arranges home stays, an airport greeting, car ride to your host's home, and a guarantee that at least one member of the host family speaks English. Some families provide evening meals as well as breakfast. The company has a London office (phone: 44-81-472-2694; fax: 44-81-964-0272).

Accommodations in Moscow hotels usually are available in three classes: first class double rooms, deluxe 2-room suites, and deluxe 3-room suites. A few hotels also have spacious super-deluxe suites — usually with 2 floors. The dramatically fluctuating Russian economy makes it difficult to provide accurate rates for hotels. Foreigners must pay for hotels in US dollars (occasionally German marks), but the Russian government periodically threatens to make the ruble the only legal tender in the country. Be sure to check the exchange rate immediately prior to your departure. Be aware, too, the Russian government has imposed a 20% sales tax on rooms, so check in advance to see whether or not that has been included in the price you are quoted. Many hotels include breakfast in the cost. Most take major credit cards, but you should confirm that in advance. Most of Moscow's major hotels have complete facilities for the business traveler. Those hotels listed below as having "business services" usually offer such conveniences as English-speaking concierge, meeting rooms, photocopiers, computers, translation services, and express checkout, among others. Call the hotel for additional information. All telephone numbers are in the 095 city code unless otherwise indicated.

For an unforgettable Moscow experience, we begin with our favorites, followed by our cost and quality choices of hotels.

SPECIAL HAVENS

Metropol Completely restored and renovated by *Intourist* and now managed by Inter-Continental hotels, this Moscow grande dame is close to the *Bolshoi* and *Maly* theaters. The façade of the turn-of-the-century building is decorated with a marvelous majolica relief that reproduces artist Mikhail Vrubel's *Dream Princess.* There are 403 rooms, including 35 suites, many of which are decorated with antique and period furniture. All the guestrooms have TV sets, mini-bars, air conditioning, radios, and computer hook-up capabilities. There are 3 restaurants, including the *Metropol Room* (where Lenin made spirited speeches and where portions of *Doctor Zhivago* were filmed) and the *Boyarskiy Zal* (see *Eating Out* for both); 4 bars; a coffee shop; and, during the warm weather months, a friendly outdoor café. The health club has a swimming pool, fitness room, and saunas. Business services. 1-4 Teatralniy Proyezd (phone: 927-6096; 800-327-0200 in the US; fax: 975-2355).

Savoy Moscow's first real nod toward Western-style luxury was this renovation of the former *Berlin* hotel, just a 5-minute walk from the Kremlin. There are 86 guestrooms with tiled baths, mini-bars, and TV sets. Also here are the first gambling casino to open in the former USSR, several designer shops, an art salon, and car rental facilities. The luxurious dining room is one of the best places in town to enjoy an elegantly presented meal of Russian, Scandinavian, or international fare (see *Eating Out*). (The surest way of obtaining a hard-to-get room reservation is to fly into Moscow via *Finnair,* which runs the hotel). Business services. The hotel now has a weekend vacation center outside Moscow at Voskresenskoye, where you can go sleighing, skiing, and skating in the winter, and top off the day with a Russian sauna. The hotel also arranges yacht cruises from May to September. 3 Rozhdestvenka Ulitsa (phone: 230-2625; fax: 230-2186).

DELUXE

Aerostar Recently opened, and one of Moscow's choice locations, it has 417 well-appointed rooms, in addition to a fully equipped fitness center. The *Borodino* restaurant features live lobster from Nova Scotia, while the more casual *Café Taiga* serves buffet breakfast along with daily crustacean specials. Business services. On the road to the international airport. 37 Leningradskiy Prospekt (phone: 155-5030; fax: 200-3286).

Baltschug It has taken 3 years and $80 million to renovate this yellow-and-cream–colored building, once the old *Bucharest* hotel. Located across the river from the Kremlin and St. Basil's, the view is great — especially from the hotel's eighth-floor *Mansard Bar*. The best of the 234 rooms (including 24 suites) are located in the "round tower" overlooking the river and facing the Kremlin. Other amenities include international direct dialing from each room; shops; a hairdresser; laundry and cleaning services; plus a swimming pool, sauna, solarium, whirlpool, and fitness studio. There's even a library on the top floor with 2,500 books in English, German, and Russian. On site are 2 restaurants, a bistro, and a nightclub in the basement that stays open until 3 AM. Business services. 1 Baltschug Ulitsa (phone: 230-6500; 800-426-3135 in the US; fax: 230-6502).

Cosmos Originally built for the *Olympics,* this huge property has 1,777 simple but comfortable rooms, including 53 two-room suites and 6 four-room suites. The 26-story hotel is an entire community in itself, with 4 restaurants, 2 bars, a sauna, a swimming pool, art and fur salons, and a car rental counter. It is near the *VDNKh* (the USSR Exhibition of Economic Achievements), which is rather far from the city center. Business services. 150 Mira Prospekt (phone: 217-0785; fax: 288-9551).

Intourist Built more than 20 years ago, this 22-story high-rise is just a short walk from Red Square. Though lacking the charm of some of Moscow's renovated older hotels, the 443 rooms are quite comfortable. There are 5 restaurants, 2 cafés, a nightclub, shops, a casino, and an art salon. On the third floor, there is a tasting room where you can sample Armenian wines and cognacs. Business services. 3-5 Tverskaya Ulitsa (phone: 203-4008; fax: 203-9475).

Novotel Sheremetyevo Located next to the international airport, this 488-room property (including 5 rooms for disabled guests) is the newest member of Europe's largest hotel chain. The *Efimoff* restaurant features fine local and international fare. Business services. At the Sheremetyevo Airport, 35 miles from downtown Moscow; free airport shuttle service (phone: 578-9401; fax: 578-2794).

Olympic Penta Recently opened, this joint venture of *Intourservice* and the Penta group has 500 rooms, including 10 suites; all have international direct-dial phones, satellite TV, and mini-bars. The 12-story establishment also offers a sauna, swimming pool, solarium, gym, and car rental office. There also are 2 restaurants;, a brasserie; and an authentic German beer hall, *Die Bierstube,* which serves draft beer and pub food. *The Bakery* offers freshly baked cakes, pastries, and croissants daily from 8 AM to 8 PM. Business services. 18 Olympiyskiy Prospekt (phone: 971-6101 or 971-6301; 800-225-3456 in the US; fax: 230-2597).

Palace Opened last year, this is a joint venture between the Austrian–Marco Polo group and the Russian Academy of Sciences, which once owned the building. There are 199 guestrooms and 22 suites (including a 2-story presidential suite decorated in an Art Nouveau style complete with gold-plated bath fixtures), 3 restaurants (including the *Anchor* seafood restaurant), and a health club. Business services. 19 Tverskaya Ulitsa (phone: 951-3152; fax: 931-3151).

Park To escape from the city bustle, locals and foreign travelers alike stay at this hotel set in forested grounds at Nahabino, about 19 miles (31 km) west of the Kremlin. Along with a boat pond, the 4-story property offers 85 rooms, a restaurant serving Russian fare, a bar, a billiard room, a sauna, massage facilities, and a hair salon. The hotel's new 18-hole Robert Trent

Jones, Jr. golf course is located nearby. Business services. 1 Nahabino (phone: 563-0598 or 561-2975; fax: 563-3456).

Pullman Iris Overlooking a beautiful atrium, this very comfortable property offers 155 rooms and 40 suites (including a presidential suite). There is a French restaurant (the *Champs-Elysées*), a coffee shop, and a bar. Other amenities include a fitness club, a swimming pool, a sauna, laundry and dry cleaning services, safety-deposit boxes, a beauty salon, and shops. Business services. 10 Korovinskoe Shosse (phone: 488-8000; fax: 906-0105).

Radisson Slavyanskaya On the banks of the Moskva River, this is Russia's first American-managed hotel, a joint venture of Radisson Hotels International, Americom International Corporation, and *Intourservice*. There are 430 rooms, 4 restaurants, a health club, a swimming pool, a car rental office, and shops. The furniture is spare but functional; the rooms are a good size. Business services. The *American Business Center,* which is open daily round the clock, is located on the second floor. 2 Berezhkovskaya Naberezhnaya (phone: 941-8020; 800-333-3333 in the US; fax: 240-6915).

FIRST CLASS

Mezhdunarodnaya I and II Known locally as the *Mezh*, this hotel attracts business travelers. Offered here are 540 rooms, 5 restaurants (serving Russian, continental, and Japanese food), 3 bars, an English pub, saunas, a swimming pool, a bowling alley, a variety of shops, and a car rental counter. Business services. 12 Krasnopresnenskaya Naberezhnaya (phone: 253-1316 or 253-6303; fax: 253-1071 or 253-1072).

Rossiya Near St. Basil's Cathedral, this is Europe's largest hotel, with 3,090 rooms capable of accommodating 6,000 guests. It is so large that it has four separate wings, each with its own entrance and dining facility. On the top floor of the 21-story tower wing (room rates are higher here than elsewhere in the hotel), the *Rossiya* restaurant provides a great view of the Kremlin and Red Square. The south wing has its own 3,000-seat concert hall and 2 cinemas. Business services. 6 Varvarka Ulitsa (phone: 298-5402; fax: 298-5541).

Ukraina One of the seven look-alike skyscrapers built during the late Stalinist period (Moscow State University is the largest), this city-owned property is on the banks of the Moskva, not far from the city center. It offers 1,009 rooms, 5 restaurants, 2 art galleries, several hard-currency shops, and a hair salon and barbershop. Business services. The lobby, which includes the service bureau, was under renovation at press time. Kutuzovskiy Prospekt (phone: 243-2388; fax: 243-2896).

EATING OUT

The number of restaurants offering good meals for hard currency (and in a few cases, rubles) has exploded since the collapse of the Soviet Union.

Japanese, French, Italian, Greek, and American restaurants are overtaking the purveyors of good old-fashioned Russian fare in places where surly service alienated visitors. Happily, there still are many hotel restaurants and other establishments that offer hearty Russian cuisine or the exotic, spicy fare of Georgia and the other former Soviet republics.

With the opening of new dining places and the quality of their cuisine as unstable as the ruble, it is advisable to check with your hotel service bureau or with friends or contacts before you go. Also be sure to find out whether payment is in rubles or hard currency, cash, or credit card.

Most Western-run hotels now offer modern dining rooms serving European or American fare, English-language menus, and English-speaking staff. Compared to Western standards, prices are often on the high side. Most traditional Russian restaurants offer prix fixe meals that usually include an assortment of appetizers, an entrée, dessert, vodka, champagne, and coffee, as well as music, dancing, and a show.

And Russian restaurants have another claim to fame: huge portions of black caviar (*chornaya ikra*), served with sour cream and pancakes called *blinis*, or large bowls of dark bread and butter, for less money than you would pay at Western-run dining spots. If you like vegetables, you'll be disappointed; even in summer, vegetables are puny compared to those available in the West. In fact, it won't take long to figure out that Moscow can truly be called "Cholesterol City," with fatty sausages, salami, sour cream, butter, and eggs on menus in the better hotels — and that's just for breakfast.

The dramatically fluctuating Russian economy makes it difficult to provide accurate prices for restaurants; we suggest that you check costs — and the operative exchange rate — immediately prior to your departure. It may be difficult to make a reservation at a Russian restaurant on your own, unless you speak some Russian. But your hotel service bureau can make the arrangements for you, and a pre-set meal can be waiting for you on your arrival. This arrangement will almost certainly mean that you will have to pay in hard currency instead of rubles, but it will eliminate any problems in ordering. Be sure to find out in advance whether your bill will be in rubles or dollars. Some restaurants do accept major credit cards. Many restaurants charge rubles to Russians and to those who know how to ask, but they are quite happy to accept dollars from foreigners for the exact same meal — and in some cases insist on it. All telephone numbers are in the 095 city code unless otherwise noted.

For an unforgettable dining experience, we begin with our culinary favorites, followed by our quality choices.

DELIGHTFUL DINING

Aragvi With its marble walls and murals, this is an oasis of luxury in a politically changed city. The bustling dining room — usually crowded with latter-day commissars, foreign journalists, ballerinas, and diplomats — does a booming business in caviar (*ikra* in Russian) and icy vodka. The dinner menu features Georgian fare, and the best dishes are hot and spicy — try the *tsiplyata tabaka* (roast chicken pressed between scalding stones) or the *shashlik po kharski* (skewered roast Georgian mutton). Sturgeon roasted on a spit is also excellent. The band plays folk music every night. Open from 11 AM to 11 PM. Reservations necessary. You can pay in rubles. Major credit cards accepted. 6 Tverskaya Ulitsa (phone: 229-3762).

Skazka The name means "fairy tale," and if good eating plus extravagant entertainment is what you're after, this is the spot. The atmosphere is warm, candlelit, and very Russian, and the acts range from performing cossacks to Gypsies to jazz musicians. *Zakuski* (cold appetizers that include herring, cold meat, tomatoes, deviled eggs, caviar, and a variety of vegetable salads) or single menu items are available. The *pelemeni* (a Siberian dish of dumplings filled with meat and floating in sour cream) is excellent here. Also recommended is boar cooked in wine, *veal perestroika* (marinated veal that is then cooked on a spit), and *pozharskiy cutlet* (slices of veal and chicken stuffed with butter). Be sure to save room for some homemade pastries. The entertainment ranges from Gypsy dancers, acrobats, and jazz musicians, to an accordionist accompanied by a musician playing spoons. Notice the thank-you note on the wall from former US Secretary of State George Schultz, who dined here in 1988. There's also an art gallery with works for sale. Open from noon to 5 PM and from 7 PM to midnight. Reservations advised. Rubles only for food; hard currency and major credit cards only for wine and hard liquor. 1 Tovarishchevskiy Pereulok (phone: 271-0998).

Alexander Blok A British-managed restaurant aboard a boat moored by the *Mezh* hotel, it offers Greek and continental fare. On the menu are Greek favorites — *moussaka* and *tiropita* (small triangles of filo pastry stuffed with feta cheese), *baklava*, and Greek coffee. There's a casino next door. Open from 7:30 to 10:30 AM; 12:30 to 3:30 PM; and 7 PM to midnight. 12 Krasnopresnenskaya Naberezhnaya (phone: 255-9284).

Arleccino A Russian-Italian venture, this upscale eatery decorated in pink and black offers a menu of good Italian dishes, including *medalyoniy telyachiy po-milanski* (fried veal medallions served with spaghetti, grated cheese, and tomato sauce), *spaghetti nizza* (spaghetti with tomato sauce), and *salat Arleccino* (greens with olive oil). The risottos are also respectable. A variety show is featured on weekend evenings. Open from noon to 3 PM and from 7 PM to midnight. Reservations advised. Major credit cards accepted. 15 Druzhinnikovskaya Ulitsa (phone: 205-7088).

Atrium A small dining establishment with a marble-columned decor reminiscent of 16th-century Rome, this cooperative specializes in Russian and continental fare. Fish eaters will enjoy the *sudak po-monastyrsky* (a pike dish);

the veal with prunes is also good. Open from noon to 4 PM and from 6 to 10 PM. Reservations advised. 44 Bolshaya Kaluzhskaya Ulitsa, just off Leninskiy Prospekt (phone: 137-3008).

Boyarskiy Zal If money is no object, this elegant dining room in the *Metropol* hotel is the place to go. An enormous stuffed bear greets guests at the entrance and a 5-piece Russian folk instrumental group serenades from the balcony, all setting an appropriately Russian tone for the traditional fare served here — *pelemeni* (meat-stuffed dumplings), *piroshki* (small meat-filled turnovers) with vintage brandy sauce, or beef Stroganoff. The bad news is that the food is a bit bland and disappointing considering the steep prices. Open Mondays through Saturdays for dinner. Reservations necessary. *Metropol Hotel,* 4 Teatralniy Proyezd (phone: 927-6452 or 927-6000).

Café Kolkhida A short walk from the *Tchaikovsky Concert Hall* and across the street from the *Puppet Theater,* this unpretentious cooperative is decorated in red and black, with crystal chandeliers and wall sconces. Live music is performed, and Georgian food is the specialty. Try the *kharcho* (spicy tomato soup with meat), *lobio krasniy* (peppery kidney bean salad), or the *satsivi* (chicken with nuts and a variety of spices). Bring your own bottle. Open from noon to 11 PM. Reservations advised. 6 Sadovaya-Samotechnaya (phone: 299-6757 or 299-3111).

Café Margarita Smack in the middle of the Margarita section of Moscow, the setting for Mikhail Bulgakov's monumental novel, *The Master and Margarita,* this little café on the corner has long been the haunt of Moscow's arty, trendy types. Patriarch's Pond, where the memorable opening scenes of the book take place, is across the street. A perfect place for coffee and homemade pastry or, if something more substantial is required, try the mushroom *plov* (pilaf). Open noon to 10 PM. No reservations (but if it's crowded and the doorman opens the door a crack and leers, try babbling a bit in English — he may let you in). 28 Malaya Bronnaya Ulitsa (phone: 299-6534).

Café Ordynka Excellent Russian pork and potato dishes in a comfortable tavern atmosphere. Occasionally such exotica as crayfish is served. All the entrées are artfully presented, and the *pelmeni Siberskiy* (a dumpling filled with spicy meat topped with a garlic and chive cream sauce) is perhaps the best version of this traditional dish in town. Prices are unusually inexpensive, and the service is topnotch, even by Western standards. Reservations advised. Rubles only for food; hard currency only for wine and hard liquor. Major credit cards accepted. 71 Bolshaya Ordynka Ulitsa (phone: 237-9905).

Café Sorok Chetiyre Customers like to linger at this comfortable little eatery serving continental fare and featuring live music most nights. The crowd is composed of Russian yuppies and foreign businesspeople. Try the

Govyadina 44 (the café's special beef dish) and finish up with some of the best Turkish coffee in town. Open from 11 AM to 11 PM. Reservations advised. 44 Leningradskiy Prospekt (phone: 248-4438 or 159-9951).

Café Taiga Fresh lobster flown in live from Nova Scotia is served in this restaurant in the *Aerostar* hotel. There are vodka and caviar happy hours daily, as well as champagne brunches on Sundays. Open daily. Reservations advised. Major credit cards accepted (phone: 155-5030, ext. 2428).

Café Viru A rather youngish crowd frequents this Estonian café, which primarily serves sandwiches, salads (caviar is usually available), cakes, ice cream, coffee, and cognac. A short walk from the Prechistenka metro stop, this is the ideal lunch spot for those who aren't conversant in Russian, since ordering requires only feverish pointing at the sample dishes. Open from noon to midnight. Reservations unnecessary. 50 Ostozhenka Ulitsa (phone: 246-6107).

Le Chalet Moscow's only Swiss restaurant, located at the *Chaika Tennis Club* on the Moskva River (although there are no river views). The menu features beef or cheese fondue, raclette, Caesar salad, carpaccio, and steak tartare. There is also an extensive, and expensive, wine list. The management provides free transportation to and from your hotel. Open from noon to whenever customers want to go home (its a good after-theater choice). Reservations necessary. Major credit cards accepted. 1-2 Korobeynikov Pereulok, on the corner of Prechistenka Ulitsa, near the Krimsky Bridge (phone: 202-0106).

Delhi Even though the lady with the snake (who used to provide the entertainment) is gone, this still can be a fun place to dine. The Indian dishes are appropriately spicy, and even if the restaurant runs out of Indian staples, like yogurt, it doesn't seem to matter much. The waiters are elegantly dressed in Nehru jackets, and the bar stocks a wide range of liquors and liqueurs. Reservations necessary. There are separate hard-currency and ruble rooms. 23B Krasnopresnenskaya Naberezhnaya (phone: 255-0492).

The Exchange The *Radisson Slavyanskaya* hotel's new steakhouse has a menu that will capture the hearts and appetites of those who can't live without beef. This is the place for prime ribs, filet mignon, sirloin for two, or a whopping porterhouse. Other touches of Americana such as iceberg lettuce and baked potatoes are served in an elegant atmosphere. Open from 11:30 AM to 11 PM. Reservations advised. Major credit cards accepted. In the *Radisson Slavyanskaya Hotel,* 2 Berezhkovskaya Naberezhnaya (phone: 941-8333 or 941-8020, ext. 3269).

Glazur An intimate dining spot featuring live jazz, this Russian-Danish joint venture specializes in seafood, including shrimp, salmon, and herring. The food is lovingly prepared and delicious. The list of international wines is also impressive. Open from noon to midnight. Reservations advised.

Major credit cards only accepted. 12-19 Smolenskiy Bulvar (phone: 248-4438).

Iberia Delicious Georgian food served in a cozy, candlelit restaurant near the *Savoy* hotel. Artwork (which is for sale) decorates the walls, and a piano player and wandering violinist provide the entertainment. Menu choices include *lobio* (marinated bean salad) and *khachapuri* (cheese-filled bread); don't try the chicken intestines unless you're an adventurous diner. Open noon to 5 PM and 6 to 11 PM. Reservations necessary. Rubles only for food; hard currency only for wine and hard liquor. 5-7 Rozhdestvenka Ulitsa (phone: 928-2672).

Imperial Regal touches, such as the double-headed eagle, a symbol of czarist Russia, accent this recently renovated dining spot in Moscow's historic Margarita section. Diners sit at tables surrounding a fountain, and partake of good Russian fare — meat Romanoff (veal cooked with cheese and tomatoes), beef Stroganoff, mutton Zhivago (mutton with mushrooms), and chicken filet Potemkin (chicken cutlets). The house specialty is the Czar's Plate — pork, chicken, and veal with vegetables and potatoes — that serves four. A pianist or violinist provides background music. Open from noon until 11 PM. Reservations necessary. The management also offers free transportation to and from your hotel. 1-2 Korobeynikov Pereulok, on the corner of Prechistenka Ulitsa, near the Krimskiy Bridge (phone: 202-0106).

Kropotkinskaya 36 Opened in 1986, this Russian-Spanish venture is both the first and one of the best of the cooperative restaurants. The Russian food is good — try the caviar, *blinis,* special salads, and sturgeon. The upstairs dining room is elegant and formal; downstairs is cozier, with strolling violinists. Open daily from noon to midnight. Reservations necessary. 36 Prechistenka (formerly Kropotkinskaya) Ulitsa (phone: 201-7500).

Lazaniya For respectable Italian food, this comfortable restaurant just across the river from the Kremlin is the place to go. The cooperative's menu features over 50 items, including its namesake, lasagna. During the warm months, there is outdoor seating amid the beauty of this ancient neighborhood. Open from noon to 5 PM and from 7 to 10 PM. Reservations advised. 40 Pyatnitskaya Ulitsa (phone: 231-1085).

Livan Exquisite Lebanese food served in a dining room within a state-run restaurant called *Baku.* You can make an entire meal of the appetizers — several kinds of hummus; tabbouleh; pastries stuffed with meat, cheese, or spinach. It's a good idea, however, to save room for delicious cakes or *baklava.* Reservations advised. Major credit cards accepted. 24 Tverskaya Ulitsa (phone: 299-8506).

Manila Continental and — what else? — Philippine fare are served in this cozy, peach-colored dining room. The menu offers a wide variety of à la carte items, including sizzling shrimp and good sweet and sour pork. Begin with a daiquiri at the bar. Open from noon to 11 PM. Reservations necessary. 81 Vavilova Ulitsa (phone: 132-0055).

McDonald's Russians and foreign travelers alike have gotten their fill of *Big Moks, kartofel* (French fries), and *kokteyli* (milk shakes), since the first of several planned franchises opened its doors in Moscow in early 1990. The grill and 29 computerized cash registers are manned by Russian employees who wait on customers at what was briefly the world's largest branch (it's been eclipsed by the one in Beijing, China), with seating for 700. Go early to avoid the lines (during the warm-weather months the wait can be as long as an hour). It's the only eatery in town with a no-smoking policy. Two more locations have opened: one seats only 35 and is located on the ground floor of the new 12-story McDonald's Building on the corner of Tverskaya Ulitsa and Ogareva Ulitsa, across from the Central Post Office. The newest outlet is a 500-seater located near the Kremlin. Open from 10 AM to 10 PM. Rubles only, but they will deliver for hard currency between 10 AM and 10 PM. Reservations unnecessary. In Pushkinskya Ploshchad (phone: 200-0590 or 200-1655).

Metropol Room Lenin once made post-revolutionary speeches to party members in this lavish dining room, with its stunning stained glass ceiling. (It was re-created for some scenes in the film *Doctor Zhivago.*) Today it is the site of what is probably the best brunch in Moscow. The buffet includes eggs florentine and benedict, smoked salmon, caviar, sausages, stuffed tomatoes, brie, fruit, champagne, and more. Take a few minutes just to stand in awe of this spread — most Russians would faint if they saw it. The feasting is accompanied by a seven-piece jazz band. Open daily for breakfast and lunch; brunch on Sundays only. Reservations advised. *Metropol Hotel,* 4 Teatralniy Proyezd (phone: 927-6452 or 927-6000).

Peking If you suddenly get the urge for Chinese food, this is where Chinese diplomats and journalists in Moscow eat. About 70 different dishes are prepared by Chinese cooks at this 600-seat Russian-Chinese venture. German beer also is available, and there is music and dancing at night. The barbecued bean curd is very hot and covered with dry spices, and the dry-fried chicken strips with lemon and five-spice marinade is also very good. Open from noon to 11 PM. Reservations advised. There are two dining rooms here — one accepts rubles; the other, hard currency. 1 Sadovaya Bolshaya (phone: 209-1865).

Pescatore A favorite of the expatriate community, this Italian restaurant features a wide selection of pasta dishes (including penne with vodka), veal, and rabbit, but as the name suggests, the emphasis is on seafood. Skip the lobster fettuccine and concentrate on the fish and prawns. White wines are moderately priced (by Moscow standards), but other wines are quite expensive. Though there is an English-language menu, the staff speaks only

Russian and a smattering of Italian — don't worry, just point. Open daily for lunch and dinner. Reservations necessary. Major credit cards only accepted. Located across the street from the *Savoy Hotel*, 7-5 Pushechnaya Ulitsa (phone: 924-2058).

Pizza Hut Another US fast-food eatery becomes part of the Russian lifestyle. You know the menu. Open from 11 AM to 11 PM. Reservations unnecessary. There are two branches. The one at 17 Kutuzovskiy Prospekt (phone: 243-1727, 243-7978, or 243-7960), near a large foreigners' compound, has a ruble section (there's a long wait to get in) and a hard-currency section (no wait), which share the same kitchen. The other branch is at 12 Tverskaya Ulitsa (phone: 229-2013 or 299-7840) and is hard currency only.

Praga Located in the center of Moscow, this huge, state-run restaurant, which pre-dates the 1917 Revolution, serves uninspired Russian, Czech, and other Eastern European dishes to as many as 970 guests at a time. The turn-of-the-century decor is impressive: You've hit pay dirt if you find yourself at a balcony table overlooking the city. A dance band plays in the evening. Open from noon to midnight. Reservations advised. Major credit cards accepted. 2 Novy Arbat Ultisa (phone: 290-6171).

Razgulya Living up to its name, which means "cheer up," this small dining place (it seats 67) has an interesting variety of creatively decorated rooms. One room has Khokloma-style folk art, including red and gold paintings on Russian lacquerware. Another room, with a blue and white color scheme and wood-beam ceiling painted with blue flowers, is reminiscent of the Gzhel region, known for its blue and white pottery. A third room, the Beresta, has red tablecloths, colorful paintings, and hanging baskets. The menu features a variety of traditional Russian dishes, such as Salad Razgulya (crab, rice, and nuts predominate). Live Russian and Gypsy music. Open from noon to 11:30 PM. Reservations advised. Major credit cards accepted. In the northeast part of the city; 11 Spartakovskaya Ulitsa (phone: 267-7613).

El Rincon Espanol As its name suggests, Spanish food is the thing in this ground floor restaurant at the *Moskva* hotel. (There is a little-known annex on the second floor, but the menu is limited.) The only place in town where you can get sangria and San Miguel beer, this trendy restaurant has become a favorite hangout for the expatriate community. Open daily for lunch and dinner. Reservations necessary. 7 Okhotniy Ryad (phone: 292-2893).

Sadko Arcade This mall next to the *Sadko* grocery store includes a spate of good, hard-currency restaurants. Best bets are the *Steakhouse* (no phone), the *German Beer House,* which offers excellent pea soup (phone: 940-4066), and the *Trattoria Italian Restaurant* (phone: 259-5656). Located along the Krasnaya Presnya Naberezhnaya, near the *Mezh* hotel. 1 Krasnogvardeisky Proyezd.

Savoy The luxurious dining room in the hotel of the same name is one of the best places in town to enjoy a quiet, elegant meal of Russian, Scandinavian, or international fare (the menu changes every 6 months). There is a prix fixe business lunch that includes an appetizer, main course, and tea. Open from noon to 11 PM. Reservations advised. Major credit cards accepted. *Savoy Hotel,* 3 Rozhdestvenka Ulitsa (phone: 929-8600).

Sedmoe Nebo (Seventh Sky) Moscow's only revolving restaurant, located atop the Ostankino TV tower. There are 3 dining rooms, all at separate levels: the Bronzovi Zal (Bronze Hall), the Zolotoi Zal (Golden Hall), and the Serebryani Zal (Silver Hall) — each completes a revolution every 45 minutes. The prix fixe menu served here is part of an excursion package that includes admission to the observation deck and an English-speaking guide who points out the important buildings (you get a chance to see all of Stalin's "wedding cake" constructions). The security is so tight, however, that foreigners must bring their passports with them, and no bags or briefcases are allowed. The food is filling, if not fancy — start with pastry snacks and sausages, continue with mushrooms in sauerkraut and chicken cutlets, and end with ice cream. Vodka, champagne, and caviar can be ordered for an additional charge. Open daily. Reservations advised. Major credit cards accepted. 15 Akademika Korolyeva Ulitsa (phone: 282-2293 or 282-2038).

Stanislavsaya 2 This petite, lace-festooned spot is a real charmer. The veal, mushroom soup, and *blinis* also are endearing. A violinist and pianist play softly in the background and, for a while, the bustle of Moscow disappears. Open from 6 PM to 1:30 AM. Book at 6 PM on the evening you wish to dine. 2 Stanislavsaya Ulitsa (phone: 291-8689).

Strastnoy-7 Chic and expensive, the most elegant of Moscow cooperatives boasts a stark neo-classical decor, warmed by lavish table accessories, quiet music, and professional, friendly service. There is no menu; diners are served daily specials, which make the most of limited ingredients. One such dish consists of tomatoes piled high with fresh herbed cream cheese, served with a tangy potato and cucumber salad; another is Old Moscow-style *roulette* — well-garnished platters of lightly fried, meat-and-ham-filled crêpes. Open from noon to 11 PM. Reservations advised. Major credit cards only accepted. 7 Strastnoy Bulvar (phone: 299-0498).

Tanganka Bar The entertainment — cossack and Russian singers who roam this dark, dungeon-like place in their elaborate garb belting out folk melodies — overshadows the food. Belly dancers slink around, slithering from one businessman to the next. Nevertheless, the ordinary Russian *zakuski* (a spread of cold meat, fish, and vegetables) is tolerable and reasonably priced. The evening is festive here and great for foreigners on a short stay. Open from 8 PM to midnight. 15 Radishchevskaya Ulitsa (phone: 272-4351).

Tren-Mos The name is a shortened version of Trenton-Moscow. Operated by a father-son team of Ukrainian descent from Trenton, New Jersey, this is a place where homesick Americans can relax over a good US meal. US state flags, along with other related memorabilia, cover the walls, and the menu offers familiar American dishes, such as chili, T-bone steaks, and apple pie. The French chef has quite a range of specialties, from cannelloni *al forno* to Texas-style boar. There's live piano music, too. Open from noon to 5 PM and from 7 to 11 PM. Reservations advised. 21 Komsomolskiy Prospekt (phone: 245-1216).

Tren-Mos Bistro The ambience is decidedly American, but the food and wine offered here are European bistro fare — individual pizzas, lots of pasta dishes, and Italian-style meat, served by efficient and courteous waiters. Open daily from 11 AM to 10 PM. Reservations unnecessary. 1-9 Ostozhenka Ulitsa (phone: 202-5722 and 202-3540).

Tsentralniy Originally opened in 1865 as *Filippov's,* then known as the *Astoria* before the 1917 Revolution, this faded dining room serves traditional Russian food, such as beef Stroganoff and *shashlik* (mutton roasted on a spit, served with marinated peppers, onions, and tomatoes) in an atmosphere of faded glory. But the variety show (performed nightly except Sundays and Mondays) is terrific. Champagne, vodka, and wines are available. Open noon to 3:30 PM and 6 PM to midnight. Reservations advised. Rubles, unless you book through your hotel, in which case hard currency only. 10 Tverskaya Ulitsa (phone: 229-0241).

U Pirosmani This Georgian restaurant is a Moscow favorite. Named after the Georgian primitivist painter Nikolai Pirosmanashvili, this cozy spot is decorated with copies of the painter's works, as well as wood beams and tables, stucco walls, an old piano and gramophone, and a fireplace. Ask for a table in the more attractive outer room. The menu offers spicy Georgian dishes including *khachapuri* (cheese-stuffed bread), *lobio* (marinated bean salad), marinated mushrooms, and pickled vegetables. There are usually only two main courses — if you still have room — *shashlik* and huge meat-stuffed dumplings. Open from noon to 11:30 PM. Reservations advised. Near Novodevichiy Monastyr. 4 Novodevichiy Proyezd (phone: 246-1638 or 247-1926).

Vstrecha A popular cooperative serving Georgian and Italian fare, it also features live music and a bar. Specialties include *shashlik* and *chakhohbili iz kuritsi* (stewed chicken with potatoes and tomatoes, cayenne, coriander, and saffron). Open 11 AM to midnight. Reservations advised. 3 Gilyarovskogo Ulitsa (phone: 208-4597).

Odessa

Such eloquent sobriquets as "Pearl of the Black Sea" or the "Western Gate of the (former) Soviet Riviera" have long been used to describe the Ukrainian seaside city of Odessa (population 1.1 million), the old Soviet Union's most culturally diverse city.

The inclination to wax poetic about Odessa is perhaps the legacy of a long line of writers and poets who for centuries have flocked to this distant landing on the Black Sea. Many, such as Gogol and Gorky, came of their own volition to experience the quickened pace and exotic mixture of people. Others, such as Pushkin, were exiled here by a czarist regime that used the distant city (532 miles/851 km from Moscow) as a sort of sultry Siberia of the southwest.

Odessa has enchanted visitors for hundreds of years, pleasing even the crusty Mark Twain, who unexpectedly visited this port city when his steam cruiser *Quaker City* made a stop to take on coal. He said the Odessa of the late 1860s looked, surprisingly, "like an American city." Indeed, Odessa is admired not for its sweeping history and its link to a fabled past, but for its energy and vitality. People visit Odessa not for its ancient architecture (the city's oldest surviving buildings were erected in the 18th and 19th centuries) but to see lovely seascapes, vibrant street scenes, and bustling markets, and to meet the city's lively inhabitants.

Odessa is at once a melting pot and mishmash of nationalities, a commercial citadel where buying low and selling high was the rule (albeit under the table) long before *perestroika,* and a raunchy seaport where sailors from scores of foreign ports carouse until the wee hours. The city's population is remarkable for its diversity: Russians, Jews, Bulgarians, Armenians, Azerbaijanis, Gypsies, Turks, Greeks, Moldavians, and Ukrainians have long made this their home.

It is for its sizable Jewish population, however, that the city perhaps has been best known. Odessa was for centuries a center of Jewish life and culture. In the years before World War II, more than half of the city's citizenry was Jewish. But the history of the Jewish people of Odessa is marred with tragedy and violence. Few have forgotten the pogroms that were inflicted on Odessa's Jews by the czarist regime in the 1880s, and again in the years preceding the Russian Revolution. Thousands of Jews also were massacred or deported during the Axis powers occupation of Odessa during World War II. Under the Soviet regime, the practice of Judaism (along with virtually all other religions) was suppressed. In recent years, however, organized Jewish religious and community life in Odessa was revived under *perestroika* and has flourished since Ukraine's declaration of independence. Odessa today still has Ukraine's largest and most cohesive Jewish community. However, as the nation's economic and political woes mounted, bringing with them the fear of a resurgence in anti-Semitism, many of Odessa's Jews emigrated to more economically stable countries. As a result, the city has seen a significant decrease in its Jewish community and a serious case of brain drain, as skilled workers, merchants, and professionals have departed for Israel, Europe, and the US. Today, as little as 15% of the city's population is Jewish. Sadly, the departure also has sapped the city's vitality: Odessa, even some locals concede, may never again be quite the same.

Though hardly a trace of them remain, there have been settlements on the site that is now Odessa since the Middle Ages. First there was Kotsubievo, a Slav village that flourished due to its proximity to the Danube, Dnieper, and South Bug rivers, which brought goods from the steppes and northern regions. In the 14th century, the village was sacked by the Tatars, who rebuilt it and named it Khadzhibei. In 1764 the Tatars gave way to the Turks, who built a fortress here as a bulwark against the Poles and the more threatening, enterprising Russians to the north.

But it was only a matter of time, however, before the colossal powers flanking this region asserted their control. The Russians arrived first, taking the fortress with a detachment of soldiers and Zaporozhian cossacks in 1789. Recognizing the site's strategic and economic importance, Alexander Suvorov, the great Russian military officer, wasted no time in building a fortress and a naval port at the request of Catherine the Great.

The following year the city was renamed after the ancient Greek settlement of Odessos, which was thought to have been located nearby. The very existence of Odessos has been questioned; many claim it was in Bulgaria.

One name closely linked to Odessa's past is that of the Duc de Richelieu, the city's first governor, who later became Prime Minister of France. Often called Odessa's founding father, Armand Emmanuel de Plessis Richelieu (1766-1822), a descendant of the famous 17th-century cardinal, came to czarist Russia at the beginning of the French Revolution, soldiered for Catherine the Great, and eventually was given the run of Odessa and the surrounding region by Czar Alexander I. Richelieu commissioned many major buildings and organized institutes and schools, and under his tutelage the city expanded rapidly. Odessa's link to Richelieu only adds to the city's worldly flair. A statue of the duke, by sculptor I.P. Martos, was the first monument erected in the city (1828). It stands on the best — and perhaps most visited — spot in the city: the very top of the Potemkin Staircase.

The rapid growth of rail transportation brought even more rapid growth to Odessa. Since the city is located at the confluence of three major rivers and the Black Sea, it is ideally situated as an outlet for the export of the fruits of the Ukrainian breadbasket, and the city enjoyed free port status for most of the first half of the 19th century. In addition, Odessa's climate permits use of its port year-round; the rivers' ice is never too thick for marine transport even during a deep freeze.

ODESSA
Points of Interest

1. Potemkin Staircase;
   Duke of Richelieu
   Monument
2. Grigory Vakulinchuk
   Monument
3. Shevchenko Park;
   Avangard Stadium
4. Count Vorontsov
   Monument
5. Railroad Station
6. Archaeological
   Museum
7. Museum of Western
   and Oriental Art
8. Pushkin Museum
9. Opera and Ballet
   Theater
10. Philharmonic Concert
    Hall
11. Krasnaya Hotel
12. Arcadia Hotel
13. Chorne More Hotel
14. Londonskaya Hotel
15. Delphin Campsite
16. Town Hall
17. Pushkin Monument

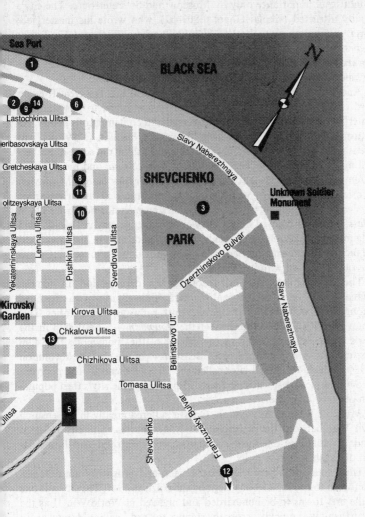

Sea Port

BLACK SEA

Lastochkina Ulitsa

eribasovskaya Ulitsa

Gretcheskaya Ulitsa

SHEVCHENKO

olitzeyskaya Ulitsa

Yekaterininskaya Ulitsa

Lenina Ulitsa

Pushkin Ulitsa

Sverdlova Ulitsa

Slavy Naberezhnaya

Unknown Soldier
Monument

PARK

Dzerzhinskovo Bulvar

Slavy Naberezhnaya

Kirovsky
Garden

Kirova Ulitsa

Chkalova Ulitsa

Chizhikova Ulitsa

Belinskovo Ulit

Tomasa Ulitsa

Ulitsa

Shevchenko

Frantzuzsky Bulvar

By the mid-19th century Odessa was czarist Russia's third city, eclipsed in industrial importance only by Moscow and St. Petersburg. The city's vitality attracted Nikolai Gogol (1809–52), who wrote his masterpiece *Dead Souls* here; satirist Ilya Ilf (1897–1937), who co-authored *The Twelve Chairs;* and the revolutionary writer Maxim Gorky (1868–1936), who worked on Odessa's docks as a stevedore, a period of his life that he later chronicled.

And then there was Pushkin. It cannot be said that the great Russian bard came to Odessa willingly, since he was banished to this southern hinterland by the czar for his controversial and contemptuous poetry. As it turned out, sending the resilient Alexander Pushkin (1799–1837) to Odessa was like exiling Hemingway to Spain. Pushkin did some of his best writing here, completing *The Fountain of Bakhchisarai* and more than 2 dozen other poems. He also worked on *The Gypsies,* about Moldavian Gypsies (he was exiled to Moldavia, too), and completed three chapters of *Eugene Onegin,* his epic work, which makes ample reference to his life in Odessa. Pushkin enjoyed his punitive-yet-productive stay in Odessa. And judging from the many monuments, plaques, and busts in his honor, and the fact that his former residence has been turned into a museum, Odessa was rather pleased with its prisoner.

The first proletarian and revolutionary organization in Czarist Russia — the Union of Russian Workers of the South — was founded among the 30,000 workers of Odessa's port, railways, and factories. This group joined with the mutineers of the *Potemkin* — a battleship in the czar's Black Sea fleet that was the subject of the eponymous 1925 film classic by Russian director Sergei Eisenstein — in the abortive revolution of 1905, which V.I. Lenin later called the Great Rehearsal. The pogroms followed immediately, causing nearly 13 percent of the city's then population of 600,000 to flee.

After the Russian Revolution, Odessa suffered greatly in the ensuing Civil War between the Bolsheviks and Mensheviks. The city changed hands several times, one-third of its houses were destroyed, and its population diminished considerably.

There followed a period of relative calm and prosperity until Odessa was forced to endure a 69-day siege by the Nazis in 1941. The city was one of the first towns to be bombarded and invaded in World War II as the Germans moved quickly across the steppes toward Leningrad (now again called St. Petersburg) and Moscow.

Today Odessa still proudly proclaims its position as one of Ukraine's most culturally colorful cities, a legacy of the writers, performers, musicians, and royalty who lived or visited here. The city is in a well-reputed wine region and is the site of a champagne winery of the *Institute of Viniculture and Wine Making.* Odessa's film studio is among the best in the country, and the biannual end-of-summer *Odessa Film Festival* — a sort of Cannes of Eastern Europe — is a must-attend event should you happen to be in town.

Odessa's history of thriving enterprise has left the city with some splendid architecture from the 18th and 19th centuries and a multifaceted, irrepressible spirit. Although Odessa might be less exotic than in years past, a new entrepreneurial force is flourishing: Street vendors and stores are better stocked than those in other Ukraine cities. Odessites — from top politicians on down to small shopkeepers and cabbies — hope that a proposed "free port" status for their city will soon be approved, spurring increased economic development and foreign investment. Although port activity and even local tourism have suffered considerably from the breakdown of Ukraine's economy, hotels are packed with foreign businesspeople looking to make a future killing as Odessa seeks to broaden its ties with the rest of the world. In fact, Odessites delight in claiming a closer spiritual kinship with the West than do their fellow countrymen. It's one reason why the welcome extended to visitors here can be forthright and unabashed.

> **NOTE** At press time, prompted by the increase in reported cases of diphtheria in Russia and Ukraine, travelers are advised to update their immunizations before entering these regions. For further information call the US State Department's *Citizen's Emergency Center* at 202-647-5225.

Odessa At-a-Glance

SEEING THE CITY

Everything you will want to see and do in Odessa is within walking distance (or a short drive) of the harbor, the focal point of Odessa's colorful and animated street scenes. From the top of the Potemkin Staircase, where it meets Primorskiy Bulvar, is a 180° panorama of Odessa's port, among the largest on the Black Sea.

The following information on sights and sites was accurate as we went to press, but it is more than possible that, given the current political situation, more statues may be toppled, streets and squares renamed, and hotels and restaurants changed hands, or even closed as Ukraine adjusts to its independence and proceeds with economic reforms. Although street names and the names of other landmarks are slowly being changed from Russian to Ukrainian, the street signs are still in Russian and the Russian names are still more commonly used by locals. Russian translations, therefore, appear throughout this chapter. "Ulitsa" means "street" in Russian; "naberezhnaya" means "seaside avenue"; "bulvar" or "prospekt" mean "boulevard"; and "ploshchad" means "square."

SPECIAL PLACES

THE CATACOMBS No visit to Odessa is complete without a romp through the catacombs. Since sandstone was quarried from beneath the city in the early

19th century for use in many buildings, there are over 500 miles of tunnels, caves, and catacombs that have been used by smugglers, revolutionaries, and, later, as a command post for the Resistance to the Nazi forces during World War II (there is a model of the command headquarters in the local *History Museum*). The Nazis, interestingly, never occupied these caves. At one time the caves contained an underground print shop. There are many entrances and many exits to the catacombs, and some passages (containing the remains of soldiers and their munitions) have only recently been discovered. Most of the entrances are on Mount Shevakhovo. The catacombs must be visited with a guide. Call the *Londonskaya* travel office (see *Tourist Information,* below) for tour information or check with your hotel.

POTYEMKINSKAYA LESTNITSA (POTEMKIN STAIRCASE) The city's Eiffel Tower, this is the site of the most dramatic and memorable scene in the 1925 film *Potemkin,* and Odessa's most visited and best-known landmark. Built between 1837 and 1841 and originally designed to be the main gateway to the city, the Potemkin Staircase is an architectural masterpiece, a long and wide stone stairway that consists of 192 steps that sharply descend from a row of palaces down to the harbor. In the Eisenstein film, czarist soldiers massacred a crowd on these steps as they made their way to the mutineers of the *Prince Potemkin Taurichevsky,* a battleship that was part of the czar's fleet moored in the bay and that took part in the 1905 Revolution (the ship's crew had joined the city's workers in the revolt). Though Eisenstein later admitted that the confrontation on the steps was purely fictional, they are still a premier tourist attraction because of the film. The steps were built narrower at the top than the bottom to give the illusion of greater length; they lead to Primorskiy Bulvar, Odessa's main seaside promenade (see below). Sitting proudly on Primorskiy, appearing always at the ready but actually hardly able to shoot, is a cannon used in the Crimean War that was taken from the *Tiger,* a sunken British frigate, when it was recovered from the bottom of the sea.

PRIMORSKIY BULVAR (SEASIDE BOULEVARD) Lying just beyond the Potemkin Staircase, this delightful seaside promenade is a nerve center of Odessa. Some of the city's best-known landmarks are found along its path: the Duke of Richelieu Monument, Vorontsov Palace, Town Hall, and the Pushkin Monument. Nearby are Kommunarov Ploshchad (Commune Square), which is surrounded by a charming cluster of buildings that were designed by Tomas de Thomon, who built the famous St. Petersburg Stock Exchange; the *Arkheologicheskiy Muzey* (Archaeological Museum; see *Museums* below); and the Sailor's Palace, the former residence of the Commandant of Odessa.

PUSHKIN MONUMENT Opposite the Town Hall on the southeastern end of Primorskiy Bulvar, this monument is dedicated to Alexander Pushkin, Russia's greatest poet. The dates 1820–24 engraved on the monument are the years Pushkin lived on and off in Odessa, both by choice and when he was forced into exile. During this time he penned *The Fountain of Bakhchisarai* (in which he wrote of Odessa in rather raving prose); several chapters of his epic, *Eugene Onegin;* and a slew of lyric poems. The house in which he lived (13 Pushkinskaya Ulitsa) is now the headquarters of the Ukrainian Writers' Association.

GORODSKAYA MERIYA (TOWN HALL) The seat of the Odessa City Council is a good example of 19th-century classical architecture; it is elaborately adorned with statues depicting Mercury, the Greek messenger of the gods, and Ceres, the Greek goddess of agriculture. The large clock on the face of the building bears sculpted figures personifying night and day. Primorskiy Bulvar.

VORONTSOVSKIY DVORETS (VORONTSOV PALACE) Completed in 1827 in classic Russian style, this palace was once the residence of Count Vorontsov, who served as Pushkin's guardian while the poet lived and worked (he was employed as a civil servant) here in exile. Pushkin considered Vorontsov to be a harsh chaperon and taskmaster, describing him as a "vandal, a cad, and a petty egoist" in letters to the writer Ivan Turgenev. The flamboyant Pushkin — known for his philandering — had an affair with Vorontsov's wife (perhaps history's most definitive case of "poetic justice"). Vorontsov was governor of Novorossiisk (New Russia), a region that surrounded Odessa. His palace became the headquarters of the Odessa Soviet (a sort of City Hall) after the Bolshevik Revolution, and later was restored and became the Palace of Pioneers. Located at the far northwestern end of Primorskiy Bulvar.

PARK IMENI TARASA SHEVCHENKA (TARAS SHEVCHENKO PARK) Named for the beloved 19th-century Ukrainian poet, this is a lush and restful oasis in the city. On the park's 225 acres is a bathing beach (caution: within city limits the Black Sea is said to be heavily polluted); a monument to Bohdan Khmelnytsky (the Ukrainian cossack leader who signed a union treaty with Russia in 1654); the 40,000-seat *Avangard Stadium,* an open-air theater; and boat rental stations with rowboats for hire. But the park's real gem is its heart-fluttering view of the Black Sea. On the extreme northeast corner of the park are the remains of the Odessa Fortress built by the Russians in 1793.

PORT OF ODESSA Before the city's economic crisis, Odessa's warmwater port was both the city's pulse and its cash cow. Many of Odessa's residents make their living in some way from the sea; ships from various countries regularly dock here, adding to the town's cosmopolitan bent. Before the advent of cranes and mechanized loading and stacking machinery, hundreds of burly men could be seen toiling from warehouse to ship. Two new seaports northeast and south of Odessa now handle the bulk of commercial cargo. One of the best vantage points from which to take in the port scene — and the semicircular bay — is from the top of the Potemkin Staircase.

DERIBASOVSKAYA ULITSA Odessa's main commercial district, this is arguably the city's liveliest thoroughfare. Nearly every building is a café or a store. The street's energy is due in no small part to the presence of nearby Mechnikov State University. Also here is Richelieu College, where Pushkin studied during his exile, and where Dmitry Mendeleyev, the scientist who created the Periodic Table of Elements, taught in the 1850s. The street, laced with several gardens and parks, leads to Preobrazhenskaya Ploshchad, formerly the Square of the Soviet Army, where a bust of Count Vorontsov stands in one corner.

USPENSKIY SOBOR (ASSUMPTION CATHEDRAL) This Russian Orthodox church incorporates Russian and Byzantine styles of architecture, and it houses the reputedly miracle-working icon of Our Lady of Kasperovskaya. The five-domed cathedral was completed in 1869. Preobrazhenskaya Ulitsa.

> **EXTRA SPECIAL** Odessa's most attractive feature is its close proximity to scores of resorts and other vacation havens along the Black Sea and the Crimea, a peninsula that juts out into the sea. One of the restful oases to be found in the Crimea is Yalta, the resort town made famous by the summit meeting held here in 1945. Yalta is best reached by water; boat cruises pass by the majestic fortress at Sevastopol and the quaint resorts along the southern coast of the Crimea. Crimean tours usually begin at Simferopol, the regional capital, which is 55 miles (88 km) from Yalta. You can go by bus, or rent a car with a driver.

Sources and Resources

TOURIST INFORMATION

Once the country's premier travel agency, *Intourist* is but a shadow of its former self. Travelers needing assistance should contact *Londonskaya* travel office (Primorskiy Bulvar; phone: 228468).

> **NOTE** Economic turmoil, including frequent and steep price increases on many goods and services, makes it impossible to provide accurate information on prices, including the cost of basic services such as public transportation and the telephone. In addition, at press time Ukraine was using the kupon, an interim currency that replaced the ruble; it was set to introduce its own national currency, the hryvnia.

TELEPHONE The country code for Ukraine is 7. The city code for Odessa is 0482. With coins out of circulation, at press time, it was practically impossible to make calls from public pay phones. Long-distance calls from Odessa are best handled through your hotel's service bureau. It is advisable to check first on the rates and in which currency you are expected to pay.

GETTING AROUND

AIRPORT Odessa's airport is about 10 miles (16 km) north of the center of the city. *Air Ukraine* serves Ukrainian cities, and *Aeroflot* makes connections to many former Soviet cities. The *Aeroflot* office in Odessa is at 17 Yekaterinenskaya Ulitsa. At press time, flight schedules were greatly reduced or canceled because of severe fuel shortages.

CAR RENTAL Cars, with or without drivers, may be rented at the *Chornoye More* hotel (59 Lenina Ulitsa; phone: 242024) or at the *Londonskaya* hotel (11 Primorskiy Bulvar; phone: 228787). Check with your hotel service bureau for the names of joint-venture car rental agencies (which may have Western autos). Travel by rental car is an excellent way to visit the various resorts along the Black Sea (if gasoline is available).

BOAT Check with the *Londonskaya* travel office (see *Tourist Information,* above) for details on the various cruise and boat trips up the Dnieper River or along the Black Sea. For more details, see *Classic Cruises and Wonderful Waterways* in DIVERSIONS.

BUS Virtually every inch of pavement in Odessa is served by bus routes. Tickets can be purchased at kiosks, which are located on nearly every street corner. Just say *adin bilet pozhaluysta* (one ticket, please). Bus maps are usually available at these kiosks.

TAXI Cabstands are located at the hotels and the major intersections throughout the city, but drivers may demand more than is actually registered on the meter. Unofficial (free enterprise) taxis will also require fare negotiations prior to heading off.

TRAIN There are many rail connections between Odessa and various cities of the former Soviet Union. The train station is located at Privokzalnaya Ploshchad. Train tickets can be purchased daily before departure and must be paid for in hard currency (unless you can convince newly made local friends to buy a ticket for you in local currency). Purchasing any ticket — airplane, boat, or train — can be a major hassle for visitors these days; you're likely to hear that all seats are sold out! Best bet is to buy tickets through a travel company, such as *Londonskaya* (see above), that specializes in dealing with foreign guests. It's well worth the small surcharge.

LOCAL SERVICES

DENTIST Most hotels have special contracts with dentists to handle emergencies. Inquire at your hotel for more information.

DRY CLEANER At all major hotels. Dry cleaning can take from 6 hours to 2 or 3 days.

FAX/TELEX The *Chornoye More* and *Londonskaya* have public fax facilities. The main post office (see below) and the *Chornoye More*, *Delphin*, and *Krasnaya* hotels offer telex services.

LIMOUSINE SERVICE Contact the *Chornoye More* hotel (59 Lenina Ulitsa; phone: 242031 or 242024). A number of Western cars, including Mercedes-Benz, are available.

MEDICAL EMERGENCY The *Medishniy Institut imeni Peragova* (2 Medishniy Provulok) handles emergencies. The medical emergency telephone number is 03.

MESSENGER SERVICE Available, for a fee, from any of the major hotels.

NATIONAL/INTERNATIONAL COURIER *DHL Worldwide Express* is offered through major hotels. The local *DHL* office is at 27 Lenina Ulitsa (phone: 244269).

OFFICE EQUIPMENT RENTAL Available at the larger hotels.

PHARMACY Call 09 for the *dezhorniy apteki* (all-night pharmacy) or ask at your hotel for the one nearest you.

PHOTOCOPIERS Available at the *Chornoye More*, *Krasnaya*, and *Londonskaya* hotels.

POST OFFICE The main post office (10 Sadovaya Ulitsa) is open 24 hours a day, 7 days a week. Telegrams and telex messages may be sent from here.

TAILOR Inquire at your hotel for the closest tailor.

TRANSLATOR Available through major hotels.

SPECIAL EVENTS

April 1, *April Fool's Day* (*Prima Aprilis* in Ukrainian, *Den Pervov* in Russian), is celebrated with a carnival and variety shows in the city's streets and concert halls. The biannual *Odessa Film Festival* takes place in August.

MUSEUMS

Odessa, which is foremost a commercial city, has never been accused of having more museum curators than merchants. But what museums the city does have are worthwhile. All museums have a nonimal admission charge. The following are several of the more interesting ones:

ARKHEOLOGICHESKIY MUZEY (ARCHAEOLOGICAL MUSEUM) An engaging collection of objects that chronicle the life and culture of the people who lived on the northern shore of the Black Sea until the 13th century. There also is an excellent display of Greek and Egyptian artifacts. The "Golden

Depository" is a grand permanent exhibit of ancient jewelry, medals, and coins. Open daily 10 AM to 6 PM. 4 Lastochkina Ulitsa.

MUZEY MORSKOVO FLOTA (MARINE MUSEUM) Artifacts, displays, and models of dozens of ships relating mostly to the Black Sea and, specifically, at the port of Odessa. Open 10 AM to 5 PM; closed Thursdays. 6 Lastochkina Ulitsa.

MUZEY ZAPADNOVO I VOSTOCHNOVO ISKUSSTV (MUSEUM OF WESTERN AND ORIENTAL ART) This museum's 23 halls fall into three categories: antiques (mainly reproductions); Western European art, including a painting attributed to Caravaggio; and Oriental art, including Persian miniatures and handicrafts from India and the Far East. Open 10 AM to 6 PM; closed Wednesdays. 9 Pushkinskaya Ulitsa.

ODESSKIY KHUDOZHESTUENNIY MUZEY (ODESSA ART MUSEUM) Houses one of Ukraine's largest collections of Ukrainian and Russian art, from 15th- to 18th-century icons to contemporary painting, sculpture, and graphics. Open 10:30 AM to 5 PM; closed Tuesdays. 5A Korolenko Ulitsa.

PUSHKINSKIY MUZEY (PUSHKIN MUSEUM) The great Russian poet lived in this former inn, called the *Hôtel du Nord,* when he first was exiled to Odessa. The building dates from 1812 but was restored after war damage caused in 1941. The museum collection consists mainly of portraits of the beloved bard. Open 11 AM to 5 PM; closed Wednesdays. 13 Pushkinskaya Ulitsa.

SHOPPING

In a country where demand consistently trounces supply, shopping more closely resembles the body bumping of sumo wrestling than the relatively tame sport we consider it to be in the West. Lingering too long over an item in a crowded shop without snatching it up only invites a blitz of body slams and elbow throwing from manic shoppers who rush the display case in droves. Even though customs may confiscate your beloved purchases upon exiting the country (check with your hotel before you buy antiques, art, jewelry, or anything else of cultural significance), you will nevertheless have sharpened your shopping skills. Generally, any object made before 1945 cannot be taken out of the country, a move the government has taken to curb the tremendous amount of artwork and antiques that has been exported in the past several years. In addition to this ruling, paintings of current vintage must also bear a special certification (ask an art gallery for specifics) to clear customs.

Deribasovskaya Ulitsa is one of the main shopping thoroughfares. *Ukrainskiy Souvenir* (16 Deribasovskaya) sells a variety of inexpensive Ukrainian and Russian folk art items such as carved woodenware, decorated *Easter* eggs, and lacquer boxes. *Budynok Knyhy* (27 Deribasovskya), reputedly the city's largest bookstore, occasionally carries art and historical books on Odessa, but it's usually pot luck; there's also a selection of sheet music at unbeatable prices. In addition, drop by the open-air book market (29 Deribasovskaya), where plenty of books in English are offered. While on Deribasovskaya, don't miss the covered *pasazh* (passage), not so much for the rather upscale boutiques, but for a look at the impressive turn-of-the-century stucco work on the walls, now being renovated. Antiques, including icons, silverware, paintings, and furniture are featured at 22 Deribasovskaya (above the cinema on the second floor). Ceramics patterned after ancient Greek vases — and among the best-known Odessan souvenirs — are sold at the private stands set up in the parks along Deribasovskaya.

Tsentralniy Univerma (Central Department Store; 72 Pushkinskaya Ulitsa) has been known to yield an occasional treasure, despite its uninspired name. The daily *tolchok* (open-air bazaar) at Malinovskovo Ulitsa is worth a visit as well as *Art Gallery* (24 Lastochkina Ulitsa; closed Fridays), which carries works by local artists at very reasonable prices (local currency only).

Regional wines are another good bargain. Look for Oksamyt Ukrainy, Starokozatske, and Alihote available throughout the city.

SPORTS AND FITNESS

Like most of the cities along the Black Sea, Odessa's physical pursuits usually involve more fitness than sport — unless you consider sunbathing and taking medicinal baths competitive events. Odessa has a slew of beaches (though the water, so close to an industrial port, is said to be heavily polluted). One of the better spots is at Chernomorka (in the city's southernmost corner), which features a quartz sand beach. There is a café and a number of therapeutic treatment centers for children at this resort, which was formerly the German settlement of Lustdorf. The golden beach at Arkadia Park (in the city's southern region) is an ideal place to catch some rays. There is a summer theater there, plus the *Yuzhnaya Palmira* restaurant (see *Eating Out*) and an entrance to the catacombs.

There are more than 30 resorts (known here as rest homes), medicinal baths, and therapeutic beauty spas in the Odessa area that feature the mud and hydro treatments so popular in the countries along the Black Sea. Locals say that the secret ingredients in Odessa's water are the magnesium, lime, iodine, and bromine. The mud is rich in sulfur and purportedly is effective in the cure of rheumatic, nervous, and skin disorders. Try the *Kuyalnitskiy* resort, located about 8 miles (13 km) from the city center, where a spa, mud baths, and a lake with the most concentrated salt solution (up to 27%) of any in the Odessa area are the attractions. Also of interest is the *Lermontovskiy* resort, located on an avenue of the same name, where there is a large park, rheumatic treatment center, and a terrace that leads down to the sea.

THEATER

The *Russkiy Dramaticheskiy Teatr Ivanova* (Ivanov Drama Theater; 48 Karla Libknekhta) features Russian-language classics and some new works, with performances nightly. Next door is a musical comedy theater. The *Teatr Yunovo Zritelya imeni Nikolaya Ostrovskovo* (Ostrovsky Youth Theater; 48 Karla Libknekhta) is named after the Russian playwright. *Musicalna Comedia* (3 Chizhykova Ulitsa) features modern operettas in Ukrainian, Italian, and other languages. Odessa is a good place to succumb to an evening at the circus, and the *Odessa Circus* is one of the best (25 Podbelskaya Ulitsa). The clowns, riders, and animals are superb.

MUSIC

The pièce de résistance is the *Opera and Ballet Theater* (8 Lastochkina Ulitsa), sometimes referred to as the *Odessa Opera House,* which was designed in the late 19th century by two Viennese architects and resembles a Vienna or Dresden court theater. The ceiling is decorated with colorful pastel scenes from the works of Shakespeare. Some of the greats, including Rimsky-Korsakov, Tchaikovsky, and Rubinstein, have performed here. The *Philharmonic Concert Hall* (15 Politzeyskaya) dates back to 1899. The hall was the original building of the merchant stock exchange and is one of the most elaborate examples of 19th-century architecture in Odessa, built in the Florentine Gothic style. As you tilt your head back, savoring the hall's sweet acoustics, notice the ceiling murals, which symbolize trade and industry.

NIGHTCLUBS AND NIGHTLIFE

Despite the fact that it's a port city, nightlife worth noting has been hard to find in Odessa in recent years. Things are slowly changing, however, as the city enacts economic reforms. Typifying this change was the opening last year of the upscale British casino *Richelieu* (15 Rosa Luxemburg Ulitsa) in the elaborate *Philharmonic Concert Hall* building. A 140-seat restaurant and a jazz café add to the late-night entertainment. Also popular are the after-hours bars (usually open until 2 AM at the *Chornoye More* and *Londonskaya* hotels.

Best in Town

CHECKING IN

Hotel accommodations in the Ukraine can be booked through your travel agent, one of the local *Intourist* bureaus, or on your own.

The country's dramatically fluctuating economy makes it difficult to provide accurate rates for hotels. At press time, Ukraine was using the kupon (coupon) as an interim replacement for the ruble, but was planning to introduce its own currency, the hryvnia. Travelers are advised to check exchange rates immediately prior to departure. Also note that most hotels in Ukraine catering to foreign tourists accept payment in hard currency only; virtually none accept credit cards. Most of Odessa's major hotels have complete facilities for the business traveler. Those hotels listed below as having "business services" usually offer such conveniences as English-speaking concierge, meeting rooms, photocopiers, computers, translation services, and express checkout, among others. Call the hotel for additional information. All telephone numbers are in the 0482 area code unless otherwise indicated.

Chornoye More (Black Sea) Near the city center but (in spite of its name) nowhere near the harbor and away from most of Odessa's prime sites, this 9-story *Intourist* hotel is used mainly for groups. It's well managed and has a friendly staff. The restaurant is air conditioned. Business services. 59 Lenina Ulitsa (phone: 242024; fax: 240031).

Delphin For the adventuresome, this is a large campground 7 miles (11 km) outside Odessa in the Luzanovka district. There is parking for 150 cars, 450 campsites, and space for 120 tents, which can be rented. Bungalows with outdoor bathroom facilities are also available. Among the facilities here are a bar, a sauna, a bathing beach, a gas station, and a large restaurant. Business services. Open June through September; bungalows open year-round. 307 Kotovskovo Dorogo (phone: 555052; fax: 552223).

Krasnaya (Red) A 4-story, rose-colored (thus its name), sandstone hotel, it consists of 90 rooms, a good restaurant, a buffet, and a bar. This late-19th-century property is among the best in town, and unlike many former great hostelries of czarist Russia, it still retains much of its former glory. White marble columns and baroque statuary add to the grandeur of the place, located near the harbor. Business services. Note: At press time it was learned that possible renovations and a name change to *Bristol* were being considered. 15 Pushkinskaya Ulitsa (phone: 258520 or 227220).

Londonskaya Considered one of the finer hostelries in Ukraine, this establishment has been refurbished in the past few years and is in top form. The location — on the seaside promenade, overlooking the harbor — is wonderful. The 60 rooms are attractive and comfortable; most are very large as well. A Swiss-run restaurant was scheduled to open at press time, and there's a delightful courtyard that allows guests to breakfast under the trees. Business services. 11 Primorskiy Bulvar (phone: 228787 or 225019).

EATING OUT

Perhaps due to its status as a trader's town, Ukrainian, Jewish, Central Asian, Caucasian, and Russian food are all popular here. As a restaurant town, Odessa, with the few exceptions such as those listed below, still lags behind other Eastern European cities. Given Odessites' traditional entrepreneurial spirit, however, the betting here is that economic reforms will bring quick change to the culinary sector as well.

The country's dramatically fluctuating economy makes it difficult to provide accurate prices for restaurants; we suggest that you check the operative exchange rate prior to your departure. At press time, a growing number of restaurants throughout Ukraine were accepting payment in hard currency only. Reservations are always advisable. Odessites customarily make dining an all-night event — reservations may be hard to come by. All telephone numbers are in the 0482 area code unless otherwise indicated.

Gold Fassl (Golden Keg) The large Austrian "Gold Fassl" beer sign prominently displayed outside this restaurant gives a good indication of what can be found inside. Popular among expatriates and cruise ship passengers, its wooden booths and checkered tablecloths are reminiscent of a German *bierstube*. The menu offers a wide variety of continental specialties including roasted quail; beer is a staple (natch). Open daily for lunch and dinner. Reservations necessary. 8A Shevchenka Prospekt (phone: 607168).

Svetlana A favorite with businesspeople, it offers first-rate Ukrainian-Jewish dishes. The dining room (there's also an adjacent bar) is dark, plush, and quite romantic with gypsy music performed nightly. Try the Ukrainian borscht. Open daily for lunch and dinner; closed Mondays. Reservations advised. 2 Varninskaya Ulitsa (phone: 618102 or 618406).

U Pechesskavo This cooperative eatery serves continental fare and local Jewish specialties. There's a variety show, too. Open daily noon to 11 PM. Halturina Ulitsa (phone: 250395).

Yeva (Eve) Managed by two Armenians, this cozy basement eatery is famous for its unusual specialties, including spicy Korean carrot salad (there's a sizeable Korean community in Odessa), tender veal shish kebab, and delicate gefilte fish. There's live music and a late (rather tame) evening floor show in the vaulted main room. If you prefer a quiet setting, ask to be seated in one of the three adjoining private rooms. Open daily for lunch and dinner. Reservations necessary. 2 Rosa Luxemburg Ulitsa (phone: 214009).

Yuzhnaya Palmira (Southern Palmyra) Worth a visit if only for its location: Set in the city's Arkadia spa region overlooking the sea, this turn-of-the-century place once catered to the summering elite. The main building looks more like a huge ballroom than an eatery. Seafood is the specialty here; the shish kebab is also superb. During warmer months, dine on the verandah amidst lush formal gardens. Dancing to live music nightly. Open daily for lunch and dinner; closed Sundays. Reservations necessary. On Arkadia Beach (phone: 684477).

Prague

Praha to its 1.2 million inhabitants, Prague is known as the "mother of cities." Its beauty has been legendary since the Middle Ages. Goethe once called it "the most precious stone in the crown of the world," and anyone who has seen the sun's rays lengthen across the city, skimming the gilded roofs and skirting the banks of the Vltava, will agree that it is aptly called Zlatá Praha, Golden Prague.

The lasting beauty of the capital of the Czech Republic is even more remarkable when one considers the turmoil it has seen over the past century. The city survived German occupation during World War II, and it emerged from 41 years of Communist rule faded and frayed but still lovely. In the years since the 1989 "velvet revolution" that led to the Communist fall, Prague has seen incredible changes. Hundreds of the city's centuries-old buildings with their pastel façades have been faithfully restored. And now that the conversion of the Czech Republic to a market economy is in place, life here is emulating the West more and more: Tourists are assaulted with advertisements touting everything from the latest diet craze to the benefits of reincarnation. Black-bereted beatniks and towheaded fraternity boys sporting T-shirts cruise Wenceslas Square. In Prague one can find not only ample evidence of Europe's fairy-tale past, but Coca-Cola, *McDonalds,* and *Pizza Express.* Hawkers and peddlers cram Charles Bridge and Old Town Square, selling Cinderella puppets, fur hats, cut-glass paperweights, and miniature portraits of the city's famous castle. Like most major cities, Prague has become an energetic and contradictory place, suffused with a new enlightenment.

First the seat of the Holy Roman Empire, then of the Austrian Empire, Prague is the capital of Bohemia, in what was Czechoslovakia's westernmost province. The first inhabitants of Bohemia were a Celtic tribe called the Boïens, who called their territory Bolohaemom. The Slavs arrived during the 5th century, and settled in what are today the three provinces of the former Czechoslovakia — Slovakia, Moravia, and Bohemia. Prague's history can be read not only in its buildings but also in the layout of the city. The earliest settlements, first recorded in the 9th century, were at the foot of two ancient castles perched high on the tops of hills — Vyšehrad on the right bank of the Vltava and Hradčany on the left; after the fall of the great Moravian empire at the beginning of the 10th century, these strongholds became residences of the Bohemian kings. On the right bank, a small settlement then formed a market center, which developed into the Staré Město (Old Town), and on the opposite bank, the Malá Strana (Lesser Quarter) grew up. Finally, Charles IV founded the Nové Město (New Town) near the Old Town during the 14th century. (The five royal towns of Prague did not officially become one until 1784, and even today each retains its distinct personality.)

Bohemia and its capital reached their full glory during the reign of Charles IV (1346–78), a man of culture and vision, who, in addition to founding the New Town, built Charles University (1348), reconstructed Prague Castle in the Gothic style, and initiated the construction of St. Vitus's Cathedral. By then, Prague — with 40,000 residents — was the third-largest city in Europe, eclipsed only by Rome and Constantinople.

In 1402, John Huss began preaching his "fighting words" from Prague's Bethlehem Chapel. An advocate of the reform of church abuses and the supremacy of Czech national aspirations in the face of German influences, he was burned at the stake in 1415; his martyrdom triggered the religious Hussite Wars. In 1526, when Ferdinand I of Austria became king, the long oppression of the Czechs under the Hapsburgs began. Ferdinand's efforts to control the city were cultural as well as political in nature. He left his imprint on Prague's architecture by rebuilding the castle in Renaissance style. Vienna's efforts to reintroduce Catholicism and Germanization by force inspired the Czechs to passionate resistance, which climaxed with the famous "defenestration" of two government officials. The men literally were thrown out of the windows of Prague Castle in 1618, sparking a revolt by the Czech Protestant nobility and, subsequently, Central Europe's devastating Thirty Years War.

After the Czechs' defeat at the Battle of White Mountain (1620), and the public execution of 27 leaders, foreign nobles confiscated Czech lands. The Germanization of Bohemia reached its height under the Austrian Empress Maria Theresa in 1749, when German was made the official language. The Czech national spirit, however oppressed, was never vanquished. In 1918, the Republic of Czechoslovakia, created from the kingdoms of Bohemia, Moravia, and Slovakia was born. But independence was tragically short-lived. Operating on the theory that their actions would keep Europe out of the war, France and England gave part of Bohemia to Germany during the infamous Munich Peace Conference in 1938. Hitler's troops occupied Bohemia and Moravia from 1939 until 1945, when the Czechs rose up against them in Prague, and held out bravely until the Soviet Army arrived 4 days later. (The Americans had already liberated western Bohemia, including Plzeň.)

Czechoslovakia emerged from its World War II occupation by the Germans only to become part of the Soviet Union's sphere of influence. The Communist state of Czechoslovakia was a direct result of the Yalta agreement. Although the Czechoslovakian Communist Party received only minimal support in the 1946 elections, within the next 2 years the party had succeeded in nationalizing the country's entire economy, and by the early 1950s demonstrated (in the travesty of justice known as the "Prague trial") its total consolidation of power.

The following decade saw some easing of centralized political, cultural, and economic control, as more enlightened party members moved to the fore. In 1968, this trend culminated in the rise to power of party chief Alexander Dubcek, who promised Czech citizens "socialism with a human

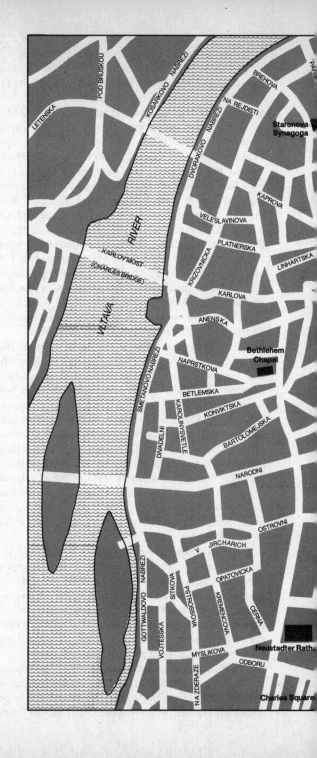

PRAGUE

Points of Interest

Staronova Synagoga
Bethlehem Chapel
Neustadter Rathaus
Altstadter Rathaus
Prasna Brana
National Museum

face." But Russian tanks quickly dashed liberal hopes, and the joy of the so-called "Prague Spring" proved very short-lived. During the period of "normalization" that followed the harsh Russian suppression, most of the proponents of freedom went to jail, were sent into exile, or accepted retirement — Dubcek himself was relegated to an obscure post in the forestry ministry. The final blow to enlightened leadership came on January 16, 1969, when Jan Palach, a despondent 20-year-old student, burned himself to death in Wenceslas Square.

Virtually all of Czechoslovakia spent the next 2 decades in a paralyzing stupor, relieved suddenly in November 1989 when Communist power in the country — and in most of the rest of Eastern Europe — collapsed like a house of cards. The leadership vacuum temporarily was filled by brave "amateurs" such as playwright Václav Havel, the dedicated champion of human rights who headed a young protest movement called Civic Forum. In June 1990, in the first free elections in Czechoslovakia since 1946, 96% of the eligible voters cast votes in an election that brought Civic Forum (and its Slovak twin, Public Against Violence) to power. President Havel earned the legal right to try to govern Czechoslovakia.

Havel's task, however, was not an easy one. While it seemed that at last the country could focus on developing its democratic institutions and jump-start its mismanaged state-owned economy, ongoing disagreements between the Czech parts of the country (Bohemia and Moravia) and Slovakia resulted in an irreconcilable rift. The differences were exacerbated by the election of two conflicting personalities in June 1992 — the Czechs voted into power the strong-willed, pragmatic economist Václav Klaus, the moving force behind the country's unique coupon privatization program. The Slovakian voters elected populist politician Vladimír Mečiar, a former Communist as well as a professional boxer, who vowed to protect his electorate from the harsher realities of economic reforms, advocating a looser "confederation" to hold the Czech and Slovak lands together. In July 1992, the Slovaks declared their sovereignty, and President Havel resigned the same day, declaring that he did not want to preside over a divided country.

Most citizens of the Czech Republic wanted the two parts of the country to stay united, but the leaders, unable to compromise, began formal negotiations and in the end, announced the impending division of Czechoslovakia. Two new countries — the Czech Republic and the Slovak Republic — were born on January 1, 1993. Weeks later, Havel was once again elected, but this time as president of the newly formed Czech Republic.

Despite all the convolutions on the political front, the 1,000-year-old city of Prague retains its historical atmosphere and flavor. The center of the city is the largest protected urban area in the world for two reasons. First, Czechoslovakia, which lay beyond the reach of Allied planes, escaped the heavy bombings of World War II, emerging almost unscathed physically. Second, almost half the 3,507 buildings now standing on Prague's original medieval ground plan are under landmark protection. The task of halting their decay — and restoring them to their former grandeur — is a dauntingly costly one, which only can be attacked piecemeal. Over the last couple of years, a good deal of scaffolding in the oldest parts of the city has come down to reveal breathtakingly beautiful façades.

A city of 500 spires, Prague is a sumptuous blend of nature and architecture. Like Rome, it is built on seven hills and is divided by a river, the Vltava (called Moldau in German), and is spanned by 18 bridges. The city, everywhere dotted with parks, waterways, and gardens, overwhelms the visitor with its architecture. As in many European cities and towns, numerous periods and styles are represented here — Romanesque, Gothic, baroque, neo-classical, Art Nouveau, and modern. The Old Town is itself a course in the architecture of the last 500 years.

But Prague is best known for its distinguished examples of the Gothic and the baroque. Gothic spires are literally everywhere, particularly in the Old Town, which boasts the Týn Church (1365) with its twin towers and flying buttresses (and, typically, a baroque interior), and the inspiring early Gothic Old-New Synagogue, majestically tall and graced with fluted pillars, pointed arches, and delicate stone embellishments.

Prague's baroque heritage includes the Wallenstein Palace, built by Italian architects between 1623 and 1630. It is an early baroque ensemble harmonizing sculptures, paintings, fountains, gardens, and a *sala terrena* (patio).

The city is as subtle as it is complex, unfolding itself leaf by leaf, and then only to the most observant and curious. To know the city, a visitor must amble through it leisurely — discovering a palace here, a tower there, a decorative touch somewhere else, and now and then lingering at one of its numerous wine cellars and beer halls for refreshment.

Slowly, Prague is emerging as a new rival to the glitter of Parisian nightlife and the hurly-burly of London's Piccadilly Circus, with new clubs and theaters opening almost daily. Indeed, it has become the destination of choice among young people from both the US and Europe (a recent report estimated that 20,000 Americans and thousands of other Westerners now reside in this suddenly trendy city).

Those who choose to stroll through the cobblestone streets, full of shadows at night, follow in the footsteps of Mozart, German poet Rainer Rilke, and French poet Guillaume Apollinaire, all of whom lived here. Franz Kafka was born here and resided for a while on Golden Lane, a crooked little street behind the forbidding castle. Characteristically, he once described Prague as "a little mother with claws," a different perspective from that of French poet Paul Valéry, who said "there is no city in the world in which magnificent wholes and valuable details and corners would be better combined, more happily situated" than in Prague.

Prague At-a-Glance

SEEING THE CITY

To experience the drama of Prague, visit the *Zlatá Praha* (Golden Prague) restaurant, on the eighth floor of the *Inter-Continental* hotel (see *Eating Out*). From here there's a spectacular view of Prague Castle, particularly beautiful at sunset when the castle is a black silhouette and the last rays of the sun splash red and gold into the Vltava River. A trip up Petřín Hill in the funicular offers a fine view in the opposite direction.

For an unsurpassed perspective on the city, consider the "Prague by Balloon" tour offered by *Buddy Bombard's Great Balloon Adventures* (6727 Curran St., McLean, VA 22101; phone: 703-448-9407 or 800-862-8537). The 6-day tour features daily treetop-level sightseeing excursions that lift off from Old Town Square. Terrestrial and aquatic tours (via motorcoach and boat) are also included in the package.

Any exploration should begin with "Historical Prague," a half-day tour of the city by motorcoach, with a multilingual guide, offered by *Cedok*, the now-privatized national tourist office. Buses leave from the *Cedok* branch office at 6 Bílkova, opposite the *Inter-Continental* hotel (phone: 231-8255 or 231-6619). *Cedok* also offers a 4-hour walking tour called "Old Prague by Foot."

Seeing the city by steamship is yet another option. The *Pražské Paroplavební Společnost* (Prague Passenger Ships; phone: 298309; fax: 205893) runs the historical steamship *Vyšehrad*, which leaves regularly from Rašínovo nábřeží, close to the Palackého Bridge, and travels to the Barrandov Cliffs, the Prague Zoo, and the Roztoky and Slapy Dam. Lunch, coffee, and dinner cruises are available.

A few Czech words that may help with your navigations: "náměstí" is the word for square or place; "ulice" and "ulička" mean street; and "trida" means avenue.

SPECIAL PLACES

Historical Prague was originally five independent towns, and each of these five districts — Nové Město (New Town), Staré Město (Old Town), Malá Strana (Lesser Town), Hradčany, and Vyšehrad — retains its individual character.

NOVÉ MĚSTO (NEW TOWN)

Prague's New Town dates from 1348, when it was established by King Charles IV. Wenceslas Square, with its profusion of shops, hotels, and restaurants, is the center of the modern city of Prague and a logical starting point for seeing the city.

VÁCLAVSKÉ NÁMĚSTÍ (WENCESLAS SQUARE) St. Václav ("Good King Wenceslas"), seated on his horse, guards this square, which is really a boulevard.

Dominated by the *National Museum,* Wenceslas Square — 2,475 feet by 198 feet — is the central thoroughfare of the city, lined with Art Nouveau hotels, restaurants, cafés, and rather pricey shops.

NÁRODNÍ MUZEUM (NATIONAL MUSEUM) The imposing neo-Renaissance façade and the interior decorations of this building reflect the spirit of late-19th-century Czech nationalism in which it was built. Its façade still bears the machine gun markings made by Russian troops, who mistook it for the Parliament during the 1968 invasion. Inside are paintings on Czech historical themes, fossils, stamps, and archaeological items. Open Mondays, Wednesdays, and Thursdays from 9 AM to 5 PM; Saturdays and Sundays from 10 AM to 6 PM. Admission charge. 68 Václavské náměstí (phone: 269451, ext. 376).

KARLOVO NÁMĚSTÍ (CHARLES SQUARE) Now a park surrounded by old buildings, the New Town's oldest square — and still Prague's largest — was the central market around which the town was proudly planned by Charles IV in 1348. On the north side is the oldest building in the New Town, the Novoměstská radnice (New Town Hall), site of the town government from 1398 to 1784. On the south side of Charles Square, at No. 40, is an 18th-century baroque building known as Faust's House. Ever since the 14th century, houses on this site have been associated with alchemy and other occult practices. (The origin of the Faust legend is uncertain; it sometimes is said to have arisen from the strange adventures of a 16th-century English alchemist named Edward Kelley.)

MUZEUM ANTONÍN DVOŘÁKOVA (ANTON DVORAK MUSEUM) This lovely baroque building, designed by the noted architect K. I. Dienzenhofer, was a summer residence called Villa America in the 18th century. Fittingly, the building now houses mementos of Antonín Dvořákova, the Czech composer of the great "New World Symphony" (which uses American folk tunes). During the summer, Dvořák's music is performed in the sculpture garden in back of the house. Open from 10 AM to 5 PM; closed Mondays. Admission charge. 20 Ke Karlovu, not far from Karlovo námĕsti (phone: 298214).

STARÉ MĚSTO (OLD TOWN)

Walk here just before dusk, when the narrow, winding cobblestone streets seem to merge into dim Gothic arcades. The Old Town, which contains most of the oldest buildings in Prague, dates from 1120. A great many medieval exteriors have been preserved in this area.

PRAŠNA BRÁNA (POWDER TOWER) This gate to the Old Town, used in the 17th century to store gunpowder, was first built in 1475, then rebuilt in the late 19th century. It marked the beginning of the royal coronation route. The view at the top (186 steps up) is delightful. At press time, the tower was undergoing renovation; there is no scheduled reopening. Na příkopě.

CELETNÁ ULICE (CELETNÁ STREET) Renovated baroque townhouses line this curving street, once part of the royal coronation route. Today, visitors can follow the route from the Powder Tower to Old Town Square, running parallel to Zelezná ulice where the Carolinum, a 14th-century building that was part of the original university founded by King Charles IV (9 Zelezná ulice), is located. Also along the way is the *Stavovské Divadlo* (Estates Theater), formerly the *Tyl Theater* (6 Ovocný), where Mozart's masterpiece *Don Giovanni* had its world premiere in 1787 and where scenes from the 1984 film *Amadeus* were shot. Recent renovations have restored the original magnificence and charm to this musical landmark.

STAROMĚSTSKÉ NÁMĚSTÍ (OLD TOWN SQUARE) The center of Prague's Old Town, this important square was given a face-lift in time for the 1988 celebration of the 40th anniversary of the Communist takeover. The monument to John Huss was erected in 1915, 500 years after the religious reformer was burned at the stake. Every hour on the hour, crowds gather to watch the Old Town Hall's astronomical clock (built in 1490), with its mechanical figures of Christ, the 12 apostles, and allegorical *memento mori* figures performing their solemn march. The Town Hall itself was founded in 1338 and rebuilt many times (parts of it were destroyed by fire during the final days of World War II). The many interesting features within include a dungeon and a well in the cellar, and a 15th-century council chamber adorned with 60 imaginative coats of arms belonging to the guilds of Prague and still used by the city government. Guided tours — some in English — are given hourly, following the clock's ritual. On the east side of the square is the Kostel Panny Marie před Týnem (Church of Our Lady at Týn), dating from 1365, with its twin Gothic spires. Once the property of the Hussites and later of the Jesuits, this beautiful church combines a Gothic exterior with a baroque interior. Tycho de Brahe, the Danish astronomer, was buried here in 1601. A pretty little café, *U Týna,* is at 15 Staroměstské náměstí (phone: 231-0525). Open daily from 10 AM to 10 PM. Nearby is the *Dům u Zvonu* (House of the Stone Bell; phone: 231-0272), a Gothic structure that serves as a municipal art exhibition hall, where concerts are performed. Open Tuesdays through Sundays from 10 AM to 6 PM.

This is "Kafka territory." A bust of the writer commemorates the site of his birth in 1883, at 5 U Radnice. He grew up in the house next to the Old Town Hall (it's now covered with graffiti), and his father ran a dry goods shop on the ground floor of the rococo Goltz-Kinský Palace on the Old Town Square. The palace is also where young Kafka attended school.

On the north side of the square is the Kostel Sv. Mikuláše (St. Nicolas); built in 1732–35 by architect Kilian Ignác Dienzenhofer, it houses statuary by Antonín Braun. This is also the site of frequent organ and choir concerts. Check a listing posted on the door for times and dates.

JOSEFOV (THE JEWISH QUARTER) Walk north from the Old Town Hall on Pařížská ulice and turn left on Cervená to see the Staronová Synagóga (Old-

New Synagogue), the oldest surviving synagogue in Europe (1270). One of Prague's most beautiful examples of the early Gothic style, it is truly inspiring, with its fluted pillars and sculptural decorations.

Jewish traders founded the Prague ghetto as early as the 9th century, and it became a center of Jewish culture by the 17th century. Parts of the ghetto were demolished in 1896 when Pařížská ulice was being constructed. Only seven synagogues and the cemetery remain. Located within several of the synagogues and public buildings are some fine collections of torah mantles and silver artifacts. In the restored Pinkasova Synagóga (Pinkas Synagogue; 3 Siroká), the names of 77,297 Jewish men, women, and children murdered by the Nazis are painted on the interior walls. Ironically, during the war, the Nazis attempted to turn the entire Jewish quarter into a museum of the very culture they were seeking to destroy.

Within the Jewish Quarter is an intensely moving collection of drawings and paintings by children in the Theresienstadt concentration camp.

Also here is the Starý Zidovský Hřbitov (Old Jewish Cemetery), with its 12,000 15th- to 18th-century tombstones. The oldest preserved tomb dates from 1438; burials continued here until 1787 when a new cemetery was built in Prague. The cemetery is the property of the *Státni Zidovské Muzeum* (State Jewish Museum; 17 Listopadu; phone: 231-0785), which houses exhibitions of religious articles and Hebrew manuscripts. The museum is open 9 AM to 5 PM; closed Saturdays.

Nearby, in the Jewish Town Hall, is the only kosher restaurant in town, the *Koscher Restaurace Shalom* (18 Maislova; phone: 231-6925). Open daily for lunch and dinner during the summer; lunch only on Saturdays and in the winter.

KLÁŠTER SV. ANEŽKY (CONVENT OF ST. AGNES) In a partly reconstructed Gothic convent, collections of 19th-century Czech paintings, porcelain, glass, silver, and pewter are on display. Look for the paintings of Antonín Mánes (1784–1843) for an artist's view of Prague and its environs before the modern age. Open 10 AM to 6 PM; closed Mondays. 17 Milosrdných ulice (phone: 231251).

BETLÉMSKÁ KAPLE (BETHLEHEM CHAPEL) Here on the southern edge of the Old Town, the church reformer John Huss preached his revolutionary ideas from 1402 until his martyrdom in 1415. To the Czechs, Huss is a symbol of freedom from oppression and is revered as a national hero. The present chapel is a painstaking 1950-54 reconstruction of the original Gothic building, and the wooden threshold of the pulpit, once trod by Huss himself, is now protected under glass. Open 9 AM to 4 PM. Betlémské náměstí.

KARLŮV MOST (CHARLES BRIDGE) One of the oldest and most beautiful bridges in Europe was built of stone between the Old Town and the Lesser Town in 1357 by Charles IV. Lined on both sides by 30 fine statues of the baroque period (1683–1714), its Lesser Town end has two towers; the higher one may be climbed for a spectacular view. The bridge is a favorite strolling place day or night, and it offers views of the castle, the Vltava River, and the lovely island of Kampa, with its chestnut trees. Vendors now sell souvenirs here, and there are usually musicians playing for contributions.

MALÁ STRANA (LESSER TOWN)

Sometimes called Little Town, this is Prague's baroque soul, founded in 1257 as the second (after the Old Town) of the royal towns. During the 17th and 18th centuries, foreign noblemen and the Catholic church engaged some outstanding architects and artists to embellish what is the city's most picturesque quarter. Full of old palaces — including the magnificent Wallenstein Palace, where concerts are held during the summer — Lesser Town is a maze of crooked cobblestone lanes lined with old churches, museums, inns, wine cellars, and charming little parks. It is best just to wander around the town and discover its nooks and crannies for yourself.

MALOSTRANSKÉ NÁMĚSTÍ (LESSER TOWN SQUARE) Surrounded by 16th-century houses with arcades, the square — like the entire Lesser Town — is dominated by the Jesuit Kostel Sv. Mikuláše (Church of St. Nicholas). Designed by famous 18th-century architects, the Dienzenhofers and Anselmago Lurago, this is the finest baroque building in Prague.

VALDŠTEJNSKÉ PALÁC (WALLENSTEIN PALACE) Northwest of St. Nicholas's Church is the magnificent baroque palace begun in 1624 by Italian architects for Albrecht Wallenstein, the great Hapsburg general. Unfortunately, the frescoes inside can't be seen because the building also houses the Ministry of Culture, but the public concerts in the garden with its *salla terrena* (patio) are an experience that should not be missed. The garden, consisting of a lake, a cave, and hundreds of roses, rhododendron, magnolias, and Japanese cherry trees, was landscaped in 1623. The statues here are actually replicas of originals created by Dutch master Adrian de Vries in 1626. Be sure to visit the Wallenstein Riding Academy (accessible from Valdštejnské náměstí), which often holds special art exhibitions. Open daily from 9 AM to 7 PM May through September. Valdštejnské náměstí.

KOSTEL PANNY MARIE VITĚZNÉ (CHURCH OF OUR LADY OF VICTORY) A favorite pilgrimage site that dates from the 17th century and houses the *Bambino di Praga* (The Infant Jesus of Prague) by an anonymous artist; it's a renowned statue that was brought to Prague from Spain at the beginning of the 16th century. 13 Karmelitská.

NERUDOVA ULICE (NERUDA STREET) Leading from the Lesser Town to Hradčany Castle and lined on both sides by baroque façades is one of the most beautiful streets in the Lesser Town. Many townhouses on this street, named after Jan Neruda, the 19th-century writer, have preserved the old signs used before numbers were introduced: a red eagle, three violins, a golden goblet, and other quaint symbols.

HRADČANY (CASTLE DISTRICT)

Near the castle of the same name, which probably was begun in the 9th century, is the Prague town of Hradčany, officially founded in 1320.

HRADČANY (PRAGUE CASTLE) Today the seat of the government, this castle has been a Slav stronghold, a residence of the kings of Bohemia, and the seat of the president of the Republic; it is the history of the Czech nation in stone. With three dizzyingly complex walled courtyards, the castle is best grasped with the help of a *Cedok* walking tour (see *Seeing the City*). Perhaps most interesting is the interior of the vaulted Gothic Vladislav Hall, where jousting tournaments once took place.

KATEDRÁLA SV. VÍTA (ST. VITUS'S CATHEDRAL) Dominating the castle is this Gothic mausoleum of the Czech kings. The original building was designed in 1344 by Mathias Arras and Peter Parléř and finally completed in 1929. It is the repository for the Czech crown jewels, which are rarely on public display. However, they were shown during the last week of January 1993 to commemorate the birth of the new Czech Republic. Pražské Hrad.

ZLATÁ ULIČKA (GOLDEN LANE) Just north of the castle, this charming cobblestone lane lined with little houses and shops is famous as the legendary street of alchemists who tried to turn lead into gold. Franz Kafka lived at No. 24 in 1917; it is now a bookstore.

NÁRODNÍ GALERIE (NATIONAL GALLERY) From European Old Masters to Picasso, a very rich collection of paintings adorns this museum in the Baroque Sternberg Palace on Castle Square. Open 10 AM to 6 PM; closed Mondays. Admission charge. 15 Hradčanské náměstí (phone: 352441).

KLÁŠTER SV. JIŘSKÁ (ST. GEORGE'S MONASTERY) An extensive collection of Czech Gothic art, which is superbly installed in the first convent founded in Bohemia. Open from 10 AM to 6 PM; closed Mondays. Admission charge. 33 Sv. Jiřská náměstí.

LORETA (OUR LADY OF LORETTO CHURCH) Built in 1626, this structure was so named because it was modeled after a pilgrimage church in Loretto, Italy. It also is famous for the 1694 carillon in its clock tower and for the "Loretto treasury," a collection of extremely valuable 16th- to 18th-century jewelry and religious applied arts. Open 9 AM to 12:15 PM and 1 to 4:30 PM; closed Mondays. Admission charge. Loretánské náměstí (phone: 536228).

PETŘÍN GARDENS The site of the newly restored 180-foot Petřín Tower (modeled after the Eiffel Tower), these captivating gardens offer the perfect respite for the weary traveler. Also located here is a mirrored *bludiště* (labyrinth), in addition to a diorama that depicts the 1648 battle between Czechoslovakia and Sweden. Open daily from 9 AM to 6 PM. To reach the gardens, take the funicular on Ujezd ulice.

THE ROYAL SUMMER PALACE OF BELVEDERE (QUEEN ANNA'S SUMMER HOUSE) Originally designed in 1537 for Anna, wife of King Ferdinand I, this is the most important Renaissance building north of the Alps. The garden contains a "singing fountain" (water drips into a bell-like metal bowl, producing a musical sound) designed by Tomáš Jaroš in 1564. The palace is now the site of numerous art exhibitions. Open from 10 AM to 6 PM; Wednesdays from 10 AM to 7 PM; closed Mondays. Chotkovaey sady (phone: 206780).

KLÁŠTER STRAHOVSKÝ (STRAHOV MONASTERY) West of the castle, high above the green slopes of Petřín Hill, is a gigantic monastery, built between 1140 and 1784, which once rivaled the castle itself in magnificence and whose garden provides a lovely view of Prague. Today, Strahov houses the *Muzeum Národního Písemnictví* (Museum of Czech Literature); two baroque library halls also may be seen. Open 9:30 AM to 12:30 PM and 1 to 5 PM; closed Mondays. Admission charge. 1 Strahovský nádvoří (phone: 538841).

VYŠEHRAD

High on the cliffs above the Vltava River on the side opposite Hradčany, this fortress and the town around it probably were founded in the 9th century. However, no one knows how old Vyšehrad really is; it may be much older.

VYŠEHRAD FORTRESS Walk around the grounds, which include a park, the 11th-century Rotunda of St. Martin, and the Church of St. Peter and St. Paul.

VYŠEHRAD CEMETERY This is the burial place of the country's greats; Antonín Dvořákova, Karel Capek, Jan Kubelik, Jan Neruda, and Bedřich Smetana are just a few of the prominent names. Next to the Church of St. Peter and St. Paul. Open daily from 8 AM to 7 PM.

ENVIRONS

KUTNÁ HORA A lovely area just 42 miles (67 km) southeast of Prague, it is a former silver mining town that boomed in the 13th century when its rich deposits were used to help create the splendor of the Bohemian court. During the 14th century, it was the second-largest town in the country. Here coins were minted by craftsmen imported from Florence. Here also is the Vlašský Dvůr, a 13th-century palace where the craftsmen worked, a fine coin museum, a church whose vault is lined entirely with human skulls, and the unusual Gothic roof of St. Barbara's Church. A one-day bus excursion — "Treasures of Bohemian Gothic" — includes a tour of Kutná Hora, as well as a stop at Cesky Sternberk, a 13th-century hilltop castle. For further information, contact *Cedok* (see *Sources and Resources*).

KARLŠTEJN, KONOPIŠTĚ, AND KŘIVOKLÁT CASTLES About 17½ miles (28 km) southwest of Prague is the most visited castle in the Czech Republic. The 14th-century Karlštejn Castle, built by Charles IV, is the depository of the great wealth he attained as a Holy Roman Emperor. The castle underwent massive reconstruction in the 19th century, and today is the site of the Chapel of the Holy Rood with its magnificent display of crown jewels. Also of interest is the Audience Hall, where the king greeted his suppli- cants, and Luxembourg Hall, which features a tapestry that traces the royal family tree. Within the palace complex is the Church of the Virgin where *Relic Scenes* (ca. 1357), one of the earliest known portraits in European art, is on display. St. Catherine's Chapel, with an oratory en- crusted in semi-precious stones, and the Chapel of the Holy Cross are also on the grounds.

Konopiště Castle, located 26½ miles (42 km) from the city, is a Renais- sance château surrounded by landscaped gardens and a park. It offers a fine collection of 15th- and 16th-century armor, porcelain, and other pre- cious objects.

About 2 miles (3 km) farther in the small town of Bonesov is Křivoklát Castle. Set in a forest preserve near the Berounka River, it was used as a hunting lodge by Czech kings from the 13th to the 16th centuries. Later, it was turned into a prison for political offenders. The permanent collec- tion on display here includes sculpture and paintings from the late Gothic period, as well as arms, carriages, and sleighs dating from the 17th to the 19th centuries.

All three castles are open from 9 AM to 6 PM; closed Mondays. There is an admission charge to all three and English-language tours are available. Tickets can be purchased in advance from the concert and tourist activities booking agency *BTI* (16 Na příkopě; phone: 228738; fax: 261889). Most major travel agencies, including *Cedok* (see *Sources and Resources*) offer half-day bus excursions from Prague. The castles also are accessible by public transportation — trains leave the Praha Hlavní Náraží train station (see *Getting Around,* below) in Prague hourly for Karlštejn, where you can transfer to trains for the other two sites. Be sure to check train schedules and information before your departure.

LIDICE Also quite popular is the village of Lidice, only 13 miles (21 km) from Prague. The town was totally destroyed by the Nazis in 1942 in reprisal for the killing of a Nazi police governor. All local men were shot on sight, all women sent to concentration camps, and all young blond children shipped to the German Reich for adoption. Today the village (a national monu- ment) has been preserved exactly as it was — so the ruins can serve as a reminder of Nazi atrocities and a memorial to its victims. *Cedok* (see *Sources and Resources,* below) offers coach trips to the area, 37½ miles (60 km) from Prague, which includes Terezín, which was set up by the Nazis as a "model" concentration camp with its own orchestra and children's school. The area is also accessible by public transportation.

Sources and Resources

TOURIST INFORMATION

For general information, brochures, maps, and tour bookings, contact the now-privatized *Cedok* (18 Na příkopě; phone: 212-7111; or 10 E. 40th St., New York, NY 10016; phone: 212-689-9720) or the Prague Information Service (20 Na příkopě; phone: 544444). The latter can arrange for private guides as well as concert and theater tickets at its office (4 Panská; phone: 223411 or 224311). *Rekrea* (26-28 Pařížská; phone: 231-1193 or 231-1591) is much smaller than *Cedok,* yet it offers many services — and a much warmer welcome. *IFB Bohemia* (25 Václavské náměstí; phone: 260333; fax: 26201), another private tourist agency, also is helpful, as is *Pragotour* (23 Obecního domu ulice; phone: 231-7281; fax: 232-2216). The *American Hospitality Center* (14 Malé náměstí; phone: 236-7486; fax: 269738) offers tourist information and will assist travelers in finding accommodations and in reserving theater and concert tickets. It also operates a small café that features excellent Chicago deep-dish pizza.

> **NOTE** Throughout the city there are numerous "Chequepoints" where travelers may exchange currency. Very often, these places charge a much higher commission rate than do banks. On the flip side, there are the ubiquitous black marketeers who are in the business of exchanging money — and ripping-off unsuspecting tourists. No matter how tempting their deals may sound — steer clear.

LOCAL COVERAGE You can find English-language newspapers in Prague in a few of the larger hotels or from street vendors in popular tourist areas. *Prognosis* is a biweekly paper that covers local news and has excellent listings of cultural events and nightlife in Prague. It can be purchased in major hotels, tourist offices, bookshops, and airline offices. The *Prague Post,* an English-language weekly newspaper produced by a group of American expatriates, also has complete entertainment listings. It is available at newsstands.

TELEPHONE The country code for the Czech Republic is 42; the city code for Prague is 2. Most public phones now operate with phone cards, which can be purchased at the Main Post Office (see *Local Services*) or at newspaper kiosks.

GETTING AROUND

AIRPORT Praha-Ruzyně Airport, about 40 minutes from downtown by taxi, handles both domestic and international flights (for information call 367814 or 367760). Cab fare is about $20 to downtown Prague. Buses connecting the airport and downtown leave from the *Vitava Travel Bureau* (25 Revoluční trida) and cost about 60¢; contact the *Czechoslovakia Airline* (*CSA*) counter at the airport. Shuttle bus service connecting the airport and major hotels costs about $8; more information can be obtained from the *Cedok* counter at the airport.

BUS/TRAM Though public transportation has been both inexpensive and good, bus and railway fares increased as the state began withdrawing its subsidies. Tickets are sold at newsstands and tobacco shops — not on the bus or tram. The ticket is punched once you are aboard. For destinations outside of Prague, buses depart from the central bus stop located at the Florenc Station. For information call 221445 weekdays from 6 AM to 8 PM.

CAR RENTAL The *Avis* office is located at 33 Opletalova (phone: 222324); the company also operates out of the *Atrium* and *Forum Praha* hotels (see *Checking In*). *Budget* has offices at Praha-Ruzyně Airport (phone: 316-5214) and at the *Inter-Continental* hotel (see *Checking In*). There are *Hertz* branches at the Praha-Ruzyně Airport (phone: 312-0717) and at the *Atrium* and *Diplomat* hotels (see *Checking In*). There's also *Prague Car Rent* (7 Malá Stěpánská; phone: 691-0323 or 295857). Limos (both Lincoln and Cadillac) are available from *Exclusive Luxury Limo Service* (4 Na marně; phone: 342791; fax: 311-5031).

CARRIAGE RIDES A ride in a *fiakr* (horse-drawn carriage) is a romantic way to see the city. The cost is about $40 per hour. You can find carriages drawn up at 5-13 Pařížská.

METRO Built in cooperation with the Russians and still expanding, the subway system, which runs from 5 AM to midnight, is fast, safe, and clean. The same 4-koruna (about 12¢) ticket used for the metro, buses, and trams can be purchased in metro stations, tobacco shops, and at hotel desks. Twenty-four-hour, 2-, 3-, 4-, or 5-day metro passes are available.

TAXI Reasonably priced taxis are available at major hotels or through *Radio Taxi* (phone: 203941 or 202951).

TRAIN The main train station, Praha Hlavní Nádraží (2 Wilsonova trida; phone: 235-3836 or 264930) is also called the Woodrow Wilson station in honor of the US president's efforts for peace at the end of World War I and his subsequent involvement in negotiating the 1919 Treaty of Versailles, which officially recognized Czechoslovakia as an independent nation.

LOCAL SERVICES

Most hotels will try to arrange for any special services a business traveler might require.

DENTIST (ENGLISH-SPEAKING) The number to call for emergency dental care is 261374, although English is not always spoken; it's best to ask the service desk at any major hotel to make the call for you.

EMERGENCY The number to call for an ambulance is 155, although English is not always spoken; it's best to ask the service desk at any major hotel to make the call for you. The 24-hour medical emergency number for foreigners is 299381; doctors on call at this facility (32 Karlovo náměstí) speak English and/or German. The *Diplomatic Health Center* (724 Na homolce; phone: 529-22146 weekdays or 529211 evenings and weekends) also treats foreign travelers. A 24-hour first-aid service is located at 5 Palckého (phone: 220081 or 268126). The police emergency number is 158. For less urgent police matters call the station (14 Konviktská; phone: 212-1111). English may not be spoken; ask at your hotel service desk for assistance. Emergency road service is provided by *Yellow Angels* (phone: 154).

LOST AND FOUND A drop-off and pick-up depot is located at 5 Bolzánov (phone: 236-8887).

PHARMACY The pharmacy at 7 Na příkopě (phone: 220081) is open around the clock. Other pharmacies alternate in staying open 24 hours a day; ask at your hotel desk for a schedule.

POST OFFICE The Hlauní Pošta (Main Post Office) is located just off Wenceslas Square, and is open 24 hours (phone: 264193).

SPECIAL EVENTS

Pražské Jaro (Prague Spring), held every mid-May to early June since 1946, offers concerts that feature internationally known soloists, orchestras, chamber ensembles, and operas (also see *Music*). Tickets range from $7 to $60. The *International Jazz Festival Prague,* one of the major European jazz festivals, takes place in even-numbered years. Previous festivals have featured Chick Corea, Stephane Grappelli, and Czech bands led by Gustav Brom and Milan Svoboda. For information, contact *Pražské Jaro Agency,* the Czech arts and entertainment agency (18 Hellichov; phone: 533474; fax: 536040). Prague also hosts several other smaller scale jazz events during the year — the *Prague Jazz Celebration Festival* in the spring, and the *Jazz on the Island Festival* in June. For further information, inquire at *Cedok* (see above) or *BTI* (16 Na příkopě; phone: 228738; fax: 261889).

MUSEUMS

In addition to the museums mentioned in *Special Places,* we recommend the following (all charge admission):

BERTRAMKA/PAMÁTNÍK W.A. MOZARTA (VILLA BERTRAMKA/MOZART MUSEUM) A 17th-century mansion in the Smíchov district where Mozart stayed is now a museum devoted to the composer and the city of Prague. Open 9:30 AM to 5 PM; closed Tuesdays. 169 Mozartová (phone: 543893).

LOBKOVICKÝ PALÁC (LOBKOVIC PALACE) Housed in an 18th-century building, this museum is devoted to the country's baroque period. Piano and orchestra concerts are held on Wednesdays, Thursdays, and Fridays during the summer. Open 9:30 AM to 6 PM; closed Mondays in summer; open 9 AM to 5 PM; closed Mondays in fall and winter. Jirská ulice, behind Prague Castle (phone: 537306).

MUZEUM BEDŘICHA SMETANY (BEDRICH SMETANA EXHIBITION) A museum devoted to the composer's life. Open 10 AM to 5 PM; closed Tuesdays. 1 Novotného lavka (phone: 265371).

MUZEUM HUDEBNÍCH NÁSTROJŮ (MUSEUM OF MUSICAL INSTRUMENTS) A must for music lovers, it has the second-largest collection of antique instruments in the world. Open 10 AM to 5 PM; closed Mondays. 2 Lázeňská, Malá Strana (phone: 530843).

SHOPPING

Bohemian glass and crystal are world famous and are available here at prices not to be found anywhere else. Try *Moser* (12 Na příkopě; phone: 221851) or *Bohemia* in the Old Town Square (16 Staroměstské náměstí; phone: 232-7771) for better items at top prices. Other shops worth exploring are *Krystal* (30 Václavské náměstí; phone: 263384) and *Crystalex* (6 Malé náměstí; 263694). For chandeliers, try *Lux* (16 Na příkopě; phone: 220619), though keep in mind differences between US and European electrical currents.

Many Europeans and Americans living in Europe buy entire sets of glass and china in Prague's department stores, which have improved dramatically in recent years. Department stores also carry clothing, hats, and other local items at incredible prices, although imported items are less of a bargain. Head first to Prague's largest department store, *Kotva* (8 Republiky náměstí; phone: 235-0001); others are *Máj* (26 Národní; phone: 262341); *Bila Labuť* (23 Na přikopě; phone: 232-0622); and *Krone* (21 Václavské náměstí; phone: 263842). All the above stores (except *Bila Labuť*) are now under *Kmart* ownership.

For costume jewelry, stop in at *Bijoux de Bohème* (8 Dlouhá; no phone); for the real stuff, try *Granát* (15 Na příkopě; phone: 220619). *Garnet* (28 Václavské náměstí; no phone) specializes in the gem of the same name, native to Bohemia.

Crafts can be bought in the Wenceslas Square area at *Krásná Jizba* (36 Národní; phone: 236-6535). At *Christmastime,* gingerbread tree ornaments are baked and sold at *Ceská Jizba* (12 Karlova; phone: 265773). Russian souvenirs can be purchased at stalls that line Na příkopě.

The *Central European Gallery* (19 Husová; phone: 236-0700; fax: 269086) offers a wonderful selection of posters and works by Czech graphic artists.

In addition, *Galerie Maislova* (17 Maislova; phone: 231-8196; fax: 231-8754) features fine antiques; *Antikvariat* (7 Dlážděná) sells used books, graphic arts, sheet music, and paper money. Sheet music can be found at

30 Jungmannovo náměstí and musical instruments at 17 Jungmannovo náměstí. For English-language and other foreign books, browse though the bookstore at 42 Malá Stěpánská (phone: 235-2827). The *Zahraniěni Literatura* bookstore (2 J. Palacha náměstí; phone: 231-9516), located at the Filozoficka Fakulta (Philosophical Faculty) of Charles University, carries the best selection of English-language classics in town.

SPORTS AND FITNESS

FITNESS CENTERS *Plavecký Stadión* (74 Podolská; phone: 439152), a 20-minute drive south of Prague in Podolí, has an Olympic-size pool, steamroom, and sauna. In addition, several larger hotels also offer guests facilities: the *Atrium* has a pool, tennis courts, and fitness center; the *Forum Praha* has a modern penthouse fitness center with gym, pool, squash courts, saunas, and solarium; the *Inter-Continental* features exercise equipment and a sauna; and the *Panorama* hotel has a pool, sauna, and solarium (see *Checking In*).

JOGGING A good place is Stromovka Park, a 15-minute walk or 5-minute ride northeast of downtown.

SOCCER Games are played at *Spartakiade* (Sparta Stadium; 98 Mílada Horaková, Letná; phone: 382441); you can purchase tickets there.

SQUASH Courts are available at the *Forum Praha* hotel (see *Checking In;* phone: 410238) and at *Club Hotel Průhoice* (400 Průhoice; phone: 643-6501).

TENNIS There are indoor-outdoor courts at *Spartakiade* (98 Mílady Horakové; phone: 325479), *Centrálni Tenisový Dvorec* (Central Tennis Courts; 7 Praha, Stauanke; phone: 213-6323 or 213-1270), and at *Tennis Club Průhoice* (400 Průhoice; phone: 643-6501).

THEATER

Although theater is usually performed in Czech, don't miss this special experience which transcends all languages:

CURTAIN CALL

Laterna Magika This unique theater experience is an amalgam of cinema, opera, theater, dance, and circus. One of the most intriguing spectacles on the Continent, its name, "Magic Lantern," conveys the swirling, kaleidoscopic style of the performances. It's not necessary to understand Czech to enjoy the hypnotic beauty of these shows; children in particular find them fascinating. This theater is also of interest because of the role it played in the 1989 "velvet revolution." In the first days of the demonstrations that overthrew the Communist regime, the *Laterna Magika* troupe offered their theater to playwright (later president) Václav Havel and the other dissidents masterminding the revolution. Every night, reporters from around the world would squeeze into the theater to hear Havel's latest words on the progress of negotiations with the Communists. 4 Národní (phone: 206260; fax: 261103).

Also popular with foreigners are the pantomime productions at the *Divadlo Na Zábradlí* (Theater on the Balustrade; 5 Anenské náměstí; phone: 236-0449). Other theaters include the *Národní Divadlo* (National Theater; 2 Národní; phone: 205364) for the classics (in Czech); the *Nová Scéna*, the *National Theater*'s architecturally controversial offshoot next door; and the *Stavovské Divadlo* (Estates Theater; 6 Ovocný; phone: 228658), which offers some simultaneous translations.

MUSIC

Prague is a city that Mozart loved, and where Dvořákova and Smetana lived and composed their music. It is still a very musical city.

HIGH NOTES

Pražské Jaro (Prague Spring) This doyen of European music festivals has been an annual event since 1945. Internationally known conductors, soloists, orchestras, chamber ensembles, and opera companies from Eastern Europe are always on the program, as are some fine Russian artists (who invariably go on to give sold-out performances at *Carnegie Hall*). The festival takes place from mid-May to early June. 18 Hellichová (phone: 533474; fax: 536040).

Concerts can be heard at the *Stavovské Divadlo*, formerly the *Tyl Theater* (see *Theater*, above), where *Don Giovanni* had its world premiere; *Dvořákova Síň* (Dvorak Hall) in the *Dům Umělců* (House of Artists; Jana Palacha náměstí; phone: 231-9164); *Smetanova Síň* (Smetana Hall) in *Obecní Dům* (Municipal House; 5 Republiky náměstí; phone: 232-5858); and *Palac Kultury* (Palace of Culture; 65 Květná ulice; phone: 416-1111), as well as the newly opened *Rudolfinum* (12 Alešovo nábřeží; phone: 286-0352). Operas are performed at the *Národní Divadlo* (see *Theater*, above), the *Smetanovo Divadlo* (Smetana Theater; 3 Wilsonova trida; phone: 269745), and the *Státní Opera Praha* (Prague State Opera; 4 Wilsonova trida; phone: 269746).

NIGHTCLUBS AND NIGHTLIFE

In the past year, Prague has seen an explosion of new clubs and discos. For a grab bag of jazz, blues, and rock, try the smoke-filled *Malostrnská Beseda* (Malostrnská náměstí; phone: 539024). Have a beer, watch TV, or dance the night away at *Borat* (18 Ujezd; phone: 538362). The *Bunkr Café* (2 Lodecká; phone: 231-0735) is a favorite among the young American crowd, and the *Rock Club Bunkr* next door features local and international live bands. For dancing, drinks, and a view of the Vltava River, there is the slick *Lávka* (1 Lávka; phone: 228234). The *Rock Café* (20 Národní; phone: 206656) is a popular high-volume rock club with live music and a disco. *Eden Palladium*'s (1 Slávie; phone: 747063) claim to fame is a huge dance floor and an oldies night. Run by Americans, the newest club on the scene is called *Radost* (120 Bělohradská; phone: 251210), with disco from 10 PM to 5 AM.

For jazz buffs, the *Reduta Jazz Club* (20 Národní; phone: 203822), a cozy jazz cellar with plush furniture and a smoky, dark atmosphere, has everything from Dixieland to swing to contemporary jazz-fusion nightly except Sundays. The *Jazz Art Club* (40 Vinohradská) offers not only jazz but a music store and an offbeat bar; open daily except Sundays at 8 PM. The *Press Jazz Club* (9 Pařížská, near the Old Town Square; phone: 224723) features live jazz and swing concerts. The large upstairs room, which patrons enter via a spiral staircase, is rarely full. In addition, *Aghartha* (5 Krakouská; phone: 224558) is a funky club, with a shop and a café.

For extravagant floor shows, don't miss *Lucerna* (61 Malá Stěpánská; phone: 235-0888) and *Revue Alhambra* at the *Ambassador/Zlatá Husa* hotel. *Club Penguin* (5 Zborovská; phone: 545660) has been known to spin waltz music if the crowd is right. For those with a penchant for gambling, try the casinos at the *Forum Praha, Ambassador/Zlatá Husa,* and *Jalta* hotels (see *Checking In*). The weekly English-language newspaper *Prognosis* and the weekly *Prague Post* include listings of pubs, clubs, and other popular Prague venues.

Best in Town

CHECKING IN

Hotel reservations may be made through *Cedok* or through your own travel agent. One intriguing Prague option is called a "botel" (boat plus hotel), several of which are anchored in the Vltava River. In addition, the newly established *Prague Travelers Service* (phone: 800-626-4160) arranges apartment rentals for $60 to $120 a night (for a 2-room unit).

Also available for considerably less are private apartments. Contact *Ave Travel Agency* (8 Wilsonova trida; phone: 236-2560 or 236-3075; fax: 236-2956). Another option is *American-International Homestays* (1515 W. Penn St., Iowa City, IA 52240; phone: 319-626-2125), which arranges for stays with Czech families in Prague and several other Eastern European cities.

For all accommodations, advance bookings are essential; the influx of tourists has created a greater-than-ever shortage of space in Prague. *Cedok* accepts bookings for non-deluxe hotels only on a half-board basis (meal vouchers can be used outside the hotel). Expect to pay from $200 to $300 for a double room at a very expensive hotel; $70 to $200 at an expensive property; $40 to $70 at a moderate place; and $20 to $40 at the inexpensive botels. Be aware that at press time, the Czech government had imposed a 23% sales tax on hotel rooms, so check in advance to see whether or not the tax has been included in the price you are quoted. Most of Prague's major hotels have complete facilities for the business traveler. Those hotels listed below as having "business services" usually offer such conveniences as English-speaking concierge, meeting rooms, photocopiers, computers, translation services, and express checkout, among others. Call the hotel for additional information. All telephone numbers are in the 2 city code unless otherwise indicated.

For an unforgettable experience in Prague, we begin with our favorites, followed by our cost and quality choices of hotels, listed by price category.

SPECIAL HAVENS

Palace Praha Offering the finest accommodations in the nation's capital, this is the city's most beautiful — and most expensive — hotel. Built at the beginning of the century in the ornate Art Nouveau style, this luxurious property near the Old Town has been renovated to its original grandeur. From the sartorially splendid doorman to the elegantly decorated rooms, this establishment does its best to pamper and impress its chic international clientele. There's a restaurant that serves excellent French fare and an upscale cafeteria with that rare find, a salad bar (see *Eating Out*). There are 125 rooms and suites (including a romantic honeymoon suite, a stately presidential suite, and a delicate pink room designed for "lady travelers"), a piano bar, a sauna, and a solarium. Business services. 12 Panská (phone: 235-9394; fax: 235-9373).

U Tří Pštrosů (At the Three Ostriches) Located at the Lesser Town end of the Charles Bridge, this pretty 16th-century house is the oldest and most charming hostelry in Prague and one of the most exclusive places in all of Eastern Europe. The 18 rooms and suites must be booked several months in advance, particularly for summer visits. The restaurant also is one of the city's most delightful; it serves Czech specialties at lunch and dinner, and features fine service. 12 Dražického náměstí (phone: 536151).

VERY EXPENSIVE

Diplomat Now managed by Vienna International, this favorite among businesspeople, only a 10-minute drive from the city center, offers 387 rooms, 12 suites, 5 rooms for the disabled, and 1 diplomatic suite. (Nonsmokers should ask for a room on the sixth floor.) There also are 2 restaurants, a club/restaurant, and a disco. The fitness center offers a sauna, solarium, whirlpool bath, and gym. Business services. 15 Evropská (phone: 331-4214; fax: 331-4215).

Jalta A favorite of Americans, it has 89 rooms, each with its own bath and shower. The service staff is friendly and helpful, and the *Jalta Club* has disco music for dancing. There's also a restaurant and a casino. The hotel's second floor has been redesigned as a business center with full business services. 45 Václavské náměstí (phone: 265541-9; fax: 265347).

Paříž Praha This lovely 100-room hotel has been recently refurbished in Art Nouveau style, with a new lobby, lounge bar, café, and the blue-tiled *Sarah Bernhardt* restaurant, which features continental fare and light, health-conscious meals. A new executive floor for the business traveler includes 10 deluxe rooms, 2 suites with mini-bars, as well as business services. The hotel also has a contract with the neighboring Municipal House office building, which allows for the use of 12 meeting rooms. 1 U Obecního domu (phone: 236-0820; fax: 236-7448).

Prague Penta Opened last year and geared toward the business traveler, this hotel is one of the best and most modern in town. The 301 rooms (including 12 suites and 1 duplex) offer satellite TV sets, mini-bars, and telephones. Guests also enjoy the *Pavilion* restaurant, a bar, and a *bierstube*. Other amenities include a fitness center with gym, swimming pool, sauna, solarium, and massage. Business services. V. Celnice (phone: 231-2422; 800-225-3456 in the US; fax: 231-3133).

EXPENSIVE

Ambassador/Zlatá Husa The *Ambassador* has joined forces with its somewhat shabbier cousin and is now a larger hotel that offers 174 rooms and 17 suites. A few of the floors have been completely renovated; others exude a somewhat faded Old World charm, with Louis XIV furniture and chandeliers. Amenities include 3 restaurants, 2 cafés, 2 wine cellars, 3 bars, a disco, a casino offering blackjack and roulette, and the popular floor show *Revue Alhambra.* 5 Václavské náměstí (phone: 214-3111 or 214-3121; fax: 236-3172 or 223355).

Atrium This huge 786-room property just outside the city center offers the most up-to-date facilities and the most services in town. Highlights include a large, airy atrium; 4 restaurants; a café; 2 nightclubs; the *Casino de France;* and a fitness center with a pool, sauna, and tennis courts. The large conference center makes this the choice for businesspeople. Business services. 1 Pobřežní (phone: 284-1111; fax: 232-3990 or 232-3791).

Esplanade One of the more evocative pre–World War II hostelries in town, this 63-room Old World establishment has a very friendly family atmosphere, a well-trained staff, an excellent restaurant, and a nightclub. There's a meeting room for up to 20. Near the *National Museum* and the main train station, 19 Washingtonova (phone: 222552; fax: 265897).

Forum Praha Opposite the *Palace of Culture* conference center/concert hall, and a short taxi ride from the city center, this large, modern, and relatively new tower has 492 doubles and 39 suites (including a "Presidential" suite), all with cable TV. Other amenities include 2 restaurants, a brasserie, 3 bars, a café, a nightclub, a casino, a fitness center and swimming pool, a squash court, a bowling alley, gift shops, and a parking garage. Business services. 1 Kongresová ulice (phone: 419-0111; fax: 420684).

Inter-Continental A 9-story, 398-room modern property, conveniently located on the river at the edge of the Old Town. The rooms on the upper floors offer superb views of the castle and the Old Town, as does the excellent restaurant, the *Zlatá Praha* (Golden Prague; see *Eating Out*). There's also a nightclub, a wine cellar, 24-hour room service, a sauna, and a parking garage. Business services. 43-5 Curieových náměstí (phone: 280-0111 or 231-1812; fax: 213-0500 for reservations).

International This monolithic building, once a base for Soviet army brass and now a hotel, has 240 comfortable, if nondescript rooms (including 69 suites). Ask for a room in one of the wings, which are larger. At press time, a portion of the hotel was closed for renovations (plans include the addition of a swimming pool and a fitness center). The hotel is 15 minutes by subway from the center of Prague. There are 3 restaurants serving Czech and continental fare. 15 Koulova (phone: 311-8201; fax: 331-9111).

Ungelt This tiny hostelry is set in a 600-year-old building that was originally a customs hall. It's located in the Týn Cathedral complex of centuries-old Romanesque and Gothic buildings. The 10 apartment-style suites are in great demand, due to this establishment's Old World ambience; reserve months ahead. There's also a restaurant and a bar on the premises. 1 Stupartská (phone: 232-0471).

Villa Voyta Located 15 minutes by taxi from the city center, this Art Nouveau–style villa offers 13 elegant rooms and 2 luxury suites. A good restaurant serves Czech and continental dishes. Business services. 124-54 K Novému dvoru, Lhotka (phone: 472-5511 or 472838; fax: 472-9426)

MODERATE

Evropa A wonderfully ornate Art Nouveau–style establishment on Wenceslas Square, it offers good value in once exquisite, now faded, surroundings. The 88 rooms are homey but clean, and the 3 suites are sparsely and eclectically furnished, making their spaciousness seem almost surreal. The lackadaisical service and offbeat ambience may not appeal to everyone, but the place has a certain quirky charm. There is a cocktail bar and gallery on the second floor, and the restaurant is a replica of the dining room on the *Titanic* (see *Eating Out*). 25 Václavské náměstí; phone: 262748/9; fax: 236-5274).

Panorama Just four subway stops from the center of town, this large (400-room) hotel offers a pool, sauna, and gym. There's a good Czech restaurant and some shops as well. Other features include a meeting room for up to 15, a solarium, coffee and snack bar, nightclub, and disco. 7 Milevská (phone: 416-1111 or 416853).

EATING OUT

Prague has thousands of eating places — outdoor cafés, wine cellars, pubs, and international restaurants. In most cases, reservations are necessary, particularly during the *Easter* holidays and in summertime, but be aware that they aren't always honored when you arrive. Czech cuisine is hearty and good, although it is weak on produce and fresh vegetables, which rarely appear on the menu. Specialties include *knedlíky* (dumplings, both plain and filled with fruit or meat); *knedlo-zelo-vepřo* (dumplings, sauerkraut, and pork); *svíčková* (beef marinated in spicy cream sauce); *uzené maso* (smoked pork with potato dumplings and spinach); and roast goose or duck. A pub favorite is *smažený sýr*, which quite literally means breaded and fried cheese; its cousin, *hermelín smžený*, is a variation using Camembert cheese.

Wines from southern Moravia are the best; sample *tři grácie* red, rosé, or white. In Prague, as elsewhere in the country, you have the choice of eating in either *pivnice* (beer halls), where the only drink is beer and dishes are quite basic, or in a *vinárna* (wine restaurant), where you can order wine and the food is a bit more distinctive. There also are the more traditional restaurants, where you have a multiple choice of drinks and food.

Restaurant prices in Prague generally are quite reasonable; we have rated a dinner for two at $30 and up as expensive; $20 to $30 as moderate; and $10 to $20 as inexpensive. Remember, too, that you always can eat for almost nothing at a street stall, or "hall in the wall," a type of fast-food place featuring grilled sausages. Approach the *parekv rohlíku* with caution, as you would New York City street hot dogs. The *bramborák,* a greasy but delicious, potato-tasting pancake is worth a try. Many restaurants do *not* accept credit cards. All telephone numbers are in the 2 city code unless otherwise indicated.

For an unforgettable dining experience, we begin with our culinary favorites, followed by our cost and quality choices, listed by price category.

DELIGHTFUL DINING

U Labutí (At the Swans) It's hard to believe that this dining spot right on Castle Square once was home to the steeds of the local princes. But the royal stables have been transformed into a charming eatery with old-fashioned nooks, vaulted ceilings, and window casings dating from the 14th century. The service is excellent, if a bit obsequious, and the Czech specialties are superb. Game dishes are featured, and venison prepared with a variety of sauces is a specialty. The Bohemian plate, which includes several different types of meat, is also quite good. Open daily for dinner. Reservations necessary. Major credit cards accepted. 11 Hradčanské náměstí (phone: 539476).

U Malířů (At the Painters) A combination of 16th-century decor and 20th-century culinary expertise makes this restaurant, a French-Czech venture opened 4 years ago, one of the finest dining experiences in Prague. The superbly prepared French-style dishes are pleasingly authentic, thanks to weekly deliveries of lobsters, asparagus, truffles, and other essentials from Parisian markets. There's also a choice selection of French wines. This is one of the most expensive places in town, but the memorable meals are worth every koruna. Open for lunch and dinner; closed Sundays. Reservations necessary. Major credit cards accepted. 11 Maltézské náměstí. (phone: 531883).

EXPENSIVE

Club Kampa This eatery, located in the Lesser Town, not far from Wallenstein Palace, is set in an 18th-century building with high vaulted ceilings. The menu (recited by elegantly attired waiters) features traditional Czech fare, done to perfection. Try the wild duck with cumin-flavored sauerkraut. Open daily for lunch and dinner. Reservations necessary. No credit cards accepted. 14 Na kampě (phone: 530636).

David Located near the US Embassy, this well-run dining spot is very popular with diplomats. A menu in every imaginable language features carefully prepared continental and Czech dishes as well as crêpes. Open daily for lunch and dinner. Reservations necessary. Major credit cards accepted. 21 Tržiště (phone: 539325).

Diplomatic Club A luxury establishment that serves international fare and caters to foreign visitors, it is complemented with a bar, a casino, and a video room. Closed weekends. Reservations necessary. No credit cards accepted. 21 Karlova (phone: 265701).

Evropa Restaurant and Café This hotel dining room was once the best in Prague. The prix fixe dinner of either Czech or French fare is still dependably good, and the decor, a replica of the main dining room on the *Titanic,* is stupendous. Food is prepared at your table, and cognac is available in fishbowl-size snifters. The decor in the café is equally marvelous, although the pastries are only so-so. Open daily for lunch and dinner. Reservations necessary in the dining room; unnecessary in the café. Major credit cards accepted. In the *Evropa Hotel,* 9 Václavské náměstí (phone: 236-5274). Note: The café is inexpensive.

Nebozízek The funicular from Ujezd ulice in the Lesser Town takes diners to this pleasant restaurant in a park facing the castle. Its terrace offers good Czech food and a gorgeous view. Open daily. Reservations necessary. No credit cards accepted. 411 Petřínské sady (phone: 537905).

Opera Grill Convenient to the *National Theater,* it offers excellent traditional Czech food and boasts a fine wine cellar. After dinner, a specialty is brandy served in a giant crystal snifter. Closed weekends. Reservations necessary. Major credit cards accepted. 35 Karolíny Světlé (another entrance at 24 Divadelní), in the Old Town (phone: 265508).

Parnas Situated near the *National Theater*, this former 1920s jazz club offers live piano music, romantic views of the Vltava River and Prague Castle, and excellent food and service. Specialties include Norwegian salmon and Czech roast duck as well as pasta dishes. The *crème caramel* is not to be missed for dessert. At press time, plans called for the addition of a Sunday jazz brunch and a pre- and post-theater menu. Open daily for lunch and dinner. Reservations necessary. Major credit cards accepted. 2 Smetanovo nábřeží (phone: 261250 or 265760; fax: 265017).

Principe This excellent dining spot, popular with businesspeople, is authentically Italian; even the menu is written in Italian. Specialties include lasagna, veal scaloppine, steak with green peppercorns and cream, and other favorites. The ambience is cheerful and contemporary, and the service is good. Open daily for lunch and dinner. Reservations necessary. American Express accepted. 23 Anglická (phone: 259614).

Reykjavik Not far from the Charles Bridge, this new, nautically styled place offers some of the best seafood in Prague. Owned by Thoris Gunnarsson, a Scandinavian expatriate, its specialty is excellently prepared salmon. Other dishes include creatively prepared vegetarian platters. One of the city's liveliest spots, the bar is crowded with folks waiting for tables. Open daily. No reservations. Major credit cards accepted. 20-180 Karlova (phone: 265776).

Svatá Klára (St. Klara) Three hundred years ago, Count Václav Vojtěch spent his evenings in the wine cellar of his baroque château. Today, foreign diplomats and others in the know frequent this *vinárna*. It's cozier now than it was in the count's day, with its fireplace, fine service, accomplished cuisine, and selection of Moravian wines. Specialties range from fondue bourguignon to *palačinky* (crêpes) *flambé,* a classic Czech dessert. Open weekdays for dinner. Reservations necessary. No credit cards accepted. 9 U Trojského zámku (phone: 841213).

U Fleků (Flek's Inn) One of Prague's most famous old pubs (no one knows quite how old it is, but it was in existence in 1499), it specializes in strong, dark beer (probably the best brew you'll ever quaff), and offers good goulash, too. A huge place, filled with music and guests who love to sing along, it's a big favorite among Germans and other tourists. Open daily from 9 AM to 11 PM. Reservations advised. Major credit cards accepted. 11 Křemencova (phone: 293245/6)

U Mecenáše (At the Patron's) A small, medieval-style wine restaurant, it has vaulted ceilings, comfortable booths, and a cozy, romantic atmosphere. Political types such as German Chancellor Helmut Kohl have dined in the elegant Queen Anne–style back room. The fare is quite good, particularly the beef and pork dishes; there's also game, duck, and goose. Open daily for dinner. Reservations necessary. Major credit cards accepted. 10 Malostranské náměstí (phone: 533881).

U Pavouka (At the Spider) Vaulted ceilings and wood-paneled rooms add to the charm. When the elegant dining room is full, as it usually is, ask to be seated in the beautifully appointed cocktail area. Classic Czech and continental dishes are served; try the Goulash Spider (beef in cheese sauce, topped off with a brandy flambé). There is also a snack bar and a garden restaurant that offer a separate menu of traditional Czech dishes. Open daily. Reservations necessary. Major credit cards accepted. In the courtyard of 17 Celetná (phone: 232-1037).

U Zlaté Hrušky (At the Golden Pear) Set in an 18th-century house near the castle, this small charming eatery is popular with tourists. Game dishes are the specialty here, but the beefsteak in wine sauce is delicious. Open daily until midnight for dinner. Reservations necessary. Major credit cards accepted. 3 Nový Svět (phone: 531133).

U Zlatého Rožné (At the Golden Skewer) A favorite of people associated with the foreign embassies nearby, its eclectic menu offers a variety of cuisines — from Icelandic fish to Chinese and Czech specialties — all superbly prepared. Try the chicken with pineapple and almonds or the broiled salmon. Open for lunch and dinner. Reservations necessary. American Express accepted. 22 Cs. armády (phone: 312-1032).

Vinárna v Zátiší Located between the Old Town Square and the Charles Bridge, this restaurant run by an Englishman specializes in roast beef, salmon, and other international dishes. Popular with businesspeople, fixed-price lunches and dinners are available. Open daily. Reservations necessary. No credit cards accepted. 1 Liliová on Betlémské náměstí (phone: 265017).

Zlatá Praha (Golden Prague) Good Czech and international fare and a spectacular view of Prague Castle are the attractions at this elegant dining room atop the *Inter-Continental* hotel. Open daily for lunch and dinner. Reservations necessary. Major credit cards accepted. 5 Curieových náměstí (phone: 280-0111 or 231-1812; fax: 213-0500 for reservations).

MODERATE

Myslivna (Hunting Lodge) True to its name, this eatery specializes in well-prepared game — deer, boar, hare, pheasant, quail, and duck — from the

Bohemian woods. Open daily for lunch and dinner. Reservations necessary. No credit cards accepted. 21 Jagellonská, Vinohrady (phone: 627-0209).

Palace Hotel Cafeteria This upscale spot has a good salad bar, making it a lifesaver for vegetarians and a refreshing change for everyone else. Open daily for lunch and dinner. Reservations unnecessary. Major credit cards accepted. 12 Panská (phone: 235-7556).

Penguin's A bit out of Prague center, this modern, elegant dining place offers continental and Czech specialties and some of the freshest vegetables in town. The turtle soup is authentic and the steaks are first-rate. A popular spot for local Czech artists and sports figures. Open daily. Reservations recommended. Major credit cards accepted. 5 Zborovská (phone: 545660).

Sumicka Vinárna In addition to the Moravian wine that you can order by the carafe, this well-run wine cellar also serves traditional pork, beef, and veal dishes. The background Gypsy music adds to the enjoyment. Open daily. Reservations necessary. No credit cards accepted. 12 Mikuldanská (phone: 291568).

U Cerveného Kola (At the Red Wheel) It may take some effort to find this small spot, located in an open courtyard, and even more to get in, since it is always crowded — but it is well worth the trouble. Steaks are a specialty. Open daily. Reservations unnecessary. Major credit cards accepted. 2 Anežská (phone: 231-8941).

U Cížků (At the Bluebird's) Popular with the business crowd and with tour groups, this classic Bohemian restaurant serves delicious and hearty portions of Czech staples. Try the pork with three kinds of dumplings. Open daily for lunch and dinner. Reservations necessary. No credit cards accepted. 34 Karlovo náměstí (phone: 298891).

U Golema A good place to lunch before or after touring the *State Jewish Museum*. Popular with literary types, it has an elegantly simple decor. Try the veal with apple slices. Closed Mondays. Reservations necessary. Major credit cards accepted. 8 Maislova (phone: 232-8165).

U Kalicha (The Chalice) A popular pilsner beer hall and restaurant, which is disappointingly modern in character (but full of literary allusions). This is where Good Soldier Svejk, a character in a series of novels by Jaroslav Hašek, arranged to meet his World War I buddies "at 6 o'clock after the war." Terrific Czech dishes are served. 12 Na bojišti (phone: 290701).

U Sedmi Andělů (At the Seven Angels) Furnished in a spare and elegant style — with a baroque accent. Try the *síp amorův*, a specialty platter of grilled meat. Open for lunch and dinner; closed Sundays. Reservations unnecessary. No credit cards accepted. 20 Jilská (phone: 266355).

U Zelené Záby (At the Green Frog) The quiet atmosphere is perfect for talking and drinking at this wine cellar housed in a building more than 8 centuries old. The house specialty is grilled meat with sauerkraut. Open daily for lunch and dinner. Reservations necessary. No credit cards accepted. 8 U Radnice (phone: 262815).

Vinárna u Maltézských Rytířu (Wine Tavern at the Knights of Malta) Located in a former hospice of the Knights of Malta religious order (it was also a dance hall after World War I), this cozy, Renaissance-style wine cellar with only 3 tables and 8 bar stools serves delicately prepared Czech and international specialties. Try the chicken with pineapple and walnuts or the excellent *staropražská panenka* (medallions of pork filled with a pâté of chopped olives, cheese, mushrooms, and ham). You can also dine downstairs in one of the two simple saloons that seat about 30. Open for lunch and dinner. Reservations advised. Major credit cards accepted. 10 Prokopská (phone: 536357).

INEXPENSIVE

Kmotra (Grandmother) Pizza served in a relaxed atmosphere plus steaks and helpings from the salad bar. Try the house pizza specialty, *kmotra.* There is a café upstairs. Open for lunch and dinner. No reservations. No credit cards accepted. 12 V. Jirchářích (phone: 203564).

Mikulka's Pizzeria This small eatery with great tasting pizza is a favorite with Americans. Also try the pasta, ice cream, and cappuccino. Open daily. Reservations unnecessary. No credit cards accepted. 16 Benediktská (phone: 231-5727).

Saté Grill Conveniently located near the castle, this small, simple grill serves Indonesian specialties including saté, noodles, and salad. It's a popular place for lunch. Open daily for lunch and dinner; closes at 8 PM. Reservations unnecessary. No credit cards accepted. 3 Pohořelec (phone: 532113).

U Cerného Slunce (At the Black Sun) Located right off the Old Town Square, this 17th-century wine cellar offers atmospheric decor and good, simple dishes made from pork, chicken, and beef. Open daily. Reservations necessary. No credit cards accepted. 9 Kamzíkova (phone: 236-5769).

U Cerveného Raka (At the Red Lobster) A small, pretty place for lunch or dinner. An international menu includes steaks, seafood, lobster and shrimp cocktails, and a variety of desserts. Open daily. Reservations necessary. No credit cards accepted. 30 Karlova (phone: 265538).

U Pavlice A cheery, traditional tavern serving hearty fare and robust brews. Open daily. Reservations unnecessary. No credit cards accepted. 1 Fügnerovo náměstí (phone: 290373).

U Radnice (At the Town Hall) Under the arcades just southeast of Old Town Square, this typical beer cellar caters to businesspeople at lunch and dinner. Though not a full-fledged restaurant, it serves one of the best duck dinners in town. Open daily. Reservations unnecessary. No credit cards accepted. 2 Malé náměstí (phone: 262822).

U Sv. Tomáše Prague's oldest beer hall — a large, vaulted room with wooden tables, lots of students, and huge steins of beer. The best dish is a plate of pork, sauerkraut, and dumplings. Open daily. Reservations unnecessary. No credit cards accepted. 12 Letenská (phone: 536262).

U Zeleného Caje (At the Green Teahouse) This charming teahouse near Hradčany Castle offers 60 different kinds of tea and coffee as well as baked goods. For nonsmokers only. Open daily. No reservations. No credit cards accepted. 19 Nerudova ulice (phone: 532683).

Vltava Located on the bank of the river, this place offers excellent fish and a great view of the castle and river from its patio. The Czech menu boasts a fairly wide variety of beef, pork, and chicken dishes. Closed Mondays. Reservations unnecessary. No credit cards accepted. 2 Rašínovo nábřeží (phone: 294964).

Riga

If weathering a tempestuous history builds community strength and spirit, then there's little wonder that the people of the once-again independent republic of Latvia are so proud of Riga, their worn but still lovely capital city. Although Latvia has been occupied by nearly every European race and creed, its resilient capital has survived as a symbol of solidarity, strength, and hope for the Latvian people, the Letts.

It is not coincidental that natives of Riga invariably suggest that first-time visitors begin their tours in Old Riga. The Old Town is Riga's historical and spiritual heart, an ancient world of cobbled streets, medieval spires, venerable churches, and cavernous, Teutonic drinking haunts. Though today the Old Town bustles with the activity of a modern metropolis, this ancient neighborhood has memories that predate the birth of Stockholm, or even venerable Prague. Old Riga has more than 80 buildings of historical or cultural value. Bits and pieces of it stood when Moscow was sacked by the Mongols, when the world's first national flag flew over Denmark, and when the jester became an integral member of the courts of Europe. Much of this historic district predates Ivan the Terrible and the first of what were to be a series of Russian invasions. In fact, even the newer buildings, those faddish baroque structures from the late 17th and early 18th century, were already in place when the restive Russian monarch Peter the Great trod these very streets after seizing the city from the Swedes in 1710 (the elm that Peter planted in Viestura Garden also still stands).

Latvia's recently restored independence has not erased the handed-down memories of life under the Livonian knights, the Poles, the Danes, the Swedes, the Russians, the Nazis, and the Soviets. The ancient buildings of the Old Town are constant reminders of the republic's tumultuous past, and of the elusiveness of lasting freedom.

Yet Old Riga is not just a barren museum piece. The ancient façades — built over the course of 700 years and ranging in style from Roman and Gothic to Renaissance, baroque, classical, and even (occasionally) Art Nouveau — belie an inner vitality. For example, in one Renaissance-era building on a side street near Doma Laukums (Dome Square) are the offices of the Popular Front of Latvia, an organization founded in 1988 to spearhead Latvia's independence movement. The organization continues to influence Latvia's future from a building steeped in its past. Similarly, the Free Trade Unions of Latvia now operate in an old Guild Hall, a popular meeting place of merchants in the Middle Ages. And in the building surrounding the Swedish Gate, built into the 13th-century city wall during Swedish occupation in 1698, members of the Society of Architects gain inspiration from their antiquated office space.

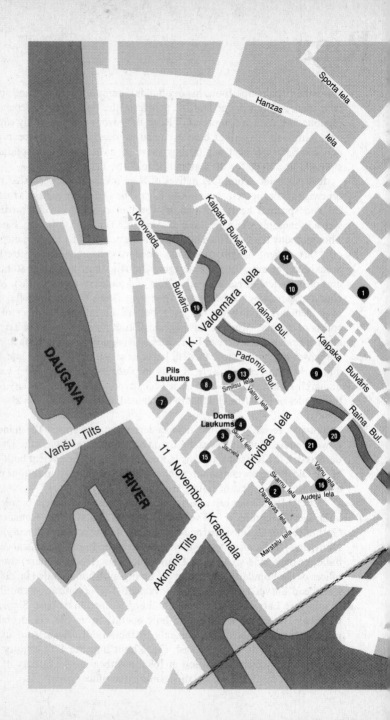

N

RIGA
Points of Interest

1. Latvia Hotel
2. St. Peter's Church
3. Dome Cathedral; Dome Concert Hall
4. Virgin's Guild Hall
5. Gunpowder Tower
6. Swedish Gates
7. Riga Castle; Museum of Latvian History; Museum of Foreign Art; Rainis Museum of the History of Literature and Art; Viestura Garden
8. St. Jacob's Church
9. Freedom Monument
10. Esplanāde; Art Academy
11. Central Market
12. Vērmanes Dārzs
13. Military Museum of Latvia
14. Latvian State Art Museum
15. Museum of the History of the City of Riga and Navigation
16. Central Department Store
17. Riga Sports Pils
18. Daugava Stadions
19. National Theater
20. State Ballet and Opera Theater
21. Riga Hotel

Tallinas Iela

K. Barona Iela

...as Iela

K. Barona Iela

Marijas Iela

Railway Station

The newer part of Riga (called Outer Riga) was only lightly touched by the stolid hand of Soviet architects. It is graced with abundant parkland, gardens, and ornate 19th-century buildings, as well as the occasional Soviet concrete monstrosity. Outer Riga is separated from the Old Town by the Pilsetas Kanalis (City Canal), a lazy spindle of water that connects with the mighty Daugava River (also known as the Western Dvina) at both ends and is shrouded by a semicircular park of linden trees, oaks, willows, and wildlife that serves as a buffer between old city and new. The City Canal was responsible for thwarting enemy attacks in its prior role as a moat that ran outside the city walls.

Though the Latvian region was originally settled by nomadic tribes of reindeer hunters many thousands of years ago, modern Latvians descended from a variety of pagan Indo-European peoples who migrated from the south about 4,000 years ago to settle what is now Lithuania and Latvia. The Latvian language is similar to Lithuanian (together with the now-extinct Old Prussian, they form a separate "Old Baltic" group of dialects), but culturally Latvia is closer to Estonia since Lithuania was enveloped by Poland for many years.

The site that is now Riga had been long occupied by these Baltic tribes when German merchants established a community at the mouth of the Daugava River in 1158. By the turn of the century, an organization of German crusaders who occupied nearby Livonia began to covet the profitable trading routes of the Daugava River. The group, the Livonian Brothers of the Sword, or the Livonian Knights, set up a trading station on the right bank of the river, where Old Riga now stands. In 1201, Bishop Albert of Livonia transferred his seat to the trading station. Riga was then formally established as a city, and it began to attract many German settlers. A defensive wall and fortifications went up and dwellings, churches, and other institutions were constructed inside. Riga was markedly German in custom, social life, religion, and architecture, and remains so today. The native Latvians lived outside the city walls and along the coast.

Some historians believe that Riga was named after a stream called the Rige, a word that means "pure" in Latvian. Others say the city's name is a Germanized version of "rija," the Latvian word for barn. Indeed, Riga was the site of a complex of barns and storehouses built by Vikings who staged attacks on the mainland from this strategic site before the Germans arrived.

For the next several centuries, Riga remained under the sway of the Livonian Knights, who allowed the city a measure of independence. In 1282, Riga joined the Hanseatic League, a group of German cities and principalities allied for the promotion of commerce and mutual protection (the city's three Guild Halls were built for merchants during this time). The city flourished as a focal point of Baltic trade and developed as a major commercial and handicraft center. In 1522 Riga accepted the Reformation, and the city's bishops lost much of their power over the populace. After the Livonian Order was dissolved in 1561, Riga enjoyed a brief period of independence before being conquered by Poland in 1582, and then by Sweden in 1621. Under Swedish rule, Riga's population grew even larger than Stockholm's and it became the biggest city among Sweden's vast holdings. For the first time, Latvians were allowed to participate in the social and cultural life of the city and cultivate their national identity. The city burst the seams of its walls and began to expand into what is now Outer Riga.

But due to a series of blunders and misunderstandings, Riga inextricably bound its fate to Russia when, in 1697, Peter I, the young Russian czar, passed through on his famous "Great Embassy" to Europe. Due to poor timing, the city's governor failed to meet the Russians outside of Riga with a customary escort, didn't pay their expenses (as was usual), provided no banquets, fireworks, or other entertainment (which Peter loved), and generally treated the Russians shabbily. Furthermore, as Peter clambered about taking notes and drawing sketches of Riga's fortifications (Riga was like a futuristic city to the backward Russians), a Swedish sentry drew his gun on the czar. Though an apology was offered, Peter was outraged. Citing the rude treatment he received in Riga, 3 years later he started the Great Northern War with Sweden, which Russia eventually won after a decade of fighting. In 1710, when the Russians had Riga surrounded and began the siege that led to over 2 centuries of Russian domination, Peter was on hand to fire the first three shells into the city. It took 13 years, but he got his revenge.

Napoleon was the next ruler to wreak havoc on the city. Though the French never actually laid siege to Riga, a number of threats and the fear of a French invasion in the early 19th century caused the city's Russian governor to burn Riga's suburbs, leaving 7,000 Latvians homeless just as Outer Riga was beginning to take shape. As they have so many times in their history, the Latvians rebuilt, and as part of the Russian empire became an important port and industrial center in the 18th and 19th centuries.

Lying like a doormat between the growing German military juggernaut to the west and the mammoth yet troubled Russian Empire to the east, Latvia in the early years of the 20th century must have sensed doom. After fighting first with Russia against the Germans and then against the Russians with the Bolsheviks, by 1918 Latvians found themselves fighting against both Germans and Bolsheviks, both of whom were intent on the annexation of Latvia while the Letts were proclaiming their independence.

After World War I, the Germans, who had occupied Latvia from 1917–19, and the Soviet Union signed a peace treaty renouncing forever all claims on Latvian territory. (Although Lenin first reneged on his wartime promise, he later gave in to Latvian independence. Consequently, Latvians despised Lenin less than other Soviet leaders — which may be why his statue stood in front of the *Latvia* hotel for as long as it did. It finally was toppled in the immediate aftermath of the 1991 Soviet coup.)

Latvia finally gained its independence in 1920. The new country adopted a constitution establishing a democratic form of government, divided the estates of wealthy landowners into small farms, joined the League of Nations, and bustled with businessmen and spies, both intent on getting a better fix on an enigmatic Soviet Union. Because of its cosmopolitan atmosphere, Riga became known as the "Paris of the North."

But the situation was not to last. After a recession severely damaged Latvia's economy, Karlis Ulmanis, its democratically elected president, dissolved parliament in 1934 and declared a state of emergency. Latvia became a dictatorship. In 1939, Germany and the Soviet Union signed the Molotov-Ribbentrop non-aggression pact, which included a secret protocol dividing Eastern Europe into spheres of influence. The pact enabled Joseph Stalin's Soviet Union to forcibly annex the Baltic republics the following year without fear of German intervention. Latvia became a battleground during World War II and again it suffered tragically, first at the hands of the Soviets (32,000 Latvians were either deported or executed in 1941), then under the Germans, who occupied Riga from 1941 to 1944 and whose concentration camps nearly wiped out Latvia's Jewish population. When the Soviets again seized control of Latvia in 1944, they carried out a second wave of repression.

Wholesale rebuilding was required after the war, and hundreds of thousands of Russians and Soviet nationalists were encouraged to move to Latvia to dilute the Latvian population. Many of these newcomers replaced Latvians in senior government and business positions. In 1935, when Latvia was last independent, Latvians made up 77% of the population. Today, only a little more than half of the country's 2.7 million people are Latvian. Most of the rest are ethnic Russians or Belorussians.

As a Soviet republic, Latvia was deprived of its national flag, its anthem, its monuments, its language — which uses Roman rather than Cyrillic script — and its history. The Soviet Union imposed a Communist government and took control of all industry and land.

Latvia's modern independence movement served as a bellwether for similar movements throughout the former USSR. The first independence rally in the Baltics was held at Riga's Freedom Monument in June 1987 in defiance of local authorities. The popular Front of Latvia, a pro-reform, pro-independence organization, was founded in October 1988, and during that same month the first church service in more than 30 years was held in the Doma Baznīca (Dome Cathedral) in the heart of Riga's Old Town. Soon afterward the flag was legalized, Latvian was reinstated as the official local language in 1989 and the traditional Latvian anthem, "God Bless Latvia," was sung lustily. These pro-independence acts were in defiance of the Communist government, yet at first they provoked no violent reaction from Moscow, a sign of some change in the Soviet mentality.

Lativa's parliament adopted a declaration of independence in May 1990, voting to negotiate a gradual withdrawal from the Soviet Union. In late 1990 and early 1991, the Soviet response to the Baltic republics' independence movement came in the form of a brutal military crackdown; bullet holes remain in the main staircase of the *Ridzene* hotel, a permanent reminder of the Latvian struggle for freedom.

In March 1991, 2 months after the crackdown, Latvia's declaration of independence was approved by 74% of the voters in a republic-wide referendum. Amid the tumultuous happenings in Moscow in August 1991, the Latvian parliament outlawed the Communist Party and announced immediate independence. It was recognized as a separate entity by the rest of the world, and by Moscow, soon thereafter. Latvia is once again its own country; Riga its proud capital.

Independence has brought bewildering changes and new possibilities to Riga. In the relatively short period since the break with Moscow, the city of 915,000 has undergone a renaissance that has greatly revived the historical and spiritual heart of the capital, the Old Town. Dilapidated buildings, that for nearly half a century stood in a permanent state of disrepair, have been restored to their former splendor.

Under a government program, Latvian citizens and their descendants who left the country before the 1940 Soviet annexation have been able to reclaim any property once owned by them. Many have returned from decades of exile determined to rebuild the capital and once again to line its cobbled streets with cozy cafés, trendy art galleries, well-stocked bookstores, and good restaurants.

Still, Latvians are struggling with economic hardship as the country continues to extract itself from the turmoil of the former Soviet economy. In 1992, the government replaced the Russian ruble with an intermediate currency called the "rublis." However, at press time, this currency was being replaced gradually with a more stable currency called the "lat."

Latvia is now proudly reclaiming its long-suppressed heritage and is in the midst of building a new economy, a new government, a new nation. Today's visitor to Riga will hear mostly Latvian — not Russian — and a smattering of English and German on the streets, and will have the unique opportunity to eavesdrop on history in the making.

Riga At-a-Glance

SEEING THE CITY

For panoramic views of Riga there are two perfect perches. *Pie Kamina* (At the Fireplace), the restaurant on the top (26th) floor of the *Latvia* hotel (on Brivibas Iela), offers a nearly 360° view of the city. An enclosed observation deck surrounds the restaurant on three sides. In addition to offering wonderful views of the Bay of Riga, 10 miles (16 km) to the north,

Old Riga to the west, and Latvia's verdant pine forests to the south, this is an excellent place from which to see the city since, by virtue of standing on its top floor, the ugly blue-and-white *Latvia* hotel itself is entirely eliminated from the picture. Another great roost is the viewing platform on the tower of Svata Pētera Baznīca (St. Peter's Church) on Old Town Square. The spire is a steel copy of an ancient wooden one that was destroyed by German bombs during World War II. This 400-foot-high vantage point allows a look straight down on the jumble of Riga's architectural styles that document its long, rich history. The viewing platform is open daily from 10 AM to 8 PM May through September; from 10 AM to 4:30 PM the rest of the year. Admission charge.

Riga street signs are still in both Latvian and Russian, so a street is either an "iela" or a "ulitsa," a boulevard a "bulvāris or a "bulvar," and a square a "laukums" or a "ploshchad" (Latvian and Russian, respectively).

> **BEWARE** The narrow streets in Riga's Old Town are a delight to visit during the day but are poorly lit and practically deserted at night. Visitors are advised to exercise caution as crime is on the rise here.

SPECIAL PLACES

Since the greatest concentration of the city's special places are inside the Old Town, Riga is best seen on foot. The Old Town is a short walk from all of the city's hotels. Special permits are needed to drive through Riga's narrow, cobblestone streets, so taxis may drop you off at its outskirts. Walking in the Old Town is much easier now that the concrete and metal barricades blocking streets leading toward the parliament building have been removed. The barricades were erected by Latvian nationalists to protect the parliament and other government buildings during the Soviet military crackdown in January 1991, and remained in place until after the August 1991 Soviet coup and the restoration of Latvia's independence. Only one — a massive concrete block wall at the foot of Pils Iela guarding the entrance to the parliament building — remains as a reminder of how tenuous democracy can be.

THE OLD TOWN

DOMA LAUKUMS (DOME SQUARE) This cobblestone central meeting area is home to ancient churches, winding streets, palaces, statues, and several comfortable cooperative cafés with a view to the embankment of the Daugava. Doma Baznīca (Dome Cathedral), one of the oldest (completed in 1226) and largest churches in the Baltics, is a commanding presence on Dome Square. It is a living chronology of Riga's architectural styles. The ultramodern foyer, where you pay an admission fee, leads into the magnificent church where Romanesque, Gothic, Renaissance and baroque reconstructions can be seen amid resplendent light streaming through stained glass panels. The elegant carved-wood altar dates from 1641. The crown jewel of the church is a world-renowned organ with 6,768 pipes, built by German craftsmen in 1884. It draws organ aficionados from around the world who delight in the church's acoustics and use the instrument for their recordings. Though the church had been used as a concert hall and museum (see *Museums*) when Latvia became a Soviet republic, the first church service in over 30 years was held here in October 1988 in connection with the founding of the Popular Front independence group. Today services are held each morning, and concerts — which should not be missed — each week.

No. 8 Doma Laukums is the headquarters of *Radio Latvia*. It still bears the bullet holes and other scars inflicted when Soviet troops used an explosive device to blow down the front door during the August 1991 coup. Down Amatu Iela, leading from Doma Laukums, are the Guild Halls, three oaken, neo-Gothic buildings with leaded windows, coats-of-arms, stained glass windows, and murals of Riga and other cities of the Hanseatic League. The Virgin's Guild Hall is the site of regular performances of the *Latvian Philharmonic*.

JAUN IELA (JAUN STREET) An ancient street that runs south of Doma Laukums, it was once Peter the Great's address (as was 11 Novembra Krastmala, the river promenade). After seizing Riga from Sweden's King Charles in 1711, Peter often stayed at the mansion at the end of the street (at Nos. 6, 7, and 9 Palasta Iela). Today it appears to be a plain residential building. The czar was said to adore this riverfront house because of its garden terrace (he liked to putter) and its hanging garden on the roof. In 1745, it was redecorated by Bartolomeo Rastrelli, the man responsible for inventing the Russian baroque style and creating much of St. Petersburg's superb architecture.

PULVERTORNIS (GUNPOWDER TOWER) This is the only surviving tower of the 28 that once fortified the Old Town. Gunpowder Tower (originally called Sand Tower because of several sand dunes nearby, it was given its current name when it became a gunpowder depot) provides a graphic illustration of Riga's turbulent history. Nine cannonballs, dating back to the Russian invasions of 1656 and 1710, are still lodged in the tower's 9-foot-thick walls. Though the exact date of its completion is not known, it was men-tioned by city chroniclers as early as 1330. During the 14th and 15th centuries it was used as a dungeon and torture chamber. Ironically, after defending Riga from foreign invaders for centuries, it became part of the *Latvian Museum of the Revolution,* an exercise in Soviet propaganda, with exhibits that described the Latvian struggle to become a Soviet republic. It's now the *Military Museum of Latvia* (see *Museums*). Close to the City Canal, just off Azpazijas Bulvāris on Smilsu Iela.

ZVIEDRU VARTI (SWEDISH GATES) At the end of a maze of streets just beyond Gunpowder Tower is a complex of buildings that includes Riga's only surviving historic gate. Built into the city wall in 1698 during the Swedish occupation of the city, this small archway cuts through a 13th-century building and into Aldaru Iela (Brewer Street), a narrow alleyway lined with houses from the 13th through the 19th century. 11 Torna Iela.

RĪGAS PILS (RIGA CASTLE) This 14th-century fortress on the Daugava River was the Livonian Order's stronghold in Riga. In the 15th century, the castle was nearly destroyed by the townspeople, who supported the papacy, and who were unhappy with the Livonian Order's efforts to loosen its ties with Rome. After the Livonians regained a semblance of order, they forced the burghers (who represented the people) to rebuild it. During the first Latvian independence in the 1930s, the castle was home to then president Karlis Ulmanis. Today, it houses three museums: the *Latvijas Vēstures Muzejs* (Museum of Latvian History), the *Latvijas Aizrobezas Mākslas Muzejs* (Museum of Foreign Art), and the *Raina Literaturas un Mākslas Vēstures Muzejs* (Rainis Museum of the History of Literature and Art); see *Museums* for details on all three. 3 Pils Laukums.

TRIS BRALI (THE THREE BROTHERS) Located just east of Pils Square, this trio of buildings is quite impressive. The white one, No. 17 Maza Pils Iela, dates from the 1400s and is the oldest surviving medieval building in Riga. Records show it housed a bakery in 1687, 200 years after it was built. Nearby is the yellow one, built in 1646 by a merchant who used the ground and first floors as living areas and the upper floor as storage space. The green one is about 150 years old. Maza Pils Iela.

VIESTURA DĀRZS (VIESTURA GARDEN) Just north of Riga Castle is the city's oldest park, created in 1721 with the help of Peter the Great himself, who enjoyed wielding a hoe and shovel almost as much as his sword. It was originally called the Czar's Garden, since the mansion where Peter the Great once lived is nearby. The 3-acre park is crisscrossed with alleys, paths, and canals, and contains over 70 species of trees, including a living elm tree planted by the czar, with a memorial plaque next to it. At the park's main entrance on Hanzas Iela is Alexander's Gate, a Roman-style triumphal arch with sandstone columns, cornices, and four bronze medallions, built in 1817 to commemorate Napoleon's defeat. Hanzas Iela.

SVATA JĒKABA BAZNĪCA (ST. JACOB'S CHURCH) Originally built outside the city walls in 1226, this is the only church in Riga with an authentic Gothic spire, erected in 1756. In its early years it was used mainly by the Latvians and Livonians who lived in the area, since they weren't allowed inside the city walls. The sanctuary and the three-nave basilica are original. Riga's first Lutheran church service was held here in 1522. In 1922 it reverted to Catholicism and, since then, has been an active Catholic church with services every morning. Across the street is an imitation Renaissance building, in the Florentine style. During the country's earlier independence, it was home to Latvia's parliament, which was dissolved in 1934. It later housed the Latvian Suprème Soviet, the republic's parliament during the Soviet period. Jēkaba Iela.

SKARNU IELA (SKARNU STREET) Svata Pētera Baznīca (St. Peter's Church), Riga's most definitive landmark, and several other ripe old buildings are found along this street, which runs into Vecrigas Laukums (Old Town Square). Originally built of wood in 1209, St. Peter's is a monument to the city's patron saint and was replaced by a stone structure in 1408. Peter the Great came running from his nearby mansion to help fight the fire when the wooden steeple burned in 1721. The steeple was repaired only to be demolished during World War II. The residents of Riga were outraged when *Intourist* built the *Latvia* hotel 3 feet higher than the church's spire, formerly the city's tallest structure. There's a spectacular view of Riga from the viewing platform. Nearby Svata Jura Baznīca (St. George's Church) was used as a chapel for Riga's first castle and dates back to 1208. Riga's oldest stone building, it is now the *Museum of Applied Arts,* where tapestries, pottery, glasswork, and sculpture are displayed in the hushed and timeless ambience of this 13th-century house of worship.

Farther down Skarnu is Svata Jana Baznīca (St. John's Church), which was part of a Dominican monastery founded in 1234. Today it operates as a Lutheran church, and from the grounds inside (which are always open) you can see part of the original fortress wall built between the 13th and 15th centuries. Next door is the Convent of Eke, originally a home for out-of-town guests in the 15th century. It was turned into a residence for widows in 1592.

MARSTALU IELA (MARSTALU STREET) Crowded with medieval houses and ware-houses in a bouquet of pastel hues, as well as an exhibition hall and a café, this lovely street, which runs down to the river embankment, is the site of the Reitern House, a 17th-century dwelling decorated with reliefs and garlands cut in stone; the House of Dannenstern, typical of the homes originally owned by the city's many rich merchants; and the Reformed Church, one of the first churches that legally conducted services for towns-people in the "other" (read Protestant) religion.

OUTER RIGA

Outer Riga is the vast area of the city outside the City Canal. It is studded with rose gardens, spacious parks, statues, fountains, monuments, the city's larger restaurants, souvenir and handicrafts shops, and fin de siècle architecture. Lacking the ancient buildings of the Old Town, Outer Riga is more functional and commercial, yet it contains pockets of pastoral charm.

BRIVIBAS PIEMINEKLIS (FREEDOM MONUMENT) The focal point of the Latvian independence movement is the liveliest spot in all of Riga, and is much more than a tall obelisk of rock and metal in the center of the city. Built in 1935 during Latvia's first modern period of independence, Rigans are still amazed that the Soviets didn't topple it when they invaded in 1940. A female bronze figure stands atop the limestone obelisk holding three stars — representing the three geographic territories of Latvia: Kurzeme, Vidzeme, and Latgale — in her outstretched arms. On the base of the obelisk, "For the Fatherland and Freedom" is inscribed in Latvian beneath several sculpture groups symbolizing events from Latvian history and mythology, including the "chain breakers" who represent liberation from foreign oppressors. Until the summer of 1987, the area around the monument was effectively off limits to locals because, Latvians claim, KGB agents were stationed in nearby parks. Anyone who tried to reach the monument was apprehended, and unacceptable political behavior (including laying flowers at the statue's base) was punished by arrest for "anti-Soviet" activity. During the struggle for Baltic freedom, this was the site of demonstrations, impassioned speeches, and candlelit vigils. Today it is still a favorite gathering place, and protests by political groups are held here. People still place flowers at the base of the monument, now patrolled by Latvian National Guards, in memory of those killed during the January 1991 confrontation with Soviet troops. It is not coincidental that Lady Liberty, who stands atop the obelisk, faces west, while the monument to Lenin — now toppled — faced east toward Moscow. Brivibas Iela, between Aspazijas Bulvāris and Raina Bulvāris.

BASTELJKALNS (BASTION PARK) Be sure to reserve some time before sundown (which can be as late as midnight during the summer) for a leisurely stroll along the Pilsetas Kanalis (City Canal) in this lovely park built on what used to be the city's fortifications. Willows seem to weep right into the idle water of the canal, crossed by 19th-century footbridges and bordered by a long path that is a tranquil place to promenade. Have a seat on one of the benches or on the grassy banks of the canal. There is a waterfall, illuminated at night, an alpine garden, and a statue of Rudolfs Blaumanis, a famous Latvian writer of comedy and tragedy. And don't forget to drop into a bakery and pick up a loaf of fresh bread to feed the hundreds of ducks who call this park home. Located between Aspazijas Bulvāris in the Old Town and Raina Bulvāris in the City Center.

CENTRALAIS TIRGUS (CENTRAL MARKET) Housed in five zeppelin hangars along the Daugava River that were used by the Germans in World War I, this is one of Europe's largest markets and a Riga landmark. With some of the produce flown in by peasants from more bountiful former Soviet republics to the south, the selection here always is better than in state shops and, with prices allowed to fluctuate, much more expensive.

BRIVIBAS IELA (FREEDOM STREET) Outer Riga's main thoroughfare has returned to its pre-Soviet name, which many old timers continued to use during the decades it was officially known as Lenin Street and was watched over by a huge bronze statue of Lenin across from the *Latvia* hotel. The statue was toppled in the days following the August 1991 Soviet coup, and all that remains is its red granite base. Whatever its name, the street runs 7 miles (11 km) through the city from the river, past the *Latvia* hotel and beyond, and contains Riga's most interesting shops, including a few good souvenir stores (see *Shopping*).

ETNOGRĀFISKAIS BRĪVDABAS MUZEJS (ETHNOGRAPHIC OPEN AIR MUSEUM)

On the outskirts of Riga to the east, this fascinating 200-acre open-air museum should not be missed. Over 90 authentic buildings re-create the old lifestyles of Latvian peasants (which in many ways remain unchanged). It was the first and largest museum of its kind in the Soviet Union, and was the model for similar museums in other former Soviet republics: Lithuania, Estonia, Ukraine, and Georgia. Along with windmills, dwellings, and other buildings, the museum features a 16th-century church moved here from Latvia's Zemgale region. An annual fair is held here during the first week in June, with handicrafts demonstrations and sales of traditional crafts. Open daily 10 AM to 5 PM. Take the No. 6 bus from the *Latvia* hotel.

VĒRMANES DĀRZS (VERMANES PARK)

This is one of Riga's most popular parks, originally built for Riga residents whose health was too poor to allow them to go to the countryside. It features a restaurant, an open-air concert platform, a bronze fountain cast in Berlin, the city's first rose garden, a sundial, a skating rink, and a playground. It is the site of concerts, book fairs, art exhibits, and other outdoor events. Near the train station, between Merkela Bulvāris and Elizabetes Iela.

ESPLANĀDE

Yet another spectacular Riga park, formerly Komunaru Park, it is separated from Vermanes Park by Brivibas Iela. The former Riga Stock Exchange (now the *Art Academy,* which exhibits works by Russian and Latvian artists; open daily from noon to 6 PM; closed Mondays) sits on its border to the north, while the Russian Orthodox cathedral (recently returned to believers) is to its south. In between is a seemingly endless bed of roses, much activity, and a statue of Janis Rainis, the great Latvian writer who ushered in the golden age of Latvian literature in the late 19th century. Located between Merkela Bulvāris and Elizabetes Iela.

EXTRA SPECIAL | A Sunday morning stroll through the Old Town is accompanied by singing and the chanting of litanies from a host of services. More than a dozen churches, from Russian Orthodox to Lutheran, make the Old Town seem like one of Eastern Europe's holiest places. There also is a synagogue on Peitavas Iela for Riga's 25,000-member Jewish community.

Sources and Resources

TOURIST INFORMATION

The breakup of *Intourist,* the once-official travel agency for the Soviet Union, has opened up opportunities for new private businesses; however, they have yet to establish themselves as offering travel services up to Western standards. Although it is best to deal with your hotel for efficient service, *Latvia Tours* (22-24 Grecinieku Iela; phone: 213652 or 220047; fax: 213666) offers package tours of all three Baltic states, plus day trips from Riga to other Latvian cities, farms, castles, and parks. The company, which has friendly and knowledgeable guides, also offers walking tours of Old Riga.

> **NOTE** Economic turmoil, including frequent and steep price increases on many goods and services, makes it impossible to provide accurate information on prices.

LOCAL COVERAGE English-language newspapers and books (including *Time, Newsweek,* the *Guardian,* the *Financial Times of London,* the European *Wall Street Journal,* and the *International Herald Tribune*) are available for hard currency at the *Latvia* and *Riga* hotels, and the *Hotel de Rome.* The *Latvia* hotel has the best selection of English-language periodicals. The main local English-language newspapers are *Atmoda,* the biweekly publication of the Latvian Popular Front, which is heavy on politics but also has good listings of art exhibits, theatrical performances, films, concerts, and other cultural events; and the *Baltic Observer,* a weekly paper with news from the three Baltic states.

Latvian television broadcasts CNN's "World News" daily between 5 and 6 PM. The *Riga* hotel's "Eurolink," a Swedish-renovated, third-floor wing that features Western-style amenities, also offers CNN; and the *Ridzene* hotel provides "Sky News," the British equivalent of CNN. A shortwave radio usually can pick up BBC programming or Radio Moscow, both in English.

English-language books are available at a branch of *Daina Books* (63 Elizabetes Iela). It's open weekdays from 9 AM to 6 PM.

TELEPHONE At press time, Latvia was scheduled to drop the telephone code of the former Soviet Union (7-0132) and adopt 371 as its international direct-dial area code; the city code for Riga is 2. Most hotel rooms in Riga now have telephones that allow visitors to dial direct within the city and to many parts of the former Soviet Union. Direct-dialing abroad is available but for a hard currency rate that ranges between $5 and $12 a minute to the US and Canada.

Public pay phones in Riga accept a token that can be purchased at any post office or newspaper kiosk. Rates are about $2 a minute to North America and $1.50 a minute to Western Europe (with a 3-minute minimum).

GETTING AROUND

AIRPORT The Riga Airport is 9½ miles (15 km) from the center of the city. There are plenty of taxis at the airport, and the No. 22 bus transports passengers and baggage into Riga. You'll need to validate one ticket for yourself and one for your baggage. Otherwise, you're subject to a fine. For more details on scheduled airlines to Latvia, see FACTS IN BRIEF.

> **NOTE** As a result of a post-independence energy crisis, at press time most flights departing from and landing at Riga Airport were international carriers that could bring in enough fuel for the return journey. *Latvias Aviolineas* flights were frequently delayed or canceled due to fuel shortages and breakdowns in the aging fleet of planes acquired from *Aeroflot,* the former Soviet airline. There's nothing to worry about if you're flying on a foreign airline, but if your itinerary includes a trip to Moscow, St. Petersburg, or some other part of the former USSR, you'll probably want to go by train.

BUS/TRAM Riga's formerly dependable public transportation system also was suffering from fuel shortages at press time (due to the fact that there is no longer a Soviet Union to provide guaranteed subsidized supplies of oil and gas). Bus service within Riga has been curtailed, as have routes to nearby cities such as Jārmala. Check the bus station or ask at your hotel for the latest schedules. The main inter-city bus terminal is at 1 Pragas Iela (phone: 213611) between the Daugava River and the train station. One ride on a trolley, tram, or bus cost 60 kopecks at press time. Tickets can be purchased at kiosks or the bus depot. Since public transportation operates on the honor system, you will need to validate your ticket in a machine usually situated by the vehicle's door. Just put your ticket in the slot and press the knob which clamps down on the ticket. If spot checks turn up an invalidated ticket, expect a fine.

CAR RENTAL Riga is best explored on foot, but if you decide to take a trip out of the city, all major hotels offer car rentals at a rate of about $30 a day; $183 a week. If you want a driver, expect to pay about $15 an hour within Riga and $22 an hour outside the city. Gas, however, is difficult to find. Motorists are best advised to fill up at the service station of the *Latvian Traffic Service.* This Finnish-Latvian joint venture has two 24-hour service stations in Riga (78 Pernavas Iela; phone: 273715, and 286 Brivibas Iela; phone: 551806). A third service station on the Riga-Tallinn highway, in Saulkrasti about 24 miles (40 km) north of the city, offers a coffee shop and car wash.

A final warning for motorists: If you park your car, be sure to remove the windshield wipers and radio antenna and hide them in the glove compartment; otherwise they could "disappear." It's also a good idea to keep any suitcases or shopping bags out of sight in the trunk. With economic reforms has come increasing crime throughout much of Eastern Europe, and Latvia is not immune.

TAXI The easiest way of getting around Riga. Hail one in the street, order a cab by telephone (phone: 334041/42/43/44), or go to the nearest taxi stand (labeled *taksometrs*). State-owned taxis are usually light green Volgas emblazoned with a black "T" on their doors with a light on top. Cabs are metered, although some hucksters will try to arrange a higher fare before accepting you. If you're hailing a taxi and an unmarked car stops and waves you in, don't panic. This is a private taxi, a way some Latvians earn a little extra income. Be sure to agree on the fare before setting out.

TRAIN The overnight train trip from Riga to Tallinn, the capital of Estonia, takes 7 hours; the trip from Riga to Vilnius, Lithuania's capital, is 6 hours. There are five trains a day to Moscow, a journey of about 14 hours. Purchase tickets in Riga's train station (at the intersection of Marijas Iela and Raina Bulvāris).

LOCAL SERVICES

DENTIST Ask at the service bureau of your hotel or contact the *Skonto Polyclinic* (38 Lachplesha Iela; phone: 281705).

DRY CLEANER Through your hotel or at Riga's only Western-style dry cleaners (39 Gamilu Dambis Iela; phone: 381879). Open 8 AM to 8 PM; closed Sundays. Your clothes will be ready in 24 hours.

LIMOUSINE SERVICE Inquire at your hotel.

MEDICAL EMERGENCY First try the service bureau of your hotel, which should be staffed 24 hours a day and can arrange transportation and interpreters. Outside the hotel, contact the newly established 24-hour *Skavya Emergency Medical Association* (25-1 Elizabetes Iela; phone: 216268). The special medical emergency telephone number is 03 (01 for the fire brigade and 02 for the police); no coins are needed when calling from a pay phone.

NATIONAL/INTERNATIONAL COURIER *DHL Worldwide Express* (5 Palasta Iela; phone: 210973).

OFFICE EQUIPMENT RENTAL Try the *Riga Business Center* (45-47 Elizabetes Iela; phone: 225189).

PHARMACY Two pharmacies offer the best selection of medicine and medical supplies for hard currency only. *Amfa* (21 Elizabetes Iela; phone: 333196) is open Mondays through Saturdays from 10 AM to 6 PM; and *Leader* (13

Vagnera Iela; phone: 216885) is open Mondays through Saturdays from 10 AM to 7 PM.

PHOTOCOPIERS At some hotels, or try the *Riga Business Center* (see "Office Equipment Rental").

POST OFFICE The main post office (21 Brivibas Iela) is open 24 hours daily. The post office next to the Riga Railway Station (Stacijas Laukums) is open weekdays from 8 AM to 8 PM; Saturdays from 8 AM to 6 PM; and Sundays from 10 AM to 4 PM. Most hotels sell stamps and will post mail.

SECRETARY/STENOGRAPHER Arrange through your hotel service bureau.

TAILOR *Rīgas Modus Nams* (Riga Fashion House; 68 Brivibas Iela; phone: 273312 or 285919) creates made-to-measure coats and jackets; payment is in hard currency.

TRANSLATOR Arrange through your hotel service bureau.

SPECIAL EVENTS

The *International Boys' Choir Festival* is held in the Dome Cathedral every year in March. An annual fair is held in early June at the *Ethnographic Open Air Museum* (see *Special Places*). The *Baltic Organ Festival* also is held annually in June. *Ligo,* also known as *Johannisfest* or the *Feast of St. Hans,* is the ancient midsummer festival commemorating the longest day of the year with song, dance, drink, and a great bonfire. It starts on June 23, or "Herb's Eve," when wildflowers and oak leaves are gathered to make St. Hans garlands, which are hung indoors and out. St. Hans beer is brewed and special cheese and pork dishes are prepared. The festival continues on June 24 when bonfires are built on local hilltops. *Riga Summer* is a series of concerts that take place in June, July, and August in the *Summer Concert Hall* in Jārmala, a popular resort 9 miles (14 km) outside of Riga. The *Church Music Festival* is held in Letgale, the eastern, Roman Catholic part of Latvia, to coincide with the feast of the Assumption on August 15. Thousands of pilgrims from near and far flock to the Aglona Basilica, the focal point for Riga's Catholics. *Riga Sings,* the annual choir festival, is held in September. *International Music Day,* October 1, is marked with a number of symphony concerts.

MUSEUMS

In addition to those listed in *Special Places,* the following museums are worth visiting. Most have a small admission charge. Check the English-language newspaper *Atmoda* for current exhibitions.

DOMA MUZEJS/RĪGAS VĒSTURES UN KUGNIECĪBAS MUZEJS (DOME MUSEUM/HISTORY OF THE CITY OF RIGA AND NAVIGATION MUSEUM) Founded in 1773, this is the oldest museum both in the Baltics and in the former Soviet Union. It offers a broad overview of Riga's historical development. *Dome*

Museum (2 Palasta Iela; phone: 213498) is open weekdays from 1 to 5 PM; Saturdays from 10 AM to 2 PM. *History of the City of Riga and Navigation Museum* (4 Palasta Iela; phone: 211358) is open Wednesdays and Saturdays from 1 to 7 PM; Thursdays, Fridays, and Sundays from 11 AM to 5 PM.

LATVIJAS AIZROBEZAS MĀKSLAS MUZEJS (MUSEUM OF FOREIGN ART) Paintings, sculpture, and drawings from France, Holland, Germany, and elsewhere. Open 11 AM to 5 PM; closed Mondays. 3 Pils Laukums, Riga Castle (phone: 220647).

LATVIJAS KARA MUZEJS (MILITARY MUSEUM OF LATVIA) Formerly known as the *Latvian Museum of the Revolution,* this museum is trying to expand its collection, which once proudly showed how Latvia became a Soviet republic. Open Tuesdays, Wednesdays, and Fridays through Sundays from 11 AM to 6 PM; Thursdays from noon to 7 PM. 20 Smilsu Iela, next to Gunpowder Tower (phone: 228147).

LATVIJAS MĀKSLAS MUZEJS (STATE ART MUSEUM) Traditional and modern paintings, sculpture, and graphics by Latvian, Russian, and Soviet artists. Open Mondays and Wednesdays through Fridays from 11 AM to 5 PM; weekends 11 AM to 6 PM. 10 Valdemara Iela (phone: 323204).

LATVIJAS VĒSTURES MUZEJS (MUSEUM OF LATVIAN HISTORY) A collection of weapons, tools, coins, textiles, and ceramics that traces the development of Latvian civilization. Open Wednesdays and Fridays from 1 to 7 PM; Thursdays, Saturdays, and Sundays from 11 AM to 5 PM. 3 Pils Laukums, Riga Castle (phone: 227429).

RAINA LITERATURAS UN MĀKSLAS VĒSTURES MUZEJS (RAINIS MUSEUM OF THE HISTORY OF LITERATURE AND ART) Exhibits and displays about Latvia's greatest poet, Janis Rainis, and other important figures in the country's literary and theatrical history. Open from 11 AM to 5 PM; closed Wednesdays. 3 Pils Laukums, Riga Castle (phone: 220349).

RĪGAS AUTOMOTO MUZEJS (RIGA MOTOR MUSEUM) Stalin's armored limo, the car Leonid Brezhnev crashed while driving to Moscow's Sheremetyevo Airport in 1981, a mini-van from the US-boycotted Moscow *1980 Olympics,* and a 16-cylinder German sports car worth $2 million are among the exhibits. Open Tuesdays through Sundays from 10 AM to 7 PM. 6 Eizeinshtein Iela (phone: 537730).

SHOPPING

Latvia's quantum leap to the free market has turned Riga into a shopper's paradise. Private handicraft shops have sprung up in the Old Town, with each store offering its own particular variety of handwoven tablecloths, wall hangings, hand-painted ceramics, woodcarvings, and wicker ware. *Paija* (Troksnu Iela) has a small collection of handmade dolls.

Several stores along Valnu Iela including *Maksla* sell pottery, amber, handwoven rugs, textiles, leathers, hand-knit sweaters, and carved wood. *Sakta* (32 Brivibas Iela) features a good selection of pottery and other crafts.

Special attention should be given to amber jewelry. Ranging in color from a smoky beige to a clear deep brown, amber is mounted on silver, polished in different sizes, and combined with other precious stones. Pieces with fossilized insects are particularly prized, and jewelry shop owners will gladly show you their collections of "amber with bugs." The most extensive selection of amber can be found at the *A & E Art Gallery* (17 Juan Iela; phone: 619989), which also creates made-to-order pieces. *Vecpilseta* (7-9 Kalku Iela; no phone) and *Tik-Tak* (corner of Skarnu Iela and Kalku Iela; no phone) also offer wide selections of amber jewelry, including bracelets and necklaces.

Probably the nicest clothing store in Riga is *VIP* (18 Basteja Bulvāris; phone: 228929), which features designer suits, dresses, sweaters, and accessories at very reasonable prices (hard currency only). And don't leave Riga without dropping in at the *Globus* bookstore (26 Aspazijas Bulvāris; phone: 226957), which has a good selection of books about Riga in English. Open weekdays from 9 AM to 4 PM.

Art aficionados will want to pick up a painting or sculpture in one of Riga's many new privately owned galleries. The *Kolonna Art Gallery* (16 Skuna Iela; no phone) boasts what is probably the best art collection in the Baltics, including paintings in oil and watercolor, sculptures, graphics, and photography. Open Tuesdays through Saturdays from 11 AM to 6 PM. Also worth a stop is the *Jana Seta* (off Skarnu Iela; no phone), which features handmade jewelry and is open daily from 11 AM to 7 PM. Antiques and art lovers should be aware that rare and historical goods (paintings, sculptures, precious stones, old books, and manuscripts) cannot be taken out of the country.

Most stores accept the local currency unless otherwise indicated. (There is a *valuts apmaina* — currency exchange bureau — on almost every street corner; open daily. Shopping hours are usually Mondays through Saturdays from 10 AM to 8 PM, with a lunch break from 2 to 3 PM. Some shops open on Sundays during the summer tourist season.

SPORTS AND FITNESS

From the stable of outstanding Latvian athletes (from which the Soviet *Olympic* teams were drawn for years) to those more corpulent souls who languish in the country's saunas, Letts cherish sports and fitness.

If language is no problem, check the back page of *Sports,* a newspaper that lists a calendar of sporting events, or call the following sports complexes: *Central Police Sports Club* (1A Melnga Iela; phone: 331211), *Daugava Stadions* (1 Augsh Iela; phone: 274815), *Riga Sports Pils* (75 Kr. Barona Iela; phone: 279669), or *Riga Sporta Maneza* (160 Maskavas Iela;

phone: 241770). If you don't speak Latvian or Russian, consult your hotel service bureau for information on sporting events. In addition, the sports center at the Riga Technical University (phone: 616989) offers 2 swimming pools, 2 saunas, and a café. Open daily from 7 to 11:30 PM.

The nearby resort of Jārmala features 30 miles of coastline. The often polluted water is unsuitable for swimming, but the sandy beach is ideal for sunbathing and walking, and tennis courts abound. In the winter, it is a popular place to cross-country ski.

HORSEBACK RIDING Can be arranged by *Latvia Tours* at Tervete, outside Riga.

SAUNA A trip to the public sauna (or bath) has been a Riga ritual since the 13th century. Ovens heat rocks to a glowing red and they are then doused with water, emitting a blast of steam. Real saunas (called *pirt* in Latvian, *banya* in Russian) provide bound-up birch branches, which bathers use to flog themselves (it's said to open the pores). Novices should start with a hotel sauna, such as the one in the basement of the *Latvia,* which has hot, warm, and cold dipping pools, water massage, and a surround shower (the spray comes from all directions). Public baths are for the more adventurous and those who really want to see how the locals live. Be aware, however, that many public baths don't live up to Western notions of cleanliness, security, or service. If you're game, the most centrally located public bath is at 98 Chaka Iela (phone: 263480). It's open 8 AM to 11 PM; closed Mondays and Tuesdays.

THEATER

In 1918, Latvia first declared its independence within the walls of the *Nacionālais Teātris* (National Theater; 2 Kronvalda Bulvāris), where occasional performances of native Latvian works and translations of classics are held today. The more modern *Dailes Teātris* (75 Brivibas Iela) often stages the works of foreign playwrights and the *Rīgas Pantomīmas Teātris* (Riga Pantomime Theater; 1 Ropazu Iela) is the only theater of its kind in Latvia. Check at your hotel service desk for specific information regarding performances.

MUSIC

Classical or modern, Riga is a hit when it comes to music.

HIGH NOTES

Doma Baznīca (Dome Cathedral) Concerts held in this ancient church are special both for the quality of music and the splendor of the architecture. Dedicated in 1211 as the Chapel of the Monastery of the Virgin, the building was expanded and altered over the centuries, and today it stands as a huge, magnificent conglomerate of architectural styles — Romanesque, Gothic, Renaissance, and baroque — and wonderful stained glass windows. The jewel in the crown is the 6,768-pipe organ, built by German craftsmen in 1884. One of the largest and finest such instruments in the world, it draws musicians from around the world, who use it in their recordings. The excellence of the acoustics, the grandeur of the organ, and the ambience of the church combine to make concerts here a memorable experience; not surprisingly, they attract music lovers of all ages, particularly young people. Concerts are weekly and tickets can be purchased before each performance. 1 Doma Laukums (phone: 213498).

Classical and modern Latvian operas are performed at the *Nacionālā Opera* (the National Opera; 30 Azpazijas Bulvāris; phone: 223817). This theater, which is also the home of the widely acclaimed *Rīgas Balets* (Riga Ballet), is closed for major renovations until next year. Meanwhile, the resident performance companies will be staging only a limited number of productions in borrowed buildings. Concerts also are held in the *Liela Gilde* (Great Guild Hall; 6 Amatu Iela), originally built in 1330, and in the *Wagnera Zal* (Wagner Hall; 4 Richard Wagnera Iela), named after the composer, who gave performances in Riga in the 1830s. On a lighter note, the *Rīgas Operetes Teātris* (Riga Musical Comedy Theater; 96 Brivibas Iela; phone: 276528) features popular cabaret-style entertainment. For performance schedules, consult the English-language newspaper *Atmoda,* or check at your hotel service desk.

NIGHTCLUBS AND NIGHTLIFE

There are basically two options for after-dinner entertainment in Riga, and luckily both are first-rate. The *Jever Bistro* (Skarnu Iela near St. Peter's Church) is both a German restaurant and beer garden. German food is served from 11 AM to 3 AM, and the well-stocked bar features authentic pilsner beer. It takes a good 5 to 10 minutes for the bartender to pour each half-liter glass of the foaming, tasty brew, stopping frequently to allow the rich head to settle. Cheesecake and apple pie, both served with cream, are available for dessert.

Only a couple hundred yards up Skarnu Iela toward Freedom Monument in a converted movie theater is *Casinos Latvia,* an Austrian-run casino that's open from 3 PM to 4 AM daily (except *Christmas Eve* and *Easter*). All gambling is conducted in English. Games include slot machines, a money wheel, and blackjack tables. At press time, local currency was the accepted payment in the afternoon; at night, the till switched over to hard currency. Befitting the elegant surroundings, men are required to wear jackets and jeans are prohibited. The casino has a free minibus service to and from the *Latvia, Rome,* and *Ridzene* hotels (for hotel guests only; book through your hotel service bureau).

Westerners will not be impressed by hotel discos in Riga, which are mainly geared for the locals and are frequented by black-marketeers and prostitutes. In addition, foreigners are routinely forced to pay a cover charge 20 times that levied on locals. If you're determined to experience every aspect of Latvian life, however, try the *Melody Bar* in the basement of the *Latvia* hotel or the disco at the *Riga* hotel. See the English-language newspaper *Atmoda* for information about the hottest discos elsewhere in the city.

During the summer months, there are outdoor evening concerts in the nearby resort of Jārmala.

Best in Town

CHECKING IN

Hotel accommodations can be booked through your travel agent or directly with the hotels listed below. The dramatically fluctuating Latvian economy makes it difficult to provide accurate rates for hotels. We suggest that you check costs — and the operative exchange rate — immediately prior to your departure. In 1992, the government replaced the Russian ruble with an intermediate currency called the "rublis." However, this currency is being replaced gradually with a more stable currency called the "lat." Also at press time foreigners were required to pay for hotels in hard currency. Most hotels have service desks that will make restaurant reservations and will arrange for tours, theater, and concert tickets. Most of Riga's major hotels have complete facilities for the business traveler. Those hotels listed below as having "business services" usually offer such conveniences as English-speaking concierge, meeting rooms, photocopiers, computers, translation services, and express checkout, among others. Call the hotel for additional information. All numbers are in the 2 city code unless otherwise noted.

Hotel de Rome Latvia's first Western-style (at least architecturally) hotel opened on the edge of Old Town in December 1991 and is operated by a German firm. It accepts hard currency only, so be prepared to run a gauntlet of security guards trying to keep curious locals out. This is one occasion when it helps to speak loudly in English as you walk through the front door. A warning to single women: The security guards adhere to the old Russian belief that an unaccompanied woman enters a hotel lobby for only one purpose, so be prepared to show your room key and complain loudly to the manager if you are embarrassed or harassed. There are 90 rooms, each with private bath, mini-bar, color TV set, radio, and direct-dial telephone; there's also 24-hour room service. The *Otto* restaurant on the top (seventh) floor serves mostly German cuisine (see *Eating Out*), and the fifth-floor *Atrium* bar makes great cappuccino. Business services. Room rates are quoted in German marks, but can be paid in US dollars. Breakfast is included in the rate. 28 Kalku Iela. For reservations, call *Latvia Tours* (phone: 213653 or 220047; fax: 213666).

Latvia Once government owned, this huge, relatively modern hotel is a comfortable place to stay. The 14th and 16th floors have recently been renovated, and guests can request one of the 34 rooms that have been upgraded to Western standards. The remaining 600 rooms are in the traditional Soviet style — clean but spartan, although most have big windows offering good views of the city. The staff is polite, and as in the other Baltic states, the hotel has several Western-style amenities. There is a sauna, a hair salon that offers massages and manicures, several restaurants (the one on the 26th floor has a great view; see *Eating Out*), and several bars, most of which take only hard currency. Business services. 55 Elizabetes Iela (phone: 212505 or 211781; fax: 283595).

Metropole One of Riga's newest hotels, it offers 85 tastefully decorated rooms and suites. A Swedish-Latvian joint venture, this hostelry is geared to businesspeople and offers a full range of business services including international direct-dial telephone. Although the hotel is in a rather run-down area of the Old Town, it does offer a good restaurant serving continental fare. 36-38 Aspazijas Bulvāris (phone: 225411/12/13/14; 469-882-0068 in Stockholm; fax: 469-882-0068 in Stockholm).

Radisson Daugava Overlooking the Old Town on the south side of the Daugava River, this new property features 350 beautifully appointed rooms and 21 luxurious suites, all featuring original paintings by local artists. In addition, guests enjoy a health spa, an indoor pool with locker facilities, a bar, 2 restaurants, 24-hour room service, and an indoor shopping complex. Business services, including international direct-dial phones. Close to all government buildings and the city center. 24 Kagu (phone: 216392 or 800-333-3333 in the US).

Ridzene This former Council of Ministers (read Communist Party) hotel was once off-limits to foreigners, but now accepts a limited number of tourists. However, many of the 49 spacious single and double rooms and apartments are rented on a long-term basis to the hordes of Western diplomats, newly assigned to Latvia, who have been unable to find offices or apartments. The Latvian government also continues to book official delegates here, and individual guests have been known to be bumped to make room for them. The hotel's restaurant is widely acclaimed, but it's open to registered guests only. Amenities include a sauna, hairdressing salon, billiard room, and a business center. Business services. 1 Endropa Iela (phone: 324433; fax: 324475).

Riga This 6-story hotel is in an ideal location, close to the Old Town, the Freedom Monument, and Bastion Hill Park. It's the domain of *Latvia Tours,* the new private Latvian travel agency. Insist on a room in the "Eurolink," the third-floor wing recently renovated to Western standards by a Swedish firm. The hotel's amenities include a sauna, a car rental counter (cars are available with or without a driver), 2 restaurants with lovely views of the park and music in the evenings, a casino, and a hard currency bar that serves German beer and cocktails. The 307 rooms (singles, doubles, and suites) all have private baths, TV sets, and telephones. Business services. 22 Aspazijas Bulvāris (phone: 216100; fax: 229828).

EATING OUT

Riga boasts a number of cozy and quaint cafés and restaurants that have somehow escaped the American Legion Hall atmosphere of many Eastern European restaurants. You'll want to avoid most of the formerly Soviet-owned restaurants as many of them have not managed to shake off their reputations for bad service and mediocre food. Over the past year, foreign investors have opened many fine restaurants, and although prices are steep, the quality offered is well worth the tab. There are several new fast-food restaurants that offer inexpensive meals that have been an instant hit with the Latvians. In general, payment varies from one restaurant to another — some accept only local currency, others accept both hard and local currencies, and only a few accept credit cards. No traveler's checks accepted.

Latvian food is typically German in character, but most restaurant menus are heavy on the Russian dishes. Latvian specialties include peas and bacon, pork dishes, and anything made from mushrooms. Non-alcoholic beverages can be difficult to find, and the mineral water is often salty, so don't hesitate to bring your own soft drinks. Latvia is not an easy place for anyone on a restricted diet: much of the food is fried, pork is often the only available meat dish, and fresh vegetables are a luxury much of the year. All numbers are in the 2 city code unless otherwise noted.

Anre The name is short for Anitas and Renar, the owners of this recently opened café, which features good pizza, spaghetti, burgers, cheese sandwiches, pastries, and fruit. Open daily from 10 AM to 7 PM. Reservations unnecessary. Local currency only. 30 Azpazijas Bulvāris (phone: 229915).

Arhitekts Riga's student hangout, this is an intimate basement bistro with only ten tables. During the day it serves light, inexpensive meals, but in the evening the menu features appetizers, coffee, pastry, and cocktails, including the "Black Latvian," a lethal mixture of champagne and Riga's black balsam liqueur. The menu is in Latvian only, but the friendly staff will make sure you get what you want. This is a good place to strike up a conversation with students who want to practice their English. A piano player plays soft, classical music in the evenings. Open daily from 11 AM to 11 PM. No reservations. Local currency only. 4 Amatu Iela in the Old Town (no phone).

Café Argentina This trendy new bistro is one of Riga's best self-serve eateries. The varied menu features pasta dishes, soup, and sandwiches in a clean, bright atmosphere. Open daily. No reservations. Local currency only. Smilsu Iela (no phone).

Café Jana Probably the best restaurant in town, and always crowded because it has only four tables. Spectacular fare, artfully arranged. The menu is printed in Latvian, Russian, and English, and the waiters make a genuine effort to speak English. The marinated mushrooms in a slightly sweet sauce are exquisite, as are the plump preserved cherries that accompany the tender beefsteaks in mushroom or spicy tomato sauce. (However, variety can be limited once the fresh vegetables go out of season.) Open 11 AM to 4 PM and 5 to 11 PM; Sundays 11 AM to 8 PM. Reservations necessary. Local currency only. 15 Skunu Iela in the Old Town (phone: 226258).

Café Senite A tiny, subterranean eatery where diners are surrounded by stained glass windows and aquariums full of tropical fish. In the summer, try to grab one of the outdoor tables lining one curve of the cul-de-sac surrounding the Church of St. Gertrude, where you can snap up bargain-priced caviar, chocolate, and champagne at an outdoor take-out counter. A menu in English is usually available; if not, there's usually a waiter who can translate. The restaurant's liquor supply is sporadic, but if you ask nicely they'll probably let you bring your own wine. Open daily from 11 AM to 11 PM. Reservations advised. Local currency only. 9 Gertrudes Iela, off Brivibas Iela.

Café Vecriga This place is a wonderful location to pass the time and get a real slice of Riga life. Locals mingle with visitors over good coffee, tea, and delicious sweet pastries. Open daily from 8 AM to 10 PM. No reservations. Local currency only. 18 Valnu Iela (no phone).

Jever Bistro Home away from home for Riga's expatriate community, this fern bar-cum-German beer garden feels just like a Western eatery, with food and service to match. This was one of the first restaurants in the former Soviet Union to use clear plate glass in its windows rather than painting them black or covering them with heavy curtains to prevent the curious from staring at food-laden tables and contented diners. It's located in the Old Town in the building where the late, great native-born photographer Philippe Halsman lived until leaving for America in 1929. Open daily from 11 AM to 3 AM. No reservations. Hard currency and credit cards accepted. 6 Kalku Iela (phone: 227078).

Juras Perle (Pearl of the Sea) A 3-story glass tower that juts out onto the beach at Jārmala, with a marvelous view of the Bay of Riga. The standard Soviet-style fare on the menu is okay — the steak in picante sauce is recommended — but the main reason to make the trip from Riga is the scenery. A broader menu and a floor show are featured in summer. Open daily from 1 PM to 1 AM. Reservations advised; book through your hotel service bureau. Hard currency only. 2 Buldari, on the beach at Jārmala (phone: 7-51198).

Lido Gothic pillars adorn this newly opened establishment where guests feast on exceptional pork and poultry dishes. Try the pork loin in orange sauce with steamed vegetables. Live jazz music nightly. During the summer months, dining on the verandah is especially inviting. Open daily for lunch and dinner. Reservations advised. Hard currency only. 6 Tirgonu Iela (phone: 222431).

Magdalena Not much to look at, but good food — and lots of it. The pickled mushrooms are outstanding, especially when washed down with the Polish cherry vodka. The house specialty is *karbonat Magdalena,* a pork cutlet with mushroom sauce. The former state-owned restaurant also provides music and dancing in the evenings. Open daily from noon until 11 PM. Reservations unnecessary. Local currency only. 4 Smilsu Iela (phone: 223090).

Otto Atop the *Hotel de Rome*, this very German restaurant has a handful of tables overlooking the canal and the Freedom Monument. The food is most definitely German, with a few Latvian specialties such as herring in a sweet sauce with vegetables and apples. Service is polite, there's live dinner music, and an extensive wine list. Open daily from 7 to 10 AM for breakfast; noon to 3 PM for lunch; 3 to 6 PM for coffee, cakes, and drinks; and 7 PM to midnight for dinner. Reservations necessary (make them at the front desk or at the restaurant itself; doormen may even refuse to allow you into the hotel until they phone upstairs and confirm that you're expected). Hard currency only. No credit cards accepted. 28 Kalku Iela (phone: 212572).

Pie Kamina (At the Fireplace) Cozy and tastefully decorated, this restaurant offers a menu that leans toward the continental. The food can be very good, particularly the mushrooms baked in sour cream and the pork stuffed with prunes. Several waiters speak English and some German and are patient about explaining the menu, which is now printed in Latvian and English. Unlike 99% of the restaurants in the former Soviet Union, they will alter a dish to suit your tastes: "Of course Madame can have sliced tomatoes and dark bread without sour cream." The view is spellbinding, and there's live piano and violin music at night. Open daily for lunch and dinner. Reservations through the ground floor service bureau are essential. Hard currency only. Top floor of the *Latvia Hotel* on Brivibas Iela (phone: 212505 or 211781).

Pie Kristapa Two restaurants in one, set in a lovely old building (notice the interesting sculptural detail on the façade). Downstairs, with seating for about 60 people, is a Latvian-style tavern featuring brown ale — somewhat like an English bitter — made especially for the place at the nearby

Lacplecis Collective Farm. Local dishes include a "peasant sausage" with sauerkraut, and moose meatballs. Upstairs, with seating for about 50, is a more formal dining room with dancing and a live band in the evenings. Both spots are open daily from noon to midnight. Reservations necessary; book in person or through your hotel service bureau. Local currency only. 25-29 Jaun Iela in the Old Town (phone: 224368).

Pinguin Latvia's answer to Baskin Robbins, featuring a dozen flavors of ice cream, all sold for local currency. Open daily from 10 AM to 8 PM. 76 Brivibas Iela.

Put, Vejni (Blow Wind!) Good food is served in an intimate atmosphere. High-backed throne chairs turn each table into a booth, providing complete privacy from the diners behind and in front of you. The menu features Latvian-Russian food, with several fish dishes and a creamy dessert called *slivky* served with nuts or berries. Reservations are necessary through your hotel (in which case you'll probably have to pay hard currency) or in person (in which case you'll likely be asked to leave a deposit). Open weekdays from 11 AM to 11 PM. Reservations advised. Local currency only. 18-22 Jaun Iela, just off Doma Laukums in the Old Town (phone: 223777).

Skonto Café A good place for breakfast, particularly after you've seen what your hotel has to offer. No bacon and eggs, but there is fresh fruit, pastry, and good espresso. Salads and open-faced sandwiches are served later in the day. Open daily from 10 AM until 9 PM. Reservations unnecessary. Local currency only. 4A Veidenbaum, just behind the *Latvia Hotel* (no phone).

Tower Bar From its opening a little more than a year ago, this split-level restaurant has become Riga's newest landmark. The first floor features a cozy bar, while upstairs caters to more elegant dining under the watchful eye of its imaginative Swedish chef. Grilled lamb sausage with roasted vegetables, and some sinfully sumptuous desserts make this worth the calories. Open daily for lunch from 11:30 AM to 1 PM; dinner from 6 PM to 1 AM. Reservations advised. Hard currency only. At the *Metropole Hotel* (phone: 225415).

Zilais Putns Pizzeria This new bistro offers 18 varieties of homemade pizza, plus salads and fresh fruit desserts. It's very popular with the young crowd, who often wait in line for hours. Open daily for lunch and dinner. Reservations advised. Local currency only. 4 Tirgonu Iela, overlooking Doma Laukums (phone: 228214).

St. Petersburg

The name St. Petersburg calls to mind the riches of imperial Russia: music, art, theater, ballet, literary salons, glittering court life. The city was the center of the lavish, reckless social milieu immortalized by Pushkin, Dostoyevsky, Tolstoy, and Turgenev. Almost inevitably, it was also the Cradle of the Revolution: Bloody Sunday, the storming of the Winter Palace, and Lenin's triumphant return from exile. As Leningrad, it was the second-most important city in the vast Soviet Union, and even after suffering near annihilation during World War II, it remained an important cultural and commercial center. Less than 290 years old, the city — once again called St. Petersburg — is relatively young to claim such a rich heritage, but what happened here has changed the course of world history.

In a city of such great beauty, where virtually every downtown building displays a plaque noting its historical significance, it sometimes is difficult to focus on the people and the life of today's St. Petersburg. But a visitor from the West is immediately comfortable here, and St. Petersburg is an easy city to explore and to get to know. When the days lengthen and dusk comes late, it is hard to resist walking among the people strolling arm in arm in the street, or relaxing in the parks in the fading light that casts its strange glimmer over the city.

St. Petersburg's glorious White Nights of summer are a consequence of its location on the Gulf of Finland, at about the same latitude as Helsinki. The city is built on a series of islands, 403 miles (645 km) northwest of Moscow. Although its climate is less harsh than the Russian capital's, the harbor is frozen 3 or 4 months of the year.

The scores of islands near the mouth of the Neva River, at a point where the Baltic Sea penetrates deepest into its eastern shore, were disputed for centuries by a succession of Finns, Swedes, and Russians. The Neva was an important early trade artery between Europe and Asia. In 1703, after defeating Sweden, Peter the Great built a fortress here to guard against future invasions. Within 9 years, Peter had built a new city, his "window on the West," and had moved the capital from Moscow.

St. Petersburg — Petrograd — as the new capital was called, was designed from the first to rival the beauty of Western Europe's finest cities. It developed in well-planned stages, acquiring an elegant façade as government buildings, cathedrals, and private residences of the nobility took their places along the Neva and the Fontanka and Moika rivers. Many of the most beautiful palaces were built in the last half of the 18th century under the direction of Catherine the Great's favorite French and Italian architects. As the excessive indulgence of the gentry increased, however, the lives of the czars' subjects became even more intolerable. Serfs were in semi-slavery. In St. Petersburg itself, overcrowded hovels, where workers lived in miserable poverty, surrounded the beautiful palaces, the lovely parks, and the great squares and avenues. This incredible contrast between the lifestyles of the nobility and the daily oppression of the workers was impossible to ignore. Change was inevitable.

On January 9, 1905, thousands of workers marched with their wives and children to the Winter Palace to petition Czar Nicholas II to intervene on behalf of better working conditions. The czar's troops opened fire at close range. The resulting massacre, known in Russian history as Bloody Sunday, was the spark that ignited the Revolution of 1905. Nicholas made some concessions that allowed him to survive this popular uprising, but only for a time. His inability to rule effectively, further economic hardship brought on by World War I, and continued revolutionary activity brought down the czar in March 1917. A new era in Russian history began in November of that year, when a Soviet government replaced the provisional government. It also meant a new era for this city: The capital was moved back to Moscow.

The city was renamed Leningrad in 1924 after the death of Lenin. Although its political importance diminished when Moscow became the seat of government, the city continued to grow as an industrial and commercial center until World War II. Almost 700,000 Russians lost their lives and some 10,000 buildings were destroyed during the 900-day German siege of Leningrad. But the city emerged from the war determined to restore its former beauty, and today St. Petersburg — its original name triumphantly restored after the extraordinary overthrow of the Communist regime — remains the loveliest and most European of Russia's cities.

The canals, rivers, and low buildings remind one of Venice (indeed, St. Petersburg's nickname is the "Venice of the North"), and Nevsky Prospekt has the air of the great boulevards of Paris. The parallels are reinforced by the 18th- and 19th-century baroque and neo-classical architecture that dominates the central city. The Yusupov Palace (where Rasputin was killed), Sheremetyev Palace, Count Orlov's Marble Palace, Prince Potemkin's Tavritcheskiy Palace, and especially the Winter Palace, are among the noble homes restored and used today as museums, offices, and meeting houses. Although they've lost some of their original grandeur, the buildings are still beautiful and eminently more useful.

Even St. Petersburg's present modernization plan is designed to preserve the beauty of the city's past. New construction in the downtown area must be completed within existing façades. No skyscrapers are permitted to mar the horizon; glass and concrete structures are prohibited in central St. Petersburg. Modern building is allowed beyond the city center, however, and numerous large apartment complexes have been built to house the city's 4.5 million people. Most of the industrial expansion — from the shipbuilding industry to factories producing hydrogenerators — has taken place in outlying areas.

St. Petersburg has an extraordinarily rich cultural heritage, with direct

ST. PETERSBURG

Points of Interest

1. Small House of Peter the Great
2. Peter and Paul Fortress
3. Peter the Great Museum of Anthropology and Ethnography
4. St. Isaac's Cathedral
5. Admiralty
6. Winter Palace
7. State Russian Museum
8. Summer Palace

JABLOCKOVA

DUBROLYUBOV

KRONVERKSKY

PROSPEKT

BIRZHEVOY MOST

NEVA

MAKAROVA NABEREZHNAYA

DVORTSOVYI

DVORTSOVAYA

MILLIONNAYA ULITSA

DVORTSOVAYA PLOSHCHAD

UNIVERSITETSKAYA NABEREZHNAYA

PROSPEKT

NEVSKY

KONNOGVARDEISKY BULVAR

ADMIRALTEJSKIJ

MALAYA MORSKAYA ULITSA

BOLSHAYA MORSKAYA ULITSA

GOROCHOVAYA ULITSA

POCHTAMTSKAYA ULITSA

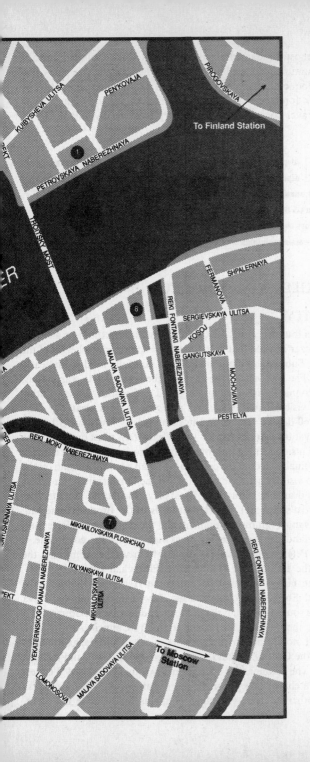

links to the most fundamental changes in Russian political history. Though not immune to the country's present disruptions, it is a city that speaks most eloquently of Russia's past. And so with the easing of travel restrictions for foreigners and the dissolution of *Intourist,* the former state-owned travel company, St. Petersburg is more inviting than ever before.

NOTE At press time, prompted by the increase in reported cases of diphtheria in Russia and Ukraine, travelers are advised to update their immunizations before entering these regions. For further information call the US State Department's *Citizen's Emergency Center* at 202-647-5225. Visitors should also be aware of increased crime in recent months; as always in new surroundings stay alert and avoid isolated areas.

St. Petersburg At-a-Glance

SEEING THE CITY

By decree of its founder, Peter the Great, this was from the start a city of low-rises. The czar insisted that no structure could exceed the height of the Winter Palace. Subsequent city officials have faithfully heeded that early building code. The best view of the city, and the best place to start a tour, is from the colonnade surrounding the gilded dome of St. Isaac's Cathedral, which is visible from at least 15 miles away on a clear day. The mesmerizing 360-degree view from the colonnade is just reward for the bracing journey it takes to get there — aerial-view fans must first climb the spiral staircase inside a cathedral tower, then negotiate the metal catwalk that covers the final 40 feet to the colonnade. Small signs in Russian on the colonnade help visitors get their bearings. To the north (*sever*), far below the cathedral's dramatic statuary, is Senatskaya Ploshchad (Senate, formerly Decembrist's, Square), a park that leads to the Bronze Horseman, St. Petersburg's most famous monument; and the mighty Neva River and Vasilyevskiy Island beyond. Moving clockwise around the colonnade, a number of St. Petersburg landmarks come into view: the Admiralty, the birthplace of the Baltic fleet; Dvortsovaya Ploshchad (Palace Square), graced with the famed Winter Palace and the *Hermitage* museum; the Peter and Paul Fortress; and the cruiser *Aurora* docked on the Neva beyond. To the south is Isaakievskaya Ploshchad (St. Isaac's Square) and Mariya Palace, the home of St. Petersburg's City Council. As you look toward the west, notice the intricate network of canals and the huge cranes towering over the Gulf of Finland, a reminder that this was and still is a busy port city. The colonnade is open from 11 AM to 5 PM; closed Wednesdays. There is a charge (steep) for the use of cameras or video cameras.

There are other interesting vantage points as well. Beside the Neva, opposite the Peter and Paul Fortress, you get a sense of where and how the city began. At the Admiralty Building, where the city's three major avenues converge, you can grasp St. Petersburg's layout and planning. In Palace Square, the site of czarist splendor and bloody revolution, you get in touch with the city's history; and on Nevsky Prospekt at Yekaterinskiy Canal, you can feel the contemporary pulse of the city.

SPECIAL PLACES

The major sites of St. Petersburg are spread out over a number of the 101 islands that interconnect to form the city, but all are easily reached by public transportation. You can sightsee on your own or arrange tours through your hotel's service bureau.

NOTE The following information on the city's sights was accurate as we went to press, but it is more than possible — given the current state of uncertainty in Russia — that some streets and squares have been renamed, and some hotels and restaurants have changed hands. Locals and visitors alike must grapple with this transitional stage. Fortunately, many buildings retain small white plaques with elegant lettering (albeit in the Cyrillic alphabet) that indicate pre-revolutionary street names that have either been revived or are expected to be.

A few Russian words to assist you in your navigating: "ulitsa" is the Russian word for street; "prospekt" means avenue; "bulvar" means boulevard; "naberezhnaya" is embankment; "proyezd" means passage; "shosse" means highway; and "ploshchad" is the word for square.

DOWNTOWN

PETROPAVLOVSKAYA KREPOST (PETER AND PAUL FORTRESS) Before Peter the Great chose this site to build a new capital for Russia, he ordered a fortress built to bar the Swedish fleet's approach. As the threat of attack decreased, the fortress, established in May 1703, came to be used as a prison for opponents of the czarist regime. The list of political prisoners over the centuries includes Peter the Great's own son, Alexei; Fyodor Dostoyevsky, before his exile to Siberia; the writer Maxim Gorky; and the anarchist Mikhail Bakunin. The Petropavlovskaya Sobor (Cathedral of Saints Peter and Paul), with its tall, extremely slender golden spire, stands in the center of the fortress. It is the burial place of the Romanov czars from Peter the Great to Alexander III, with the exception of Peter II. (Grand Duke Vladimir Kirillovich Romanov, the most recent head of the Romanov dynastic house, died in April 1992 and was buried in a special Romanov vault in the fortress, although not in the cathedral.) In 1924, the Peter and Paul Fortress became a museum. (The main branch of the *State Museum of the History of St. Petersburg and Petrograd* is also on the premises; see

Museums.) There is a cannon salute fired here at noon daily, a tradition carried on from the 18th century, when it was used to notify citizens of the exact time. Open 11 AM to 6 PM; closed Wednesdays and the last Tuesday of the month. Admission charge. 3 Petropavlovskaya Krepost on Zayachy Island, just over the Troitskiy Most (Trinity Bridge) near Kamennoostrovskiy Prospekt (phone: 238-4540).

LETNIY SAD; DVORETS-MUZEY PETRA I (SUMMER PALACE; GARDEN OF PETER I)

Across the Neva from the fortress, on Naberezhnaya Kutuzova (the Kutuzov Embankment), is a 30-acre park, laid out in 1704, and an unpretentious summer palace built in the Dutch style for Peter the Great. The park, filled with classical sculptures, is a favorite open space for St. Petersburgers, particularly during the summer's long White Nights. The palace is open from noon to 7 PM May through the first week of November; closed Tuesdays. Admission charge (phone: 312-9436 or 312-9666). The park is open year-round, although the outdoor sculpture is covered during the winter. The park's entrance is at 2 Pestelya Ulitsa.

GOSUDARSTVENNIY ERMITAZH; ZIMNIY DVORETS (STATE HERMITAGE; WINTER PALACE)

Built as a home for the czars and czarinas during the 18th-century reigns of Elizabeth and Catherine the Great, the *Hermitage* was designed by Bartolomeo Rastrelli, the Italian architect. The grandiose baroque palace and four adjacent buildings now house one of the finest art collections in the world. The splendor of the room decorations — patterned parquet floors, molded and painted ceilings, elaborate furniture, and decorative objects of malachite, lapis lazuli, and jasper — dazzle the eye as much as works such as Gainsborough's *Duchess of Beaufort;* Renoir's *Girl with a Fan;* Ingres's *Portrait of Count Guriev;* Breughel's *Fair;* Rembrandt's *Old Man in Red;* Titian's *Danaë;* Holbein's *Portrait of a Young Man;* and a wonderful, little-known Michelangelo sculpture, the *Crouching Boy.* Don't overlook the private dining room, where members of the provisional government were arrested on the evening of November 7, 1917. A great deal of space is allotted to Russian history and culture, and exhibits run the gamut from exquisite antique silver and a map of the Soviet Union in semi-precious stones to turn-of-the-century paintings with such fetching titles as *The Dairymaid Spurned* and *The Volunteer Shall Return No More.* Unfortunately, the dazzling Gold Treasure Room — which holds the exquisite jewels of Catherine the Great and a spectacular collection of Scythian gold — was closed at press time, so check before you go. There are no museum tours conducted in English, but you can book an English-speaking guide through your hotel. The museum is open Wednesdays through Saturdays from 10:30 AM to 6 PM; Tuesdays from 10 AM to 5 PM; and Sundays from 10 AM to 5:30 PM. Admission charge. 36 Dvortsovaya Naberezhnaya (phone: 219-8625 or 311-3420).

DVORTSOVAYA PLOSHCHAD (PALACE SQUARE)

Between the *Hermitage* and the great curve of the Admiralty Building, the former general staff headquarters, is the central square of the city. The red granite Alexander Column in the center was erected in 1832 as a monument to the victory over Napoleon in 1812. This square, the site of Bloody Sunday in 1905, is closely associated with the revolutionary movement. The climax of the October Revolution in 1917 was the storming of the Winter Palace from this square. Each year there are parades and demonstrations to mark the event, although, not surprisingly, these gatherings have diminished in intensity in recent years. Several enterprising local souls will rent horses to tourists for a gallop around the square and a dramatic photo.

MEDNIY VSADNIK (THE BRONZE HORSEMAN/PETER THE GREAT MONUMENT) The famous bronze statue of Peter the Great, designed by French sculptor E. M. Falconet, stands in the center of the grassy Senatskaya Ploshchad (Senate, formerly Decembrist's, Square) to the west of the Admiralty Building. The statue, commissioned by Catherine the Great, depicts Peter astride a horse whose hoofs are trampling a writhing snake (said to be a symbolic representation of Sweden). The monument inspired Pushkin to write *The Bronze Horseman,* and the statue in turn takes its nickname from the poem.

ISAAKIEVSKIY SOBOR (ST. ISAAC'S CATHEDRAL) St. Petersburg's largest church — and one of the world's largest domed structures — stands to the south of Dekabristov Ploshchad, across the street from the *Astoria* hotel. The cathedral is filled with mosaics and decorated with various kinds of minerals and semi-precious stones. Malachite and lapis lazuli columns form a part of the massive gilded iconostasis before the altar. A museum under the Soviet regime, it's now used as a church on Russian Orthodox holidays and other special occasions. Open from 11 AM to 6 PM; closed Wednesdays. The colonnade around the dome offers the best views of the city. It's open 11 AM to 5 PM; last tickets sold at 4:30 PM. Closed Wednesdays. Admission charge. Isaakievskaya Ploshchad (phone: 315-9732).

ALEKSANDRO-NEVSKAYA LAVRA (ALEXANDER NEVSKY MONASTERY) The monastery's Troitskiy Sobor (Trinity Cathedral) was built in 1722 to house the remains of St. Alexander Nevsky, which were brought here from Vladimir. In 1922, the silver sarcophagus containing the saint's ashes was moved to the *Hermitage.* The monastery also has ten other churches, four cemeteries (known here as necropolises), and a seminary. The *Muzey Gorodskikh Skulptur* (Museum of Urban Sculpture), which has models and site photographs of most of the city's monuments, is under renovation, and at press time, there was no date set for its reopening. The 18th-century necropolis includes the graves of Peter I's sister and Mikhail Lomonosov, the scientist and poet who founded Moscow University. The 19th-century necropolis includes the graves of Dostoyevsky, Tchaikovsky, Mussorgsky, Rimsky-Korsakov, and Borodin. You must buy a ticket to enter these cemeteries, but you may visit the interesting modern necropolis opposite the cathedral without charge. Note its unusual grave markers, such as the propeller of the plane in which a pilot met his death and a miniature oil rig for three oil field workers. The monastery is open 11 AM to 4:30 PM; Tuesdays to 3:30 PM; closed Thursdays. Admission charge for both the monastery and the museum. Since the grounds are never closed, they are a nice place to walk during *White Nights,* the June arts festival. (For additional details on *White Nights,* see *Quintessential Eastern Europe* in DIVERSIONS.) There are daily services in the cathedral at 9 AM and 6 PM. Near the Aleksandra Nevskovo metro stop. 1 Aleksandra Nevskovo Ploshchad (phone: 277-1716).

VOLKOVSKOYE ORTHODOX CEMETERY This necropolis, also known as Literatorskiye Mostki (Literary Stage), holds the graves of several famous Russian writers (Alexander Kuprin, Ivan Turgenev, and Alexander Blok), scientists (Dmitri Mendeleyev and Ivan Pavlov), and other prominent native sons. Open from 11 AM to 5 PM; closed Thursdays. No admission charge. 30 Rastanniy Proyezd (phone: 166-2383).

GOSUDARSTVENNIY RUSSKIY MUZEY (RUSSIAN STATE MUSEUM) After the *Tretyakov Gallery* in Moscow, this is the largest collection of Russian art in the world. There are some 300,000 examples of Russian painting, sculpture, decorative art, and folk art, all housed in the former Mikhailovskiy Palace. You need not have a PhD in Russian art to appreciate this museum, since many works are interpretations of classical themes. Open 11 AM to 6 PM (last tickets sold at 5 PM); closed Tuesdays. Admission charge. 4-2 Inzhenernaya Ulitsa (phone: 314-3448 or 314-4153).

KHRAM SPASA NA KROVI (CHURCH OF THE BLOOD OF THE SAVIOR) This church was built in the Old Russian style, similar to St. Basil's in Moscow, at the end of the 19th century on the spot where Alexander II was assassinated. The exterior is covered with mosaics. The church was temporarily closed for renovation, and at press time it was still unclear whether it would reopen as a mosaic arts museum or a church. The best views of the church are from the pleasant Mikhailovskiy Garden just to the east beyond the elegant wrought-iron fence, or from one of the footbridges spanning the Yekaterinskiy Canal to the south. Just north of the *Russian State Museum.* 2A Yekaterinskovo Kanala Naberezhnaya (phone: 314-4053).

KAZANSKIY SOBOR (KAZAN CATHEDRAL) Freed from its previous role as a dubious museum devoted to the history of religion and atheism (not necessarily in that order), this majestic cathedral is once again holding religious services. Originally modeled on St. Peter's in Rome and named for the famous icon of *Our Lady of Kazan* that was once on the premises (its current whereabouts is unknown), the Kazan Cathedral's most noticeable features are its distinctive Corinthian columns. The dramatic architecture and enormous dome are best appreciated inside, where there are a number of trophies and banners from the Napoleonic Wars. The great Russian Field Marshal Kutuzov prayed here before going off to war and is buried on the spot where he prayed. No admission charge, but a donation for restoration is appreciated. Open 11 AM to 5 PM; Saturdays and Sundays from 11:30 AM to 4:30 PM; closed Wednesdays. Services are held on Saturdays and Sundays from 9 AM to 6 PM. 2 Kazanskaya Ploshchad, off Nevsky Prospekt (phone: 311-0495).

BRIDGES OF ST. PETERSBURG From the large, impressive Troitskiy Most (Trinity Bridge) over the Neva to the multitude of smaller spans connecting the islands, St. Petersburg's bridges are not only useful but beautiful and historic as well. The stone turrets and chains of the Lomonosov Bridge over the Fontanka are an example of the earliest bridges. This heavy style soon gave way to light, airy ironwork decorated with lions, gilded griffins, sphinxes, and other delightful creatures. There are hundreds of these bridges, large and small, and they give a unified aspect to the city. The most famous, perhaps, is the Anichkov, which spans the Fontanka River at Nevsky Prospekt and has four sculptures by Peter Klodt. To allow ships to pass, the bridges are raised at various times during the night.

SMOLNIY MONASTYR (SMOLNY MONASTERY AND INSTITUTE) The cathedral and convent of the monastery were built in the 18th century by Czarina Elizabeth, and the institute was founded during the reign of Catherine II as a school for young ladies of the nobility. The room at the institute where Lenin later lived has been turned into a museum featuring paintings by several St. Petersburg artists. Tours of the interiors are available by special arrangement, but the park may be visited at any time. Classical musicians and the church choir perform at the Cathedral and Exhibition Complex here on Saturday and Sunday nights at 7 PM. The complex is open from 11 AM to 5 PM; closed Thursdays. Admission charge. 3 Rastrelli Ploshchad (phone: 311-3690). The museum is open from 9:30 AM to 6 PM; closed Sundays. Admission charge to the exhibitions. Along the Neva between Smolnaya Ulitsa and Smolny Prospekt, about 7 blocks east of the Sernysevskaya metro stop (phone: 278-1461).

PISKAREVSKOYE KLADBISHSCHE (PISKAREVSKOYE MEMORIAL CEMETERY) An eternal flame and small museum are located at the entrance to these memorial grounds commemorating the 900-day siege of St. Petersburg (then called Leningrad) during World War II. Some 500,000 of those who died before the ring of the blockade was broken in 1943 were buried in mass graves here. The museum contains photographs and documents chronicling the heroism of the city's residents during the siege. North of the Smolny Monastery, across the Neva in the northeast sector of the city. Open daily 10 AM to 6 PM in summer; 10 AM to 4 PM in winter. 74 Nepokorennykh Prospekt (phone: 247-5716).

KREYSER *AVRORA* (CRUISER *AURORA*) The Communists claim a blank shot fired from this cruiser signaled the start of the October Revolution. But local journalists say the original *Aurora* was sunk and this is just a replica. The cruiser is permanently moored in the Neva, opposite the *St. Petersburg* hotel. Open 10:30 AM to 4 PM; closed Mondays and Fridays. Admission charge. 4 Petrovskaya Naberezhnaya (phone: 230-8440 or 230-5202).

ENVIRONS

PUSHKIN This town, once known as Tsarskiy Selo (the Czar's Village), is the site of the Yekaterinskiy Palace, named for Peter the Great's wife, Catherine I. Built during the reigns of Elizabeth and Catherine II and set in a 1,482-acre park, the palace has a stunning aqua façade, decorated with gold and white ornaments. Part of the building now is a museum, with exhibitions of furniture and china, and displays explaining the palace's history. The *Pushkinskiy Litsey Muzey* (Pushkin Lyceum Museum for Noblemen's Children; 2 Komsomolskaya Ulitsa; phone: 276-6411), located near the railroad station, about a half mile from the palace, is filled with manuscripts, rare books, and the personal belongings of Alexander Pushkin, who studied at the school for the nobility attached to the palace. The village was renamed for the poet in 1937 on the 100th anniversary of his death. Both museums are open from 10 AM to 5 PM; closed Tuesdays and the last Monday of every month. Admission charge. Trains and taxis are available at the Vitebskiy Station in St. Petersburg; trains leave Vitebskiy every 20 minutes. The trip takes about 30 minutes (get off at the Detskoe Selo Station in Pushkin/Tsarskiy Selo). From Detskoe Selo, buses and taxis are available to take you to the museums. But first-time visitors will probably find it more enjoyable to arrange for an English-speaking guide and taxi driver through their hotel concierge. The palace is at 7 Komsomolskaya Ulitsa, 14 miles (22 km) south of St. Petersburg along Zabalkanskiy Prospekt.

PAVLOVSK One of the most beautifully restored palaces in Russia is less than 2 miles (3 km) from the Pushkin museum. The 1,500-acre palace grounds, originally the village's hunting grounds, is now one of the largest landscaped parks in Europe. The land and palace were a gift from Catherine II to her son Paul in 1777. After crossing a quaint wooden bridge, visitors enter the park through cast-iron gates. The palace was occupied by the Germans during World War II; they set fire to it when they were forced to flee in January 1944. In every restored room is a black-and-white photograph showing the condition of the room after the Nazis left, which makes the restoration work all the more impressive. During the winter, the grounds are popular with cross-country skiers. The palace is open Saturdays through Thursdays from 10 AM to 5 PM; closed the first Monday of every month. Admission charge. (Check with your hotel before going since many hotels offer combined tours of Pushkin and Pavlovsk.) 20 Revolyutsii Ulitsa (phone: 470-2156). The palace grounds are 15 miles (24 km) south of St. Petersburg along Zabalkanskiy Prospekt.

EXTRA SPECIAL On the southern shore of the Gulf of Finland, Peter the Great built Petrodvorets, the Grand Palace, which he hoped would rival Versailles. Originally designed by the French architect Alexandre Jean-Baptiste Leblond, today the building reflects the Russian baroque style of architect Bartolomeo Rastrelli, who altered the original building under the direction of Peter's daughter, Elizabeth. It was Peter himself, however, who drafted the layout of the 300-acre park, and the spectacular system of fountains that cascade through the park and gardens. The 129 fountains in this elaborate system begin on the Ropshinskiy Heights 13 miles (21 km) away; unfortunately, most of the fountains are currently under renovation and it is not clear when the entire system will be fully operative again. The most impressive is the Samson Fountain, directly in front of the Grand Palace, depicting Samson ripping open the jaws of a lion as a spray of water rises from the lion's mouth. Three other palaces stand on the grounds. Montplaiser, completed in 1723, is said to have been Peter the Great's favorite palace; it was later the residence of Catherine the Great. The Hermitage Pavilion and the Marly Palace date from the same era. All the builings were badly damaged during World War II but have been carefully restored by art historians and craftsmen following photographs and original plans. Petrodvorets is about 20 miles (32 km) southwest of the city. It can be reached by car (leave the city via Stasek Prospekt), taxi, or, in summer, by hydrofoil down the Neva into the gulf (board at the dock across from the *Hermitage* museum). The palace is open from 11 AM to 5 PM; closed Mondays and the last Tuesday of every month. Admission charge. 2 Kominterna Ulitsa (phone: 427-5390 or 427-9527).

Sources and Resources

TOURIST INFORMATION

Intourist's so-called successor, the *St. Petersburg Tourist Company* (11 Isaakievskaya Ploshchad; phone: 315-5129 for information; 272-7887 for guides; fax: 312-0996), still operates out of the old *Intourist* headquarters opposite St. Isaac's Cathedral. Its services include reserving hotel rooms; booking tickets for concerts, exhibitions, and special events; arranging tours of museums, palaces, and other special attractions; and providing English-speaking guides. It is no longer essential (as it once was) to make all travel arrangements through this company. The major hotels and the burgeoning number of private companies associated with them often offer better deals and with less red tape.

It is best to buy comprehensive guides to St. Petersburg before you leave the US. The *Blue Guide* to St. Petersburg and Moscow (W. W.

Norton; $19.95) is particularly useful. In addition, although good transportation and city maps are available in hotels and at news or book kiosks for very reasonable prices, it is helpful to take along a Falkplan map of St. Petersburg (Falk-Verlag; $6.95), available in the US. This pocket map is designed to be used in sections and includes a street name index and gazetteer for monuments, museums, hotels, and theaters. Another highly recommended book is *Where in St. Petersburg* (Russian Information Services; $13.50), which includes directories of emergency services as well as lists of the numerous places — among them streets, squares, and theaters — that have officially changed names since the collapse of Communism in 1991. Many have reverted to their pre-revolutionary names. The problem is that many taxi drivers and even locals still know only the Communist-era names.

> **NOTE** Economic turmoil, including frequent and steep price increases for many goods and services, makes it impossible to provide accurate information on prices, including the cost of basic services such as public transportation and the telephone. At press time, the Russian ruble's exchange rate was determined by twice-weekly currency auctions, and its value was plummeting. The Russian government periodically announces plans to ban domestic commercial transactions in currencies other than the ruble, putting an end to the common practice of charging foreigners hard currency at shops, restaurants, and hotels. (The ruble is still a nonconvertible currency, worthless outside Russia, and while there are restrictions against taking rubles out of the country, no one is going to confiscate a few souvenir bills.)

LOCAL COVERAGE The *International Herald Tribune, USA Today,* British daily newspapers, and some weekly magazines are occasionally on sale in some hotels and hard currency stores. Delivery has been spotty in the past, but is gradually improving.

TELEPHONE The country code for Russia is 7; the city code for St. Petersburg is 812.

Telephone directories are nearly impossible to find in St. Petersburg, but *Where in St. Petersburg* (se - above) has extensive listings of everything a tourist may need. Your hotel service bureau or business center also can help find a number.

Only some — mostly Western — hotels have switchboards, allowing you to dial direct. To make a long-distance call from your room, dial "8" and wait for a second dial tone. Then dial "1" and then "0" for an international line (followed by the city code and local number). In most hotels built during the Soviet era, you will have to place such calls through your hotel operator, service bureau, or business center. But beware: The costs of international calls range from high to excessive, so check carefully before making the call.

GETTING AROUND

St. Petersburg has a small but exceedingly good subway system, called *Metro,* which is supplemented by a network of bus, trolley, and tram routes that enable visitors to move about the city with relative ease. Good, inexpensive transportation maps are generally available in hotels and at street kiosks, although English-language versions may be hard to find.

AIRPORT St. Petersburg's Pulkovo-2 International Airport is about 45 minutes from downtown by taxi; the fare can cost from several dollars up to $15 depending on who you ask, so bargain before entering a taxi (see *Taxi* below).

BOATS In summer, hydrofoils and excursion boats ply the Neva River, the canals, and the smaller rivers. There are two docks opposite the *Hermitage* museum on the Neva River. One is for Neva cruises to the Smolny Convent (about 1 hour), the other for hydrofoils to Petrodvorets, Peter the Great's summer palace (about 25 minutes). Boat trips on the Neva are also available from a dock in front of the *St. Petersburg* hotel. The boat trip along the Fontanka and Moika rivers and Kyukov Canal (about 2 hours) leaves from the dock near the Anchikov Bridge, where Nevsky Prospekt crosses the Fontanka. Cruises are inexpensive and may be paid for with rubles — although many operators are asking for hard currency from foreigners. In the summer, tickets should be purchased in advance at kiosks near the docks. For more details, see *Classic Cruises and Wonderful Waterways* in DIVERSIONS.

BUS/TROLLEY/TRAM The costs of tickets for St. Petersburg's public transportation system are rising all the time, but they still remain a bargain for tourists because of the falling value of the ruble. Tickets must be bought in advance either from vending machines located near the bus stops or from nearby kiosks. Bus stops are marked by the letter "A," tram and trolleys by the letter "T." Route numbers are posted on signs and match the number on the front of the bus. Maps showing the various bus, tram, and trolley routes are available at hotels and street kiosks. However, for those without at least a passing knowledge of Russian, the public transit system can be confusing.

CAR RENTAL There are now many places to rent cars and chauffeured cars, including at major hotels. Rates can be exorbitant, so shop around. Fords are available through *Svit Automobile Rental* (*Pribaltiskaya Hotel;* phone: 356-9329 or 356-1074; fax: 356-0094 or 356-3845) and Nissans through *Innis Automobile Rental* (*Astoria Hotel;* phone: 210-5858, fax: 210-5859). At press time, *Hertz* was the only major Western agency in St. Petersburg, located at the *Grand Hotel Europe* (see *Checking In*) or at its affiliated

Interavto office (9-11 Ispolkomskaya Ulitsa; phone: 277-4032; fax: 274-2662 or 277-4677). The main car rental agency is *Intourist Transport* (5 Sedova Ulitsa; phone: 567-8246). It's highly recommended that visitors, particularly first-timers, rent a car with a driver. St. Petersburg's roads are absolutely horrible — many have crater-sized potholes, particularly those near the trolley tracks. In addition, Russian drivers pay little, if any, attention to traffic laws or rules of common driving courtesy. Street patterns, especially near the canal and the Neva River, are hard to fathom.

METRO The subway system runs daily from 5:30 AM to 1 AM, and the fare is inexpensive. Since St. Petersburg is built on marshy land, the stations for the 25-mile metro are exceptionally deep. In fact, some escalator rides up from the platforms can take a full 2 minutes. Stand to the right on down escalators; the left lane is for "runners." Coming up, however, you can stand on either side.

TAXI Once the easiest way to get around town, cabs have become expensive and unsafe for foreigners. Requesting limousine service is preferable, since many limousines are owned either by the hotels or private companies. In addition, make sure you agree on the fare *before* you get into a cab — bargaining is essential. Away from hotels and tourist haunts, you can often pay for cabs or private cars in rubles, although the driver will often ask for dollars first.

| **BE ALERT!** | There have been an increasing number of reports of tourists being robbed by bands of young people, commonly known as Russian "mafia," who lurk outside major hotels and restaurants posing as taxi drivers. The best advice is to never get into a cab with other passengers, and walk away if anything looks or sounds suspicious. |

TRAIN The five railway stations are Moscow Station (2 Vosstaniya Ploshchad; phone: 168-04374 or 277-0800); Finland Station (6 Lenina Ploshchad; phone: 168-7685); Warsaw Station (118 Obvodnovo Kanala Naberezhnaya; phone: 168-2611 or 259-1972); Baltic Station (120 Obvodnovo Kanala Naberezhnaya; phone: 168-2259); and Vitebskiy Station (52 Zagorodniy Prospekt; phone: 168-5390). Train station names indicate the primary destination of trains leaving from that station. For example, trains leaving from Moscow Station travel to Moscow. Tickets can be purchased at the above stations or at the Rail Kassa (24 Griboyedova Kanala Naberezhnaya), Mondays through Saturdays from 8 AM to 7 PM; on Sundays to 3 PM. For general information about train arrival and departure times, call 168-0111. For ticket information and advance reservations call 162-3344 (for trains within the former Soviet Union) or 274-2092 (international).

For those who want to explore St. Petersburg and beyond, *Cox & Kings* provides a 14-day tour from the city on their *Bolshoi Express* steam locomotive that includes stops at Volgograd, Sukhara, Samarkand, and Moscow. Accommodations and meals are provided. For more information contact *Cox & Kings,* 511 Lexington Ave., New York, NY 10017 (phone: 212-935-3854).

LOCAL SERVICES

All major hotels now have their own business centers, with services including fax and photocopying machines, typing, translation, and direct-dial international telephones. Some also offer conference and audiovisual facilities. See individual hotel listings in *Checking In.* (You don't have to be a guest at most hotels to use their business services.)

DENTIST *Dental Polyclinic No. 3* has 24-hour emergency service, with an English-speaking staff (phone: 213-7551 days; 213-5550 nights). *Polyclinic No. 2* (see *Medical Emergency,* below) has a dental facility that is open during clinic hours. The private company *Nordmed* (12-5 Tverskaya Ulitsa; phone: 110-0206, fax: 522-2006) is open Mondays, Tuesdays, Wednesdays, and Fridays from 9 AM to 5:30 PM; on Thursdays to 8 PM. They have an "on call" dentist available nights and weekends (phone: 110-0654). All facilities have Western-trained personnel and equipment. Patients must pay in hard currency only.

HAIR SALON There are facilities in all major hotels. The best non-hotel outlet is *Debut* (54 Nevsky Prospekt, corner of Malaya Sadovaya Ulitsa; phone: 312-3026 or 298-7235), a joint venture with Wella, the German beauty products company, and a reliable spot for a haircut, facial, or manicure. The shop has a professional staff, modern equipment, Wella skin- and hair-care products, and perfumes. Open Mondays to Saturdays 9 AM to 9 PM; closed Sundays and holidays.

MEDICAL EMERGENCY All major hotels have a doctor on call, and translators are provided for those doctors who do not speak English. *Polyclinic No. 2* (22 Moskovskiy Prospket; phone: 292-6272, fax: 292-5939) has its own ambulance service, and its medical staff will make house/hotel calls. The 24-hour emergency number is 110-1102. Clinic hours are weekdays from 9 AM to 9 PM; Saturdays to 3 PM; closed Sundays. Hard currency only.

For extreme medical problems, *Lenfinmed* (77 Reki Fontanki Naberezhnaya; phone: 310-9611), a joint Russian-Finnish venture, will airlift patients to Helsinki for treatment. Also, contact the US Consulate for further information (15 Furshtadtskaya Ulitsa; phone: 274-8235).

PHARMACY Most hotels now have a good selection of over-the-counter drugs and health-care products available in their shops. For prescription drugs, try *Polyclinic No. 2*'s *Damian Pharmacy* (phone: 110-1744 or 110-1272; fax: 292-5939), open weekdays from 9 AM to 8 PM; closed weekends and public holidays. *Lenfinmed* (see above) operates its own pharmacy.

SPECIAL EVENTS

St. Petersburg Spring, March 31 to April 7, is a week of festivities celebrating the end of winter. The major annual arts festival in St. Petersburg is called *White Nights,* and is held the third week in June to coincide with the longest days of the year. This far north, the sun does not set until 10 or 11 at night and rises again at 2 or 3 in the morning. Since the collapse of the Soviet Union information on what will be offered during the festival is spotty at best; traditionally there have been performances by the *Kirov Academic Theater of Opera and Ballet* (see *Theater*), by the *Maly Theater Opera and Ballet,* and by various top Russian singers and musicians. Evening cruises to watch the sun "set" for its brief rest are becoming increasingly popular.

The *Goodwill Games* will take place in St. Petersburg this year, with up to 2,500 athletes from 50 countries expected to participate in various competitions. The main events will take place from July 23 through August 7 at the *Kirovskiy Stadion* and the *Dvorets Sporta Yubileiny* (see *Sports*).

MUSEUMS

St. Petersburg is a major art center; many of the best-known museums are listed in *Special Places*. In addition, you may enjoy visiting — either individually or on a guided tour — some of the following. (Note: The hours for many of these museums can change with little or no notice; be sure to check before you go. Most museums charge either a nominal entrance fee or ask for a donation for upkeep or repair.)

BOTANICHESKIY MUZEY (BOTANICAL MUSEUM) Founded in 1824, the garden has more than 3,000 varieties of tropical and subtropical plants. There is a separate Orangerie with varieties of trees. Both are open from 11 AM to 4 PM; closed Fridays. 2 Professora Popova Ulitsa (phone: 234-1764, 234-8470 or 234-0673).

ETNOGRAFICHESKIY MUZEY (ETHNOGRAPHIC MUSEUM) Located near the *Russian State Museum,* this museum houses a beautiful collection of clothing, household goods, and folk articles associated with the daily life and customs of the peoples of the republics that once made up the Soviet Union. Open from 11 AM to 5 PM; closed Mondays and the last Friday of every month. 4-1 Inzhenernaya Ulitsa (phone: 219-1174 or 210-3652).

KITAYSKIY DVORETS (CHINESE PALACE) Commissioned by Catherine the Great (who lived here for only 2 months), this exotically adorned building, located in the suburb of Oraninbaum (known as Lomonosov in Soviet times), is considered just as important — and impressive — as the Summer Palace. Peter the Great also lived here before he was crowned. Off the usual tourist track, this palace was spared during the Nazi occupation of World War II, and its splendid original details are still intact. Open from

11 AM to 5 PM in summer only (exact dates vary from year to year depending on the weather, so it's best to check before you go); closed Tuesdays and the last Monday of the month (phone: 422-3753 or 422-4796).

KREPOST ORESHEK (ORESHEK FORTRESS) A former czarist prison where Lenin's older brother was executed, this out-of-the-way museum offers exhibitions on the fortress's history and on modern life in Schliesselburg, its suburban island home. Take the train from Finland Station to Petrokrepost Station and then a hydrofoil to the island. Open from 10 AM to 6 PM from mid-May to mid-September (dates vary depending on the weather, so call ahead); closed Tuesdays and the last Monday of each month. Schliesselburg (phone: 238-4686 or 238-4720).

LITERATURNY-MEMORIALNIY MUZEY ANNI AKHMATOVOI (ANNA AKHMATOVA LITERARY AND MEMORIAL MUSEUM) In a wing of the illustrious Sheremetyev Palace, the apartment where the famous Russian poetess lived for many years is now a museum. English audiotapes are for sale at the entrance. Open from 10:30 AM to 6:30 PM; closed Mondays and the last Wednesday of the month. 34 Reki Fontanki Naberezhnaya (phone: 272-5895 or 272-1811).

MEMORIALNIY LITERATURNY MUZEY-KVARTIRA DOSTOYEVSKOVO (DOSTOYEVSKY LITERARY MEMORIAL APARTMENT-MUSEUM) Home of the celebrated writer during the last years of his life. Open from 10:30 AM to 5:30 PM; closed Mondays and the last Wednesday of the month. 5-2 Kuznechniy Pereulok (phone: 164-6950).

MEMORIALNIY MUZEY-KVARTIRA A. BLOKA (ALEXANDER BLOK MEMORIAL APARTMENT-MUSEUM) The furniture and rooms have been re-created as they were when the distinguished Russian poet lived — and died — here. Open from 11 AM to 5 PM; closed Wednesdays. 57 Ofitserskaya Ulitsa (phone: 113-8616 or 113-8633).

MEMORIALNIY MUZEY-KVARTIRA A. S. PUSHKINA (PUSHKIN MEMORIAL APARTMENT-MUSEUM) The house where Pushkin lived during the last months of his life (he died from wounds received in a duel). Open from 10:30 AM to 6 PM; closed Tuesdays and the last Friday of each month. English-speaking guides must be arranged for in advance. English-language books and audiotapes are available at the entrance for an additional charge. Special shoe coverings (located in bins on the way upstairs to the museum) must be worn in the apartment. 12 Reki Moiki Naberezhnaya (phone: 311-3531).

MENSHIKOVSKIY MUZEY-DVORETS (MENSHIKOV PALACE) St. Petersburg's most recently restored treasure, this branch of the *Hermitage* offers insights into the Russian domestic scene — palatial style — along with art from the time of Peter the Great. Open from 10:30 AM to 5:30 PM; closed Mondays. 15 Universitetskaya Naberezhnaya (phone: 213-1112).

MUZEY ANTROPOLOGII I ETNOGRAFII IM PETRA VELIKOVO (PETER THE GREAT MUSEUM OF ETHNOGRAPHY AND ANTHROPOLOGY) An exhibition of rarities, curiosities, and oddities of nature, started by Peter the Great, and occupying the building that formerly was the *Kunstkamera* (Chamber of Curiosities). Open 11 AM to 5:30 PM; closed Fridays, Saturdays, and the last Thursday of every month. 3 Universitetskaya Naberezhnaya (phone: 218-1412).

MUZEY ARKTIKI I ANTARKTIKI (MUSEUM OF THE ARCTIC AND THE ANTARCTIC) The only museum of its kind in the world, it offers an introduction to the history of the exploration of the North and South Poles. Open Wednesdays through Sundays from 10 AM to 5 PM. 24A Nikolayevskaya Ulitsa (phone: 311-2549).

MUZEY ARTILLERII, INZHENERNIKH VOISK I VOISK SVYAZI (MUSEUM OF ARTILLERY, ENGINEERS, AND SIGNALS) A military museum of old arms, including a good collection of 16th-century weapons that belonged to the czars. Housed in the city's former arsenal, built in 1860. Open Wednesdays through Sundays from 11 AM to 5 PM; closed the last Thursday of every month. 7 Park Lenina (phone: 232-0209).

MUZEY DOMIK PETRA I (MUSEUM OF THE HOUSE OF PETER I) The modest dwelling used by Peter the Great while the Peter and Paul Fortress was being constructed nearby in the early 18th century. A must-see for history buffs, the small cottage has been refurbished with period antiques and replicas of maps and implements Peter used when he was redesigning the city. Open 10:30 AM to 4:30 PM; closed Tuesdays and the last Monday of every month. 6 Petrovskaya Naberezhnaya (phone: 232-4576 or 238-9070).

PUSHKINSKIY DOM/MUZEY RUSSKOI LITERATURIH (PUSHKIN HOUSE/MUSEUM OF RUSSIAN LITERATURE) The most comprehensive collection in Russia of manuscripts by Russian poets from the 12th to the 20th centuries. Open from 11 AM to 5 PM; closed Mondays. Basil's Island, 4 Naberezhnaya Makarova (phone: 218-0502).

TEATRALNIY MUZEY (THEATRICAL MUSEUM) A variety of exhibits and descriptions of Russian theater and theatrical life. Open from 11 AM to 6 PM; closed Tuesdays and the last Friday of the month. 6 Ostrovskiy Ploshchad (phone: 311-2195).

TSENTRALNIY VOENNO-MORSKOI MUZEY (CENTRAL NAVAL MUSEUM) A collection of ship models begun by Peter the Great in 1709 and more, housed in the former stock exchange building. Open 10:30 AM to 4:30 PM; closed Mondays, Tuesdays, and the last Thursday of the month. 4 Pushkinskaya Ploshchad (phone: 218-2501).

SHOPPING

St. Petersburg does not offer the variety of goods that Moscow does, and the prices are a bit higher, but it is a good source for souvenirs. Department stores and souvenir shops as well as an outdoor crafts market near the State Circus (be careful of pickpockets in this area) all offer a wide selection of Russian mementos: gaily painted wooden dolls that are stacked one inside the other, amber jewelry from the nearby Baltics, wooden toys, balalaikas, painted wooden eggs, shawls, vodka, caviar, and china and crystal from St. Petersburg's famed porcelain factory. This is also an excellent place to look for furs — coats, hats, muffs, and pelts — as Russia's main fur auctions are held in this city three times a year.

Located in all of the major hotels, hard currency stores sell souvenirs as well as toiletries, soft drinks, film, alcohol, snacks, and the most essential item for tourists — bottled water. The best of these outlets are in the *Astoria* and *Pribaltiskaya* hotels (see *Checking In*).

A recent phenomena on the Russian shopping scene is the non-newsstand kiosk. These tiny outlets, which resemble oversized phone booths, have been popping up on every street corner. Though the emphasis is on Western goods, some surprisingly good deals can be found on spirits, caviar, hats, lacquered objects, and other souvenirs.

Be sure to make time to go to the *Kuznechiy Rynok* (3 Kuznechnaya Ulitsa), St. Petersburg's best farmers' market, where merchants from all parts of the former Soviet Union come to sell their wares under a big tent. Georgians stand over what looks like an alchemist's selection of obscure spices; gold-toothed *babushkas* proffer their prized pickles, pickled garlic (a Russian phenomenon), homemade goat cheese, and honey; and Uzbeks are on hand with bright bouquets of fresh flowers. Prices at the farmers' market are traditionally much higher than in the stores, but the array is impressive. The market is open daily from 7 AM to 6 PM.

Most of St. Petersburg's department stores are open Mondays through Saturdays from 10 AM to 9 PM. *Gostiny Dvor* (35 Nevsky Prospekt; phone: 312-4165 or 312-4174), a large old-fashioned establishment that dates from the 18th century, is St. Petersburg's version of Moscow's *GUM* department store. At press time, parts of the store were undergoing extensive renovations. Other major department stores include *Dom Leningradskikh Torgovel (DLT)*, which specializes in everything related to children, including clothes and toys (21-23 Bolshaya Konyushennaya Ulitsa; phone: 312-2627); *Moskovskiy* (205-220 Zabalkanskiy Prospekt; phone: 293-4455), not far from the *Pulkovskaya* hotel; and *Tsentr Firmennikh Torgovel* (Trade Firm Center; 1 Oktyabrskiy Prospekt; phone: 352-1134). Most shops, except for department stores, close for lunch from 2 to 3 PM.

The following are some of St. Petersburg's finer small shops.

ARIADNA A cooperative that sells contemporary works by local artists. Open from 11 AM to 7 PM; closed Wednesdays. 32 Reki Moiki Naberezhnaya (phone: 312-7831).

DOM KNIGI (HOUSE OF BOOKS) The largest bookstore in St. Petersburg, with posters, reproductions, and postcards on the second floor. The building itself is of interest because it was the Russian headquarters of the Singer

Sewing Machine Company early in this century. It has some wonderful Art Nouveau details as well as distinctive metalwork sculpture on its roof. Open from 10 AM to 8 PM; closed Sundays. 28 Nevsky Prospekt (phone: 219-9443).

FABERGÉ Located on the site where the famed Frenchman made his baubles and jewel-encrusted eggs for Russian royalty, this store features a wide selection of amber necklaces and gold and silver jewelry. Open from 10 AM to 2 PM and 3 to 7 PM; closed Sundays. 24 Hertzon Ulitsa (phone: 314-6447).

GALEREYA Drawings, Russian boxes, wooden dolls, ceramic sculptures, painted samovars, and folk art by talented young Russians. Open from noon to 7 PM; closed Sundays and Mondays. 10 Pushkinskaya Ulitsa, apartment 10 (on the third floor — no elevator; phone: 164-4857).

GRIFFON Paintings, drawings, and photographs by professional artists, as well as souvenirs. Open from 11 AM to 2 PM and from 3 to 7 PM; closed Sundays. 38 Bolshaya Morskaya Ulitsa (phone: 314-4815).

IZDELIYA KHUDOZHESTUENNIKH PROMISLOV (ARTS AND HANDICRAFTS) Traditional Russian handicrafts including ceramics, wooden dolls, and lacquered boxes. Open from 11 AM to 8 PM; closed Sundays. 51 Nevsky Prospekt (phone: 113-1495).

KOMISSIONNIY ANTIKVARNIY MAGAZIN (ANTIQUARIAN SECONDHAND BOOK-SHOP) Old and rare books in a variety of languages. There's also an excellent collection of antique ruble notes and maps. Open from 11 AM to 7 PM; closed Sundays. 18 Nevsky Prospekt (phone: 312-6676).

LANCÔME A branch of the famous French cosmetics firm. Open from 11 AM to 8 PM; closed Sundays. 64 Nevsky Prospekt (phone: 312-3495).

LENINGRAD A good selection of artwork, books, and some souvenirs, all of which can be bought for rubles. Open from 10 AM to 2 PM and 3 to 7 PM; closed Sundays. 52 Nevsky Prospekt (phone: 311-1651).

NASLEDIE (HERITAGE) The art shop of the St. Petersburg branch of the Russian Cultural Foundation offers superior quality souvenirs including painted eggs and nesting dolls as well as paintings, drawings, and jewelry. Open from 10 AM to 2 PM and 3 to 7 PM; closed Sundays and Mondays. 116 Nevsky Prospekt (phone: 279-5067).

NEVSKY 20 GALLERY Attached to the Blok Library, this place features a good variety of works by amateur St. Petersburg artists. One side is primarily a gallery; paintings may be purchased on the other side (signs in English explain which is which). Open from 11 AM to 9 PM, to 6 PM on Saturdays and Sundays. 20 Nevsky Prospekt (phone: 311-0106).

NORKA (MINK) A cooperative offering a wide choice of opulent fur coats, hats, and muffs, along with other small fur souvenirs — all made in the traditional Russian style. Open from 11 AM to 2 PM and from 3 to 7 PM; closed Sundays. 34 Bolshaya Morskaya Ulitsa (phone: 273-4404).

NOTY (NOTES) For sheet music. Open from 10 AM to 7 PM; closed Saturdays and Sundays. 26 Nevsky Prospekt (phone: 312-0796).

PALITRA (PALETTE) A cooperative selling works of fine and applied art. Open from 10 AM to 8 PM; closed Mondays. 166 Nevsky Prospekt (phone: 274-0911).

PASSAGE A very old, beautiful department store, catering mainly to women. Open weekdays 10 AM to 9 PM; Saturdays 10 AM to 6 PM. 48 Nevsky Prospekt (phone: 311-7084).

PETERSBURG An exquisite antiques shop, with everything from furniture, icons, and paintings to silverware, porcelain, and toys. Drop in for a browse, even if you can't afford the hefty price tag, or don't have the patience for the paperwork you would have to do to get a purchase through customs. Open daily from 11 AM to 2 PM and from 3 to 7 PM. 54 Nevsky Prospekt (phone: 311-4020).

PLAKAT (POSTER) St. Petersburg's best selection of posters, and a reasonable selection of paintings, greeting cards, and other graphics. Open daily 10 AM to 9 PM. 38 Lermontovskiy Prospekt (next to the *Sovietskaya* hotel).

POLYARNAYA ZVEZDA (POLAR STAR) A fine selection of semi-precious stones, such as malachite, tiger's-eye, and carnelian. Open from 10 AM to 2 PM and from 3 to 7 PM; closed Saturdays and Sundays. 158 Nevsky Prospekt (phone: 277-0980).

RAPSODIYA Musical paraphernalia, including recordings and books in Russian, German, English, and French. Open from 10 AM to 7 PM; closed Saturdays and Sundays. 13 Bolshaya Konyushennaya Ulitsa (phone: 314-4801).

SEVER (NORTH) A popular pastry shop noted for its excellent tortes, cakes, and other sweets. Locals say it's the best in town. Open daily. 44 Nevsky Prospekt (phone: 311-2589).

SOUVENIRS More traditional Russian and Central Asian handicrafts. Open from 11 AM to 7 PM; closed Sundays. 92 Nevsky Prospekt (phone: 272-7793).

VOSTOCHNIYE SLADOSTI (FAR EAST SWEETS) Specializing in Middle Eastern sweets, including that all-time favorite, halvah. Open daily 9 AM to 9 PM. 104 Nevsky Prospekt (phone: 273-7436).

YELISEYEV'S This grand old food emporium, unimaginatively labeled *Gastronom No. 1* during the Soviet years, has regained its former name and has been restored to its original splendor. At the turn of the century this was St. Petersburg's showcase for imported European and Asian delicacies, but don't visit the early Art Nouveau building expecting to find the brimming cornucopia it was when the millionaire Yeliseyev brothers were in charge. In fact, today the opulent stained glass, ornate tile-hung interior, and bronze façade seem downright overblown when compared with its limited selection of goods. Open daily 9 AM to 1 PM and from 2 to 9 PM. 52 Nevsky Prospekt (no phone).

SPORTS

Hundreds of sporting events are held each year in St. Petersburg's major sports arenas: the *Sankt Petersburgskiy Sportivno-Kontsertniy Kompleks* (St. Petersburg Sports and Concert Complex; 8 Yuria Gagarina Prospekt; phone: 298-4847 or 298-2164), which seats 25,000; *Kirovskiy Stadion* (Kirov Stadium; 1 Morskoi Prospekt; phone: 235-4877 or 235-5494); *Dvorets Sporta Yubileiny* (Jubilee Palace of Sports; 18 Dobrolyubov Prospekt; phone: 238-4122 or 238-4067); and *Zimniy Stadion* (Winter Stadium; 2 Manezhnaya Ploshchad; phone: 210-4688 or 315-5110). Soccer and ice hockey are the two main professional sports in town. Your hotel service bureau can provide schedules and tickets for events.

For those who prefer participating over spectating, the *Kirovskiy Stadion* (see above) offers (for a fee) horseback riding, track and field facilities, tennis courts and equipment, and bowling. In winter, you also can rent cross-country skis and ski the surrounding grounds.

Tennis courts and equipment also can be rented at the *Pulkovskaya* hotel (see *Checking In*), where the staff speaks English; *The Tennis Club* (23 Konstantinovsky Proyezd; phone: 235-0407); or *BAST Sports Centre* (16 Raevskovo Proyezd; phone: 552-5512 or 552-3936).

The *World Class Fitness Centre* at the *Astoria* hotel (phone: 210-5869) offers gym facilities, sauna, swimming pool, solarium, and massage facilities. Open weekdays from 7:30 to 10 AM and from 3 to 10 PM; Saturdays from 9:30 AM to 9 PM; closed Sundays. The same company operates the *World Class Health Club* at the *Grand Hotel Europe* (phone: 312-0072), which offers a sauna, swimming pool, gym, solarium, massage, hairdresser, and sports shop. Open weekdays from 7 AM to 10 PM; Saturdays and Sundays from 9 AM to 9 PM. The *BAST Sports Centre* (see above) also has an exercise room, sauna, and massage facilities, as well as an English-speaking staff.

For true fitness freaks, the world's only nighttime marathon is run during White Nights, in the third week of June, when the sky stays light well past midnight. The date and route vary from year to year, so it's best to check in advance.

THEATER

It's easiest to arrange tickets through your hotel service bureau, which will also have schedules of performances at all the theaters in town. Performances begin early, usually 7 PM for the theater and 7:30 PM for the circus and puppet shows. During intermission, be sure to try the theater buffet, which includes open-faced salami and sturgeon sandwiches, cakes, cookies, soft drinks, and other snacks.

Many of the best resident theater, ballet, and opera companies tour Western countries, other parts of Russia, or parts of the former Soviet Union during the summer months. However, their stand-ins are just as talented. Here are some of our favorites.

CURTAIN CALLS

Kirov The most famous troupe in St. Petersburg is the theater and ballet troupe simply known as the *Kirov* during Soviet times (formally known as the *Akademicheskiy Teatr Operi i Baleta im S. M. Kirova* — Kirov Academic Theater of Opera and Ballet). Such legends as Nijinski, Pavlova, Nureyev, and Baryshnikov have danced with this company, which is noted for its adherence to strict classical ballet traditions. In fact, many critics regard the *Kirov* as the foremost European ballet company — in the East or West — even better than Moscow's *Bolshoi.* Originally the *Imperial Russian Ballet,* the company performed in St. Petersburg until 1889, when it moved to the *Maryinskiy Teatr* in Moscow. Under the direction of Marius Petipa, the company gave the premiere performances of Tchaikovsky's *Sleeping Beauty* and *Swan Lake* in 1890 and 1895, respectively. The company declined after the Russian Revolution, then experienced a rebirth under storied ballet teacher Agrippina Vaganova. Named the *Kirov* in 1935, today, its performances are held in the beautiful *Kirov Theater.* Tickets can be difficult to get, so book as far in advance as possible. (Some people have had luck just showing up at the theater or at the booking desk in their hotel early on the day of the performance and asking for a *single* ticket.) 1 Teatralnaya Ploshchad (phone: 314-9083 for general inquiries; 114-5424 for administration; 114-4344 for the box office).

Pushkin Whether or not you understand Russian, this is the top theater in St. Petersburg. Recent productions have often been satirical and have touched on topics strictly forbidden only a short time ago. 2 Aleksandrinskaya Ploshchad (phone: 312-1545).

Other major theaters include *Sankt Petersburgskiy Konservatoriya imeni Rimskovo-Korskikov* (St. Petersburg Rimsky-Korsikov Conservatory — but tell your taxi driver the "Konservatoria"; 3 Teatralnaya Ploshchad; phone: 312-2519 or 312-2507); *Akademicheskiy Maly Teatr Operi u Baleta* (Small Academic Theater of Opera and Ballet [but simply tell your taxi driver "Maly Teatr"]; 1 Mikhailovskaya Ploshchad [better known as Arts Square]; phone: 312-2040 or 314-3758); *Bolshoi Teatr Kukol* (Grand Puppet Theater; 10 Nekrasova Ulitsa; phone: 273-6672 or 272-8215); the *Tsirk* (Circus; 3 Reki Fontanki Naberezhnaya; phone: 210-4411 or 210-4390); and the *Bolshoi Konsertniy Zal* (Grand Concert Hall; 6 Ligovskiy Prospekt; phone: 277-7400 or 277-6960).

MUSIC

Tickets and performance schedules for concerts can be obtained through your hotel service bureaus. Concerts usually begin at 7:30 PM. The major concert halls are the *Sankt Petersburgskiy Filarmoniya* (St. Petersburg Philharmonic; 2 Mikhailovskaya Ulitsa; phone: 311-7353 or 312-2201); the *Maly Zal Imeni Glinki* (Glinka Small Hall) of the *Sankt Petersburgskiy Filarmoniya* (30 Nevsky Prospekt; phone: 312-4585); the *Sankt Petersburgskiy Kontsertny Zal* (St. Petersburg Concert Hall; 1 Lenina Ploshchad; phone: 542-0944); the *Dzhaz Tsentr* (Jazz Center; 27 Zagorodniy Prospekt; phone: 164-8565); the *Gosudarstvenniy i Vistavochnii Kompleks Smolniy Sabor* (Smolny Cathedral and Exhibition Complex; 3-1 Rastrelli Ploshchad; phone: 271-9182 for the box office, or 311-3560 for administration); and the *Sankt Petersburgskiy Sportivno-Kontsertniy Kompleks* (St. Petersburg Sports and Concerts Complex; phone: 298-4847 or 298-4659).

NIGHTCLUBS AND NIGHTLIFE

Although by Western standards there is still not that much nightlife here, there has been a relative boom in the number and variety of nightspots compared to the bleakness of Soviet times. All the major hotels usually have a bar that stays open late, a disco, a casino, and one or more giant dance halls with shows (see *Checking In*). The *Dzhaz Kafé* (Jazz Café; 27 Zagorodniy Prospekt; phone: 164-8565 or 113-5343) is a hot venue for some cool jazz performed by local artists until the wee hours of the morning (some of the best in Russia play here as well). Sip cognac in an atmosphere that is mellow and, unlike most places in Russia, refreshingly smoke-free. Tickets should be purchased at the door earlier in the day. The *Troika Klub* (Troika Club) is attached to the *Jazz Café* and advertises itself as the "Moulin Rouge of St. Petersburg." In general, though, opt for nighttime entertainment close to your hotel as there has been a tremendous rise in street crime. Also be warned that the "night bars" are targets for St. Petersburg's growing number of prostitutes. The *Kareliya* hotel has a discotheque; the *Pribaltiskaya* hotel has a nightclub that features live jazz, and a new "international class" casino (see *Checking In* for both). Casinos also can be found in the *Chayka, Vostok,* and *Vityaz* restaurants (see *Eating Out*).

Best in Town

CHECKING IN

During the Soviet era, all hotel accommodations in St. Petersburg had to be booked through *Intourist*, the state monopoly. Now the major hotels accept direct private bookings or those made through Western travel agencies. The *Grand Hotel Europe* and the *Astoria* have both been recently remodeled and are the city's best — and most expensive. But package deals, arranged in advance through a travel agent, offer the best value. Most hotels have banks, hard currency shops, postcard and stamp kiosks, service bureaus, beauty parlors and barber shops, newsstands, restaurants, and business centers.

Youth hostels do exist; it is best to arrange for these in advance. An inexpensive hostel for travelers of all ages also has opened in a former dormitory 2 blocks from the Moscow train station off Nevsky Prospekt. For information, contact *Russian Youth Hostels and Tourism* (409 N. Pacific Coast Highway, Building 106, Suite 390, Redondo Beach, CA 90277; phone: 310-379-4316 or fax: 310-379-8420). For bed and breakfast accommodations, contact *Room With the Russians,* which has an office in London (Station Chambers, High St. N., London E611E, England; phone: 44-81-472-2694; fax: 44-81-964-0272). The organization provides a driver who will greet you at the airport and take you to your destination; all of the participating families have at least one English-speaking member and some provide evening meals. The agency can arrange for apartment rentals as well. *American-International Homestays* (1515 W. Penn St., Iowa City, IA 52240; phone: 319-626-2125) arranges for stays with Russian families in St. Petersburg and several other Eastern European cities. *IBV Bed & Breakfast Systems* (13113 Ideal Dr., Silver Spring, MD 20906; phone: 301-942-3770; fax: 301-933-0024) can also arrange for a home visit with a local family.

Accommodations in St. Petersburg hotels usually are available in three classes: first class double rooms, deluxe 2-room suites, and deluxe 3-room suites. The dramatically fluctuating Russian economy makes it difficult to provide accurate rates for hotels; we suggest that you check costs — and the latest exchange rate — immediately prior to your departure. Be aware that the Russian government has imposed a 20% sales tax on rooms; check in advance to see if the tax is included in your room rate. Most of St. Petersburg's major hotels have complete facilities for the business traveler. Those hotels listed below as having "business services" usually offer such conveniences as English-speaking concierge, meeting rooms, photocopiers, computers, translation services, and express checkout, among others. Call the hotel for additional information. All telephones numbers are in the 812 city code unless otherwise noted.

For an unforgettable experience, we begin with our favorites in St. Petersburg, followed by our cost and quality choices of hotels.

SPECIAL HAVENS

Astoria Built in 1912 in the heart of downtown St. Petersburg, and extensively refurbished in 1991, this is still one of the city's best. The 436 rooms in the hotel, which incorporates the former *Angleterre* hotel next door, are decorated with antique furniture; many of them afford good views of St. Isaac's Cathedral and the Mariya Palace on St. Isaac's Square. Potted plants dot the elegant public rooms, and everything and everyone, including the doormen, are impeccable and impressive. Hitler planned to hold his victory banquet here after his armies captured the city; the arrangements, however, were premature (the invitation once hung in the lobby). There are 3 restaurants (the *Winter Garden* is the most elegant, although the ambience outshines the bill of fare), 3 bars, 2 cafés, 24-hour room service, an art salon, a fitness center with pool and sauna, a hair salon, and 3 shops. Business services. 39 Gertsena Ulitsa (phone: 311-4206, 210-5010, or 210-5020; fax: 315-9668).

Grand Hotel Europe Simply the best. With a fleet of Volvo limousines that greets guests at the airport, a glass-enclosed atrium shining with marble, a bar with a harpist and 33 types of vodka, this hotel is rivaled only by Moscow's *Metropol* as the country's finest. Formerly the *Evropeyskaya,* it was designed by Swedish architect Fyodor Lidvall at the turn of the century. The Swedish-Russian joint venture that restored the building has made it one of Europe's premier hotels. There are 301 guestrooms, some decorated with antiques, others in an Art Nouveau style. Even if you're not a guest, be sure to stop for coffee or a drink at the hotel's first-floor bar, an elegant respite from the sometimes overwhelming crush of shoppers that roam Nevsky Prospekt around the corner. In addition to European grandeur, the hotel has its own water-cleaning system (tap water in St. Petersburg is unfit to drink), 3 restaurants (including the *Europe,* which features European and Russian fare), a nightclub, 2 cafés, a health club, a sauna, a wood-paneled billiard room, 24-hour room service, and a row of boutiques and shops. Business services. Located off Nevsky Prospekt, it is next door to the *Sadko,* one of St. Petersburg's best restaurants (see *Eating Out*). 1-7 Mikhailovskaya Ulitsa (phone: 312-0072 for information/switchboard; fax: 312-0354 for reservations; 1-800-THE-OMNI in the US).

DELUXE

Pribaltiskaya This huge (1,200 rooms — including a number of 3-room suites) hotel is located on Vasilyevskiy Island, overlooking the Gulf of Finland. Although it's about 4 miles (6 km) from the city center, this vast, Swedish-built hotel is exceptional. Of special note are two 2-story corner suites, complete with spiral staircases, pianos, chandeliers, kitchens, and dining areas. There are several restaurants with floor shows and dancing, a bar, a nightclub with live jazz, a casino, a sauna with a massage room, a beauty salon, a duty-free shop, car rental facilities, a plane/train ticket desk, and dry-cleaning services. In addition, this establishment is distinguished from every other hotel in town by its bowling alley. Business services. 14 Korablestroitelaya Ulitsa (phone: 356-0158, 356-0207, or 356-0263; fax: 356-0094).

St. Petersburg A small plaque near the entrance to this hotel (formerly the *Leningrad*) reads "St. Petersburg" in English, a sign that it's trying to keep up with the times. Completed in 1970, this 736-room former *Intourist* property overlooks the Neva River and the cruiser *Aurora* from its comfortable B-floor lounge area (if you're lucky, they will have just washed the windows — but don't count on it). There is an 800-seat concert hall, 2 restaurants (one was under renovation at press time), 3 bars, a billiard room, a sauna, a duty-free shop, and 24-hour room service. Business services. 5-2 Pirogovskaya Naberezhnaya (phone: 542-9123; fax: 542-9042).

FIRST CLASS

Helen This Finnish-Russian joint venture property on the banks of the beautiful Fontanka River is ideal for the budget-conscious traveler in search of Western-quality accommodations. A favorite of many British, German, and Scandinavian travelers, the hotel projects a clean and modern atmosphere and has a personable staff — it's a welcome relief from the sprawling, dingy, and chaotic atmosphere of most Russian-managed hotels. The 275 rooms are quiet, cozy, and tastefully decorated, but the bathrooms can be a bit spartan. A breakfast buffet is included in the price. There's a modest cafeteria, a typically loud Russian restaurant, and a swinging bar on the fifth floor (open until 5 AM) with a good view of the Fontanka River. Rooms are furnished with cheerful prints, Finnish furniture and fixtures, radios and color TV sets. The hotel has several buses and minibuses and offers tourist excursions and sightseeing tours. Business services. 43-1 Lermontovskiy Prospekt (phone: 251-6101; fax: 113-0859). Reservations also can be made in Helsinki (phone: 694-8022; fax: 694-8471).

Kareliya This bare-bones hotel located in the northern part of town (a 30-minute drive from the city center) is popular with visiting students. It offers 429 rooms, 2 restaurants, 2 cafés, a disco, and a hair salon. Business services. 27-2 Marshala Tukhachevskovo Ulitsa (phone: 226-3515).

Pulkovskaya A mammoth, modern, Finnish-built property located between the airport and central St. Petersburg about 5 miles (8 km) from the center of town. An eternal flame monument to World War II victims is nearby. There's an impressive lobby, 840 serviceable rooms, 2 restaurants (the *Meridian* and the *Turku;* see *Eating Out*), 2 bars, 2 saunas, a duty-free shop, a hair salon, car rental, and a plane/train ticket desk. Business services. The hotel staff can be rude at times, and though you can't make direct-dial local or international calls from your room, even the switchboard personnel are less than helpful. 1 Pobedy Ploshchad (phone: 264-5122 or 264-5111; fax: 264-6396).

EATING OUT

The food situation throughout Russia is getting better, and the advent of independent, cooperative restaurants has added a competitive edge to the city's dining scene. Food, service, and atmosphere in St. Petersburg dining establishments have improved over what was offered just a year ago.

Russia has many notable dishes — although many are heavy on oil and sour cream — from the familiar beef Stroganoff, chicken Kiev, and borscht, to *pelemeni* (Siberian dumplings stuffed with spicy meat) and *shchi* (cabbage soup). Most Russian meals start with an array of appetizers known as *zakushi,* such as caviar, canned crab, sliced meats, smoked fish, marinated mushrooms, mushrooms baked in a sour cream sauce known here as *julienne,* sliced tomatoes and cucumbers, and *salad stolichnaya* (a potato salad with meat). Be sure to save room for the main course; you could easily fill up on appetizers alone.

Wise travelers do not drink water from public fountains, tap water, or the water served at restaurant tables; a parasite, called *giardia lambia,* is prevalent in the St. Petersburg water system. It can cause violent intestinal illness that can require hospitalization if not properly treated. There is an incubation period of about 2 weeks; therefore, this illness should not be confused with the usual travelers' maladies. You can avoid this parasite by taking minimal precautions; cooked food, tea, coffee, bottled water, and soft drinks are quite safe. If you order the local mineral water, be warned that it is often very salty. Russian restaurants rarely serve wine, but they often have local champagne, which is often quite good, especially if you insist on the dry variety (ask for brut or *suhoy*).

Meals at major restaurants in St. Petersburg can be booked in advance through your hotel service bureau, or you can book them on your own — that is, if you speak Russian. You can request a prix fixe menu, or you can order à la carte. Most of the St. Petersburg hotels have dining rooms with live bands, dancing and, occasionally, a floor show. Reservations for hotel restaurants also should be made in advance with your hotel service bureau. There are many cafés in St. Petersburg, providing a good opportunity to mix with local residents. As in other Russian cities, private or cooperative cafés and restaurants have become popular here. You can make your own reservations at co-ops — but remember that English isn't always the lingua franca. Otherwise, book through your hotel service bureau, which will do the honors at some, if not all, restaurants.

All restaurants below are open daily and all variety shows are offered nightly, unless otherwise indicated. The dramatically fluctuating Russian economy makes it difficult to provide accurate prices for restaurants; we suggest that you check costs — and the going exchange rate — immediately prior to going. Also check before you order whether or not you'll be expected to pay in rubles or in hard currency. All telephone numbers are in the 812 city code unless otherwise noted.

For an unforgettable dining experience, we begin with our culinary favorites, followed by our recommendations of cost and quality choices.

DELIGHTFUL DINING

Literaturniy Kafé In this city rich in culture and vibrating with social change, there's no better place to get a feel for the current arts scene than this, the favorite gathering spot of St. Petersburg's cultural elite, both past and present (Pushkin left the café to fight his fatal duel). The white-walled first-floor room is elegant and serene, with meals accompanied by a classical quartet; St. Petersburg's best poets, writers, and artists congregate upstairs. The food is good, although the selection can be rather limited, and the service is notoriously slow. Pass on the soups, which tend to be watery and rather greasy; stick with the cold appetizers and the steak with mushrooms. Also try *salat slavyanskiy* (a salad of sliced beef and potatoes mixed with a variety of fresh vegetables, hard-boiled eggs, and mayonnaise). Open from noon to 11 PM. Reservations necessary. Rubles accepted; there is a small cover charge. 18 Nevsky Prospekt (phone: 312-6057).

Metropol One of St. Petersburg's oldest dining establishments, it was founded in the 19th century and still tries to maintain that era's charm — although it's becoming increasing more difficult to justify that effort as prices rise and upkeep does not keep pace. Russian fare is served in baroque surroundings, and live music adds to the ambience. The place is as large as an airplane hangar (10 halls); however, since it is resting on laurels earned when there was little competition, food and service can be erratic. The prix fixe menu generally consists of a huge selection of cold appetizers (including crab and caviar), soup, a choice of hot entrées such as chicken Kiev, and dessert, all washed down with champagne or vodka. Specialties include *kotlety po-Kievskiy* (chicken-fried steaks served with mashed potatoes) and *file pikantnoye* (beef stew served with boiled cabbage and carrots). The desserts are wonderful. Open from noon to midnight. Reservations advised. Rubles accepted. 22 Sadovaya Ulitsa (phone: 310-1846).

Austeria Located in the Peter and Paul Fortress, this eatery recalls the era of Peter the Great. The fare, too, has an Old Russian flavor. Try the *file austeria* (fried beef stuffed with onions and nuts and served with fried potatoes, onions, and carrots) or the *rulet starorusskiy* (roast veal roll with hard-boiled eggs, onions, and carrots). Live music is played most nights. Open from noon to 11 PM. Reservations advised. Hard currency only. Ioannovskiy Ravelin, Peter and Paul Fortress (phone: 238-4262).

Chayka The first foreign-owned restaurant in the city, this Russian-German joint venture specializes in German fare (beefsteaks and sausages) and German beer. The interior has a nautical decor (*chayka* is Russian for seagull). It's also a popular nightspot, since it's open into the wee hours. No reservations. Hard currency only; major credit cards accepted. 14 Yekaterinskovo Kanala Naberezhnaya (phone: 312-4631).

Daugava Set in the *Pribaltiskaya* hotel, this dining room with modern decor specializes in roast chicken and grilled meat. Open from noon to 11 PM.

Reservations necessary. Hard currency only; major credit cards accepted. *Pribaltiskaya Hotel,* 14 Korablestroitelaya Ulitsa (phone: 356-4409).

Demyanova Ukha A small spot with rustic decor, it's highly recommended for vegetarians; the inexpensive fare consists primarily of fish and seafood. Open from noon to 10 PM. Rubles and hard currency accepted. Reservations unnecessary. 53 Gorkova Ulitsa (phone: 232-8090).

Diamond Jack A relaxing dining spot not far from the Peter and Paul Fortress, this genteel place offers elegant Russian decor, soft piano music in the background, and solid Russian and Italian fare. Open from noon to midnight. Hard currency only. 32 Lenina Ulitsa (phone: 230-8830).

Fortezia A Russian-Belgian venture, this cozy spot seats only 45 in 3 small dining rooms (the smallest of them has only 2 tables set under portraits of Peter the Great and his wife, Catherine). Traditional Russian food is the bill of fare. Open from noon to midnight; closed Mondays from noon to 7 PM. Reservations advised. Food for rubles; drinks for hard currency only. 7 Kuibysheva Ulitsa (phone: 233-9468).

Fregat The food and decor here are right out of Peter the Great's era. Try the Russian specialties *myaso Fregat* (roast beef with cheese and mushrooms) or *kury po-Kupecheskiy* (roast chicken in sour-cream sauce). Open from 11 AM to 10 PM. Reservations unnecessary. Hard currency only. 39 Bolshoi Prospekt (phone: 213-4923).

Gino Genelli Originally opened as an ice cream shop (a mysterious decision considering that ice cream is a Russian specialty and the selection at this place is not wide), this glitzy little subterranean joint now serves a variety of hamburgers. An Italian-Russian joint venture, it's not a bad place to go to satisfy a sudden hankering for a cheeseburger and to pretend you never left the USA. Open from noon to midnight. Reservations unnecessary. Hard currency only; major credit cards accepted. 14 Yekaterinskovo Kanala Naberezhnaya (no phone).

Goluboy Delfin Specializing in a variety of fish dishes, this place is a favorite of seafood lovers and vegetarians. Open from noon to 11 PM. Reservations advised. Hard currency accepted. 44 Sredneokhtinskiy Prospekt (phone: 227-2133).

Hermitage For good traditional Russian fare and old-fashioned decor, stop in this café located in Pushkin, a mile from Yekaterinskiy Palace and its park. Try the *zharkoye russkoye* (roast meat). Open from noon to 11 PM. Reservations advised. Major credit cards accepted. 27 Kominterna Ulitsa (phone: 476-6255).

Imperial Traditional Russian dishes are served in this ornately decorated dining room (the walls are covered with paintings and photographs of Russian nobility and other pre-Revolution bigwigs). Try the *suvorov* (a beef and mushroom stew baked in a clay pot). The service, from tuxedo-clad wait-ers, is fast and efficient. Open from noon to midnight. Reservations ad-vised. Rubles or hard currency is taken, depending on what you can negotiate in advance. 53 Kamennoostrovskiy (formerly Kirovskiy) Pros-pekt, on the main road to Vyborg on the "Petrograd" side of the river (phone: 234-1594 or 234-1742).

Ismailov Some of the best traditional Russian food in town — and the best floor show (Gypsy love songs, cossack dancing, and Russian folk songs). The prix fixe menu starts with a groaning table of cold *zakushi*, hot *blinis*, caviar, and creamed mushrooms crêpes. There are usually three entrées to choose from, followed by dessert and coffee. Open from noon to midnight. Reservations necessary. The only sour note here is that foreigners are asked to pay in hard currency, while the Russian natives sitting next to you pay in rubles for a fraction of the cost. Corner of Sovietskaya Ulitsa and Krasnoarmeyskaya Ulitsa (phone: 292-6838).

John Bull Pub Located in what used to be an ice cream parlor, this English-style pub offers draft beer (John Bull bitter) on tap and snacks. Traditional Russian meals are served in the adjacent dining room, but be warned that the service can be very slow. The pub is open daily from noon to midnight; the restaurant serves from 10 AM to 10 PM. Reservations advised. Hard currency only. 79 Nevsky Prospekt (phone: 164-9877).

Meridian In the *Pulkovskaya* hotel, this 450-seat dinner-theater features a variety show, along with Russian and continental fare. The *schnitzel Pulkovskiy* (pork fried in herbs and bread crumbs) is a specialty. Open from 7 PM to midnight; closed Mondays. Reservations advised. Hard currency only. 1 Pobedy Ploshchad (phone: 264-5134).

Na Fontanke Located in the center of St. Petersburg, this is one of the best cooperative dining spots in town. The menu offers such specialties as *langet na-Fontanke* (fried beef served with boiled potatoes and peas) and the *salat St. Petersburghskiy* (salad prepared from an old Russian recipe). The prix fixe menu is determined by what's fresh in the market that day, but generally includes a full table of cold appetizers (the marinated mush-rooms are the best in town), a choice of hot entrée (the steak topped with tomatoes and cheese is good), and dessert. You can request a vegetarian meal in advance, but more than likely you'll wind up with fried fish. There's a piano player and violinist. Open from 1 to 11:30 PM. Since there are only 10 tables in the restaurant, reservations are essential. Food for rubles; drinks for hard currency. 77 Reki Fontanki Naberezhnaya (phone: 310-2547).

Nevsky For traditional Russian food and hospitality offered in modern sur-roundings, visit this first class dining establishment located in the city center. Specialties include *eskalop* (veal served with fried potatoes and olives). There's a variety show, along with live music performed by different orchestras in three separate dining rooms. Open daily from noon to midnight. Reservations necessary. Hard currency only; major credit cards accepted. 71 Nevsky Prospekt (phone: 311-3093).

Petrovskiy An old ship that has been permanently moored and transformed into a restaurant and bar. The dark blue decor recalls the 18th century, as does the food. A house specialty is the *myaso po-preobrazhenskiy* (fried, beef-filled pastry, served with peas, onions, and tomato sauce). Open from noon to midnight. Reservations advised. Major credit cards accepted. Opposite house No. 3 on Mytninskaya Naberezhnaya (phone: 238-4793).

Pizza Express A Russian-Finnish venture, this eatery offers 13 kinds of pizza from "Americano" (ham, pineapple, and blue cheese) to "Milano" (tuna, clams, onions, and capers), made from Finnish products and served in Russian surroundings (or — astonishingly — delivered to your hotel door). The menu also includes a full range of other entrées, including pork dishes and beef Stroganoff. Cocktails are served. Paintings by local artists are for sale, too. Open from 10 AM to midnight. Reservations advised. Major credit cards accepted. 23 Podolskaya Ulitsa (phone: 292-2666).

Sadko Still one of the best restaurants in St. Petersburg, with traditional Russian fare and a flashy, predominantly Russian clientele. Try the beef Stroganoff, *lyulya kebab* (skewered meatballs), and *blinis* (crêpes stuffed with caviar, smoked salmon, or other delicacies). A balalaika orchestra, singers, and occasionally folk dancers provide entertainment. Open from 11 AM to midnight. Reservations advised. Hard currency only. Next to the *Grand Hotel Europe,* Mikhailovskaya Ulitsa and Nevsky Prospekt (phone: 210-3198).

Saint Petersburg This first class dining spot is located on the Yekaterinskiy Canal, one of the city's prettiest streets, between Nevsky Prospekt and the Church of the Blood of the Savior. A German-Russian joint venture (the flags of both countries billow over the entrance), it is outfitted in brass and wood with a clubbish feel of a New York steakhouse, although the prix fixe menu consists of page after page of traditional Russian fare. Specialties include Peter's soup (cabbage), chicken Nicholas I (cutlets stuffed with mushrooms, cheese, and nuts), and a *White Nights* dessert (a cream and fruit concoction). The wine list features a wide assortment of French and Italian wines. The folk orchestra that performs throughout the evening gives way to a floor show featuring impersonations of Peter the Great, Empress Catherine I, and other early Russian royals. Open noon to midnight. Reservations essential; it is sometimes necessary to book a day or 2 in advance. Hard currency only. 5 Yekaterinskovo Kanala Naberezhnaya (phone: 314-4947).

Schvabskiy Domik Also known as the "Schwäbisch Hut," this stylish eatery serves genuine Schwäbisch food and light German wines from Baden and

Württemberg. There are two separate dining rooms with different menus and entrances. Open from 11:30 AM to 3:30 PM and from 6:30 to 10 PM. Reservations necessary. Hard currency only. 28-19 Krasnogvardeyskiy Prospekt (phone: 528-2211).

Tbilisi Café A little out of the way on the "Petrograd side" of the city (across the river and north of the Peter and Paul Fortress), this festive Georgian cooperative is a favorite with foreigners and tour groups. Georgian art and tapestries adorn the stone walls, and there are many ceramics and miniatures on display. The staff seems genuinely delighted to serve foreigners, but the food can occasionally be bland and uninspired. (Purists in search of authentic Georgian fare will not find it here — too many Russian dishes appear among the Georgian specialties.) Open from 11 AM to 11 PM. Hard currency only; major credit cards accepted. Reservations advised for dinner. 10 Sytninskaya Ulitsa (phone: 232-9391).

Tête-à-Tête This former barbershop has become a luxurious dining room that is intimate, lamplit, and graced with plenty of antiques and chandeliers with real candles — all of which make diners feel as though they've stepped back into Old St. Petersburg. The menu features continental fare, including sturgeon, a house specialty. A tail-coated jazz pianist works wonders on the grand piano in the corner. "Evening dress" is requested (translation: jacket and tie are required for men and the improperly attired will be turned away). Open from 1 PM to 1 AM. Reservations necessary. Hard currency only. 65 Bolshoi Prospekt, Petrogradskaya Storona on the Petrograd side (phone: 232-7548).

Troika Excellent food and first-rate entertainment served up in a red and gold baroque setting. There are several courses offered here, from caviar to crab, right through to the ice cream and vodka and champagne. The nightly variety show is one of the best in town — traditional Russian folk songs, dancing, and music; after intermission, however, the whole thing turns into a tacky sex show. Open daily 2 PM to 1 AM. Reservations essential. Rubles and hard currency accepted. 27 Zagorodniy Prospekt (phone: 133-5343).

Turku A Gypsy variety show is performed for up to 300 guests in this dinner-theater decorated in shades of red. The chicken leg stuffed with mushrooms is one of the best dishes offered on the continental menu. Open from 8:30 PM to midnight. Reservations necessary. Major credit cards accepted. *Pulkovskaya Hotel,* 1 Pobedy Ploshchad (phone: 264-5716).

U Petrovicha Old Russian game dishes — elk, wild boar, and rabbit — are the specialties at this cozy little spot. Live music is performed most nights. Open from noon to 11 PM. Reservations necessary. Major credit cards accepted. 44 Sredneokhtinksiy Prospekt (phone: 227-2135).

Vityaz Not far from Yekaterinskiy Palace in Pushkin, this Russian-Italian venture offers Russian fare and a variety show (except Tuesdays). An especially tasty dish is the *myaso Vityaz* (beef sirloin covered with shredded onions and bread crumbs) and served with sour cream, fried potatoes, and whortleberries. There also is a bar and a casino. The restaurant is open from noon to midnight; the casino operates from midnight to 5 AM. Reservations advised. Major credit cards accepted at the restaurant only. 20 Moskovskaya Ulitsa, Pushkin (phone: 466-4316).

Vostok This is still the only dining establishment in St. Petersburg serving Indian fare. A joint Russian-Indian venture, it offers good and spicy dishes prepared over an open fire. There is a variety show and casino. Open from noon to 4 AM. Reservations advised. Major credit cards accepted. Primorskiy Park Pobedy, near the lake (phone: 235-5984 or 235-2804).

Winter Garden The Doric columns, marble floors, fountain, and lush foliage are quite enough to ensure a delightful experience at this dining room in the *Astoria* hotel. Add an orchestra and well-prepared traditional Russian fare and you've got the makings of a truly memorable meal. Reservations advised. Rubles and hard currency accepted. At the *Astoria Hotel,* 39 Bolshaya Morskaya Ulitsa (phone: 315-9637).

Sofia

For many years, Sofia suffered from a desperately sinister reputation. To many, the city wasn't just the sleepy capital of Bulgaria, the former Soviet Union's most faithful ally (though that was bad enough); it also conjured up images of drug dealing, arms smuggling, and political terrorism.

In recent years, however, some of the tarnish has been rubbed from Sofia's negative image, thanks in great part to Bulgaria's impressive strides toward democracy. Todor Zhivkov, the longtime Communist leader, was thrown out at the end of 1989 and put on trial for corruption 2 years later (he was convicted in 1992 and received a 7-year prison sentence, which he is appealing). The Bulgarians rejected the string of Communist puppets who succeeded him, and in 1990, Zhelyu Zhelev, a former dissident, was appointed president by the Bulgarian Parliament. In January 1992, Zhelev retained his job when he emerged the victor in the country's first free presidential election. Although Bulgaria still faces daunting economic problems, including growing inflation and unemployment, Zhelev and his non-Communist government have had one major success: They seem to have stemmed the flow of drugs from Bulgaria to Western Europe. But arms are a different story. Being so close to the border of Yugoslavia (Serbia) and the ongoing civil war there, Sofia has been less successful in stopping the shipments of arms across the border. Ironically, the UN–sponsored boycott of its former trading partner to the west has frustrated its moral intentions of doing away with the "business" of arms smuggling.

Sofia's dubious reputation was always a bit at odds with reality, for it is a surprisingly pleasant city. It lies in a broad, high valley, hemmed in by the Stara Planina Mountains to the north, the Ljulins to the west, the Sredna Gora range to the southeast, and snow-capped Mt. Vitosha to the southwest. Graceful baroque buildings line the boulevards in the old parts of town, and houses are clustered around grassy parks and squares. The skyline is dominated by the gold-domed Alexander Nevsky Memorial Church, a neo-Byzantine cathedral completed in 1912. (The Bulgarians built the church to show their gratitude to Russia, which helped to free Bulgaria from Turkish rule.) Yellow cobblestone sidewalks give Sofia a romantic air, and the absence of cars in some parts of the city center — only taxis are permitted — gives this bustling metropolis of slightly more than 1 million people a semblance of calm.

Sofia was founded in the 8th century BC, when a Thracian tribe known as the Serdi settled here. The Romans, who conquered the settlement in 29 BC, named it Serdica. Then, as now, the city stood at the crossroads between East and West. Its strategic location was a mixed blessing, for it attracted both merchants and invaders, including the Greeks, Romans, Goths, Huns, and Byzantines. Huns sacked the town in AD 441, but it was

SOFIA

Points of Interest

1. Sv. Nedelia Square;
   Sheraton Sofia Hotel;
   Balkan Holidays
2. National History
   Museum (2 Vitosha
   Blvd)
3. National Gallery of Art
   and the National
   Ethnographic Museum
4. National Archeology
   Museum
5. Sv. Petka Samardjiiska
   Church
6. Ivan Vasov National
   Theater
7. Sofia National Opera
8. Banja Basi Mosque
9. Union of Bulgarian
   Artists Gallery
10. Alexander Nevsky
    Memorial Church
11. Synagogue of Sofia
12. National Palace of
    Culture
13. Church of St. George
14. Sv. Sofia Church

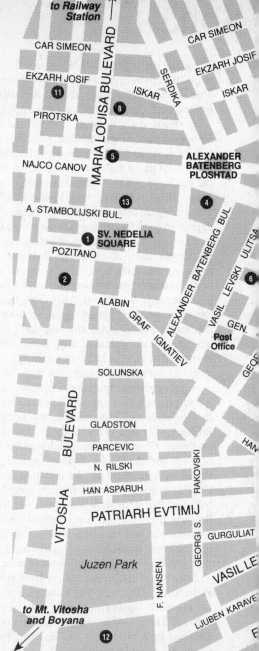

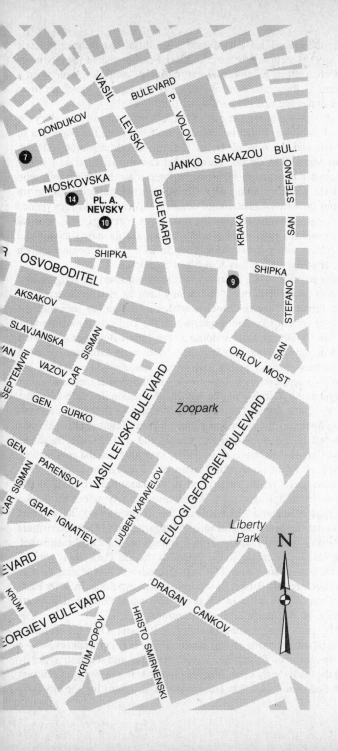

rebuilt by the Byzantines, who named it Triaditsa. The Bulgars, a Slavic people from the steppes north of the Black Sea, conquered the city in AD 809, and changed its name to Sredets, meaning "central." Aside from a brief return to Byzantine control (1018–86), the bustling merchant town remained under the rule of the Bulgars until 1382.

The city thrived during the early Middle Ages, a time of rare glory for Bulgaria. Prosperous Bulgarian colonies stretched from the Black Sea to the Adriatic and the Aegean. In AD 865, two Greek missionary monks, Cyril and Methodius, devised an alphabet known thereafter as Cyrillic, and, through their evangelical work, brought it to the Bulgarians, who accepted the alphabet along with Christianity. Monasteries sprang up throughout the newly Christianized country, and their workshops yielded fine paintings, illuminated manuscripts, icons, carvings, and musical scores. Some of the monasteries, such as the one at Rila, have survived and today attract a steady stream of tourists. In 1376 the city became known as Sofia, after the 6th-century Church of St. Sophia.

Disaster struck in 1382. Invading Turks overwhelmed the Bulgars, and for the next 5 centuries many Bulgarians lived as virtual slaves of the Ottoman Empire. Turkish colonists settled on Bulgarian soil, and the Orthodox church of Constantinople, which the Turks declared sovereign over all the Christians in their domain, suppressed Bulgarian Orthodox Catholicism and the Bulgarian language. In the early 19th century, when other countries such as Serbia and Greece managed to shake off the Ottoman yoke and declare independence, the Bulgarians remained sullen and resigned. As Turkish power waned, the region fell into anarchy, ravaged by roving armies and rapacious officials. As Bulgarian nationalism grew, however, the country's culture revived; intellectuals rekindled their interest in the Bulgarian vernacular, and in 1870, the Bulgarian Orthodox Catholic church received official sanction from the government.

In 1874, a violent insurrection broke out. The Turks, aided by Bulgarian converts to Islam, suppressed it, massacring more than 15,000 Bulgarians. In the spring of 1877 Russia invaded, driving out the Turks. Russia granted Bulgaria independence the following year, an act that earned Russia the perpetual gratitude of Bulgaria, with which it continues to share many common bonds. Both countries use the Cyrillic alphabet, and both have historical ties to the Orthodox church. The bond is symbolized by the equestrian statue of Czar Alexander II that stands on Car Osvoboditel (formerly Ruski) Bulevard in downtown Sofia. In other Eastern European cities, a statue of a Russian hero would be defaced, but here no graffiti mars the image of the "Liberator."

In 1879, Sofia became the capital of free Bulgaria. Over the centuries, the city had grown more or less haphazardly, and its architecture — a curious amalgam of Byzantine, Greek, Roman, and Turkish styles — reflected the hurly-burly of successive conquests. In the late 19th century, however, Sofia took on a less amorphous shape. Plans for the city were drawn up in 1880, and many new buildings were constructed. The new structures were built in a turn-of-the-century Viennese style of architecture, reflecting Bulgaria's growing interest in the West.

The city soon became a pleasant, if provincial, outpost of Europe. In the vicious Balkan Wars of 1912 and 1913, Bulgaria was forced to cede much of its territory, and in both world wars it had the misfortune of allying itself with the losers. King Boris III managed to keep some distance from the Nazis, however, saving Bulgarian Jews from deportation, and he refrained from declaring war on the Soviet Union. But after an angry meeting with Hitler (who wanted to keep Bulgaria firmly under the Nazi heel) in the fall of 1943 Boris died, suddenly and mysteriously, at the age of 49. As the Soviet armies advanced, the Bulgarian government tried to avert occupation by seeking an armistice with the Allies. The gambit failed, and in September of 1944 Soviet troops marched into Sofia.

The key figure in the Sovietization of Bulgaria was revolutionary Georgi Dimitrov. Exiled from Bulgaria in 1923 for his pro-Communist activities, Dimitrov was arrested in Berlin for allegedly attempting to set fire to the Reichstag. (The Nazis actually staged the incident themselves.) Dimitrov's brilliant self-defense captured worldwide attention, and he was eventually acquitted. In 1934, he went to Moscow, where he was offered honorary citizenship and, soon thereafter, the post of secretary-general of the Comintern. At the end of the war, Dimitrov returned home to lead the Bulgarian Communist Party. In 1946, the burly, mustached Dimitrov became Bulgaria's Lenin, Trotsky, Stalin, and Tito all in one. He nationalized Bulgaria's industries, collectivized its farms, and brutally eliminated any opposition. He died in Moscow in 1949. His body was brought to Sofia and interred in a white stone mausoleum across the street from the shady lawns of the City Gardens. There it remained until July 1990, when the new government, responding to pervading anti-Communist sentiment, had the body removed and buried in one of the city's cemeteries.

Dimitrov's successors toed the Soviet line. Todor Zhivkov, who assumed control over the Bulgarian Communist Party in 1954 and remained in power for 35 years, expressed the bond between the two countries succinctly. "The Soviet Union and Bulgaria breathe through the same lungs," he liked to say. When Khrushchev fell in 1964, Zhivkov adopted Leonid Brezhnev's line, sent tanks to help crush Czechoslovakia in 1968, and supported détente. In the 1980s, Zhivkov adopted Mikhail Gorbachev's policy of *perestroika.* The result was chaos. Sofia, for instance, was carved up into 24 municipalities, each with its own budget.

The Communist Party loosened its reins somewhat in 1989, when Zhivkov was deposed. Petar Mladenov, his successor, tried to undo some of the repression of the past, restoring to ethnic Turks their religious rights and promising free elections. The meager reforms weren't enough. Demonstrators gathered daily in front of the Parliament building in downtown Sofia, demanding a faster transition to democracy. Mladenov resigned, as did his successor, and by the end of 1990, Bulgaria had its first non-Communist president and prime minister since the war.

Sofia, meanwhile, is bursting at the seams. Forced industrialization has tripled the city's population in 3 decades. Public transportation consists of a fleet of aging trams and buses. (Before the political upheavals in Moscow in the summer of 1991, there were plans to build a subway, with Soviet help, but that source of aid has disappeared and local funds now are short.) Beyond the pedestrian zone downtown, Russian Ladas and Moskviches and Czech Skodas look comical beside new Western cars as they all zoom around the crowded streets, filling the air with fumes. Taxis add to the pollution; once scarce, they're now everywhere, thanks to a recent ruling that allows workers to supplement their incomes by hiring themselves out as part-time drivers.

The worst problem, however, is housing. Three generations of families often are squeezed into tiny 2-bedroom flats. Newer buildings frequently are shoddy and unsafe.

Rather than building more apartments, the government has responded by curbing the city's growth. Its job policy, for example, has created a Bulgarian catch-22. To get a city resident card, an applicant must first have a job, but to get a job he needs a resident card. The results are often absurd: Some medical doctors from centers outside Sofia will toil as construction workers in order to get their residency permit.

Many Bulgarians prefer Sofia to other centers because its amenities — theaters, parks and museums, and, above all, stores and supermarkets — are the best in the country. There are more goods in the smart shops along Vitosha Bulevard than in all the other towns and hamlets in Bulgaria, and Sofia's markets are better stocked than those anywhere else in the country. Few of the city residents, however, can afford anything but the most basic goods.

The economic picture was particularly grim in 1990, as politicians bickered over the future of the country. Things improved somewhat when the government freed prices early in 1991. Overnight, grocery shelves were restocked. The International Monetary Fund approved the country's budget, the first step toward loosening credit, which was halted after the country stopped payments on its $11 billion debt. But the costs of economic reform have been high. Prices have soared, and at press time unemployment remains at about 10%. In addition, the dissolution of the Soviet Union has cut off Bulgaria's previous source of inexpensive fuel, resulting in an energy shortage that's just short of desperate.

Visitors can sense the grim side of reform on their first night in Sofia. Streetlights are often dimmed at 10 PM to conserve energy. Restaurants and nightclubs close early, and few people venture out into the street. But in the daytime, there's a new liveliness about the place. Merchants hawk their wares, and people gather in parks and cafés to exchange the gossip of the day and debate the country's future and its infant market economy.

Despite the problems of the present and the uncertainty of the future, there is a sense of hope in the changing city of Sofia.

Sofia At-a-Glance

SEEING THE CITY

Mt. Vitosha, 5 miles (8 km) from the center of town, affords the most spectacular view. Two chair lifts climb the mountain, which is the site of a number of ski resorts. Its highest peak, Cherni Vrâh (Black Peak), is 7,500 feet. There is a restaurant on the northwest slope where visitors can sip a cup of coffee and enjoy the scenery — unless the view is blocked by a blanket of smog. On smoggy days, take a bus to the Aleko ski resort on the northeastern part of the mountain, where the air usually is clear. To get to Mt. Vitosha, take tram No. 2 or 9 to the southern terminal and transfer to bus No. 61, 62, 122, or 261. Weekdays are the best time to ski, since Sofia residents fancy spending Saturdays and Sundays on snowy slopes.

SPECIAL PLACES

Sofia is a fine place for a stroll. Be sure to get a map before heading out, however, because street signs are lettered in Cyrillic and can be tough to decipher. "Ulitsa" is the Bulgarian word for street, "bulevard" means boulevard, and "ploshtad" means square.

DOWNTOWN

SV. NEDELIA PLOSHTAD (ST. SUNDAY SQUARE) Formerly Lenin Square, this is both the geographical and the psychological heart of the city. The square is formed where Vitosha Bulevard meets Maria Louisa Bulevard. To the left as you face the *Sheraton Sofia* is the *National History Museum* (2 Vitosha Bulevard), which specializes in archaeological artifacts and folk art (see *Museums*). To the right is *TSUM,* the state's central department store (there are plans for its privatization), which can be reached via a pedestrian passageway. Located in this underpass, which is partially open-air, is a small shopping center and a busy flea market. Excavators discovered some ancient Roman ruins while digging the passageway and incorporated them, encased in glass, into the structure. Also located here is the 14th-century St. Petka Samardjiiska Church, which contains some fine murals, and is open to visitors in the summer.

TSŘKVATA SV. GEORGI (ST. GEORGE CHURCH) Located immediately behind the *Sheraton Sofia* — in fact, partly surrounded by it — this is Sofia's oldest building. Built by the Romans in the 4th century, the brick building (the stone tiles originally on its façade were probably removed to be used as building material over the centuries) is celebrated for its fragments of frescoes that date from the 5th to the 14th centuries. The 14th-century

Angels mural is of particular interest. Remains of Roman buildings may be found outside the church. Sv. Nedelia Ploshtad

ALEXANDER BATENBERG PLOSHTAD (ALEXANDER BATENBERG SQUARE) Known as Ninth of September Square under the Communists, and in recent years as Democracy Square, this place has reverted to its pre-Communist name. For decades the block-long white stone mausoleum of Georgi Dimitrov, the founder of Communist Bulgaria, dominated this spot (though the structure was still standing at press time, its destruction was imminent). The mausoleum held Dimitrov's embalmed body until July 1990, when the new government — responding to public pressure — had the body removed and buried in one of the city's cemeteries. The uniformed soldiers who once watched over the tomb, and who were changed with much fanfare and goose-stepping every hour, have vanished. Many Bulgarians, weary of the semi-canonization of the onetime revolutionary, want to see the monument demolished.

Behind the mausoleum are the City Gardens, the perfect place to sit and people watch. The former Royal Palace, which stands directly opposite the tomb, is hardly Versailles, but it does have a certain provincial charm. It is now the site of the *National Art Gallery* and the *National Ethnographic Museum* (see *Museums*).

HRAM-PAMETNIK ALEKSANDÜR NEVSKI (ALEXANDER NEVSKY MEMORIAL CHURCH) This imposing neo-Byzantine structure is the most famous building in Sofia, its gold-leaf dome visible throughout the city. Built between 1882 and 1924, it was named after Czar Alexander II's patron saint, a 13th-century prince from Novgorod, and was dedicated to the 200,000 Russian soldiers who died fighting in the 1877–78 war for Bulgarian independence from Turkish rule. Its ornate interior, which can hold 5,000 worshipers, is decorated with onyx, marble, alabaster, and mosaics, and is graced with the works of many Russian and Eastern European artists. The crypt, now a branch of the *National Art Gallery,* has exquisite displays of icons and ecclesiastical garb. The choir is excellent; several of its members sing with the *National Opera.* Open daily. Car Osvoboditel Bulevard.

TSRKVATA SV. SOPHIA (ST. SOPHIA CHURCH) Across the square from the Alexander Nevsky Memorial Church, but a much simpler structure, this church is nonetheless important because the city was named after it in the 14th century (it was previously called Sredets, meaning "center"). A domed, three-nave basilica of red brick, it was built during the time of the Byzantine Emperor Justinian, at the beginning of the 6th century. Aleksandür Nevski Ploshtad.

BANJA BAŠI MOSQUE Located just beyond the *TSUM* department store on Maria Louisa Bulevard, this mosque, built in 1576, is one of the few surviving monuments from the Ottoman occupation. It is closed to worshipers and visitors alike, however, due to long-standing tensions between Bulgars and the Turkish minority. Animosity between the two groups goes back 600 years, when Bulgaria was absorbed by the Ottoman Empire. During the Communist era, Bulgaria's 1.5 million ethnic Turks were severely persecuted. Mosques and Turkish schools were closed, and in 1985, Turks were forced to adopt Bulgarian surnames and abandon the public practice of their religion. Since the advent of democracy, the Turks have had most of their civil rights restored, and though tensions still remain high, the mosque may soon reopen.

SYNAGOGA SOPHIA (SYNAGOGUE OF SOPHIA) Just behind the main market is Sofia's main synagogue, built in 1910. Unlike the rest of Eastern Europe's Jews, who are Ashkenazi, the Jews of Bulgaria are Sephardic and speak a dialect that is similar to Spanish. The Jewish population of Bulgaria, always relatively small compared to many other Eastern European countries, owes its survival in large part to the policies of the Bulgarian government during World War II. Under pressure from the Nazis to deport the country's 48,000 Jews, the Bulgarian government procrastinated. Some Jews were sent to live in villages, but none were surrendered to the Nazis. Members of Parliament, government ministers, intellectuals and professionals, and King Boris III himself protested against Jewish deportation. (Bulgaria did deport Jews from its occupied territories in Macedonia, however.) By September 1944, all anti-Jewish decrees had been abolished. Since the war, Sofia's small Jewish community, which numbers about 5,000, has lived in relative tranquillity. Bulgaria recently restored diplomatic ties with Israel, and many young Jews are emigrating there, leaving aging parents and grandparents in Sofia. 16 Eharh Iozif Ulitsa (phone: 831273).

ENVIRONS

MT. VITOSHA Five miles (8 km) from the center of town, this mountain is a favorite destination for vacationing Sofians, who come here to ski or to hike its many trails. The Aleko ski resort is the largest on the mountain. Located on its northeastern face, it has several beginners' slopes and six runs, the longest of which is 11,670 feet. The center has a ski school, and is the site of national and European competitions. There's a cable car lift from the suburb of Simeonovo to Aleko, as well as a chair lift from the suburb of Dragalevtsi. The resort also is accessible by car, mountain paths, and rope tows. At the foot of the mountain stands a charming monument: bells of different sizes and shapes from 89 different countries, dedicated to peace and the children of the world. To get to Vitosha via public transportation, take tram No. 2 or 9 to the southern terminal and transfer to bus No. 61, 62, 122, or 261.

BOYANA For a pleasant half-day excursion, take bus No. 63 to this small village near Mt. Vitosha, only 6 miles (10 km) from the city center. Hidden among the trees is the famous Boyana Church. Only six visitors at a time are allowed to enter this medieval structure, as the temperature and humidity must be strictly controlled to preserve the frescoes that cover the walls and ceiling. Painted by an anonymous Boyana master in 1259, they are among the oldest frescoes in Bulgaria. Some depict real people, including King Constantine Assen and Queen Irina. Check the visiting hours with the *Balkan Holidays International* office (phone: 831211) before setting out, as the church often is closed for repairs. 153 Bukston Bulevard (phone: 685304).

DRAGALEVTSI The Dragalevtsi Monastery, with its 14th-century church and 15th-century frescoes, is located in this village in the foothills of Mt. Vitosha. There is a chair lift from Dragalevtsi to the Aleko resort complex (see above). To reach Dragalevtsi, take bus No. 93 from Sofia.

Sources and Resources

TOURIST INFORMATION

The main *Balkan Holidays International* office is at 5 Triaditsa Ulitsa (phone: 831211; fax: 883739) and there are branch offices in all the main hotels. Maps and brochures are available at the main office, which also will provide a translation of the Cyrillic alphabet into Roman script. *Balkan Holidays International* offers a useful half-day bus tour with a bilingual guide, and will provide individual guides for walking tours. The *Bulgaria Tourist Information and Reservations* travel office (22 Lovele Ulitsa; phone: 880139; fax: 803201) makes tour arrangements and hotel and restaurant reservations.

TELEPHONE The country code for Bulgaria is 359; the city code for Sofia is 2. International telephone service from Bulgaria is surprisingly good.

GETTING AROUND

AIRPORT Vrâzdebna Airport is 7½ miles (12 km) east of the city center and can be reached via bus No. 84 or 284. The main *Balkan Airlines* office is at 12 Narodno Sobranie Ploshiad, off Car Osvoboditel Bulevard (phone: 451113 or 884989; or 79321 at the airport). In wintertime, the airport often is closed due to fog.

BUS AND TRAM For the moment, buses and trams are the only forms of public transportation within the city. Although work has begun on a new subway, Bulgaria's economic straits will undoubtedly delay its completion. Buy tickets in advance from special kiosks by the streetcar stop. The trams operate from 4 AM to 1 AM. While downtown Sofia is best negotiated on foot, many of Bulgaria's best tourist spots — Rila Monastery, Gabrovo (see Bulgaria in DIRECTIONS), Troyan, and Vidin — are most easily reached by bus. The city has several bus terminals. Buses to Rila and points west leave from the terminal at 9 September Bulevard (phone: 553047); buses to points south depart from the terminal at 22 Dragan Tzankov Bulevard (phone: 720063); buses heading for northern towns depart from Zahorna Fabrika (phone: 383191); buses heading for towns to the east, including Troyan and Gabrovo, leave from the Podujane bus station at Pirdop Ploshtad (phone: 453014). The international bus station is at 23 Christo-Mihailov Bulevard (phone: 525004).

CAR RENTAL *Balkan Holidays International* holds a *Hertz* franchise and rents everything from luxury Mercedes limousines to Renault subcompacts. Reservations can be made with the *Hertz* world reservation center (phone: 800-654-3001) or locally (phone: 833487). The main rental office is at 1 Vitosha Bulevard (phone: 874480); there are also offices at the airport (phone: 791506 or 796041) and the *Pliska* hotel (phone: 723957). Since car rental prices are high, particularly in the summer, visitors may prefer to hire a taxi for a day, which often is less expensive. Agree on the rate before setting off.

TAXI In the old days, it was almost impossible to find a taxi in Sofia. Since economic reform, however, taxis can be seen lining up at stands throughout the city. You also can call *Radio Taxi* (phone: 142). Be sure to agree on a price with the driver before you set off.

TRAIN The main station is at 23 Maria Louisa Bulevard, just north of downtown (phone: 870222 or 313111). It is reached by tram No. 1, 6, 7, 8, 9, 12, or 15, and by bus No. 74, 77, 85, 213, 285, or 313. Express trains run frequently between Sofia and Varna, a resort city on the Black Sea. Most other domestic trains are locals, and are slow and crowded. Night trains link Sofia with Moscow, St. Petersburg, Berlin, Warsaw, Istanbul, Athens, and Belgrade. For tickets, call 593106. For sleeping car reservations, call 597124. Reservations and tickets also are available from the Rila international travel office (5 General Gurko Ulitsa; phone: 870777 for information; phone: 875935 for reservations) and *Wagon-Lits International* (10 Legue Ulitsa; phone: 873452).

SPECIAL EVENTS

Sofia is most crowded during *Music Weeks,* which run from May 24 to June 15. The festival offers a full schedule of concerts, opera performances, and musical competitions. The *Kukeri Festival,* which is somewhat similar to Rio's *Carnaval,* featuring music, dance, food, and general revelry, is held before *Lent* begins.

MUSEUMS

Museums generally are closed on Mondays. Most are free or have a nominal admission charge. There are seldom any museum catalogues or pamphlets, and descriptions are often in Cyrillic script only.

ART GALLERY OF THE UNION OF BULGARIAN ARTISTS Features temporary exhibitions of works by contemporary Bulgarian artists. Open 9 AM to 8 PM. 6 Shipka Ulitsa (phone: 446121 or 43351).

EXHIBIT ON THE SAVING OF THE BULGARIAN JEWS An interesting permanent exhibit on a little-known chapter in the story of the Holocaust, the period from 1941 to 1944 when the Bulgarian government resisted pressure from the Nazis to deport the country's 48,000 Jews. Open 9 AM to noon and 2 to 5 PM; closed Saturdays and Sundays. 40 Alexander Stambolijski Bulevard, fifth floor (phone: 870163).

NATIONAL ARCHAEOLOGY MUSEUM Changing exhibitions of Bulgarian and foreign treasures. Open 10 AM to noon, and 2 to 6 PM. 2 Saborna Ulitsa (phone: 875129).

NATIONAL ART GALLERY Located in the old Royal Place, this gallery showcases Bulgarian art from medieval times to the present. Open 10:30 AM to 6:30 PM; Fridays from 2:30 to 6:30 PM. Alexander Batenberg Ploshtad (phone: 883559 or 877697).

NATIONAL ETHNOGRAPHIC MUSEUM Also housed in the old Royal Palace, the museum specializes in folk art, particularly costumes from the country's different regions. Open 10 AM to noon and 1:30 to 6 PM; closed Mondays and Tuesdays. 6A Moskowska Ulitsa (phone: 885117 or 884036).

NATIONAL HISTORY MUSEUM Located in the former Palace of Justice, it chronicles the country's story from prehistory to 1878, when Bulgaria won its independence. Don't miss the Panagyurishte gold treasure, which dates from the 4th century BC, and the silver treasure of Rogozen from the pre-Christian period. Open 10:30 AM to 6 PM; Fridays from 2:30 to 6:30 PM. 2 Vitosha Bulevard (phone: 8571 or 884160).

NATIONAL MILITARY HISTORY MUSEUM A collection of over 100,000 items related to combat and armaments in Bulgarian history. Open 9:30 AM to 12:30 PM and 1:30 to 6 PM. 23 General Skobelev Bulevard, near the *National Palace of Culture* (phone: 512574 or 523869).

NATIONAL SCIENCE MUSEUM Four floors house 500,000 species of flora and fauna native to Bulgaria and other countries. Open 9 AM to noon and 1 to 6 PM; Saturdays and Sundays from 9 AM to noon and 3 to 6 PM; closed Mondays and Tuesdays. No admission charge on Thursdays. 1 Car Osvoboditel Bulevard (phone: 885115).

SHOPPING

Vitosha Bulevard, Sofia's main shopping street, begins at Sv. Nedelia Ploshtad and leads to the *Narodniyat Dvorets na Kulturata* (National Palace of Culture), a concert and conference hall built in 1981. The best bet here is folk art. The boutique at 14 Vitosha Bulevard sells silver jewelry, leather goods, and embroidered blouses, as well as rugs, wooden articles, ceramics, and copper coffee sets. For fashion, try *Rila* (35, 52, and 63 Vitosha Bulevard); for knitwear, *Yanitsa* (1 Vitosha Bulevard); and for crystal and china, *Quarta* (8 Vitosha Bulevard). *Maestro Atanassov* (8 Car Osvoboditel Bulevard) is a good place to buy recordings of Bulgarian folk music, which also make fine souvenirs. Right next door is another good folk art store, *Mineralsouvenir* (10 Car Osvoboditel Bulevard), and down the street is the company store of the Union of Bulgarian Artists (4 Car Osvoboditel Bulevard), which sells pottery, filigree silver jewelry, and handmade items of wood, leather, and wrought iron. Most shops are open from 9 AM to 7 PM and are closed Sundays. The city's main outdoor market, where vendors sell Oriental spices, handmade woolens, and pottery, is located on Maria Louisa Bulevard.

SPORTS AND FITNESS

In addition to the skiing and hiking trails on Mt. Vitosha (see *Special Places*), Sofia offers a variety of athletic facilities.

FITNESS CENTERS All the major hotels have gyms. Basketball and volleyball courts and weight lifting facilities are available at the *Universade Sports Club* (Alfred Nobel Prohod; phone: 722148) and at the *Slivnitsa Sports Hall* (186 Slivnitsa Bulevard; phone: 833964).

SWIMMING There are pools at the *Sheraton Sofia,* the *Vitosha,* and *Rodina* hotels, as well as at Liberty Park (phone: 653169).

TENNIS Courts are available at the *Vitosha* hotel, or at the different sporting clubs in Liberty Park (phone: 653169).

THEATER

The level of theater in Sofia is high. The *Ivan Vasov Theater* (5 Levski Ulitsa in the City Gardens; phone: 874831) is Bulgaria's largest. Performances (in Bulgarian) generally start at 7 PM, and tickets are inexpensive. Most visitors are delighted by the *Central Puppet Theater* (14 Gurko Ulitsa; phone: 877288). You don't have to be an expert in Bulgarian to understand the puppets, and the plays are popular and well executed.

MUSIC

The quality of opera and orchestral performances in Sofia also is high. The leading concert halls are *Bulgaria Hall* (1 Aksakov Ulitsa; phone: 874073) and *Slavekov Hall* (Slavekov Ploshtad; phone: 882349). Also popular are performances of the *Sofia National Opera* (58 Dondukhov Bulevard; phone: 871366) and the *Stefan Makedonski Musical Theater* (4 Vasil Levski Bulevard; phone: 441979). Curtain time is 7:30 PM, and tickets can be bought at the Concert Office (2 Car Osvoboditel Bulevard; phone: 871588).

NIGHTCLUBS AND NIGHTLIFE

Sofia is not a swinging town. Those who can't survive without a nightclub and floor show should try their luck at the gambling casino at the *Vitosha New Otani* hotel, which is open nightly until 4 AM. There is a disco at the *Grand Hotel Sofia* and the *Sheraton Sofia* has a nightclub called *Fantasia*.

Best in Town

CHECKING IN

Outside of the few Western-built hotels, lodging in Sofia is substandard. Decent rooms can be had only for a high price. The most commendable spot is the *Sheraton Sofia,* which might not shine in most Western European capitals, but does here. Managed by Westerners — the last manager was a Dane — it imports almost everything, from the toilet paper in the bathrooms to the black bread on the breakfast table.

Bulgaria used to be among the most inexpensive destinations in Europe, but while group package tours are still reasonably priced, hotel rates for individual travelers have skyrocketed in recent years. A double room in an expensive hotel will cost up to $200 a night; a double room in a moderate hostelry will run from $100 to $150; and places that charge less than $150 a night for a double are considered inexpensive. One money-saving alternative is to rent a room in a private apartment for about $25 a night. The *Balkan Holidays International* office (37 Dondukhov Bulevard; phone: 880655) lists private rentals; it is open weekdays from 7 AM to 10 PM. All hotels listed below take major credit cards. Most of Sofia's major hotels have complete facilities for the business traveler. Those hotels listed below as having "business services" usually offer such conveniences as English-speaking concierge, meeting rooms, photocopiers, computers, translation services, and express checkout, among others. Call the hotel for additional information. All telephone numbers are in the 2 city code unless otherwise indicated.

For an unforgettable experience in Sofia, we begin with our favorite, followed by our cost and quality choices of hotels, listed by price and category.

A SPECIAL HAVEN

SHERATON SOFIA Once the landmark *Grand Hotel Balkan,* the property is now managed by the well-known American chain. At the same time, the staff was trained to meet Western expectations; today the service is excellent by any standard. It has 188 air conditioned rooms, 16 suites, and 3 restaurants — including *Preslav* (see *Eating Out*), the best restaurant in town, offering formal dining and exceptional international fare. Guests also enjoy a nightclub and a health club. Business services. 2 Sv. Nedelia Ploshtad (phone: 876541; fax: 871038).

EXPENSIVE

Grand Hotel Sofia A well-located if undistinguished property, with 172 rooms, a complex of shops and restaurants, and a nightclub. 4 Narodno Sobranie Ploshtad (phone: 878821; fax: 800965).

Novotel Europa A 600-room French hotel near the main railway station. Although architecturally bland, it's modern and comfortable, and offers a restaurant and several bars. 131 Maria Louisa Bulevard. (phone: 31261; fax: 320011).

Park Hotel Moskva A 390-room Stalinist-style hotel well outside the center of town. It's surrounded by landscaped gardens, but the building is far from pretty. It hosts many international conferences and has several restaurants, a nightclub, and a folk tavern. 25 Nezabravka Ulitsa (phone: 71261; fax: 656737).

Rila Formerly the *Europa Palace,* this well-appointed hostelry was once reserved for members of the Communist Party. Now open to the public, it offers 120 comfortable rooms and a restaurant. 6 Kaloyan Ulitsa (phone: 881861; fax: 65105).

Vitosha New Otani The priciest place in town after the *Sheraton,* this Japanese venture lacks the latter's charm and is located outside the downtown pedestrian zone, but its views of Mt. Vitosha and the surrounding forests are wonderful. The 485 rooms are comfortable, but more functional than luxurious. The *Sakura* restaurant serves Japanese fare, and 3 other dining rooms offer international and Bulgarian dishes. There's also a nightclub, a casino, a Viennese café and garden, and several cocktail lounges. For the fitness-mined, there's a gym and bowling alley. 100 James Baucher Bulevard (phone: 62451; fax: 681225).

MODERATE

Bulgaria Once a classy 80-room hotel, it still has a great downtown location and a beguilingly seedy Old World flavor. But don't expect luxury. Its eponymous restaurant is worth a visit for the atmosphere (see *Eating Out*). 4 Car Osvoboditel Bulevard (phone: 871977; fax: 880136).

Rodina About a 10-minute walk from the city center, this huge Swedish-built high-rise has 536 rooms, a restaurant, several bars, a nightclub, a pool, saunas, a gym, and a solarium. 8 Totleben Bulevard (phone: 51631; fax: 543225).

INEXPENSIVE

Slavianska Beseda The best of the relatively inexpensive hotels. Not far from the *Ivan Vasov Theater,* it has 100 rooms but lacks a restaurant. 3 Slavianska Ulitsa (phone: 880441; fax: 875638).

Most of the hotels in this region cater to tour groups. The moderately priced *Prostor* (phone: 654881) is the best on Vitosha, with 100 rooms, a nightclub, a restaurant, and an indoor pool and sauna. The *Stastliveca* (phone: 665024) is an inexpensive hostelry with 70 rooms and a folk tavern.

EATING OUT

Bulgarian cuisine, like most cooking in the Balkans, relies heavily — and often tediously — on grilled lamb and pork kebabs. But the fresh vegetables and fruits — particularly the cherries and strawberries in season — are very good, and the yogurt is fantastic. The Bulgarians claim to have invented yogurt, and the thick, creamy sort served here really does taste superior to Western knock-offs. Desserts, like the ubiquitous Turkish baklava, tend to be cloyingly sweet. Bulgarians make good red wines, especially the *gamzas,* and coffee is traditionally served Turkish-style, thick and sweet, in tiny china cups. If you don't read the Cyrillic alphabet, remember that "PECTOPAHT" means restaurant. Restaurant prices are very reasonable. Dinner for two will cost about $25 at expensive establishments, $15 at moderate places, and less than $15 at inexpensive spots. All telephone numbers are in the 2 city code unless otherwise indicated.

EXPENSIVE

Budapest This eatery features decent Hungarian food and music. Open daily for lunch and dinner. Reservations advised. Major credit cards accepted. 145 Rakovski Ulitsa (phone: 872750).

Forum A handsome dining place serving Bulgarian and international classics such as onion soup, omelettes, and leg of lamb. It also offers a wide selection of Bulgarian wines. Open daily for lunch and dinner. Reservations advised. Major credit cards accepted. 64 Vitosha Bulevard (phone: 521119).

Preslav Located in the *Sheraton Sofia,* this is perhaps the fanciest and most expensive restaurant in all Bulgaria. Its chefs dabble in haute cuisine, and the results aren't shabby, though the pretensions seem a bit out of place in modest Sofia. Try the snail soup, caviar omelettes, and kiwi salads. Open daily for lunch and dinner. Reservations advised. Major credit cards accepted. 2 Sv. Nedelia Ploshtad (phone: 876541).

MODERATE

Bulgaria Go for the music, the dancing, and the atmosphere in this 1930s-era building, not for the food. There is a good café downstairs. Open daily for lunch and dinner. Reservations advised. Major credit cards accepted. In the *Bulgaria Hotel,* 4 Car Osvoboditel Bulevard (phone: 871977).

Rubin Local favorite with 1960s decor, Italian-style food, and good wines. Visitors may dine in the somewhat upscale restaurant or at the low-priced snack bar. Open daily for lunch and dinner. Reservations unnecessary. No credit cards accepted. Sv. Nedelia Ploshtad (phone: 874704).

Zheravna Bulgarian specialties served in a folksy atmosphere. Open daily for lunch and dinner. Reservations unnecessary. No credit cards accepted. 26 Vasil Levski Bulevard (phone: 872186).

MT. VITOSHA

There are folk-style restaurants serving traditional local fare located in the Vitosha area on the outskirts of the city. *Boyansko Hanche* (Sofia Boyana Zboriste; phone: 563016), near the historic church in the suburb of Boyana, is a moderately priced dining spot featuring local specialties and wines, as well as a folk orchestra and a floor show. *Vodenicarski Mehani* (phone: 671001 or 671021), at the foot of Mt. Vitosha above the town of Dragalevtsi, is another moderately priced traditional eatery. It serves local specialties and features a floor show. Both restaurants can be reached by taking bus No. 63 from Sofia.

Tallinn

Like its sister Baltic capitals, Tallinn is living through dramatically historic times. In the wake of the failed Kremlin coup of August 1991, Estonia (known as Eesti to its proud citizens) once again became an independent state, and its capital city is spinning with all the changes that such independence entails.

Estonia is struggling with the formidable task of regaining control of a country and an economy that have spent the last 5 decades held in a tight Soviet embrace. The newly untethered republic has established diplomatic links with the outside world, become a member of the International Monetary Fund, and joined the United Nations (on September 17, 1991). It also introduced its own currency, the "kroon," in 1992.

As the political, industrial, and cultural center of this 17,143-square-mile country, Tallinn is at the heart of all these changes. As it struggles to adapt to a market economy, however, the city has managed to retain its appeal. In fact, even during its half century as the capital of a captive Soviet republic, Tallinn was among the most charming, scenic, and westernized cities of the USSR. A seaport on the Gulf of Finland with a population of about 600,000 people, its clean, cobblestone streets, cozy cafés, and relatively well-stocked shops often looked as if they belonged in Helsinki or Heidelberg rather than on the pinched edge of the beleaguered Soviet Union.

To a great extent, Tallinn was spared the grim, cement-block high-rises endemic in other Soviet cities (with such notable exceptions as Lasnamäe, a suburb where some 200,000 workers live in just such charmless housing). In general, the city has a graceful, relaxed feel to it, with winding streets, shady parks, and low wooden buildings sometimes crowned by red tile roofs, turrets, spires, and steeples. Much of Tallinn's architecture has a Germanic feel, the legacy of its medieval membership in the Hanseatic League of German trading towns. The Old Town, crisscrossed by narrow medieval streets, possesses a wealth of well-preserved Gothic buildings and an ancient fortress.

Despite the Soviet government's efforts to resettle Russians in the Baltic cities — which left the capital city's population about 60% Estonian — Tallinn managed to preserve its Estonian identity and heritage. When the country declared its independence, city street signs, shop signs, and the language on the street switched back to Estonian almost overnight.

Perhaps the reason that the city bears the mark of a half century of Soviet rule so lightly (at least outwardly; there's still a lot of ill will beneath the surface) is that its pre-Soviet history is so long. Tallinn first appears on a map drawn in 1154 by al-Idrisi, an Arab geographer working for the King of Sicily, who called the settlement Kolyvan (after Kalev, an Estonian folk hero still lauded in legends and ballads. Among the Estonians, too, it was known in early times as "Kalev's City"). After the Danes conquered the settlement in 1219, Estonians called the city Tallinn, from the Estonian *Taani Linn,* or "Danish Town." Until 1918, however, the German name for the city was Reval.

Tallinn has been affected by outside influences since its earliest days, and the ties of Estonia to Western Europe (Scandinavia and Germany in particular) are even older and more deeply ingrained. This is reflected in the physical and cultural characteristics of the natives, who call themselves *eestlane* and are most closely related to the Finns. The Estonian language is very much like Finnish, and the similarities extend to the people, many of whom have blond hair and blue eyes.

The whole of Estonian history, in fact, is a tale of interaction with invaders and outsiders. For this reason, a familiarity with the country's past helps visitors to understand present-day Tallinn, and sheds light on what the future may hold for the city and its citizens.

Estonia's roots are ancient: Its clan-based society was first mentioned in the 1st century BC by Tacitus, the Roman historian, who called the inhabitants Aesti. From the start, invasion, migration, and trade brought a host of foreign influences that helped shape Estonian culture. First came the Vikings in the 9th century; then the Danes and Swedes; still later, the Russians and Germans. In 1227, the German Brethren of the Sword, a militant Christianizing order that later became known as the Teutonic Knights, captured Tallinn and built a stone fortress. Eleven years later, Tallinn changed hands again, with the Danes once more becoming its masters until 1346, when Denmark sold its Estonian duchy to the Teutonic Order for 500 kilograms of silver. Tallinn became a major trading town, and prospered as a member of the mercantile Hanseatic League of German cities. Lutheranism became the religion of most Estonians, and German became the language of culture and intellectual life, with the Estonian tongue relegated to the countryside. (German is still widely spoken as a second language today.)

Ivan the Terrible invaded in 1558, and to escape his rule, Tallinn took an oath of allegiance to Sweden, while southern Estonia yielded to Poland. By 1583, the Russian armies were forced out of Estonia, and as a result of the Swedish-Polish wars, all of mainland Estonia became Swedish territory in 1629. Sweden spent the next several decades trying to curb the power of Estonia's Baltic German nobility (which dated from the days of the Teutonic Knights) and to improve the conditions of the peasants. In 1631, King Gustavus II of Sweden founded the first high school in Tallinn where, besides other subjects, Estonian was taught.

Swedish reforms in Estonia came to a grinding halt with the Great Northern War, which started in 1710 and ended in 1721 with the defeat of Sweden by the Russian forces of Peter the Great.

In the 1800s, a Russification campaign wiped out a good deal of the

TALLINN

Points of Interest

1. Town Hall
2. Kadriorg Park
3. Peter the Great's Cottage; Kadriorg Castle/Estonian Museum of Art
4. Luhike Jalg tower; Pikk Jalg tower
5. St. Nicholas Church
6. Toompea Castle
7. Museum of Theater and Music
8. Tallinn Historical Museum
9. Church of the Holy Spirit
10. Kalev Sports Hall
11. Dynamo Stadium
12. Kadrioru Stadium
13. Sport Hotel; Olympic Center; Yachting Center
14. Swimming Pool
15. Estonia Drama Theater
16. Hotel Viru
17. Hotel Palace
18. Hotel Olümpia
19. Alexander Nevsky Cathedral

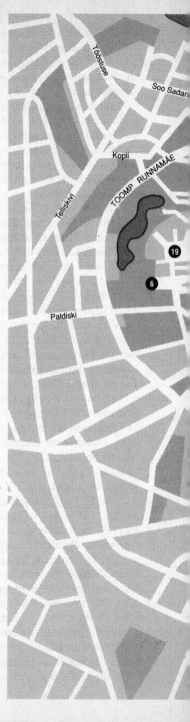

GULF OF TALLINN

PIRITATEE

Regati Pues

13

PIRITATEE

Pikktee

Venetee

Ujuta

14 Mere

Antri Tuurkri

Uus Sadama

8

9

Pikk tee

Raekoja plats

Vana-Viru

1

Virutee

Viru Väljak

Muu-nava

Suur-

Karia

Harju Kullassepa

liste

PÄRNU MAANTEE

16

NARVA MAANTEE

3

2

Jõe Pronksi

7

15

Estonia Puiestee

abados Väljak

17

Roheline aas

11

Tartu Maantee

18 Liivalaia

TARTU MAANTEE

Lennuki

Liivalaia

Junkentali

10

Siaadioni

Herne

12

Herne

Järvevanatee

N

Herne

PÄRNU

Ülemiste
Lake

German influence that had dominated Estonian life since the Middle Ages, and created some concern among Estonians that their own culture would be threatened. When uprisings in St. Petersburg in 1905 led Czar Nicholas II to allow a degree of democracy within his empire, Estonian nationalist leaders such as Konstantin Päts demanded Estonian autonomy, a movement that was bloodily suppressed.

When the Bolsheviks seized power in Russia in November 1917, they imposed their own regime in Tallinn, only to have it routed by the invading troops of Germany's kaiser 3 months later. After Germany's defeat, however, the Estonian government of Konstantin Päts proclaimed the country's independence on February 24, 1918, a day still celebrated as *Independence Day*. When the Red Army tried to reconquer Estonia, they were repelled by local forces, and Estonia became an independent state.

In 1939, the secret Nazi-Soviet Motolov-Ribbentrop Pact divided Eastern Europe into spheres of influence, and a secret protocol ceded the three Baltic states to Moscow. The following year, Stalin's army invaded Estonia, annexed it to the Soviet Union, and installed a puppet government. In 1941 it deported almost 11,000 Estonians to Siberia, two-thirds of them women, children, and the elderly. Estonia was invaded by the Nazi German Wehrmacht that summer and was occupied until 1944 when the Red Army took control again, after a battle that included the bombing of Tallinn on March 9, 1944, by the Soviet Air Force. After the war, the Soviet Union again sent thousands of Estonians to Siberia. But although Stalin's regime sought to purge many elements of Estonian culture from the capital city in particular, the people of Tallinn possess a powerful national consciousness that has enabled them to retain their own identity and culture, despite nearly 5 decades under the Soviet system.

When Estonia sought finally to free itself from Communist rule in the late 1980s, it took a somewhat slower and less strident approach to negotiating its freedom from Moscow than did Lithuania, and its more reserved people held fewer demonstrations than either Lithuanians or Latvians. The country also escaped the worst of the bloodshed and Soviet military crackdowns imposed on the rest of the Baltics. Estonia's Popular Front independence movement was formed in April 1988, and on November 16 of that year the Estonian parliament passed a declaration of sovereignty that was overwhelmingly endorsed by voters in the March 1991 referendum. On August 20, 1991, at the height of the Kremlin coup, the Estonian parliament declared outright independence, and was soon recognized as a sovereign nation by the rest of the world.

The most interesting parts of Tallinn are within the Old Town, which is divided into two sections: the Lower Town and the Upper Town, or Toompea, which means Castle Hill in Estonian. The Lower Town, the city's most picturesque area, was traditionally the mercantile district and continues to be a bustling market quarter today. The Upper Town, site of the old Danish fortress and palace, was the town's original seat of government (and still continues in that role, housing the republic's Council of

Ministers). For many years the two towns had separate mayors and were often at odds, to the point where walls were built to divide the settlements and residents had to pass through a single sturdy gate along the Pikk Jalg (Long Leg), which was bolted fast each evening. Parts of the wall and the gate still remain. The walls surrounding the entire Old Town also still stand, as do the town's ancient towers and bastions, which bear such colorful names as Paks Margareeta (Fat Margaret), Pikk (Tall) Herman, and Kiek-in-de-Kok (Peep-in-the-Kitchen). The newer section of the city is dominated by Vabaduse Väljak (Freedom Square), formerly Victory Square. Lovely Kadriorg Park is on the outskirts of town, and the district of Pirita, some 6 miles (10 km) from the center of Tallinn on the Gulf of Finland, is a popular beach and resort area.

Estonian independence has brought prosperity to the capital, evidenced by the growing number of new shops, cafés, restaurants, and businesses that now line its streets. The risky introduction of a new convertible currency, the "kroon," in June 1992 has been dubbed a success; its value remains stable on foreign money markets. All establishments, from four-star hotels to fast-food cafés and even taxis, accept the kroon. And most importantly, the tourism industry is booming, prompting city officials to open a fully equipped tourist bureau.

Visitors to Tallinn today will find an ancient city whose medieval town, Gothic architecture, and many works of art and religious artifacts are much as they were before Communist rule, but whose atmosphere is infused with a new sense of vitality and hope. Tallinn's excitement over its newfound freedom is contagious, and Estonians, traditionally gracious hosts, are now even more welcoming toward foreign guests.

Tallinn At-a-Glance

SEEING THE CITY

The most beautiful view of Tallinn is from the crest of the ridge of the Upper Town, or Toompea (Castle Hill), which can be reached by climbing one of two steep stairways located along Pikk Jalg and Lühike Jalg, or by walking up Komandanditee and turning right past the Kiek-in-de-Kok cannon tower. There are at least four good viewing platforms, the most spectacular of which is located at the end of Kohtutee, where visitors can gaze down at the red rooftops and towering church spires of the Lower Town. Two other platforms at the end of Toompea offer views of the city center, the newer section of Tallinn. There is also an observation platform near Toompea Loss (Toompea Castle), opposite Kiek-in-de-Kok looking west toward the city, with a park and the old fortress moat directly below.

SPECIAL PLACES

Tallinn's Old Town, which is divided into the Lower Town and the Upper Town, or Toompea (Castle Hill), is the city's most interesting and picturesque area. Toompea was the seat of feudal power, while the Lower Town was the home of merchants and artisans. Be sure to poke your nose into the Old Town's many delightful small coffee shops, which serve sinfully rich cream-filled pastries. Note that "tee" is a suffix meaning street in Estonian, "puiestee" means boulevard, "maantee" is the Estonian word for road, "plats" means place, and "väljak" means square.

We would be remiss not to caution foreign travelers about the growing incidence of street crime. Tourists walking on dimly lit streets are an appealing targets to muggers.

THE LOWER TOWN

Walk through the Viru Gates near Tammsaare Park and the *Estonia Theater* to enter the lower part of Old Tallinn, a maze of lovely cobble-stone streets, turreted houses, shops, cafés, and bakeries. Founded in 1154, the Old Town, which has been beautifully preserved, has some of the city's finest medieval architecture. Walk slowly, for there are many small details to savor, from the elaborately carved architectural elements to the pretty dried-flower arrangements that decorate nearly every shop.

FORTRESS WALL A mile-and-a-half-long wall as high as 52 feet and as thick as 8 feet once surrounded the entire Lower Town, but today only about three-quarters of it still stands. Most notable are the two remaining tow-ers — Kiek-in-de-Kok (Peep-in-the-Kitchen; 1 Komandanditee; phone: 446686) and Paks Margareeta (Fat Margaret; 70 Pikktee; phone: 601803). The name Kiek-in-de-Kok is Low German, and probably derives from the tower's height, which afforded a view into the kitchens of the houses below. Built between 1475 and 1483, it now contains a museum with exhibits on Tallinn's fortifications. Paks Margareeta was built in the begin-ning of the 16th century, and her dimensions give away the source of her name: 78 feet in diameter, with walls more than 13 feet thick at the base. The tower now houses the *Meremuuseum* (Maritime Museum), a perma-nent exhibition of the history of shipbuilding and fishing in Estonia. The tower museums are open 11 AM to 6 PM; closed Mondays.

RAEKOJA PLATS (TOWN HALL SQUARE) Located in the center of the Lower Town, this cobblestone square was the heart of the city in the Middle Ages and is once again lined with good restaurants, shops, and architectural monu-ments. The square comes alive with dancing and a handicrafts fair in June during *Vanalinnapaevad* (Old Town Festival).

RAEKOJA (TOWN HALL) Located in the middle of Old Town Square, this nearly intact example of Gothic architecture was built between 1371 and 1404. It is crowned with a replica of a 16th-century weather vane nicknamed Vana Toomas (Old Thomas) because elections were traditionally held here on *St. Thomas Day,* December 20. The original weather vane is in the build-ing's museum, which features a fine array of late-medieval furniture and artwork, including paintings and friezes. On a grimmer note, there's also a collection of torture instruments. No admission charge. Raekoja Plats.

RAEAPTEEK (TOWN COUNCIL'S APOTHECARY) This superb Gothic structure is one of the oldest registered pharmacies in Europe. It's thought to have been open more than 150 years before it was officially registered in 1583 by Johnann Burchart Belvary de Sykvary, a Hungarian. The apothecary was run by the Burchart family for more than 300 years and is still in business today. Restoration work on the building in the 1960s returned the façade to its 17th-century appearance. No admission charge. 11 Raekoja Plats.

SAIAKANG (WHITE BREAD PASSAGE) The shortest street in Tallinn (only about 50 paces long), it leads from Raekoja Plats to Pikktee. It's so narrow that cars cannot pass down its cobblestones. There's a flower shop, and a handicrafts store at No. 2.

MUSTPEADE VENNASKONNA MAJA (HOUSE OF THE BROTHERHOOD OF THE BLACK-HEADS) The Brotherhood of the Blackheads was Tallinn's second most important organization of merchants after the Great Guild. First mentioned in 1399, it was an organization of unmarried merchants, mostly foreigners, who were obliged to take part in the town's defense by patrolling the towers and other elevated locations. The patron saint of the Brotherhood was St. Mauritius of Mauretania, and the head of a Moor carved out of stone sits above the doorway of the building, which is now a youth club. Admission charge. 24 Pikktee.

HOONERÜHUM KOLMÖDE (THE THREE SISTERS) These three restored buildings are exquisite examples of the style of Tallinn residences from the 14th through the 16th centuries. Built by a merchant for his three daughters, each of the houses is made of a different kind of stone. A coat of arms is carved over each doorway, and one building has a large stained glass window with an icon above it. Admission charge. 71 Pikktee.

PÜHAVAIMU KIRIK (CHURCH OF THE HOLY SPIRIT) This 15th-century Gothic landmark, an active Lutheran church, houses some spectacular works of religious art, including a wooden altar carved in 1483 by Bernt Notke, a well-known painter and sculptor from Lübeck, Germany. In the baroque tower, originally known as the Town Hall Chapel, is an ornate blue clock and bell dating from 1433. The bell is said to be the oldest in Estonia that's still chiming. 4 Pühavaimutee.

PÜHA KATARUNA KLOOSTER (MONASTERY OF ST. CATHERINE) Founded by the Dominicans in the 13th century, the monastery was destroyed in a fire in 1531 and has only been partially restored. The artistic portals of the church are particularly noteworthy. 12/18 Venetee.

RATASKAEVUTEE One of the Lower Town's main streets, it was laid with oak pipes in the 1400s, providing Tallinn with its first public water supply (the wooden pipes were replaced with lead ones in 1616). Many tall, white-washed stone medieval homes with peaked tile roofs and arched doorways line this charming byway.

NIGULISTE KIRIK (CHURCH OF ST. NICHOLAS) This beautiful baroque structure, built between 1316 and 1350 for Swedish merchants, contains paintings and carvings from the 15th century, including an elaborate wooden altarpiece depicting the lives of St. Victor and St. Nicholas (the latter is the patron saint of sailors and an important figure in seaports). The original altar from the Church of the Holy Spirit is also located here, as is a fragment of the famous painting *Danse Macabre* (Dance of Death) by Bernt Notke, the 15th-century painter and sculptor from Lübeck, Germany. Organ concerts are performed each morning, and there are frequently evening chamber music recitals. Rataskaevutee and Rüütlitee.

THE RUINS In a fenced-off area next to the Church of St. Nicholas are the remains and rubble of several demolished buildings. Signs in four languages (Estonian, German, Russian, and English) explain that the Old Town was bombed by the Soviet Air Force on the evening of March 9, 1944. More than 3,000 bombs were dropped, killing 453 people and injuring 659. In addition, more than half of the district's residences were destroyed, leaving more than 20,000 people homeless. Located on Harjutee.

TOOMPEA (CASTLE HILL)

There are three paths that lead to Tallinn's original fortress in the Upper Town, or Toompea (Castle Hill), the highest point of elevation in the city. The first, Lühike Jalg ("Short Leg"), begins just across from the entrance to the Church of St. Nicholas in the Lower Town and continues up a steep flight of stone steps to the Upper Town. The second, the Pikk Jalg, is a longer and less steep path that begins at the Gulf of Finland and follows the 15th-century stone wall that divided the two parts of town. The third path, which runs through a small park near the south end of Rataska-evutee (one of the Lower Town's major thoroughfares), is the longest and most picturesque of the three.

Smaller than the Lower Town, Toompea is also quieter, although it does house several government buildings. Many of its oldest structures have been destroyed by fire, although some medieval streets and courtyards remain. Several interesting 18th- and 19th-century buildings still stand, too. Toompea is a pedestrian zone; only those with special permits (granted to local residents and workers) may drive here.

HARJUMAGI (HARJU HILL) This park, which sits near the top of the hill, is the site of the 100-year-old statue of Linda, a central figure in Estonian folklore. She was the wife of Kalev, and according to legend, created the hill by piling stones upon her husband's grave. The park is a favorite rendezvous for lovers. Shows for children are performed here in the summer.

TOOMPEA LOSS (TOOMPEA CASTLE) The old defensive parts of this citadel were erected by the Knights of the Sword in 1229, and were rebuilt in the second half of the 14th century. The massive stone structure, which looks out over the Lower Town, is remarkably well preserved. The observation platform between the castle and the cathedral affords a good view looking west toward the city, with the park and the old fortress moat directly below. The castle was built in 1773 and renovated from 1935 to 1937; it now houses the Estonian parliament. Behind the castle you can see Pikk (Tall) Herman, the 150-foot ancient tower that has stood guard over Tallinn for 5 centuries. Above the tower flies the blue, black, and white flag of Estonia (blue for the sky; black, originally for the soil and now to mourn the thousands deported to Siberia; and white for hope). Open daily from 9 AM to 4 PM. Admission charge. Located on Lossi Plats (Castle Square) near Komandanditee.

TOOMEKIRIK (DOME CATHEDRAL) Located atop the Upper Town's hill, this is one of the district's most impressive edifices. The Gothic structure originally was built in the early 13th century, and while much of it — including its baroque-style tower — was rebuilt after a fire in 1684, some 13th- through 17th-century monuments and architectural elements remain. The white-walled interior is simple, although a late-17th-century carved altarpiece and the more than 300 mostly Renaissance-era tombs and memorials are noteworthy. The most outstanding is the tomb of Swedish Field Marshal Pontus De La Gardie and his wife, Sophie, daughter of Swedish King Johann III. The life-size figures of the couple carved in stone and the bas-reliefs on the sides of the sarcophagus are especially interesting. Admiral Adam John Johann Krusenstern, the first Russian seaman to sail around the world (in 1846), is also buried here. Special permission was required for his burial, as all internments in the church were prohibited at the end of the 18th century. The wooden pews are built into individual booths, with doors at either end. Lutheran services are held Sundays, and the rest of the week the church is open to the public. Concerts are held every Saturday, usually at 11 AM.

OIGEUSU PÜHA ALEKSANDER NEVSKI KATEDRAAL (ALEXANDER NEVSKY CATHE-DRAL) Located on Castle Square, this mustard-colored Russian Orthodox church was built from 1894 to 1900 in the Russian Revival style, complete with onion domes. Services are held daily at 10 AM and 6 PM. Photography is prohibited inside the church. Lossi Plats.

LARGE FORTRESS In the Middle Ages, the part of Toompea where the castle stands was called the Small Fortress, and the rest of the hill, with its administrative buildings and homes of nobles, the Large Fortress. Today many of the old buildings of the Large Fortress still stand, making it an interesting place for a stroll. It's easy to get lost among the narrow cobblestone streets and alleyways here.

NEW TOWN

The sections of Tallinn beyond the Old Town and the waterfront are primarily modern, with some structures dating from the 19th century. While there is little of architectural or historic interest here, these areas offer a glimpse of how Estonians live today.

VABADUSE VÄLJAK (FREEDOM SQUARE) Formerly called Victory Square, this site dominates the newer part of the city. In recent years, Estonians gathered here by the tens of thousands to demand greater freedom from Moscow. Large rallies, complete with waving flags and scores of flowers, are held here every February 24 to commemorate the day in 1918 when Estonia declared its independence from Russia's Bolshevik regime.

KADRIORG PARK

Located on the outskirts of the city on Tallinn Bay, this lovely green stretch of land — dotted with trees, fountains, and a lake — was once a favorite retreat of Peter the Great, who built a summer palace here for his wife, Catherine, as well as a modest cottage for himself. A stately soft-pink palace is located about 100 yards from Peter the Great's cottage, housing the offices of parliamentary leaders. The ride aboard trams No. 1 and No. 3 from Vabaduse Väljak in downtown Tallinn to Kadriorg Park takes only 15 minutes and travels through a nice residential area. Some of the most charming homes in Estonia, mostly 19th-century wooden buildings with whimsical gingerbread trim and lovely landscaped gardens, are located here.

KADRIORG LOSS (KADRIORG PALACE) This grand Italianate baroque palace, built between 1718 and 1724 by Peter the Great for his wife, Catherine, now houses the *Estonian Museum of Art.* The collection of some 17,000 works features 19th- and 20th-century Estonian and other European art, including paintings by Ilya Repin, the late-19th-century Russian realist, and Jan Breughel the Elder, the 16th-century Flemish master. Closed at press time for renovations.

PIRITA

This waterfront district, about 6 miles (10 km) from the center of Tallinn, takes its name from the 15th-century Convent of St. Bridget (Pirita in Estonian). It has a nice shoreline and offers a bracing view across the Gulf of Finland, where windsurfers and sailboats skim across the waves. The area was spruced up for the *1980 Summer Olympics,* when several sailing and regatta events were held here; today the *Pirita Olympic Sailing Center* has kayaks, rowboats, sailboats, and powerboats for rent.

PÜHA BRIGITA NUNNAKOOSTER (CONVENT OF ST. BRIDGET) Built in the early 15th century as a token of gratitude to the saint, who was believed to have saved the town from invading Lithuanians. The convent was largely destroyed in the 16th century during the Livonian War, but the walls still stand. During the summer, concerts and plays are performed here. Open daily; admission charge.

PIRITA BEACH Just east of the *Pirita Olympic Sailing Center,* this popular 3-mile white sand beach offers bathhouses, small shops, and a kiosk that rents surfboards. The water is a little chilly but clean enough for swimming. On *New Year's Eve,* the celebrations here include an incredible display of fireworks over the gulf. There are quite a few large, fairly new restaurants overlooking the water, including the *Pirita,* one of the most popular dining spots in the area. Its scenic location makes it the site of many state dinners (see *Eating Out*). Downstairs is the very popular *La Playa* nightclub and disco, open Fridays through Sundays from 9 AM to 2 AM.

MÁLESTUSMÄRK NÕUKOGUDE VÕIMU EEST LANGENUTLE IGAVENE TULI (MONUMENT TO THE FIGHTERS FOR SOVIET POWER) This memorial — one of the least clunky of its ilk — honors the Estonian heroes of World War II, which is probably why, in this era of strong anti-Soviet sentiment, it remains (thus far) unmolested. Erected in 1960, it stands in a quiet park on the gulf near the *1980 Olympic* regatta site. The granite sculpture follows the contours of the hill, and is divided in the center by a walkway. Suspended over the path is a stone sculpture of dying birds, representing Estonian sailors who died at sea, and at the path's end is a pavilion shaped like the bow of a ship. To the right of the pavilion an eternal flame burns, symbolically sheltered by a sculpture of two cupped hands. Fresh flowers and wreaths are placed by the flame every day, and the sculpture is dramatically lit at night.

Across the road, the graves of Estonians who died in World War II stretch out in endless rows. One granite monument, which stands beside a dead tree transplanted here from a nearby island, marks the grave of a man who refused to collaborate with the Nazis and was hanged from one of the tree's branches.

Sources and Resources

TOURIST INFORMATION

The *Tallinna Turismiamet* (Tallinn Tourist Office) offers a range of information materials and services including city maps, pamphlets on special events, and an English-speaking staff. During the summer months, the tourist office conducts 2-hour walking tours of the Old Town for less than $2. Helpful guides also will arrange special tours of the city with advance notice. The tourist office also will book theater tickets, make restaurant reservations, and arrange trips outside of Tallinn. Open daily from 10 AM to 8 PM. 8 Raekoja Plats (phone: 666959 or 448886; fax: 441221).

LOCAL COVERAGE *Radio Estonia* broadcasts a 10-minute English-language news bulletin at 6:20 PM. *Estonian TV* airs 1 hour of *CCN* weekdays from 5 to 6 PM. Visitors can obtain foreign newspapers and magazines at kiosks in all major hotels, but the best selection is found at the *Viru* hotel. There are several local English-language publications, including the *Tallinn City Paper;* published bimonthly, it has events listings and restaurant reviews as well as news and feature stories. In addition, the *Baltic Independent* and the *Baltic Observer*, both weekly newspapers, are available at newsstands. Books in English are sold at two shops, *Virivarava Raamatukauplus* (23 Virutee) and *Lugemisvara* (1 Harjutee).

TELEPHONE Estonia now can be dialed directly from the US using the 372 international area code; the city area code for Tallinn is 6. Phone books are impossible to find in Tallinn, but local newspapers have up-to-date listings of major establishments in the city. Most hotels have international direct-dial telephones. Although more expensive (much more) than the calls booked through the *Long Distance Telephone Exchange* (10 Lomonossov-tee), the lines are better, clearer, and there is little risk of being disconnected. To use a public pay phone, you must purchase a token, available at newsstands or post offices. Deposit the token in the pay slot before lifting the receiver; then dial when you hear a long buzz.

GETTING AROUND

AIRPORT Tallinn Airport is located on Tartu Maantee, about 4 miles (6 km) southeast of the city (10 to 15 minutes by car from the city center). For more details on scheduled airlines, see FACTS IN BRIEF.

BOAT The following operators have offices in the Tallinn Harbor Building: *Estonian New Line* (phone: 428382) operates three hydrofoils and a large passenger ferry that travel daily between Tallinn and Helsinki. *Estline* (phone: 602010; fax: 428382) operates the ferry *Nord Estonia* between Tallinn and Stockholm. In addition, *Tallink* (16 Pärnu Maantee; phone: 442440) has two large boats traveling daily between Tallinn and Helsinki. For additional information on operators leaving from Scandanavia, see FACTS IN BRIEF.

BUS The city has extensive bus and tram lines, some of which reach the outlying suburbs. They are very inexpensive and run from 5 AM to midnight; 6 AM to midnight on Sundays. Minibuses leave daily from the parking lot of the *Viru* hotel (14 Viru Väljak) from 3 PM to 3 AM. They seat eight and follow 20 different fixed routes.

CAR RENTAL You don't really need a car to see Tallinn, because the Old Town is best explored on foot and the Upper Town is off limits to cars except those with special permits. But if you want to go farther afield, car rental rates are approximately $40 per day. *Refet Ltd.* (20 Magasinitee; phone:

661046 or 682607; fax: 448525) rents cars and minibuses, with and without drivers. *Refet* reservations may also be made through the *Olümpia* hotel (phone: 602427 or 602434).

TAXI Official state-owned cabs, marked by a yellow or white card on the right-hand side of the front windshield, can be reserved by calling *Taksopark* (phone: 444856). Two smaller private firms, *Taksokeskus* (phone: 603044) and *Esra* (phone: 602340), also offer taxi services. Official taxis can be booked at your hotel for a slight service charge. Rates are higher in the evening and on weekends. For information, call 603044.

TRAIN The city train station is located just beside the entrance to the Upper Town at 39 Paldiski Maantee (phone: 446756). It's about 9 hours by rail from Tallinn to St. Petersburg, and there's an overnight train to Moscow that takes about 15 hours, depending on the length of the stops at the border for passport and customs checks.

LOCAL SERVICES

DENTIST (ENGLISH-SPEAKING) *Baltic Medical Partners* (phone: 602200) or *Olümpia* hotel (phone: 602290).

DRY CLEANER/TAILOR The *Olümpia, Palace,* and *Viru* hotels offer dry cleaning services. Inquire at their service bureaus about tailoring.

MEDICAL EMERGENCY Call your hotel service bureau, or try the medical center on the fourth floor of the *Olümpia* hotel (phone: 605761).

NATIONAL/INTERNATIONAL COURIER *DHL Worldwide Express* (6 Ravela Puiestee; phone: 454489; fax: 4544880). Also try the new *Tallinn Business Center* on Rüütlitee in the Old Town (phone: 441197; fax: 445159).

OFFICE EQUIPMENT RENTAL Try your hotel service bureau, or the *Tallinn Business Center* (see above). *Frens, Ltd.* (phone: 446987; fax: 441932), a new Swedish-Estonian company specializing in travel arrangements for business groups, also rents a variety of equipment.

PHARMACY *Apteek* (4 Tartutee; no phone) offers prescriptions and a selection of vitamins and medical supplies. Open Mondays through Saturdays from 8 AM to 8 PM.

POST OFFICE The main post office (1 Narva Maantee, opposite the *Viru* hotel) is open weekdays from 8 AM to 8 PM; Saturdays from 8 AM to 5 PM. Estonia has direct mail service with Finland, so if you write "via Finland" on an overseas letter it stands a better chance of reaching its destination.

SECRETARY/STENOGRAPHER Inquire at the service bureaus of the *Olümpia, Palace,* or *Viru* hotels; *Tallinn Business Center* (see above); and *Frens, Ltd.* (see above).

TRANSLATOR Try the *Palace* hotel, *Tallinn Business Center* (see above), or *Frens, Ltd.* (see above).

SPECIAL EVENTS

The equivalent of the Russian *White Nights* festival in June is called *Jaanipaev* (St. John's Day) here and is the most celebrated event of the Estonian calendar. *Jaanipaev* has pagan origins and used to mark the end of spring planting. Nowadays it is celebrated on June 24, highlighted by the age-old tradition of lighting bonfires. Also in June is the *Vanalinnapaevaed* (Old Town Festival), a joyous celebration of singing, folk dancing, and street theater centered around Town Hall Square. One very special event is the *Song Festival,* which has been held in Tallinn every 5 years since 1880. As many as 30,000 people come together from all over the Baltics to perform songs, folk dances, and a wide range of music at a 100,000-spectator stage in Kadriorg Park. The next festival will be held this year (one year early) in commemoration of the 125th anniversary of the song festival. Events begin in Tartu, the original site of the festival. For more information, contact *Estonian Song Festival Managing Board,* 12 Väike-Karja, Tallinn EE0106 (phone: 449262; fax: 440963). The next festival is due to be held in 1995.

MUSEUMS

Tallinn's wealth of small museums are worth visiting, if only to view the spectacular medieval towers and buildings that house them (often of much greater interest than the exhibits themselves). This is especially true of the *Maritime Museum* in Paks Margareeta and the Kiek-in-de-Kok, both located in the Old Town. Most museums are closed on Mondays unless otherwise specified. Also, exhibits are identified in Estonian with some Russian, but there is no English. However, you can book a tour with an English-speaking guide in advance. Unless otherwise indicated, the museums listed the are open Tuesday through Sundays from 9 AM to 4 PM, and charge a nominal admission.

AJALOOMUUSEUM (HISTORICAL MUSEUM) Located in the early-15th-century building that housed the city merchants' Great Guild. The permanent exhibit of current Estonian history is small, but the museum also features interesting temporary exhibits. Note the gabled façade. Open from 10 AM to 6 PM. 17 Pikktee, two doors down from the new Russian Embassy at No. 19 (phone: 443446 or 602163).

KIEK-IN-DE-KOK (PEEP-IN-THE-KITCHEN) The permanent exhibit in this museum traces the history of Tallinn's fortifications, built between 1475–83. Recently, the Estonian Union of Photographers has held several good exhibits here. Visitors can admire a view of the Old Town from the top floor of the museum. Open from 11 AM to 5:30 PM; closed Mondays and Thursdays. 1 Komandantitee (phone: 446686).

MEREMUUSEUM (MARITIME MUSEUM) Housed in the Paks Margareeta (Fat Margaret) tower, it offers a collection of drawings, pictures, and navigation equipment. Note the 1920s hard-shell diving suit in the entryway. There is a viewing platform on the roof. Open Wednesdays through Sundays from 10 AM to 6 PM. 70 Pikktee (phone: 601803).

TEATRI-JA MUUSIKAMUUSEUM (MUSEUM OF THEATER AND MUSIC) A collection of musical instruments, costumes, set designs, programs, scripts, and literature relating to the history of Estonian theater and music. 12 Müürivahetee (phone: 442884).

VABAÕHUMUUSEUM (MUSEUM OF ETHNOGRAPHY) This open-air museum, situated in Rocca al Mare (Cliff by the Sea) about 2 miles (3 km) west of downtown Tallinn, is a collection of traditional rural dwellings brought from villages throughout the country. Folk dance ensembles and handicrafts fairs and exhibitions are held here on Saturdays. The museum is open only during the warm-weather months. 12 Vabaõhumuuseumitee, Rocca al Mare (phone: 559176).

SHOPPING

Estonian handicrafts, among the highest quality in the Baltics, include hand-knit sweaters, caps, socks, and mittens of thick, coarse wool (dyed in patterns differing from region to region), national costumes, dolls in folk costumes, knit cobweb-patterned shawls of woolen lace from Haapsalu, contemporary jewelry, leatherwork, woven baskets, and woodenware similar to that found in Finland. The Estonian island of Muhu specializes in colorful floral embroidery stitched onto slippers, sweaters, blankets, and dresses.

With the introduction of the kroon, all payment is now in the local currency; credit cards are not widely accepted.

Visitors should explore the many stores in the Old Town, the main shopping district. Walk through Raekoja Plats (Town Hall Square) and along the narrow streets of the square including Pikktee, Venetee, and Virutee. There are several good arts and souvenir shops in Toompea (Castle Hill). Most stores are open from 10 AM to 6 PM, closed on Sundays and Mondays. A fine selection of ceramics, leatherwork, and eye-catching jewelry is available at *ARS* (8 Vabaduse Väljak) and *Complex Firmakauplos* (9 Pikktee; phone: 443280). *Bogapott* in Toompea (9 Pikk Jalg) has beautiful candles, hand-painted postcards, and ceramics. Also in Toompea, *Patkor* and *Estars* (both located at 5 Rakhukohtee) have stunning amber jewelry and leatherwork. Both are open on Sundays. At *Salong Dunkri* (Dunkritee at Rataskaevutee Plats), there are painted lacquer boxes, old crystal decanters, and a lot of pleasant surprises. The store itself is a gem, with merchandise displayed on antique 19th-century tables and in huge, wooden-arched glass showcases along one wall.

Don't miss the *Nuku Pood* doll shop (18 Raekoja Plats) on Town Hall

Square with its hundreds of traditional Estonian costumed dolls. Also, the *Flea Market* (Paldiski Maantee) is open Saturdays and Sundays from 8 AM to 3 PM and features everything from refrigerators to old Soviet paraphernalia. Among Tallinn's best bookstores is *Lugemisvara* (1 Harjutee; phone: 443565), which features a large selection of titles in Estonian, Russian, and Finnish. There also are a few volumes — mostly children's books — in English. In the far corner of the shop is an array of nicely framed original works of art and topical cartoon drawings, and local crafts. Estonian and Russian calendars, prints, cards, and postcards also are sold here. Open weekdays from 9:30 AM to 6:30 PM; Saturdays from 10 AM to 5 PM.

SPORTS AND FITNESS

A variety of sporting events is held at the *Linnahallis* (Center of Culture and Sports; 20 Mere Puiestee; phone: 425158). The massive limestone structure, located right beside the international ferry terminal, was built for the *1980 Summer Olympics.* It has two main halls, the *Konserdsaal* (Concert Hall), site of musical performances, and the *Jaahall* (Ice Arena), which is used year-round for hockey games and figure skating. The *Jaahall* is sometimes used for large dances (the ice is covered with wooden floorboards). There's also a bowling alley. In addition, the complex is the site of a popular nightclub, *Lucky Luke's* (see *Nightclubs and Nightlife*). The *Linnahallis* is open daily except January 1, *Good Friday,* May 1, and *Christmas Day.*

The other main sports complex in the area is the *Olümpiakeskus* (Olympic Center; 1 Regatitee, Pirita, next to the *Sport* hotel), which was also built for the *1980 Summer Olympics.* It's about 6 miles (10 km) from the center of Tallinn. Facilities here include the *Tallinn Jahtklub* (Yacht Club; see *Sailing*) and the *Universaal* building, which features a large gymnasium with facilities for weight lifting, wrestling, and boxing, as well as locker rooms and showers. Hours of operation vary, so check in advance. The *Soltrim Solarium,* a tanning studio, is also located at the *Universaal;* it's open weekdays from 9:30 AM to 7:30 PM; Saturdays and Sundays from 10 AM to 7 PM. Next to the *Universaal* is *West Sport,* a small sporting goods store that sells bathing suits, sports clothes and shoes, bicycles, and some racquet sports equipment. It's open Tuesdays through Saturdays from 10 AM to 6 PM; Sundays from 11 AM to 3 PM.

BASKETBALL The Estonian *Kalev* basketball team plays at the *Kalev Sports Hall* (12 Junkentali; phone: 661187) during the winter months. Volleyball matches also are held here.

CROSS-COUNTRY SKIING This sport is very popular in the Baltics. There are ample trails — but no rental equipment — at Nomme, a beautiful park just southwest of the center of Tallinn. Ottepa, a lovely spot some 124 miles (200 km) outside of Tallinn, rents skis. "Unified Team" (former Soviet) *1992 Olympic* contenders trained and practiced here.

GOLF There are no real links in Tallinn, but there is *Adam Golf,* a miniature golf course, at the *Olümpiakeskus.* It's open from May through August.

HOCKEY AND ICE SKATING Hockey games and figure skating competitions are held at the *Jaahall* (Ice Arena) of the *Linnahallis* (see above) and at *Talleks Stadium* (1 Pirnitee; phone: 532628).

SAILING The *Tallinn Jahtklub* (Yacht Club; phone: 237300) is located at the *Olümpiakeskus.* It possible to rent sailboats or yachts from *TopSail,* a company based at the club (phone: 237055; fax: 237044); reserve in advance. The *Jahtklub* has a small café with microwaveable hot meals and snacks, and champagne and vodka as well. There are saunas, showers, and changing rooms on the premises. The *Tallinn Sailing Service* (phone: 237655) offers assistance to those who want to sail in the port.

SAUNA The *Olümpia* hotel has the best sauna in Tallinn. Located on the 26th floor, the glass-doored sauna is big enough for eight people and features a spectacular view of the city.

SOCCER Matches are played at *Dynamo Stadium* (4 Roheline aas; phone: 425158) and at *Kalev Stadium* (3 Staadionitee; phone: 661665).

SWIMMING Try the indoor pool at the *Kalev Sportshall* (18 Aiatee; phone: 440545) or at the *Dynamo Sports Complex* (3 Aietee; phone: 446617). During the summer, there's swimming at Pirita Beach (see *Special Places*).

TENNIS There are excellent outdoor clay and asphalt courts opposite the *Palace* hotel (2 Kaarli Puiestee; phone: 441269) and at the *Tennisekeskussini-Valge,* a tennis club in Kadriorg Park (38 Koidula; phone: 430638 or 430389). The *Kalev* courts (28 Hernetee; phone: 443461) also can be booked. Operating times vary depending on the season.

THEATER

Though concerts are more popular here than plays, there's still a fairly lively theater scene in Tallinn. All performances are in Estonian except for the *Russian Drama Theater* (5 Vabaduse Väljak; phone: 443716). The *Eesti Noorsooteater* (Estonian Youth Theater; 23 Laitee; phone: 448579) has good productions presented in a small intimate auditorium. *Eesti Draamteater* (Estonian Drama Theater; 5 Pärnu Maantee; phone: 443378), founded in 1916, stages both foreign and domestic productions in Estonian. The Estonian coat-of-arms once again graces the exterior of the theater (it had been removed by Soviet authorities). The *Eesti Riiklik Nukuteater* (Estonian Puppet Theater; 1 Laitee; phone: 441252) presents plays for adults as well as children.

MUSIC

The Estonian love of song and dance reaches the level of passion in the capital city. The most joyous expression of this fervor is the massive music festival held every 5 years in Tallinn (see *Special Events*), but performances and recitals of every kind are held in the city throughout the year. The *Estonia Teater* (Estonian National Theater; Estonia Puiestee; phone: 449040) is home to the local opera and ballet companies, and also hosts touring companies from the other Baltic countries, Russia, and even farther afield. The box office is open Mondays and Wednesdays through Saturdays from 1 to 7 PM, and Sundays from 11 AM to 7 PM. The *Estonia Concert Hall* (phone: 443198) features Estonian music, organ recitals, and performances by the *Estonian Symphony Orchestra* and other groups. The box office is open daily from 1 to 7 PM. Evening musical performances are frequently held at the Church of St. Nicholas. In addition, organ recitals are held each day at 10:15 AM before services.

NIGHTCLUBS AND NIGHTLIFE

After-dark life in Tallinn is mostly hotel-centered, though the capital boasts one good club, *Eestitall* (4 Dunkri), which often features live jazz music. Other nightspots can sometimes border on tacky if not seedy. You should be aware that the city is a popular weekend destination for Finns who like to party — long and loud. For them, Tallinn offers bargain prices on wine, women, and song. The *Kuma* bar in the *Kungla* hotel is especially popular with this crowd (and thus is best avoided).

The *Sky* bar atop the *Palace* hotel (3 Vabaduse Väljak; phone: 451510) has taped music from 9 PM to 3 AM, a small dance floor, and a casino. *Lucky Luke's* (20 Mere Puiestee; no phone), which is open from 11 PM to 3 AM, features country music.

Best in Town

CHECKING IN

Hotel reservations in Tallinn are best made through your travel agent or directly with the hotel. Estonia is currently undergoing a tourism boom and there is a shortage of hotel space, so visitors are advised to book early and to confirm reservations before departure. Expect to pay $70 and more for a double room in an expensive hotel; $40 to $70 in one listed as moderate; and $20 to $40 for an inexpensive place. Payment is almost always in Estonian kroons; credit cards are not widely accepted. Most of Tallinn's major hotels have complete facilities for the business traveler. Those hotels listed below as having "business services" usually offer such conveniences as English-speaking concierge, meeting rooms, photocopiers, computers, translation services, and express checkout, among others. Call the hotel for additional information. All telephone numbers are in the 6 city code unless otherwise noted.

EXPENSIVE

Olümpia This recently renovated 378-room property, now one of Tallinn's best, was built by *Intourist* for the *1980 Summer Olympics,* and it's the tallest building in Tallinn after the TV Tower. A small bar/café on the 14th floor offers a nice view of the harbor; an airy, plant-filled bar on the second floor attracts those seeking something more familiar. Also on the premises: a spectacular sauna (see *Sports*), beauty and barber shops, a shoe repair service and dry cleaner, and a gift shop. There is also a service bureau, where travelers can book tours and reserve rail and airline tickets. Business services. 33 Liivalaia (phone: 602346 or 602438; fax: 601907).

Palace A joint venture with Finland's Arctica chain, this hotel is simply one of the best in the Baltics. All 91 rooms have color TV sets with Britain's "Sky News" satellite channel, international direct-dial telephones, and mini-bars. Two deluxe suites have a private sauna. Local artwork and stained glass in the hallways is for sale through the service bureau. There are 2 restaurants: *Linda,* which serves continental fare, and the *Pizzeria Margarita* (see *Eating Out* for both). There's also a small lobby bar and a casino bar on the top floor. Business services. 3 Vabaduse Väljak (phone: 444671; fax: 443098).

MODERATE

Kungla Located in the center of town, this modern, though unpretentious, 160-room establishment has a large, Soviet-style restaurant and a small café serving snacks. The *Kuma* bar features both taped music and a live band nightly, and an "erotic show" on Thursdays, Fridays, and Saturdays (it's very popular with visiting Finns). 23 Kreutzwalditee (phone: 421460 or 427040; fax: 425594).

Peoleo A well-run Canadian joint venture located just south of Tallinn, this motel features 44 rooms with private baths, color TV sets, and telephones. In addition, there are tennis courts, a good restaurant, a shop, and shuttle bus service into the city. Business services. 555 Pärnu Maantee, Tallinn Laagri (phone: 556469; fax: 771463).

Viru Tallinn's main Soviet-era hotel is a 22-story gray cement structure adjacent to the Old Town. Each of the 458 rooms has a private bath with shower, as well as a telephone and TV set. A Soviet-style restaurant on the 22nd floor offers a great view of the port and the Old Town (see *Eating Out*). There's also a pseudo-English pub and a tiny grill on the first floor that serves incredibly tasty grilled meat. (Don't be discouraged by the heavy security at the door, which is, inexplicably, always locked. Just ask for a table.) Business services. 4 Viru Väljak (phone: 652081; fax: 444371).

INEXPENSIVE

EMI Run by the Estonian Management Institute (EMI), this 89-room establishment is located about 6 miles (10 km) from the city center in a rather run-down residential section of Tallinn. Its saving grace is that the rooms are clean and modern, and the young staff is charming and ready to help at the drop of a kroon. All rooms feature TV sets and private baths, there's also a sauna, hair salon, bar, and restaurant. Business services. 21 Sutistetee (phone: 521611; fax: 521624).

Pirita Once known as the *Sport,* this clean, functional hotel has 300 rooms. Originally built for athletes attending the *1980 Summer Olympics,* the rooms can best be described as spartan, although they do have TV sets and small refrigerators. The beds are small, low to the floor, and unsuitable for anyone over 6 feet tall. You can send and receive international faxes at the business center. 1 Regatitee, about 6 miles (10 km) from the center of Tallinn in Pirita (phone: 238615; fax: 237433).

EATING OUT

Estonian food, which reflects Germanic, Scandinavian, Hungarian, and Russian influences, can be very good, particularly if you're fond of fish. Estonians also make some of the best pastries east of Vienna — light, cream-filled, and not overly sweet. The Old Town has dozens of cafés where you can stop for small sandwiches, excellent cakes, ice cream, coffee, or tea.

With the introduction of the kroon in 1992, Estonia's old system of payment in either hard currency or local currency has been abolished. All payment is now in kroons, and credit cards are not widely accepted.

Reservations are necessary in almost every restaurant in town, so book as soon as you can. In recent months, many visitors have stayed close to their hotels at night because of a growing incidence of street crime. Do take the necessary precautions: Arrange return transportation to your hotel, and be careful not to drink too much. Dinner for two, not including wine and tip, will cost $50 and over at restaurants described as very expensive; $35 to $50 at restaurants in the expensive category; $20 to $35 at places listed as moderate; and less than $20 at inexpensive spots. All numbers are in the 6 city code unless otherwise noted.

VERY EXPENSIVE

Astoria Tallin's fanciest restaurant, the former buffet of the *Russian Drama Theater,* has been restored to its original 1926 elegance. The menu, available in English, features Estonian and continental food, including a number of fish dishes such as salted trout and *balokk* (a smoked Siberian fish), as well as beef and pork. The dining room is laid out in a circle around a dance floor. There's great entertainment: a singer from 2 to 4 PM and an orchestra starting at 10 PM. Attached to the restaurant is an elegant casino with blackjack and roulette tables. Be sure to dress up. Open daily 1 to 7 PM and 9 PM to 2 AM. Reservations are necessary and sometimes must be made days in advance. 5 Vabaduse Väljak, in the basement next door to the *Palace* hotel (phone: 448462).

Linda A pleasant, well-appointed dining room on the ground floor of the *Palace* hotel, this is Tallinn's priciest, but well worth it. The continental menu includes salmon marinated in lemon and oil, and wild boar shashlik. Wine is available by the bottle and the glass (a rarity in the former Soviet Union). There are menus in English and the waiters speak enough English to get by. Open daily for breakfast, lunch, and dinner. Reservations necessary. 3 Vabaduse Väljack (phone: 451510).

Toomkooli Very popular with Estonia's emerging capitalist crowd, this new restaurant is housed in the building adjacent to the Canadian Embassy in Toompea. The menu includes chateaubriand and various pork and poultry specialties. There's also a good selection of wines and excellent desserts. Request a table near a window overlooking the Upper Town. Open daily from noon to midnight. Reservations advised. 11 Toomkooli (phone: 446613).

EXPENSIVE

Maharaja Yes, an Indian restaurant in Estonia, and a pretty good one at that. Opened in 1991, this British-Estonian venture is presided over by a charming restaurateur from Bombay. The atmosphere is quiet and elegant and the eastern Indian dishes are authentic and spicy. The curry and rice dishes are highly recommended. Open daily for lunch and dinner. Reservations advised. 13 Raekoja Plats (phone: 444367).

Pirita A beautiful establishment with a spectacular view of the Gulf of Finland, it is frequently booked for official government functions. During the summer there's alfresco dining on a second-floor patio that overlooks the water. The food is good and reasonably priced, and there's a band for dancing. This is the place of choice for taking in the *New Year's Eve* fireworks over the bay. Open daily from noon to 5 PM and 7 PM to midnight. Reservations advised. 5 Merivaljatee (phone: 238102).

MODERATE

Du Nord Seafood, fondue, and Estonian fare are featured in this 3-story, renovated house in the Old Town. On the first floor is the Hunting Hall dining room, which serves local game, such as venison and boar, in season. On the top floor is a fondue restaurant, plus a grill for fish, chicken, and meat. Open daily for lunch and dinner. Reservations advised as a lot of tour groups are booked here. 5 Rataskaevutee (phone: 441695).

Gnoom A snug, medieval-style dining hall that has a cellar with taped music, a grillroom with live music, and a series of cozy rooms upstairs decorated with old-fashioned wallpaper, chandeliers, and a mixture of small, round intimate tables and formal dining room antiques. Grilled meat is the specialty in the grillroom downstairs; the upstairs café features coffee and pastries but also serves some traditional Estonian dishes. Upstairs open 9 AM to 9 PM; Sundays noon to 9 PM; downstairs open daily noon to 5 PM and 6 to 11 PM. Reservations necessary. 2 Virutee (phone: 442488).

Peetri Pizza This new eatery offers the best pizza this side of Italy. Varieties include cheese, seafood, and vegetarian; there's even a Hawaiian-style pizza, smothered with pineapple. Open daily from 10 AM to 3 PM. No reservations. Pärnu Maantee (phone: 666711).

SubMonte A popular eatery in a medieval cellar in the Old Town. Specialties include international cuisine and Estonian dishes prepared with pork and poultry. Also, a good selection of wines and terrific desserts. Open daily noon to 11 PM. Reservations necessary. 4 Rüütlitee (phone: 666871).

Viru Located on the 22nd floor of the *Viru* hotel, this Soviet-style restaurant serves typical Russian fare (read: potato salads, greasy meat dishes, and no dessert), but there is a spectacular view of the harbor and the Old Town. Open daily for breakfast, lunch, and dinner. Reservations advised. 4 Viru Väljak (phone: 652270).

INEXPENSIVE

Bogapott (Artists's Jug) Located in Toompea, this café serves tasty, light snacks and delicious pastries. Handicrafts and hand-painted postcards are sold in the adjoining shop. A pleasant stopover while exploring the Upper Town. Open daily. No reservations. 9 Pikk Jalg (phone: 443220).

Café Neitsitorn (Maiden's Tower Café) Located in a 14th-century tower of the Fortress Wall, this is a delightful place to stop for refreshments on a tour of the Upper Town. There are 3 floors and a wine cellar (try the hot spiced wine). In the summer you can relax on the outdoor balcony perched off the upper floor. Liqueurs, coffee and tea, juice, and small snacks and pastries are available upstairs, but not hot dishes. No smoking is allowed. Open daily from 11 AM to 10 PM. No reservations. 9A Lühike Jalg, behind Kiek-in-de-Kok (phone: 440896).

Eeslitall Very popular with the locals, so reservations are a must. The menu is limited, but the fare is better than average; try the spaghetti smothered in creamy Estonian cheese au gratin. The bar upstairs is a big attraction with live jazz music. Open daily for lunch and dinner. Reservations necessary. 4 Dunkritee, off Town Hall Square (phone: 448033).

Gloria This large dining spot offers good, inexpensive meals (although it has lost its cachet as the best place in town because it can't shed the once-prevalent Soviet attitude that customers exist only to irritate waiters). Try the chicken Kiev or bouillon with meat turnovers. There's a choice of well-lit tables near the front, where a band performs most evenings for dancing, or darker, quieter booths near the bar in the back of the room. Open from noon to 7 PM and 8 PM to midnight; until to 2 AM on Fridays and Saturdays. Reservations necessary. 2 Müürivahetee (phone: 446950).

Kannike Tallinn's first private restaurant, this is a big, barn-like building where beer, light snacks, and a sauna all can be enjoyed. The owners often display the works of local artists. Open daily from 11 AM to 10 PM. Reservations advised. 108 Vabaduse Puiestee (phone: 447888).

Maiismokk (Sweet Tooth) Bakery Café Five small rooms on the upper floor of an 1806 coffee shop, each decorated in a different color. Green plants, big glass windows, and bright curtains make this one of the most popular places to linger for coffee, tea, pastries, and light snacks. Open daily from 11 AM to 10 PM. Reservations necessary. 16 Pikktee, across the street from the Church of the Holy Spirit (phone: 601250 for same-day reservations; 601396 for future reservations).

Maiustused Pastries and coffee to die for, both to take out and to eat at a small, sit-down counter. Open 9 AM to 8 PM; Sundays 9 AM to 2 PM. No reservations. 8 Vanaturu Kael (no phone).

Pizzeria Margarita Clean and comfortable, with lots of ivy-covered trellises and ersatz Tiffany lamps perched over cozy booths, this eatery serves a good, thin-crusted pizza at reasonable prices. There's take-out service available. Open daily noon to 11 PM. Reservations advised. In the *Palace Hotel,* 3 Vabaduse Väljak (phone: 451510).

Toidutare Café This roadside eatery located near the *Peoleo* motel is very popular with the local traffic police who stop in for good food. Service is strictly cafeteria-style, and the menu features homemade soups, sandwiches, hamburgers, and fries. Open from 8 AM to 10 PM. No reservations. 555 Pärnu Maantee (no phone).

Vilnius

One of the most salient characteristics of the Lithuanian people is that they are predominantly and fervently Roman Catholic. This powerful underlying force has dominated their past, fueled their successful drive for independence from the former Soviet Union, and stands as one of the cornerstones of their future.

Nowhere is this more obvious than in Vilnius, Lithuania's capital city, a metropolis of 570,000 people that has long been the political, religious, economic, and cultural center of this southernmost Baltic state. It is no coincidence, then, that Vilnius's churches represent the architectural soul of the country, and also function as a sort of social center and rallying point for political ferment and debate. The rarely subtle Soviet overlords bluntly tried to ignore this fact. Under the atheistic regime, many lovely monasteries and cathedrals in the city were converted to museums and theaters, and the Communists even went so far as to turn St. Casimir's Church — one of Vilnius's most beautiful houses of worship — into the *Museum of Atheism.* A sure sign that Lithuania has regained its independence is the fact that St. Casimir's is once again a working Roman Catholic church.

In fact, today the city is filled with working churches. Didzioji Gatve (Large Street), one of the city's ancient thoroughfares, is studded with both Catholic and Russian Orthodox churches, and during services music pours like holy water into the street. In addition, during the last several years the Catholic church has begun to reclaim the various churches-turned-museums and slowly is returning them to their original function. It is a cumbersome and costly process, though, and after more than 50 years of official, state-sanctioned atheism, many priests have to be taught the necessary skills to assume control over the dioceses.

Another source of strength for the long-suffering Lithuanian people has been their rich history and the memory of independence and, at one time, hegemony in the region. When you consider that a settlement on this site was noted in written records dating from 1323 (archaeologists have found evidence of habitation here as early as the 5th century), and that Vilnius was being compared favorably with the great capitals of Europe by the 15th century, a short spell under German fascism followed by 5 decades of Soviet Communism may eventually be seen as a brief historical interruption.

Lithuanians are one of the oldest peoples of Europe. Their language (along with Latvian, which is similar) is one of the oldest living Indo-European tongues. (After years of Russian being the "official" language, Lithuanian again became the republic's mother tongue in 1989). Lithuania was a powerful state in the 13th century, a time of glory that saw this upstart nation extend its reach to the Black Sea, including parts of Russia, Ukraine, and Belorus. But Gediminas, Lithuania's national hero, did not appear on the scene for another 100 years. He was the legendary founder of the settlement of Vilnius, a warrior and a duke who is credited with much of the expansion of the Lithuanian territory in the 14th century. Gediminas ruled from 1316 to 1341, and during this time Old Vilnius consisted of two parts: the grand duke's court and castles, and the main city area. The state's power was further increased in the late 14th century by the marriage of the Polish Queen Jadviga and the Lithuanian Grand Duke Jagaila. The two states were united, Catholicism was formally introduced into Lithuania, and the country reached what would be the apex of its influence.

Then began a long process of absorption into Poland, beginning with the founding of Rzeczpospolita (a united Polish state) in 1569, that started to sap Lithuania's landmass and political power. However, as a Polish city, Vilnius prospered. What it lost in political and geographical influence it gained in beautification. Wealthy merchants and feudal knights built their palaces in the town, and there were so many monasteries, churches, and administrative buildings that Vilnius was compared with Prague and Cracow. The likeness still remains. Many Renaissance and, later, baroque buildings began to sprout like Polish sugar beets. But these strong ties with the juggernaut to the west were also the cause of the city's political decline. Vilnius lost its significance as the capital when the elected Polish kings, who were also Grand Dukes of Lithuania, stopped frequenting the city.

The following centuries were calamitous. The plunder of the country began with the war between Russia and Poland in 1655, and continued with the Northern War involving Russia, Sweden, and Poland in the early 18th century. Throughout these years Vilnius was a victim of devastating fires and plagues. Damaged by war and neglect, the city's castles and fortifications began to decay and crumble, and the town fathers were forced to sell or demolish many of them.

Until the mid-1800s, Vilnius remained a town of artisans and small businesses, most of which dealt in the processing of raw materials. In 1860, Lithuania's first railway linked Vilnius with St. Petersburg and Warsaw, and later with other towns and seaports of Europe and the Baltics, giving the city a renewed and (this time) more solid economic status.

By the late 18th century, Lithuania's land had been divided among the Russian Empire, Austria, and Prussia. In 1812, it was occupied by Napoleon's armies. A national liberation movement against the Russian czars grew, and Vilnius was the center of uprisings in 1831 and 1863. Throughout, Lithuanians maintained such a sense of culture and individuality that they were able to establish an independent republic in February, 1918. Lithuania was its own sovereign state, with Kaunas as its provisional capital, as Vilnius was then occupied by Poland.

But independence would be short-lived. In 1926, a right-wing dictator-

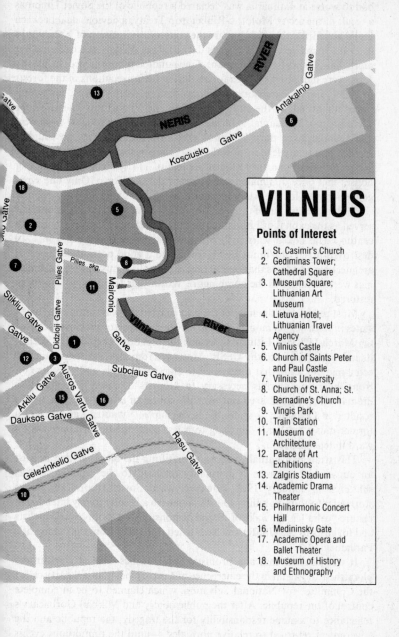

VILNIUS

Points of Interest

1. St. Casimir's Church
2. Gediminas Tower; Cathedral Square
3. Museum Square; Lithuanian Art Museum
4. Lietuva Hotel; Lithuanian Travel Agency
5. Vilnius Castle
6. Church of Saints Peter and Paul Castle
7. Vilnius University
8. Church of St. Anna; St. Bernadine's Church
9. Vingis Park
10. Train Station
11. Museum of Architecture
12. Palace of Art Exhibitions
13. Zalgiris Stadium
14. Academic Drama Theater
15. Philharmonic Concert Hall
16. Medininsky Gate
17. Academic Opera and Ballet Theater
18. Museum of History and Ethnography

ship supplanted the democratic government and, in 1940, things went from bad to worse as Lithuania was declared a republic of the Soviet Union as a result of the secret Molotov-Ribbentrop Treaty, a devious deal between Stalin and Hitler that didn't spare the country the invasion of Nazi troops in 1941. These were the republic's darkest days. Vilnius was occupied for more than 3 years by the Germans. One hundred thousand people, mostly Jews, were murdered by Nazi forces during mass executions in the forests of Paneriai, on the outskirts of Vilnius. Before World War II, Jews comprised about half of the city's population and Vilnius was known as the "Jerusalem of Lithuania." During the war, more than 200,000 Jews were killed in the more than 100 mass execution sites all over the country. Jewish community leaders nowadays say the forests of Lithuania are Jewish "cemeteries" and they mourn the loss of 114 synagogues and prayer houses that once dominated the streets of the Old Town. Only one synagogue remains for the 5,000 Jews now living in Vilnius.

With the exception of the years between the two world wars, Vilnius has served as the capital of Lithuania since the founding of the city in the 14th century. The Polish wars with Moscow and Sweden and a fire in 1710 destroyed much of Vilnius's Old Town, and a good portion of the city's architecture postdates that fateful time. Many of Vilnius's historical buildings were damaged in the bombings of World War II and have since been restored.

Most recently, Lithuania set the pace and led the way among the Baltic states in releasing its moorings from the sinking dock of the Soviet Union. On March 11, 1990, Lithuania became the first Soviet republic to declare its independence from the USSR. Moscow's response was to institute an economic blockade that threatened to starve its people and cut them off from the raw materials necessary to keep its economy running. This drama, which played itself out over the course of several months, finally resulted in Lithuania — under the leadership of Vytautas Landsbergis, a former music teacher — agreeing to a less confrontational approach toward independence.

This strategy eventually succeeded in lifting the blockade and at least an outward appearance of normality returned to the republic. It was shattered in January 1991, however, when Soviet troops and tanks stormed into Vilnius, killing 13 Lithuanians in a bloody frenzy intended to restore "calm" in the wake of several demonstrations (both by nationalists and loyalists to the USSR) and threatened price rises from the democratic Parliament.

It was obvious that anachronistic Soviet tactics were at work in the bloodshed and again in the emergence of a pro-Soviet political party called the Committee for National Salvation, which claimed to be in complete control of the republic. After the public outcry and Mikhail Gorbachev's reluctance to assume responsibility for the tragedy, the republic and the government returned to relative normalcy — until the tumultuous events in Moscow in August 1991.

In the days following the unsuccessful military coup in the Soviet capital, events in Lithuania unfolded at a rapid pace. Its government declared outright independence and outlawed the Communist Party. The "Sovietized" streets and squares were renamed, statues of Lenin were toppled, and the Lithuanian flag now flies throughout the capital of this reborn country.

It seems unfair that Lithuania, which spearheaded the Baltic independence movement, should have to suffer more hardship than its two Baltic sisters in pulling out of the turmoil of the Soviet economy. Since its break with Moscow, Vilnius has been rocked by an energy crisis due to a dispute with Russia, which demands Lithuania pay world prices for fuel. The result for citizens of Vilnius has been two winters spent with little heating and an unreliable public transport system dependent on gas deliveries from Russia. It is not surprising then that on February 14, 1992, Lithuanians elected the former head of the reformed wing of the Communist Party, Algiradas Brazauskas, as president on the promise that he would mend fences with Russia. He replaced Vytautas Landsbergis, father of Lithuania's independence, and until the energy crisis, an overwhelmingly popular leader.

In the fall of 1992, the Lithuanian government introduced a transitional currency, called the "talonas," or coupon, which replaced the Soviet ruble. Plans to launch a fully convertible currency have been under discussion since 1991, but that may not come until later this year, due to the instability of the economy, still weakened by inflation and low production.

Despite its economic woes, Vilnius has always been more cosmopolitan than the rest of Lithuania. Only 48% of its residents are ethnic Lithuanians, compared with 80% throughout the country. As you stroll about the streets of Vilnius today, absorbing its lovely atmosphere, its vibrant mood, and Westernized feel, it may seem as though this ancient city at the confluence of the Neris and Vilnia rivers does indeed have more in common with Prague or Paris than with Perm (a city in central Russia). And the highly charged independent atmosphere should only enhance a visit since, in a city that for many years has enthralled tourists with its rich history, it is exciting to witness the next chapter unfold before your eyes.

Vilnius At-a-Glance

SEEING THE CITY

Gediminas Tower on Castle Hill offers the best vista of this photogenic city. Just climb the spiral staircase in the tower wall to the top, where there is an observation platform. The view from the tower is almost like an aerial photograph, down into Katedros Aikšte (Cathedral Square, also known as Gediminas Square). Conversely, the view of Gediminas Tower and Castle Hill from the square is inspiring, the Lithuanian flag billowing in the wind atop the octagonal Western Tower of this ancient stone fortress. From

Cathedral Square, notice the monument of three white crosses that overlooks the city. This was erected a few years ago in memory of the thousands of Lithuanians who died during Stalin's brutal purges.

There is also an excellent view from the *Panorama* restaurant on the 21st floor of the *Lietuva* hotel (see *Eating Out*). From this roost, the vista stretches across the Neris River and into the Old Town, with its red tile roofs and the clusters of churches and spires that dot the area.

The Lithuanian television tower (10 Suderves Gatve) now has an observation deck, as well as a revolving restaurant and bar 540 feet up, offering a view reaching 30 miles in any direction around Vilnius on a clear day.

SPECIAL PLACES

The lion's share of Vilnius's historical attractions are tucked snugly into the Old Town, the most fascinating section of the city. In fact, Vilnius boasts the largest Old Town in Eastern Europe, and visitors can literally spend days wandering about, discovering magnificent churches, quaint cafés, curious narrow streets, and a plethora of shops. In a bid to curb traffic in the Old Town, city authorities now charge motorists a toll (best to park your car beyond Old Town and explore the area on foot). Since the Old Town buildings have emerged over the course of 5 centuries in myriad styles, they offer a unique jumble of interesting architecture. Though a visitor is likely to notice the baroque flavor of the architectural design — with its emphasis on the ornate — Vilnius originally was built according to the principles of Gothic construction. However, much of the city was destroyed by fire in the early 18th century and has been rebuilt.

At press time, many of the buildings in the Old Town were undergoing renovation, receiving well-deserved face-lifts after years of neglect under the previous Soviet regime. This applies to several sections along Didzioji Gatve and Pilies Gatve. The Lithuanian word for street is "gatve," the word for prospect is "prospektus," and the word for square is "aikšte."

SENAMIESTIS (OLD TOWN)

KATEDROS/GEDIMINAS AIKŠTE (GEDIMINAS OR CATHEDRAL SQUARE) Originally named Cathedral Square, this central plaza in the heart of the Old Town was named Gediminas Square in 1951. It is now reverting back to its original name. Because of its proximity to many Vilnius attractions — including Gediminas Castle and the Central Cathedral — and its link with the Lithuanian nationalist movement, it is the best place to begin an exploration of the city.

Cathedral Square is situated where the lower castle, one of Vilnius's original castles, once stood. The square itself began to take shape in the 19th century, when markets and the famous fairs of St. Casimir (the city's patron saint) were held here. When the markets moved on, the southern end of the square was turned into a public garden. At the rear of the 14th-century Arkikatedra (Central Cathedral) is a small semicircle of stones surrounding a cross and small crucifix. Hunger strikes and protests against Soviet rule were held here, and the square was packed with people in early October 1988 as the red, green, and yellow flag of the Lithuanian republic was hoisted above Gediminas Tower in place of the Soviet flag. In January 1991, Soviet troops opened fire on Lithuanian nationalists who were demonstrating at the Central Cathedral, causing a flood of Lithuanians to pour into the square several days later for the funerals of their fallen compatriots. Today, Cathedral Square has become something of a shrine to Lithuanian independence. A huge boulder with the dates 1323-1973 anchors one corner of the square, commemorating the 450th anniversary of the founding of Vilnius. In fact, settlers were here earlier, but that date was chosen by historians because the first written record of the city — letters from Gediminas to European leaders, which refer to Vilnius as a royal city — date from 1323.

ARKIKATEDRA (CENTRAL CATHEDRAL) Dominating Cathedral Square, this church, originally called the Church of St. Stanislav, was founded in 1387 when Poland and Lithuania were united, and just after Christianity had been introduced to the country. A castle originally stood here, but it was destroyed (except for one of its towers, which has become the cathedral's belfry). Earlier, this was the site of a pagan shrine where, from the tower, the head priest announced the will of the gods to the people below. Sacrifices were offered here to the god Perkunas (whose name is evoked as a swear word by Lithuanians), and grass snakes were kept in a basement since they were considered to be holy by the Lithuanian people.

Over time, the cathedral has been damaged, restored, and reconstructed repeatedly; its style has changed from Gothic to baroque. Only tokens of the original baroque structures have stood the rather tough test of time; St. Casimir's Chapel, which is graced with Italian frescoes, remains one of the city's best examples of this design. Note the engraved reliefs of Noah after the Great Flood and the lives of the apostles on the cathedral's pediments. A nearby bell tower, originally built in the 13th century, contains a clock installed in the 17th century that has truly taken a licking and, remarkably, still keeps on ticking. Under Soviet secular rule, the cathedral served as the *Art Museum of Lithuania* from 1956 to 1988. Its reconsecration in early 1989 received worldwide news coverage, and was another crucial step in the re-emergence of the Lithuanian identity. Roman Catholic services are held daily. The cathedral and bell tower are open Mondays through Saturdays from 7 AM to noon and 3 to 8 PM; Sundays and holidays from 7 AM to 2:30 PM and 5:30 to 9 PM. Katedros Aikšte (phone: 610731).

GEDIMINO PILIES (GEDIMINAS CASTLE) This imposing fortress, known more generically as Vilnius Castle, dominates the skyline. Originally built of wood, it was replaced with a more modern, stone castle by Grand Duke Vytautus in the early 15th century. The only remaining structure of a trio of castles, it took a heavy pounding during 7 years of war between Russia and Poland in the mid-17th century and was never restored. The castle was last used as a bastion during the reign of Peter the Great when, in 1701, the Russian czar stored food and munitions here. The octagonal Gediminas Tower is the best-preserved relic of this castle's former glory, from which the Lithuanian flag proudly flies again. A modest museum devoted to the history of Vilnius is found in the tower. It's open from 11 AM to 5 PM in winter, and from 9 AM to 8 PM from May through August; closed Tuesdays. Even if the museum causes your eyes to glaze over, the view will bring you back to life. Located at the top of the hill in the center of town (phone: 617453).

SVEBTUJU PETRO IR POVILO BAŽNYČIA (CHURCH OF SAINTS PETER AND PAUL)

The best-known baroque building in a city that is rich in examples of this style, this church stands on the original site of a pagan temple to Milda, the goddess of love. The church took more than a century to complete, and though the exterior is not terribly elaborate, the interior is saturated with stucco carvings and intricate ornamentation. After being greeted by the figure of Death — scythe in hand — at the entrance, and huge Turkish war drums, captured in 1673, you will see over 2,000 life-size statues standing throughout the church. The interior is divided into a series of small chapels, each depicting a historical, mythological, or biblical scene. An enormous crystal chandelier, shaped like a ship, hangs from the ceiling. The Roman Catholic Church of Saints Peter and Paul is Vilnius's most important house of worship. Tourists cannot enter during services (usually held 7 to 8:30 AM and 7 to 8 PM on weekdays and 7:30 AM to 2:20 PM and 7 to 8 PM on Sundays and holy days). Otherwise, the church is open to the public. 1 Antakalinio Gatve.

GEDIMINO GATVE (GEDIMINAS STREET)

Formerly called Lenino (Lenin) Street, the headquarters of the Lithuanian Communist Party once stood at one end of this thoroughfare, and the offices of Sajudis, the Lithuanian independence movement, at the other. The street is now dotted with crafts shops, bookstores, a number of large, Soviet-style restaurants, and a monument to Zemaite, a famous Lithuanian classical writer. The *Literary Café* is at No. 1, opposite Katedros Aikšte (see *Eating Out*).

DIDZIOJI GATVE (LARGE STREET)

Formerly called Gorky Street, and now primarily a pedestrian zone, Didzioji harks back more than any other Vilnius street to the city's medieval past. It contains about a third of the architectural monuments of the Old Town. The centerpiece of Didzioji is the 17th-century St. Casimir's Church. Other prime attractions are the Gates of Dawn, also known as Medininsky Gate; the Church of St. Theresa; the Gate of the Basilian Monastery (73 Didzioji), currently under renovation; and a group of four 16th-century houses.

AUŠROS VARTAI ("GATES OF DAWN" OR MEDININSKY GATE)

The gate is the best entrance to the Old Town and the only remaining city gate of nine built in the 16th century. Above it is a bas-relief depicting two griffins holding the emblem of the Lithuanian state, and a small head of the Greek messenger god Hermes, who was also god of commerce and education. The five round spaces for cannon in the gate were last used in 1812 when Vilnius was occupied by Napoleon's army. The gate houses a tiny 17th-century chapel (the entrance is on the right and up 40 stairs), where the Renaissance painting *Our Lady of Vilnius* is located. The chapel holds only 30 to 40 people and is often crowded with worshipers since the painting is thought to work miracles. The walls are covered with small silver hearts and other ornaments placed by people hoping to cure illness — their own or a loved one's — through prayer. Connected to the chapel by a gallery on the right is the Church of St. Theresa, completed in 1650, which has an extensive number of paintings, sculptures, and bas-reliefs. Frescoes on the ceiling illustrate scenes from St. Theresa's life. Didzioji Gatve.

JUS AIKŠTE (MUSEUM SQUARE) Traveling south from Castle Hill, Didzioji Gatve broadens into this triangular (oxymoronic though it may be) square, at the start of Pilies Gatve. This was the junction of trade routes linking Riga, Moscow, and Cracow, and thus was once the site of a thriving market and the liveliest spot in Vilnius of old. Formerly called Rotušés Aikšte (Town Hall Square), it was also, more significantly, the site of Vilnius's first Town Hall, and is where the reconstructed Town Hall stands today. The old Town Hall, a 2-story Gothic building, was built in the 15th century. Its bells rang out to announce the commencement of war, the arrival of a diplomat or visiting VIP, or the death of a local dignitary. Until the 17th century there was a pillory in the center of the square, and gallows would be erected for public executions. In the 18th century, a series of fires destroyed the old Town Hall. A new one was constructed in 1785–99; that neo-classical structure now houses the *Lithuanian Art Museum* (31 Didzioji Gatve; phone: 628679), featuring the works of 19th-century Lithuanian artists. It's open from noon to 6 PM; closed Mondays.

SVENTO KAZIMIERAS BAŽNYČIA (ST. CASIMIR'S CHURCH) Built in 1615 and named for the patron saint of Vilnius (St. Kazimieras or St. Casimir), it is the oldest baroque church in the city, and its playful pink-and-white façade is topped with a dome in the shape of a crown, the symbol of St. Casimir's lineage. The Soviets exhibited no subtlety in 1966 when they chose to turn this church into the *Museum of Atheism of the Lithuanian Republic*. The building reverted to its ecclesiastic purpose in March 1991, and today is a working Roman Catholic church. Mass is held at 6 AM daily; on Sundays and holy days, there's mass with a homily in Russian at 8:30 AM, mass for students at 10:30 AM, and high mass — followed by a concert of religious music — at noon. 34 Didzioji Gatve (phone: 221715).

SERMINES OR TSERKOV PYATNIDESYAT (PENTECOST CHURCH) This Russian Orthodox church was built in 1345 and took the place of a pagan temple. It was here that, in 1705, Peter the Great had an Ethiopian named Hannibal baptized. Hannibal, who took the name Abraham, rose to become a full general in the czar's army, and is best remembered as Alexander Pushkin's great-grandfather. Formerly an icon museum, it has been converted back into a house of worship; a reopening date had not been announced at press time. 2 Didzioji Gatve.

SVENTO MIKOLAJAUS BAŽNYČIA (ST. NICHOLAS CHURCH) A functioning Russian Orthodox church, steeped in incense and the memory of centuries of worshipers. It was built in 1514, probably on the site of a wooden church. Open to the public weekdays from 10 AM to 5 PM; Saturdays, Sundays, and holidays from 10 AM to 8 PM. Services are held at 5 PM on Thursdays and Saturdays (6 PM in summer) and 10 AM on Sundays. 4 Sv. Mikolajaus (phone: 623069).

VILNIAUS UNIVERSITETAS (VILNIUS UNIVERSITY) Founded in 1579, this is the oldest university in the Baltics and among the oldest in Eastern Europe. The best entrance to this ancient school is through the gates between the bell tower and the Church of St. John. Gothic when it was built in 1387, St. John developed some Renaissance characteristics when the Jesuits took it over in 1571. The church's 121-foot belfry offers an excellent view of the city. The *Museum of Scientific Thought,* formerly housed in the church (to the consternation of churchgoing Lithuanians) was closed in 1992 following a vote by students and faculty. Since it was built and expanded regularly over the course of centuries, the university, which has been responsible for the education of almost every important historical figure in Lithuanian history since its founding, is an ensemble of architectural styles. The oldest buildings are situated opposite the church and to the right of the courtyard entrance. There are 12 inner courtyards, hallowed halls saturated with frescoes, ample statuary, and libraries and bookstores with impressive collections of old books and manuscripts. At the corner of Universiteto and Skapo Gatve.

DAUKANTO AIKŠTE (DAUKANTO SQUARE) During the 15th century, this square was the site of the Episcopal Palace, which was rebuilt several times over the years. What finally emerged from the persistent renovation and reconstruction is the present palace, last rebuilt in 1832 in the Empire style. Sitting on this square is the late-18th-century Palace of the Governor General, one of the finest buildings in the city. Napoleon stayed here for a while when the French entered Vilnius in 1812. At the end of the Russo-French War, Kutuzov, the great Russian field marshal, used the palace as his residence. France has now unabashedly reclaimed the palace as its embassy. Across from Vilnius University, at the corner of Universiteto and Skapo Gatve.

SVENTO ONOS BAŽNYČIA (CHURCH OF ST. ANNA) When Napoleon first saw this church on his march to Moscow, he reportedly said, "I want to carry this church back to France in the palm of my hand." Said to be the most beautiful Gothic church in Lithuania, it is sculpted from 33 different forms of red and yellow brick that wind and bend to create a complex yet graceful façade and majestic spires, towers, arcs, and pinnacles. Though it originally was built in 1500, the ceiling vaults collapsed in 1563, and the church was reconstructed 20 years later. Photo buffs may want to bring a wide-angle lens to capture the church, but it may be difficult to get a full, clear shot because of its size (73 feet long, 33 feet wide). The church is open to the public except during services, which are held weekdays at 7:30 AM and 7:30 PM; Sundays at 9 and 11 AM and 7:30 PM. 8 Maironio Gatve.

SVENTO MYKOLD BAŽNYČIA (ST. MICHAEL'S CHURCH) Across the street from the Church of St. Anna, this is the only Renaissance-style church in Vilnius. It was built in the late 1500s and now contains the *Museum of Architecture,* although the Catholic church wants it back. Sv. Mykolo Gatve, near the intersection of Maironio Gatve and Volano Gatve.

SVENTO BERNADINES BAŽNYČIA (ST. BERNADINE'S CHURCH) Though cast in the shadow of St. Anna's and not nearly as striking, this 15th-century fortress-style church contains beautiful Gothic frescoes. It was built as part of the defensive wall that surrounded Vilnius, and is currently under restoration, although for use as a ceremonial, secular building, rather than as a house of worship. Near the intersection of Maironio Gatve and Volano Gatve.

JYDU GETAS (JEWISH GHETTO) Before World War II, 70,000 Jews lived in Vilnius and comprised about half the population of the city. In 1944, following mass executions by Nazi and Lithuanian troops, only 800 were left. Under Nazi occupation, most Jews were forced to live in two ghettos that occupied most of the Old Town. Three plaques written in Yiddish and in Lithuanian have recently been placed in the Old Town on Gaono Gatve, on Ligonines, and on Rudininku. They read: "Between July 1941 and September 1943, here stood the gates to the Jewish ghetto through which 20,000 Jews walked to their deaths." Most of the Jewish quarter was destroyed during World War II bombings, and the remaining traces of what was then called the "Jerusalem of Lithuania" disappeared under Stalin's "reconstruction plan." One of the last traditional courtyards of the Jewish quarter can be visited on 2 Zydu Gatve off Stikliu Gatve.

ELSEWHERE IN THE CITY

ZALIAS TILTAS (GREEN BRIDGE) Formerly called Chernyakhovsky Bridge, it crosses the Neris River. The lifelike statues on either end attest to the work ethic of the Lithuanian people. Unfortunately, the statues were commissioned under Stalin, and the people of Vilnius consider them merely another example of the platitudes the now banned Communist government imposed on their country. (They may well be gone by the time you read this.) Even so, the sculptures of a man and woman, soldiers, and peasants bearing sheaves of wheat are beautiful. To the right of the bridge is a medieval-style castle with a tower. This was once a private home and, at one time, served as the offices of the Singer Sewing Machine Company. Between Kalvariju Gatve, near the *Lieutva* hotel, and Vilniaus Gatve on the other side of the Neris.

SINAGOGAS (SYNAGOGUE) This still-functioning synagogue must be one of the world's few to sport a Byzantine onion dome. It's the only surviving synagogue of dozens that existed in Vilnius before World War II. The synagogue has irregular hours due to ongoing renovations. 39 Plylimo Gatve.

TELEVIZIJOS BOKŠTAS (TELEVISION TOWER) Lithuania's 1,070-foot TV tower was the focal point of the brutal Soviet military crackdown in the Baltics in January 1991. Thirteen Lithuanians died on January 13, 1991, trying in vain to defend the tower from Soviet takeover. In one sense they failed, as the tower was occupied by Soviet troops until the August 1991 coup attempt against Mikhail Gorbachev, but in a larger sense, it became one of the symbols of the fading power of the Kremlin hard-liners, which climaxed in the failed coup. There are memorial markers to those who were killed and a small museum explaining the dramatic events. Lithuanians come to lay flowers daily at the foot of the tower. Several tours are offered daily, some in English. The small admission price includes a visit to the observation deck at the 540-foot level, with a view extending 30 miles around Vilnius. 10 Suderves Gatve.

VINGIO PARKAS (VINGIS PARK) This, the largest park in Vilnius, is surrounded on three sides by the Neris River, and has been a popular spot for Lithuanian nationalist rallies. A folk music festival is held here every 5 years on a stage that can hold up to 20,000 singers (the next festival is set for 1995). In the Middle Ages, the park belonged to the Jesuits, and later to the Russian czars. More recently it was a popular spot for Lithuanian nationalist rallies. Enter from the main entrance on Ciurlionio Gatve, and proceed up the walk to the center of the park for a spectacular view of fields next to the concert stage. Botanical gardens are located near the children's railway on the riverbank. The *Lakstingala Café,* an outdoor eatery open mid-May to mid-September, sits near the stage and is a fine place for rest and refreshment. For information on concerts and events call 632869.

Sources and Resources

TOURIST INFORMATION

The former *Intourist* office, now known as the *Lithuanian Travel Agency,* has its home base on the ground floor of the *Lietuva* hotel (20 Ukmerges Gatve; phone: 614612). Service is only fair as the agency is geared primarily toward organizing group sightseeing tours and will offer little assistance to individual travelers. There are a few other agencies in Vilnius that with advance notice will arrange for sightseeing: *Aliso* (34 Savaboriu Gatve; phone: 230676; fax: 230788), *Baltic Tours* (9-1 Vaizganto Gatve; phone: 227979; fax: 226767), and *Lithuanian Tours* (18 Seimyniskiu Gatve; phone: 353931; fax: 351815).

> **NOTE** Economic turmoil, including frequent and steep price increases on many goods and services, makes it impossible to provide accurate information on prices, including the cost of basic services such as public transportation and telephone calls. In the fall of 1992, Lithuania introduced its own transitional currency, the "talonas," or coupon, and was hoping to move toward a fully convertible currency, the "litas," later this year.

LOCAL COVERAGE Next-day English-language newspapers, including *USA Today* and the *International Herald Tribune,* are available at the *Astoria, Draugyste,* and *Lietuva* hotels. Local publications such as the *Lithuanian Weekly,* the *Baltic Independent, Baltic News,* and the *Baltic Observer* can be purchased at newspaper kiosks. The *Lietuva* hotel offers "Sky News" (Britain's all-news satellite channel), as well as "MTV" and a German entertainment channel. *Radio Vilnius* broadcasts a 30-minute news report in English at 10 PM. Some English-language books on Vilnius and Lithuania can be purchased for hard currency at the *Penki Kontinental* (Five Continents) bookstore (39/6 Vilniaus Gatve); open weekdays from 10 AM to 7 PM, Saturdays from 10 AM to 3 PM.

TELEPHONE Lithuania now uses a 370 international direct-dial country code; the city area for Vilnius is 2. Several hotels provide international direct dialing to the US (see *Checking In*). Public phones require a *zetonas* (token) that can be purchased at any post office.

GETTING AROUND

AIRPORT Vilnius Airport (phone: 630201 for information 24 hours a day) is about 5 miles (8 km) from the center of the city. The main terminal was undergoing renovations at press time with plans for a duty-free shop to be completed later this year. Bus No. 2 travels from the airport to the city center; it's often easier (and fairly inexpensive) to take a taxi, especially if you have luggage. Taxi drivers may ask for hard currency. The fare should not exceed $10. For more details on scheduled airlines to Lithuania, see FACTS IN BRIEF.

BUS AND TROLLEY Public transportation is very inexpensive but rather irregular and crowded due to the fuel shortage. It's much simpler — and also inexpensive — to take taxis.

CAR RENTAL Automobile travel is becoming an increasingly popular mode of transportation in Lithuania. Cars can be rented for hard currency through

Eva (14 Jacionu; phone: 649419). Cars with a driver can be rented at the *Astoria* or *Lietuva* hotels; and the *Litofinn* service station (24 Aguonu Gatve; phone: 226504) has plenty of gas for hard currency only.

TAXI The easiest and most inexpensive way of getting around Vilnius. Taxi stands are scattered throughout the city, but beware of cabs parked outside hotel entrances. They often charge three or four times the usual amount, which still might end up costing you less than $10 for a ride across town. Don't be afraid to negotiate. Better still, ask your hotel to order a private taxi.

TRAIN There is rail service to Moscow, most Baltic cities, and many other destinations from Vilnius. The overnight train from Vilnius to Riga (Latvia) is a 6- to 7-hour ride, depending on the number of stops; the trip to Tallinn (Estonia) takes 13 to 14 hours; the journey to Moscow, 13 hours on the express train but as many as 23 hours on the milk run. Tickets for destinations in Lithuania must be purchased at the station (16 Gelezinkelio Aikšte; phone: 630088 or 630086). Tickets to the former Soviet Union can be bought at the sales office (3 Sopeno Gatve; phone: 623044). Travelers are advised to buy tickets in advance as train travel is popular here. To avoid complications, contact the *Lithuanian Travel Agency* (see *Tourist Information,* above) or your hotel service bureau. They will charge you hard currency but again, the price far outweighs the hours of waiting in line.

LOCAL SERVICES

DENTIST *SBT Private Clinic* (24 Seskines; phone: 468583) has an English-speaking staff. Open weekdays from 1 to 6 PM. Also the *Red Cross Hospital* (6 Zygimantu; phone: 616258).

DRY CLEANER Inquire at your hotel.

MEDICAL EMERGENCY First try the service bureau of your hotel, or contact the clinic and hospital listed above.

NATIONAL/INTERNATIONAL COURIER *Express Mail Service* run by the Lithuanian Post Office (7 Vokieciu; phone: 625670) will deliver parcels weighing up to one-half pound to the US within 5 days. Hours are weekdays from 8 AM to 8 PM; weekends from 11 AM to 7 PM.

OFFICE RENTAL EQUIPMENT Check with your hotel service bureau.

POST OFFICE The main post office is located at 7 Gedimino Gatve and is open weekdays from 8 AM to 8 PM; weekends from 11 AM to 7 PM.

SECRETARY/STENOGRAPHER Inquire at your hotel.

SHOE REPAIR *While-U-Wait* repair shop (22 Vilniaus; phone: 618232). Open weekdays from 8 AM to 7 PM.

TRANSLATOR Contact your hotel service bureau, or call *Litinterp* (10 Vokieciu; phone: 612040; fax: 222982).

SPECIAL EVENTS

Lithuanian Independence Day — marking Lithuania's first period of independence — is celebrated on February 16 with special masses in the churches, street fairs, folk dancing, more than an earful of music, and theatrical productions. Lithuanians also celebrate March 11, the anniversary of their 1990 declaration of independence from the Soviet Union. July 6 is a state holiday commemorating the anniversary of the coronation of the Grand Duke Mindaugas of Lithuania. The country also observes Roman Catholic church holidays.

MUSEUMS

In addition to those described in *Special Places,* other museums worth visiting include the following:

APHITEKTĀROS MUZIEJUS (MUSEUM OF ARCHITECTURE) Housed in the Church of St. Michael, this museum is devoted to Lithuanian architecture and the construction and reconstruction of historic monuments. Open from 11 AM to 7 PM; closed Tuesdays. Admission charge. 13 Sv. Mykolo Gatve (phone: 616409).

DAILES PARODOS RĀMAI (PALACE OF ART EXHIBITIONS) This modern structure won the 1973 USSR Council of Minister's Award for architecture (a dubious honor, considering the building style generally favored by the Soviets). Inside are a number of art exhibitions and the *Gelezinis Vilkas II* (Iron Wolf II) café (see *Eating Out*); there's a permanent open-air sculpture garden in the courtyard. American movies are shown with subtitles in Lithuanian. Next door, the *Daile Centrinis Salonas* (Central Art Shop) boasts the best selection of paintings and drawings in Vilnius. Open daily from 11 AM to 7 PM. Admission charge. 2 Vokieciu Gatve (phone: 617097).

ISTORIJOS IR ETNOGRAFIJOS MUZIEJUS (MUSEUM OF HISTORY AND ETHNOGRAPHY) A collection of more than 300,000 items covers everything you possibly could want to know about Lithuanian archaeology, ethnography, folk art, and history. Open from 11 AM to 6 PM; closed Tuesdays. Admission charge. 1 Arsenalo Gatve, at the foot of Castle Hill (phone: 627774).

LIETUVOS VALSTYBINIS ZYDU MUZIEJUS (LITHUANIAN STATE JEWISH MUSEUM) A small green wooden building housing an impressive exhibit on the Holocaust. Many of the documents on display, including rare records from the Gestapo, were obtained after the Soviet KGB handed over archives to the Lithuanian government in late 1991. All exhibits are identified in Lithuanian, Yiddish, and English; but there are also English-speaking guides, some of them Holocaust survivors who give truly informative tours. Open weekdays from 10 AM to 5 PM. Admission charge. Plylimo Gatve (phone: 620730).

MEMORIALINIS BUTAS ADOMO MICKEVIČIAUS (ADAM MICKIEWICZ MEMORIAL APARTMENT) Paintings, sculpture, photos, documents, and other personal effects from the time this 19th-century Polish poet lived here. Open Fridays from 2 to 6 PM; Saturdays from 10 AM to 2 PM. Admission charge. 11 Bernadinu Gatve.

SHOPPING

The Baltic states are known for their vast quantities of beautiful amber. You can find chunks of it for sale in most souvenir shops for talonas or dollars. These golden nuggets are an especially good buy in Lithuania (don't be put off by the small "flaws," such as pieces of trapped insects or twigs — Lithuanians prefer this because then they know the amber is real, not manufactured). Linen and folk handicrafts are also good souvenir choices. Permission is needed to export some artwork, antiques, rare books, and other articles of historic, artistic, scientific, or cultural value. Check with your hotel service bureau if you have any doubts. Many stores are closed Sundays and Mondays. Some accept only hard currency and only a few accepted credit cards.

Several shops in the Old Town have excellent selections of amber jewelry including *Amber and Sage* (Aušros Vartu; no phone) and *Daile Centrinis Salonas* (2 Vokieciu; phone: 619516); both are open Tuesdays through Saturdays from 10 AM to 7 PM. Also worth a visit is the *Paroda-Pardavimas Sauluva* (22 Pilies Gatve; phone: 221696), known for its wide array of amber jewelry; a good selection of ceramic masks, paintings and drawings; and the traditional *verba* (a bouquet of dried flowers and twigs blessed on *Palm Sunday*). Open daily from 10 AM to 7 PM. At *Verba* (10 Saviciaus; phone: 224249) the collection of jewelry is smaller, but the prices are quite reasonable.

The Old Town is also the place to pick up a beautiful drawing, water-color, or oil painting available at the *Arka Art Gallery* (7 Aušros Vartu; phone: 221319), open Tuesdays through Saturdays from 11 AM to 7 PM, Saturdays from noon to 5 PM. The *Langas Art Gallery* (8 Asmenos; phone: 221505) is another fine place to browse and is open Mondays through Saturdays from 11 AM to 7 PM. Both *Daile Centrinis Salonas* (see above) and *Vilnius ir Daile* (6 Barboros Radvilaites; phone: 226611) specialize in landscapes and are open Tuesdays through Saturdays from 10 AM to 7 PM.

Try the *Dizaino Salonas* (4 Mesiniu; phone: 220179) for leather wear, jewelry (including amber and precious stones), as well as paintings, ceramics, and some original handmade clothing. Open weekdays from 11 AM to 7 PM.

SPORTS AND FITNESS

The athletic traveler will want to stay at the *Villon* hotel (see *Checking In*), which offers a broad range of sports and leisure activities including horseback riding, boating, swimming, and fishing. Vilnius has a *Palace of Sports and Culture* (21 Sporto Gatve; phone: 698468) that offers daily aerobics classes as well as use of all fitness equipment. Unfortunately, the city's two pools were closed at press time due to the energy crisis. Inquire nevertheless at the *Vandens Sporto Rumai* (Vandens Sports Palace) with locations at 13 Erfurto Gatve (phone: 269041) and 1 Pakrantes Gatve (phone: 758923) where swimming, aerobics, and other sports facilities can be found. Tennis fans will enjoy the facilities at the *Sports Center* (6 Zemaites Gatve; phone: 660055), which features two indoor courts.

THEATER

Vilnius offers a fair amount of cultural diversity. Check your hotel service desk or the *Lithuanian Travel Agency* for specific information regarding performances.

The *Akademinis Dramos Teatras* (Academic Drama Theater; 4 Gedimino Gatve; phone: 629771) is known for its presentation of familiar works in traditional style. Innovative, experimental works are a rarity on the main stage, though they are the raison d'être of the smaller, more intimate stage in the back of this Scandinavian-style building. Plays are presented in Lithuanian only; closed Mondays. Performances at the *Akademinis Operos ir Dramos Teatras* (Academic Opera and Drama Theater; 1 Vienuolio Gatve; phone: 620636) are confined to a standard fare of Russian and Western classics, with a few diversions into contemporary works. At *Jaunimo Teatras* (Youth Theater; 5 Arkliu Gatve; phone: 626732), housed in a 17th-century palace, performances are more experimental; the resident troupe frequently sells out. If you call in advance, you can make arrangements for an English translation of the play's script. In the same building as the *Juanimo Teatras* is the *Teatras Lélé* (Children's Puppet Theater; phone: 616012), with performances daily except Mondays. The *Rusu Dramos Teatras* (Russian Drama Theater; 13 Basanaviciaus Gatve; phone: 620552) stages works based on Russian classics, but only in the Russian language. It's also closed Mondays. Many local theater troupes go on tour in summer.

MUSIC

Every *New Year's Eve,* the *Akademinis Operos ir Dramos Teatras* (Academic Opera and Drama Theater; see above) packs in a full house for its performance of Verdi's *La Traviata*. The acoustics could be better here, but the comfortable, high-backed seats and eclectic architecture compensate. Most interesting is the tradition of walking arm-in-arm in a circle during intermission. The *National Philharmonic* (Nacionaline Filharmonija; 5 Aušros Vartu; phone: 627165) offers weekly performances after a year-long break.

NIGHTCLUBS AND NIGHTLIFE

Vilnius now boasts some of the best jazz clubs in the Baltics; although they appeal to music lovers of all ages, they attract mostly the twentysomething crowd. Check out the *Galerija Langas* (8 Asmenos; phone: 221505), a smoke-filled basement club with a great saxophone player. Open Wednesdays, Fridays, and Saturdays from 7 PM to the wee hours. The *Leandra Café* (10 Labdariu; no phone) and the *Galerija Arka* (7 Aušros Vartu; phone: 221319) sometimes feature jazz concerts. And for dancing and the late-night bar scene, try *Zirmunai* (67 Zirmanu; phone: 779939), open nightly from 11 PM to 7 AM.

Best in Town

CHECKING IN

Hotel accommodations in Lithuania can be booked through the *Lithuanian Travel Agency* or your own travel agent. Compared to its two Baltic sisters, Vilnius lacks a true luxury class hotel (with the possible exception of the *Marbre*). But what the establishments listed below lack in Western-style comfort, they make up for in friendliness and good service. At press time, all hotels were requesting payment in hard currency from foreigners until the government introduces a fully convertible currency, expected sometime later this year. (That move is not, however, expected to dramatically influence room rates as hotels will charge the equivalent of the dollar room rate in local currency.) Most hotels accept credit cards. Due to the energy crisis, the winter room temperature in hotels is kept at a chilly 65F, which makes winter travel to Lithuania a bit uncomfortable. Insist that the hotel provide you with an electric heater if the room is too cold. The smaller hotels are more obliging than their larger counterparts.

The fluctuating economy makes it difficult to provide accurate rates for hotels. We suggest that you check costs — and the operative exchange rate — immediately prior to your departure. Most of Vilnius's major hotels have complete facilities for the business traveler. Those hotels listed below as having "business services" usually offer such conveniences as English-speaking concierge, meeting rooms, photocopiers, computers, translation services, and express checkout, among others. Call the hotel for additional information. All telephone numbers are in the 2 city code unless otherwise noted.

Astoria Built in 1901 and recently taken over by a Norwegian firm, this lovely establishment in the heart of the Old Town gets high marks for friendly service. The 37 rooms are small and cozy; all feature baths and showers, TV sets, and international direct-dial phones. Ask for a room with a view of St. Casimir's Church. There are no business services in the hotel, but the staff can direct guests to places where there are conference rooms, photocopiers, and English-translation services. Car rental with driver is available. Guests are greeted at the airport when requested. Make reservations well in advance: This hotel is very popular and booked solid for weeks during the summer season. There is restaurant, bar, and café. 35/2 Didzioji Gatve (phone: 224031; fax: 220097).

Draugyste (Friendship) Formerly reserved for Communist Party officials, this drab, 114-room Soviet-style establishment is desperately lacking in charm and character. Rooms have private baths and are equipped with cable TV sets and refrigerators. However, international calls must be arranged through the hotel. Business services. 84 Ciurlionio Gatve (phone: 662603; fax: 263101).

Lietuva (Lithuania) Not bad for a hotel built by the Soviets; there are flashes of Western comfort and attention to detail. Several floors of the 24-story property were being renovated at press time. There are 335 rooms equipped with private baths, 2 restaurants, including a grill and a bar with an excellent view of the city from the 21st floor (see *Eating Out*). Business services. International calls must be arranged through the hotel. 20 Ukmerges Gatve (phone: 356018; fax: 356270).

Mabre With a bit of luck, you might be able to get a reservation at this small German hotel located in a former monastery. Each of the 4 duplex suites is beautifully decorated and features a bar, satellite TV, refrigerators, and bath. Business services. 13 Maironio Gatve (phone: 614162; fax: 613086).

Sarunas Opened last year, this hotel — owned by Lithuanian basketball star Sarunas Marciulionis — is geared to business travelers. The 26 large rooms are equipped with TV sets, phones with direct international dialing, and full bathrooms. Guests also enjoy a restaurant complete with basketball sneakers dangling from the ceiling. The one drawback is its location: A bit far from the Old Town and the city center, its guest have to rely on either car rental or taxi to get around. 4 Raitininku Gatve (phone: 354888; fax: 290072).

Villon Located about 20 minutes (15 miles) outside of Vilnius, this new hotel and recreation complex has a country club atmosphere. The 73 rooms are small but cozy and include satellite TV. The main attraction here, however, is the range of recreational activities, including an indoor swimming pool, a sauna, horseback riding, boating, and fishing. Business services. There is also a shuttle bus service available for sightseeing in Vilnius. Villon (phone: 651385; fax: 616582).

EATING OUT

If for no other reason, it's worth visiting Vilnius just to eat. The city boasts some of the best restaurants in the Baltics. The best dining can be found in the small, mostly privately owned cafés in the Old Town, some in the city's oldest and most historic buildings. Hotel restaurants are still typically Soviet — loud, boisterous, and with fairly limited menus.

Traditional Lithuanian food is similar to Polish fare. It consists of heavy peasant bread, a slew of potato dishes such as *bulvinai blynai* (potato pancakes), *cepelinai* ("zeppelins" — cylindrical-shaped potato dumplings), and *vedarai* (a potato croquette served with a lot of sour cream). The main course is pork more often than not, but many restaurants have started offering a wider selection of meat and many are experimenting with game.

The dramatically fluctuating economy makes it difficult to provide accurate prices for restaurants. Lithuania introduced a transitional currency, called "talonas," or coupon, in 1992 and was hoping to stabilize the economy before launching its own fully convertible currency, the "litas." Some restaurants request only hard currency; call ahead and check. Meals in local currency are very inexpensive. A hearty meal for two, including wine and dessert, usually costs less than the equivalent of $20. Note: No credit cards are accepted for payment in local currency. All telephone numbers are in the 2 city code unless otherwise noted.

Arka This outdoor café located in the Old Town has live jazz music during the summer and is a favorite spot for Vilnius's thriving arts community whose works are often on display in the adjoining art gallery. The menu features light snacks and drinks. Open daily from 11 AM to 11 PM. No reservations. Local currency only. 7 Aušros Vartu (phone: 221319).

Gelezinis Vilkas II (The Iron Wolf II) Locals favor this café, which offers delicious salads plus such hard-to-find specialties as mussels, escargots, and avocados. The menu is in Lithuanian and English. Open daily from 11 AM to 10 PM. No reservations. Local currency only accepted. 2 Vokieciu Gatve in the Old Town (no phone).

Golden Dragon The first Chinese restaurant in the Baltics has a limited but authentic menu. Dishes, including fried chicken, hot spicy salad, and a variety of shrimp and fish specialties, are prepared by Oriental chefs. Service is excellent. Open daily from noon to 10 PM; closed Wednesdays. Reservations advised. Hard currency only. 10 Aguonu Gatve (phone: 262701).

Ida Basar Located in a the cellar of a lovely stone building in the Old Town, this German restaurant is a favorite among diplomats and other members of Vilnius's foreign service community. The menu includes delicious soups and such traditional German fare as sausage and stews. The friendly waiters speak only German, although the menu is in English, German, and Lithuanian. Open daily from noon to 1 AM. Reservations advised. Hard currency only. 3 Subaciaus Gatve in the Old Town (phone: 628484).

Literatu Svetaine (Literary Café) Once a hip place for Vilnius's intellectual crowd, this café is now mostly frequented by locals who enjoy the convenience of its central location on Gedimino Gatve, the city's main shopping street. In the evening, there's soft piano music. The menu is strictly Lithuanian and Russian and the waiters do their best to welcome guests — although they don't speak very good English. Open daily for lunch and dinner. Reservations necessary. Hard currency and major credit cards accepted. 1 Gedimino Gatve (phone: 611889).

Lokys (Bear) A comfortable café where you can get a fine meal and local spirits. It is very popular with the younger set and frequently crowded. Some tables are set in intimate nooks in the brick and stone walls of this 16th-century cellar. As its name suggests, this eatery specializes in wild game such as boar and elk that the restaurant manager obtains from a local hunting club, although you can also choose from tamer cuts of chicken, beef, pork, or fish. No dessert is offered, only coffee. Open daily from noon to midnight. Reservations advised. Local currency only. 9 Ktikliu Gatve in the Old Town (phone: 629046).

Medininkai Wonderfully located in a 16th-century multi-arched, stone structure just beyond the entrance of the Old Town. When reconstruction began on this building several years ago, the 18th-century plaster was removed to reveal the original Gothic design and Renaissance-style details underneath. This is a cozy place with several small, intimate rooms, heavy wooden furniture, and a spiral staircase leading to a second-floor balcony. One tiny room is just big enough for two. The food is good but very heavy and the menu is limited — potatoes, potato pancakes, pork, and stuffed meat are common. In summer, there is outdoor dining in a wonderful sculpture garden. Open daily for lunch and dinner. Reservations for dinner only. Local currency only. 4 Aušros Vartu in the Old Town.

Panorama The dining room on the 21st floor of the *Lietuva* hotel serves typically Soviet-style food — a pre-set menu of *doktorskaya* (meatloaf) and *kartofyel tushoniy so svyezhimi gribami* (potatoes stewed with mushrooms). It affords a great view of Vilnius, so try for a table near the window. The weekend floor show is bad, but borders on kitsch. Open daily for lunch and dinner. Reservations advised. Local currency only for food, but hard currency only for alcoholic beverages. 20 Ukmerges Gatve (phone: 356038).

Pauksciu Takas (Milky Way) At the 540-foot level of the TV tower (better known as the symbol of the violent Soviet military crackdown in January, 1991), this revolving dining room and bar offers a panoramic bird's-eye view of

Vilnius. The restaurant makes one full turn every 50 minutes. Traditional fare is served, but the view is the real draw here. Open daily 10 AM to 10 PM. Reservations necessary. Local currency only. 10 Suderves Gatve (phone: 458877).

Senasis Rusys (Old Cellar) One of the most popular restaurants in Vilnius, the decor here features a vaulted ceiling, stained glass windows, and heavy wooden furniture. The bar adjacent to the basement restaurant is a great spot for a drink or cappuccino. The service can be slow, but the traditional fare can be very good (stuffed pork a specialty). Smoking is not permitted in the restaurant. Open daily from 10 AM to 8 PM. Reservations advised in the summer. Local currency only for food, but hard currency only for alcoholic beverages. No credit cards accepted. 16 Sv. Ignoto Gatve (phone: 450777 or 458877).

Stikliai This privately owned dining spot, awash with antiques, crystal, and crisp white linen tablecloths, is hands down the best in Vilnius, if not in the Baltics — some even say it's tops in all of the former Soviet Union. The continental menu is extensive, offering many dishes — such as veal and goose — rarely available in this part of the world. The owner travels throughout Europe looking for new dishes to add to his repertoire. Waiters dressed in tuxedos and white linen aprons are attentive but not cloying. Piped-in classical music is a regular accompaniment to the meal (the restaurant sponsors the *Lithuanian Chamber Music Orchestra*). The menu is available in English, and the waiters speak English, though with some difficulty. No smoking permitted. Open noon to midnight; Mondays noon to 5 PM. Local currency only for food, but hard currency only for alcoholic beverages. 7 Gaono Gatve (phone: 627971).

Stikliai Yes, it's the same name as the place above. It's a beer bar just around the corner from the above-mentioned restaurant and owned by the same people. Beer — particularly the German variety — is the big attraction here. The fare is designed to complement the beer and it's a lot more creative than peanuts and pretzels — there's the *salatk pivu* (beer salad), for example, cubes of bread and cheese combined with mayonnaise. Even American-style cheeseburgers are available. There are two halls — one smoking and one nonsmoking. Open 11 AM to 9 PM daily. No reservations. Local currency only. 7 Gaono Gatve (phone: 222109).

Warsaw

Warsaw, like its people, is a surprise, and it takes a little effort to get to know them both. On first impression, the capital seems as gray and forbidding as the poured-concrete buildings with which the Poles rebuilt their city after it was reduced to rubble during World War II. Though pollution is a fact of life, the skyline, dominated by the Stalinesque Palace of Culture and Science and a few glass structures housing the city's latest hotels, seems as no-nonsense and functional as the almost 2 million people who live in the Polish capital.

Poland (pop. 38 million), much larger than its Eastern European neighbors, was the first of the Soviet satellites to shed the yoke of Communism in 1989. It also took the most radical route toward dismantling its centrally controlled economy. Under the new Economic Reform Plan (started in January 1990), price controls were lifted, subsidies to state-owned industries were withdrawn, and barriers to private business and foreign investment were removed. The new democratically elected officials warned that the going would be tough and they were right. Disappointment that Western living standards were not immediately evident was heightened by wages freezes in the state sector, spiraling inflation, and fear of unemployment. With the captive East Bloc market freed, and more desirable goods pouring in from the West, Polish industries fell into a deep recession. A gap between rich and poor opened, and social ills such as crime, homelessness, and joblessness — all officially nonexistent under the Communists — surfaced. In a country that had longed to taste the sweet joys of Western freedom, euphoria was not spontaneously erupting on every street corner.

There were positive signs, however. The days of spending hours waiting on line for shoddy goods were over. With their extra time, many Poles went into private business, if only "tailgate" enterprises that flourished from the backs of cars and trucks. By last year, Warsaw was the first among the Eastern European cities to emerge from the post-Communist recession. And today, despite their very real economic struggle and the poverty level of the country as a whole, most Poles find pleasure not only in all the products and services available, but also in their vibrant free press, the end of the secret police, democratic elections, and Poland's re-emergence as a member of the European community.

Visitors will find Warsaw a city at the heart of a nation in transition. It is possible to see a horse-drawn cart heading down a traffic-congested main thoroughfare to deliver a single crate of vegetables to a modern supermarket. The capital is blooming with new hotels, restaurants, and shops — although with prices high and salaries low by Western standards, many Poles cannot yet partake of the bounty. Western investors and Polish companies are working toward a new standard of quality and

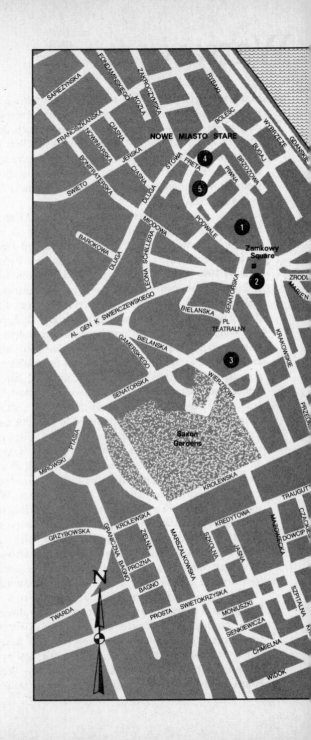

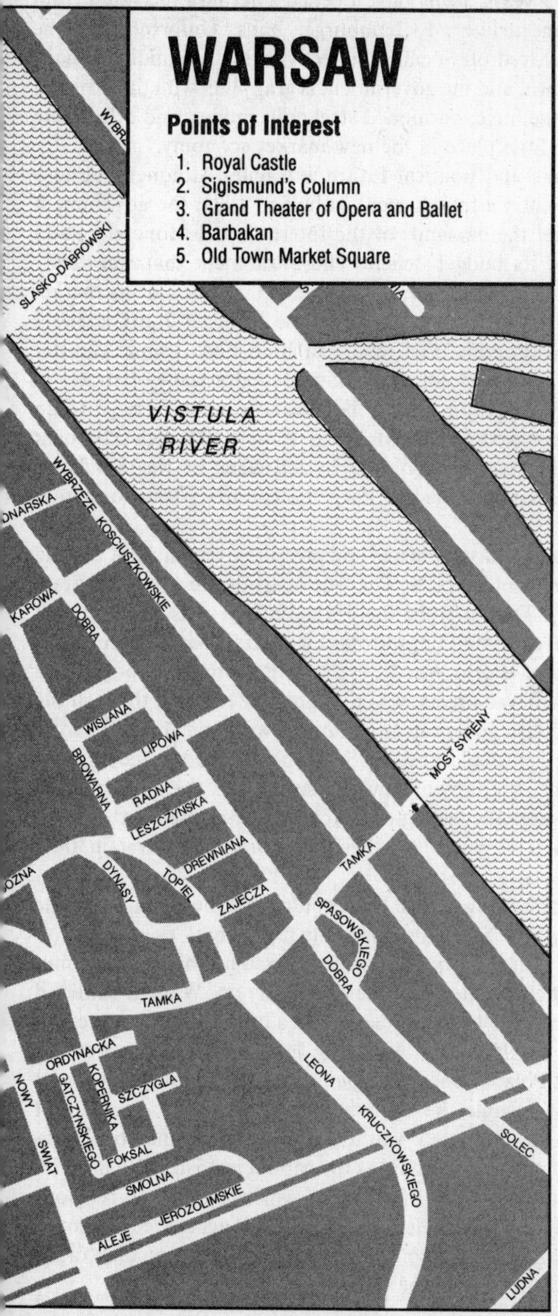

WARSAW

Points of Interest

1. Royal Castle
2. Sigismund's Column
3. Grand Theater of Opera and Ballet
4. Barbakan
5. Old Town Market Square

WYBR

ŚLĄSKO-DĄBROWSKI

VISTULA
RIVER

DONARSKA

WYBRZEŻE KOŚCIUSZKOWSKIE

KAROWA

DOBRA

WIŚLANA

LIPOWA

BROWARNA

RADNA

LESZCZYŃSKA

MOST SYRENY

DYNASY

TOPIEL

DREWNIANA

TAMKA

ZAJĘCZA

SPASOWSKIEGO

OZNA

DOBRA

TAMKA

LEONA

ORDYNACKA

KOPERNIKA

SZCZYGLA

NOWY

GAŁCZYŃSKIEGO

KRUCZKOWSKIEGO

SOLEC

ŚWIAT

FOKSAL

SMOLNA

JEROZOLIMSKIE

ALEJE

LUDNA

service. In the last 3 years, firms have opened offering everything from international package delivery to hamburger buns. Unfortunately, the small farmers who staved off Socialist collectivization are finding it hard to make it on their own, and the government is grappling with the problem of what to do with the huge, outmoded steel mills, mines, and other state industries that have little place in the new market economy.

Poland's economic and political future is fragile. Although Western creditors cut the country's foreign debt in half in 1991, the government has struggled to meet the demands of the International Monetary Fund for strict control of its budget deficit. The Parliament that was freely selected in October 1991 was deeply fragmented. A turn from market reforms to appease public protest under Prime Minister Jan Olszewski proved disastrous, ending his brief tenure in June 1992. Prime Minister Hanna Suchocka promised political stability, ended a wave of strikes in late 1992, and scored a major victory last year with the passage of an austerity budget approved by international lenders. Though President Lech Wałęsa has not electrified Poles as he did when he was Solidarity union chairman, he has managed to keep the country's transformation under control.

Despite these modern-day problems and pressures, remnants of the Old World curiously persist in Warsaw. The true heart of the city is the Stare Miasto (Old Town). Dating from the 13th century, it is a mixture of Renaissance and baroque buildings around a central marketplace. After the Nazi destruction of World War II, everything, from the wrought-iron shop signs to the medieval streets, was thoughtfully restored through the joint efforts of the Polish government, volunteer workers, and Poles from all over the world — particularly the US — who donated money for the restoration. To some, the now-mellowing newness of the buildings has given the renovated area the feeling of a Hollywood set. But to the Poles, the new Old Town is a symbol of their determination to retain their heritage.

The village of Warszawa was on a trade route from the Black Sea to the Baltic in the 13th century. Some historians say it goes back even farther to the founding in the 10th century of Stare Brodno, a neighboring community that later was incorporated into the city. Early on, Warsaw achieved prominence, probably due to its protection by a castle, and its successful administration by a bailiff and a city council. In 1526, it was incorporated into the kingdom of Poland. Soon the *sejm,* or parliament, began to meet here, and in 1573 it became the site where the kings were elected (not surprisingly, the castle ultimately was transformed into the royal residence), and Warsaw replaced Cracow as the capital in 1596. Also in 1573, the *sejm* approved the Compact of Warsaw, which guaranteed religious freedom to all non-Roman Catholics in Poland. This act spared the country the religious wars pitting Protestants against Catholics that raged across many parts of Europe at the time.

The Poles have had to work hard to preserve their past and their identity as a people. Three times in Warsaw's long history there have been attempts to annihilate the city. The Swedes razed Warsaw in the 17th century, and Russia sacked it in 1794 while suppressing an insurrection. Poland ceased to exist as a nation when it was partitioned in 1795 and Warsaw was given to Prussia. Napoleon captured the city in 1806 and formed the Duchy of Warsaw, but it was retaken by the Russians in 1813. Poland was not restored as a nation until after World War I. During the period between the two world wars, however, Warsaw came into its own as the capital of Poland, and with the birth of such prestigious events as the *International Chopin Competition* for pianists in 1927 and the *Henryk Wieniawski International Competition* for violinists in 1935, it emerged as one of Central Europe's leading cultural lights.

Then came the German occupation of World War II and the oppression of the Warsaw ghetto. At the turn of the century, the city contained the largest urban concentration of Jews in the world, a population that greatly increased when German and Polish Jews were shipped to Warsaw while Hitler's Nazis were pondering the details of the "Final Solution." From 1940 to 1943, almost half a million Jews died of starvation or were executed in Warsaw or were transported to death camps. The Jews of the Warsaw ghetto, which was surrounded by a high wall, inspired the world in 1943 by rising up in a fierce, albeit futile, battle against the Germans, who burned down the ghetto. The following year, all the underground groups in Warsaw united in a 63-day battle against the Nazis, which is remembered as the Warsaw Uprising. When that failed, the Nazis began their systematic destruction of the city. Hitler issued an order that not one stone be left standing. More than 200,000 people were killed, and most of those who survived were deported.

Warsaw and its people were devastated by the war. And the city remembers. Plaques and monuments are everywhere; the *Historical Museum of the City of Warsaw* shows visitors Nazi films documenting the destruction of the city. Nevertheless, only one of the city's synagogues, near Grzybowki Square, was restored, and it is often the object of anti-Semitic graffiti. After the war, the Polish Communist government used the rebuilding of the capital as an opportunity to move industrial and warehouse facilities to the city's outskirts. Park areas tripled in size; streets were widened — and renamed for socialist heroes, a process now being reversed. While the Old Town was lovingly restored, the heart of the pre-war city was replaced by Stalin's Palace of Culture and the empty square around it, only now being filled by ranks of private kiosks. With the explosion of new businesses, Warsaw today is a city incorporating the past and looking with hope toward the future.

The Wisła (Vistula) River splits the city, with the downtown area on the left, higher bank, and the Praga housing suburb on the right. The symbol of Warsaw is Syrena, a winged mermaid armed with a sword and shield, whose statue stands guard on the Kościuszko embankment. For Varsovians (as residents of Warsaw are called), she personifies the city's proud motto: "Defies the Storm."

Warsaw At-a-Glance

SEEING THE CITY

For a general sense of Warsaw's postwar reconstruction and continuing modernization, take the elevator to the 30th-floor terrace of the Pałac Kulturi i Nauki (Palace of Culture and Science) on Plac Defilad (Defilad Square). From here, on a clear day (rare in this heavily polluted metropolis), you can see beyond the outskirts of the city, which are marked by heavy industry, modern buildings, and new housing estates. There is a small charge for the elevator ride. The best view of the Old Town and the castle is from the east side of the river.

SPECIAL PLACES

The Old Town is west of the Wisła (Vistula) River and just north of Sląsko-Dąbrowski Most (Slasko-Dabrowski Bridge). Most sights and activities of interest to tourists are found between this area and Lazienki Park, south of Plac na Rozdroźu.

As you make your way through the city, it's helpful to remember that "ulica" is the Polish word for street, "aleja" is the word for avenue, and "plac" means square. Though streets renamed by the Communists are being changed again, taxi drivers and locals are aware of both names and are happy to help confused visitors.

STARE MIASTO (OLD TOWN)

ZAMEK KRÓLEWSKI (ROYAL CASTLE) Warsaw's most important historical monument, its Royal Castle, built between the 14th and 18th centuries, was blown up by the Nazis in their campaign to wipe Poland off the map. Painstakingly rebuilt, its imposing silhouette forms an impressive background to Kolumna Zygmunta (King Sigismund III Column) in the middle of Plac Zamkowy (Castle Square). The Royal Castle has rejoined the ranks of the most beautiful palaces in Europe. In addition, the castle boasts 17th-century paintings of Warsaw by Canaletto. Guided tours are offered Tuesdays through Saturdays. Admission charge. Adjacent to Plac Zamkowy (phone: 635-3995).

KOLUMNA ZYGMUNTA (KING SIGISMUND III COLUMN) This, the oldest monument in Warsaw (1644), stands in the center of Plac Zamkowy at the edge of the Old Town. At the top is the bronze statue of the 16th-century Polish king who built his castle here. The column was nearly destroyed by the Nazis, but the statue survived and the monument was re-erected shortly after the war.

POD BLACHĄ A tin-roofed baroque palace noted for its attic crowned with a richly ornamented cartouche bearing coats-of-arms. Near Plac Zamkowy.

RYNEK STAREGO MIASTA (OLD TOWN MARKET SQUARE) The most beautiful square in Warsaw, it is enclosed by 17th- and 18th-century baroque burgher houses that were re-created using bits of ornamentation recovered after the Nazi destruction (No. 28, housing the *Historical Museum of the City of Warsaw,* and Baryczka House at No. 34 are considered among the best preserved). The square is filled with flowers, and alive with little shops and cafés. Each side of the square is named for a Warsaw burgher of the late 18th century who fought for civil rights.

KATEDRA SW. JANA (ST. JOHN'S CATHEDRAL) The site of a parish church since the early 14th century, the cathedral was virtually destroyed by the Nazis, then rebuilt in the Gothic style. It is beloved by the city's deeply religious Roman Catholics. The crypts contain the remains of illustrious Poles, including romantic novelist Henryk Sienkiewicz (1846–1916), who won the Nobel prize for his *Quo Vadis?.* In 1992, 51 years after his death, the remains of pianist Ignacy Jan Paderweski were interred here, fulfilling his wish to be buried in a free Poland. Ulica Swiętojáńska.

BARBAKAN (BARBICAN) This brick wall with turrets was built to encircle and defend the Old Town in the mid-16th century and later reconstructed. Today it marks the dividing line between the old and the newer sections of the city. There are fine views of the Vistula River from the top.

TRAKT KRÓLEWSKI (ROYAL ROUTE) About 6 miles (10 km) long, this thorough-fare begins at Plac Zamkowy (Castle Square) and heads south to Łazienki Park and on to Wilanów Palace. The street, whose name changes from Ulica Krakowskie Przedmieście, to Ulica Nowy Swiat, to Aleje Ujaz-dowskie along the way, is lined with palaces of Poland's nobility, baroque houses, museums, government and university buildings, embassies, churches, restaurants, and shops. Located near the statue to the romantic 19th-century poet Adam Mickiewicz is the Radziwiłł Palace (46-48 Ulica Krakowskie Przedmieście), now the Council of Ministers, where the Soviet bloc's Warsaw Pact was signed, and years later where the "round-table" agreement transferred power from the Communists to the Solidarity-led opposition.

ELSEWHERE IN THE CITY

NOWE MIASTO (NEW TOWN) New in relative terms only, it was built adjacent to the expanding Old Town in the early 15th century. At 16 Ulica Freta is the house where physicist Marie Curie was born in 1867. The long *Rynek Nowego Miasta* (New Town Market Square) boasts a beautiful well in its center.

WORLD WAR II MONUMENTS So extensive was the heroic resistance to the Nazis that even the churches and cemeteries of Warsaw were scenes of fierce fighting. Bullet holes still can be seen on many façades. The city's *Monument to the Heroes of Warsaw* stands in Plac Teatralny (Theater Square) in front of the *Wielki Theater* (see *Music*). It is sort of a new version of the mermaid Syrena, a fighting goddess with sword raised. The *Więzienia Pawiak* (Pawiak Prison; 24-26 Ulica Dzielna; phone: 311317), where 35,000 Poles were executed and another 65,000 were detained, is today the *Muzeum Walki i Meczenistwa* (Museum of Struggle and Martyrdom). At the intersection of Ulica Długa and Ulica Miodowa on Plac Krasińskich is a striking monument to the heroes of the 63-day Warsaw Uprising in 1944. Still intact near the middle of the intersection is the manhole through which the fighters escaped from the Old Town. The ghetto where the Jewish population was walled up in 1940 is remembered by the *Pomnik Boharterów Getta* (Monument to the Heroes of the Ghetto) on a grassy square at Ulica Zamenhofa and Ulica Anielewicza. The *Zydowki Institut Historyczny* (Jewish Historical Institute; 79 Aleje Solidarnosśći; phone: 271530) has an exhibit on the ghetto as well as an extensive archive on Jews in Poland. A marble monument marks *Umschlagplatz* (Ulica Stawki at Ulica Dubois), the square where hundreds of thousands of Jews were loaded onto railway cars en route to death camps.

CMENTARZ ZYDOWSKI (JEWISH CEMETERY) Somehow this large cemetery survived the Nazi destruction of the city. Though overgrown, it is possible to walk among the headstones, many of which go back 2 centuries. Of the hundreds of thousands of Jews who once called Warsaw home, there are now only about 300 left. A visit to this final resting place, which had no succeeding generation to tend it, is heartbreaking, but a must. There is often an English-speaking caretaker at the entrance. 49-51 Okopowa (phone: 382622).

CMENTARZ WOJSKOWY (ARMY CEMETERY) The memorial to the Polish officers massacred by the Soviets at Katyn in 1940 is here, as well as the birch crosses marking the graves of young couriers who died in the resistance to the Nazi occupation. 43-45 Powązkoska (phone: 332140).

PARK LAZIENKI AND PAŁAC NA WODZIE (LAZIENKI PARK AND PALACE ON THE WATER) The splendid Palace on the Water in Warsaw's loveliest park was built in the 18th century for Stanisław August Poniatowski, last of the Polish kings. The Nazis plundered its collections and devastated the palace, but the interiors have been carefully copied and restored. There are some 18 other buildings and monuments in the spacious park, including the Biały Domek (Little White House), once the residence in exile of the future King Louis XVIII of France. In warm weather, the monument to Chopin at the southern end of the park is the scene of Sunday afternoon Chopin concerts in warm weather. At the southern end of the gardens is the conservatory, a place to enjoy a cup of coffee, a slice of chocolate cake, and piano music. Park open daily to dusk; palace closed Mondays. Admission charge to the palace. The Belvedere Palace, official residence of the President of the State Council, is in Belvedere Park, adjacent to Lazienki Park. Southeast of Plac na Rozdroźu, along Aleje Ujazdowskie (phone: 218212).

OGRÓD SASKI (SAXON GARDENS) In the center of the city, next to Plac Piłsudskiego and the *Grób Nieznanego Zołnierza* (Monument to the Unknown Soldier), this is the oldest garden in Warsaw. Built at the end of the 18th century in the orderly style of an English garden, it has many rare trees and an artificial lake. Open daily. No admission charge.

WILANÓW PALACE AND PARK This Polish version of Versailles was built in the late 17th century as a summer residence for King Jan Sobieski III and his French-born wife, Marysiénka; it is now a branch of the *Muzeum Narodowe* (National Museum). The baroque palace was restored after World War II and contains period furniture, china, old clocks, portraits, and other mementos of the Sobieski family. The French-style gardens are lovely, with baroque terraces leading to a small lake. The *Muzeum Plakatow* (Poster Museum; phone: 422606), with an interesting collection of Polish graphic art, is in a building on the palace grounds. The palace is closed Tuesdays; the museum is closed Mondays. Admission charge to palace and museum. Ulica Wiertnicza, just south of the city, less than 6 miles (10 km) from the Old Town. Reached by express bus B or bus No. 180 from Ulica Marszałkowska (phone: 420795).

ENVIRONS

OJCIEC POPIŁUSZKO JRÓB (FATHER POPIELUSZKO TOMB) Next to the Kościół Sw. Stanisława Kostki (Church of St. Stanislawa Kostka) in the Zoliborz section, due north of central Warsaw, is the tomb of Father Popieluszko, a national hero and martyr, who fought for workers' rights and national independence alongside the Solidarity trade union. He was killed by the state police in 1984, and a simple granite cross has become a pilgrimage site for many Poles and visiting dignitaries. Ulica Hozjusza, off Ulica Krasińskiego, Zoliborz.

POD CHOPIN (CHOPIN'S HOME) Thirty-three miles (53 km) west of Warsaw in Zelazowa Wola is the Chopin family manor, where the composer was born in 1810. The house, set on lovely grounds, has been turned into a museum, and concerts of the composer's work are held on the lawn on Sundays during the summer. Usually performed by a four- or five-piece chamber ensemble, the concerts are presented in a delightful Renaissance setting, and the music is sublime. Die-hard Chopin fans may want to travel 6 miles (10 km) north of Zelazowa Wola to the village of Brochów to see the mid-16th-century Renaissance church where Chopin was baptized. Leave Warsaw by Route E30 (2) in the direction of Pozan (phone: 828-22300). For more information contact *Orbis* (see *Sources and Resources,* below).

Sources and Resources

TOURIST INFORMATION

Maps and information have become widely available, especially at gift shops in hotels and the Old Town. The *Informacja Turystyczna* (*IT* Center; 1-13 Plac Zamkowy; phone: 310464) is across from the Royal Castle. *Orbis*, the Polish national tourist agency, also can be helpful (142 Ulica Marszalkowska; phone: 278031).

Several good English-language guidebooks to the country and city are available. The 120-page *Destination Poland* is free from the Polish National Tourist Office (275 Madison Ave., Suite 1211, New York, NY 10016; phone: 212-338-9412). Also look for *A Guide to Warsaw*, by Anna Wasilkowsk (Interpress; about $4); *Warsaw, A Pocket Guide* (Penna; about $3); and the detailed *The Old Town in Warsaw Atlas of Architecture*, by Maria Lewicka (Arkady; about $2.50). The complex street layout makes a city map useful, and several have been published updating the street names. We also recommend carrying a Polish-English dictionary; a pocket *Say It in Polish* (Polfact; about $3) is helpful.

LOCAL COVERAGE The *Warsaw Voice* is an English-language newspaper. The *International Herald Tribune*, *USA Today*, *Time*, *Newsweek*, and other major English-language periodicals are available in hotels and larger bookshops. *What, Where, When Warszawa* and *Welcome to Warsaw* are monthly English-language magazines with useful listings distributed free at major hotels and travel agencies.

For suggestions on local eateries, consult the tourist information centers, hotel staff, or the English-language *Restaurants of Warsaw* guide on sale in hotels (about $5).

TELEPHONE The country code for Poland is 48; the city codes for Warsaw are 22 (for six-digit numbers) and 2 (for seven-digit numbers).

GETTING AROUND

The Old Town, the Vistula River embankment, and the whole Royal Route of Ulica Krakowskie Przedmieście, Ulica Nowy Swiat, and Aleje Ujazdowskie are best seen on foot. But Poland's capital is a very big city, so at some point you will probably want to use cabs or municipal transportation.

AIRPORTS Warsaw's new international terminal and its domestic airport are collectively known as Okęcie (phone: 606-7381) and are about 5 minutes apart by shuttle bus. Okęcie is about a 20-minute cab ride from downtown; the fare can vary widely, but expect to pay anywhere from $20 to $40. Some hotels have courtesy buses. Regular buses between the airport and major hotels are provided by *AirportCity* (phone: 268211); the fare is about $1.50.

BUS/TRAM Avoid them if possible during rush hours, but they are the least expensive way to get around. Route signs are at each stop. Buy your ticket before boarding at a nearby tobacco or newspaper kiosk, then cancel it in a special machine on the coach. It's a good idea to buy extra tickets since kiosks often are closed.

CAR RENTAL The major rental car companies now operate in Poland, although better rates can be obtained by making reservations in advance. Most are located at the airport and several hotels. The main *Orbis S.A./Hertz Rent-a-Car* location is near the *Forum* hotel (phone: 211360); *Avis* is at Okęcie Airport (phone: 650-4872).

TAXI Cabs may be hailed on the street or more easily at taxi stands. To order a taxi by phone, call 919. Make sure the driver turns on the meter at the outset of the ride. Be aware, too, that because of inflation, the price that appears on the meter is multiplied several hundred times; a sign on the taxi window will tell you which figure is used. Cabs also are fine for extended sightseeing surveys of the city; rates are reasonable if you agree on them before setting off. Roman Cichecki has his own Mercedes cab and is a good English-speaking guide. Contact him at *Taxi Osobowe* (18 Ulica Woronicza; phone: 625).

TRAIN The main train station is on Aleje Jerozolimskie, in the center of town (phone: 200361 for local train schedules and fare information, 204512 for international train schedules and fare information). A PolRailPass is available in Poland at *Orbis* travel agencies. Although there is an increased police presence, be aware of professional bands of pickpockets who lie in wait for Western travelers as they board the trains.

LOCAL SERVICES

Most hotels will try to arrange any special services a business traveler might require, such as a translator.

DENTIST (ENGLISH-SPEAKING) Ask the service desk at any major hotel to recommend a dentist in an emergency.

MEDICAL EMERGENCY The number to call is 999. English generally is not spoken, so it's best to ask the service desk at any major hotel to make the call for you.

PHARMACY Some pharmacies stay open 24 hours a day; ask at your hotel desk.

POST OFFICE The main post office is in the center town and is open 24 hours daily, 31-33 Ulica Swiętokrzyszka.

SPECIAL EVENTS

An *International Book Fair* is held here each May, and there is an *International Poster Biennale* in June during even-numbered years. The *"Warsaw*

Autumn" International Festival of Modern Music is an important September event, and the *Jazz Jamboree* held in late October is the oldest jazz festival in Central and Eastern Europe. The *International Chopin Competition* for pianists (held every 5 years) will next take place in October 1995, and the *Henryk Wieniawski International Competition* for violinists is held annually in September.

MUSEUMS

In addition to those described in *Special Places,* Warsaw has a number of other interesting museums. Most are closed Mondays or Tuesdays and charge admission.

CENTRUM SZTUKI WSPÓŁCZESNEJ (CONTEMPORARY ART MUSEUM) Exhibits of modern art and installations with a partially renovated castle as the dramatic backdrop. Admission charge. 6 Aleje Ujazdowskie (phone: 628-1271).

JOHN PAUL II COLLECTION Formerly the *Museum of Revolutionary Politics,* it now houses an exhibition of Old Masters' paintings contributed by the Porczyński family. Plac Bankowy — once named Plac Dzierzynskiego after the Polish-born founder of Tcheka, forerunner of the Soviet KGB (phone: 202725).

MUZEUM ARCHEOLOGICNZE (ARCHAEOLOGICAL MUSEUM) Tools and other relics of prehistoric Baltic peoples, as well as changing exhibitions. 52 Ulica Długa (phone: 313221).

MUZEUM ETNOGRAFICZNE (ETHNOGRAPHIC MUSEUM) Exhibits on peasant life, folk art, and costumes. 1 Ulica Kredytowa (phone: 277641).

MUZEUM HISTORYCZNE WARSZAWY (WARSAW HISTORICAL MUSEUM) Pictures and exhibitions trace the history of Warsaw through the centuries. A 20-minute presentation compiled from captured Nazi film (narrated in English) documents the devastation of the city; shown daily at noon. Admission charge. 28 Rynek Starego Miasta (phone: 635-1625).

MUZEUM MARII SKŁODOWSKIEJ-CURIE (MARIE SKŁODOWSKA-CURIE MUSEUM) The Polish chemist's home before she moved to Paris. 16 Ulica Freta (phone: 318092).

MUZEUM NARODOWE (NATIONAL MUSEUM) Poland's greatest art collection. Above all, don't miss the huge painting of the *Battle of Grunwald* by Jan Matejko, which shows the defeat of the Knights of the Teutonic Order in the 15th century. During World War II, the Polish government ordered that the painting, like all other national treasures, be hidden, and though the Nazis offered a whopping reward for its return, there wasn't a single taker. 3 Aleje Jerozolimskie (phone: 211031).

TOWARZYSTWO IM. FRYDERYKA CHOPINA (CHOPIN'S DRAWING ROOM) Composer Frederic Chopin lived briefly in a second-floor room of the former Raczyński (or Czapski) Palace, now the Akademia Sztuk Pieknych (Academy of Fine Arts). Concerts are occasionally held in the room, which is decorated with Empire-style period furnishings. Nearby, on Ulica Krakowskie Przedmieście, is Kościół Sw. Krzyza (Holy Cross Church), where Chopin's heart is buried in one of the columns. 1 Ulica Okólnik (phone: 275471).

SHOPPING

Shops in Warsaw generally are open from 11 AM to 7 PM, but department stores open earlier and close later. Avoid the crowds by shopping before 3 PM. Leather, linens, and folk art, which ranges from wonderful woodcarvings to handsome handwoven rugs, are good buys here. Amber and sterling silver jewelry are the best buys. A good place to look for old and new jewelry is along the side streets of the Old Town. Check the small shops as well as the new larger ones. Warsaw's Fifth Avenue is Ulica Nowy Swiat (New World Street), not terribly elegant by Western standards but getting there. On Sunday mornings, there is an interesting antiques flea market in the Wola district on Ulica Obozowa near Ulica Ciołka. (There are restrictions on the quantity and types of items you can take out of Poland, particularly on things made before 1945; check with authorities before your trip.)

While the dollar used to carry extraordinary value in Poland, the country's national currency now is its own złoty. Dollars and other Western currency can legally and most easily be exchanged for złotys at the many private exchanges marked *kantor*. Hotels and banks also generally have exchanges.

AREX A good collection of Polish folk crafts and paintings. 5A Ulica Copina (phone: 296624).

ART Stylized folk art and works of modern art. 1-7 Ulica Krakowskie Przedmieście (no phone).

ARTEON Located behind the *Marriott* hotel, this shop offers beautiful silver and amber jewelry. 65-79 Aleje Jerozolimskie (phone: 650-5053)

BAZAR RÓZYCKIEGO Sought-after items such as fur coats are for sale here; prices are negotiable. Ulica Targowa (no phone).

CANALETTO A good shop for amber and silver jewelry. 89 Ulica Krakowskie Przedmieście (no phone).

CEPELIA Shops that sell souvenirs and folk art. Several locations: 2 and 5 Plac Konstytucji, and 10 Rynek Starego Miasta (no phone).

DESA Specialists in Polish antiques. Locations at 34-50 Ulica Marszałkowska (phone: 628-7705), and 48 and 51 Ulica Nowy Swiat (phone: 274760).

EDWARD MAGDZIARZ One of finest collections of stained glass lamps in Warsaw. 64 Ulica Nowy Swiat (no phone).

SILVER LINE Amber and silver jewelry in traditional and modern settings. 59 Ulica Nowy Swiat (phone: 266355).

STADION DZIESIĘCIOLECIA (10TH ANNIVERSARY STADIUM) One of the largest weekend bazaars in Eastern Europe, favored by traders from the former Soviet Union. The stadium is on the east side of the Vistula River on Wybrzeże Szczecińskie (no phone).

ZAPIECEK In the Old Town, this modern art gallery features work of local artists. 1 Ulica Zapiecek (phone: 319918).

SPORTS AND FITNESS

HORSE RACING The *Sluzewiec* race course, on the southern extremity of the city, is one of the largest in Europe. Races are held on Wednesdays, Saturdays, and Sundays in summer.

SOCCER Played at *Skra* and *Warszawa* soccer stadiums. *Legia,* the best and most popular Warsaw team, also plays its matches at various stadiums around the country.

SWIMMING In summer there is swimming at the *Legia* pool (Ulica Łazienkowska) or the indoor pool at the *Palac Kultury i Nauki* (Palace of Culture and Science; 6 Plac Defilad). Also the *Marriott* hotel (see *Checking In*) has a pool (there's a fee for non-guests). There are no public beaches, and swimming is not permitted in the badly polluted river.

THEATER

Advance booking for theater or cinema tickets can be made at the box office or through one of the tourist information centers (the branch at 1-13 Plac Zamkowy; phone: 635-1881), the *ZASP* ticket office (25 Aleje Jerozolimskie; phone: 266164 or 285995), or at the ticket office in *Kino Wisla* (Plac Wilsona; phone: 392365). The city's foremost drama theaters include *Polski* (2 Ulica Karasia; phone: 267992), *Dramatyczny* (in the Palace of Culture and Science, Plac Defilad; phone: 263872), *Ateneum* (2 Ulica Jaracza; phone: 625-7330), and *Zydowski* (12-16 Plac Grzybowski; phone: 207025). There are several children's theaters in Warsaw, including the *Lalka* puppet theater (in the Palace of Culture and Science, Plac Defilad; phone: 204950).

MUSIC

Opera and ballet are performed at Warsaw's *Teatr Wielki Opery i Baletu* (Grand Theater of Opera and Ballet; Plac Teatralny; phone: 263001). The prestigious international *Chopin Piano Competitions* are held every 5 years at the *Filharmonia* (5 Ulica Jasna; phone: 267281), and there are operettas staged at the *Operetka* (49 Ulica Nowogrodzka; phone: 628-0360).

NIGHTCLUBS AND NIGHTLIFE

You'll need a fairly sophisticated knowledge of Polish to appreciate the humor at one of Warsaw's popular satirical cafés, but you might try one for the atmosphere.

For jazz and some international food, try *Akwarium* (49 Ulica Emilii Plater; phone: 205072), a modern nightspot near the *Palace of Culture and Science*. One of the city's best private clubs is *SARP* (13 Foksal; no phone), which is run by the association of Polish architects and artists. However, you must be taken there by a member. Young crowds frequent *Riviera Remont* (12 Ulica Waryńskiego; phone: 257497).

Though Las Vegas has nothing to fear, gambling is popular at the casinos at the *Orbis-Grand, Marriott,* and *Victoria Inter-Continental* hotels (see *Checking In*), where there are slot machines, blackjack, and roulette tables. There is an admission charge; gambling is in hard currency.

Best in Town

CHECKING IN

Recent openings have improved the Warsaw hotel situation, but with less than a dozen recommendable properties, booking well in advance is strongly advised, especially during the summer months. Expect to pay more than $200 a night for a double room in one of Warsaw's very expensive hotels; from $120 to $200 in the expensive range; $70 to $120 in the moderate category; and under $70 for an inexpensive place. Prices include breakfast and can be paid in hard currency or złotys. All hotels listed below accept major credit cards.

Another housing option is the bed and breakfast type of accommodation, but in Warsaw, such places don't offer the breakfast. What they do provide, however, is the rare chance for a glimpse into the lives of typical Poles. Bookings and information are available through the *Syrena* travel agency (17 Ulica Krucza; phone: 287540 or 217864). Most of Warsaw's major hotels have complete facilities for the business traveler. Those hotels listed below as having "business services" usually offer such conveniences as English-speaking concierge, meeting rooms, photocopiers, computers, translation services, and express checkout, among others. Call the hotel for additional information. All telephone numbers are in the 22 or 2 city code unless otherwise indicated.

For an unforgettable experience in Warsaw, we begin with our favorite hostelry, followed by our cost and quality choices of hotels, listed by price category.

A SPECIAL HAVEN

Marriott It may not have the patina of age, but the creature comforts and convenience offered by this hotel provide a welcome Western respite in this

European capital. The hotel occupies the top 20 stories of a 40-story skyscraper smack in the middle of town. Its 525 spacious rooms — complete with color TV sets (CNN, too) — are decorated in soft pastel tones; its bathrooms come complete with thick terry cloth towels and hair dryers. Best of all is the English-speaking staff, which is unfailingly polite and helpful (it's said that none of the employees ever worked in a hotel or restaurant before — *Marriott*'s way of avoiding the surly service that was common in Communist Poland). There are several restaurants from which to choose: The *Lila Weneda* coffee shop — where plenty of East-West wheeling and dealing takes place — serves a truly first-rate buffet breakfast that is included in the room rate. Afternoon tea (try the pastries) or snacks can be enjoyed on the mezzanine lounge overlooking a large, light-filled atrium and the lobby. And for those who crave a game of chance, there's a hard-currency casino. Business services. 65-79 Aleje Jerozolimskie (phone: 630-6306; fax: 300050).

VERY EXPENSIVE

Bristol This 1901 Art Nouveau establishment reopened in late 1992 after being left unattended under Communist-government management. Now a Forte property, it is regaining its status as the country's grande dame (it boasts such famous former guests as Marlene Dietrich, Douglas Fairbanks, Charles de Gaulle, and John F. Kennedy). Lovingly restored, all 163 rooms and 43 suites feature marble baths, air conditioning, direct-dial telephones, and satellite TV. There's also a health club with a swimming pool, a gym, a sauna and solarium, as well as beauty treatment facilities. There are 3 restaurants: the *Malinowa* features traditional Polish specialties, the *Marconi* has an Italian menu, and the *Café Bristol* serves morning coffee and afternoon tea. Business services. 42-44 Ulica Krakowskie Przedmieście (phone: 625-2525 or 800-225-5843 in the US).

EXPENSIVE

Forum The Inter-Continental chain's second link in Warsaw is bigger than the *Victoria* (see below), but not as nice. Its 751 rooms are of modest size and sparsely decorated. It has a casino and a central location near the Palace of Culture and Science. Business services. 24-26 Ulica Nowogrodzka (phone: 210271; fax: 258157).

Jan II Sobieski A splash of color on the Warsaw cityscape, this recent addition is cheerful and well appointed. Conveniently located a few blocks from the city center, its 419 rooms and suites are attractive in a streamlined way, with satellite TV, direct-dial telephones, and other amenities. The large restaurant features Polish and international fare. Business services. Plac Artura Zawiszy (phone: 658-4444; fax: 659-8828).

Mercure Opened last year, this ultramodern French venture is in a less congested area of Warsaw, located between the city center and Old Town. There are

250 well-appointed rooms, which feature satellite TV, direct-dial tele-phones, and 2 restaurants. Business services. 22 Aleja Jana Pawła II (phone: 200201 or 800-221-4542 in the US).

Novotel A joint venture with the French hotel chain, this hotel offers 150 simple but comfortable rooms, along with shops and restaurants. On the down side, the location near the airport is not attractive or convenient to the city center. Business services. 1 Ulica Sierpnia (phone: 464051; fax: 463686).

Orbis-Europejski For some sense of Old World Warsaw, this is the place to stay. The 279 rooms — including singles and doubles, with and without bath, and suites — are functionally modern, although the 4-story building is over 100 years old. A café looks out on the Saxon Gardens and the *Grób Nieznanego Zolnierza* (Monument to the Unknown Soldier). Business ser-vices. 13 Ulica Krakowskie Przedmieście (phone: 265051; fax: 26111).

Orbis-Holiday Inn One of the first joint ventures of US and Polish capital, it boasts 338 rooms, spartan by most Western standards, but adequate. There also are 3 restaurants, a sauna, and a swimming pool. Business services. 2 Ulica Złota (phone: 200341; fax: 300569).

Victoria Inter-Continental One of Warsaw's top hotels, it is close to the *Wielki Theater* and the Saxon Gardens. Its 370 rooms are comfortable (although the furniture is a little frayed at the edges), and the *Canaletto* restaurant specializes in Polish dishes. There is a swimming pool and a casino. Busi-ness services. 11 Ulica Królewska (phone: 279271; fax: 279856).

MODERATE

Orbis-Grand The more than 410 rooms here are rather plain, but the midtown location is a plus. It has a rooftop café with glass-enclosed terrace and a swimming pool. On the eighth floor is a disco, making seventh-floor rooms places to be avoided, due to the noise. 28 Ulica Krucza (phone: 294051; fax: 219724).

Orbis-Solec Located near the Vistula River embankment, this hotel features 147 rooms with baths and showers. A restaurant offers delicious Polish fare. The decor is minimal motel-modern. 1 Ulica Zagórna (phone: 259241; fax: 216442).

INEXPENSIVE

Maria A small private hotel, a bit out of the way but quickly accessible by taxi or public transportation. The 22 rooms and suites are modern, all with private baths. There's good Polish fare at the restaurant. 71 Aleje Jana Pawła II (phone: 384062).

EATING OUT

Food shortages are no longer a fact of life in Poland, and while not yet a culinary wonder, Warsaw is brimming with restaurants. Some of the new ones are excellent, but those that probably interest city residents the most are the *McDonald's* and *Burger King* chains that finally opened in 1992.

Warsaw restaurants serve dinner relatively early, and by 10:30 PM most of the kitchens are already dark. Dinner for two, with wine, will cost $50 to $60 at restaurants described as very expensive; $25 to $50 at restaurants in the expensive category; $15 to $25 at places listed as moderate; and under $10 at inexpensive spots. All telephone numbers are in the 22 or 2 city code unless otherwise indicated.

VERY EXPENSIVE

Belvedere Elegant continental dining in a lovely setting in Lazienki Park. Open daily for lunch and dinner. Reservations necessary. Major credit cards accepted. Nowa Oranzeria (phone: 414806).

Fukier Traditional Polish and continental fare as well as some vegetarian dishes are featured in this Old Town dining room. The favorite dish here is *bigos* (traditional Polish hunters' stew of pork, beef, and sauerkraut). Live music most nights. Open daily for lunch and dinner. Reservations advised. Major credit cards accepted. 27 Rynek Starego Miasta (Old Town Market Sq.; phone: 311013).

Zajazd Napoleonski In a neighborhood not meant for strolling, this is a small, private hotel and restaurant. The uniformed, white-gloved staff serves superb food with great style. Open daily; dinner only on Sundays. Reservations advised. Major credit cards accepted. Ulica Płowiecka (phone: 153454 or 153068).

EXPENSIVE

Bazyliszek Easily Warsaw's premier restaurant, best known for its wild game and Old Town location. It's on the second floor over a snack bar and has an Old Warsaw ambience, with a decor that features hussars' armor and wooden beams. A horse and carriage usually is waiting outside to take you for a romantic ride through the city after dinner. Open daily for lunch and dinner. Reservations necessary. No credit cards accepted. 5 Rynek Starego Miasta (Old Town Market Sq.; phone: 311841).

Gessler Lovely, especially in the summer when the restaurant opens into the Saxon Gardens. The menu is traditional Polish. Try the smoked trout soup, herring, and other fresh fish dishes. The homemade ice cream is also worth a taste — or two. Open daily for lunch and dinner. Reservations necessary for dinner. Major credit cards accepted. 37 Ulica Senatorska (phone: 270663).

Montmarte Fine French bistro food in a pleasant setting across from the old Communist Party headquarters. The steaks are first-rate, as are the soups and salads with cheese and bread. Open daily for lunch and dinner. Reservations advised. No credit cards accepted. 7 Ulica Nowy Swiat (phone: 628-6315).

Swiętoszek An Old Town cellar restaurant where Polish fare is well represented. Don't miss the blini with caviar — it's unbeatable. Open daily for lunch and dinner. Reservations necessary. No credit cards accepted. 6-8 Jezuicka (phone: 315634).

MODERATE

Da Elio One of Warsaw's many new Italian eateries specializing in homemade pasta (the gnocchi is great), with a salad bar. Open daily for lunch and dinner. Reservations advised. Major credit cards accepted. 20A Ulica Zurawia (phone: 625-5457).

Nowe Miasto Warsaw's first vegetarian restaurant boasts a pleasant wicker dining room and patio on the New Town Market Square. Ingredients used in all dishes, including salads, soups, and vegetable crêpes, are made from organically grown produce. Open daily for lunch and dinner. Reservations advised. Major credit cards accepted. 13 Rynek Nowego Miasta (phone: 314379).

Rycerska Good — yet popularly priced — Polish fare is served in a rustic atmosphere with medieval armor and original paintings. Open daily for lunch and dinner. Reservations advised. Major credit cards accepted. 9-11 Ulica Szeroki Dunaj (phone: 313668).

Wilanów Traditional Polish cooking served in a modern setting. This eatery is some distance from the town center, near the Wilanów Palace. Open daily for lunch and dinner. Reservations advised. No credit cards accepted. 27 Ulica Wiertnicza (phone: 421852).

INEXPENSIVE

Bambola Poland's first home-grown restaurant chain serves first-rate pizza. Open daily for lunch and dinner. No reservations. No credit cards accepted. Locations at 111 Aleje Jerozolimskie and 42B Ulica Nowy Swiat serve pasta as well as salad. Pizza only at 16 Ulica Puławska, 27 Ulica Wspolna, and 36 Ulica Przemysłowa.

Staropolska Near the university, this restaurant is a mainstay among academic types. Although the menu is limited, it has one of the best cold buffets in Warsaw, with veal in aspic and steak tartare. Also sample the broth with hard-boiled egg and sausage, called *zurek staropolski.* Old *Beatles* tapes or European disco music plays continuously. Open daily for lunch and dinner. Reservations advised. No credit cards accepted. 8 Ulica Krakowskie Przedmieście (phone: 269070).

VERY SPECIAL One corner of the Old World still thrives in this otherwise drab culinary capital. It's called *E. Wedel* (8 Szpitalna; it's on the corner of Wojciecha Górskiego). The name is stenciled on the front window, and there is a sign that says *"Pijalnia Czekolady,"* which roughly translates as "Chocolate Pump Room." The place consists of two small rooms right out of a *mittel* European stage set: one is mint green, the other is pink. The *only* thing served here is very good thick hot chocolate (in porcelain cups), for 22¢ per cup. No smoking is allowed. (Also see *Quintessential Eastern Europe* in DIVERSIONS.) Right next door (on Szpitalna) is a faded but still elegant (by local standards) candy shop, also owned by *E. Wedel.*

Also not to be missed is the tiny bakery *A. Bikel* (35 Ulica Nowy Swiat; phone: 226-4568), an enduring Warsaw tradition since 1869. The *mazurki* and *babkas* are Polish classics, and the *paczki* (light, spongy jelly doughnuts) are simply irresistible.

Diversions

Exceptional Experiences for the Mind and Body

Introduction

It's hard to imagine a more intriguing area than today's Eastern Europe. The collapse of Communism is turning a world that slumbered anonymously behind the Iron Curtain into an extraordinary travel opportunity.

The new freedom and openness that now exists from the Baltic to the Black Sea mean greater choices for travelers in a host of fascinating countries. Gone are the strictly supervised itineraries and regimented arrangements for even the most basic requirements of eating and sleeping. Strictly guided tours to only the best-known historical sights in the largest cities have given way to journeys that take advantage of the enormous range of available activities. Great museums are still on most itineraries, certainly, but a trip to this part of the world now may also include a seacoast village, a turn-of-the-century spa, a world class ski resort, or even some serious shopping.

Many of the streets and much of the landscape still will seem gray and grim, the legacy of long decades of failed Communism. But there are unspoiled baroque cities, great Gothic churches, and splendid castles. Above all, there is the spell of special people, curious, friendly, and impassioned. In many ways this region's history, culture, values, and way of life are not unlike those in the West; yet it is a place that remains largely unknown.

The sheer wealth of attractions now open to travelers to Eastern Europe poses a challenge. Combining the right setting with the right activity is an art even back home, and this area, with its dozens of tempting cities and hundreds of districts and regions (all with distinct cultural features), can cause even the savviest traveler some uncertainty. The pertinent question is: Where is the quality of experience highest? On the following pages, we suggest the best places in Eastern Europe in which to pursue its many offerings: shops, beaches and mountains, ski resorts and spas. This section represents a distillation of the best at the moment from Prague to Moscow, from Tallinn to Kiev, a selective guide to the region at its most intriguing, calculated to make your visit the most memorable experience possible.

Quintessential Eastern Europe

Even before Communist governments isolated this region and made traveling difficult, Eastern Europe was an exotic location for Westerners, mysterious, intriguing, and largely unknown. Today, with Communist rule gone, all the sights, sounds, traditions, foods, and arts of the Baltic states, Bulgaria, the Czech Republic and Slovakia, Hungary, Poland, Romania, Russia, and Ukraine are waiting to be discovered by those with a sense of adventure and curiosity. Eastern Europe offers travelers a rich mosaic of experiences, but as in any place, there are some activities that uniquely capture the spirit of the people and the place, crystalizing them and helping visitors understand why they are like no other. The following are some such activities in Eastern Europe. Experience them now, while they still retain the exotic flavor of the almost unexplored.

ORIENT EXPRESS, Paris to Budapest There is no better way to relive the grand age of European travel than to take a trip on that most fabled of trains, the *Orient Express.* The original train, indisputably one of the most luxurious in the world, began making its run from Paris to Budapest (then on to Istanbul) in 1883, and it was the favorite of sophisticated travelers — princes and playboys, actors and adventurers, heads of industry and all manner of society's elite — for decades. The train stopped running in 1977, but since 1983 the *Venice Simplon–Orient Express* — re-creating its original splendor — travels every 2 weeks from London to Budapest, stopping at Paris, Munich, Innsbruck, Salzburg, and Vienna.

The cars are nothing short of sumptuous, with inlaid wood walls, thick carpets, stained glass, and velvet upholstery. The elegance of the dining car rivals that of the finest restaurant dining room; the tables are set with silver and crystal, and the preparation and white-glove presentation of the food is nothing short of superb. So faithfully is the original train re-created that, as you travel past the glittering capitals of Europe, there is little to remind you that the year is 1994, not 1894. In this, the realm of romance, intrigue, and Agatha Christie plots, it's difficult not to let your imagination run wild. Your elegantly clad dinner partners must certainly be European royalty, sipping champagne and arranging secret assignations in their private compartments. That mysterious woman in the black hat is unquestionably a spy. What mystery — or romance — awaits at your final destination? Information: *Venice Simplon–Orient Express,* 1520 Kensington Rd., Oak Brook, IL 60521 (phone: 800-524-2420).

WHITE NIGHTS OF ST. PETERSBURG, Russia Once a year, during the last half of June, the sun leaves the horizon over this beautiful city for only a few hours, and in place of the darkness of night, a mysterious chalky haze hangs over the horizon. Even the most stolid Russians go giddy and sentimental, and in a kind of metropolitan tribal rite that celebrates the return of the White Nights, they flock to Strelka, on Vasilyevskiy Island. The delicate pastel façades of structures built along the Neva River in the brilliant heyday of the Court of St. Petersburg glow in the eerie light. The great past of Mother Russia comes splendidly alive: the opulence of the czars' Winter Palace, the brooding mystery of Dostoyevsky in the Peter and Paul Fortress,, the romance of Tchaikovsky.

HOT CHOCOLATE AT E. WEDEL, Warsaw, Poland Despite much of the dismal history of this century, there are still some all too rare spots in Eastern Europe where time has stood still. One of these is *E. Wedel,* a special corner of the Old World in Warsaw, which is a slice of prewar Poland carefully preserved. The sign in the window reads *"Pijalnia Czekolady,"* which roughly (and charmingly) translates as "Chocolate Pump Room." Inside, seated at the tiny tables scattered through the two small rooms — one pink, one green — are self-possessed and proper ladies in their best silk dresses and pearls, languid hand-holding lovers, and intense young members of the intelligentsia, black clad and in deep discussion. One and all are sipping from pretty porcelain cups the only item on the menu — thick hot chocolate, rich, creamy, and of precisely the right degree of sweetness. Smoking is not permitted, yet another reason why this elegant little café is a breath of fresh air in an otherwise smog-filled city. Information: *E. Wedel,* 8 Szpitalna, corner of Wojciecha Górskiego, Warsaw, Poland (no phone).

THE BANI, Kiev, Ukraine What the sauna is to Helsinki inhabitants, the *bani* (baths — known as banya to Russians) is to their neighbors far south of the Gulf of Finland. It is here that Kiev residents, young and old, male and female (separately), go to truly relax. You'll find young mothers and *babushkas* at the *bani;* idealistic young men and grizzled World War II veterans; you might even see a red-faced former Communist apparatchik sweating it out now that the party has been outlawed. Here people sit naked in the steam, sip vodka, languidly exchange the latest gossip, and revel in an atmosphere of all-out lethargy. Bathers alternate between lounging in steam-filled rooms, feverishly scrubbing themselves with special brushes and soap, thrashing their bodies with birch branches (to open the pores), and finally, taking an exhilarating plunge into a pool so cold that it seems like runoff from a glacier. Afterward, there's usually a buffet in the changing room, where snacks or beverages may be purchased (alcohol is not officially condoned, but the locals simply bring their own). For the visitor, the *bani* is a place particularly conducive to forging friendships with the locals. The relaxed atmosphere encourages congenial conversation, and there's something about stripping, sweating, and swigging (vodka) with someone that fosters a common bond. But aside from the opportunity for social exchange, for travel-weary visitors and for hardworking natives alike, the *bani* is a sensuous luxury, a muscle-relaxing, foot-soothing, head-clearing treat.

AUSCHWITZ, Poland Less than an hour's drive from Cracow stands a sad and stark reminder of the power of evil in the world, and the depth of man's inhumanity to man. The horror that pervades this place hits with immediate, chilling force. Above the entrance to the former military barracks is a sign, worked in iron: it reads *"Arbeit Macht Frei"* (Work Makes One Free). Inside these gates is Auschwitz (the German name for the Polish town of Oświęcim), the first and the largest of the Nazi concentration camps. The principal center for the extermination of Jews, Poles, Slavs, and others between 1940 and 1945, the camp encompassed several square miles, including an extension known as Birkenau, site of horrendous housing, gas chambers, and crematoria. At one point, some 140,000 prisoners were held here; and in the 5 years that the camp was in operation, some 1.5 million people perished here. Under today's non-Communist Polish government, the camp places new emphasis on the fact that most of the victims here were Jewish. New plaques, erected near the main monument at Birkenau in 1992, read (in 18 languages): "Let this place remain for eternity as a cry of despair, and a warning to humanity. About one and a half million men, women, children, and infants, mainly Jews from different countries of Europe, were murdered here. The world was silent. Auschwitz-Birkenau 1940-1945."

When the camp was liberated by the Russians in 1945, the gas chambers and crematoria were, for the most part, destroyed. What remains — the vast grounds and the rows of buildings — have been made into a national museum in memory of those who died. The extent and viciousness of the Nazi extermination is perhaps most vivid at the unrestored Birkenau, where the railway track ends at the gas chambers. A collection of the victims' personal possessions is heartbreakingly housed in Auschwitz's tidy stone barracks — one floor-to-ceiling glass case is filled with eyeglasses; another with children's toys; another with hair shorn from prisoners and destined to be sold as pillow stuffing; still another with suitcases packed for the trip to this hell, nametags and travel stickers still legible. These everyday items survive as horrifying reminders of the crimes committed here. There are photographs, too, haunting faces of the men, women, and children who lost their lives. A film shot by the Soviet army just after the liberation is shown several times a day. Although it is translated into several languages, including English, the images are far more moving and shocking than any words. After a visit to Auschwitz, no one — regardless of background or belief — is ever the same. Information: *Auschwitz Museum* (phone: 381-32022).

ORIGINAL BORSCHT BELT No, we're not talking about Catskill Mountain summer resorts, with their endless stream of comedians bellowing, "Take my wife — please!" What we have in mind is the true home of the traditional soup that has been a staple of Jewish, Russian, and Slavic family meals for centuries. What most folks don't realize is that borscht, that quintessentially "Russian" dish, is actually Ukrainian. Lovers of the ruby-red, sweet-sour beet soup shouldn't miss the opportunity to experience it at its source. Stop into almost any restaurant in Kiev, the Ukrainian capital. The borscht in this city is almost always delicious. But don't expect to find the same all-beet broth that you enjoy at your favorite New York City delicatessen. There are almost as many recipes for borscht as there are chefs, and in Ukraine the soup is a hearty combination of beets, meat, and cabbage, often prepared with mushroom stock rather than meat stock, and sometimes with stewed prunes added to the vegetables. If Ukraine is not on your itinerary, sample borscht in Moscow, St. Petersburg, or in any of the other former Soviet republics. In all its endless varieties — warm or cold; with whatever ingredients the chef of the day has at hand; and almost always topped with a generous dollop of *smetana* (sour cream) — borscht was (and is) the closest the old USSR ever came to a national dish.

GYPSY VIOLINS: A ROMANTIC DINNER IN BUDAPEST, Hungary You're seated at a table for two in an elegant Old World restaurant or an intimate wine cellar in Hungary's ancient capital. Candles flicker gently, the soft light playing off the dark, wood-paneled walls, the white tablecloth, and the face of your dinner companion. The meal is traditionally Hungarian, rich and spicy, a memorable mix of flavors and textures: a hearty bowl of goulash, tender veal with a sprinkling of paprika, or perhaps a perfectly cooked piece of *fogas,* the sweet-tasting pike-perch found only in the nearby waters of Lake Balaton. As you linger over a glass of tokay, the native brandy-like dessert wine, the music begins. A small band of Gypsies, dark and handsome, their black and white attire accented by traditional bright-colored sashes, strolls through the dining room, their music in turns flamboyantly lively and tragically melancholy. In time, the Gypsies make their way to your table and pause to play a haunting love song just for you. The adventure and passion of the Gypsy soul seem captured in their violin strings — and the romance of their songs lingers long after the meal is forgotten.

RED SQUARE All that is Russian in the Western mind is embodied in a 2,280-foot-long, 426-foot-wide newly repaired cobblestone stretch in the center of Moscow known as Red Square. Bounded by the thick red brick walls and towers of the Kremlin, the familiar onion domes of St. Basil's Cathedral, the baroque façades of the *GUM* department store, and the *State History Museum* (scheduled to reopen by the end of this year); site of the red and black tomb of the now out-of-favor Vladimir Lenin (who may one day soon be buried in a less glorious spot), guarded by young soldiers who march in lockstep, Red Square is much more than the eye can see. The physical center of Moscow, and the symbolic heart of Mother Russia and yesterday's Soviet Union, much of the dramatic and tumultuous history of this land has been focused here.

Established as the city's marketplace in the 15th century, it was already the center of Moscow's political life by the 16th century, the site of ceremonies, imperial decrees, demonstrations, and executions. It was called *krasnaya*, a Russian word that means "beautiful," as well as "red," in the 17th century, long before the color had any political significance. A sense of history and power pervades Red Square, its vast expanse evokes a hundred different images and ideas. To walk in the square is to walk in the footsteps of Ivan the Terrible, Peter the Great, Catherine the Great, the Romanovs, and every subsequent Russian leader from czar to Communist. The square has been filled with the revolutionary adherents of Lenin and Trotsky waving the hammer and sickle, and with scores of the faithful standing in line for hours to view the body of the revolution's secular saint. It has been the site of parades of tanks and soldiers passing before Stalin, Khrushchev, Brezhnev, and Gorbachev on innumerable *May Days,* now called the *Day of Spring and Labor.* On *Christmas Day* 1991, the old Russian tricolor flag was raised above the square, replacing the Communist hammer and sickle, drawing to a close yet another act in the drama that is Russian history. The final act on this historic stage has yet to be performed. But no matter what flags fly over its buildings, Red Square will always conjure up Russia in the world's imagination.

Eastern Europe for the Savvy Shopper

Unlike most of Western Europe, shopping and Eastern Europe *do not* go hand in hand. You'll find precious few designer clothing shops, and as for bargains in fine leather and suede — forget it. What the savvy shopper will find, however, is an unlimited range of items that generally are difficult to find in the West or simply unavailable — hand-embroidered clothing from Poland, the distinctive pottery of Romania, amber jewelry and lacquerware from Russia and Ukraine, the beautiful crystal of the Czech Republic, hand-painted porcelain from Hungary, and myriad examples of traditional craftswork. It is to these unique expressions of the Eastern European marketplace that the shopper should look.

Remember, too, that shopping is part of the *experience* of travel. Buy because it brings you into contact with people and places, customs and creativity. Shop for those things you couldn't find elsewhere, remembrances that will call to mind your trip when you are back home. Then your purchase becomes a three-dimensional snapshot, and the pleasure of the experience lingers.

What follows is a list of the best buys and the best places at which to buy them, arranged by country.

A final note for lovers of antiques: There are wonderful places to shop for antiques in Eastern Europe, and more have opened especially in the last few years. Do be aware, however, that many countries in the region forbid the export of any item over 50 years old, and some have restrictions on other items as well. Be sure to check with the proper tourist authorities.

But even if you must limit yourself to window shopping, antiques stores offer a wonderful glimpse into a country's culture.

For listings of the best shops in Eastern Europe's major cities, see the *Shopping* sections of the individual reports in THE CITIES.

THE BALTICS Handicrafts and jewelry are the best buys in the Baltics. Latvian specialty goods include heavy, painted ceramics; hand-knit socks and mittens; embroidered blouses and other native clothing; woodcarvings; wickerware; and amber jewelry. Particularly exquisite knitwear is found in Estonia — each area of the country has a unique pattern, color, and tradition for sweaters, mittens, socks, and blankets. Also available are fine crystal, leather goods, porcelain, wickerware, dolls in folk costumes, knit cobweb-patterned shawls of woolen lace from Haapsalu, woodenware, and creative jewelry by contemporary Estonian artists. The Estonian island of Muhu specializes in colorful floral embroidery stitched onto slippers, sweaters, blankets, and dresses. The best buy in Lithuania is amber — it may be purchased at most souvenir shops either in unset pieces or made into jewelry. Lithuanian amber often has a bit of twig or an insect trapped inside; such flaws are prized by Lithuanians because they indicate that the piece is authentic, not manmade.

> **NOTE** As the new currencies are introduced in Latvia and Lithuania, it is expected that hard currency shops will no longer accept foreign money but will require payment in local currency or by credit card.

Riga, Latvia Shops that sell alcohol are the place to go for Riga's famous black balsam liqueur, Rigas Melnais Balzams. Also, look for fine carved wood items, glassware, and handmade jewelry.

Tallinn, Estonia Look for all kinds of chocolates, especially a delicious variety of truffle bonbons; as well as hand-knit sweaters, caps, socks, and mittens of thick, coarse wool; national costumes; knit shawls; linens; contemporary jewelry and leatherwork; and woven baskets.

Vilnius, Lithuania Shopping is not the Lithuanian capital's strong suit; the selection of crafts and gift items is limited. The most-wanted items on visitors' lists include amber and liquor and liqueurs. Other traditional Lithuanian goods, including the long, colorful, heavy cotton belts worn with traditional folk costumes, and small *tabochki* (souvenir pins) can be found in most shops.

BULGARIA The most popular souvenirs here are dolls dressed in folk costumes, brass plates and cups, pots for making Turkish coffee, ceramics painted in bright florals and native ornamental designs, and *rakija,* the national (and potent) drink made from plums.

Sofia There are numerous places to browse and buy along Vitosha Bulevard. Look for shops that specialize in silver jewelry, leather goods, and embroidered blouses, as well as rugs, wooden articles, ceramics, and copper coffee sets. At the city's main outdoor market (on Maria Louisa Bulevard), vendors sell Oriental spices, handmade woolens, and pottery.

CZECH REPUBLIC This country is known for its beautiful Bohemian crystal and lavish gold-rimmed china, particularly tea sets. Other special items include Moravian pottery and handmade ornaments of braided and glazed *vižovice* dough, and hand-painted *Easter* eggs. Another great buy is classical music on cassette tapes and compact discs.

Prague Visitors should look for fine crystal, glassware, and handicrafts in or near the Wenceslas Square area. Also, the city is noted for its festive gingerbread tree ornaments in all shapes and sizes at *Christmastime.*

HUNGARY Beautiful hand-painted Herend and Zsolnay porcelain, hand-painted pottery, handmade lace, tableware, crystal, and cut glass, Matyó and Kalocsa embroidery, dolls in regional costumes, embroidered sheepskin jackets, and herdsmen's carvings in wood and horn are among the sought-after items here. A packet of authentic Hungarian paprika, available at any grocery store, also makes a great souvenir, as does a bottle of Hungarian wine, sold at many delicatessens.

Budapest A number of shops and cooperatives are devoted to traditional folk art. Try those specializing in Hungarian classical and folk music or perhaps ethnographic prints. There is a small flea market near the Astoria metro stop where Eastern European migrants sell their goods.

Szentendre This charming village on the Danube, about 20 minutes north of Budapest, has long been a renowned artists' colony. In 1986, *Arteria* (1 Varisgaz tér), Hungary's first private art gallery, was founded by 20 painters. Right around the corner from the main village square, it offers high-quality abstract art at fantastically low prices (first-rate lithographs for as little as $20).

POLAND Vodka is a specialty, as are glassware, woodcarvings, handwoven rugs, leather, linens, and embroidered clothing. Handmade sterling silver and amber jewelry are also good buys.

Cracow This is not a city of high fashion or luxury goods, but visitors may find good buys in leather, linens, and folk art. The best place to look is Cloth Hall in Ryneck Główny (Main Market Square), which houses numerous stalls and shops selling native wares.

Warsaw This city's version of Fifth Avenue is Ulica Nowy Swiat (New World Street). Look for old and new jewelry along the side streets of the Old Town.

ROMANIA Handicrafts include lead crystal from Transylvania; handmade lace; woodcarvings; pottery (including the beautiful shiny black Margina pottery); wool sweaters; hats; handwoven rugs; beautifully woven long-haired sheepskin blankets of Maramures; and embroidered tablecloths, linens, blouses, skirts, and native costumes. Most of these items are available at major hotels in Bucharest and throughout the country. These shops offer some decent bargains, especially for crystal. Stores where Romanians shop (and pay in lei) also can offer some interesting finds.

Bucharest Look for handmade wool rugs, scarves, and national costumes and blouses. Also, most stores carry a wide selection of wonderful woodcarvings and ceramics at low prices, as well as record albums and cassette tapes of native music.

RUSSIA Among the Russian treasures to be found are *matryoshka* dolls, those families of gaily painted wooden figures hidden one inside the other (Yeltsin dolls with Soviet leaders back to Lenin nested inside are particularly popular these days); black and red lacquer boxes, chess sets, spoons, and bowls; blue-and-white ceramic Gzhel pottery; painted trays; hand-carved wooden toys; art books; silverware; china tea sets; printed scarves; amber jewelry; fur hats and coats; samovars; balalaikas; caviar; vodka and champagne; and chocolate.

Moscow In addition to *GUM* on Red Square, there are three shopping areas of particular interest. The Arbat is a pedestrian shopping street with numerous interesting stores selling books, posters, antiques, and handicrafts, and plenty of street vendors. The churches directly behind the *Rossiya* hotel (Varvarka Ulitsa) all have wonderful little souvenir shops. And on weekends there's an outdoor flea market at Izmailovskiy Park on the northeast edge of the city, where some of the early czars, including Peter the Great, spent their childhoods.

St. Petersburg Nevsky Prospekt is the main shopping street, perhaps the most elegant thoroughfare in Russia. It is lined with shops selling crystal, china, paintings, ceramics, jewelry, recordings, and lacquered boxes. A number of shops throughout the city carry traditional Russian crafts, as well as furs and jewelry.

If time permits, be sure to go to the *Kuznechiy Rynok* (3 Kuznechnaya Ulitsa), St. Petersburg's best farmers' market, where merchants from every corner of the former Soviet Union come to sell their wares under a big tent. Prices at the farmers' market are traditionally much higher than in the stores, but the array of goods is impressive. The market is open daily from 7 AM to 6 PM.

SLOVAKIA While glass and crystal from the neighboring Czech Republic can still be found here, look for samples of regionally produced *majolica* plates, jugs, bowls — decorated with the traditional blue-and-white flowers and other colorful motifs. Traditional Slovak craftsmen are well known for their woodcarving, weaving, and hand-sewn folk costumes. Slovakia also sells and produces some religious icons. Modern artisans favor beautifully glazed ceramics, boutique clothes, and unusual jewelry.

Bratislava The city is brimming with wide choices and reasonable prices for crystal, colorful pottery, and general merchandise. Shops in the Old Town are your best bet for souvenirs, musical recordings, books, and crystal.

UKRAINE Local crafts to look for include woodcarvings and woodenware, china, dolls, kilims, and embroidered shirts; books and musical recordings also make nice souvenirs.

Kiev Look for a wide array of furs, handicrafts, foods, and liquor, as well as woodcarvings and Ukrainian arts and crafts. Also popular are dolls in native costume, woodenware, embroidered shirts, and other souvenir items.

Spas: Eastern Europe's Unique Watering Spots

Long before travelers even dreamed of the pleasures of sea bathing and suntanning, spas like *Marienbad* and *Vichy,* blessed with mineral-rich waters thought to have healing powers, were important stops on a European travel itinerary — every bit as important as Paris, Rome, and St. Petersburg.

Taking a cure — a favorite pastime of so many historic and fictional characters — is still a possibility in Eastern Europe. Several countries have a fair sampling of mineral baths — most comfortable, a few luxurious — where visitors can find peace for both body and soul.

Here's a selection of places to sample the spa experience. It's best to check with your travel agent or your hotel's information desk for up-to-the-minute details.

CZECH REPUBLIC *Mariánské Lázně* and *Karlovy Vary,* (*Marienbad* and *Carlsbad,* respectively, in German) are Eastern Europe's principal spa centers. The grandiose hotels, pastel façades, elegant palm trees, and crystal chandeliers are from an earlier, more gracious period that was at odds with the communized monotony of postwar Bohemia. The winds of political change have blown good news this way, however, particularly to *Karlovy Vary.* The *Pupp* and the *Imperial* hotels, after undergoing rigorous renovations, have returned to their pre-Stalin splendor. In addition to enjoying the waters and other spa pleasures, visitors may take tours through the beautiful nearby hills, and visit Count Metternich's superb castle (though you'll have to go to Schloss Nymphenberg near Munich if you want to see where *Last Year at Marienbad* really was filmed). Bookings in the Czech Republic are necessary well in advance, since hotel facilities are limited. The most practical approach is to sign up for one of the comprehensive tours that include airfare, full room and board, and access to all health facilities; arrangements can be made through *Cedok*. Information: *Cedok*, 10 E. 40th St., Suite 1902, New York, NY 10016 (phone: 212-689-9720).

HUNGARY The country offers more than 600 mineral water springs with curative claims for everything from rheumatism to heart disease. The natural, warm-water spas of Budapest are known throughout Eastern Europe, although they have not been widely publicized in the West. Within the city are a dozen or so baths, where you can enjoy a tradition of taking the waters that dates back to the Roman occupation. The *Thermál Margitsziget* and the *Gellért* are the best-known spas in Budapest. The *Margitsziget* — a luxury hotel from a bygone era — is on Margaret Island, which sits in the middle of the Danube. Its thermal waters were brought to the surface in 1866. The *Gellért* hotel, located at the foot of the Buda Hills at the edge of the Danube River, has been in operation since 1918; its spa features natural mineral springs.

There are Turkish baths throughout the country as well, the Ottomans having continued the bathing tradition through the 16th and 17th centuries. Some of the older hotels have their own spa facilities. One of the best-known spas outside Budapest is the 12-acre thermal lake at Hévíz, southwest of the capital. Fed by a natural hot spring, it has been known since Roman times, and those with rheumatic complaints and other health problems have long sought treatment here. The enormous spa at *Balatonfüred* on Lake Balaton is known internationally for its treatment of cardiac ailments. There are plenty of hotels nearby, although many of them are rather drab, Soviet-style accommodations. Information: *IBUSZ Hungarian Travel Co.*, 1 Parker Plaza, Suite 1104, Ft. Lee, NJ 07024 (phone: 201-592-8585).

ROMANIA The country's Black Sea spas combine medical treatment with first class hotels and white sand beaches. The strip of seacoast from the Danube Delta and south is dotted with resorts and spas for treating arthritic and rheumatic conditions, lung and respiratory ailments, heart trouble, and other health problems. Mamaia, Eforie Nord, Mangalia, and Constanţa are just a few of the resorts offering anti-aging treatments. Most spas have their own hotels, with swimming pools, restaurants, air conditioning, and other amenities; some of them extend treatment to visitors as "outpatients." Book through *Carpaţi*, the Romanian Tourist Board. Information: *Carpaţi*, 152 Madison Ave., New York, NY 10016 (phone: 212-447-1537).

Classic Cruises and
Wonderful Waterways

Eastern Europe is graced with some of the world's most spectacular rivers, lakes, and waterways. Whether you explore them by ship, sailboat, ferry, or rowboat, the experience is unforgettable.

LAKE BALATON, Hungary With some 122 miles (195 km) of coastline, this is one of Europe's largest lakes and one of Hungary's greatest tourist attractions. Surrounded by spacious parklands and lined with resort towns, it has been a famous recreation area since the 19th century. The best way to experience the lake's vast beauty is to rent a sailboat or rowboat (motorboats are not permitted) at one of the many establishments along the shore. As you sail along, traditional farmhouses, beautifully preserved, will appear along the North Shore, and several lakeside castles will slip into view. For those interested in a little onshore exploration, the castles in the towns of Sümeg, Veszprém, Balatonszentgyörgy, and Keszthely have interesting museums. Other intriguing onshore spots are the open-air ethnography museum at Tihany, which includes ruins of a Celtic wall, a Roman tower, and a 900-year-old abbey crypt; and the 18th-century palace at Keszthely, which houses a museum and an extensive library. When dining in the area, be sure to sample *fogas,* a sweet-tasting, nearly boneless whitefish found only in the waters of Lake Balaton. It is best served poached in bouillon. Also try the very small fish called *sullo,* grilled and served hot and crisp. Other fish native to the water are catfish, bream, carp, and trout. To accompany your meal, try one of the local wines. Appropriately enough, given its festive, vacation atmosphere, Balaton is renowned for its excellent vintages. The Badacsony region just north of the lake produces sweet white varietals, tramini and sauvignon blanc, which are aged first in the cask and then in the bottle.

DANUBE While it is certainly not blue, this celebrated waterway is long — 1,770 miles/2,832 km — and immeasurably historic: The geography of the river was a factor in much of the movement of European history, as it passes some of Europe's most important and glittering cities and forms the borders between a number of Eastern European countries. From its two sources in Germany's Black Forest, the Danube flows southeast across Germany, then into Austria, where it passes Linz and Vienna. It then forms the border between Slovakia and Hungary, passing Bratislava. At Szob it turns south into central Hungary, where it flows past Budapest. The river enters Yugoslavia (Serbia) northwest of Belgrade, then flows southeast, to form the border between Yugoslavia and Romania. The Danube then continues on to form the Romanian-Bulgarian border, turns north, and passes though eastern Romania to the port city of Galaţi, where it empties into a delta before flowing into the Black Sea. Day cruises depart from most of the major cities along the river, but perhaps the best way to see the many beautiful sights and cities is to take a luxury cruise. *European Cruises* offers a 22-day sail from Austria to Istanbul, with stops in Vienna; Bratislava in Slovakia; and Esztergom and Budapest in Hungary from March through October. A number of other tour operators also offer Danube tours; check with your travel agent. Information: *European Cruises,* 241 E. Commercial Blvd., Ft. Lauderdale, FL 33334 (phone: 800-5-DANUBE).

DNIEPER This is Europe's third-longest river (1,364 miles/2,182 km), beginning in Russia near the city of Smolensk and ending in the Black Sea in Ukraine. During the warm weather months, cruises down the Dnieper River (Dnipro in Ukrainian) stop at a dozen or so small Ukrainian towns and are a delightful way to enjoy the beautiful countryside. Nine-day cruises sail from Kiev to Odessa, or vice versa. Don't count on all the comforts of the *QE2,* but do expect lovely sights and a sense of adventure. Information: *River Passenger Transport Agency,* Rich Kovy Vokzar, Kiev (phone: 044-416-1268); *Londonskaya Travel,* Primorsky Bulvar, Odessa (phone: 0482-228468).

WATERWAYS OF ST. PETERSBURG Peter the Great's showcase city is built on a network of rivers and canals that snake in, out, and through the town, reflecting on their surfaces the splendid architecture that makes St. Petersburg one of the most beautiful cities in the East or West. It's pleasant to walk along these waterways, crossing over the many ornate bridges, but for a special perspective on this lovely metropolis, don't pass up the 2-hour cruise along the Fontanka, one of the city's prettiest rivers. The Fontanka, which circles the center of St. Petersburg, was the southern boundary of the city until the mid-18th century. Many fine townhouses and palaces were built here, including the brilliant red Anichkov Palace on the corner of Nevsky Prospekt. From May through October, boat tours depart every 15 to 30 minutes from the dock near the Anichkov Bridge, where Nevsky Prospekt crosses the Fontanka. Boat trips on the Neva are also offered; they leave from a dock in front of the *St. Petersburg* hotel. Information: For a tour with an English-speaking guide, buy tickets through your hotel service bureau. Tickets for tours without guides, however, are much less expensive and can be purchased at the pier.

Good Sports

The variety of landscape and climate in Eastern Europe — balmy sea coasts, towering mountain ranges, dense forests, fertile plains — allows for a wide range of sports and outdoor activities. In fact, although they're little known in the West, many of Eastern Europe's resorts and natural preserves rival their Western European and American counterparts in both beauty and facilities. The following are some of the best in the region.

MOUNTAIN RESORTS FOR SKIING AND HIKING

Aside from the splendor of the mountains of Eastern Europe and the abundance of fresh snow, the culture into which the sport takes you is almost a vacation unto itself. Ski down the steep Carpathians in Romania and you're likely to pass a shepherd with his flock crossing a frozen pond. The skiing itself is spectacular, with long drops, challenging but comfortable runs, and decent hardware. Prices are right, too, as no one here has yet heard of the $50-a-day lift ticket. Hotels and restaurants in all these resorts offer comfort, diversity, and lots of fun.

ZAKOPANE, Poland The mountains of Poland have been getting some extra attention in recent years, thanks to native son and avid skier Pope John Paul II. As a result, the rest of the world is discovering the beautiful mountains that the Poles (and the pope) have long enjoyed. Zakopane, a charming town nestled between the Gubałowka Ridge and the towering Tatras, is Poland's most popular mountain resort. There's skiing from November through May, but the beauty of the mountains and valleys draw Poles to Zakopane year-round. There are numerous ski trails, and cable railways and lifts to nearby peaks, as well as nicely maintained trails for walking and hiking during the spring, summer, and fall. At Kuźnice, a little more than 2 miles (3 km) south of Zakopane, there is a funicular to Kasprowy Wierch (6,451 feet), the region's most famous ski mountain. There are plenty of *Orbis*-run hotels and lodging houses in the area and a lively après-ski life. The town of Zakopane itself is a museum of regional folk culture, with wooden gingerbread houses that look like Victorian valentines against the backdrop of pine forests and snow-peaked mountains. Information: *Orbis*, 22 Ulica Krupówki, Zakopane, Poland (phone: 165-5051) or 342 Madison Ave., New York, NY 10173 (phone: 212-867-5011).

POIANA BRAŞOV, Transylvania, Romania Near the city of Braşov in the Transylvanian Carpathians is Poiana Braşov, one of Romania's best ski resorts. Skiing here is spectacular, with trails for all levels of ability. For cross-training enthusiasts there's also cross-country skiing, ice skating, indoor swimming, and other indoor and outdoor activities. A ski school and a nursery are on site, and rental equipment is available, although even semi-serious skiers will want to bring along their own equipment. Buses shuttle skiers between the hotels and the slopes. At the foot of a 2,625-foot vertical drop is a complex of restaurants, discos, and at least half a dozen good hotels. Après-ski also is fun in Poiana, with an array of theme restaurants (Gypsy, Transylvania, Dacian) and nightlife that features folk dancing, live music, and discos. Bran Castle, of *Dracula* fame, is nearby, and the 13th-century city of Braşov offers good shopping, restaurants, and interesting sights. The best Romanian folk show is at the *Cerbul Carpatin* (Carpathian Stag; Stradă Republicii; no phone) restaurant in Braşov.

In the summer, Poiana Braşov offers hikers the same array of comfortable accommodations, good restaurants, and nightlife, plus the chance to tramp through some of Romania's wildest countryside and most beautiful mountains. Book through a travel agent or *Carpaţi,* the Romanian National Tourist Office. Information: *Carpaţi,* 152 Madison Ave., New York, NY 10016 (phone: 212-447-1537).

VYSOKÉ TATRY (HIGH TATRAS), Slovakia Like most of Eastern Europe, this magnificent mountain district is generally overlooked by Americans, though the resort areas are less developed and less expensive than their Western cousins. Eastern Europe's best skiing is found at Starý Smokovec, in the heart of the High Tatras. Located in a national park rich with deep woods, frozen lakes, and craggy peaks, the ski resort offers jumps and slalom runs, as well as long, gentle cross-country trails. The base elevation is 3,280 feet, and the mood is pastoral and low-key. Skiers can opt for the fine, old, but pricey *Grand* hotel (Starý Smokovec; phone: 969-2154 or 969-2229).

There is also a century-old tradition of climbing in the High Tatras, and a well-maintained network of huts and hotels. Starý Smokovec, Strbské Pleso (4,428 feet), and Tatranská Lomnica (2,788 feet) are the main starting points for area excursions. Guided tours, maps, and information can be found at the Dom Horskéj Služby (Mountain Rescue Service; phone: 969-2820 or 969-2855) and at the Tatras National Park (TANP) Information Center in Starý Smokovec. The *Patria* hotel (Strbské Pleso; phone and fax: 969-92591) is a fine starting place for trips into the popular Rysy mountains. Cave lovers should stop by to view the stalactites at Belianskájaskyňa. Among the best high *chata* (mountain huts) are the Zbojnička, the Terryho, the Zamkovský, and the Pod Rysy, at 7,380 feet, the highest hut in Slovakia. Information: *Cedok,* 5-9 Jesenského ulica, Bratislava, Slovak Republic (phone: 7-499142; fax: 7-499591) or *TatraTour,* 25 Bajkalská ulica, Bratislava, Slovak Republic (phone: 7-63128; fax: 7-212722).

SUN AND SAND

The resorts on the Black Sea, the Aegean Sea, the Adriatic, and the Baltic are the most developed areas for tourism in Eastern European countries with coastlines, and the amenities are surprisingly close to what you'll find at seaside resorts in the West.

JĀRMALA, BALTIC SEA, Latvia For sunbathing, Jārmala is Latvia's best-known health resort. It's a delightful coastal spot 9 miles (14 km) outside Riga, set on low, rolling hills, where sports opportunities abound. Unfortunately, swimming isn't one of them. Local authorities regularly close the beach because of pollution, much of it from a nearby pulp-and-paper mill. But the beach itself is paradise, with fine, golden sand. Flanked on one side by the Baltic Sea and the other by Latvia's second-largest river, the Lielupe, Jārmala is made up of 12 fishing villages strung along more than 19 miles

(30 km) of coastline. It's home to 70,000 people and 300 different varieties of plants. Boats cruise along the coast several times a day in summer. Ask at your hotel for the schedule, which is sometimes erratic. Jārmala's main street, Jomas Iela, is a pedestrian mall dotted with small shops, art galleries, and outdoor cafés. Spas, sanatoriums, children's camps, and small, pastel-colored *dachas* decorated with gingerbread trim abound (by law all buildings must no taller than the surrounding treetops). Summer concerts are held in the outdoor *Dzintaru Koncertzāle* (Amber Concert Hall). In winter, cross-country skiers flock to the area's pine forests, as do the swans that in warm weather patrol Riga's City Channel. When the channel freezes, the swans migrate to Jārmala, where they gather along the beach and will tamely eat from your hand.

MAMAIA, BLACK SEA, Romania The Black Sea is one of those bodies of water that American children learn about in geography but never associate with swimming. Yet the Romanian, Bulgarian, Ukrainian, and Russian Black Sea coasts are to Eastern Europe what the Riviera is to France. Mamaia, a 5-mile stretch of beach and rich vegetation between the Black Sea and Lake Siutghiol, offers a wide choice of hotels with rooms and facilities that are fully satisfactory. The crowd is international, with a preponderance of Eastern Europeans, and the sports and nightlife are abundant and varied. Prices are reasonable, and there are many Romanian restaurants serving fish and other good food and wine (also see *Romania* in DIRECTIONS).

HUNTING

There are abundant opportunities for hunting large and small game, and for enjoying some of the serene, unspoiled parts of Eastern Europe. Game include deer, pheasant, partridge, and wild boar. Foreign hunters are subject to strict regulations; and permits to bring guns into most countries are required. Copies of the regulations can be obtained from national tourist boards. Here are two of your best bets for hunting adventures.

ZIDLOCHOVICE, Southern Moravia, Czech Republic Practically one giant game reserve, Southern Moravia offers some of the finest hunting on the Continent; the pheasant preserve at Zidlochovice, near Brno, is a rich and unique area, attracting hunters by the hundreds every autumn. Northern Moravia also has two excellent reserves in the Jeseniky and Beskydy districts. Prague, incidentally, has a number of specialty shops where you can buy excellent hunting equipment. Information: *Cedok,* 18 Na příkopě, Prague, Czech Republic (phone: 2-212-7111); or *Cedok,* 10 E. 40th St., Suite 1902, New York, NY 10016 (phone: 212-689-9720).

GAVRILOVKA, Ukraine This beautiful piece of land, located in the Ukraine near the city of Kherson on the banks of the Dnieper River, is reserved for hunting expeditions. Guided group or individual tours are arranged during the deer-hunting season, September through October. Information: Tours can be booked through your travel agent, or the *Intourist* office in Kherson (phone: 055-222-2619).

WILD EASTERN EUROPE

The wildlife reserves in Eastern Europe are spectacular, home to hundreds of species of large and small animals and birds, wildflowers, and even such edibles as mushrooms and berries. The following is one of the best — an extraordinary place where you'll find clear lakes and streams, quiet places for walking, and flora and fauna flourishing in lands almost untouched by civilization.

PUSZCZA BIAŁOWIESKA, Poland One of the last strongholds of the majestic bison, this deep wilderness — the largest virgin forest area in central Europe — also shelters wild boar, stags, lynx, wolves, elk, and more than 200 species of birds. Giant 500-year-old trees still flourish here, and in late September, during the mating season, the bucks go antler to antler and put on quite a spectacle. Access to the forest is restricted, but guides can be hired for a horse-drawn cart tour, often best done very early in the morning. Culinary highlights of a visit to the area include mushrooms (eat only those served at restaurants or by Polish hosts), wild blueberries, and *zubrówka,* an aromatic vodka made from a local grass. Information: *Orbis,* 342 Madison Ave., New York, NY 10173 (phone: 212-867-5011); or in Warsaw, 142 Marszalkowska (phone: 22-278031).

HORSEBACK RIDING

PUSZTA, Hungary Horse breeding and riding are a specialty of this agricultural Great Plains area. A day-long excursion from Budapest to the town of Lajosmizse includes close looks at the farms and the horses (Lipizzaners are among the breeds here). A popular tour includes a stunning horse show. The day concludes with a traditional Hungarian dinner at a *csarda,* or peasant inn, which features Gypsy music and dancing, and plenty of wine and *palinka,* the national drink made from plums and apricots. Tours are held March through October. Information: *IBUSZ Hungarian Travel Co.,* 1 Parker Plaza, Suite 1104, Ft. Lee, NJ 07024 (phone: 201-592-8585).

SOCCER

DYNAMO, Kiev, Ukraine While visitors to Eastern Europe are more likely to be found at a theater or opera house than a sports arena, attending a Ukrainian soccer match is a great way to meet the natives and to gain a greater understanding of their lives. Kiev is the home of *Dynamo,* a soccer (they call it *futbol*) team that is a multi-championship winner. (In fact, *Dynamo* won the *1986 European Club Championships*.) Games are held in spring, summer, and fall at the *Republican Stadium* (55 Chervonoarmiyska Vulytsia), which seats more than 100,000 *futbol* fans. If *Dynamo* is playing when you're in town, by all means try to get a ticket (they're inexpensive) through *Intourist* and join the locals in cheering their team to victory.

Directions

Introduction

The dramatic and extraordinary changes that have occurred in Eastern Europe during the past few years have made driving tours through this region both more feasible and more attractive to Western travelers. No longer are strictly policed itineraries and regimented arrangements the rule; most countries are allowing foreign travelers greater freedom and flexibility in exploring areas outside the major cities. Westerners may now journey through rural areas, crisscrossing the lesser known parts of the region. Such trips are both interesting and illuminating, enabling travelers to experience not only the beauty of Eastern Europe's mountains, seasides, valleys, and plains, but to see how the people of the countryside — with their varied ethnic backgrounds and traditions — live.

On the following pages are touring routes through 11 Eastern European countries. The tours lead to those areas of greatest scenic and historic interest, with each route organized to cover 3 to 5 days of traveling. From Poland's High Tatras to Moravia and Bohemia in the Czech Republic, from the fascinyating medieval monasteries of Bulgaria to the Russian and Ukrainian resorts along the Black Sea, from the colorful Hungarian towns along the Danube River to the Transylvanian region of Romania, home to the Dracula legend, these tours capture Eastern Europe at its most intimate, historic, and dramatic.

Where possible, tours begin at major cities, and though our routes are most easily negotiated by car, tour operators with local buses often cover the same territory, freeing you from the necessity of driving.

Entries are organized by country or region; an introduction provides some perspective and explains the routes that follow. Entries are not exhaustive or comprehensive; they discuss the highlights of each route and can serve as starting points for longer journeys. The *Best en Route* section of each tour provides hotel and restaurant recommendations along the way (under each city, they are listed in order of expense). There is no effort to cover absolutely everything in these selections; our choices are made on the basis of places that offer the most memorable experiences.

Since most countries are divided into several routes, it is often possible to string these together to form longer itineraries. But if you are pressed for time, you will find that by following any single itinerary you will see the most notable sights in the area.

The Baltic States

Until recently, most Westerners viewed the Baltic states — Estonia, Latvia, and Lithuania — as just another unknown portion of the vast entity called the Soviet Union, three small republics in the northwest corner of the USSR, separated from Scandinavia by the Baltic Sea.

The anti-Soviet movements of the late 1980s, however, brought the Baltic states to the world's attention, and since the three republics achieved their independence in 1991, interest in travel there has increased significantly. At the same time, travel to and through the Baltics has become easier. While large areas of these countries were off-limits to foreigners under Communist rule, today almost the entire Baltic region is open for travelers to explore.

While the capital cities — Tallinn (Estonia), Riga (Latvia), and Vilnius (Lithuania) — offer the most to travelers, excursions outside the major urban centers provide additional insight into the Baltic states. There are no dramatic vistas or awesome historical landmarks along the routes described below. But there are ancient castles, medieval towns, 17th- and 18th-century churches and mansions, small museums of local art and folklore, rolling hills, fields dotted with cows, gleaming lakes and rivers, acres of forest and green parkland, and charming seaside resorts. These routes offer scenic land and seascapes, a greater understanding of the history and culture of the Baltic states, and the opportunity to meet the people of the countryside and to see how they live.

Be aware, however, that driving in the Baltics is still more of an adventure than a usual European tour. Many of the roads (often unlit at night) are in disrepair. Restaurants, restrooms, and other facilities along the road are few and far between; many fall far below Western standards; and there are few that are truly first-rate outside the main cities. In addition, the Baltic states — Latvia and Lithuania in particular — were facing a serious energy crisis at press time. Shortages of fuel often translate as *no* heat or hot water during the winter months. Gasoline is not always available, and even when it is, you may have to stop at several gas stations or wait in long lines until you get that gas gauge up to "F." Be sure your tank and the biggest metal gas canister you can find are both full before embarking on any of the following routes. Be aware also that in the transition to a market economy, many formerly state-owned hotels and restaurants are closing, only to reopen later under private ownership. Due to this unpredictability factor, travelers are advised to call ahead to check whether a hotel or restaurant is still in operation.

Also be sure to bring along the most detailed and up-to-date road map you can find (most probably available in the US). The Baltic states are erasing the Soviet-era names of their streets and towns and returning to their former names, but at this point these countries lack the resources to keep their maps up to date. Many maps printed during the Soviet era were deliberately falsified to hide military and other closed zones. Note, too, that in many areas, only the main roads have numbers, and they are not well marked.

Other necessities for a driving trip in the Baltics: a funnel (for refueling); two spare tires (you can easily blow two tires on a sharp pothole); bottled water and snack food; and, perhaps most important, your senses of curiosity, humor, and adventure.

Each of the eight routes below begins in one of the Baltic capitals and can be covered in a day or two. This approach enables travelers to see the countryside without having to spend too much time searching for fuel and lodging.

Estonia

In many ways, Estonia is the envy of its Baltic brothers, Latvia and Lithuania. The easternmost of the Baltic states, lying between the Baltic Sea and the Gulf of Finland (with Russia to the east and Latvia to the south), Estonia has benefited from its proximity to Finland and Sweden. Now that the country's tourism industry, once rigidly controlled from Moscow, is in the hands of flourishing local businesses, Finnish and Swedish entrepreneurs have been quick to cross the Gulf and set up new, Western class hotels and restaurants.

But the switch to a market economy has been difficult for Estonia, and the process is far from over. The smallest of the Baltic states (roughly the size of New Hampshire and Massachusetts combined, it covers an area of 17,400 square miles), Estonia's size has made it particularly vulnerable to economic change. The country has faced severe food and energy shortages, a sharp fall in production levels, and skyrocketing prices. Despite these difficulties, however, Estonians are still filled with pride over their renewed independence, and they welcome the travelers who have begun to flock to this land with its wealth of history and rich cultural tradition. The introduction of its own currency, the convertible Estonian "kroon" in 1992, has given some stability to the economy and stores are now crammed with domestic and foreign goods, albeit expensive by local standards.

Estonians belong to the Finno-Ugric group of peoples, which includes the Finns and the Hungarians. They trace their roots to an ancient people whom the Roman geographer Tacitus, writing in the 1st century BC, called Aesti. Beginning in the 9th century, the Estonians were conquered by the Vikings, the Danes, the Swedes, the Russians, and the Germans. In 1227, the German Brethren of the Sword, crusaders later called the Teutonic Knights, captured the country and remained in control for over 3 centuries. Under the rule of the knights, four Estonian towns — Tallinn, Pärnu, Narva, and Tartu (then called Dorpat) — became prosperous members of the Hanseatic League. The legacy of this period is still evident in modern Estonia. A number of the churches and stone fortresses built in this era still stand; Lutheranism is still the dominant church; and German is widely spoken as a second language today.

During the 16th and 17th centuries, Estonia was nearly destroyed by ongoing feudal wars between Russia, Sweden, and Poland. Sweden controlled the country from 1629 to 1710, an era considered important by Estonians because the Swedes allowed the Estonian language to be taught in schools and in 1632 the Swedish King Gustavus II founded Estonia's first university.

The Northern War between Russia and Sweden (1710–21) almost wiped out the population of this tiny territory, which has always held strategic importance because of its access to the sea. In 1721, Estonia was incorporated into Russia, although Estonians continued to cling to their national identity. When the Russian Empire began to collapse in 1905, the Estonian independence movement, born in the 1860s, gained momentum. Parties were formed and an Estonian Parliament was elected.

The move toward nationhood was soon thwarted, however, first by the Bolsheviks, who established a government in Tallinn after they seized power in St. Petersburg, and then by the Germans, who occupied the country during World War I. Estonia declared its independence immediately after the war, although it fought the Soviet Union for nearly 2 years before its sovereignty was recognized in 1920.

Political stability eluded the new nation, however. In 1934 President Konstantin Päts abolished political parties and instituted an authoritarian regime. A more democratic government took control in 1938, but a year later the secret Molotov-Ribbentrop pact between Germany and the USSR placed the Baltics under Soviet control. Germany occupied the region during World War II, but after the war the Soviets regained power and for the next 4 decades Moscow controlled almost every aspect of Estonian life.

In the 1980s, *perestroika* gave rise to a new wave of Estonian nationalism. On November 16, 1988, the Estonian Supreme Soviet declared sovereignty for Estonia, a move that set the stage for the following years of struggle. In a March 1990 referendum, an overwhelming majority of Estonians voted in favor of independence. A year and a half later, following the unsuccessful coup in Moscow, Estonia declared its independence. Finally, in September 1992, the US and other Western nations recognized the free nation of Estonia; the newly independent country elected its first president after an interval of 50 years.

The following three driving routes through Estonia are all easily accessible from Tallinn, the capital. The first excursion is to Pärnu, a summer resort; the destination of the second route is Tartu, an academic city and the cradle of Estonian culture; and the third route leads to Narva, on Russia's border.

TALLINN TO PÄRNU

The seaside city of Pärnu is about 80 miles (129 km) — less than a 2-hour drive — from the capital. A bus to Pärnu leaves Tallinn every hour, and there's a daily round-trip train. Although an excursion from Tallinn to Pärnu and back can easily be made in a day, there are several pleasant hotels for those who'd like to spend the night by the sea.

TALLINN For a complete description of the capital and its hotels and restaurants see *Tallinn* in THE CITIES.

En Route from Tallinn Take Route M12, the Pärnu Maantee (Pärnu Highway), which starts at the *Viru* hotel (14 Viru Väljak), and head south. The highway has been renamed "Via Baltica" (the Baltic Way) because it passes through all three Baltic capitals. About 12 miles (19 km) out of Tallinn, the four-lane boulevard becomes a two-lane highway, which leads through evergreen forests and farm fields.

PÄRNU In the 1930s, this seaside resort was known as the "pearl of the Baltic" because of its white sandy beaches, which stretch for miles. In the wake of Estonian independence, this town of 56,000 people is trying to regain its reputation as a trendy, popular resort area. Western businesses have jumped in to assist, and Pärnu now boasts the Swedish-managed *Victoria* (see *Best en Route*), whose restaurant serves the best food in the city. A newly renovated beachhouse along with a second Western-style hotel, the *Bristol* (see *Best en Route*), are other good choices. In addition, the long strands of sand, polluted and neglected during the Soviet years, have been cleaned up, and many Estonians now say that Pärnu has the best beaches in the country.

Pärnu is the fourth-oldest town in Estonia. "Perona," as it was called in 1251, was founded by Bishop Heinrich of the Livonian Order, who built the first harbor. In the middle of the 14th century, Pärnu joined the Hanseatic League and played an important part in the trade between Russia and the western towns of the League. Most of Pärnu's buildings were destroyed during World War II, when the town was occupied by the Nazis. Unfortunately, only a few structures of real historical and architectural value remain.

Under Soviet rule, Pärnu became a "workers' holiday center" and four sanatoriums complete with mud baths were opened in the 1970s. About 50,000 people from across the former Soviet Union came to Pärnu each summer. The town is also renowned for its quiet parks. There are 18 in all — two of the loveliest are the Lydia Koidula Park, across from the *Victoria* hotel, and the Rannapark (Beach Park) on Mere Puiestee (Sea Boulevard).

Architecture and history buffs may want to take the walking tour offered by the Pärnu Tourist Bureau (32 Kuningatee, across from the *Victoria* hotel; phone: 1444-42750); English-speaking guides are available. Among Pärnu's historical structures is Mohr House (21 Rüütlitee — note that "tee" is a suffix meaning street in Estonian). Now a post office, in the 17th century it was the home of a wealthy merchant. Fastened to the eaves of the house is a horseshoe that belonged to the steed of King Karl XII of Sweden, who visited the town in 1700. Russian Empress Catherine the Great stayed at Mohr House when she visited Pärnu in 1764. Nearby is Schmidt House (8 Pühavalmutee), another 17th-century home, which is now a youth center. Two of the nicest buildings in Pärnu house the Town Hall. The yellow baroque-style building on Yyctee dates from the end of the 18th century, while a second structure around the corner on Nikolaitee was built in the early 1900s. Also noteworthy is Catherine Church (on Veetee). Built from 1764 to 1768, this Orthodox church is named in honor of Catherine the Great, who donated the money for the building and also selected its site. Also of interest is the *Folk Art Museum* (8 Rüütlitee; no phone), which gives visitors a glimpse into Pärnu's history through a collection of old photographs and period costumes. Open from 11 AM to 5 PM; closed Mondays.

The town's main attraction, however, is Pärnu Beach, a 2-mile-long strand of fine white sand. There's plenty of room for sunbathing, but due to pollution, swimming is not advised. To reach the beach, follow Supelusetee (Bathing Street) to Ranna Puiestee (Beach Boulevard); there's plenty of parking. A bus also provides transport from the city center. On Mere Puiestee (Sea Boulevard), there's a beach the locals call "Women's Paradise"; no men are allowed, so women can sunbathe in the nude freely here.

Pärnu also has a good yacht club (6 Lootsitee) with experienced sailors. Some members rent out their boats to visitors. For information, contact Peeter Sober (phone: 1444-41948), the director of the yacht club.

A Swedish firm recently began the renovation of the 1930s beachhouse overlooking the bay. At press time it was scheduled to reopen with a café in the daytime and a more formal dining room complete with a live band and dancing in the evening.

Also new on the Pärnu scene is the slew of bars that have opened in the basements of many of Pärnu's buildings and houses (look for signs that say "baar"). Some of these are dark, unpleasant places, but many are more like neighborhood cafés. For a look at the "baar" scene, stop by the *Roosikelder* (Rose Cellar; 18 Kuningatee) or one of the many others along Rüütlitee.

Finally, no trip to Pärnu Beach is complete without a long walk along the pier in the evening, especially in June during *Jaanipaev* (St. John's Day), the Estonian equivalent of Russia's *White Nights.* Night lasts only about 30 minutes around the summer solstice (June 22) in this, the northernmost Baltic state, and festivals with dancing and singing are held here and throughout the country.

BEST EN ROUTE

BEST EN ROUTE

With the demise of *Intourist* in Estonia, hotel reservations are best made through your travel agent or directly with the hotel. In 1992, the Estonian government introduced a new national currency, the "kroon," which has remained stable on foreign markets. Expect to pay $60 and more for a double room in an expensive hotel; $40 to $60 in one listed as moderate; and under $40 for an inexpensive place. Payment is almost always in Estonian kroons; credit cards are not widely accepted. Also be sure to ask what kind of currency is expected before ordering a meal.

Most local restaurants serve Estonian fare, which features a variety of simple but tasty pork dishes made with good quality meat. Try the *seapraad,* a special oven-cooked pork often served with potatoes and turnips, and smoked forrel (trout). Dinner for two, excluding wine and tip, will cost $25 to $40 at restaurants in the expensive category; $20 to $35 at places listed as moderate; and less than $20 at inexpensive spots.

For each location, hotels and restaurants are listed alphabetically by price category.

TALLINN LAAGRI

Peoleo (Oriole) Located about 10 miles (16 km) outside of Tallinn in a quiet, wooded area along the Pärnu Highway, this Estonian-Canadian venture is the best roadside café in Estonia. It's very popular with local highway patrol officers, who stop here for good soup, coleslaw, sausages, fries, hamburgers, pork chops, fresh pastries, homemade cheesecake, and coffee. Service is cafeteria-style. There's also a comfortable motel, opened in 1990, with 44 rooms and 5 cottages. Each room is equipped with a color TV set, a telephone with direct access to international lines, a mini-bar, and private bath. The *Old Saku* restaurant serves tasty soups, pasta, and steaks. There's also a jazz band and dancing most nights. Major credit cards accepted. 555 Pärnu Maantee (phone: 142-556469). Moderate.

BETWEEN TALLINN AND PÄRNU

Camp Kernu This motel is about 23 miles (37 km) from Tallinn on the Pärnu Highway. It has 7 double rooms with a shared shower, and 2 "lux" suites with private bathrooms. There also are 13 cottages and a restaurant serving meat dishes and salads. Pärnu Maantee (phone: 142-771630; fax: 142-214941). Moderate.

PÄRNU

Pärnu's four sanatoriums are now privatized, with some being converted into hotels. Travelers, however, may find these "luxurious" spas quite spartan. *Sanatorium Tervis* (6 Seedri; phone: 1444-43935 or 1444-43127; fax: 1444-42103), considered the most comfortable of Pärnu's spas, resembles an American hospital built in the 1960s, while its main restaurant may remind some of a summer camp cafeteria. The Estonian government maintains 23 apartments for officials at *Tervis,* which offers mud and water "cures," a warm-water swimming pool, and underwater massage. Inquire at the Pärnu Tourist Bureau (see above) or directly at the sanatoriums, located near the beach on Ranna Puiestee.

Bristol Newly opened, this 41-room hostelry on Pärnu's main street is a Swedish-Estonian venture. The dining room serves well-prepared Estonian meals — salads, pork dishes, and good desserts. There's a live band and dancing on weekends. On Rüütlitee, near the *Pärnu* hotel (phone: 1444-44700). Expensive.

Victoria Located in the former *Voit* hotel building, which dates from the early 1900s, this Swedish-managed hotel, opened in June 1991, is among the best in Estonia and ranks first in Pärnu. It has 13 single rooms, 8 doubles, and 2 junior suites nicely decorated in pastel shades. Each room has a color TV set featuring MTV and CNN, and a telephone with access to international lines. (One drawback: Guestrooms are located on top floors and there are no elevators.) There's also a sauna. The elegant restaurant, which has large windows overlooking the Lydia Koidula Park, serves the best food in Pärnu and is particularly strong on Estonian national and Swedish dishes. Try one of the pork dishes for a taste of authentic Estonian fare. In summer, there's dining on an outdoor patio. The English-speaking staff, which is very helpful, organizes fishing trips, boar hunting parties, and sightseeing tours. 25 Kuningatee (phone: 1444-43412; fax: 1444-43415). Expensive.

Emmi Not far from one of the town beaches, this establishment caters to groups, but individual travelers are also welcome. There are 21 bright, clean rooms, 1 suite, and a sauna. The suite has 2 bedrooms, a kitchen, and a bathroom — particularly convenient for families. Rates include breakfast, but the restaurant does not serve lunch or dinner. 2 Lainetee (phone: 1444-22043; fax: 1444-45472). Moderate.

Pärnu At one time the main hotel in town, this 88-room Soviet-style establishment now is only recommended for the budget-conscious. The accommodations are simple, but the location is convenient, close to shopping and the Old Town. The restaurant serves good food. There's a band and dancing most evenings. 44 Rüütlitee (phone: 1444-42142; fax: 1444-43100). Inexpensive.

FROM TALLINN TO TARTU

This 118-mile (187-km) route passes through Estonia's farmland and evergreen forests.

TALLINN For a complete description of the capital and its hotels and restaurants see *Tallinn* in THE CITIES.

En Route from Tallinn Head southeast on Route A202, the Tartu Maantee. The 2-hour drive cuts through the country's dairy heartland. Note the *piimapukk* — little wooden milk stands that look like staircases — along the highway. Containers of milk, left on the stands at the crack of dawn, are picked up by trucks and transported to Tallinn.

TARTU Life in this city of 100,000 people, the second-largest in Estonia, revolves around the university. Founded in 1632 by Swedish King Gustavus II, Tartu University (originally called the Academia Gustaviana) is one of the oldest institutions of higher learning in Europe. It has trained generations of noted scientists, doctors, lawyers, theologians, and historians. Karl Boer (1792-1876), the founder of embryology, studied here, as did German chemist and Nobel Prize winner Wilhelm Ostwald (1853-1932).

Tartu owes its vitality to its large student population. Aside from the university, which has a student body of about 6,000, it is also the site of the Estonian Agricultural Academy, a smaller institute of physics, and a veterinary school. The best time to visit Tartu is in the fall, when students converge from across Estonia. A number of festivals are held then and the city is at its liveliest. During the summer, there are outdoor cafés and music in the main square.

Tartu is the oldest city in Estonia. Russian Prince Yaroslav the Wise established a fortress town called Yuriev here in 1030, and in the 14th century, the city — then called Dorpat — flourished as a key member of the Hanseatic League. Very little of the medieval town remains, however. The city was destroyed during the Northern War (1700–21) and later rebuilt by the Russians. As a result, most of the present-day buildings are in the classical style of the late-18th and 19th centuries.

The city was given its present name in 1919; a year later, the Treaty of Tartu, in which the Soviet Union recognized Estonian sovereignty, was signed here. Tartu has always been fiercely nationalistic — the country's first independence movement was founded here in the 19th century. The city was also the cradle of modern Estonian culture: The first Estonian-language newspaper *Tarto maa rahwa Naddali-Leht* (Tartu Estonian Weekly) was published here in 1806; the first Estonian song festival took place in Tartu in 1869; and the first Estonian theater group, *Vanemuine,* was founded here in 1870. And the Estonian flag was both born and resurrected here: Tartu University students first chose the blue-black-and-white striped banner as the national flag in 1870. Under Soviet rule, the flag was banned, but during an April 1988 demonstration, so many students carried the tricolored banner that the police were powerless and the ban was never again enforced. Today, despite 5 decades of Soviet domination, Tartu remains authentically Estonian. Russian is hardly ever heard on Tartu's streets and practically no Russian signs remain.

The best place to start a tour of the city is at Toomemagi (Cathedral Hill). Located in the center of town, it is easily reached via the stairs that climb up from Jakobitee near the statue of King Gustavus II of Sweden.

The site of the original fortress of Yuriev, Toomemagi is now a wonderful park, green and serene. Many of the city's festivals are held here, and its pleasant paths, lined with statues of noted Estonian writers and scientists, are ideal for long walks. Toomemagi is named for the 13th-century Cathedral of St. Peter and St. Paul, one of the city's two remaining medieval structures (the other, the 14th-century St. John's Church, is at the foot of the hill). The cathedral stands mostly in ruins, although one section has been converted into the *Tartu University Museum*. Also located in the park is the *Theatrum Anatomicum* (Dissecting Theater), where generations of Estonian doctors have conducted anatomical research. The centerpiece of Toomemagi is the observatory built by the Russian astronomer Vassili Struve in 1822.

Tartu's Raekoja Plats (Town Hall Square, formerly called Soviet Square), lined with 18th- and 19th-century buildings, is dominated by one of the city's most impressive edifices, the pink 18th-century Raekoja (Town Hall). Souvenir hunters might want to stop in at the *Kunstisalon* (Art Store; 8 Raekoja Plats), which sells Estonian paintings, pottery, leather, and knitted handicrafts. Also try *Raë* (12 Raekoja Plats), which offers national crafts and costumes. The square is also the site of folk fairs and political demonstrations.

Another imposing structure is the main building of Tartu University on Ulikoolitee (University Street) not far from Raekoja Plats. Distinguished by its tall white columns, it houses administrative offices, the *Tartu University Classical Art and Antiquities Museum*, and a lovely concert hall.

Also worth a visit is the *Estonian National Museum* (32 Veskitee; phone: 1434-32254), which mounts exhibits related to Finno-Ugric history, and houses the world's largest collection of Estonian folk art. The museum is open Wednesdays through Sundays from 11 AM to 6 PM.

The Tartu Reisiburoo (Tourist Bureau; 35 Laitee; phone: 1434-31533) can provide information on accommodations, restaurants, and sightseeing in the city. It's open weekdays from 9 AM to 5 PM; weekends from 9 AM to 3 PM.

BEST EN ROUTE

Hotel reservations are best made through your travel agent or directly with the hotel. Expect to pay $50 or more in a hotel listed as expensive; $35 to $50 in a place listed as moderate; and under $35 for an inexpensive place. Dinner for two, excluding wine and tip, will cost $20 to $35 at places listed as moderate; and less than $20 at inexpensive spots. Payment is almost always in Estonian kroons; credit cards are not widely accepted — be sure to ask what kind of currency is expected before ordering a meal.

For each location, hotels and restaurants are listed alphabetically by price category.

ADAVERE

Adavere Tuulik (The Windmill) This interesting eatery in a historic windmill features good food and a quaint atmosphere. House specialties cater to the hunter's palate and include smoked quail, wild boar, trout, and mackerel. Open daily from 7 AM to midnight. Reservations unnecessary. American Express and Diners Club accepted. Tartu Maantee, about 75 miles (120 km) from Tallinn (phone: 1434-57311 or 1434-57351). Moderate.

MAO

Presto This 24-hour café — located halfway between Tallinn and Tartu in the tiny town of Mao — serves soups, salads, sandwiches, sausages, pork dishes, and coffee and desserts. Closed Sundays. Reservations unnecessary. No credit cards accepted. Tartu Maantee (phone: 8234-94148). Inexpensive.

PAIDE

Paide Good, traditional Estonian food is served at this dining spot in the city of Paide, about 60 miles (96 km) from Tallinn. A jacket and tie are required for men in the evenings. Open Tuesdays through Sundays for lunch and dinner. Reservations advised. No credit cards accepted. Raekoja Plats (phone: 1438-41330). Moderate.

TARTU

Park An older 3-story hostelry conveniently located next to Toomemagi, this is Tartu's best, with a lovely decor and an exceptionally friendly staff. No two of the 20 immaculate rooms are alike, although all feature high ceilings, antique furniture, color TV sets, telephones, and vases of fresh flowers. The suites have balconies overlooking a park. The dining room, open to hotel guests only, is graced with a lovely old fireplace. There's also a sauna and an indoor swimming pool. Breakfast is included. 23 Vallikraavi (phone: 1434-33663). Expensive.

Taru Opened in 1989, this Finnish-run property offers 40 clean and comfortable (but a little drab) rooms, with heavy brown curtains and Soviet-style furniture. The location, about a mile from the city center, is a bit inconvenient. But the place has one outstanding feature: the *Fox* restaurant, which serves the best food in Tartu. Specialties include a delicious seafood salad and a croquette filled with spiced ground meat and topped with a tangy carrot-garlic sauce. For dessert, try the brandied apple cooked in meringue with a light custard. The restaurant is open daily for lunch and dinner. Reservations advised. Major credit cards accepted. 9 Rebasetee (phone: 1434-73700; fax: 1434-74095). Expensive.

Tavern Located in the basement of the "Leaning Tower of Tartu," a sloping white edifice on the main square, Tartu's newest restaurant is surprisingly modern in design with red tablecloths and napkins, and sparkling silverware. The strictly European fare includes soups, pasta, and meat and fish dishes. Open daily. Reservations advised. No credit cards accepted. 20 Raekoja Plats (phone: 1434-31222). Expensive.

Tarvas This city-owned dining spot is popular with the locals, who arrive in formal evening wear. The bill of fare features such Estonian specialties as pork rolls and beet salad. There is music and dancing every night except Monday. Open for lunch and dinner; lunch only on Mondays. Reservations advised. No credit cards accepted. Close to the bus station and the market. 2 Riiatee (phone: 1434-52253). Moderate.

Pussirohukelder (The Gunpowder Magazine) The food is nothing to write home about, but what this place lacks in culinary flare it more than makes up for in atmosphere. A gunpowder cellar built by the Swedes in 1774, it was restored and opened as a restaurant in 1982. The menu features caviar, soup, and pork dishes, accompanied by wine, vodka, and champagne. It's a popular spot with the city's students (especially after exam time), who sit in the adjoining bar until the band starts playing in the dining room on Wednesday, Friday, and Saturday nights. Open daily for lunch and dinner. Reservations advised. No credit cards accepted. 28 Loositee (phone: 1434-34231). Moderate to inexpensive.

Remark Opened in 1992, this small, Estonian-owned establishment has 4 guestrooms and a nice atmosphere. Breakfast (included in the room rate) is served in a small café with a fireplace. There's also a bar and a sauna. The staff is friendly and speaks English. 94 Tahetee (phone: 1434-77720; fax: 1434-76911). Moderate to inexpensive.

Pro Studiorum This 14-room, no-frills residence hotel is inconveniently located on the outskirts of the city. The rooms have no phones, although some have color TV sets and refrigerators. 13 Tuglasetee (phone: 1434-61853; fax: 1434-31481). Inexpensive.

FROM TALLINN TO NARVA

This 133-mile (212-km) route along the Gulf of Finland leads to the city of Narva on the Russian border, about halfway between Tallinn and St. Petersburg. The 3-hour drive through farmland and birch forests, with a few unforgettable glimpses of the Gulf of Finland, is really the main attraction of this excursion. Be sure to stop at the beautiful Lahemaa National Park along the way. Visitors to this area should be advised that the route to Narva passes through the town of Sillamäe, a site of uranium production and a dumping ground for nuclear waste materials. Although production has long since ceased, the scientific community has documented radiation in the air as far as 37 miles (60 km) away.

TALLINN For a complete description of the capital and its hotels and restaurants see *Tallinn* in THE CITIES.

En Route from Tallinn Leave the city via Virutee, which becomes Route M11, the Narva Highway. The Lahemaa National Park visitors' center is about 40 miles (64 km) from Tallinn.

LAHEMAA NATIONAL PARK Established in 1971, this was the first national park in the old Soviet Union. A wide expanse (386 square miles) of government-protected territory on the south coast of the Gulf of Finland, it is the perfect place to enjoy Estonia's natural beauty. There are 15 natural and 21 manmade lakes, several impressive bogs, and dense pine forests inhabited by elk deer, wild boar, fox, lynx, hare, and other wild animals. Given a few days' notice, the park visitors' center (phone: 232-45659 or 232-93651) will organize hiking tours through the forests or up to Altja, a small fishing village along the coast. Less ambitious visitors can stroll along a 2-mile boardwalk, or tour one of several 18th-century mansions, once inhabited by German barons, on park grounds. The most impressive of these is the Palmse Manor. For those who'd like to linger in the wilderness for a day or two, the visitors' center rents rooms in six 12-room cottages (see *Best en Route*). Private cottages are available for rent across the highway from the park, and a motel is currently under construction about 2 miles (3 km) farther along the road.

En Route from Lahemaa National Park Follow the Narva Highway to the city of Narva, about 93 miles (155 km) away.

NARVA Although geographically located in Estonia, this border city of 75,000 people is, in many ways, Russian. About 98% of Narva's citizens are of Russian descent and there is very little here that seems Estonian. It is one of the few cities in Estonia (or in Eastern Europe, for that matter) that still has a Lenin statue standing in the town square.

Estonian independence has made Narva's mostly Russian population uneasy. Ineligible for Estonian passports under a new law that grants immediate citizenship only to those non-ethnic Estonians who lived in the country before 1938 (a 2-year period of naturalization and tests in the Estonian language and constitution are required for others), many of the city's residents have crossed the bridge over the Narva River to Russia. Those who remain are unsure about their future as a Russian-speaking minority in the new, proudly nationalistic nation. (Estonia's population of 1.6 million is about 66% ethnic Estonian and 28% ethnic Russian, with smaller groups of Poles, Ukrainians, and Belorussians.) Residents of Narva have also been hard-hit by the transition to a market economy; difficulties in negotiating with Russia over raw materials have led to factory slowdowns, and Narva's unemployment rate recently topped 50%.

Although founded in 1240 by the Danes, Narva's links to Russia are old and strong. In the 15th century, the Russian fortress of Ivangorod was constructed on the riverbank opposite Narva, and for the next 3 centuries, the city was passed back and forth between the Swedes and the Russians. In 1704, Peter the Great's troops conquered Narva and it remained part of Russia until 1918, when it became part of independent Estonia. The city came under Russian influence once again when Estonia was annexed by the Soviet Union after World War II.

Narva's main attractions are Narva Castle and Herman Tower, which are among Estonia's most interesting medieval monuments. The Danes began construction of the stone castle, located on the bank of the Narva River, in 1240, and it was later completed by the Knights of the Livonian Order and the Swedes. The Herman Tower was added in the 16th century. Both structures were heavily damaged during World War II and are currently being restored, although they're still open to the public. Be sure to make the climb up the Herman Tower for a good view of the city. The tower also houses an interesting museum where a copy of Peter the Great's death mask is on display, along with numerous artifacts from the 17th century. The castle and tower are open from 10 AM to 6 PM; closed Mondays and Tuesdays; admission charge. To book a tour in English, call at least a day in advance (phone: 1435-31163). The castle grounds are often the site of summer crafts fairs and music festivals.

The Narva Tourist Bureau (8 Noukogufetee; phone: 1435-99294) can provide information on accommodations, restaurants, and sightseeing in the city.

BEST EN ROUTE

Hotel reservations are best made through your travel agent or directly with the hotel. Expect to pay $50 or more in a hotel listed as expensive; $35 to $50 in a moderate establishment; and under $35 for an inexpensive place. Dinner for two, excluding wine and tip, will cost $20 to $35 at places listed as moderate; and less than $20 at inexpensive spots. Payment is almost always in Estonian kroons; credit cards are not widely accepted — be sure to ask what kind of currency is expected before ordering a meal.

For each location, hotels and restaurants are listed alphabetically by price category.

LAHEMAA NATIONAL PARK

Lahemaa Cottages Six 12-room pine cottages are run by the park visitors' center. Single and double rooms — all with shared bathrooms and showers — are available. There's also a sauna, and a communal kitchen in which guests may store and prepare their own food. In summer, boats are available for rent and there's swimming in a nearby lake. In winter, the cottages, which are heated, are ideally suited for cross-country skiers. Lahemaa National Park Visitors' Center, Narva Maantee (phone: 232-45659 or 232-93651). Moderate to inexpensive.

Vanalinn Built in the 17th century, this historic inn once belonged to a well-heeled publisher who had a printing press in the basement. Converted into a hostelry in 1983, it has 15 clean and comfortable rooms (with telephones); ask for one with a view of the Ivangorod fortress across the river in Russia. 6 Koidulatee (phone: 1435-22486; fax: 1435-24120). Expensive.

Rondel (Gun Turret) The best restaurant in Narva is located in a charming round whitewashed room in a tower on the grounds of Herman Castle. The house specialty is beef rondo, an unusual blend of meat cooked with melted cheeses and apples, and served with thin slices of kiwi fruit. The ham and cheese salad is also quite good. Open daily for lunch and dinner. Reservations unnecessary. No credit cards accepted. 2 St. Petersburg (phone: 1435-33244). Moderate.

Baltika Russian food is featured in this Soviet-era restaurant. The *salianka* (beef and vegetable soup served with sour cream) is excellent, and omelettes, blinis, and meat dishes are also on the menu. There's a band and dancing in the evenings. Open for lunch and dinner; closed Mondays. Reservations unnecessary. No credit cards accepted. 10 Pushkinskaya (phone: 1435-31531 or 1435-22253). Moderate to inexpensive.

Latvia

Latvia is the second-largest of the Baltic states, tucked between Estonia and Lithuania on the eastern shore of the Baltic Sea. At only 38,400 square miles — roughly the size of West Virginia — it is one of the smallest countries in Europe.

Until Latvia regained its independence in August 1991, most of the country was closed to Western tourists, and large swaths of land were closed even to Latvians themselves. Of the country's 56 cities and towns, only four outside Riga, the capital, were on the officially sanctioned *Intourist* list.

Now more than 95% of the country is "open," and Latvians are scrambling to attract tourists from home and abroad. The push is on to build Western-style hotels and restaurants, to promote local scenery and wildlife, and to restore castles, monuments, and other sites reflecting Latvia's nearly 2,000-year-old history. In the meantime, however, travelers should be prepared for a few inconveniences. Like many Eastern European countries making the transition to a market economy after decades of Communism, Latvia is experiencing every economic woe — inflation, a devaluating currency, and shortages of consumer goods.

But Latvians say it's a price worth paying for independence after nearly 50 years of forced annexation by the Soviet Union. And despite the occasional difficulties these economic problems may cause travelers, most visitors will find that Latvia is one of the most pleasant and most Westernized of the 15 countries that emerged from the old USSR.

Latvia is bordered by Estonia to the north, Lithuania to the south, the Baltic Sea to the west, and Belorus and Russia to the east. Part of the large coastal plain of Northern Europe, it is a land of forests (which cover 40% of the country), low rolling hills, and shallow valleys, with many small lakes and swamps. The highest point in Latvia is only 1,024 feet above sea level. The country's highest waterfall (of which Latvians are quite proud) is a mere 6½ feet. The main river is the Western Dvina (Daugava in Latvian), which flows northwest from Belorus through central Latvia and empties into the Gulf of Riga just beyond the capital.

The first people arrived in Latvia during the Stone Age, as early as 8000 or 9000 BC, although the first recorded mention of Baltic tribes was in the chronicles of Roman geographer Tacitus. The Vikings raided Latvia during the AD 800s, and Russian forces attacked several times in the 900s. Christianity was brought to the pagan tribes in the region on orders of Pope Innocent III, who summoned the Teutonic Knights on a crusade in 1199 against "the barbarians who do not worship God but dumb animals, leafy trees, clear waters, green grass, and pagan spirits instead."

War between the knights and the tribes lasted until the late 1200s, when the Latvians surrendered. For more than 200 years, the Teutonic Knights governed Latvia as part of a larger state called Livonia. By 1562, most of Latvia had come under the rule of Poland and Lithuania, although part of the country became the German-ruled Duchy of Courland. Sweden conquered northern Latvia in 1621 and Russia took control of this area in 1710. In 1795, the entire territory of Latvia was incorporated into the Russian Empire.

During the late 1800s, Latvians began to organize an independence movement; it became stronger in the 1900s as the Russian Empire crumbled under the weight of war and revolution. On November 18, 1918, one week after the end of World War I, the independent republic of Latvia was proclaimed, although it was not formally recognized by Russia until 1920. Latvia adopted a constitution that established a democratic form of government, formed its own army, and joined the League of Nations.

But the days of democracy were short-lived. In 1934, Latvia's democratically elected president, Karlis Ulmanis, dissolved Parliament and seized power. Five years later, the secret Molotov-Ribbentrop Pact was signed, leading to the annexation of the three Baltic States by the Soviet Union the following year. In 1941, the Nazis invaded Latvia and occupied it for 3 years. After the war, Latvia was controlled by the Soviet Union, which set about transforming this mainly agricultural land into an industrial one and imposed tight controls on the Latvian people.

Latvia's independence movement was revived in the late 1980s, and in May 1990 the republic declared it would become independent after an unspecified transition period (this was an attempt to avoid the bloodshed that characterized neighboring Lithuania's efforts to break free of Soviet control). In a March 1991 referendum, 73% of the voters cast ballots in favor of nationhood, and after the Moscow coup, Latvia declared outright independence in August 1991.

Latvia moved quickly to abolish unwanted Soviet links — renaming streets, reclaiming churches, and negotiating the withdrawal of former Soviet armed forces. As in Estonia, however, nationalism has created some tensions in this ethnically mixed nation. The number of ethnic Latvians or "Letts" living in Latvia has declined sharply over the last 4 decades, from 77% of the population in 1940 to 52% today, and some Letts fear that they will soon become a minority in their own country. As of January 1993, residents living in Latvia before 1940 and their descendants were automatically entitled to Latvian citizenship. A law now under consideration would require non-Latvians to pass a Latvian language test before becoming citizens, this despite the fact that less than half the population currently speaks Latvian, which is related to Sanskrit. Russian is still spoken on the streets here, and — unlike the other Baltic states — visitors will not be shunned for trying to communicate in that language.

A visit to Latvia today can be both an enjoyable and an educational experience, as the country revives its rich, centuries-old traditions of good food, folklore, and hospitality. Latvians are friendly by nature, and they welcome foreign visitors as a way of learning more about the outside world.

For those who would like to see more of Latvia than its capital, we offer three driving routes. The first heads south toward the Lithuanian border to the town of Pilsrundale, site of Latvia's most beautiful baroque castle. The second route leads to the city of Sigulda in Gaujas National Park, Latvia's "Switzerland," and the third route goes to the Hanseatic town of Kuldīga via the beach resort of Jārmala.

RIGA TO PILSRUNDALE

The city of Pilsrundale, site of the spectacular Rundale Palace, is about 48 miles (79 km) south of Riga.

RIGA For a complete description of the capital and its hotels and restaurants see *Riga* in THE CITIES.

En Route from Riga Head south on Route M12, the Pärnu Highway also known the Baltic Way. Bauska is about 41 miles (66 km) away.

BAUSKA The ruins of a castle are visible as the road crosses the Memele River at Bauska. The castle, built between 1443 and 1452 for the Dukes of Courland, who once ruled much of the southern half of Latvia, was damaged in 1706 during the war between Russia and Sweden and is currently undergoing massive renovation; the 3-story tower offers splendid river views. Bauska is famous — at least in Latvia — for its textile industry, sugar beets, and beer. Three rivers converge here; two become the Leilupe (Big) River, which flows on to the Baltic Sea resort of Jārmala. Bauska's big showpiece collective farm, Uzvara (Victory), was recently disbanded by the government and its *Tractor Museum,* which displays all the foreign and Soviet tractors ever used in Latvia, is open only sporadically. However, the *Museum of Latvian Crafts* (8 Kalna Iela) is worth a visit. Exhibits of farm tools and period costumes offer a view into the past. Open Tuesdays through Saturdays from 10 AM to 5 PM; admission charge.

En Route from Bauska Continue on Route M12 to Pilsrundale, 7 miles (11 km) west of Bauska and only 7 miles (11 km) from the Lithuanian border.

PILSRUNDALE This town's claim to fame is Rundale Palace (phone: 8-239-62197 or 8-239-62271), the most outstanding example of baroque architecture and rococo decorative art in Latvia. The palace resembles a miniature version of the *Hermitage* in St. Petersburg, which is not surprising since it is the work of Italian architect Bartolomeo Rastrelli, who later designed the czars' Winter Palace. The castle was built for Ernest Johann Biron, a notorious lover of wealth and luxury, when he was appointed Duke of Courland. Construction was begun in 1736, but Biron was subsequently exiled to Siberia and the building was not completed for another 30 years. The palace was used as a hospital during both world wars, and later as a school. Restoration began in 1972, and the palace was opened as a museum in 1981. The Gold (Throne) Hall is the most luxurious of the 17 rooms open to the public. Local newlyweds often dance their first dance in the White Room — so named for its delicate stucco reliefs of allegorical pastoral scenes. The palace is open from 10 AM to 6 PM in summer; 10 AM to 5 PM from October through April; closed Mondays and Tuesdays; admission charge. A small café on the palace grounds serves sandwiches and drinks (same hours as the palace).

BEST EN ROUTE

Hotel accommodations in Latvia can be booked through *Latvia Tours* travel agency (22-24 Grecinieku Iela, Riga; phone: 2-213652 or 2-220047; fax: 2-213666); your own travel agent; or, in some cases, directly through the hotel. The fluctuating Latvian economy makes it difficult to provide accurate rates for hotels and restaurants. In 1992, Latvia introduced an interim currency called the "rublis," and is plans to gradually introduce its own currency, the "lat." In the meantime, most hotels, and more and more restaurants, are accepting payment only in dollars and other foreign currencies. Credit cards are accepted in few places, and when travelers' checks are accepted, they are subjected to very high commission fees, so bring a good supply of cash. Also be sure to check the latest exchange rate before leaving home and to ask what kind of currency is expected before ordering a meal.

Latvian food is typically German in character, but most restaurant menus are heavy on the Russian dishes. Latvian specialties include gray peas and bacon, pork dishes, and anything made from mushrooms. Desserts rely heavily on fruits and include *klingeris,* a pretzel-shaped coffee bread stuffed with almonds and raisins.

BRENCIS

Brencis This modern, chalet-style complex is set in the woods off Route M12. There are 20 spartan but clean rooms and 10 suites. Facilities include a restaurant and bar, a sauna, a billiard room, a conference room, and a car repair center. Off Rte. M12, about 23 miles (37 km) south of Riga (phone: 8-239-42262).

RIGA TO SIGULDA

The medieval town of Sigulda, gateway to the scenic Gauja National Park, is only 32 miles (52 km) from Riga.

RIGA For a complete description of the capital and its hotels and restaurants see *Riga* in THE CITIES.

En Route from Riga Leave Riga via Brivibas Iela, which becomes the four-lane Route A212. The route to Sigulda passes through pine and birch forests; during the summer it's not uncommon to see people picking mushrooms and berries by the roadside.

SIGULDA This town on the steep banks of the Gauja River offers a glimpse into the Middle Ages. Founded in 1207, Sigulda is today a community of 11,000 people, but its several medieval structures — most notably the ruins of the Sigulda Castle (built between 1207 and 1221) and Turaida Castle (built in 1214) — give it an air of timelessness.

The ruins of Sigulda Castle are on the upper, or main part of the town, on the grounds of a 19th-century red-and-gray brick sanatorium. Built by the Livonian Order of German knights, the castle was badly damaged during the war with the Poles in the 16th century and was never repaired. The walls of the main building and two watchtowers are all that remain today; they currently are under renovation, but visitors can still view the crumbled stone edifices and walk around the castle grounds. In front of the ruins is an amphitheater where open-air folk concerts are held in the summer.

To reach Turaida Castle, drive down a very steep winding road from the residential area and cross the bridge over the Gauja River. The road will pass Gutmana Cave, the largest (60 feet deep) and most visited cave in Latvia (spelunkers may want to stop for a brief tour). Legend has it that its waters possess curative powers. Past the cave, Turaida Castle is visible above the road to the right, its red brick façade standing out brightly against the trees.

Turaida Castle comes complete with a legend. According to the tale of the Rose of Turaida, a beautiful young girl named Maya was killed here by a Polish nobleman in 1620 because she refused to become his mistress and betray her true love, a lowly gardener who worked at the castle. What is said to be Maya's tomb is located on the path to the castle in the shade of a linden tree, supposedly planted by the gardener at the time of her burial. Newlyweds often come here to place flowers at the tomb.

The first fortress to be built on this rugged outcropping overlooking the River Gauja was a wooden structure erected at the end of the 12th century by the Livs. It was destroyed by the German crusaders in the 13th century and replaced with a stone castle. All that remains now are two round towers and a large red brick building that houses a collection of artifacts uncovered during archaeological digs in the area, but other buildings are currently under reconstruction. Be sure to climb the winding staircase in one of the towers for a spectacular view of the surrounding countryside and the river below. The castle is open daily from 10 AM to 5 PM in winter; 10 AM to 7 PM in summer; admission charge.

Near the castle grounds is a park known as Dainu Hill, which features 15 sculptures illustrating the old Latvian folk songs known as the *Dainas*. Folkloric groups from all over Latvia give concerts here on summer Sundays.

Sports buffs will be interested in the state-of-the-art bobsled run — built for the former Soviet *Olympic* team — that dominates Sigulda's skyline. Sigulda is also a popular place for cross-country skiing and boating. The Gauja River, which flows through the town on its meander to the Baltic Sea, is one of the most beautiful waterways in the country.

Before leaving the area, be sure to drive or hike in the lovely Gauja National Park, which covers about 500 square miles. It is known (just a touch optimistically) as "Latvia's Switzerland" because of its undulating hills and many chalet-style buildings.

About 15½ miles (25 km) from Sigulda on Route A212 is the National Park's Ligatnes Zone, a recreational area with animal trails where visitors can catch a glimpse of deer, fox, and moose.

BEST EN ROUTE

The fluctuating Latvian economy makes it difficult to provide accurate rates for restaurants. Be sure to check the latest exchange rate before leaving home and to ask what kind of currency is expected before ordering a meal.

Café Senite The name of this not-to-be-missed restaurant means little mushroom and it's built in that shape, with a white domed roof forming the cap and a brown entrance tunnel for the stem. Located about 24 miles (40 km) from the capital, it features traditional fare prepared with ingredients fresh from a local farm; there is live music and dancing on weekends. The bakery/delicatessen next door is a good place to stock up on picnic supplies — the selection of smoked meat, cheese, and cookies and cakes is superior to that in any Riga shop. Open daily for lunch and dinner. Reservations advised (they may be made through your hotel service bureau). No credit cards accepted. On Rte. M12 (phone: 1359-77563 for restaurant; 1359-77305 for bakery).

SIGULDA

Turaida Café This small stone eatery with heavy wooden tables serves traditional Latvian food such as peas and bacon, and small pastries stuffed with bacon, along with the local black balsam liqueur. Open daily from 10 AM to 5 PM in summer and from 10 AM to 6 PM in winter. Reservations unnecessary. No credit cards accepted. On the path to Turaida Castle (no phone).

RIGA TO KULDĪGA

The first stop on this route is Jārmala, a lovely resort town on the Gulf of Riga, and the final destination is Kuldīga, one of the oldest towns in Latvia, 97 miles (155 km) west of the capital.

RIGA For a complete description of the capital and its hotels and restaurants see *Riga* in THE CITIES.

En Route from Riga Leave Riga via Valdemaras Iela and the suspension bridge and follow the signs to Jārmala, 9 miles (14 km) west. To drive through Jārmala itself, purchase a special pass at the militia booth at the entrance to the town. In summer, Jārmala also can be reached by hydrofoil from Riga. Ask your hotel service bureau for the schedule.

JĀRMALA This is one of the most popular spa towns in the Baltics, although its azure coastal waters have been off-limits to swimmers since 1988 because of pollution. A delightful coastal town, it is actually made up of 12 fishing villages — the main one is Majori (Major) — built on a narrow strip of land between the Leilupe River and the Gulf of Riga.

The beach here is beautiful, with fine, golden sand and lots of space for sunbathing, and the town, which has a population of 70,000 people, is charming. The streets are lined with summer homes known as *dachas,* 1- and 2-story wooden buildings painted in pastel colors and decorated with gingerbread trim, lace curtains, and stained and etched glass windows. Jomas Iela, the main street, is a pedestrian mall lined with small shops and boutiques, plus art galleries and outdoor cafés.

Jārmala abounds with tennis courts, biking and walking trails, and sanatoriums once reserved for high-ranking bureaucrats and Communist Party bigwigs. In summer, boats cruise along the coast, and concerts are held in the outdoor *Dzintaru Koncertzāle* (Amber Concert Hall). In winter, cross-country skiers flock to the area's pine forests. For additional information, see *Good Sports* in DIVERSIONS.

En Route from Jārmala Take Route A220 west through the fir and pine groves known as the "dark forests of Kurzeme." Before independence, much of this region was closed to both foreign and Latvian travelers. The road passes through fields full of the country's own breed of chocolate-colored cows known as "Latvian Brown." At the town of Kandava, turn left off A22 and follow the right bank of the Abava River to the town of Sabile, about 72 miles (120 km) from Jārmala. Sabile is listed in the *Guinness Book of World Records* as having the most northerly vineyard in the world. A little more than 2½ miles (3 km) from the town is the Abava waterfall, a nice place for a picnic. The road also passes the Ventas Rumba, a scenic waterfall on the Venta River, before reaching Kuldīga, which is about 28 miles (47 km) from Sabile.

KULDĪGA Founded in the 12th century, this is a city of narrow alleys, red-tiled roofs, and 17th- and 18th-century architecture. The best way to experience its charm is to walk through the Old Town, noting the eclectic array of Renaissance, baroque, Gothic, and Germanic buildings. Among the city's most noteworthy structures is the Roman Catholic Trinity Church (10 Raina Iela), built in 1640, which has an Italian Renaissance-style exterior and a richly decorated baroque interior. Note the Madonna and Child sculpture, which dates from the early 16th century. The church's altar was a gift from Russian Czar Alexander I. The church is only open to the public by prior arrangement; check with your hotel service bureau.

A small house that once was home to the guard of Kuldīga Castle can be found at 4 Pils Iela, across the street from a small park containing works by Latvia's best-known sculptress, Livija Rezevska, who was born in Kuldīga.

Be sure to buy some Laima brand chocolate while in Kuldīga. Said to be the best in the country, it's available at the *Laima* store (on Ratslaukums Iela). The "zodiac," a milk chocolate bar loaded with nuts, is an unforgettable treat.

BEST EN ROUTE

Hotel accommodations in Latvia can be booked through *Intourist* (see above); the new, private *Latvia Tours* travel agency (see above); your own travel agent; or in some cases directly through the hotel.

The dramatically fluctuating Latvian economy makes it difficult to provide accurate rates for hotels and restaurants. Be sure to check the latest exchange rate before leaving home and to ask what kind of currency is expected before ordering a meal.

JĀRMALA

Jārmala Really the only place for an overnight stay in town, this 259-room establishment was built by *Intourist* and still operates in the Soviet tradition. Several 3-room suites with balconies are available. The restaurant menu is fair, but good coffee and ice cream are served at the outdoor café. 47-49 Jomas Iela (phone: 7-61340 from Riga; 132-761455 from elsewhere; fax: 132-780132).

Orients Fish dishes, as well as Soviet-style shish kebabs and spaghetti, are served at this eatery. The specialty of the house is *carbonade* (pork stuffed with cheese, eggs, and peas and served with French fries). The location — in the middle of the shopping district — makes it a good spot for lunch or a light snack. Open daily for lunch and dinner. Reservations advised on Saturdays and Sundays. 86 Jomas Iela (phone: 132-764473).

KULDĪGA

Aijas Pagrabias (Small Cellar) This intimate 4-table eatery, dominated by brick decor, is the best Kuldīga has to offer. The menu emphasizes salads — rice and sausage, fruit and nut, peas and onion — as well as hot meat dishes, including *shashlik*. Open daily for lunch and dinner. Reservations advised for large groups. 5 Pasta Iela (phone: 133-22246).

Venta The odd combination of a typically Soviet menu (salad, fried meat, potatoes) and an American Southwest decor (potted cacti and pine floors) make this restaurant on Kuldīga's central square worth a visit. The smartly dressed waiters are quick and efficient. A live band provides nighttime entertainment. Open daily for lunch and dinner. Reservations advised. 1 Pils Laukums (phone: 133-24966).

Lithuania

Politically, Lithuania has joined liberated Eastern Europe. Geographically, it remains smack dab in the center of the continent of Europe. The geographic center of Europe is considered to be the village of Bernotai, 15 miles (25 km) north of Vilnius, capital of the largest and southernmost Baltic state.

Lithuania is bordered by Latvia to the north, Belorus to the east, the Baltic Sea to the west, and Poland and the Russian enclave of Kaliningrad to the south. The country stretches 172 miles from north to south and 233 miles from west to east.

Most of Lithuania is lowland, and while there are hills in the east, the country's highest point, Juozapine Hill, is only 970 feet above sea level. Lithuania lies in one of Europe's most abundant lake districts and its 2,500 lakes make up 1.5% of its territory. It also has more than 700 rivers; the Nemanus and its tributary, the Neris, are the longest.

The region that is now Lithuania has been inhabited at least since 1500 BC and, like the other Baltic states, Lithuania began to emerge as a kingdom in the 9th century. Unlike Latvia and Estonia, however, Lithuania was not conquered by the crusading Teutonic knights. Instead, the various Lithuanian tribes were united into a single state by Grand Duke Minduagas in 1240. He became king in 1251 but was assassinated in 1263.

In the 14th and 15th centuries, the Grand Duchy of Lithuania became one of the largest states in Europe, stretching from the Baltic Sea to the Black Sea. The marriage in 1386 of Grand Duke Jagiello and the daughter of Poland's king led to close ties between the two countries. Lithuania was forced to embrace Christianity, the last European country to do so. In 1569, Lithuania was absorbed into the united Polish state of Rzeczpospolita, where it remained until 1795, when all the Baltic lands became part of the Russian Empire.

Situated between Germany and Russia, Lithuania's history is inextricably linked with the expansionist aims of both countries. Lithuania was the site of battles for more than a year at the start of World War I, and was then occupied by German troops for 3 years. The unexpected collapse of both the Russian and German empires at the end of World War I, however, allowed it to become an independent republic.

The sovereign republic of Lithuania was born on February 16, 1918 — an anniversary still celebrated — although it was not formally recognized by Russia until July 1920. Vilnius was occupied by Polish troops at the time, so Kaunas was named Lithuania's provisional capital. Lithuania's first period of independence lasted only a little more than 2 decades, however, and democracy in the country had an even shorter life-span. Following a 1926 coup, an authoritarian president ruled the country by decree.

The Molotov-Ribbentrop Pact of 1939 originally consigned Lithuania to the German sphere of interest, but it was later transferred to the Soviets in exchange for a chunk of Poland and some cash. In 1940, Lithuania was forcibly annexed by the Soviet Union. The Nazis occupied it from 1941 to 1944, but after the war the Soviets regained power.

Soviet authorities maintained tight control over Lithuania in the 4 decades following World War II. But the spirit of nationalism lived, due in part to the country's homogenous population (80% of its 3.8 million people are Lithuanians) and the people's strong allegiance to the Roman Catholic church. In the 1980s, Lithuania led the independence drive of the three Baltic states, and consequently suffered most from Kremlin crackdowns and backlashes. After the Lithuanian Parliament declared independence on March 11, 1990, Moscow sent tanks into the streets of Vilnius and imposed a near-crippling economic blockade. The blockade remained in force for several months until Lithuania agreed to negotiate the terms of its independence with Moscow. The talks went nowhere, however, and in a desperate move to crush the independence movement, Soviet forces stormed the television tower in Vilnius on January 13, 1991. Fourteen people died and more than 500 people were injured in the confrontation. Lithuania declared outright independence during the August 1991 coup. The same year, Lithuania rejoined the United Nations, and in 1992, after a hiatus of 50 years, Lithuanian athletes participated under their own colors at the *Olympic Games*. Romas Ubartas, a Lithuanian discus thrower, garnered the gold. In October 1992, Lithuania introduced its own interim currency, the "talonas" (coupon), with the hope of introducing a fully convertible currency called the "litas" later this year.

Lithuania has moved quickly to erase the vestiges of its Soviet past, restoring Lithuanian names to its streets and cities, and opening areas that had been closed to foreigners. Although Russian is still spoken occasionally, it's no longer the day-to-day language here; some Lithuanians become quite hostile when addressed in Russian, even if it's obvious you're a foreigner.

Below are two driving routes through Lithuania. The first heads from Vilnius to Trakai, the ancient capital of Lithuania, and then to Kaunas, Lithuania's second-largest city, both in population (450,000 people) and significance. From there it continues to the Baltic seaport of Klaipeda, with two optional side trips. The second route leads to the river spa town of Druskininkai in southern Lithuania, near the border with Belorus.

VILNIUS TO KLAIPEDA

Trakai is only 17.5 miles (28 km) from the center of Vilnius, and Kaunas, at the confluence of the Nemunas and Neris rivers, is 62 miles (100 km) west of the capital. From Kaunas the route heads 134 miles (214 km) west to Klaipeda, the country's main seaport and third-largest city. Those who'd like to continue on can then drive north to Palanga, Lithuania's main seaside health resort, or south along all or part of the narrow, 63-mile (105-km) causeway from Klaipeda to the Russian territory of Kaliningrad, one of the most scenic drives in the country.

VILNIUS For a complete description of the capital and its hotels and restaurants see *Vilnius* in THE CITIES.

En Route from Vilnius Drive west on Route A227. The well-maintained road passes through low, rolling hills.

TRAKAI The ancient capital of Lithuania now consists of a series of castles built on and around an artificial island in Lake Galve. There are acres of lovely woodlands and, in the summer, concerts of folk and classical music are held outdoors and in the castle. The imposing red brick Trakkai Castle contains a museum of local history including ancient metalwork, weapons, tools, 19th-century silver and gold jewelry, and religious objects. Open from 10 AM to 7 PM; closed Mondays; admission charge. In good weather, rent a rowboat or take a steamboat cruise on the lake. Trakai also is the site of a community of Karaite Jews who were transplanted from the Crimea in the 15th century to serve as palace guards for the Grand Duke Vytautas. They have established a temple and an ethnographic museum (22 Karaima; open daily; no admission charge), which houses ancient ritual objects and colorful national costumes. The small black wooden house at 65 Karaima is *Kybinine,* a restaurant featuring *kybinai* (a national meat cake) and other Karaite dishes.

En Route from Trakai Continue west on Route A227. Just past Trakai, a small yellow house on the right-hand side of the road marks the old border between Poland and Lithuania. Farther along, you won't be able to miss the city of Elektrenai, which every *Intourist* tour guide once pointed out as an example of Soviet industry at its best. The city was built around a power plant whose three ugly, towering smokestacks are visible on the left. Kaunas is about 44 miles (70 km) from Trakai.

KAUNAS In addition to being among the most scenic of Lithuanian cities, Kaunas, located in the very center of the country, 125 miles (200 km) east of the Baltic Sea, is also among the most historic. Founded in 1361 (some say earlier), it was the first city in Lithuania to resist the attacks of the German knight crusaders and the first to give battle to Napoleon's army in 1812. Kaunas was the provisional capital during Lithuania's first independence — Vilnius at the time was occupied by Polish troops — so it was here that Soviet power was proclaimed in Lithuania in 1940. Kaunas was severely damaged during World War II, with 800 of its buildings destroyed. Access to the city was restricted until September 1991. Foreigners could visit on day trips from Vilnius, but were forbidden to stay overnight.

Rotuses Aikšte (Town Hall Square) is the nucleus of medieval Kaunas. It's dominated by the 16th-century Rotuses (Town Hall), known as the White Swan because of its graceful tower. Now used as a wedding palace, it's a splendid blend of Gothic, Renaissance, baroque, and classical architectural features. A number of interesting buildings line Rotuses Aikšte, including Arkikatedra Bazilika, a 15th-century cathedral that is Lithuania's largest Gothic church, and a 17th-century Jesuit church that is now a Jesuit school. A number of 2-story buildings also stand along the square. Built centuries ago as homes for merchants, they are now museums, cafés, and small boutiques.

Near the confluence of the Nemunas and Neris rivers are the remains of Kauno Pils (Kaunas Castle), built in the 13th and 14th centuries. Many of the castle's stones and bricks were removed in the early 1800s and used for homes and roads. St. George's Church, built in the Gothic style in the 15th century, stands empty next to the castle ruins.

On the banks of the river Nemunas is Vytautas Church (ca. 1400), with its larger-than-life statue of Lithuanian King Vytautas the Great and a wall map showing Lithuania under his reign, stretching from the Baltic Sea to the Black Sea. The church's stained glass windows depict the symbols of Lithuanian cities. Look for the black buffalo, the symbol of Kaunas.

Kaunas has several museums worth visiting. Perhaps the best known is the *Devil Museum* (64 Putvinskio Gatve; phone: 127-203514 or 127-208472). Formally called the *Museum of Antanas Zmuidzinavicius*, it's named after a painter who bequeathed his private collection of 260 devil figures to the museum. (An atheist, Zmuidzinavicius is said to have received his first devil from an exasperated Roman Catholic priest). The collection now boasts 2,000 items — sculptures, carvings, paintings, candlestick holders, ashtrays, anything made in the shape of a devil — from all over the world. Also here is a collection of 19th- and 20th-century Lithuanian folk art. Zmuidzinavicius's paintings are displayed on the first floor. The museum is open from noon to 6 PM, with the last entry at 5:30 PM; closed Mondays and the last Tuesday of the month; admission charge.

Many tourists visit Kaunas to get acquainted with the works of Mikalojus Konstantinas Ciurlionis (1875–1911), Lithuania's most famous artist and composer, who has been called the founder of symbolism (a label he rejected). The *M.K. Ciurlionis Art Museum Gallery* (55 Putvinskio Gatve) is the repository of all of the artist's original works, some 350 paintings. It's open from noon to 6 PM; closed Mondays and the last Tuesday of the month; admission charge.

The *Mykolo Zilinsko Dailes Galerija* (M. Zilinskas Art Gallery; 12 Nepriklausomybes) has a good collection of Western European paintings from the 14th to 20th centuries — including a Rubens — and a valuable porcelain collection. The gallery is open from noon to 6 PM; closed Mondays; admission charge.

For sightseeing information or assistance with hotel reservations, contact the *Kaunas Travel and Excursion Office* at 11 Rotuses Aikšte (phone: 127-208880 or 127-220532).

En Route from Kaunas Follow the signs out of Kaunas to Route A227, which leads to the Baltic Sea port of Klaipeda, 134 miles (214 km) away.

Just outside the Kaunas city limits, the IX Fortas (Ninth Fort) Nazi death camp looms on the left side of the road. It's now the site of a museum and an imposing stone monument to the 80,000 people killed here in the two World Wars.

The *Kalnuju Serviso Komplex*, a café, gas and service station, is located about 49 miles (78 km) from Kaunas and 86 miles (138 km) before Klaipeda. A small shop sells local car parts and will provide emergency service for Western cars; the café is open daily.

KLAIPEDA Now Lithuania's main seaport and third-largest city, Klaipeda was originally the old German trading center of Memel. Founded in 1252, it became part of independent Lithuania in 1923. The city was nearly leveled by the Nazis in 1939 — about one-third of its houses and public buildings were destroyed and many others were damaged.

Klaipeda has a small but charming Old Town, which radiates from a cobblestone square dominated by a restored theater. The city's most interesting sights, however, are a short ferry ride away on Kuršiu Nerija (Curonian Spit), a narrow strip of land separating the Baltic Sea from an inland lagoon. At the north tip of the spit, a few hundred yards to the right of the ferry terminal, are the remains of Klaipeda Castle and the *Juru Muziejus it Askvariumas* (Sea Museum and Aquarium; phone: 1261-35732 or 1261-91125). The museum, located inside part of a 19th-century fortress, focuses on the history of Klaipeda's fishing and shipbuilding industry, and on local sea life. Several old fishing boats and trawlers are displayed outside. The aquarium is home to Baltic seals and sea lions, plus a massive shell collection; a separate building for dolphins is currently under construction. The museum is open from 9 AM to 4 PM; closed Mondays; admission charge.

Only 15 miles (24 km) north of Klaipeda on Route A223 is Palanga, Lithuania's main seaside health resort, known for its sandy beaches and sanatoriums. It's also the site of an amber museum, *Palangos Gintaro Muziejus* (phone: 1236-51319), housed in a 19th-century mansion in the middle of Palangos Botanikos Parkas, a scenic botanical park. There are exhibits on how amber is formed and a huge display of amber objects, including some stunning jewelry. Open from noon to 6 PM, last admission at 5:10 PM; closed Mondays; admission charge.

En Route from Klaipeda One of the most scenic drives in Lithuania — if not *the* most scenic drive — is the narrow, 63-mile (105-km) causeway from Klaipeda to the Russian territory of Kaliningrad. The causeway separates the Baltic Sea from Kuršiu Lagoon, a freshwater inland lagoon fed by the Nemanus River; the land on either side of the road is a protected nature reserve.

To reach the causeway, take the small open-deck ferry from the foot of Danges Gatve in Klaipeda. The ferry leaves for the 7-minute voyage across a strait between the lagoon and the sea every half-hour. After departing the ferry, head left onto the causeway, a narrow, two-lane road that twists through graceful groves of birch and sweet-smelling pine trees. You must pay a small toll at the police checkpoint a couple of miles down the road. The causeway first hugs the lagoon to the left, offering glimpses of nesting birds among the rushes. Later, the lagoon and the sea are visible at the same time, although the Baltic often is hidden from view by huge sand dunes towering over sandy beaches that stretch for miles.

The causeway crosses the Lithuanian-Russian border, so if you plan to travel its entire length, be sure to obtain a Russian visa in advance, and a return visa for Lithuania. Otherwise, drive to the Lithuanian border town of Nida, roughly halfway down the causeway, and retrace your route.

BEST EN ROUTE

Hotel accommodations in Lithuania can be booked through the *Lithuanian Travel Agency* in Vilnius (at the *Lietuva Hotel,* 20 Ukmerges Gatve; phone: 2-614612); through *Aliso,* a new private travel agency also based in Vilnius (34 Savaboriu Gatve; phone: 2-230676; fax: 2-230788); or through your own travel agent. The fluctuating Lithuanian economy makes it difficult to provide accurate rates for hotels and restaurants. At press time, Lithuania had introduced the "talonas" as an interim currency but was planning eventually to introduce its own currency, the "litas." In the meantime, most hotels in Lithuania charged foreigners hard currency, while restaurants charged either talonas or foreign currency. We suggest that you check costs — and the operative exchange rate — immediately prior to your departure, and be sure to ask what kind of currency is expected before ordering a meal.

Traditional Lithuanian fare is similar to Polish food. It features heavy peasant bread, a variety of potato dishes, and main courses of meat, usually pork.

TRAKAI

Nendre (Bullrush) Located across from Trakai Castle, this is a convenient place to get a bite to eat while sightseeing. The food is simple Lithuanian fare. Open daily for lunch and dinner. Reservations unnecessary. 40 Karaimu Gatve (phone: 1238-52085 or 1238-52008).

KAUNAS

Gildija You'll feel like royalty in this restaurant set in a castle-like brick tower and furnished with throne-size chairs, chandeliers, and beautiful stained glass windows. The menu features Lithuanian food, including a tasty chicken soup and potatoes done every way imaginable. This is one of the only eateries serving *ooshi,* a very light cookie made with thin pastry. There's a café adjacent to the dining room, and a bar — frequented almost exclusively by men — downstairs. Open daily for lunch and dinner. Reservations advised. 2 Rotuses (phone: 127-200804).

Metropole Very popular in pre-World War I Lithuania, this restaurant — with its huge chandelier, red-and-white decor, and continental cuisine — remains a hit today. Opt for *barovikas,* a pork cutlet fried in batter and served on a potato stalk resembling a mushroom. Open daily for lunch and dinner. Reservations advised. 68 Laisves Aleja (phone: 127-204427 or 127-204745).

Neris The town's sole hostelry has 319 simple but comfortable rooms and a restaurant. 2 Simkaus Aleja (phone: 127-203863 or 127-203612; 127-205207 for restaurant reservations; fax: 127-205289).

Ugne Café Upstairs there's a bar with stained glass windows, a post-and-beam ceiling, and handwoven wall hangings; downstairs there's a cave-like café with low ceilings and very small rooms where coffee, champagne, and cakes are served. There are outdoor tables in summer. Open daily. Reservations unnecessary. 24 Rotuses (phone: 127-208634).

KLAIPEDA

Klaipeda The only hotel in town, this modern establishment, which can accommodate 400 guests, was built primarily for visiting Soviet businesspeople and military men. The rooms are clean and spartan. Although the restaurant serves decent food, the waiters are so surly that you should avoid it. 1 Naujo Sodo (phone: 1261-16971; fax: 1261-53911).

Meridianas This dining spot, located on a boat moored just behind the *Klaipeda* hotel, serves traditional Lithuanian fare in the ship's dark wood-paneled hold. Music nightly on weekends. Open daily for dinner. Reservations necessary (phone: 1261-16851).

VILNIUS TO DRUSKININKAI

This route leads 90 miles (144 km) from Vilnius to southeastern Lithuania and the spa town of Druskininkai, near the Belorussian border.

VILNIUS For a complete description of the capital and its hotels and restaurants see *Vilnius* in THE CITIES.

En Route from Vilnius Turn left onto Ukmerges Gatve as you leave the *Lietuva* hotel, take the first bridge across the Neris River, then follow the road out of the city.

As the scene turns from industrial to rural, the road forks; bear left, following the signs for Druskininkai. A few miles along the road is Paneriai, a forested area that was the site of Nazi massacres. Tens of thousands of Jews were executed here. The *Museum of the Genocide* (17 Agrastu; closed Tuesdays; admission charge) provides documentation of the atrocities. Continue along the road, which becomes Route A233, to Pirčiupai, 27 miles (43 km) from Vilnius.

PIRČIUPAI At the entrance to this tiny village is a statue of a grieving mother, a memorial to the 119 people burned to death when the Nazis razed the village on June 3, 1944. Behind the monument is a stone wall listing the victims' first names, and a few hundred yards off the road is a museum (open Wednesdays through Sundays from 10 AM to 5 PM) describing the plight of Pirčiupai and about 20 other Lithuanian villages similarly destroyed during World War II.

En Route from Pirčiupai The stretch of Route A233 from the town of Varena to Druskininkai is known as Ciurlionis Road in honor of Mikalojus Konstantinas Ciurlionis, Lithuania's best-known painter and composer, who was born in Varena in 1875 and grew up in Druskininkai. In 1975, on the centenary of his birth, 100 sculptures representing Lithuanian folktales and Ciurlionis's paintings were carved from oak trees by the republic's best folk artists and erected in 15 groups along the road.

DRUSKININKAI Located in the southeastern corner of Lithuania near the confluence of the Merkys and Nemunas rivers, this town owes its development in the 18th century to its mineral springs and mud cure sources. The town has only 23,000 residents, but more than 80,000 visitors arrive annually to "take the cure," to stroll through its landscaped parks and surrounding pine forests, and to ride along its many bicycle paths. Dozens of sanatoriums and spas offer modern facilities and promise cures for everything from aching joints to digestive problems and bad nerves. Druskininkai also is famous for its handicrafts. Nearby on the Ciurlionis Gatve is what locals fondly call the *House on Chicken Legs,* a 3-story Swiss Family Robinson–type wooden museum that houses a collection of wood sculptures and other forest art; admission charge. The museum is currently setting up an outdoor forest park and sculpture mall. Directly behind the museum is *Girios Aidas* (Echo of the Forest), a small café serving terrific *shaslik*. Closed Mondays (no phone).

Most of Druskininkai's sights are located between a large, beautiful lake in the center of the city and the banks of the Nemunas River, which once formed the border between Poland and Prussia. The lake, known both as Didzioji Ežeras (Large Lake) and Drushka Ežeras (Salt Lake — even though it's not salty) is home to a flock of swans, who spend the winter in local yards, returning to the lake when the ice melts.

The *Ciurlionio Museum* (41 Ciurlionis Gatve; phone: 1233-52755) consists of three small wooden buildings, including one that was once the eponymous artist's home. Ciurlionis insisted in his will that his more than 350 paintings be kept together; they are displayed in a gallery in Kaunas (see *Vilnius to Klaipeda,* above). The collection here includes memorabilia, reproductions and slides, several pianos, and tapes of Ciurlionis's musical compositions. In summer, piano concerts are held in the main museum building. The museum is open from noon to 6 PM; closed Mondays and the last Tuesday of the month. Behind the museum is the *55 Gallery* (55 Ciurlionis Gatve; no phone), which sells paintings, ceramics, leather goods, and jewelry.

On the edge of the lake on Ciurlionis Gatve is a huge mustard-colored building used as a summer cottage in the 19th century by a Polish nobleman. During the Soviet era, it was a Communist Party headquarters, and it now belongs to Sajudis, the Lithuanian independence organization. Stretching from this building to the river bank is Vilniaus Gatve, a pedestrian mall dotted with ceramic fountains. Parallel to Vilniaus, on the other side of the park, is Kudirkos Gatve, site of the city's 19th-century Roman Catholic church. Its walls are only two bricks thick, giving the Gothic building a light and graceful appearance.

Be sure to stop at the small round souvenir shop at 5 Vilniaus Aleja on the banks of the Nemunas. Originally built to shelter a mineral spring, its walls are lined with stained glass panels depicting scenes from a Lithuanian fairy tale, and the floor is covered with a superb mosaic. Behind the shop is *Dzukija,* a small café where different varieties of local mineral water are sold by the glass.

BEST EN ROUTE

Accommodations in Druskininkai are limited to the town's sanatoriums and spas. For information and reservations, contact the *Lithuanian Travel Agency,* (see above); the private travel agency *Aliso* (see above); or your own travel agent. The fluctuating Lithuanian economy makes it difficult to provide accurate rates for restaurants. We suggest that you check costs — and the operative exchange rate — immediately prior to your departure, and be sure to ask what kind of currency is expected before ordering a meal.

DRUSKININKAI

Alka This restaurant on the banks of the Nemunas River just outside the city is literally carved out of the forest. Chairs and tables are made out of tree stumps and logs, and real trees grow up through the floor. The traditional, first-rate Lithuanian fare is highlighted each night with costumed dancers performing to ethnic music. Open daily. 13 Veisieju, off Rte. A233 (phone: 1233-52849).

Astra Decorated entirely in black and white, this dining spot in the center of Druskininkai serves traditional Lithuanian food. Closed Mondays. 10 Vilniaus Aleja (phone: 1233-53335).

Bulgaria

Bordered by Romania, Yugoslavia (Montenegro), the former Yugoslavian republic of Macedonia, Greece, Turkey, and the Black Sea, Bulgaria is 325 miles wide and 250 miles long — only slightly larger than Ohio. Though it has a population of about 9 million, Bulgaria is one of the smaller Eastern European countries, with an ancient history that predates even that of Crete.

Bulgaria is the rose capital of the world, exporting more than 80% of the world's supply of rose attar (oil). It is credited with the discovery of yogurt, and its people until very recently were among the most long-lived anywhere in the world. In antiquity, the legendary Orpheus sang of Bulgaria's flower-covered meadows, the imposing Balkan and Rhodope massifs, and the deep forests of pine and walnut.

What is now Bulgaria was once the territory of Thracian tribes, whose 1,000-year-old civilization was influenced by the Greeks and the Persians before it eventually succumbed to Roman conquest and later to successive waves of Slavic immigration to the Balkans. The name "Bulgaria" comes from the Bulgars, a Slavic people from the steppes north of the Black Sea who came to the region in about the 7th century. The Thracians were completely assimilated into the Slavic culture. Today Bulgarians have a strong awareness of their Thracian heritage, as evidenced by the country's intense archaeological activity, yielding dazzling finds for its museums.

By the 9th century, Bulgaria was an empire and the cradle of Slav literature. The work of two Greek missionaries, the brothers Constantine (later Cyril) and Methodius, who advanced the use of the Slavic vernacular in religious practice, found a warm reception in the Bulgarian state, which officially adopted Christianity in 865. The script that Cyril invented to transcribe church texts became the basis for the Cyrillic alphabet, used today by Russians, Ukrainians, Serbs, and Macedonians, in addition to the Bulgarians.

During the 14th century, when its arts and trade flourished, Bulgaria was the most powerful country in southeastern Europe, largely because of its borders on the Black and Aegean seas. Bulgaria was the envy of its neighbors, which led to an invasion by the Ottoman Turks between 1371 and 1396. Through the next 500 years, the Bulgarians tenaciously held onto their culture through a network of monasteries where artists and writers were sheltered, producing paintings, books, frescoes, icons, carvings, and musical scores. Today, about half a dozen of these former spiritual and cultural centers, the most famous of which is Rila, attract legions of visitors to their secluded mountain sites. Although Bulgarians managed to preserve their cultural heritage, many remnants of the era of Turkish rule remain. For example, Bulgarians follow the Turkish custom of shaking their heads from side to side to express "yes" and nodding up and down for "no" — mannerisms that take some getting used to.

During the 15th century, to increase Bulgaria's revenues, the Turkish rulers encouraged the production of native crafts and improved trade. They also welcomed refugees, including Jews, from then intolerant Spain. When Isabel "the Catholic" ordered conversion or expulsion for Spanish Jews at the end of the 15th century, the Turkish Sultan Bayazit II said that the "arrival of Jews is a Spanish loss and a Turkish gain." Although most Jews settled in Constantinople and Thessaloníki, many Bulgarian towns acquired small Jewish communities.

In the 19th century, the small but energetic Bulgarian intelligentsia propelled the development of a "National Revival" of culture and patriotism. Vasil Levski, one of the leaders of the anti-Turkish resistance, was caught and hanged in Sofia in 1866, thus becoming the greatest hero of the movement. The "National Revival" eventually led to the April 1876 uprising against Ottoman domination. Although cruelly crushed, it provoked a larger conflict — the Russo-Turkish War of 1877, known in Bulgarian history as the War of Liberation. The 1878 Treaty of San Stefano gave birth to an independent state with strong bonds to Russia; in 1978 Bulgaria celebrated 100 years of independence. It's interesting to note that the Bulgarian-Russian connection was well established long before the Russian Revolution, so the ties between the two countries are based not so much on ideology (although Bulgaria spent most of the post-World War II period as a Soviet satellite) as on invocations of "traditional friendship." The two countries also have similar Slavic languages, both of which use the Cyrillic alphabet.

With the aid of the Soviet Red Army, the Communists took power in Bulgaria in 1946, expelled the 9-year-old King Simeon II and his mother, and nationalized Bulgaria's economy. The new government "encouraged" some 50,000 Jews to emigrate to Israel, and forced 200,000 Turks to flee to Turkey. In 1984, the country's remaining 800,000 Turks were forced to "Bulgarize" their names. (Thousands more Turks have fled, but the current government has restored their civil rights.)

In an inevitable extension of the recent dramatic political changes in the rest of Eastern Europe, Todor Zhivkov, the former Communist (renamed Socialist) Party leader, was ousted. Bulgaria's first free elections in 58 years were held in June 1990, and although there was stiff competition from the Union of Democratic Forces, the Bulgarian Socialist Party won a majority of Parliamentary seats. But in the 1992 elections, the Socialists lost their Parliamentary majority. However, the new government, headed by a coalition of democratic opposition parties, still faces severe economic problems, including a $12 billion debt.

In a move to encourage tourism, the Bulgarian government re-evaluated the leva (the local currency) to give visitors more spending power and concurrently to help eliminate the thriving black market. Unfortunately, this measure has not been of much help to the Bulgarian people, since most salaries have dwindled as prices have skyrocketed. Gas lines last for hours when the few stations are open; travelers should fill up their tanks at any opportunity.

Our first Bulgarian driving route starts in the capital city of Sofia on the western plain; climbs through the surrounding pine-forested mountains, home of the beautiful Rila Monastery; runs south and east to Plovdiv and Bachkovo in the historic center of the country; continues farther east to the friendly city of Gabrovo; and concludes in Veliko Târnovo. Our second route starts in Varna, Bulgaria's main port on the Black Sea, and covers the resorts that dot the coastline.

For specific information on traveling in Bulgaria, contact the official tour agency in the US, *Balkan Holidays* (41 East 42nd St., Suite 606, New York, NY 10017; phone: 212-573-5530). Make hotel reservations in advance (also book car rentals in advance, and be sure to agree on a fixed price; prices can fluctuate wildly if negotiated within Bulgaria).

Sofia and the Mountains

This route, which starts in Sofia, skirts the country's major ski resorts and heads into the Rila Mountains, the highest range on the Balkan Peninsula and the fourth-highest in Europe. The route ends in the Thracian plains. This 200-mile (320-km) stretch plunges you into the heart of the country's dramatic historic and cultural past. While the asphalt roads are good (as they are throughout Bulgaria), go slowly to experience the somewhat mysterious ambience of this ancient country.

En Route from Sofia The Rila Monastery is 75 miles (120 km) southwest of Sofia. Get an early start so you can enjoy Rila before proceeding to Plovdiv, which has better accommodations. Leave Sofia on Route E79, the road for the Greek frontier and Thessaloníki. It's an easy route, mostly through open rolling country, with the Rila Mountains and the 9,600-foot Musala peak beginning to appear on your left. In about 40 miles (64 km) you'll come to Stanke Dimitrov, where you turn left. On the way, you can visit Sapareva Banja, the largest thermal hot springs in Bulgaria, where temperatures reach as much as 212F (100C). Return to Stanke Dimitrov and continue south on Route E79 for 16 miles (26 km) to the village of Kočerinovo. Here the road starts to wind and climb. The hills are thickly wooded, and the valley falls away below. As you make your way through the dark pine forest, you'll cross a bubbling brook, turn a bend, and then high up on the side of the mountain, you'll see an imposing stone wall over 80 feet high — the Rila Monastery.

RILA Founded in AD 927 by John of Rila, who fled the excesses of court life to found a hermitage, the Rilskiyat Manastir (Rila Monastery; phone: 876-

946) has always been the cultural shrine of Bulgaria, the protector and preserver of its cultural values against the pressures of the Ottomans. Destroyed several times, it was rebuilt in the National Revival style after a devastating fire in 1833. Hrelyo's stone tower, built in 1335, is all that remains of the ancient monastery; it dominates the huge inner courtyard of the 4-story, eccentrically shaped building.

Behind the imposing gates, the inside courtyard boasts an amazing array of delicate architecture, brightly painted porches, winding staircases, beautiful arches, and frescoed walls. There are 300 rooms here. Look for the Chapel of the Transfiguration, with 14th-century murals, on the top floor of Hrelyo's Tower, and the monastery church in the courtyard, with its lovely woodcarvings and elaborate frescoes. For a small donation, visitors can light a candle on the elaborate candelabrum. The first level of candles are for happiness and good fortune, and the second level for remembering loved ones. The monastery houses a museum containing 16,000 manuals, Bibles written on sheepskin, icons, old weapons, coins, and a crucifix on which are carved 140 scenes with 1,500 figures — each no larger than a grain of rice — representing the decades of work by one monk, who became blind from his labors. For the practical-minded, there's a vast early 19th-century kitchen (with a flue 62 feet high and a soup pot large enough to hold two oxen) that once catered to the brisk pilgrim trade. As you exit the monastery, there is a complex of bakeries and snack bars frequented by Bulgarians. The wood-oven baked bread is delicious, and there are fine cheeses, too.

To get to Plovdiv, you have to return to Stanke Dimitrov and take Route 62 east, a crossroad via Samokov-Borovets to get to Route 8, the main road to Plovdiv. A stopover can be made at the Borovets resort in the thickly wooded Rila Mountains, where accommodations include the *Rila* hotel (phone: 99725-2203) winter sports complex, the *Sokoletz* hotel (phone: 99725-508), and the Finnish-designed *Yagoda* bungalow and sauna community (phone: 99725-343 or 99725-454).

PLOVDIV Bulgaria's second-largest city and home to many of the country's leading contemporary writers and painters, Plovdiv dates from Thracian times. The name is derived from Philipolpolis, a name given it by Philip II of Macedonia, who conquered the city in 314 BC. Built on six hills, it is the gateway to the Rhodope Mountains. The *Balkan Holidays International* office in Plovdiv is at 34 Moskva Bulevard (phone: 032-552807).

By day, Plovdiv is a bustling, modern industrial city with an important annual trade fair; at night, it turns into a stroller's paradise — quiet and tranquil. Roman stone structures and Turkish mosques, reminders of its former rulers, remain throughout the city. Divided by the Maritsa River, Plovdiv boasts an old section reached by climbing hundreds of stone steps. (You'd be well advised to wear sensible shoes; after the climb up, you've still got to negotiate the ancient cobblestone streets.) At the top are the remains of a Roman amphitheater; today, visitors can attend opera, dance, and theater performances here. On the other side of the Hissar Kapiya Gate is a world of exquisite houses from the 19th-century National Revival period. Their façades are decorated with eaves in the form of waves, and bay windows overhanging far into the streets, making the houses look top-heavy. The overhanging bays were a method of extending the house without impinging on pedestrian space in busy thoroughfares.

The *Charshiya* (Crafts Bazaar) on Strâmna Ulitsa (Street) is a group of five restored houses in which ten workshops sell handmade tufted rugs, embroidery, copper vessels, and carvings. You also can visit the *Kăshtata na Kuyunddzhioglu* (Argir-Koyumdjioglu House; 2 Dr. Chomakov Ulitsa; phone: 032-224260; closed Monday and Friday mornings), now an ethnographic museum with extensive displays of rare Thracian gold treasures. More gold artifacts are exhibited at the *Natsionalniyat Arheologicheski Muzei* (National Archaeological Museum; Sâedinenie Ploshtad; phone: 032-224349; closed Mondays). A nice ending to the tour is a stop at the open-air market for some peaches, cherries, and grapes. You can eat these comfortably ensconced on one of the terraces overlooking the city. Also worth visiting are the Djoumaya (Friday) mosque (on Stamboliiski Ploshtad) and the Imaret mosque (on Sâedinenie Ploshtad), both from the 14th century.

BACHKOVO The 11th-century Băchovskijat Manastir (Bachkovo Monastery), 18 miles (29 km) south from Plovdiv on the old Roman road connecting the city to the Aegean coast, is Bulgaria's second-largest monastery. The monastery complex is on the right bank of the Chepelarska River. Seen from the road, it looks like an ancient fortress with two courtyards; in the center of each is a cruciform church. Founded in the 11th century, this massive building is decorated with frescoes of exceptional quality. The main Church of the Holy Virgin (c. 1604) has rare, silver-clad icons and a wooden iconostasis of the finest workmanship. Nearby is the 17th-century St. Nicolas Church with its ceiling fresco of *The Last Supper* by Zacharie Zographe. This is also Bulgarian wine country; you'll find both red and white wines, some of the best this side of France.

En Route from Bachkovo Return to Plovdiv, then continue on Route 64, the road north to Karlova, then head east on Route 6. The trip to Kazanlâk is about 60 miles (96 km).

KAZANLÂK Situated between the Balkan Range and the Sredna Gore Mountains, this city is the site of the Dolinata na Rozite (Valley of the Roses), where traditional rose festivals are held at the beginning of June. The *Museum of the Rose* (phone: 0431-25170) has exhibits describing the technology of rose attar (oil) extraction, and a garden of "rosely" delights. Just up the road is the Kazanlâk Tomb, a famous Thracian monument dating back to the 4th century BC. It was discovered in 1944 during the construction of an air-raid shelter, and is now under the protection of UNESCO. A replica of the tomb — which can be visited — has been built nearby.

GABROVO This town, about 30 miles (47 km) north of Kazanlâk via Route E85 (5), is worth a stop to visit the *Museum of Humor and Satire* (64 Brianska Ulitsa; phone: 066-27229), a former factory that now houses a collection of paintings and prints from artists around the world.

Just 5 miles (8 km) south of Gabrovo, hugging the banks of a mountain stream, is the *Etara Ethnographic Museum-Park* (phone: 066-4282), Bulgaria's largest re-created historical village. Here, on cobblestone streets overhung with flower-filled balconies, dozens of handicrafts and trades — from colorful textiles to copper and tinware — are demonstrated in a fascinating display of the skills of village artisans and 19th-century rural technology.

En Route from Gabrovo Head north on Route E85 (5). Veliko Târnovo is about 25 miles (40 km) away.

VELIKO TÂRNOVO Truly the heart of Bulgaria, this medieval fortressed city was the country's capital for nearly 200 years (starting in 1197), as well as a major political and intellectual center. In 1393 the Turks took the city after a 3-month siege. In the 19th century, it became one of the leading centers of the National Revival Movement and was liberated from the Turks in 1877. The city suffered a major earthquake in 1908. Veliko Târnovo is surrounded by the churning waters of the Yantra River, and its distinctive houses are framed by verdant hills. Be sure to walk up Tsarevets Hill, where numerous 12th- to 14th-century city walls, buildings, and churches have been unearthed. The city is particularly noteworthy for its 19th-century architecture, produced during the National Revival Movement. In the 1960s, Veliko Târnovo was targeted by the government to become a showcase of traditional Bulgarian architecture. Today, the city is the country's best preserved 19th-century town. Among the restored buildings in the National Revival Quarter is Bulgaria's first pharmacy (at 13 Ivan Vazov Ulitsa; phone: 062-33921), which opened here in 1823.

BEST EN ROUTE

While Bulgaria used to be among the most inexpensive destinations in Europe, rates recently have risen dramatically. Double rooms are around $200 per night in expensive places (a bit higher during festival times) and about $100 to $150 in moderate places. Meals, however, almost always are reasonable. Food and wine prices are much higher at hotels, but in the country you'll get more than you can eat and drink for just $5 to $10 per person. Bulgarians have hearty appetites, so don't be surprised to find meals consisting of at least five courses. Bulgarian dishes are always very meaty, so vegetarians will have a hard time finding acceptable fare. Reservations are advised at all restaurants, unless otherwise noted. All restaurants accept major credit cards, unless otherwise indicated.

For each location, hotels and restaurants are listed alphabetically by price category.

BOYANA

Boyansko Hanche Tavern Near the historic church, this dining spot has delicious specialties and Bulgarian wines. There's also a folk orchestra and a floor show. Open daily. Reservations necessary (phone: 032-563016). Moderate.

RILA

Elesnica This plain, clean restaurant serves excellent Bulgarian food. Try *shopska* salad with roasted sweet red peppers, cucumbers, small tomatoes, onions, olive oil and vinegar, topped with mounds of feta cheese or *tarator* soup (made of yogurt, walnuts, garlic, dill, and cucumbers). Main courses include grilled or roast beef, lamb, or pork. Open for lunch and dinner. No reservations. On the left side of the road as you enter the Rila Monastery (no phone). Inexpensive.

PLOVDIV

Novotel Plovdiv A member of the French chain, with pleasant accommodations, including 322 rooms, a sports center, pools, outdoor tennis courts, saunas, and a nightclub. The dining room features a large selection of Bulgarian dishes. 2 Zlatyu Boyadjiev Ulitsa (phone: 032-55892; fax: 032-551979). Expensive.

Alafrangite Good Bulgarian dishes are served in an old house with a garden in the old part of town. Open daily. Reservations advised on weekends. 17 K. Nektariev Ulitsa (phone: 032-229809). Moderate.

Trimontium A fine 4-story, 163-room hotel with an Old World atmosphere, first class accommodations, and a garden. At the beginning of the pedestrian zone. 2 Kapitan Raicho Ulitsa (phone: 032-225561; fax: 032-238821). Moderate.

Zlatniya Elen This folk tavern has good food and Bulgarian dancers. Open daily. Reservations unnecessary. 13 Patriarch Eftimi Ulitsa (phone: 032-226064). Moderate.

KAZANLÂK

Kazanlâk Located in the center of town, this 200-room establishment has a dining room, a panoramic bar, a swimming pool, a sauna, and a hard currency shop. Complimentary breakfast is served, and there is free parking. Svoboda Ploshtad (phone: 0431-27210 or 0431-27431). Moderate.

VELIKO TÂRNOVO

Arabanasi Villa This mansion on a hill overlooking Veliko Târnovo was originally built for Todor Zhivkov, the former Communist dictator of Bulgaria, who ruled the country with an iron fist for 35 years. Located about 2½ miles (4 km) from the city, it has been converted into a luxury hotel. Visitors now stay in 23 rooms once reserved for foreign dignitaries and the Communist elite, or even in what were once Zhivkov's private quarters, a huge suite complete with a large office, bedroom, anteroom, and bath. The villa is set on spacious grounds with well-groomed lawns and immaculate gardens, all surrounded by a high fence. Rooms have views of the lawn and the medieval fortress in the valley below. The villa (and some of the other 40 Zhivkov palaces, villas, and mansions across the country) can be booked through *Balkan Holidays* (phone: 212-573-5530 in New York). Expensive.

Interhotel Veliko Târnovo Centrally located overlooking the old heart of the city and the banks of the Yantra River, this 195-room hotel has many modern conveniences. Complimentary breakfast is offered, and there is a dining room, bar, gym, swimming pool, and sauna. 2 Emil Popov Ulitsa (phone: 062-30571; fax: 062-39857). Moderate.

Yantra Although the *Interhotel Veliko Târnovo* (above) offers more comforts, this charming 60-room establishment offers the best view — of an old fortress and the green hills. 1 Veltchova Zavera Ploshtad (phone: 062-30391). Moderate.

Bulgarian Black Sea Coast

The Greeks called it Pontos Euxinos — the Hospitable Sea — but the Turks, who feared its storms, renamed it the Black Sea. Whatever its name, the Black Sea coast of Bulgaria — a 235-mile (376-km) stretch of sandy beach now boasting numerous hotel colonies — is fast becoming known as the Riviera of Eastern Europe. These modern resorts have sprung up relatively recently (most were built during the past 35 years) and were frequented primarily by tourists from Eastern Europe. Visitors from Western Europe and the US have only begun to discover this area in recent years.

The major coastal town, however, is anything but young. Varna, now an industrial center and Bulgaria's main commercial outlet to the sea, was founded by the Greeks in 585 BC. Some 290 miles (464 km) from Sofia, and only a little more than an hour's drive south from the Romanian border, Varna is Bulgaria's summer capital and a perfect starting point for trips up and down the coast as well as for longer excursions across the sea to Istanbul or inland to the eastern monastery towns of Bulgaria.

VARNA The Greeks founded this city, which they named Odessos (it was renamed by the Bulgarians in the 7th century), but traces of other inhabitants also remain. The Roman Thermae, a public bathhouse built by the Romans in the 2nd century, still stands in the middle of the city; and outside the city limits are the remains of a Byzantine basilica, and the Aladja Rock Monastery, built in the Middle Ages.

Tours to the modern resort towns north and south of Varna should be booked through *Balkan Holidays International* in Sofia (phone: 2-831211; fax: 2-883739), in Varna (3 Musala St.; phone: 052-225524), or through *Balkan Holidays/USA* (41 E. 42nd St.; New York, NY 10017; phone: 212-573-5530). For the most part, the hotels are quite similar — modern buildings facing the sea — but the amazing thing about these resorts is that in season, hotel accommodations right on the sea, including three meals a day, cost between $60 to $100 per day for a double room, and various package arrangements are offered. The beach towns are small and generally have uncomplicated layouts. (Unless otherwise noted, the address of a hotel or restaurant is nothing more than the establishment's name.) From Rusalka, north of Varna, to Nesebâr in the south, the beach towns are all connected by Route E85 (5), or by *Kometa,* a hydrofoil (contact *Balkan Holidays International* for schedule information).

RUSALKA Near the Romanian border, this *Club Méditerranée* holiday village caters to families seeking sun and sports. There are three bays in which to swim, and 15 tennis courts on which to play, plus diversions for the kids. For information, contact *Club Med* (phone: 359-5184, or 800-CLUB-MED in the US), *Rusalka Travel* (phone: 0570-3105; fax: 0570-3105), or your travel agent.

ALBENA Named after one of the most attractive female characters in Bulgarian literature, this town caters to a predominantly younger set, who crowd the many hotels, bars, folk taverns, and 4-mile-long beach. You can play tennis or golf or even brush up on your equestrian skills at the riding school. The town hot spot is the beachside *Starobulgarski Stan* nightclub, with an architectural style that recalls old Bulgarian Gypsy tents. It offers music and floor shows until 2 AM. The *Balkan Holidays International* office is in the *Bratislava* hotel (phone: 0427-2710 or 0427-2268).

ZLATNI PYASÂTSI Zlatni Pyasâtsi (Golden Sands) is about 8 miles (13 km) from Albena and probably the resort most popular with Americans, having often been compared to Long Beach, California. Again, you'll find an abundance of bars and hotels. The favorite here is a nightclub called the *Kukeri,* which has a wonderful view of the sea and entertainment by the *Kukeri Dancers,* masked men performing stylized pagan routines. For tourist information, contact *Balkan Holidays International* (phone: 052-856035).

DRUZHBA This town, whose name means "friendship," is only 6 miles (10 km) from Varna. It's one of the older resorts, better suited to low-key vacationers, and is the home of the Swedish-built *Grand Hotel Varna,* the most famous of all the Black Sea hotels, with a complex of restaurants and nightclubs and two sub-floors of spa facilities, including exercise and massage rooms, and mud baths (phone: 052-861491; fax: 052-861920). If the *Grand* nightclubs are too expensive, consider stopping at the *Monastery Cellar* (phone: 052-861328), a nightspot that serves a memorable wine called Monastery Whispers. The *Sveti Constantine Holiday Village* (phone: 052-861005 or 052-861045) is also a popular resort.

SLUNCHEV BRYAG About 60 miles (96 km) down the coast from Druzhba, Slunchev Bryag (Sunny Beach) is a 2½-mile stretch of sandy shores surrounded by a deciduous forest on three sides. This family resort has day care facilities and supervised children's activities, which leave parents free to roam into places like *Khan's Tent Tavern,* another tent nightclub on the beach, or the *Pirate Ship,* a restaurant built like a ship and offering Bulgarian specialties and folk entertainment. Also worth a visit is the nearby city of Burgas and its international music and folklore festival, held every other year (in odd-numbered years) during the second half of June. An attractive alternative to the high-rise resorts is the Finnish-built *Elenite Holiday Village* (phone: 0554-51571), a hillside bungalow complex, including the 100-bed *Emona* (phone: 0554-2325), about 6 miles (10 km) north.

NESEBÂR Nesebâr is a vintage fishing village on a peninsula near Slunchev Bryag, where old Greek churches and wooden fishermen's houses along narrow cobblestone streets transport visitors back in time. Nesebâr is an architectural gem and should be included on any Black Sea tour — but just for a visit, not an overnight stay. The *Balkan Holidays International* office is at 18 Jana Laskova (phone: 0554-52571).

SOZOPOL Another charming collection of 19th-century houses with grapevine-shaded patios along winding lanes. There is a *Balkan Holidays International* office (2 Chervenoarmeiska; phone: 5514-251 or 5514-2207), and several restaurants, but no major hotel. Stay at one of the three communities making up the *Djuni Holiday Village,* 6 miles (10 km) to the south. Like *Elenite, Djuni* was built by the Finns during the mid-1980s (phone:05514-260 or 05514-401).

The Czech Republic and Slovakia

Located at the geographic heart of Europe, what was once known as Czechoslovakia has long been at a crossroads traveled by both colonists and conquerors. As a result, the region's history is one of religious, cultural, and political strife. The latest manifestation of that discord was the division of Czechoslovakia into separate Czech and Slovak nations on January 1, 1993.

When the Republic of Czechoslovakia was created in 1918, it joined the predominantly Czech regions of Bohemia and Moravia with Slovakia. Disputes between the two prime population groups within Czechoslovakia — the Czechs (who comprised 95% of the nation's population) and the 5 million fiercely independent Catholic Slovaks — led to the creation of the Czech Republic and Slovakia. The Slovaks had advocated separatism since the Communist government was overthrown in 1989. And so the peaceful "velvet revolution" of 1989 turned into the "velvet divorce," which occurred January 1, 1993.

While *New Year's Eve* was a somber occasion for many and a joyous one for others, the Czech Republic has moved on, working to develop a viable democracy supported by the economic reforms advocated by Prime Minister Václav Klaus. Unemployment in the republic remains at 2.5%, and the country continues to have one of the lowest rates of inflation in the former Eastern Bloc. In 1992, the Gross Domestic Product (GDP) reached the equivalent of $9,000 per person, making the Czech Republic the richest in Eastern Europe. The same year, the first wave of the unique coupon privatization program initiated by the government put the stock of previously state-owned companies into the hands of the country's citizens with some success.

With change, though, comes sacrifice and for the majority of the Czech Republic's citizens — Czechs, Moravians, Hungarians, Germans, Poles, Ruthenians, and Romanies (Gypsies) — these concerns are compounded by a new Value Added Tax (VAT), a severe housing shortage, the privatization of health care, and the burden of new social and insurance taxes.

Václav Havel's first official duty as president of the Czech Republic was to visit Slovakia. Relations between the two former partners are cordial, if somewhat strained, by the remaining issues that divide them: Most recently the impending devaluation of the Slovak crown (at press time) has prompted much speculation as to the stability of this new country; many Czech companies are avoiding trade with their neighbor and Slovakia is suffering a severe shortage of goods.

Struggle for national identity and suppression under other nations have marked Slovak history since the first recorded mention of the Slavs in the region of modern Slovakia in AD 512. First the neighboring Avars, then the Magyar invaders took over Slovak lands. The Magyars made it a part of the Hungarian Kingdom until their defeat by the Ottoman Turks in 1526. The Austrians defeated the Turks, but while that defeat gave autonomy to various other nationalities in the late 19th century, Slovakia was claimed by the Hungarians. Despite strict Hungarian language laws, it was in this period that Slovak Slavs began to think of themselves as a separate people, and linguists such as Anton Bernolák and L'udvít Stur worked to develop the Slovak language.

After the collapse of the Austro-Hungarian Empire in 1917, T. G. Masaryk, Edvard Beneš, and M. R. Stefáník drew international support for the formation of the Czechoslovakian Federal Republic in 1918. Under Hungarian rule, the Slovak educated classes had been ruthlessly repressed, resulting in tens of thousands of Czechs pouring into rural Slovakia and creating a Czech governing class. On March 14, 1939, the Slovak National Assembly, under German pressure, voted to secede from Czechoslovakia and form a separate state. Thus Slovak autonomy existed only under the Nazi puppet nation, run by Fascist president Jozef Tiso. In 1944, the Slovak Uprising was the largest armed resistance outside of Marshall Tiso's partisans, although the revolt was quashed by the Germans. With the collapse of the Reich, the two republics were once again joined in 1945, and were subdued under the domination of the Communists until the "velvet revolution" in November 1989.

But while the Slovaks have achieved nationhood, the new country, despite its desire to improve its image abroad, has been persistently plagued with problems similar to those facing the Czech Republic, most importantly the reluctance of foreign investors. In 1993 Prime Minister Vladimir Mečiar announced that Slovakia would go its own way with economic reform, abandoning the coupon privatization program in favor of direct sales of companies to foreign bidders. In addition, criticism has been aimed at Slovakia for its treatment of Hungarian minorities: A law was passed banning the use of any language other than Slovak in schools; all town nameplates written in Hungarian were ordered removed; and all broadcasts formerly in Hungarian began using Slovak. Relations with Hungary have been further strained by the controversy over the Gabčíková Dam project to divert the flow of the Danube River, which the Hungarians claim will have a serious environmental impact. Both sides have agreed to let the World Court in the Hague decide the issue.

The Czech Republic

Despite its present difficulties, the Czech Republic is a particularly appealing destination for travelers because of its natural beauty and its many well-preserved historic sites. Although it is now half its original size, the Czech Republic boasts some 54,000 monuments, 2,000 castles (105 of which are open to the public), and a number of old towns rich in Gothic, Renaissance, and baroque architecture. Throughout the country, scaffolding bears witness to a national commitment of renewal, restoring structures that fell to ruin under the former Communist regime.

Known as the "Heart of Europe," the country is composed of two areas: the Bohemian plateau in the west (including Bohemia, North Bohemia, West Bohemia, and South Bohemia) and the Moravian lowlands in the east (including Moravia and North Moravia). The territory of Bohemia and Moravia was the center of European culture in the 14th century, when Charles IV made Prague the capital of the Holy Roman Empire. He initiated a building boom that produced such Gothic wonders as the Charles Bridge in Prague and Karlštejn Castle, located south of Prague, near the town of Beroun.

Despite its attention to the past, the Czech Republic is a developed country with the vast majority of its population of 10 million involved in commerce and industry and only 10% involved in agriculture. Czech companies produce everything from Skoda cars (now owned by Germany's Volkswagen) to bentwood chairs and Bohemian glass. Only 16% of the population lives in the two largest cities — Prague, the capital of Bohemia (pop. 1.2 million), and Brno, capital of Moravia (pop. 390,000). The rest is scattered among some 6,000 small towns.

This predominantly small-town culture opens up some appealing possibilities for those interested in folk traditions, which can be found in the wine-producing regions of Moravia and the lake country of southern Bohemia. If you visit in the spring and the summer, you will surely encounter (indeed, become part of) at least one of the many folk festivals held in the countryside. Although many of them feature professional and semi-professional troupes wearing standardized folk costumes, they do attract folk enthusiasts from all over the world. The colorful festivities usually include dance and music competitions, parades, wine tastings, and open-air markets selling handsome homemade crafts.

Spring and summer in the Czech Republic are also well-suited to sightseeing, sports, and other leisure activities. The country is in a temperate zone, so it is warm and sunny in the spring and summer, with an average May temperature of 64F (18C), and July getting no warmer than a comfortable 77F (25C). Though the Czech Republic is landlocked, it has thousands of ponds and lakes, many developed for swimming, boating, and fishing. A preponderance of these lakes are in southern Bohemia, while the Krkonoše (Giant) Mountains are in northeastern Bohemia. The Beskydy Mountains in South Moravia offer downhill and cross-country skiing, tobogganing, and sleigh riding.

The Czech Republic is a relatively easy country to explore. English is understood in the better restaurants and hotels, although German is the lingua franca for the tourist sector. Hotel reservations are essential even in the off-season (particularly in smaller towns) because the tourist traffic exceeds the population. Make arrangements through your travel agent or through *Cedok* (18 Na příkopě, Prague; phone: 2-212-7111), or in the US (10 E. 40th St., New York, NY 10016; phone: 212-689-9720).

This route begins in Prague, the nation's capital, works its way to the spa towns of West Bohemia, then down to the rich cultural monuments and natural beauty of South Bohemia and the capital city of Moravia.

PRAGUE TO OLOMOUC

This 454-mile (730-km) route links Bohemia and Moravia — the Czech Republic's two major regions — and takes in the country's capitals as well as its most famous spas, castles, and medieval towns. The route heads west out of Prague, circles through Plzeň, turns south to Tábor, Ceské Budějovice, and Ceský Krumlov, then finally east to Brno and Olomouc. You can spend several days touring, for all of the places along the route have acceptable overnight accommodations.

Since you will be passing through two distinctive areas of the country, be alert to subtle changes in traditions and customs. These regional differences will be most obvious at the spring and summer folk festivals. You'll find that the cooking also differs: In Bohemia, try roast pork, goose, or duck with dumplings accompanied by pilsner or any other local beer. In the lake country of southern Bohemia, keep an eye out for menus offering fresh trout and carp. In Moravia, be sure to sample the local wines.

The highlights of the route include the renowned spa of *Karlovy Vary;* the Burgher's Brewery in Plzeň, where pilsner beer has been produced since the Middle Ages; the preserved historic town of Tábor; the unique historical preserve of Ceský Krumlov, the formidable Spilberk Castle in Brno; and the diversified architectural mix of Olomouc. (It's possible to take a day-long bus excursion from Prague to *Karlovy Vary,* Plzeň, or Ceský Krumlov. For further information, contact *Cedok* (see above).

PRAGUE For a complete description of the city and its restaurants and hotels, see *Prague* in THE CITIES.

En Route from Prague Drive west on Route E48 (6), which passes through some of Bohemia's loveliest countryside, with deep forests and rich farmlands where hops are grown. Hillside castles dot the landscape. *Karlovy Vary* is about 83 miles (133 km) away.

KARLOVY VARY In the narrow valley at the juncture of the Teplá and Ohře rivers lies the most famous Czech spa. It has 12 developed hot springs, and more than 100 springs in all. Legend has it that *Karlovy Vary* (*Carlsbad* in German) was discovered in 1358 by Charles IV — actually by his dog, who stumbled into a hot spring while chasing a stag. Built as a leisurely resort, *Karlovy Vary* also is a walker's delight. Walk up Sadová Street, lined with classic and Art Deco villas, stop to view the golden spires of the 17th-century Byzantine-style St. Peter and Paul's Orthodox Church with its plaque commemorating Peter the Great's visit here, or hike up the trail to Jelení Skok (Stag Leap) for a beautiful view of the city. Less intrepid travelers may wish to take the *lanovka* (funicular) located next to the *Grand Hotel Pupp*. The huge spa building is reserved for guests taking the waters, but visitors can stroll along the ornate Colonnade, built in 1871–81, following in the footsteps of kings and queens and such notables as Beethoven, Goethe, and Mozart.

While visiting the spa, indulge in a few *Karlovy Vary* rites. Taste the hot bitter waters from a special mug with a long clay straw. Buy a box of *Karlovarské oplatky* — delicious large round chocolate and vanilla wafers. Order *becherovka,* a liqueur known jokingly as "the thirteenth spring." Visit the world-famous *Moser Glassworks* (19 Jaroše Dvory; phone: 17-416111) and the *Karlovy Vary Porcelain Exhibition* (3 Fjoerstrová; phone: 17-23821). Although tours are given in Czech only, the model of the city in the *Karlovarské Muzeum* (Museum of Karlovy Vary; 23 Nová Louka; phone: 17-24433) has a taped English version on the development and growth of the spa from 1650 to the present. Open Wednesdays and Thursdays from 9 AM to noon; admission charge.

In 1990, the city reinstated festivities commemorating Charles IV's discovery of the spa. A costumed procession heralds the reopening of the spa season in early May, led off by a 2-day festival. Those interested in sports can enjoy swimming, hiking, golf, tennis, or fishing. For further information, contact KUR-INFO Tourist Office, Vřídelní Colonnade (phone: 17-24433). See also *Spas: Eastern Europe's Unique Watering Spots* in DIVERSIONS.

En Route from Karlovy Vary Drive southwest on Route E48 (6) in the direction of Cheb for 25 miles (40 km), turn southeast to Route 21. Off Route 21 is the regal Kynžvart, the former summer residence of Count Metternich, the 19th-century Austrian statesman. Constructed in baroque and Empire styles, the château contains valuable collections of furniture, art, china, glassware, and arms. Continue on Route 21 for 37 miles (60 km) to *Mariánské Lázně.*

MARIÁNSKÉ LÁZNĚ Established in 1808, this spa (*Marienbad* in German) was a favorite with such notables as Richard Wagner and King Edward VII. It is nicely designed, with parks and colorful façades lining Goethe Square. The Russian writers Turgenev, Gogol, and Gorky also came here, along with such composers as Chopin, Beethoven, Liszt, Johann Strauss, and Dvořák. Spa yellow, the soft yellow of the exteriors of the major buildings and hotels, can be seen here and at retreats throughout the country. Of the 40 springs, the best known are Křížový, Lesní, and Rudolf. When you're not soaking, you can take advantage of the spa's many other recreational facilities: movies, concerts, a golf course, tennis courts, a pool, cafés, restaurants, casinos, and nightclubs. There also are numerous interesting 19th- and early 20th-century buildings: the Cross Spring Pavilion (1818), the Rudolf Spring Building (1823), the English church in neo-Gothic style (1879), the Maxim Gorky Colonnade in neo-baroque style (1889), and the Russian Orthodox church (1901). Take a side trip 10 miles (16 km) east to Teplá to see the 12th-century monastery, with an impressive collection of rare books, manuscripts, and prints.

En route from Mariánské Lázně Continue southeast on Route 21 to Sribro Mies, then head east on Route E50 (5) for 46½ miles (75 km) to Plzeň.

PLZEŇ With large factories and a very smoky skyline, this city of 173,000 contrasts sharply with the other small Bohemian towns en route. But it is worth a visit to see the Burgher's Brewery, which has produced Pilsner Urquell beer since the Middle Ages. Begin the tour at the *Beer Museum* (13 Veleslavínová ulice), located in an old brewing house. It has a fine collection of beer mugs, jugs, pewter tankards, and glasses produced during the last 6 centuries. Also on display is an iron collar — the collar of dishonor — worn by brewers whose beer didn't make the grade. The town's beer stewards will tell you that pilsner should be drunk from a sparkling clean glass, accompanied by sharp cheese, smoked meat, and dark bread. They're right. The museum is open year-round from 9 AM to 4:30 PM; closed Mondays; admission charge.

Republiky náměstí, the square in the center of town, is lined with houses that have Renaissance, baroque, Empire, and neo-Gothic façades. Two particularly lovely Gothic buildings are St. Bartholomew's Church, with its 340-foot tower, and the Abbey Church of the Virgin Mary.

In 1990, for the first time since World War II, Plzeň celebrated the anniversary of its liberation by American troops on May 5, 1945. This is now an annual event, with a number of breweries handing out free beer to celebrants throughout the day.

En Route from Plzeň Head southeast on Route E49 (20) in the direction of Písek. From this point take Route 33; Tábor is about 70 miles (112 km) away.

TÁBOR Set on the Lužnice River, amid the forests and lakes of southern Bohemia, this Gothic town is one of the best-known fortifications in the Czech Republic. Tábor was founded in 1420 by the Hussites, an army of antichurch and anti-state rebels whose struggle was set off by the death of the Czech religious reformer John Huss (Jan Huss). Huss was burned at the stake as a heretic in 1415, but the Hussite struggle continued for the next 19 years. There's a saying here that "Nothing is mine and nothing is yours, because the community is owned equally by everybody." It is this philosophy that has given rise to the false association between the words "Bohemian" and "Gypsy," and has led people to think of Bohemians as poor, homeless wanderers or struggling artists.

Tábor, which has a population of 36,000 is a modern, growing town with an interesting history. An equestrian statue of military leader Jan Zižka, who commanded the Hussite forces, stands in the middle of Zižka náměstí, the main square. The most notable building is the Town Hall, which houses a museum documenting the Hussite movement (closed Mondays). Underneath the museum are 10 miles of medieval catacombs. These tunnels and cellars were built as living quarters and later used to store beer and wine. The narrow, winding streets off the main square, laid out to confuse attackers, lead to the Old Town. Originally surrounded by ramparts and bulwarks, the Old Town still has remnants of those fortifications, such as the Bechyně Gate and the adjacent Kotnov Tower, once part of a medieval castle that was turned into the town brewery in the 17th century.

En Route from Tábor Follow Route E55 (3) heading south. Along the route is the 19th-century replica of Windsor Castle, known as Hluboká nad Vltavou. The castle is noted for Gothic and Renaissance stained glass windows, 17th-century Flemish tapestries, Venetian glass chandeliers, and a library of more than 12,000 rare books. Open from 9 AM to 4 PM; closed Mondays (phone: 38-965045). About a mile farther south is the baroque Ohrada Castle; once used as a private hunting lodge, today it houses a forestry museum. The walls are covered with trophies of all shapes and sizes, including a single set of antlers with 26 tines. In the central hall are round deerskin carpets and chairs made of heavy antlers with scrimshaw inlays. Follow Route E55 (3) south for 35½ miles (57 km) to Ceské Budějovice.

CESKÉ BUDĚJOVICE A major city of Southern Bohemia, Ceské Budějovice is the home of "Budvar" beer (better known by its German name Budweis). A definite stop is the original *Budweis Brewery* (4 Karoliny Světlé ulice; phone: 38-24237), built in 1895 and founded on a brewing tradition dating back to the 14th century. Today, the brewery still produces a rich, slightly sweet beer. Group tours and samplings of the brew are available.

In addition to its beer, Ceské Budějovice is renowned for its cobblestone square; named for the city's founder, King Přemysl Otakar II, it is the largest square in the Czech Republic. Located here is the 18th-century Samson's Fountain, built to supply the town with water from the nearby Vltava River; the pipe system running under the square was a major technological achievement for its time.

Also worth a visit is the Dominican Monastery and Church of the Self-Sacrifice of Our Lady (Piaristická ulička). Founded in 1263, it is the oldest historical monument in Ceské Budějovice. Most noteworthy are the baroque cloister, its 17th-century organ box, and the 1759 rococo pulpit. On the west end of the square is the Renaissance-style Town Hall (with its strange protruding bronze griffins); there is a small information center located inside the hall.

Before leaving, climb the 236-foot Cerná Věž (Black Tower), once a belfry and watchtower, which today affords panoramic views of the city. Built from 1549 to 1578, it was reconstructed in 1982. The lower part is Gothic, the upper tower is Renaissance (open daily from April through October). Located near the tower is the 13th-century baroque St. Nicolas's Cathedral (Kanovnička ulice), which contains impressive frescoes by J. A. Schöpfl. For tours, information, and accommodations in Ceské Budějovice and Southern Bohemia contact *Nimbus Travel* (3 Žižková; phone: 38-58028).

En Route from Ceské Budějovice Take Route E55 (3) south to Route 159. Off Route 159 is the Zlatá Koruna (Golden Crown), a Cistercian monastery first established by King Přemysl Otakar II in 1263. After a fire completely destroyed the structure in 1613, the interior was rebuilt and now houses a beautiful rococo altar and frescoed ceilings. Return to Route E55 (3) for 12 miles (19 km) south to Ceský Krumlov.

CESKÝ KRUMLOV About 15½ miles (25 km) south of Ceské Budějovice, in the foothills of the Sumava Mountains, lies the small medieval town of Ceský Krumlov. It is considered by many travelers as the most picturesque spot in all of Europe primarily because of the 13th-century Krumlov Castle, the largest in Southern Bohemia.

The town was founded in 1253 by the Vítkovec family, who built their magnificent Gothic castle overlooking the Vltava River. In 1302, the noble Rožmberks claimed the town and castle as their own. Vilém of Rožmberk, a devotee of Italian Renaissance, rebuilt the castle and inspired much of the elaborate fresco work seen throughout the town. After Vilém's death, Peter Vok managed the town and castle until he sold it to Emperor Rudolph II in 1602. Until World War II the town was populated primarily by Germans, and between 1938 and 1945, it was completely cut off from the rest of Czechoslovakia. After the Nazis withdrew, throngs of immigrants from Poland and Hungary settled here, making this one of the most diversified places in the Czech Republic.

The most ancient part of Ceský Krumlov's famed castle is the 13th-century Round Tower. Affording a beautiful view of the town's brick-colored rooftops, its interior contains many splendid rooms, including the Masquerade Hall with its wall paintings of court jesters who actually seem to leap as you pass by. Also in the castle is a theater which frequently stages theatrical productions, and an exhibit of vintage 13th- and 14th-century costumes. The Lower Courtyard contains large cannons and the former guardhouse. Oddly, live bears were kept in the castle's moat during the 16th century, perhaps indicative of the hunting prowess of the noble families who once lived here. The castle is open Tuesdays through Sundays from 9 AM to 4 PM; admission charge (phone: 38-38563).

En Route from Cesky Krumlov Return to Ceské Budějovice, head northeast on Route E551 (34) to Humpolec. From here continue east on Route E50 (D1) to Brno, a total of 119 miles (190 km).

BRNO The capital of Moravia, Brno is a combination of the historic and the contemporary. Here you'll find castles, museums, an outdoor market, a fairgrounds, a racetrack, and some of the best *vinárnas* (wine cellars) in the republic.

Spilberk Castle, which dates to 1287, was built as a fortress to resist invaders and was later turned into a prison. Its sinister history is deeply engraved on the collective conscience of the country. Here, political dissenters were detained and tortured by the ruling Hapsburgs. During World War II, Nazi forces reopened the prison, and Spilberk once again became a dungeon and death trap. Instruments of torture are on display. Now part of the *Museum of the City of Brno,* the castle is open from 9 AM to 4 PM; closed Mondays; admission charge; no phone.

Hradní, the castle restaurant (phone: 5-26203 or 5-24170), offers game dishes, Moravian wines, and a view of the city. The park outside the castle is a romantic strolling place for couples, and its covered benches make it a pleasant spot to rest.

The main streets in Brno all converge on Svobody náměstí (Freedom Square), which is flanked by splendid baroque and Renaissance buildings. From the square you can see Petrov Hill, with the Cathedral of Saints Peter and Paul, a reconstructed Gothic structure built on the site of a Romanesque basilica. The cathedral on the hill is a welcome refuge from the urban bustle below. Open Tuesdays through Saturdays from 9 AM to 4 PM; Sundays from 11 AM to 4:30 PM.

The nearby Capuchin Monastery, with its specially ventilated crypt containing 150 mummified bodies of monks and local nobility, is also of interest. The bodies originally were preserved "naturally" by placing them on the monastery's cold floor, where the flow of air, coupled with the building's unusual dryness, prevented them from decaying. This practice was outlawed in 1784 for reasons of hygiene — as well as the Hapburg's fear that the body of some local freedom-loving Moravian might wind up the object of an anti-Hapsburg pilgrimage.

From the cathedral, descend the steps to the outdoor Zelný trh cabbage market, where you'll find hundreds of locals selling fruits, vegetables, handicrafts, and kitchen utensils. The market sprawls around Parnassas Fountain, which features a baroque sculpture depicting Cerberus, the Watchdog of Hell, and four continents (its designer, Johann Fisher von Erlach, apparently was unaware of three other continents). Nearby is the Diettrichstein Palace, the largest in Brno and the site of the *Moravian Land Museum* (6 Zelný trh). On display are a reconstructed iron furnace, a jeweler's shop, as well as centuries-old weapons and tools. Among the area's other notable buildings are the old Town Hall and the Gothic

Church of St. James, both in the Old Town. Also of note is nearby Slavkov, or Austerlitz, where Napoleon defeated an Austro-Russian/anti-French coalition in 1805. An enormous monument built in 1905 commemorates the event.

Brno's *Exhibition Fairground,* down the hill and past the railway station, is the site of events all year, highlighted by the *Consumers' Fair* in April. While here, have lunch at the *Myslivna* (Gamekeeper's Lodge; 12 Pisárky; phone: 5-335911 or 5-383247), reached by crossing a wood on the south side of the Svratka River. Try the broiled trout à la Brno.

For a taste of the city's nightlife, be sure to visit the *Modrá Hvězda,* which houses a fine restaurant, winery, and snack bar. In the cellar is a brick-vaulted dance club with the American flag tacked onto the wall. (The vaults are part of the labyrinth of basements and cellars forming a complex underground system beneath the city.) 7 Siligrovo náměstí (phone: 5-27910 or 5-27919).

En route from Brno Drive northeast 50 miles (80 km) on Route E462 (46) to Olomouc.

OLOMOUC Despite the presence of spouting smokestacks and gray factories just outside the city's perimeter, Olomouc (as residents proudly boast) is second only to Prague in the number of its historical and cultural landmarks. The city's 11 churches not only represent the various religious influences throughout the region (Jesuits, Dominicans, Capuchin, Czech brethren, Russite, and Orthodox), but they also dramatically encompass every significant period in architectural history from early Gothic to late baroque.

The most interesting sights are clustered around two main areas, Horní (High) and Dolní (Lower) Squares, and Republiky náměstí. Horní Square is the venue of the main city market with a beautiful Renaissance and baroque Town Hall and clock in the center. Within the square are the fountains of Hercules and Caesar, constructed between 1688 and 1725 by sculptor F. Sattler. Of the houses and palaces that surround the square, the one particularly worth seeing is the Petráš Palace, where the oldest educational society in Central Europe was founded in 1746.

Although smaller than Horní, Dolní Square is no less interesting. A statue of the Virgin, erected in 1723, stands in the center along with two baroque fountains representing Neptune and Jupiter. Dolní is the main shopping district and it bustles from dawn to dusk. A short distance away is Republiky náměstí, which leads to Přemyslid Palace (Václavské; no phone). Originally called the Bishop's Palace, it is the most important Romanesque monument from the mid-12th century. Open Tuesdays through Fridays from 9 AM to 5 PM. Also visit St. Wenceslas Cathedral, a 12th-century church that was rebuilt in the late 19th century.

Of special interest is the Old University (1-3 Universitní), founded by the Jesuits in 1573. This complex of baroque buildings was acquired by the state in 1773. Visitors are welcome to see parts of what were once theological facilities; since 1946 it has been the home of Palacký University.

The environs of Olomouc offer a variety of side trips of particular interest to castle lovers. About 11 miles (18 km) north of Olomouc is Sternberk Castle. Built in 1241, it contains a fine collection of arms and period furniture as well as a clock museum. Open daily from 8 AM to 7 PM May through September. Náměšt na Hané is just 9½ miles (15 km) west of town and is more a fairy-tale neo-classical château, where Cinderella might have lived. Inside the castle is an interesting display of 17th-century vestments once used by Olomouc's high clergy. Open daily from 8 AM to 7 PM May through September.

BEST EN ROUTE

Southern Bohemia has an extensive network of private homes and pensions offering accommodations superior to many of the hotels in the area. For further information contact *Cedok* (18 Na příkopě, Prague; phone: 2-212-27111), which provides lists of lodgings, some located in historic buildings all throughout the Czech Republic.

Expect to pay $70 to $110 per night for a double room in hotels in the expensive range; $40 to $60 at places described as moderate; and around $30 at inexpensive spots. Prices, except at deluxe hotels, always include breakfast. (Meal vouchers can be used outside the hotel.) Be aware that at press time, the Czech government had imposed a 23% sales tax on hotel rooms, so check in advance to see whether or not the tax has been included in the price you are quoted. A dinner for two will cost $30 and up at expensive restaurants, between $20 and $30 at moderate places, and less than $20 at inexpensive spots. All restaurants below accept major credit cards, unless otherwise indicated. Reservations are advised for all restaurants.

For each location, hotels and restaurants are listed alphabetically by price category.

KARLOVY VARY

Grand Hotel Pupp Built in 1701, this recently renovated property offers the glamour of baroque architecture and a history of famous visitors, including Paganini and Goethe. The 270 rooms and 15 suites have private baths, color TV sets, telephones, and mini-bars. The *Grand* restaurant specializes in continental fare and offers a vegetarian menu. In addition, guests enjoy a fitness center with sauna, golf, tennis, and a casino. 2 Mírové náměstí (phone: 17-209111 or 17-209631; fax: 17-24032). Expensive.

Dvořak Managed by Vienna International, this hotel offers the best of modern European comforts. There are 86 rooms and 3 suites, as well as a fine restaurant featuring continental fare. Facilities include an indoor swimming pool, fitness center, and hydrotherapy sauna. The popular *Casino Karlovy Vary* is nearby. 11A Nová louka (phone: 17-24145; fax: 17-22814). Expensive.

Centrál Built in 1910 and later renovated, this frayed hotel has 60 rooms, all with balconies and private baths. There's a restaurant and a wine bar. No credit cards accepted. 17 Divadelni náměstí (phone: 17-25251 or 17-27572; fax: 17-290086). Moderate.

Elwa With 17 nicely furnished rooms, a reading room, and a bar, this comfortable new hotel offers all the amenities for guests interested in sampling a spa "cure": special dietary meals, hydrotherapy, massage, beauty- and skin-care programs, and a fitness center. There is a physician on the premises as well. 29 Zahradní (phone: 17-28473; fax: 17-28473). Moderate.

Heluan This restored 18th-century villa, which opened last year, is the only hotel in town with its own private mineral spring. All 12 rooms and 3 suites feature private baths. There's also a quaint wine cellar with nightly entertainment as well as the fine *Lovecká* restaurant, which specializes in wild game. 41 Tržiště (phone: 17-25757). Moderate.

MARIÁNSKÉ LÁZNĚ

Esplanade This 3-story complex boasts 100 rooms, all featuring color TV sets and mini-bars. Other amenities include a complete fitness center, an indoor pool, a sauna, and spa facilities. Guests also enjoy a fine restaurant, a bar, and nightly entertainment in the wine cellar. 43 Karlovarská (phone: 165-2162; fax: 165-4262). Expensive.

Interhotel Golf A pretty and gracious small hotel in a park setting with a golf course on the property. There are 24 rooms (No. 102 is the only room with a terrace overlooking the grounds) and 2 well-appointed suites. Dining in the French-inspired *Restaurace* is a must. There's an indoor swimming pool, and a solarium and massages are available with spa treatments. 55 Zadub (phone: 165-2651/4; fax: 165-2655). Expensive.

Palas Praha Built in 1875, this small, pleasant hotel in the center of town has recently undergone renovations. The 40 rooms and 5 apartments are all decorated in Louis XIV style with marble accents. There is a French restaurant and a bar. 67 Hlavní (phone: 165-2222). Expensive.

Koliba With all the charm of a mountain chalet, this hotel has 10 cozy rooms, each with satellite TV and private bath. The restaurant serves traditional Czech fare. Facilities include a skin- and beauty-center providing massages. Dusiková ulice (phone and fax: 165-5169). Moderate.

Hostinec Ceský Dvůr This small, pleasant "Bohemian-style" property is located just 15 minutes from town. All 8 rooms have private baths and satellite TV. Hearty Czech meals, including wild game, are featured in the *Lovecká Jizba* (Hunter's Lodge) restaurant. 35 Zavišin (phone: 165-4702). Inexpensive.

Continental Located in the center of town, this renovated 19th-century hotel has 53 rooms. There is a restaurant, a café, a wine bar, and a casino. 8 Zbrojnická (phone: 19-221746). Moderate.

TÁBOR

Palcát Conveniently located, this 6-story building has 68 rooms and 5 suites. There is a restaurant serving continental and Chinese dishes, a bar, and a nightclub with live music and dancing. 9 Května (phone: 361-22901; fax: 361-22905). Moderate.

HLUBOKÁ NAD VLTAVOU

Parkhotel This small, 2-story hotel offers 50 rooms and a hunting lodge restaurant specializing in wild game and fish. 602 Masaryková (phone: 38-965281). Inexpensive.

CESKÉ BUDĚJOVICE

Royal Canon A tastefully decorated hotel located in a less scenic part of town, it offers 22 large and comfortable rooms; the third floor accommodations have skylights. There is a restaurant with garden terrace dining in the summer. 103 Pražská (phone: 38-38975; fax: 38-38995). Moderate.

Zvon Located directly on the square, this modest 56-room hotel with vaulted ceilings is currently undergoing renovations which include plans for a new wing. Ask for a room overlooking the square. There's a café and 3 restaurants all serving some combination of Czech and continental dishes. 28 Přemysla Otakara II (phone: 38-58940; fax: 38-58940). Moderate.

Bohemia Built on the foundations of an old burgher house, this charming hotel-pension offers 10 spacious rooms with satellite TV and telephones. The cozy, wood-paneled bar and restaurant serves well-prepared and inexpensive local fare. 20 Hradební (phone: 38-56263). Moderate to inexpensive.

CESKÝ KRUMLOV

Růže Originally built in 1586 to house the Jesuits, this beautiful hotel offers rooms with wood-beamed and vaulted ceilings and breathtaking views of the Vltava River. There are 31 rooms with 4 luxurious suites as well as a Czech restaurant, café, wine bar, and nightclub. Other facilities include horseback riding, swimming, and tennis. 153 Horní ulice (phone: 337-2245 or 337-5481; fax: 337-3381). Expensive.

Krumlov Although the service is somewhat lackadaisical and the 30 rooms are a bit too plain, the hotel is located in the heart of historic Krumlov. Some of the spacious Louis XIV suites feature white furniture, crystal chandeliers, and marble baths. (No. 105 offers the nicest view of the town.) There is a Southern Bohemian restaurant and a wine bar. Svorností náměstí (phone: 337-3498; fax: 337-2225). Moderate to inexpensive.

BRNO

Continental This modern 212-room tower on the edge of town has a restaurant, a wine bar, and a nightclub. During summer months there's a relaxing terrace garden serving a light menu. 21 Kounicová (phone: 5-744232). Expensive.

Grand Now part of the Austrotel chain, this first class, 114-room hotel has an excellent restaurant serving Moravian specialties and wines. Facilities include a bar, casino, and nightclub. The view, however, leaves something to be desired: The front overlooks a power plant and the city's southern industrial complex; the back faces an abandoned building site. 18-20 Tř. Benešová (phone: 5-26420/9; fax: 5-22426). Expensive.

Holiday Inn Located near the fairgrounds, this new hotel caters to business travelers. It features 205 rooms and 10 executive suites (2 equipped for the disabled). Facilities include a good restaurant serving Czech specialties, a lobby bar, sauna, and business center. One floor is designated for non-smokers. 20 Krížkovského (phone: 5-336693; fax: 5-336990). Expensive.

International A deluxe modern hotel with 291 rooms, it has a good view of Spilberk Castle and the Old Town. Among the facilities are 2 restaurants serving international and regional specialties, a bar, café, and a lively nightclub. 16 Husová (phone: 5-213-4111; fax: 5-23051). Expensive.

Voroněž I & II A two-building modern hotel, it features a health club, pool, and sauna. The beautiful *Moravská Chalupa* (Moravian Cottage) restaurant serves excellent fare and shouldn't be missed. 47 and 49 Krížkovského (phone: 5-35111 or 5-431411; fax: 5-334528). Expensive.

Myslivna Located outside of town, near the Pisárky Forest, this secluded and quiet 120-room hotel is a favorite of the US Ambassador to the Czech Republic. The restaurant serves quality game, fish, and light meals, and the garden terrace overlooks dense woodlands. Facilities include a bar, a nightclub, and a fitness center. 12 Pisárky (phone: 5-383247; fax: 5-383745). Moderate.

Slovan While the bright red reception area and pastel-colored rooms are a little overpowering, this pleasant 105-room hotel is built into an arcade that boasts a wine bar, beer hall, nightclub, and casino. Guests enjoy the frequent special wine and beer parties, as well as sightseeing excursions to the nearby Dyje River valley. 23 Lidická (phone: 5-745455 or 5-745505; fax: 5-746543). Moderate.

OLOMOUC

Flora This gray tower with 175 comfortable rooms and 5 suites overlooks the town park and gardens. For a view of the city spires ask for No. 110.

Facilities include a restaurant, a café, 2 bars, a nightclub, and a souvenir shop. 34 Krapková (phone: 68-412021; fax: 68-412129). Expensive.

Obecní Dům In the town center, this 108-year-old hotel was once the favorite of the local elite. Many of the 55 rooms are on the faded side, although some have been renovated and the owners plan additional changes. The casino is new; there's also a restaurant and a café. 31 Svobody trida (phone: 68-27936). Moderate.

Sigma Across from the train station and 5 minutes from the city center, this glass-and-steel tower boasts 93 rooms and 7 suites. The rooms are plain and have showers only. There's a restaurant and café. 36 Jeřemenková (phone: 68-26941; fax: 68-28962). Moderate.

Zámek Just 8 miles (13 km) outside of the city, this hotel, designed as a castle, offers good service and pleasant surroundings. Its 16 rooms and 2 suites have satellite TVs and mini-bars. The restaurant features both Moravian specialties and Chinese food. Vélká Bystrice (phone: 68-95451/4; fax: 68-95754). Moderate.

Slovakia

The Slovak Republic is a nation of 5 million people — including a Hungarian minority of 600,000 and a large Romany (Gypsy) population — living in a territory of about 45,870 square miles. It is a land of natural beauty, crossed by the Carpathian ranges of the Malá Fatra (Little Carpathians), Vysoké Tatry (High Tatras), Nízke Tatry (Lower Tatras), and the Slovenské Rudhorie (Slovak Ore Mountains), running generally east-west. The High Tatras extend in a narrow ridge to the Polish border, and with dozens of small resort towns dotting the landscape, the area is popular with hikers and sports enthusiasts year-round. The 74-mile (118-km) long Lower Tatra range also has extensive ski and sporting facilities. The forests of the High Tatra, Lower Tatra, and Pieniny National Parks, as well as nature preserves such as the Slovenský Ráj are well-known destinations. Slovakia boasts fresh-air spas in the Vysoké Tatry, and thousands travel to "take the waters" in the modern resort towns of Piešťany and Trenčianské Teplice.

After the Communist takeover in 1948, money was pumped into the predominantly agrarian republic to establish and improve the industrial base. As a result, many of Slovakia's cities and villages are both newer and in better condition than those in the Czech Republic. About 10% of the population lives in the capital city of Bratislava (pop. 440,000) and the second-largest city of Košice (pop. 99,000); the rest is scattered in about 2,000 small towns, many of which preserve the cottage industries that keep the region's arts and crafts alive, particularly in Eastern Slovakia. Crafts fairs and folk festivals have long been a Slovak tradition.

Late spring and summer are well suited to sightseeing, sports, hiking, and other leisure activities in Slovakia. Average May temperatures are in the mid-50s F (13C), and July temperatures run up to the high 70s F (25C), with August traditionally being the warmest month. The winter season brings downhill and cross-country skiing, snowboarding, tobogganing, and sleigh riding in the region's winter resort centers.

BRATISLAVA TO THE HIGH TATRAS

Slovakia is a relatively easy country to explore. English is spoken in the major cities and resort towns, although you might have to search for an English translator in some of the smaller villages. Travelers should remember that although the Czech and Slovak languages are mutually intelligible, they do use slightly different alphabets.

The route includes the capital city of Bratislava and takes in the resort towns and mountain villages of the Tatras and the Spiš region. The drive from Bratislava to Poprad is about 205 miles (330 km). There are flights available to Poprad from both Prague and Bratislava as well as regular rail and bus connections from Bratislava.

BRATISLAVA For a complete description of the city and its restaurants and hotels, see *Bratislava* in THE CITIES.

En Route from Bratislava Drive northeast on Route E571 to Banská Bystrica. From this point take Route E77 north to Poprad. Using Poprad as a base, this journey takes in the nearby resorts of the High Tatras, the highest mountains of the Carpathian range, and the rural villages of the Spiš region.

POPRAD One of the larger cities in the region, Poprad has benefited from its strategic location in the southern foothills. In addition to being the starting point for forays into the High Tatras, the town has several historic monuments worth seeing, including the 1655 Renaissance belfry and the 14th-century early-Gothic Church of St. Egidius, which contains a fresco of a biblical scene with the Tatra Mountains in the background. The medieval streets of the Old Town are lined with baroque and neo-classical buildings, although many are coated with the thick soot of industrial pollution.

Located north, east, and south of Poprad are the several small towns and villages considered part of the Spiš region. If you venture off the main roads into some of the remote rural villages, you may get a glimpse of life as it was centuries ago. Highlights include Levoča, the medieval town of Bardejov, and Hervartov, which has one of the oldest wooden churches in the Carpathians.

Hiking is especially popular in this area, and as a part of the Tatras National Park (TANP), it boasts over 180 miles (288 km) of trails, which wind their way through the mountains and connect almost all the villages, towns, valleys, and lakes in the area. The *Cedok* office in Bratislava (5-9 Jesenského ulica; phone: 7-499142; fax: 7-499591) will make travel and hotel arrangements. For general information, tours, and accommodations in pensions and private homes, contact *TatraTour* (25 Bajaklská ulica, Bratislava; phone: 7-63128; fax: 7-212722).

One unique way to experience the spectacular beauty of the High Tatras is a plane ride over its peaks and valleys. *Cassovia Air* at the Poprad Airport offers 30-minute charter flights ($30 per person). Make arrangements through *TatraTour* (see above) or *Aeroklub Poprad* (phone: 92-22634).

KEŽMAROK Located 8 miles (13 km) north of Poprad, Kežmarok — along with Levoča — was once the center of political, economic, and cultural life in the Spiš region. Stop by the restored Renaissance castle (phone: 969-2780), which also houses a museum, and the hradní vináreň (castle wine cellar). Also take time to view the Town Hall and its Renaissance bell tower, or stroll down Hradní námestie (Castle Square), with its restored Gothic and Renaissance houses (the Gothic arch of No. 1 Hradní provides a gorgeous frame for a photographic view of the Tatras). In July, the *European Folk Craftsmanship Festival* comes to town, and it is a good opportunity to see authentic Slovakian workmanship up close.

STARÝ SMOKOVEC Founded in 1793, this is the largest and the oldest of the resort centers, located about one mile (1.6 km) north of Kežmarok with a complex of chalets, restaurants, and hotels. At heights of 3,280 feet, it's considered a first class facility for downhill skiing, cross-country skiing, and ski-jumping (at the *Na Jámach Center*). In the summer, mountaineers can climb Mt. Gerlach or take a side trip to the Vodské Vodopády (Cold Water Falls) or the Obrovské Vodopády (Giant Falls). Hikers should check on their route and local weather conditions with either the Dom Horskej Služby (Mountain Rescue Service; phone: 969-2820 or 969-2855) or the Tatras National Park Information Center. Guides can be hired at the Mountain Rescue Service. A railway leads up to Hrebienok, a small village with a toboggan run and a beginner's ski slope with night lighting.

STRBSKÉ PLESO Translated as Lake Strba, this is a modern, year-round resort town perched more than 4,000 feet high in the Tatras. About 11 miles (18 km) from Starý Smokovec, it is the site of a fresh-air spa and an extensive ski complex built for the *1970 World Ski Championships*. Spectacular Lake Strba covers more than 40 acres. On its shore stands the *Patria,* one of the finest hotels in the area; the rooms offer views of the lake or the mountains (see *Best en Route*).

ZDIAR About 25 miles (40 km) north of Poprad, in a valley that lies between the Belánské and Spisská Magura mountain ranges, this picturesque village was founded by the "goral" or mountain people. Their log homes were built fortress-style with enclosed courtyards, and blue paint was dabbed in the crevices. A unique feature is the lack of chimneys; smoke was released through the chinks in the walls. The best examples of the ornamental folk-style — brightly painted red shutters covered with geometrical designs — can be found on the houses located at the upper end of the village on Krissakov Hill above the church. The *Zdiarský Dom* (Folk Architecture Museum) is the site of "goral weddings" — visitors can don authentic costumes and participate in the feasting and dancing. For further information contact *TatraTour* in Poprad (phone: 92-63712; fax: 92-63889).

TATRANSKÁ LOMNICA The most elegant of the resort centers, about 5 miles (8 km) south of Poprad, this village is set in the second-highest park in the Tatras. Restaurants and hotels here are open all year; the favorite is *Grand Hotel Praha,* which opened in 1905 (see *Best en Route*). It offers sleigh rides in the winter and an excursion (daily except Tuesdays) on the overhead cable railway to the gorgeous Skalnaté Pleso (Rocky Lake), located at an altitude of 5,255 feet. The downhill skiing on Lomnické Sedlo (Lomnica Mountain) is the best in the Tatras. The *Tatra National Park Museum* has excellent exhibitions documenting the area's past and its natural history.

LEVOČA For centuries one of the most important commercial centers in Slovakia, this small Spiš town, about 10 miles (16 km) east of Poprad, is a treasury of Gothic architecture. The town is surrounded by 13th-century ramparts, and the older section has well-preserved buildings dating from the Middle Ages through the 16th and 17th centuries.

Laid out around a central square, the town plan still follows the chessboard pattern of its original design. Town Hall (built in 1615) is outstanding, as are the old burghers' houses with arched Gothic entries. The Thurzo House (No. 7, on the main square) epitomizes the local Renaissance style, with characteristically elaborate balconies and loggias. The interior of St. James's Church on the main square has magnificent wooden altars. The celebrated limewood-carved Gothic main altar, by Master Paul of Levoča in 1507–17, depicts the *Last Supper* in fascinating detail.

En route from Levoča The dramatic hilltop ruins of the 13th-century Spiš Castle, built to protect the inhabitants from Mongol invaders, are visible from the main highway (Rte. E50) as you head east from Levoča; the view from the hilltop is breathtaking. This is the largest castle complex in the country and is now partially restored. Continue on Route E50 to Presšov, where you will turn north on Route E371 to Bardejov.

BARDEJOV Tracing its history to the 12th century, this medieval town affords visitors a look into the past with its Gothic and Renaissance architecture and cobblestone streets. The main architectural monuments line the town square: The Gothic Church of St. Egidius, built in the 14th, 15th, and 16th centuries, has a splendid Gothic altar, intricately hand-carved pews, and shimmering rose windows. Constructed in 1506 at the dawn of the Renaissance in Slovakia, the Town Hall is an interesting transitional blend of

Gothic and Renaissance features. Also notable is the Humanistic Gymnasium (1435).

HERVARTOV Five miles (8 km) southwest of Bardejov, this village has a beautiful 16th-century wooden church with its original painted ceiling; it is considered the oldest of Slovakia's wooden churches. Ask a local to direct you to the house where the church keys are.

BEST EN ROUTE

Because the High Tatras are popular year-round, it's absolutely necessary to make hotel reservations at least a month in advance in the spring and summer months. If you are planning to visit during the winter, make reservations at any of the resort hotels at least 3 months prior to your trip. Expect to pay $60 and up per night for a double room with half board in hotels in the expensive range; $40 to $50 at places in the moderate category; and around $30 at inexpensive spots. Be aware that at press time, the Slovak government had imposed a 23% sales tax on hotel rooms, so check in advance to see whether or not the tax has been included in the price you are quoted. A dinner for two will cost $30 and up at expensive restaurants; between $20 and $30 at moderate places; and $10 and under at inexpensive eateries. For additional information on mountain resorts for skiing and hiking, see *Good Sports* in DIVERSIONS.

For each location, hotels and restaurants are listed alphabetically by price category.

POPRAD

Satel The newest hotel in town, this modern 9-story tower offers first class service and 132 rooms with satellite TV and mini-bars. There is a fitness center with solarium and sauna; the *Zdiarská Izba* restaurant, serving fine Slovak fare; and a nightclub sporting pink neon lights. Marxová ulica (phone: 92-471111; fax: 92-62075). Expensive.

Europa Its prime location next to the train and bus station makes this 73-room hotel worth considering if the others are booked. However, the rooms are small and a bit on the shabby side, and the clientele in the café is questionable. There is a restaurant and a wine bar. Wolkrová (phone: 92-32744). Moderate.

Gerlach Although it suffers from drab pre-revolution decor, this boxy tower nevertheless has 143 plain (but comfortable) rooms and 2 suites. There is a café, a restaurant, and a disco. The *Panorama* bar on the 8th floor offers a terrific view of the Tatras. 2 Hviezdoslavová (phone: 92-33759; fax: 92-63663). Moderate.

STARÝ SMOKOVEC

Grand Opened in 1898, this large alpine chalet, is the most comfortable hotel in the area. The 83 rooms are first class, and the atmosphere is old-fashioned.

There are 2 restaurants, a wine bar, a pool, and a sauna (phone: 969-2154 or 969-2229). Expensive.

STRBSKÉ PLESO

Patria This 11-story lakefront hotel, which is a bit off-kilter, either complements its mountain backdrop or wrecks the scenery, depending on your point of view. It has 150 rooms and 15 suites, all with private baths. Among the facilities are the *Sun* and *Slovenka* restaurants, a café, a bar, a snack bar, and the *Vatra* nightclub. A fitness center includes a pool, sauna, gym, and solarium (phone and fax: 969-92591). Expensive.

Panorama Near Strbské Pleso and the rail terminal, this modern, 96-room hotel has a restaurant, a café, and gamerooms (phone: 969-92111). Moderate.

TATRANSKÁ LOMNICA

Grand Hotel Praha Opened in 1905 and remodeled in 1973, this classic hotel is the favorite in the area. Its 96 rooms are convenient to ski lifts, and many offer great mountain views. There's a restaurant and a wine bar (phone: 969-967941). Expensive.

Zbojnická Koliba A cozy shepherd's hut restaurant serving barbecued meat, mulled wine, and tea, and featuring folk music. Near the *Grand Hotel Praha* (phone: 969-967630). Moderate.

Hungary

This small, landlocked country near the geographic center of Europe, with its blend of Eastern and Western traditions, has long appealed to travelers. It is a land of beautiful landscapes, romantic music, decorative folk art, historic monuments, and excellent — if occasionally rich — food.

Despite its size — it is not quite as big as Indiana — and its relative flatness, the country has an extremely colorful and varied landscape. Hungary is bisected by the Danube River (called Duna in Hungarian), which rushes south after carving a sharply angled route through mountains along the country's northwestern border.

To the west of the Danube is Transdanubia, a picturesque area of rolling hills, cultivated vineyards, old towns, and Balaton, Europe's largest warm-water lake. Within the Great Hungarian Plain, east of the Danube, are abundant fruit orchards; fields of waving wheat, sunflowers, and corn; and the prairie-like *puszta*. This vast granary is the historic home of Hungary's famous *csikos,* whip-cracking herdsmen on horseback. In addition to the scenic mountains of the Danube Bend in the northwest, there are low, forested mountains along the northeastern frontier, which is also famous for its wine-growing regions. Deer, wild boar, and spiral-horned mouflon (wild sheep) roam freely in state game reserves.

Hungary is bordered on the west by Austria; on the north by Slovakia; on the east by Ukraine and Romania; and on the south by Croatia, Slovenia, and Yugoslavia (Serbia). Foggy weather is common in fall; winters can be bone-chillingly damp or Siberian-cold with much snow; and summers are hot, dry, and dusty.

The fact that Hungary has an extremely homogeneous population today — 90% of its 10.6 million people are ethnically Hungarian or, in their language, Magyar (the rest are German or Austrian, Slavs, Serbs, Croats, Slovaks, and Romany people or Gypsies) — is the result of this century's two world wars. On the losing side in World War I, Hungary was forced to give up vast territories that had been part of its kingdom. Today, many ethnic Hungarians reside in what is now Romania, and their plight is a concern in Hungary. Some 600,000 Jews, nearly two-thirds of the country's Jewish population, were murdered during World War II.

Adding to Hungary's singularity is its language, which is unlike any other in Europe although, as part of the Finno-Ugric language group, it is distantly related to Finnish and Estonian. The first inhabitants of this part of Europe were the Celts, who were conquered by the Romans in AD 10. The Romans founded Aquincum (Budapest) as a frontier post and in AD 106 it became the capital of Panonia; they also established thermal baths there, precursors to the city's modern-day spas. The ancestors of today's Magyars were fierce bands of mounted tribesmen from the Ural

Mountains who staged forays deep into Western Europe. Seven of these tribes, under the leadership of Arpád, were check ⁝ by the forces of the Holy Roman Empire in the 9th century, and they eventually settled in the area that now is Hungary.

István (Stephen), a descendant of the legendary Magyar leader Arpád, became the first King of Hungary in AD 997 and worked strenuously to convert his people from paganism to Catholicism. For his efforts, he received a crown from the pope and was canonized in 1081. St. Stephen's Crown has been a symbol of Hungarian nationhood ever since. (The crown was taken to the US for safekeeping during World War II, but was only returned in 1978, some time after tensions between the church and the local Communist government eased.) About two-thirds of Hungary's population is at least nominally Roman Catholic, and the majority of the rest is Protestant.

After the Arpád line died out in 1301, various royal houses of Europe struggled for control of Hungary. The coronation of King Mátyás Hunyadi (Matthias Corvinus in Latin) in 1458 brought prosperity and national glory to Hungary. This Renaissance king, famous for his dazzling court at Visegrád, restored public finances and reduced the power of masters over serfs. But after his death, central Hungary fell under the yoke of the Turks for some 150 years, while the northern and western sections were drawn into the Austrian Hapsburg domain. The Turks finally were forced to withdraw from the capital of Buda in 1686, but the following year, the Hungarians were compelled to accept Austrian succession to the Hungarian throne. The Hungarians rose up against Austrian absolutism several times. They succeeded in establishing the first Hungarian republic in 1848 but were defeated by the Austrians, led by a Croatian general, Josip Jelačić, the following year. The repression that followed caused the first mass exile of thousands of Hungarians. In 1867, however, their persistent battle for more independence led to the establishment of a dual monarchy in which Austria and Hungary were partners.

After the fall of the Austro-Hungarian Empire in World War I, Hungary went through a short period as a Soviet republic, and then, from 1920 to 1944, it was governed by Admiral Miklós Horthy de Nagybanya, a right-wing strongman and, in due course, a fascist. Hungary's alliance with Nazi Germany was followed by German occupation, which lasted until the Allied liberation of Budapest by Soviet troops in 1945 after a horrendous 2-month battle. In 1949, the government was taken over by the Hungarian Workers Party (which later changed its name to Magyar Szocialista Munkáspárt — MSZMP, the Communist Party in Hungary), and Hungary became politically, economically, and militarily aligned with the Soviet Union. In 1956, Soviet forces were called in to help crush an uprising, and more than 200,000 Hungarians fled into exile. However, starting in the early 1960s, the government of János Kádár enacted a number of reforms that took some of the sting out of the defeat of liberal elements. Kádár's blend of socialism and capitalism became known as "goulash Communism."

In 1989 Hungary made a dramatic dent in the Iron Curtain by opening its borders to (then) East German refugees who wished to emigrate to (then) West Germany. Seeing that their policies had led the country to near economic and political ruin, the Communist authorities decreed political change. While changes in other Soviet-controlled countries resulted in protests in the streets, the Hungarian Communists sensed the inevitability of their demise, and in March 1990 organized — and lost — the first free elections in Hungary since 1947. In August 1990, Hungary's first post-Communist right-of-center Parliament elected Arpád Göncz to a 5-year term as president. Göncz, a writer and translator, had been a prisoner of the Communist government. Hungary's current government is perhaps the most stable in Eastern Europe.

Today the country, very much aware of its economic shortcomings, is attempting to develop free enterprise as quickly as possible. Many Hungarians fear that change might be happening too quickly, however, and that the country's industries might be sold to Western investors for far too little. Hungarians also fear that inflation and a 15% unemployment rate could further destabilize the country, but few question the need to pursue the road to free enterprise and democracy.

A visit to today's Hungary is an intellectually heady experience, as well as a pleasure for the senses. Two senses in particular — taste and hearing — are indulged here, often simultaneously. Dinner in a Hungarian restaurant accompanied by the performance of an accomplished Gypsy orchestra is a memorable experience.

The Magyar musical heritage comprises classical as well as folk music. It was dramatically expressed in the romantic rhapsodies of Ferenc (Franz) Liszt in the 19th century and in the modern music of the 20th-century masters Béla Bartók and Zoltán Kodály, both of whom devoted years of intensive study to Hungarian folk songs.

The special Hungarian harmony of flavors has earned the country's cuisine, based on a superb marriage of meat, spices, and fresh vegetables, international appreciation. The special sweet Hungarian paprika, used in many dishes and found in a shaker at every table, is one of the world's most versatile condiments.

Historical, cultural, and gustatory riches, along with the brightest and most romantic capital of central Europe — indeed, one of the loveliest cities in Europe — have increased tourism to the point where the number of visitors to Hungary each year exceeds the country's population.

For those who would like to see more of the country than its wonderful capital, we have provided three tour routes. If you have only a short time to spend outside Budapest, a visit to the nearby Danube Bend offers an opportunity to enjoy some of the country's most breathtaking scenery while encountering its royal and ecclesiastical past. Our second route, into

Transdanubia, is through a softer landscape, also rich in history, to Hungary's busiest center of recreation and relaxation, Lake Balaton. The third route, through the Great Hungarian Plain, allows you to explore the Hungary of peasant folk legend and to see some of Europe's most desirable farmland.

The Danube Bend

As it heads east from its route along the Slovakia border, the Danube River makes an elbow bend through the wooded Pilis and Börzsöny hills, divides into two channels that will unite again at Budapest, and gracefully curves south to begin its long journey to the Black Sea.

This scenic, history-rich area about 31 miles (50 km) north of Budapest is called the Danube Bend and is a favorite excursion destination for residents of the capital, many of whom have built small weekend homes there, as well as for visitors. Its picturesque environs can be explored leisurely, and most pleasantly, by steamer on the river or by car. The main towns along the route also can be reached by train.

If you drive north, Route 11 follows the general contour of the right bank of the river between Budapest and Esztergom, an early seat of Hungarian kings and an ancient ecclesiastical center. To the west, all along the route, is the Pilis Park Forest, which harbors wild boar and deer. You can make the trip upriver along one bank and downriver along the other, or you may prefer to crisscross the river, visiting key cities on either bank as they appear on the route. For the purposes of description, this route will take the latter course, beginning at Budapest and ending at Esztergom, 40 miles (65 km) away.

***

BUDAPEST For a detailed report of the city and its hotels and restaurants, see *Budapest* in THE CITIES.

En Route from Budapest The highway leaves the capital on the Buda side of the Danube, which divides into two channels around the huge Szentendre Island just north of the city. The route upriver along the Szentendre channel, to the west of the island, offers the most rewards for tourists and is one of the busiest roads in Hungary on weekends.

SZENTENDRE This old Roman market town, where the great Hungarian painter Károly Ferenczy worked for the greater part of his life, is filled with interesting churches and art museums. Many artists have settled here in the old merchant houses of the original Serbian and Dalmatian settlers, who came here during the 17th century, fleeing the Turkish occupation. Today, the city's character largely reflects the 18th and 19th century, with distinguished Serbian architecture in the lower parts, and Dalmatian style in the higher part of the city.

The small main square, Fö tér (formerly Marx tér), is lined with lovingly restored, 18th-century baroque houses. Each summer a theater festival is held in the square. The *Ferenczy Múzeum* (6 Fö tér; no phone) contains works by the Ferenczy family as well as paintings by members of the artists colony established here in 1928. Another museum (1 Vastagh György utca; no phone) displays the ceramics of Margit Kovács, and a collection of paintings and drawings by Lajos Vajda is on view at 1 Hunyadi János utca. Both museums are open Tuesdays through Saturdays from 9 AM to 4 PM; admission charge.

The *Szabadtéri Néprajzi Múzeum* (Outdoor Village Museum) in the north of town contains original examples of folk architecture, brought here from Hungary's 23 regions. Craftsmen here demonstrate milling, candlestick making, scone and honeycake baking, and other oldtime crafts, on the first Sunday of each month. There also is a very good restaurant, *Uj Etterem,* in the surrounding park. To reach the museum, which is open from April through October, follow Szabadság forrás utca for about 3 miles (5 km) uphill.

The *Szerb Egyháztörténeti Gyüjtemény* (Serbian Museum of Ecclesiastical History; 5 Engels utca) contains Eastern Orthodox religious art from the 14th through the 18th century. One of the finest carved wooden iconostasis (a screen with tiers of icons) in Hungary is found in the Greek Orthodox Belgrade Church on Alkotmány utca. There is an interesting medieval Roman Catholic parish church on Templom Hill, near the main square. This church was rebuilt in 1710, but parts of it date from the 12th century. A panoramic view of red rooftops and the Danube River is offered from the square surrounding the church.

Traces of Stone Age men have been found in caves in the vicinity, and the largest Bronze Age cemetery in central Europe was excavated in nearby Budakalász.

En Route from Szentendre At Pomáz, an unnumbered road in the direction of Esztergom leads to the popular mountain resort of Dobogókő in the Pilis forest. At Leányfalu, you can hike to the 1,500-foot Vörös-kő Szikla (Red Stone Cliff) for a wonderful panoramic view of the plain and the Danube Bend.

North of Szentendre, the town of Tahitótfalu spreads along both sides of a channel parallel to the Danube, and the bridge here is a good place to cross over to the island for some swimming, canoeing, or rowing. The river is quite shallow near the village of Kisoroszi, at the northern tip of the island. It has a good beach and a ferry that can take you back across the channel.

At this point the route leaves the plain and enters the mountain area, and the two channels of the Danube reunite as the river is forced into a more constricted course.

VISEGRÁD The setting of this small village among the mountains at the center of the Danube Bend, and the relics of its illustrious past as a royal stronghold during the Middle Ages, make Visegrád an immensely popular tourist center. Its 9th-century Slavic name "high fortress" perfectly describes its position above the Danube.

During the past few decades, a magnificent summer palace that flowered during the reign of King Matthias Corvinus (1458–90) has been excavated and reconstructed on a hillside on the main street (27 Fö utca). A fine Renaissance fountain of red marble in the ceremonial courtyard bears the king's coat of arms.

Located on Castle Hill are the remains of the Fellegvár (Citadel) and the hexagonal Salamon Tower, a typical 13th-century fortified dwelling built by King Béla IV, with walls 9 feet thick to resist prolonged attacks. On a clear day, the view over the Danube to Slovakia is absolutely spectacular. On another hill (Sibrik) are the remains of a Roman camp from about the 4th century.

Some of the discoveries of modern excavations and exhibitions of Visegrád's royal past can be seen at the *Mátyás Király Múzeum* (King Matthias Museum; 41 Fö utca), in an 18th-century baroque mansion that once was a royal hunting lodge. The mansion is open daily from 10 AM to 3 PM; admission charge.

En Route from Visegrád Dömös is at the southernmost point of the bend the Danube makes around the southern foothills of the Börzsöny Mountains. From the slopes of the little town's hills, there is an impressive view of the V-like path of the river. This popular resort is frequently used as a starting point for hiking into the Pilis Mountains.

Pilismarót, near the start of the Danube Bend, has a wonderful 2-mile beach and numerous small bays. Zebegény, the picturesque town across the river, is an artists' colony and popular summer resort that can be reached by ferry.

Upstream from Zebegény is the frontier station of Szob, on the Slovak Republic border. Here you can visit two baroque castles or enjoy the town's pleasant beach before taking the ferry back to the right bank of the Danube. From there it's only a few miles to Esztergom.

ESZTERGOM This city actually sits on a narrow side channel of the Danube, separated from the main river by a long island connected to the mainland by bridges. The philosopher-emperor Marcus Aurelius is said to have written some of the books of his *Reflections* here when this was an important Roman outpost. Esztergom is best known, however, as the residence of Magyar kings in the 12th and 13th centuries and the seat of the primate of the Hungarian Catholic church.

The largest cathedral in Hungary (390 feet long) was built here, on Várhegy (Castle Hill), between 1822 and 1856. Liszt's *Esztergom Mass* was performed at the cathedral's consecration. A Renaissance chapel adjoins the south side of the cathedral, whose treasury includes numerous works of art, including a 13th-century gold cross upon which the Kings of Hungary took their coronation oaths. Behind the cathedral is the *kincstár* (treasury), full of religious relics, including objects used by the archbishops during the past 800 years, and a small-scale model of the cathedral complex. In May 1991, the body of Hungary's Cardinal József Mindszenty was buried here. He died in 1975 in exile because of his fierce nationalism and anti-communism.

The *Vár Múzeum* (Castle Museum) next to the cathedral contains fragments of a royal palace that had been destroyed during the Turkish occupation and nearly forgotten until this century, when large-scale excavations were undertaken. The palace was begun in 972 by St. Stephen's father, but its most glorious period came in the late 12th century, during the reign of King Béla III.

The *Keresztény Múzeum* (Christian Museum; 2 Mindszenty tér; no phone) contains one of Hungary's most important fine arts collections. It includes excellent examples of Hungarian paintings, minor medieval Italian works, fine Flemish and French tapestries, and a remarkable 15th-century altar. The museum is open Tuesdays through Sundays from 9AM to 7 PM; admission charge.

For music buffs, the annual two-week *Guitar Festival* is held in early August in this ancient and picturesque town. Every kind of guitar music is featured, from classical to pop to rock. Performers come from Hungary and from across Europe.

BEST EN ROUTE

Hotels in the Danube Bend area are relatively simple places. Expect to pay about $25 or $35 for a double room (including breakfast) in a moderate place, less than $25 for inexpensive accommodations. There are a number of excellent camping sites along the route, including one on Pap Island, near Szentendre, which accommodates up to 500 campers. At area restaurants, expect to pay $10 to $12 for a dinner for two without drinks, wine, or tip for restaurants listed as moderate; less than $10 at inexpensive eateries. The restaurants below accept major credit cards unless otherwise noted.

For each location, hotels and restaurants are listed alphabetically by price category.

SZENTENDRE

Rab Ráby The name means "prisoner Ráby" (a 19th-century local literary figure), and the house, which is now an eatery, was built by a Serbian merchant about 150 years ago. Each table is graced with a unique piece of 19th-century memorabilia, such as an 1843 newspaper, an old teapot, a bronze sculpture, or a pair of prison foot chains. The menu includes Hungarian fish and meat dishes. Closed Mondays. Reservations necessary during summer. 1 Péter Pál utca (phone: 26-10819). Moderate.

DOBOGÓKÖ

Nimród A modern hotel with 70 rooms set high in the woods of the Pilis Mountains. The restaurant serves game in season. Reservations advised. 2 Eötvös sétány (phone: 26-27644). Moderate.

VISEGRÁD

Matthias Corvinus Panzio Occupying an old manor, this private pension has 15 delightful rooms (some with balconies) and a restaurant that serves traditional Hungarian cooking. 47 Fő utca (phone: 26-28309). Moderate.

ESZTERGOM

Esztergom This small, modern 36-room hostelry overlooking the Danube has its own sports center. Primás Sziget (Primate Island), Nagy-Duna sétány (phone: 33-12555). Moderate.

Sötétkapu Söröző Situated at the foot of the cathedral, this eatery offers traditional Hungarian dishes. Open daily for lunch and dinner. Reservations necessary. No credit cards accepted. Béke tér (phone: 33-13495). Moderate.

Fürdő An 89-room hotel near the spa with swimming pools, a restaurant and bar, and central heating. 14 Bajcsy-Zsilinszky utca (phone: 33-11688). Moderate to inexpensive.

Korona Káve A pleasant coffeehouse, it serves a variety of rich Hungarian cakes and pastries, along with coffee, tea, and wine. Open daily. Reservations advised. No credit cards accepted. 16 Széchenyi tér (phone: 33-11517). Inexpensive.

Lake Balaton

The sandy beaches of Lake Balaton, where water temperatures range from 68F (20C) to 79F (26C) in the summer, attract a solid stream of vacationers, both Hungarian and foreign, from May to September. Since World War II, the Hungarian government has developed the area around Balaton — central Europe's largest lake — into a mass recreation center; the 122-mile (195-km) shoreline is virtually one continuous resort. For visitors, a knowledge of German is extremely useful here.

The southern shore generally is flat, with only an occasional steep hill overlooking the lake, and the water is extremely shallow, making it an ideal beach for families with small children. The towns of the north shore are older and facilities are geared more toward adults. The north shore is characterized by a chain of long-extinct and now-eroded volcanoes. Gently undulating vineyards cover the basalt hills, producing the grapes for some of the finest wines of Hungary. The area is also known for its effervescent mineral springs.

If you don't like crowds, it is best to visit the lake area in early spring or fall; rates are cheaper then, too. There are good rail connections for most of the larger resort towns, and in summer there are frequent fast trains from Budapest. The following route, beginning and ending in Budapest, explores the various resort areas around the lake (see also *Classic Cruises and Wonderful Waterways* in DIVERSIONS).

BUDAPEST For a detailed report of the city and its hotels and restaurants, see *Budapest* in THE CITIES.

En Route from Budapest The outskirts of Budapest give way to undulating hills as you travel southwest on Route 70. The Brunswick Mansion, a must for music lovers, is located in a beautiful old park at Martonvásár, about a half hour from Budapest. A part of the 18th-century mansion is now the site of a museum dedicated to Ludwig van Beethoven, who composed some of his important works while visiting here in the early 1800s; the *Moonlight Sonata* purportedly was composed here. Concerts of his music are given here during the summer.

Almost one-third of Lake Velence, which begins some 6 miles (10 km) beyond Martonvásár, is thick with reeds and dotted with swampy, marshy islets. In spring and autumn its grassy knolls are stopping places for thousands of migrating birds, including rare waterfowl. The 6-mile-long and very shallow lake, most commonly referred to as Kis-Balaton (Little Balaton), is a rapidly developing holiday resort, with good beaches, yachting facilities, hotels, restaurants, and camping sites, particularly along the southern shore near Gárdony and Agárd. The northern shore attracts anglers, hunters, and other sportsfolk. It also is possible to drive directly to Székesfehérvár from Budapest on Route E71 (M7).

SZÉKESFEHÉRVÁR Called Alba Regia by the Romans, during the Middle Ages this town was a thriving royal seat where 37 Hungarian kings were crowned and where later 15 were buried. Hungarian legend says that the country's first prince, Great Magyar Prince Árpád, set up camp near or in the city and claimed the territory for his tribe. Today it is an important industrial center in the Mezőföld (Meadowland), where three-fourths of the population is engaged in agriculture. Most of the medieval town was destroyed during the Turkish occupation (1543–1688). However, a number of interesting buildings remain in the inner city. The main square of the inner town is Szabadság tér, site of the 17th-century baroque Town Hall, the former Zichy Palace, with its attractive rococo and baroque interior, and the Romkert (Garden of Ruins), on the site of the excavations of the former cathedral, where coronations were held.

The *István Király Múzeum* (King Stephen Museum; 3 Országzászló tér; no phone) has interesting exhibitions on local archaeology, history, and folklore. The museum is open Tuesdays through Fridays from 8 AM to 4 PM; admission charge.

Siófok, the biggest tourist center on Lake Balaton, is about an hour's drive from Székesfehérvár on Route E71 (M7).

SIÓFOK The shores of Lake Balaton are virtually one long string of beach resorts, but Siófok is the largest town on the southern shore and is continually expanding to take in neighboring communities. In the 3rd century, Romans built the Sío Canal to take excess water from Balaton to the Danube. Siófok developed around a bridge on the canal. It has the most sophisticated tourist operations, some of the best beaches, and crowded facilities from *Easter* until the season ends in September.

Although the obvious attraction of Siófok is its long sandy beach, there are a few interesting churches and an excellent riding academy nearby. There also is an open-air theater in Dimitrov Park and many pleasant garden restaurants in which to relax. The *IBUSZ* travel office here can even arrange for you to take a cooking class with a chef from one of the top resort hotels. For more information, contact *IBUSZ* (13 Kele utca, Siófok; phone: 84-12011 or 84-13412) or *Siótour* (2/6 Batthyany utca; phone: 84-13111).

There are ferries to the north shore peninsula of Tihany from Szántód Harbor, near Siófok. Inland from the lake, on Route 65 at Ságvár, are interesting ruins of a fortified Roman camp, dating from the 3rd century.

En Route from Siófok The shore road winds through numerous resort towns. About 10 minutes west on Route 71 in the town of Zamárdi is *Szántód Puszta,* a folk and horse museum featuring buildings typical of the *puszta* (Hungarian plains), horse shows, and horseback riding. At Balatonföldvár a road south leads to Köröshegy, site of an interesting 15th-century, single-naved Gothic church. Many of the original features of the church remain, despite restoration work in the 18th century. The taverns here are good places to sample the regional wine and listen to Gypsy music.

After carefully negotiating several dangerous sudden curves through the town of Balatonszemes, the shore road reaches Fonyód, the site of Stone and Bronze Age settlements and now a busy resort area. At Balatonkeresztúr, Route 7, which has paralleled the lake since Zamárdi, veers south, and Route 71 curves around to the north shore.

KESZTHELY The largest of the lake towns, Keszthely has been a municipality since the early 15th century. Its charming old streets have a pleasant ambience, and there are a number of interesting sights to divert you from the pleasures of the beaches. The Georgikon (on Georgikon utca) was founded in 1797 and was the first agricultural college established on the European continent. The first inhabitants of the area were neolithic peoples, followed by Celts and Romans, who built a bridge across the lake near here. In 1742, Count György Festetics, who was of Serbian origin, bought 250,000 acres around Lake Balaton and developed the land into one of Europe's largest stud farms, supplying various royal houses on the Continent, as well as the Republican Cavalry of the US. Festetics built himself a palace, the third-largest in Hungary, which is as fine as any built in Europe. Its wonderful Helikon Library has some 90,000 books representing most European languages. The palace's collection of valuable art and antiquities, its wonderful park, and the impressive view from the terraces make it a must-see in this region (1 Szabadság utca; closed Mondays). The *Balaton Múzeum* (2 Múzeum utca; no phone) has interesting historical and ethnographical exhibitions. The museum is open daily from 9 AM to 4:30 PM; admission charge.

Hévíz, the most famous spa in Hungary is a few miles west of Keszthely. It's the site of Lake Hévíz, Europe's largest warm-water (82–93F) lake, and indoor and outdoor thermal and mud baths. The spa offers medical and cosmetic advice.

En Route from Keszthely The shore road passes through the Badacsony, a district of basalt terraces where lava from long-extinct volcanoes has created bizarre rock formations. The area also is known for its fruit growing and for the excellence of its vineyards. The ruins of Szigliget Castle, dating from the 13th century, stand on a hill just west of the town of Badacsony.

Beyond Balatonszepezd, a favorite retreat of artists and writers, a mile-long road leads up a hillside to Zánka, where there is a fisherman's lodge in the woods and a 13th-century church that was remodeled in the baroque style in 1786. Medieval pageants are sometimes held in summer in the 15th-century castle in Nagyvázsony, a town about 10 miles (16 km) farther north.

TIHANY The small, delightful peninsula of Tihany, a series of hills covered with poplar and acacia trees and the scent of lavender, is one of the loveliest spots on Lake Balaton. Its long history as a stronghold can be read in the remains of a 3,000-year-old earthenwork fortification and in Celtic and Roman ruins. A beautiful 18th-century yellow abbey church with twin spires stands on a hill overlooking the peninsula. Several houses that once belonged to the lake fishermen now make up the small *Open-Air Museum of Ethnography* (11 Pisky sétány; closed Mondays and in off-season). Exhibits of furniture, costumes, and art are testimony to the rich local history of Lake Balaton.

There is excellent fishing in Lake Belsö — high on a hill above Balaton, it is, in effect, a lake within a lake — and the villagers' unusual thatch-roofed houses of dark gray volcanic tufa add charm to the landscape. Government institutes have been set up on Tihany to study its wealth of geological and botanical rarities. *Club Tihany,* a family holiday village, occupies the tip of the peninsula (see *Best en Route*). The *Tihany Tourist Center* (20 Kossuth utca; phone: 86-48519) rents sailboats, among other services.

BALATONFÜRED The oldest and one of the most renowned health resorts in the area, Balatonfüred is the last large town on Lake Balaton. There are several sizable and recently built hotels here, an attractive poplar-lined promenade along the lake, and an inviting central park. There is also a neo-classical Kerek (Round) Church on Blaha Lujza utca, built in 1846. Yachting races frequently are held here, and the harbor is the busiest on the lake.

In the main square, Gyögy tér, there is a colonnaded pavilion built over the bubbling waters of a volcanic spring. In all, the town has 11 medicinal springs that for hundreds of years have attracted those seeking cures, particularly for heart and nerve disorders (see also *Spas: Eastern Europe's Unique Watering Spots* in DIVERSIONS). Hills around the city are covered with vineyards that produce very drinkable wines

En Route from Balatonfüred The shore road can be followed through a dozen or so small communities around the lake back to a connection with Route E71 (M7) to return to Budapest. Another alternative is to take Highway 73 north from Balatonfüred into the Bakony hills to Veszprém before heading back to Budapest.

VESZPRÉM Built on five hills, this picturesque town of cobblestone streets, old gateways, and arches is Bakony's cultural and economic center. It is an old settlement rich in historical monuments. The *Vár Múzeum* (Castle Museum), in the Hösök kapuja (Heroes' Gate) near Ovaros tér, contains old weapons, armor, and historical documents. The late 18th-century baroque Püspöki palota (Episcopal Palace; 12 Vár utca) is next to the early Gothic Gizella kapolna (Gizella Chapel), built in the 13th century.

The *Bakony Múzeum* (Megyekas tér), on Kálvária Hill, has exhibitions that detail the Bakony region's history, customs, and crafts.

BEST EN ROUTE

Lake Balaton is Hungary's most popular resort, so hotel reservations should be made well in advance if you plan to visit during the summer. Depending on the month and resort chosen, expect a double room listed as expensive to cost $65 or more; $30 to $55 for moderate accommodations; and less than $55 for an inexpensive stay. Most hotels provide breakfast in their rates. All the hotels listed are open from May to September unless otherwise noted. It also is possible to rent cottages or apartments on the lake, and *IBUSZ* (phone: 84-12011, 84-13412, or 84-13955) can arrange for the rental of sailboats that can sleep four at $200 to $400 per week. Dinner for two will cost $40 and up at restaurants in the expensive category; anywhere from $20 to $40 at places described as moderate; and under $20 for inexpensive spots. Prices do not include drinks, wine, or tip. The restaurants below accept major credit cards unless otherwise indicated. Reservations are advised at all restaurants.

The wines of the Balaton region, particularly the spicy white ones, are justly famous. Among the best are the *Badacsonyi kéknyelü* (Badacsony Blue Stalk), *Badacsonyi szürkebarát* (Badacsony Gray Friar), and *Badacsonyi rizling* (Badacsony Riesling). The food specialty is the perch-pike-type fish known as *fogas*.

For each location, hotels and restaurants are listed alphabetically by price category.

SIÓFOK

Balaton This modern hotel is set in an attractive location on the lake. All 137 rooms have balconies with terrific views. There is an espresso bar, and the hotel is within walking distance of some good restaurants. 9 Petöfi sétány (phone: 84-10655). Moderate.

Európa A lakeshore setting, private beach, pool, sauna, and restaurant are among this 138-room hotel's amenities. 15 Petöfi sétány (phone: 84-13411). Moderate.

Fogas Excellent food served in a garden setting. Open daily. No reservations. 184 Fő utca (phone: 84-11405). Moderate.

Hungária Eighty-four balconied rooms, a private beach, a restaurant, and a bar are offered here. 13 Petöfi sétány (phone: 84-10677). Moderate.

Ménes Csárda Very good — and very spicy — local specialties are served in this restaurant, actually a restored old stable decorated with antique folk art. Open April through October. In Szántódpuszta, about 6 miles (10 km) west of Siófok on the main highway to Balatonföldvár (phone: 84-31352). Moderate.

Napfény A small (57 rooms), family-type hotel near the beach, with balconied rooms. No restaurant. 8 Mártírok ut (phone: 84-11408; fax: 84-10628). Inexpensive.

KESZTHELY

Helikon This establishment faces the beach and has its own "island," connected to the hotel by a bridge. There are spa facilities, a restaurant and bar, tennis courts, and a yacht marina. The staff is very friendly. 5 Balatonpart (phone: 82-18944; fax: 82-18403). Expensive.

Halász Csárda (Fishermen's Inn) Fish dishes are the specialty at this casual eatery. Open Tuesdays through Sundays from 11 AM to 9 PM. Reservations advised. South of Keszthely on the lakeshore (phone: 82-12751). Moderate.

Helikon Tavern Good food and wine and Gypsy music are featured at this spot about 5 miles (8 km) east of town. Open daily for dinner. Make reservations through the *Helikon* hotel (see above). Moderate.

Hévíz Aqua Thermál Hotel A large modern hotel spa with 213 rooms set in a calm, wooded area, this is the place to come for a variety of health and beauty treatments. 13-15 Kossuth Lajos utca, Hévíz (phone: 82-18947; fax: 82-18970). Moderate.

Hullám This small, flower-bedecked hotel, with a pool and wide-ranging sports activities, consciously tries to evoke the leisurely atmosphere of bygone days. No restaurant. 1 Balatonpart (phone: 82-18950). Moderate.

Park One of the first private restaurants to open in the Balaton area, this dining spot is located in the home of the proprietors, the Horvath family. It's a very pleasant eatery serving a rich variety of Hungarian dishes. During the summer the garden is a favorite of natives and tourists alike. Reservations necessary during summer. Open April through October. 1-9 Vörösmarty (phone: 82-11654). Moderate.

TIHANY

Club Tihany Hungary's first vacation village, this complex includes a 330-room hotel and 161 Scandinavian-style bungalows. Geared to families, it has a private beach, a pool, boutiques, a restaurant, and a variety of sports activities. 3 Rév utca (phone: 86-48088 or 86-44170). Expensive.

Fogas Csárda Excellent fish dishes are served on a terrace or in one of four dining rooms. Gypsy music accompanies your meal. Open for dinner only. Reservations advised. Off Hwy. 71 (phone: 86-48658). Expensive to moderate.

BALATONFÜRED

Annabella A modern 391-room hotel with picturesque surroundings on the lakeshore. There's a private beach, a restaurant and terrace, a nightclub, and a pool. Open mid-April through October. 25 Beloiannisz utca (phone: 86-42222). Expensive.

Marina On the lake with a private beach, this 374-room property has a pool, a health club, a nightclub, and a restaurant featuring Gypsy music. Open May to October. 26 Széchenyi utca (phone: 86-43644). Expensive.

Baricska Csárda The perfect spot to sample *halászlé,* an all-fish chowder with paprika, or baked *fogas,* the local fish specialty. Open for lunch and dinner. Reservations necessary. No credit cards accepted. On the lakefront (phone: 86-43105). Moderate to inexpensive.

The Great Hungarian Plain

The Nagy Alföld (Great Hungarian Plain), east of the Danube, is the heart of Hungary and one of Europe's richest larders. During the past century, the thousands of acres of the drifting sand and needle grass that characterized this seemingly endless flat expanse, called the *puszta,* have been transformed into lush orchards and vineyards, and modern machinery now cultivates the corn and wheat fields.

At the same time, however, the government has taken steps to preserve the heritage of the rural Hungarian peasant, long romanticized by poets and painters: the isolated whitewashed crofts, the special *puszta* gray cattle and herds of horses, the traditional arts and crafts. They still can be seen in places such as the National Park of Hortobágy, although, like the American prairie, the *puszta* of old is only a memory.

This circular route from Budapest takes you to some of the most important towns of the area of the Great Hungarian Plain, sometimes referred to as Little Cumania, and to some of its art centers. Most of the towns are on main railway lines and can be visited on a train journey through the region. There also are bus connections.

BUDAPEST For a detailed report on the city and its hotels and restaurants, see *Budapest* in THE CITIES.

En Route from Budapest After about an hour's drive southeast on Route E60, head south on Route 40 to Cegléd, an old peasant community that was the birthplace of István Tömorkény, one of the great chroniclers of peasant life. The *Lajos Kossuth Múzeum* (on Rákóczi utca and Károly utca) contains the patriot's death mask. Farther south is Nagykőrös, the center of a rich market-gardening region famous for its Kőrös Morello cherries and other fruit. A splendid morning market is held here. Another alternative is to take Route E75 (M5) directly from Budapest to Kecskemét, stopping off at Lajosmizse, 13 miles (21 km) before Kecskemét, to visit the *Farmhouse Museum,* or to watch the horse shows at the *Gerébi* country house and motel (see *Best en Route*).

KECSKEMÉT This is the hometown of Zoltán Kodály, the famous composer. Like its famous son, who wrote modern music but also collected and wrote about Hungarian folk music, this sprawling town of 100,000 people seems to blend two worlds.

Since World War II, Kecskemét has become an important food-processing center, and modern housing estates have replaced many single-story dwellings. But the old peasant architecture can be seen along Bánk Bán and János Hoffman streets. Two examples of Hungarian Art Nouveau that should not be overlooked are the Városháza (Town Hall) on Kossuth Lajos tér and the Cifrapalota (Ornamented Palace) on 1 Rákóczi utca. On the Kossuth Lajos tér there are three churches: a 15th-century Franciscan church, a 17th-century Protestant church, and a late 18th-century Catholic church. A bit southwest of Kossuth Lajos tér, behind the 16-story county council building, is a unique double-gated peasant house with a fine verandah. Beautiful examples of shepherds' cloaks and embroidered clothing of the region are on display at the *József Katona Múzeum* (1 Bethlen körút). The *Játékmúzeum* (Toy Museum; 11 András Gáspár utca) is a must for children. At the same address is the *Magyar Maiv Testok Múzeum* (Museum of Native Artists), which features the works of Hungarian naïf artists from 1910.

An artists colony, where many of Hungary's best painters and sculptors of the 20th century have worked, is in a large park on Mártírok utca, southeast of the center.

The Kecskemét area is famous for its apricots and apricot brandy, called *barack,* and a grape harvest (Kecskeméti Szüret) is held each September. In odd-numbered years there is a *Kecskemét Folk Music Meeting* of singers and musicians and the International Kodály Seminar for music teachers; an International Creative Camp of Musicians takes place every July. A more recent event is the March music festival held in conjunction with the *Budapest Spring Festival.*

The Kecskemét riding school, just outside the city on Highway 44, has excellent horses selected from the famous stud farms of the *puszta.*

En Route from Kecskemét Drive south on Route E75 (5) to Kiskunfélegyháza, an important cultural center of Kiskunság (Little Cumania). The *Kiskun Múzeum* has a good archaeological collection and an interesting penology display.

A road to the west of town leads to the Kiskunság National Park and its major section, the Bugacpuszta. The gray cattle and branch-horned *racka* sheep of the region graze here in pastures surrounded by trees, marshes, and sand dunes. The *Shepherd Museum,* a glass-walled, circular building resembling a Mongolian yurt, has displays that detail the old nomadic way of life and animal breeding in the *puszta.* Nearby, a refurbished old inn called *Tanya-Fogado* provides an ideal setting for sampling Hungarian specialties and regional wines (phone: 76-72688).

Another detour off Route E75 (5), this one to the east just before you reach Szeged, leads to Fehér-tó (Lake Fehér), the home of red heron, ducks, and other fish-eating birds. (Permission to visit the bird sanctuary and view some 200 varieties of winged creatures must be obtained in advance; travel agents usually can make these arrangements.)

One of the typical sights of the Great Hungarian Plain is storks nesting in the chimneys of farmhouses along the road.

SZEGED The economic and cultural center of the southern region of the Great Hungarian Plain straddles the Tisza River near the Yugoslav border. Every May the international *Hungaropan Cup,* featuring kayak-canoe races, is held on the Tisza River. The present town was laid out after a devastating flood in the last century, but Szeged has a long, rich history.

The town was occupied by the Ottoman Turks for 144 years, until the end of the 17th century, and it was plundered and burned in 1704 in retaliation for its support of the freedom struggle against the ruling Hapsburgs of Austria. During the 1848–49 war of independence from the Hapsburgs, Szeged was, for a short time, the capital of the country. During the great Tisza flood of 1879, the town was almost completely swept away.

The central town square, Széchenyi tér, has a pleasant promenade of old plane trees and is lined by a number of public buildings. A few blocks south is the impressive Dóm tér, a square surrounded by arcaded buildings of dark red brick and dominated by the twin-spired Fogadalmi-templom (Votive Church) at its center. The neo-Romanesque church has the second-largest organ in Europe (the largest is in Milan's cathedral). The church was built by survivors of the 1879 flood between 1912 and 1930. The medieval tower of St. Demetrius is at its side. Part of the huge square is the site of the *Szeged Open-Air Theater,* where the *Szegedi Szabadtéri Játékok* (Szeged Festival) of opera, drama, and ballet is held every year in July and August. Hungary's finest Serbian Orthodox church, known for its outstanding iconostasis, is on the north side of the square.

Szeged is famous for beautifully embroidered slippers; *szegedi halászlé,* a delicious fish soup; and for its salami products. Visit the *Salami Factory Museum* (10 Felső-Tiszapart; phone: 62-24814). Open Tuesdays and Thursdays; admission charge. In Tápé, an outer district of the town noted for the artistic mats woven by its women, villagers have retained their picturesque folkways and dress. A collection of folk dress and everyday articles can be seen at 4 Vártó utca. A park 3 miles (5 km) outside Szeged, inhabited by monkeys and crocodiles as well as by animals native to Hungary, was designed with young visitors in mind.

Traditional as well as newer styles of pottery are made in workshops at Hódmező-vásárhely, a small 18th-century town 16 miles (26 km) northeast of Szeged on Highway 47. Modern and traditional ceramics are displayed and sold at *Lajos Gulácsy* (Lajos Gallery; 17 Kárász utca). The *János Tornyai Múzeum* (16-18 Szanto Kovács utca) has interesting archaeological and ethnographical collections.

En Route from Szeged About halfway to Baja on Route 55 you can turn north on Route 53 to reach Kiskunhalas, home of the famous Halas lace, *halasi csipke.* You can see the lace makers at work at the *Cottage Industry Cooperative,* and the *Csipkeház* (Lace House; located at the intersection of Kossuth Lajos utca and Route 53) has a large exhibition of the fine craft that has won the town a worldwide reputation.

BAJA This picturesque town on the banks of the Danube and Sugovica rivers has numerous islands with sandy lidos and fine parks, lovely old churches, and an artists colony in a former nobleman's mansion at 1 Arany János utca.

It also has one of the few bridges over the Danube south of Budapest. The folklore and folk art collections of the *István Türr Múzeum* (on Deák Ferenc utca) are typical of the region.

KALOCSA Twenty-one miles (34 km) north of Baja on Route 51, this town, founded in the 11th century by Stephen I, is one of the most important centers of folk art in Hungary. The women of the town are famous for the primitive, ornamental painting with which they decorate the walls of their houses and for the designs they paint on furniture and door panels. The finest examples of their work can be seen at the *Népművészetiház* (1-3 Tompa Mihály utca), in the same building as the *Folk Art Cooperative,* where some of these "painting women" work with outsiders interested in learning this folk art. The *Károly Viski Múzeum* (25 Szt. István utca) exhibits folk art of the Kalocsa Sárköz region.

In quaint little villages nearby, whitewashed houses often are strung with garlands of the red peppers that are grown in the area and used to make fine Hungarian paprika. The *Paprika Museum* (on Marx tér) is at Kalocsa's open-air vegetable market.

Northeast of Kalocsa is Kiskörös, home of the 19th-century revolutionary poet Sándor Petőfi.

The highway back to Budapest parallels the Danube, passing through Dunapataj, a village near pleasant Szelidi Lake, and through two towns where the poet Petőfi lived and worked — Dunavecse and Szalkszentmárton.

BEST EN ROUTE

First class hotel accommodations are limited, but prices are relatively low. At the places mentioned, a double room with bath and breakfast will cost about $40 to $50 a night in a moderate hostelry; less than $40 in an inexpensive place. Meals also are quite inexpensive in the towns of the Great Hungarian Plain. Dinner for two, with a local wine, will cost between $15 and $25 at moderate restaurants. The restaurants below accept major credit cards, unless otherwise indicated. Reservations are advised at all restaurants.

For each location, hotels and restaurants are listed alphabetically by price category.

KECSKEMÉT

Aranyhomok This 5-story modern hotel on one of Kecskemét's central squares is the best in the area. It has a large restaurant that features excellent goose liver, a coffee shop, and a bar. The hotel also organizes horseback riding excursions. 2 Széchenyi tér (phone: 76-481195). Moderate.

Gúnár A 34-room hotel, converted from an old inn. 3 Batthyány utca. (phone: 76-483611). Moderate.

Szélmalom Csárda This restaurant is in a replica of the traditional whitewashed windmills of the Great Hungarian Plain. No credit cards accepted. Open daily for lunch and dinner. Reservations advised. Just outside town on the E5 motorway, in the direction of Szeged. 167 Városföld (phone: 76-322166). Moderate.

Gerébi Situated in a park with a pool, tennis courts, and a riding club, this 18th-century mansion has been converted into a hotel with 11 double rooms and 2 suites; there is also a motel with 39 rooms. In Lajosmizse, on Highway 5, 13 miles (21 km) north of Kecskemét. 224 Alsólajos (phone: 76-356555). Moderate to inexpensive.

SZEGED

Alabárdos Set in a cellar, this eatery provides a romantic atmosphere, including Gypsy music, with your food. Open daily for dinner. No reservations. No credit cards accepted. 13 Oskola utca (phone: 62-312914). Moderate.

Hungária A modern hotel near a shady park on the bank of the Tisza River, next to the *Szeged National Theater*. The 138 rooms all have private baths. 1 Maros utca (phone: 62-480580). Moderate.

Kis Virág Café Pastries and ice cream are served in an elegant, old-fashioned setting. Open daily from 11 AM to 8 PM. No reservations. Klauzál tér (phone: 62-21040). Inexpensive.

Napfény Motel and Camping Site Simple accommodations in a 134-room pension, a 44-room motel, and a large campground. 4 Dorozsmai utca (phone: 62-325800). Inexpensive.

Poland

To visit Poland today is to visit a country in flux. Since sloughing off Communism in 1989, the Poles no longer have to endure the repression that marked life under that regime. They now enjoy unfettered travel and the sort of self-determination that was unknown only a few years ago. But the euphoria of newfound freedom has faded somewhat as Polish citizens tackle the difficult task of economic reform. While people may now speak their minds without worrying whether they'll be in jail the next day, and the censorship of the press has been replaced with a variety of lively dailies and weeklies, many Poles are now more interested in finding ways to make ends meet than in having ideological discussions.

The transition from a closely controlled, state-run system to one of free enterprise has not been easy. Unlike other countries in Eastern Europe, Poland chose a far more drastic route to economic reform. Beginning in 1990, government subsidies were immediately removed to allow prices to rise to market levels, and the country cracked down on the easy credit that previously had kept the antiquated Communist system afloat. As might be expected in such a dramatic transformation, the results were harsh. Wages in the state-run sector were kept in check while prices rose. Factories that could not compete closed and unemployment increased. Many small private businesses opened, but others closed almost as quickly. There were periodic strikes and considerable grumbling. The government had trouble adhering to the tight money policy set by the International Monetary Fund to reduce Poland's staggering foreign debt. The freely elected Parliament was divided as to how to proceed with economic reform, and the country went through political turmoil in 1992. But last February, the Parliament passed a strict national budget that was approved by Western financiers, and Poland became the first Eastern European country to emerge from the post-communist industrial recession. Shortages of food and other basic necessities were a thing of the past, and with a growing private sector, signs boded well for the future. Then last June, without warning, Lech Wałęsa used his constitutional power to dissolve Parliament 2 years before the end of its scheduled term. Parliamentary elections followed in September. In a surprise turn of events, Poland's former Communists won a majority of seats, led by the Democratic Left Alliance Party leader, Aleksander Kwaniewski. The election results reflected the widespread discontent with increased unemployment in the 4 years since the collapse of Communism.

From the imperial rule of kings and princes to present-day economic difficulties, Poland has rarely known a day free from strife. But in spite of a succession of invasions since the beginning of its history, it has managed to survive, with both its spirit and identity intact.

The Poles are descended from tribes of western Slavs, who were unified in the 9th century by a plains-dwelling tribe, the Polany, in order to resist increasing invasions from the west by Germanic tribes. In AD 966, Poland's first king, Mieszko I, put the new state under the protection of the Holy Roman Empire and accepted Christianity for himself and his people. Roman Catholicism became virtually synonymous with Polish nationhood only later, after the country was partitioned off the map in the late 1700s. During the intervening centuries, Poland was a multi-religious nation with Protestants, Orthodox Christians, Jews, and Moslems worshiping freely within its borders.

Most of Poland lies in the north European plain. Its 120,727 square miles stretch south from the Baltic Sea to the Sudety and Carpathian mountains, which separate it from the Czech Republic and Slovakia. It is bordered by Germany on the west and Russia, Lithuania, Belorus, and Ukraine on the east. Temperatures are higher than normal for Poland's latitude, but weather conditions vary from region to region and can change from hour to hour. Winters can be severely cold, and there are frequent showers in summer. However, pleasant warm weather continues through October, although often with brisk winds and under heavy gray skies (often polluted in the major cities).

Prevailing winds and tidal action have resulted in few good harbors along the Baltic coast, but they have created wonderful long sandy beaches that attract tens of thousands of vacationers to the 325-mile seacoast, also sadly threatened by pollution. Below the sand dunes and forests of the coastal belt, there is a stunning postglacial region of thousands of lakes and heavily wooded hills rich in wildlife. Poland has 13 natural parks and some 500 wildlife preserves. The wild European bison is protected here, along with chamois, bear, grey wolf, moose, boar, elk, wildcat, and the swift, dun-colored tarpan, one of the smallest horses in the world.

The central lowlands are mostly flat and, although they do not have the richest soils, are the most extensively cultivated region. About 40% of Poland's 38 million people live in rural areas. Poles privately own 80% of the country's arable land, but mechanization has been very slow. In general, heavy industrial development was emphasized by the former Communist government at the expense of agriculture. The foothills region paralleling the two mountain ranges along the southwestern border contains most of the country's mineral wealth and its best agricultural land. The Upper Silesia region is the most industrial, the most heavily populated, and one of the most polluted areas of Europe.

The mountains themselves, not particularly rugged except in the High Tatra range of the Carpathian Mountains, have long been populated by farmers and shepherds. Outdoor activities, the beauty of the scenery, picturesque architecture, and the charm of local folk art, particularly woodcarving, make the mountains an important tourist destination.

The borders of modern Poland are strikingly similar to those of the first

Polish state, although the country's history has been one of constant struggle to hold its own against larger, more aggressive neighbors. At one point — from 1795 to 1918 — Poland ceased to exist as an independent state, having been partitioned by Austria, Prussia, and Russia. During that 123-year period and throughout Communist rule, the Roman Catholic faith has served as an element of cohesion and unity for the Polish people.

World War II began with the German invasion of Poland on September 1, 1939. On September 14, the Soviet army invaded from the east, after Stalin allied with Hitler. Following 6 weeks of fierce resistance, in part by Polish horse cavalry against German armored cavalry, the country was conquered. Poland remained under foreign occupation for 5½ years. The devastation and loss of life were among the worst suffered by any of the war's victims. It was in Poland that the Nazis started their Final Solution, subjecting all European Jews to genocide. Today, some of the concentration camps (including Auschwitz) are maintained as museums, and serve as reminders of the horrors of war. Cracow, nearly alone among Polish cities, escaped massive destruction, but nationwide 6 million Poles — half of them Jews — were killed.

In the early 14th century, during the reign of Kazimierz III (Casimir the Great), one of Poland's greatest rulers, Jews were welcomed into Poland as immigrants; before World War II, Poland had some 3 million Jewish residents — Europe's largest Jewish population. After the war, most of those who survived the Holocaust emigrated, many to Israel where sectors of Jerusalem today are reminiscent of pre-war Poland. The few who stayed behind left when an anti-Semitic campaign provoked by Communist Party infighting became virulent in 1968. It is estimated that there are now only about 3,000 Jews in all of Poland.

Throughout the war, Jews and other Poles opposed the Nazis through various resistance organizations. The culmination of the Jewish struggle was the uprising in the Warsaw Ghetto in April 1943, when 15,000 Jews were killed and 55,000 survivors were sent to concentration camps. The following year the Polish Home Army organized the Warsaw Uprising, in which more than 200,000 Poles were killed. After their defeat, Hitler gave instructions for the total annihilation of the city. The Red Army entered on January 17, 1945 to liberate what had become a city of smoldering ruins.

The Soviet-backed Provisional Government of Poland was formed in Lublin in 1944. The Potsdam peace conference in August 1945 established Poland's western frontiers along the Oder-Neise line; that same month Moscow's Polish-Soviet Treaty confirmed the 1918 Curzon Line (drawn by British diplomat George Curzon at the Versailles conference in 1919) as the country's eastern frontier. Poland lost 69,290 square miles on the east and gained 39,596 square miles on the west. Consequently, more than 3 million ethnic Germans left Poland, joining some 4 million who already had left ahead of the advancing Red Army during the closing days of World War II.

After the war, Stalin undertook the sovietization of Poland through the puppet leadership of Bolesław Bierut. Farms with more than 124 acres of land were expropriated, and all businesses with more than 50 workers were nationalized. A Soviet marshal, Konstantin Rokossovsky, who had liberated Warsaw, became Poland's defense minister from 1949 until 1956. The 1947 elections were rigged and "won" by a coalition led by the Polish Communist Party. On July 22, 1952 a Soviet-type constitution was installed and the People's Socialist Republic of Poland proclaimed.

The people's republic, however, did little to please the people, and Poles took to the streets in 1956, 1970, 1976, and again in 1980 to protest their living conditions. In 1980, Eastern Europe's first independent union, *Solidarność* (Solidarity), was founded in Gdańsk's Lenin Shipyards, under the leadership of Lech Wałęsa, an apprentice electrician. Within months, 10 million workers became members, while 3 million peasants joined Rural Solidarity. The strength of Solidarity and the recurrent strikes and demonstrations, and the implicit threat of a Soviet invasion led the head of the government, General Wojciech Jaruzelski, to impose martial law. Wałęsa and thousands of Solidarity activists were jailed, and the spirit of the nation was crushed.

Martial law was lifted in 1983, but Solidarity remained outlawed. An extensive underground developed, with a vibrant press and widespread support from workers and intellectuals alike. The Socialist economy continued its steep decline, shortages were epidemic, and unrest grew. Finally, after a series of strikes in 1988, the Communist government was forced to turn to the movement it had outlawed. Government-opposition "round-table" talks were held in 1989 and within months there were partially free elections. The Solidarity-backed candidates did so well, the Communists were forced to turn over the government; and Tadeusz Mazowiecki became prime minister of the country, now known as the Republic of Poland. In its wake, the rest of Eastern Europe shook loose from its Soviet shackles. Poland's dramatic economic reforms were introduced on January 1, 1990, the Communist Party disbanded, and after December elections, Lech Wałęsa replaced General Jaruzelski as president. The Solidarity movement began to splinter into parties, and a deeply fragmented but fully democratically elected Parliament was formed in late 1991. In 1992, Hanna Suchocka became the fifth post-Communist (and first woman) prime minister. Her governing coalition was shaky, but she pledged her commitment to the capitalistic transformation and to the political stability needed to back it up.

Poles are understandably proud of both their heritage and their pantheon of authentic heroes: Nicolaus Copernicus, whose theories about the universe provided the foundation for modern astronomy; Marie Skłodowska-Curie, whose research with her husband led to the discovery of radium; Frederic Chopin, whose mazurkas and polonaises seem to embody the Polish spirit; the Nobel Prize winners Lech Wałęsa, Henryk Sienkiewicz, Władysław Reymont, and Czesław Miłosz; and Karol Cardinal Wojtyła of Cracow, who became Pope John Paul II in 1978.

The religious shrine of Our Lady of Częstochowa, Cracow — Poland's third-largest and loveliest city — and the breathtaking Tatras draw hundreds of thousands of visitors to southern Poland each year. This first route, an almost 300-mile (480-km) trip south from Warsaw, travels through heavily industrialized Upper Silesia to the medieval beauty of Cracow, and then beyond to the serenity of the mountains where the centuries-old traditions of farmers and herdsmen survive intact. It offers the traveler a continuum of Polish history. The second route journeys some 270 miles (450 km) through the medieval cities of Toruń, Chełmno, Kwidzyn, and Malbork, on the way to Gdańsk. Be aware that driving in Poland can be arduous as the roads are often narrow. Gas stations, however, are now plentiful. Some route numbers are being changed. The new number is given first; the old one is in parentheses. There also are rail, bus, and plane connections.

Warsaw to Zakopane

WARSAW For a detailed report on the city and its hotels and restaurants, see *Warsaw* in THE CITIES. The capital is the usual point of departure for tours to other parts of Poland. From Warsaw, head southwest on Route E67 (8), then Route E75 (1); Częstochowa is about 135 miles (216 km) away.

CZĘSTOCHOWA The huge monastery complex on top of Jasna Góra (Shining Mountain; phone: 833-45087) has dominated this drab Warta River town since Paulist monks founded it in 1382. The monastery is the focal point of a religious cult devoted to Our Lady of Częstochowa, the so-called Black Madonna.

Each year, enormous numbers of pilgrims come to pay homage to the sacred portrait of the Madonna, said to have been painted by St. Luke and brought here in 1384. In 1430, according to legend, the painting was attacked by dissident Protestants, and to this day the Madonna still has a scar on her face. The portrait, with its darkened paint, hangs over an exquisite altar of wrought silver and ebony wood in a chapel in the monastery church. Its silver curtain is opened several times daily. In 1655, when the monastery was under siege from Swedish invaders and the force was held off by the heroic efforts of Polish soldiers and monks, legend has it that the defense was aided by the Black Madonna. In the following months, the Poles rallied together and drove the Swedes out of the country. More than 500,000 people take part in two pilgrimages each year on the *Feast of the Assumption* (August 15) and *St. Mary's Day* (August 26). Over the centuries, monarchs and others seeking blessings from Our Lady of Częstochowa have donated priceless art, jewelry, and heirlooms to swell the monastery's treasury. Many of the offerings are on permanent exhibition. Only VIPs, by special permission, are allowed to visit the monastery library, which contains some 20,000 valuable documents and records pertaining to Polish history.

Częstochowa itself is one of the chief towns of Poland's largest iron-ore mining region and an important textile industry center. Since World War II, there has been extensive urban and industrial development here.

En Route from Częstochowa Head south on Route E75 (1) toward Cracow, which is about 90 miles (144 km) away. The road passes some of the region's iron-ore mines before reaching Siewierz, where you can visit the ruins of the medieval castle of the Bishops of Cracow who once ruled here. Katowice, the capital of the Upper Silesia industrial region, is a modern industrial center and home of the renowned *Grand Symphony Orchestra* of Polish radio. The route continues south to Tychy, once a popular resort center on nearly dry Lake Paprociańskie. There, turn east to Oświęcim (Auschwitz), site of the largest Nazi concentration camp of World War II.

AUSCHWITZ The Poles call it Oświęcim, but whatever the name, there is no mistaking that some 4 million people (most of them Jews), representing 28 nationalities, were exterminated at the two camps that the Nazis operated here from 1940 to 1945. The site of Auschwitz (about an hour's drive from Cracow) has been made into a national museum. Pictures of the victims, the gas chambers in which they died, and the enormous display cases containing their personal belongings — even hair shorn from prisoners and destined to be sold as pillow stuffing — are chilling reminders of the grisly crimes committed here. A film (narrated in English) about Auschwitz and the starving inmates who were alive when the camp was liberated in 1945 is shown several times a day. Equally shattering is a trip to Birkenau, some 2 miles (3 km) away, the site of the largest crematoria. After a visit to either site — regardless of background or belief — you will never be quite the same. The museum is open daily 8 AM to 3 PM; young children are not admitted. For information, call 381-32022. Also see *Cracow* in THE CITIES and *Quintessential Eastern Europe* in DIVERSIONS.

CRACOW Kraków is almost everyone's favorite Polish city. Travelers destined for the Tatra resorts to the south almost always stay here longer than they had planned. Unlike Warsaw and other Polish cities, Cracow was untouched by the bombs and massive destruction of World War II. Its medieval charm is still apparent on every street, although the pollution caused by the nearby Nowa Huta (New Mill) steelworks is almost overpowering. For a detailed report of the city and its hotels and restaurants, see *Cracow* in THE CITIES

ZAKOPANE Nestled between the Gubałówka Ridge and the towering Tatras, this popular town some 66 miles (106 km) south of Cracow is an extremely charming holiday center. In winter, skiing and ski jumping are important attractions, but the beauty of the mountains and valleys and the rich folk culture preserved by the highlanders draw Poles and other travelers to Zakopane year-round.

Fir, beech, and spruce grow in the subalpine woods of the Tatras. As you go higher, there are spruce forests and dwarf mountain pine, and alpine pastures with little vegetation. Edelweiss and stone pine are among the 260 species of plants here, and the region is a natural habitat for lynx, marmot, chamois, brown bear, various deer, and, sometimes, the golden eagle.

The town itself is a museum of regional folk culture. The wooden gingerbread houses are similar to Norwegian stave churches but more complicated in design. The lacy look of the carved façades is reminiscent of Victorian valentines. Against the backdrop of pine forests and snow-peaked mountains, these homes seem most idyllic. At the lower end of Ulica Krupówki, near Kościeliska, there are a small mid-19th-century church, several typical highlanders' houses, and a cemetery where nearly every monument is a masterpiece of folk art. The local museum, *Dr. Tytus Chałubiński Tatrzanskie Museum* (10 Ulica Krupówki), includes a reconstruction of a highlander's cottage interior, specimens of plants, birds, and animals native to the Tatras, and a collection of local costumes. *Tea Cottage* (39 Ulica Bulwary Słowackiego) is another museum with typical regional flavor.

On Sundays, to the delight of the tourists, many men of the area still wear white woolen trousers with distinctive black and red embroidery called *parzenica,* and richly embroidered, cape-like outer garments, known as *cucha.* In the outdoor market, country women sell hand-knit mohair cardigans, the simple leather moccasins worn by highland people, and special local cheeses.

There are horse-drawn carriages available to take visitors to the surrounding areas, such as the village of Jaszczurówka, where a small wooden church stands as an almost perfect example of elaborate Zakopane architecture, and Harenda, which has an 18th-century church built of squared larch trunks.

For a magnificent panorama of the town and the Tatras, you can take a chair lift from near the *Orbis-Kasprowy* hotel to the top of Gubałówka Hill. At Kuźnice, a little more than 2 miles (3 km) south of Zakopane, there is a funicular to Kasprowy Wierch (6,451 feet), the region's most famous ski mountain. Go early or reserve through *Orbis* (22 Ulica Krupówki, Zakopane; phone: 165-5051; in the US, 212-867-5011). There are ski routes down to Zakopane and to Kuźnice. At the southeastern corner of the Tatras National Park complex are two beautiful lakes — Morski Ono and Czarny Staw — and Mt. Rysy, which, at 8,247 feet, is the highest peak in the Polish Tatras. Also see *Good Sports* in DIVERSIONS.

The Dolina Białego (White Valley), where the crystal Biały Potok (White Stream) flows through steep crags, is just a 15- or 20-minute walk from the center of Zakopane.

Some hotel restaurants serve such regional specialties as braised boar, elk, and rabbit (although during the summer these items often come from the freezer). Nighttime entertainment in Zakopane ranges from folk music and dancing to discotheques.

BEST EN ROUTE

Rooms in this region can be hard to come by at the height of the tourist season; they are virtually impossible to get at Częstochowa during the August pilgrimage. If you can book one, a double room will cost from $85 to $150 a night at an expensive hotel; $40 to $85 at a moderately priced one; and $30 to $40 at an inexpensive hotel. For information on lodging and hotel reservations in Zakopane, call the local tourist office at 165-2211. *Orbis* (22 Ulica Krupówki, Zakopane; phone: 165-5051; 212-867-5011 in the US) also will arrange accommodations in private homes in the area.

Dinner for two with wine at an expensive restaurant will cost $25 to $50; at a moderately priced restaurant, $15 to $25; and at an inexpensive one, as little as $5.

The introduction of private enterprise has allowed Poles to venture into the hotel and restaurant trades, and new establishments open regularly in tourist regions. Local tourist offices or branches of *Orbis* can supply information on the newest places and will assist in making reservations.

For each location, hotels and restaurants are listed alphabetically by price category.

CZĘSTOCHOWA

Orbis-Patria A relatively modern, medium-size hotel (180 rooms) on the main avenue to Jasna Góra. Its restaurant and nightclub are good bets for dining. 2 Aleje Ks. Jerzego Popiełuszki (phone: 833-47001/9; fax: 833-46332). Expensive.

Orbis Motel Simple — yet inviting — this small hostelry is about 1½ miles (2 km) from the monastery. 287 Aleje Wojska Polskiego (phone: 833-55607). Moderate.

ZAKOPANE

Orbis-Kasprowy Beautifully situated on a mountainside, this Communist-modern 288-room establishment is a 10-minute drive (half-hour walk) from town. Each room has a terrace with a lovely view. Rooms are small but bright. The restaurant serves excellent food. Polana Szymoszkowa (phone: 165-4011; fax: 165-5272). Expensive to moderate.

Gazda A comfortable hotel with a restaurant. 2 Ulica Zaruskiego (phone: 165-5011). Moderate.

Gubałówka A restaurant serving delicious Polish fare that is 5 minutes by funicular up Gubałówka Hill. No reservations. No credit cards accepted. Look for the discreet door (no sign) next to the funicular station (no phone). Moderate.

Orbis-Giewont Built in 1910 in the center of town, this hostelry has 48 rooms, a restaurant, and a cocktail bar that serves good tap beer. 1 Ulica Kościuszki (phone: 165-2011). Moderate.

Pan Tadeusz A simple but clean guesthouse once owned by the Interior Ministry, it features 15 comfortably furnished rooms. Beautifully located abutting the mountainside and within an easy 10-minute walk of the town center. Meals served. 20 Droga do Białego (phone: 165-2228). Inexpensive.

Pod Krokwia The best campground in the Zakopane area. South of the city on Ulica Zeromskiego (phone: 165-2256). Inexpensive.

Telimena Another good choice, this guesthouse has 20 comfortably furnished rooms. 7B Droga do Białego (phone: 165-2223). Inexpensive.

U Wnuka This café is in an old inn that has typical regional decor. No credit cards accepted. 8 Ulica Kościeliska (no phone). Inexpensive.

Poland's Medieval Cities

It is hard to envision the meandering, polluted Vistula River as a trading route upon which great fortunes were built, a crucial economic and cultural link for the lands between the Black Sea and the Baltic. Yet this waterway and the flatlands that surround it have been Poland's strategic heart from the start its very beginning.

In AD 980, Poland's king, Mieszko, established the city of Gdańsk at the confluence of the Vistula River and the Baltic Sea. The river had long been vital to the trade in precious amber; later it carried grain from the estates of the Polish nobility to the local populace. To protect these shipments from attack by the pagan Prussian tribes to the east, in 1226 Duke Konrad of Mazovia sought the help of the Teutonic Order, mainly Germanic knights returning from the Crusades. This monastic order was chaste and ascetic, but hardly without ambition. Sworn to fight the heathen, they also sought their own land. The duke had unwittingly played right into their hands. By 1283, they had eliminated the threat of Prussian attack, but instead of accepting the duke's initial offer of Chełmo as a reward, they set up strongholds all along the Vistula, established a massive fortress at Marienbury (now Malbork), and finally took Gdańsk. Linking Toruń to the Hanseatic League of trading cities, the order prospered as heads of the state of Prussia.

The 14th century was a period of great territorial and cultural expansion for Poland under King Kazimierz III. But the worrisome Teutonic might remained to the north. The conflict came to a head in 1410 at the great battle of Grunwald. But though the Teutonic Knights were soundly beaten, they remained at Malbork until 1457. Following the Treaty of Toruń in 1466, the Grand Master retreated east to Konigsberg (now Kaliningrad). And with trade on the Vistula finally reopened, Poland became the breadbasket for Europe.

But it would be another 4 centuries, after Germany's defeat in World War I, that the lands along the Vistula from Toruń to Gdańsk would be returned to Poland. Hitler fueled his rise to power by fanning nationalist aspirations for this lost territory, and the brutality of the World War II occupation of Poland is unrivaled.

Gdańsk would have its place again in Polish history in 1980, when shipyard strikes forced the Communist regime to recognize Solidarity as the first independent trade union in the Soviet Bloc. Though suppressed by martial law in December 1981, Solidarity continued to fight.

This trip along the Vistula River traverses about 280 miles (450 km) through Poland's history, traveling from Warsaw through the fortified cities of Toruń, Chełmno, Grudziądz, and Kwidzyn to the Teutonic stronghold of Malbork and finally into Gdańsk.

Because some main Polish roadways are being renumbered, the new number is given first, followed by the old numbers in parentheses. Gas stations are plentiful along the entire route. There are also train connections to Toruń and Gdańsk, as well as flights to the latter.

WARSAW For a complete description of the city and its restaurants and hotels, see *Warsaw* in THE CITIES.

En Route from Warsaw Head northwest on Route E77 (7) in the direction of Gdańsk. Near the Vistula River crossing is Modlin, where the remains of a Napoleonic fortress echo memories of one of the most bitter battles of the German's 1939 invasion. At Płonsk, about 37 miles (60 km) away, turn west on Route 10 and continue to Toruń about 90 miles (145 km) through the flat Polish countryside.

For an interesting alternative take Route E77 (7) northwest from Warsaw but turn west after 22 miles (35 km) onto Route 62, to Czerwińsk, where a fine twin-towered Romanesque church and monastery rise from the riverside bluff. Inside the 12th-century abbey are frescoes only discovered in 1951. Return to Route E77 (7), the main road to Toruń.

TORUŃ Halfway between Warsaw and Gdańsk is the remarkable city of Toruń, with its red brick warehouses, imposing churches, and high-gabled houses. Astronomer Nicolaus Copernicus was born here in 1473; his family mansion is now a museum (15-17 Ulica Kopernika; phone: 856-26748) where visitors can view his research equipment and other memorabilia. Open Tuesdays, Wednesdays, and Thursdays from 10 AM to 4 PM; admission charge.

The Old Town Market Square retains its 14th-century splendor. Its

Town Hall, a Gothic block of brooding brick, houses a museum of medieval church art, including an impressive collection of stained glass windows. Off Market Square is the red brick Gothic Kościół Najświętszej Marii Panny (Church of the Blessed Virgin Mary), which was begun in 1350 and boasts a Gothic façade and vibrant baroque interior. Nearby on Ulica Zeglarska is the oldest church in Toruń, Kościół Sw. Jana (St. John's Church), dating back to 1260, and best known for its 13th- and 14th-century Gothic frescoes, stained glass windows, and 7-ton bell. The churches are open only during daily services.

Once a Slav settlement on the Vistula River, Toruń prospered as a fortified trading city when it was chartered by the Teutonic Order in 1233 and joined the Hanseatic League in 1280. A remnant of this era is the castle built by the Teutonic Knights who originally founded the city. Although most of the castle is gone, its walls have miraculously endured centuries of grime and pollution.

Before leaving, don't miss Toruń's famous *pierniki* (gingerbread) — a real treat in any language. The Toruń Tourist Office is located in Market Square and is stocked with English-language guides to the city and environs (phone: 856-10931).

En Route from Toruń Leaving the city take Route E75 (1) north 28½ miles (46 km) to Chełmno. Along the way are tiny 12th- and 13th-century farm towns where the land is often tilled by horse-drawn plow, and political turmoil seems the stuff of another world.

CHEŁMNO Once the center of the territory originally offered as payment to the Teutonic Knights, Chełmno typifies what a fortified city must have looked like centuries ago. Entering through the 14th-century Grudziądz Gate, visitors immediately get a sense of the Stare Miasto (Old Town) with its narrow streets lined with houses that have survived many invasions and wars. In the center of the wide Market Square, often the site of an open-air bazaar, is the 16th-century Ratusz (Town Hall; phone: 856-1641), considered by many to be a fine example of Polish Renaissance architecture. A small museum inside offers painted beam ceilings as well as World War II memorabilia, including a large collection of pictures and postcards chronicling the Nazi occupation. Several Gothic brick churches dot the Old Town, including the oldest, Kościół Najświętszej Marii Panny (Church of the Blessed Virgin Mary), which dates from 1280. Just off Market Square.

Although there is no tourist office in Chełmno, a town map can be purchased at the Town Hall museum.

En Route from Chełmno Continue north on Route E75 (1), crossing to the left bank of the Vistula River. About 15½ miles (25 km) along the road, turn east on Route 16 for 3 miles (5 km) to the once-fortified town of

Grudziądz, where centuries-old mansions can be seen as well as a grain storehouse, still in use today. Once a Teutonic stronghold, the city is the home to a Benedictine monastery with a museum that is open daily. Located near the Rynek (Market Square).

Continue east on Route 16 to Route 514 just outside of Grudziądz and drive north 22 miles (35 km) to the town of Kwidzyn. The scene of heavy fighting as the Soviet army advanced on the Germans in 1945, many markers along the country roads commemorate the battles.

KWIDZYN A medieval city in a border region populated by both Slavs and the original Prussians, Kwidzyn was a Teutonic stronghold from the 1230s. Centuries later, during World War II, most of the city was totally destroyed. Still standing are the red brick Castle of Bishops and its adjoining cathedral, built between 1320 and 1360. The castle has been transformed into a museum, with exhibits of priceless 12th- and 13th-century artifacts; the cathedral houses a fine mosaic of St. John the Evangelist dating back to 1380. Both the castle and cathedral are open Tuesdays through Sundays; no admission charge (phone: 850-073889).

En Route from Kwidzyn Continue north on Route 514 for 23 miles (37 km) to Malbork.

MALBORK A one-time feudal complex, Marlbork offers castle dungeons, cobblestone courtyards, arcades, and a moat. As befits the headquarters of the powerful Teutonic Knights, it exhibits fine 14th- and 15th-century sculpture, shields, swords, armor, and helmets, along with crossbows and a collection of amber-inlaid pistols. From the forbidding portal entrance can be seen a carving of the order's patron, the Virgin Mary. Construction began in the 1270s with the Higher Castle, including the main church, the dormitory, the treasury, and a defense bastion. The Middle Castle was built during the 14th century, culminating with the Grand Masters' Palace, which affords a penthouse view from its airy tower, and the Great Refectory. The Lower Castle contained the warehouses, stables, and workshops that served the fortified city, the whole of which was surrounded by a massive defense system. When Malbork passed into Polish hands in 1457, it continued to serve as an arsenal and royal residence. It became Prussian again when Poland was partitioned in 1772 and fell into disrepair until a German conservator took over in the late 1800s. Rebuilt again after World War II, the castle underwent further repairs as recently as last year. There are English-language guidebooks on sale which offer help in negotiating the warren of passages and exhibits. The castle interiors are open Tuesdays through Sundays from 9 AM to 4 PM year-round. During the summer months, a spectacular sound-and-light show begins at dusk. For further information contact, *Museum Zamkowe,* 1 Ulica Hibnera (phone: 55-3364).

En Route from Malbork Leave Malbork on Route 50 heading west in the direction of Tczew. About 11 miles (18 km) after this point, turn north on Route 75 (1) for the 25-mile (40-km) journey into Gdańsk.

GDAŃSK The Baltic port city of Gdańsk has played a key part in Poland's history for a millennium — from its establishment at the mouth of the Vistula River by the first uniter of Poles, King Mieszko, in AD 980 to the rise of Solidarity in 1980. For centuries the destination of traders from across Central and Eastern Europe, this city became an economic power and the strategic focus of the struggle between Poles and Germans. It emerged from World War I as the Free City of Danzig (German for Gdańsk), the end of Poland's corridor through Prussia to the Baltic.

It was here that Hitler unleashed the first salvos of World War II. *Westerplatte,* where a small Polish garrison was the target of the German warship *Schleswig-Holstein* on September 1, 1939, is today a memorial. By 1945 the city was in rubble. In its postwar years, Gdańsk has been rebuilt, with its oldest sections thoughtfully restored. Ulica Długa (Long Street) is the main thoroughfare with the Flemish Renaissance Town Hall and its 269-foot tower the principal attraction. Much of the original interior, including the elaborate wrought-iron grilles, stucco unicorns, and intricately carved spiral staircase, was removed in 1943 after the American bombing of neighboring Gdynia. The Town Hall has been carefully restored, including the 16th-century allegorical paintings and carvings in the Red Room and the Fireplace Room. Open Tuesdays and Wednesdays from 10 AM to 4 PM; Thursdays and Fridays from 11 AM to 4 PM; Saturdays and Sundays from noon to 6 PM; admission charge.

For a sweeping view of the city and shipyards head to Kościół Mariacka (Church of Our Lady), the largest Gothic church in Poland. The cavernous white interior, which still holds 25,000 worshipers, was seriously damaged during World War II. Now entirely rebuilt, its 245-foot tower has become a landmark, affording visitors a splendid view of the city and the Baltic shipyards. Church services are held daily.

The Stocznia Gdańska (Gdańsk Shipyard), where Solidarity was born, is no longer named for Lenin; now it struggles to find a place in the free market. In front of the gates at Plac Solidarnośći Robotniczej (Solidarity Worker's Square) is a towering monument erected by the union in 1980 to honor strikers killed during the 1970 food riots. Close by on Ulica Profesorska is Kościół Sw. Brygidy (St. Bridget's Church) where Solidarity leader Lech Wałęsa worshiped; the church also provided sanctuary for union activities outlawed under martial law.

A few miles from Gdańsk is the suburb of Oliwa, which is well worth a trip. Its enormous 13th-century cathedral (a former abbey) contains an extraordinary 8,000-pipe rococo organ. When it is played, it begins an almost surrealistic fantasy as the woodcarved angels adorning the organ come to life, playing trumpets and ringing bells. There are daily recitals;

an annual organ festival takes place in August. For more information, contact *Orbis* (22 Ulica Heweliusza; phone: 58-314944).

BEST EN ROUTE

Since private enterprise has been encouraged here, bed and breakfast establishments can be found in every town, city, and village along the route. These lodgings can be booked either through the local tourist offices or travel agencies, or just look for vacancy signs.

For hotels, a double room will cost from $75 to $125 a night at an expensive property; $40 to $75 at a moderately priced one; and $25 to $40 (sometimes considerably less at bed and breakfast establishments) at inexpensive places. For a dinner for two including wine expect to pay between $25 and $50 at an expensive restaurant; $15 to $25 in a moderate place; and as little as $10 at an inexpensive one.

For each location, hotels and restaurants are listed alphabetically by price category.

TORUŃ

Orbis-Helios Typical Soviet-style modern, this 108-room hotel is the largest in the city, and within walking distance of the Old Town. There is a café, a bar, and a restaurant featuring pork and veal dishes. 1 Ulica Kraszewskiego (phone: 856-25033). Moderate.

Orbis-Kosmos The other big hotel in town, but not quite as large. It features 79 comfortable rooms, a restaurant, café, and bar. Within easy reach of the city center. 2 Ulica K. Jerzego Popiłuszki (phone: 856-28900). Moderate to inexpensive.

Staromiejska This vaulted eatery offers an unlikely mix of Italian and Polish dishes. Best bets are the homemade pasta dishes, and *bigos* (sauerkraut with smoked meat and onions). Don't pass up the cappuccino — it's the best this side of Italy. Open daily for lunch and dinner. Reservations advised. 2-4 Ulica Szczytna (phone: 856-26725). Moderate to inexpensive.

Zajazd Staropolski Not fancy by any stretch of the imagination, but a nicely located hotel/restaurant in the Old Town. The hostelry offers 33 comfortable rooms (many with private baths) overlooking the Vistula River. Its popular eatery is open daily for lunch and dinner. Reservations advised. 10-14 Ulica Zeglarska (phone: 856-26060). Moderate to inexpensive.

Bambola First-rate pizza and salad. Open daily for lunch and dinner. No reservations. No credit cards accepted. 36 Ulica Mostowa (no phone). Inexpensive.

KWIDZYN

Pensjonet Miłosna A simple 12-room country guesthouse in the woods on the edge of town. The restaurant is open daily for lunch and dinner. Horseback riding is available. No credit cards accepted. Ulica Sportowa (phone: 850-074052). Inexpensive.

GDAŃSK

Grand Although a ghost of its former self, this 19th-century hotel still recalls its glory days, when fortunes were won and lost in the resort's plush gaming halls. It offers 250 rooms, a popular restaurant, and a casino. Major credit cards accepted. Located 7½ miles (12 km) from downtown Gdańsk in an adjoining town. 8-12 Ulica Powstańców Warszawy, Sopot (phone: 58-511696). Expensive.

Hewelius This Communist-era high-rise is located between the shipyards and the historic city center. Upper floor rooms have the best views of the Baltic coastline. There's also a restaurant, a café, and a bar. Major credit cards accepted. 22 Ulica Heweliusza (phone: 58-315631). Expensive to moderate.

Pod Łososiem A good restaurant serving first-rate fish dishes. Open daily for lunch and dinner. Reservations advised. Major credit cards accepted. 54 Ulica Szeroka (phone: 58-317652). Expensive to moderate.

Tan Viet Choose from Chinese, continental, and Polish dishes at this centrally located restaurant. Although the service is mediocre, the food is quite good, especially the steamed vegetables with rice, and curry chicken. Open daily for lunch and dinner. No reservations. 1-5 Ulica Podmłyńska (no phone). Inexpensive.

Romania

Romania covers some 91,700 square miles, bordered by Ukraine to the north, the Black Sea and Moldova to the east, Hungary and Yugoslavia (Serbia) to the west, and Bulgaria to the south. Its population is almost 23 million (under the Ceauşescu regime, which outlawed birth control, Romania had the highest growth rate in Eastern Europe); the country's largest concentration of people (2.2 million) is in the capital city of Bucharest.

There are several major historic and geographic areas in Romania. Walachia is on the flat Danube Plain in the south. The Danube itself is a natural southern border with Bulgaria, and historically it has brought trade and culture to the valley from the west. Bucharest sprang up here as a major center of government and industry. The Danube flows into the Black Sea, and the only Romanian seacoast stretches below the river delta there, primarily a resort area with many beaches and a major seaport at Constanţa.

The country is fairly mountainous north of the Danube Plain. Transylvania is encompassed by the Carpathian Mountains, crossing the country's center from north to southwest. The area has had a turbulent history, having been overrun from time to time by various hordes — the Germans and Magyars from the west and the Ottomans from the south. During more peaceful times, however, Transylvanian rulers often invited Germans and Magyars to share their trading knowledge and business skills in order to help local economic development. As a result, the historical centers of most Transylvanian towns are inhabited by German or Hungarian minorities, while the suburbs and surrounding villages are populated by Romanians. At present, Transylvania has a large Hungarian population (2 million) and the remnants of a German minority depleted by postwar emigration.

The region that is now Romania was originally occupied by the Thracians. In the 4th century BC, the Greeks established a trading center along the Romanian coast of the Black Sea and began to exploit the Thracian tribes who lived there. They recruited Thracians for their armies and brought them to Greece as slaves. The first Thracian slaves sold at the Athens slave market were named "Daos" (*Davus* in Latin), a name frequently used for slaves in Greek tragedies. From this word, the Roman names for the people and their country — Dacia and Dacians — were derived.

Various Roman generals waged wars and Roman consuls practiced politics against the Dacians from 112 BC until AD 16, when the emperor Trajan finally succeeded in subduing the entire area. His success was marked by two celebrated columns, one in Rome and one (the Tropaeum Trajani) in Adamclisi in the Dobrogea area of east Romania. Although the

Romans left the country after the collapse of their empire, their language, though somewhat modified, endures. Romanians claim to be descended from Latin-speaking Daco-Romans, and the Romanian language is a Romance tongue, akin to French and Italian.

The Romans probably coined the expression *divide e impera* (divide and rule) when they conquered the Thracian tribes north of the Danube and south of the Carpathian Mountains. In fact, the concept of *divide e impera* was practiced through the centuries by all successful invaders of present-day Romania. Romania's frequent internal feuding helped the Turks, Hungarians (and Austro-Hungarians), Nazis, and Russians to divide and rule with relative ease.

Since the end of the Roman Empire, many tribes and nations have influenced Romania — culturally, socially, and economically. Goths and Slavic tribes were the first, Hungarians and Russians, the last. Christianity was introduced by the Bulgarians in 846. Magyars invaded Romania during the 9th century before settling down farther west (in present-day Hungary). They returned with King Stephen in the 11th century. In 1241, a Tatar-Mongol invasion swept the countryside. Around the same time, Vlach tribes, who lived south of the Danube, moved north and became integrated with Daco-Roman inhabitants, acquiring their language.

After the period of Mongol rule in the 13th century, the region was divided into two Danubian principalities — Moldavia and Walachia, and Transylvania, which was a Hungarian dependency. Until 1859, when the autonomous Danubian principalities formed Romania, the area's inhabitants lived more separately than together, divided and ruled by different neighbors. The Turks fought hardest and stayed the longest. It was during the 14th and 15th centuries, at the time of legendary rulers such as Mircea the Old, Vlad (the Impaler) Tepeş, Michael the Brave, and Stefan the Great that the foundations for the Romanian nation were established. Vlad became known as the Impaler when his custom of cutting off the heads of his defeated enemies and putting them on stakes became infamous throughout the Ottoman Empire and the Hungarian kingdom. Vlad's story inspired the classic vampire tale, *Dracula,* by Bram Stoker, the 19th-century Irish novelist.

Although Moldavia and Walachia were reunified in 1859 under the leadership of Prince Alexandru Ioan Cuza, Romania still was prey for its neighbors. The country managed to maintain its autonomy much of the time, however, and even augmented its territory after the dissolution of the Austro-Hungarian Empire at the end of World War I. Transylvania and Bukovina (in Moldavia) were "prizes" granted to Romania for entering the war on the side of the Entente, even though Romania's army was soundly beaten by German troops in August 1917.

Before World War II, the reign of Romania's King Carol II was marked by continued attempts to please both Germany and Russia. Eventually, Romania (with the strong-arm help of the pro-Nazi Iron Guards) fell into the pro-German camp. Half a million troops were allowed to enter the country in 1940, and in June 1941 the Romanian army joined the Germans in their attack on the Soviet Union. However, on August 23, 1944, victorious Soviet troops invaded Romanian soil. King Michael, son of King Carol II (who by now was exiled), organized a coup, captured more than 50,000 German troops, joined the Allies, and declared war on Nazi Germany.

In the 1946 elections the National Bloc Party, a coalition of the prewar National Peasant, Liberal, Social Democratic, and Communist parties, won 71% of the vote. The Communists "secured" key ministries, and through intimidation, political maneuvering, and a wave of arrests, they forced King Michael into exile after his abdication in 1947. The following year, the Communists won the majority of seats in Parliamentary elections. A constitution was adopted on March 28, 1948.

The Communist regime nationalized all of Romania's industry and agriculture, and created a nation of uniform wage earners. The peasant population was employed in huge factories built in the suburbs of all Romanian cities, and all the land was collectivized and converted into enormous agro-industrial complexes.

When Nicolae Ceauşescu was elected leader in 1965, the pace of industrialization increased, and his megalomaniac visions turned the country into Europe's largest unfinished work site. The country experienced shortages in every part of its economic, social, cultural, and private life. Romania was culturally and politically strangled, but any growing dissent was quashed quickly by the all-powerful Securitate, the feared secret police. Virtually all of Romania's ties with the outside world — except tightly controlled sporting events — were cut off during Ceauşescu's last 10 years.

At the end of 1989, after riots in Timişoara sparked 2 weeks of nationwide unrest in which hundreds were killed, the Romanian army joined an ad hoc alliance of dissidents and rogue secret police and Communist party elements to topple Ceauşescu. While trying to flee, Ceauşescu and his wife, Elena, were captured; they were summarily tried and executed on *Christmas Day*. But even after Ceauşescu fell, hundreds more people were killed in shootings and fighting that remain unexplained and still fuel myriad Balkan-style conspiracy theories.

The National Salvation Front, headed by one-time leading Communist Ion Iliescu, was installed, and political parties revived. In May 1990, Iliescu and the Front won the first free elections since 1937 by a landslide. But many Romanians were suspicious of the Front's commitment to democracy and market reforms since many of its leaders were former Communists and much of the state and police apparatus remained in place, albeit in a far more benign role. Opposition groups continued to demand Iliescu and other ex-Communists resign. Pro-government miners stampeding through Bucharest to suppress demonstrators under the glare of TV cameras cemented Romania's — and Iliescu's — unfavorable image internationally. Iliescu maintains he abandoned Leninist ideology and has allowed the reformist wing of the Front to pursue significant free market reforms under premiers Petre Roman and Teodor Stolojan. Most collectivized farmland has been returned to former owners, prices and salaries were freed, and much commerce has been privatized. But the huge, inefficient state industry — much of it an ecological disaster — remains in state hands and provides a source of power and privilege for ex-Communist managers who today support Iliescu. And although foreign investment is encouraged, foreigners still cannot own property and the bloated bureaucracy and courts remain painfully slow and corrupt.

Romania continues to be beset by crippling social and economic ills, and many Romanians feel and act like orphans searching for the right direction while fearing to risk the little they have. In 1992, the opposition parties won municipal elections, but after the disoriented Front split in two, its conservative wing — supported by Iliescu — narrowly won elections; and Iliescu was re-elected to a 4-year term.

The Democratic National Salvation Front, as it is called, now heads a minority government under Nicolae Vacaroiu, a previously anonymous economist. He is able to govern with the consent of extremist parties, including the semi-Fascist Greater Romania Party and the rabidly anti-Hungarian Romanian National Unity Party (whose leader, Cluj Gheorghe Funar, has tried to ban any public use of the Hungarian language). Although reforms continue at a slow pace, the coalition between fiscal conservatives and extreme nationalists — that has proved so explosive elsewhere in the Balkans — has raised fears of possible Hungarian-Romanian violence in ethnically mixed Transylvania.

Our first route in Romania starts with a tour from Bucharest, the spacious capital city with its lovely parks and lakes, and then leads north to Braşov, a well-preserved medieval city in Transylvania. The route goes west to Sighişoara and Sibiu (also Transylvanian cities), then on to Hunedoara, Arad, and Timişoara (the latter two located on the Banat Plain). The second route is a tour of the famous monasteries of Bukovina, a small area near the Ukrainian frontier and the historic seat of the Moldavian monarchy. These folk churches, adorned with dazzling 16th-century wall paintings, are nestled in isolated valleys and are not easy to reach. But their unique beauty rewards those who seek them out. The last of our routes takes us to the beautiful sun-filled resorts along Romania's Black Sea coast.

Travel in Romania during the winter months can be very uncomfortable because of food and energy shortages (the latter resulting both in underheated rooms and an uncertain supply of gasoline). The better hotels in the capital, however, are always well heated, and their restaurants operate reasonably well at any time of the year. When traveling through the Romanian countryside, plan to arrive at your destination at least 1 hour before sunset, since street lights are extremely rare. Note, too, that restaurants close very early, so if you're planning to arrive late at night, you might want to bring along something to eat.

Bucharest to Timişoara:
From Walachia to the Banat Plain

This route includes two of Romanian's larger urban centers, Bucharest and Braşov, as well as some interesting cities farther west, including Timişoara. Bucharest and Braşov are separated by about 105 miles (168 km) of good road. The route passes through countryside of seemingly endless wheat and cornfields, and hills covered with apple, plum, and pear trees. There are endless groups of athletes in fashionable warm-up suits jogging along the roadside (Romania has produced a number of international sports heroes, including Nadia Comăneci and Ilie Nastase, and the whole country is very sports conscious), but in the more rural areas you still can see groups of women laundering the week's wash in the streams. There also are cows, water buffaloes, herds of geese, and sheep tended by lonely shepherds wrapped down to their ankles in wool cloaks. Handmade clothes with beautiful embroidery can be bought from roadside vendors. Drive carefully, especially at night, because roads are crowded with animals, Gypsy wagons, and pedestrians. Chronic gas shortages lead to endless lines at those pumps that are working, but foreigners (who must buy gas coupons at the border or in hotels) can jump the queue. Take care not to let the tank run low, or you may end up stranded. Gas stations usually close for the night between 7 PM and midnight.

Bucharest is a flat city on the northern Danube Plain, but the drive north to Braşov ascends the Carpathian Mountains of Transylvania, where the skiing is good and the winter resorts are plentiful. Later on, driving west, you will arrive at Banat, the "breadbasket" of Romania.

BUCHAREST For a complete report on the capital and its hotels and restaurants, see *Bucharest* in THE CITIES.

En Route from Bucharest From Bucharest, drive north on Route E15 (1) to Braşov, an early medieval city at the foot of Mt. Tîmpa in the Carpathians. The road leads along the Prahova and Timiş river valleys, and passes through old Dacian settlements (founded as early as 70 BC) that now are winter ski spas. The best is located about 70 miles (112 km) north of Bucharest in Sinaia along the Olt River valley. Offering fine skiing in winter — especially on the 6,600-foot Omul Mountain — and mountain hiking in the summer, Sinaia is one of the few Romanian resort cities open year-round. In 1870 the German-born prince Carol I chose Sinaia as his summer retreat and built Peleş Castle and its two smaller palaces, Pelişor and Faison. The 160-room main castle was built in the German neo-

Renaissance style and features wall coverings of ebony and mother-of-pearl. Though open to the public, the castle does not have any set hours; check with the *Carpaţi* National Tourist Office in Bucharest (phone: 1-614-5160) for the schedule. Continue on Route E15 (1) for another 20 miles (32 km) to Braşov.

BRAŞOV This red-roofed town is famous for its winding streets and small squares. A cable car ride up the mountainside lets you absorb all the views. During the Middle Ages, when it was known as Kronstadt, Braşov was a prosperous trading center inhabited by Transylvanian Saxons, Protestant merchants who had emigrated from German lands. It's now one of the nation's chief industrial centers (pop. 320,000), but the well-preserved Old Town offers no hint of the city's modern occupations.

One of the city's most famous structures is the 15th-century Biserică Neagră (Black Church). Behind an imposing Gothic façade, it houses, unexpectedly, a collection of Oriental rugs (donated by merchants offering thanks to God for safe trips to the Middle East). The church, located just behind the Market Square, is closed Sundays. Also of interest on Market Square is the *Casă Sfatului* (Council Hall), which dates from 1420. It's now a history museum (closed Mondays). The square itself is an inviting pedestrian hub. Visitors should also see the *Weaver's Bastion,* one of seven original bastions of the town's 15th-century fortress and now the site of a museum that recounts the history of the fortress, which was frequently under siege.

The trip from Braşov up into the Carpathian Mountains to the resort town of Poiana Braşov and the 14th-century Bran Castle makes for an interesting day's excursion. About 10 miles (16 km) south of Braşov, Poiana Braşov ("Sunny Glade") is a wonderful stop for summer hikes or winter skiing and skating (also see *Good Sports* in DIVERSIONS). The restaurants here feature hot, homemade dishes cooked over open fires. Bran, about 20 miles (32 km) southwest of Braşov, is mistakenly touted as Dracula's home base, but in truth Vlad only occasionally vacationed there (generally depending on how much of a lead he had on his pursuers). Still, the hilltop castle is worth a visit, with its thick, fortified walls, dramatic peaked towers, and clammy, narrow passageways.

SIGHIŞOARA From Braşov, drive 76 miles (121 km) northwest on the road marked Tirgu Mureş to Sighişoara. This medieval town has a beautifully preserved historical center within its intact city walls and 11 watchtowers. Sighişoara also is the birthplace of Vlad Tepeş. In fact, the town flourished during Tepeş's rule, as he invited German (Saxon) and Hungarian traders and artisans to help develop his country's economy. Here the Saxons developed the iron mines and foundries, and laid a base for the town's present-day porcelain industry. Even today, the German-speaking population is very proud of its Saxon origins.

Entry to the Old Town is through the gate under the monumental

14th-century Clock Tower. At midnight, wooden marching figures emerge from the clock, which dates from 1648. The building is now a museum (closed Mondays). Nearby is a 1515 monastery church with fine hanging Oriental rugs, and across Piaţă Muzeulii (Museum Square) is the house where Vlad Tepeş lived from 1431 to 1435; it's now a restaurant (see *Best en Route*). Just behind Tepeş's house, in the center of the Old Town, the Stradă Scolii leads from Piaţă Cetatii (Citadel Square) to a covered wooden stairway built in 1642. The 172 stairs lead to the Gothic Bergkirche (Hill Church), built in 1345. After the Reformation, the fine frescoes in the church were covered with plaster (at press time the frescoes and the church's façade were being restored). The church keeper, who lives in a cottage in front of the church, has the keys and is sometimes willing to give guided tours (in German only). In front of the church is an old German cemetery with fascinating tombstones under centuries-old trees.

SIBIU To reach this city, drive 58 miles (93 km) southwest on the road marked Sibiu. Originally a Roman colony called Cibinum, Sibiu was refounded and named Hermannstadt by Germans from Saxony during the 12th century, when the city was ruled by Hungarian King Geza II. Today, it is one of the most beautiful places in Transylvania. A lovely collection of painted pastel baroque façades line Piaţă Republicii (Republic Square). On the square is the city's *Historical Museum* and Council Tower, as well as the *Brukenthal Museum,* Romania's oldest and, perhaps, finest art gallery (closed Mondays). Samuel Brukenthal was the city governor from 1777 to 1787, and his personal art collection is the backbone of the museum's collection. Behind the Piaţă Republicii is the Piaţă Griviţa with the Gothic Evangelical Church (1300–1520), which has an interesting 1772 organ with 6,002 pipes, as well as a beautiful Crucifixion fresco (1445). In front of the church is a 13th-century staircase passage leading into the picturesque lower part of town. Before heading down, admire the rooftops of the houses below.

Near Sibiu are the Făgăraş Mountains, with some of Romania's best hiking grounds.

DEVA AND HUNEDOARA Located 10 miles (16 km) from each other, these two cities were Transylvania's gateways to the Turkish empire and the ramparts against it. Iancu de Hunedoara, a legendary figure who fought the Turks, had his headquarters in these two cities during the 15th century. To reach them from Sibiu, head west on the Hunedoara road for 81 miles (130 km). In Deva, the 13th-century citadel is worth seeing. Be aware that you must pass through some of the country's most polluted areas on the way from Deva to Hunedoara. Romania's first "modern" iron mills were built here in 1750, and the industry still exists. The pride of Ceauşescu's industrial development, the Hunedoara steel mills are spread over 6 miles (10 km) of land north of the city. Brace yourself for almost deafening noise, black smoke, and red sparks emitted from the mills, which at night resemble Dante's *Inferno*. But if you can find your way along the disastrously marked roads, Hunedoara's 15th-century Corvin Castle definitely is worth seeing. The castle's walls, almost 100 feet thick in some sections, were built by Turkish prisoners. Its Gothic architecture, high towers, and fancy drawbridge are among Romania's finest.

ARAD From Hunedoara, drive 98 miles (157 km) west (and slightly north) on the road marked "to Arad." Built on the Mureş River, the city has an attractive neo-classical *State Theater* (103 Bulevardul Republicii) and an interesting *History Museum* (in the Palace of Culture, 1 Piaţă Enescu). Its impressive citadel, shaped like a six-pointed star, was built between 1762 and 1783. Never used in war, it was a prison during the Hapsburg rule (until 1918). In 1848, 13 Hungarian generals were executed here after they were captured during an uprising against Austrian rule. The event is marked by a monument near the citadel.

After Arad, take the road marked "to Timişoara." The city is 32 miles (51 km) south.

TIMIŞOARA The December 1989 uprising against Ceauşescu's Communist regime began in Timişoara. Inhabited by a mixture of Hungarians, Germans, and Serbians, the city is a showcase of Banatian baroque architecture, with its wide squares and streets and low, colorful houses. The capital of Romania's agricultural region of Banat, Timişoara has a variety of cultural monuments that reflect the town's ethnic population.

At Piaţă Unirii (Unity Square) is the baroque Catholic cathedral (1754), attended by the German-speaking population, and on the opposite end is the Serbian church (1774). At the nearby Piaţă Libertăţii (Liberty Square) is the Old Town Hall (1734), and just south of it is Hunaides Palace, with the local history museum (closed Mondays). Two blocks east of Hunaides Palace is Piaţă Opera (Opera Square), with the *Opera House* and the Serbian Orthodox cathedral (1936). In the middle of the square is a column with figures of Romulus and Remus, a gift from Rome. Piaţă Opera, with its restaurants, shops, and turn-of-the-century buildings, is the heart of the city today. It was here that the first demonstrations were held in December 1989 against the Communist regime. Behind the Serbian Orthodox cathedral is a lovely park on the banks of the Bega Canal.

BEST EN ROUTE

Expect to pay anywhere between $75 to $100 per night for a double room in hotels listed as expensive, between $40 to $70 for those in the moderate category. Meals are a much better deal. Most restaurants charge only about $12 for even the most lavish three-course extravaganza for two; at a restaurant described as moderate, expect to pay between $6 and $8. Be aware, though, that unless you travel in summer, the choice of dishes will be severely limited. Prices do not include drinks, wine, or tips. In most places, restaurant reservations always are necessary. Also, it is best to eat dinner early, since Romanian cooks are known for running out of ingredients as the evening wears on. Note: The telephone numbers below should be used when calling from within Romania; when calling from elsewhere, delete the initial "0."

For each location, hotels and restaurants are listed alphabetically by price category.

SINAIA

International Clean and modern, this 170-room hotel features TV sets, a bar and disco, and an exceptionally good restaurant. Well-situated on Sinaia's main thoroughfare. 1 Avram Iancu (phone: 0973-13851; fax: 0973-14853). Expensive.

BRAŞOV

Aro Palas The former *Carpaţi* hotel, it's still the place of choice in Braşov. It's very fancy, with 312 big comfortable rooms and a well-supplied restaurant. 9 Bulevardul Aroeler (phone: 0921-42840; fax: 0921-51427). Hotel: expensive; restaurant: moderate.

Cerbul Carpatin Housed in a 16th-century building that once belonged to a wealthy merchant, this 30-room establishment offers well-heeled residents and tourists grilled meat platters, good wine, and a "folklore" floor show, as well as music and dancing. No credit cards accepted. 14 Piaţă Sfatulue (phone: 0921-43981 or 0921-42840). Moderate.

Chinezesc If you tire of eating Romanian food, try this Sino-Carpathian eatery just 3 blocks away from the *Aro Palas* hotel. Formerly a palace and then a bank, it has been converted into a pleasant restaurant. No smoking allowed. Closed Wednesdays. Major credit cards accepted. 2 Piaţă Sfatulue (phone: 0921-44089). Moderate.

Orient There's a café on the left (where for a fixed price you get the best cup of coffee in town along with a pastry) and a tea house on the right (where for the price of tea you also get hors d'oeuvres and cakes). Although the place opened in 1987, the lovely decor has a turn-of-the-century feel. Don't miss it. No smoking allowed. No reservations or credit cards accepted. Stradă Republicii, a main shopping street off Piaţă Sfatulue (phone: 0921-26208). Moderate.

Postăvarul Built in 1906, this hotel was expanded in 1926 and now has 160 rooms, 80 with private bath. It's located in the pleasant pedestrian part of town, and unlike many of the city's other establishments, this place has some character. There is a good restaurant, too. 62 Stradă Republicii (phone: 0921-44330). Moderate.

POIANA BRAŞOV

Ciucas One of the best hotels in Poinana Braşov, it has 210 modern rooms equipped with TV sets. There's also a restaurant and a disco. Major credit cards accepted. (phone: 0922-62111). Expensive.

Sport Modern and pleasant, this 243-room hostelry near the ski lifts has a restaurant, bar, disco, and shops. Major credit cards accepted (phone: 0922-62313). Expensive.

Coliba Haiducilor Nestled in the woods off the main thoroughfare, this beautiful mountain cabin eatery offers the best grilled meat in Romania. A menu of wild game includes fresh bear, sheep, and venison cooked to order. Less gamey dishes such as smoked pork, chicken, and beef are also available. Open daily. No reservations. No credit cards accepted. (phone: 0922-62137). Moderate.

Sura Dacilor This traditional Romanian restaurant offers a magnificent mountain setting. The pleasing aroma from the kitchen will whet even the most reluctant appetite. Open daily. No reservations. No credit cards accepted. In the middle of town (phone: 0922-62327). Moderate.

SIBIU

Împăratul Romanilor This beautiful 96-room hostelry incorporates a building that dates from the 14th century. Rebuilt in 1890 in the grand European style, it was renovated in 1989 when former dictator Nicolae Ceauşescu's son Nikki, who governed this region, decided he needed a place in which to entertain dignitaries and friends. The ancient courtyard is the focal point and the site of an excellent restaurant, which offers first-rate service, good food, and piano music; a beautiful etched glass roof opens to the sky in warm weather. There is no air conditioning, but all the rooms have color TV sets and telephones. The bathrooms are adequate. 4 Stradă N. Bălcescu (phone: 0924-16490). Expensive to moderate.

SIGHIŞOARA

Cetate From 1431 to 1435, Vlad Tepeş lived in this house with thick walls and small doorways. On the first floor is an eatery serving good Romanian food, and there is a beer cellar downstairs. Piaţă Muzeulii (phone: 0950-71596). Inexpensive.

TIMIŞOARA

Continental A modern cement structure that dominates the city, this 160-room hotel has all the basics. Major credit cards accepted. 2 Bulevardul Revolutiei (phone: 0961-34144). Moderate.

Cofetaria Unirea Adjacent to the baroque Catholic cathedral, this recently redecorated coffeehouse serves ice cream and a variety of cakes. Pleasant outdoor tables offer a grand view of the Piaţă Unirii. No smoking allowed inside. Open daily 11 AM to 10 PM. No reservations. No credit cards accepted. 13 Piaţă Unirii (no phone). Inexpensive.

The Moldavian Monasteries: Bukovina

Bukovina is a small tract of land in the northern Carpathian foothills, which gradually rise from the Siret River valley farther north and east. The area, in the northeast corner of Romania, is a Moldavian reservation of beautiful mountain scenery with knobby, green-carpeted hills spotted with dense fir stands. The Moldavians still sport their traditional dress whites, and the almost total lack of English-speaking people (except for tour guides) makes a trip here an adventure. Bukovina is not heavily visited and is not really convenient to any place that is. There's minimal nightlife, few wines of distinction, and travelers are advised to bring along extra canisters of gasoline and food supplies. Nonetheless, the five churches and monasteries here, with exterior walls covered by frescoes, are like no other structures in the world.

The buildings all are relatively simple and took months rather than generations to build. They are, however, the epitome of folk architecture, built to an unwieldy and large scale that makes them look from a distance like squat, one-story bungalows. It is only when you approach them that you realize how enormous they are. They have few windows and are covered by peaked-cap roofs that descend steeply and then suddenly bow out, creating wide eaves over thick walls, the outsides of which are covered with artwork. Virtually every façade is bathed in color with frescoes illustrating the Bible, classical philosophy, and local folklore — a historic library of pictograms.

Moldavian history's medieval golden era was overseen by its greatest monarch, Stephen the Great, who, though he never rated a title higher than prince, reigned from 1457 to 1504. Because of the turbulence of the times and the violence of the populace, a reign the length of Stephen's was uncommon. He managed to stay in power by fighting Ottoman invaders and appealing to the local people's deep-rooted Catholic faith. He was a master tactician who encouraged cultural pursuits, and all the churches here were built during his era or shortly thereafter. He is credited with the development of the Moldavian style, which combines rough-hewn, hand-building techniques (that were at the same time structurally primitive and colorfully folksy) with the far more sophisticated architectural concepts of the southern Byzantine and the European Gothic. The frescoes, however, were added later. One of Stephen's successors, Petru Rares (1530-1547), had the churches and monasteries painted with biblical stories as a way of teaching religion to the largely illiterate populace. These priceless frescoes are surprisingly well-preserved. Although they've been exposed to the elements since the mid-1500s, their colors are so rich and true that the blue on the sides of the Voroneţ Church has been given a name of its own, Voroneţ blue. Though the art world has many times attempted to copy it, this blue has never been accurately duplicated in its total richness.

It's best to plan your tour with the Romanian Tourist Board in Bucharest (7 Magheru Blvd.; phone: 1-614-5160), where you can arrange to hire an English-speaking guide, but it's also possible to just get a good road map of Bukovina and wander on your own.

If you have a lot of time, sufficient gasoline, and extensive food supplies, consider extending your tour of northern Romania westward to the Maramureş region, near the Ukraine border. The villages dotting the hilly green countryside are of special interest to ethnographers; here folk art and traditional customs have been preserved as nowhere else in Europe. In Maramureş, many people wear their handmade folk costumes, not only at festivals and on special occasions but every day. Friendly villagers may invite visitors into their wooden houses for home-distilled spirits and a glimpse of a way of life that has hardly changed for centuries.

SUCEAVA This town of 100,000 is the major hub of the area — and very polluted. It's the jumping-off point for any tour of the monasteries. Suceava is 270 miles (432 km) from Bucharest, and the distance can be covered in 1 hour by plane or 6 hours by train (arrangements for a car and driver upon your arrival can be made in Bucharest), or you can drive the distance yourself in a day. This was the seat of Moldavian power from 1388 to 1564, and there are still vestiges of the medieval citadel, which was often attacked, but never conquered — not even by the Ottoman armies commanded by Mohammed II after they overran Constantinople.

There are several interesting churches in town, but since the rest of the route is predominantly architectural, time here is better spent examining (and perhaps buying) the folkwares — mostly handmade fabrics and pottery — for which Bukovina is famous. In the 16th-century *Princely Inn* you'll find the *Folk Art Museum* (5 Stradă Ciprian Porumbescu), with a restoration of the interior of an authentic peasant house and exhibitions of national costumes, dolls, masks, wedding regalia, black pottery from Marginea, and carpets.

The monasteries are spread out over the 56 miles (90 km) or so, directly west of Suceava; to stop at all five, plan on a day out and a day back. If you want to spend less time, make sure to plan your route carefully so that when night falls you don't find yourself in a town where nobody speaks a language you can understand and it takes you an hour to find out that there aren't any hotels in the vicinity. Most important of all, start out with a full tank of gas. Driving northwest out of Suceava on Route 2, turn left at Milişăuţi and you'll soon come to Arbore, the first of the famous churches.

ARBORE This is the smallest and the simplest of the 16th-century churches. Though the interior is only dimly lit, the outside walls are covered with frescoes that tell the story of Genesis and also depict the lives of the saints. The predominant color here is green, and there are five distinct shades of it, along with reds, blues, and yellows. In the courtyard there are two stone slabs with 15 even gouges that the artists used for holding and mixing their paints. The best-preserved works are on the western wall and the buttressing. Unlike most primitive wall painting, there is an abundance of detailing here involving the use of perspective, animated figures, and literal facial expressions.

SUCEVIȚA Continue west from Arbore, then turn north at the town of Solca and travel through Clit to Marginea, where black pottery has been made since Dacian times. From there it's only another 6 miles (10 km) west to Sucevița. The monastery, built between 1582 and 1596, is surrounded by thick stone walls and guarded by five imposing towers. There are more well-preserved frescoes here than at any of the other churches. They are everywhere, inside and out, except on the northern wall, which was left blank (legend has it) as a tribute to a painter who fell off his scaffold there and died. In addition to the religious paintings, there are portraits of Sophocles, Plato, and Aristotle along with Eastern images from the *Arabian Nights*. The village of Sucevița is one of the most picturesque in all of Romania — the houses' verandahs have carved wooden pillars, and townspeople dress in national costumes.

MOLDOVIȚA About 18 miles (29 km) west of Sucevița on Route 17A is the commune of Vatra Moldoviței, in the shadow of Rarău Mountain. Moldovița has another large monastery (1532) in the center of the town. The paintings here have a less religious flavor than those at the other monasteries. The most striking series is of the siege of Constantinople, with details of the entire city. The painting is something of a falsification, however, since the Persians attacked the city, but in the painting the invaders are dressed like Turks. In an even more blatant exercise of artistic license, the invaders are soundly defeated in the painting, when in fact they were victorious. There's a small museum here, housed in Clisiernita, a former princely mansion. The collection includes engraved and painted furniture, including Prince Petru Rareș's black ornamental throne. The manicured grounds are neatly laid out with flagstone paths that run from fortification to castle to church.

Just south of Moldovița is the town of Cîmpulung Moldovenesc, which has simple accommodations (see *Best en Route*). You might consider stopping for the night before returning east to Suceava on the southern half of the route.

VORONEȚ Heading east along the Moldova River on Route 17, the route passes through the towns of Vama, Molidu, and Frasin, on the way to Gura Humorului (18 miles/29 km from Cîmpulung Moldovenesc), where you can go north to the Humor Monastery or south to Voroneț. The latter is the most famous and the oldest of the monasteries (1488) and was built by

Stephen the Great himself. The 16th-century paintings here began a style that took elements from the Byzantine art of the south and gave them a more Gothic flavor. The building itself is the most elegant of all these structures, more involved and animated, with rows of repeating pilasters capped by round arches, crenelated friezes, and round windows. The famous blue is breathtaking, and the paintings, especially those of the Last Judgment, are simultaneously humane and barbaric, with pretty women, musicians, and people being torn apart by wild beasts.

HUMOR Less than 4 miles (6 km) north of Gura Humorului, the Humor Monastery is the last of the churches. Built in 1530, it has a unique large verandah, arched on three sides. One of the frescoes here depicts the devil as a woman with wings. From Humor it's only another 22 miles (35 km) back to Suceava on Route 17.

BEST EN ROUTE

Expect to pay anywhere between $20 and $30 per night for a double room in the hotels listed below. Meals are a much better deal. Most restaurants charge about $12 for even the most lavish three-course extravaganza for two. Prices do not include drinks, wine, or tips.

SUCEAVA

Arcaşul You might be a little wary of a place that brags about its parking lot, but if you've just driven 8 hours from Bucharest, you'll find this conveniently located hotel is just what you want. Besides 100 comfortable rooms with big, soft beds, it's also got a disco/bar and a good restaurant. 4-6 Stradă Mihai Viteazul (phone: 0987-10944).

Căprioara This rustic restaurant sits in the Adîncata Forest just outside of town. Beautiful surroundings for a good Moldavian meal of hearty goulash, with brandy to wash everything down. There are also a few guestrooms and a campground. Open daily for lunch and dinner. No reservations. No credit cards accepted. 5 miles (8 km) from Suceava (phone: 0987-10975).

SUCEVIŢA

Hanul Suceviţa Close to the monastery, this first class inn has small bungalows as well as rooms. The restaurant is small but serves great food. The people will make you feel as if you are Prince Stephen's long-lost brother-in-law (no phone).

CÎMPULUNG MOLDOVENESC

Zimbrul A simple, modern hotel with 90 rooms (phone: 0988-12441).

The Black Sea Coast

The Romanian coastline on the Black Sea stretches for about 150 miles (240 km) from the Danube Delta at the Ukraine border, all the way south to the Bulgarian frontier. Roughly 165 miles (264 km) east of Bucharest, this area can be reached by plane in about half an hour or by train or car in about 3 hours. (You ferry across the Danube at the midpoint of the trip.) Sandy beaches and fancy resort spas (the most famous is Mamaia) line the coast; the tideless sea assures delightful swimming. First discovered by the Romans in the 1st century, the area offers bathing in the mineral-rich waters and therapeutic mud that has been soothing tired bodies and minds for centuries. Should you tire of toasting on the Black Sea strands, you can drive into Constanţa for a taste of civilization or cruise into the Danube Delta for a glimpse of wilderness. Also see *Spas: Eastern Europe's Unique Watering Spots* in DIVERSIONS.

THE DANUBE DELTA The 2,500-year-old town of Tulcea is situated where the Danube trisects and fans into its delta. The Greeks called the city Aegyssus, and the *Danube Delta Museum* (32 Stradă Progresului; no phone) chronicles their comings and goings, as well as the flora and fauna of the area. The town is now the main departure point for tourists who want to take river cruises into the delta to see the nature preserve there. The museum is open Tuesdays through Sundays from 10 AM to 4:30 PM; admission charge. Tours can be arranged by the *Carpaţi* National Tourist Office (*Delta Hotel;* 2 Stradă Isaccea; phone: 0915-14720) or the Regional Tourist Office (Stradă Garii Faleza; phone: 0915-11607). The land is wildly beautiful here: marshes crisscrossed by canals and brooks; islands bristling with rushes and reeds; clumps of trees sheltering otters, foxes, wildcats, and boars. During migratory periods, over 300 species of birds nest in the delta.

MAMAIA About 75 miles (120 km) south of Tulcea on Route 22 lies the 5-mile (8-km) strip of Mamaia beach, which separates the Black Sea from Lake Siutghuol. The resort has a quiet elegance that attracts a fairly huge crowd year-round. Nearby is Onidiu Island, a patch of land just waiting to be explored. Many species of birds migrate to this location and are a spectacle to watch. To get there take the boat that leaves daily from the landing across from the *Albatros* hotel (no scheduled departures; the boat leaves when the captain is ready). Once there, stop in at the only restaurant (no name/phone); it serves delicious fish platters.

CONSTANŢA About 2 miles (3 km) south of Maimia, Romania's main port city occupies the site of the ancient citadel, Tomis, founded by Greek merchants during the 5th century BC. The city is an architectural mix of early Greek, Roman (Ovid was exiled here, and the square bearing the poet's name features his pensive statue), and Byzantine. There's also a mosque with an Arabian mosaic dome and a lighthouse-like minaret.

EFORIE NORD Just 10½ miles (17 km) south of Constanţa is Romania's most serene Black Sea resort. Although there are no museums or churches, most visitors come here to enjoy the peaceful, pristine beaches or flock to Lake Techirghiol for the ultimate mineral mud bath. Thought to heal all ills — from arthritis to skin conditions — this natural way of healing is performed directly on the banks of the lake. Visitors are slathered with what resembles thick fudge. After the mud has dried, it is hosed off. This alfresco activity is probably a nudist's delight: No bathing suits are permitted. Open Mondays through Saturdays from 9 AM to 4 PM.

MANGALIA This resort, located 34 miles (54 km) farther south, has become a magnet for the younger crowd since the 1989 Revolution. Along with its beachfront discos, the area boasts an extensive exhibit of Roman jewelry, vases, and artifacts discovered in 1955. The collection is housed in the *Callatis Archaeological Museum* (Stradă Constanței; no phone), open Mondays through Saturdays from 10 AM to 6 PM; admission charge.

BEST EN ROUTE

The hotel and restaurants listed below are moderately priced; accommodations will probably run about $30 per night for a double room; dinner for two, about $12.

MAMAIA

Rex One of the best hotels in this Black Sea resort town, it manages to provide near-Western–style luxury. The 102 rooms, half of which overlook the sea, feature private baths and satellite color TVs. Other amenities include a health spa complete with natural springs and mud baths, aerobics, and an indoor/outdoor pool. There's also a good restaurant, a bar, and a huge shopping complex adjacent to the hotel. Mamaia (phone: 0918-31520).

CONSTANȚA

Casă Cu Lei This hotel's restaurant is an architectural monument, and each of its dining rooms has a different structural design — Brâncovan (a Romanian style), Venetian, and Spanish. It's worth having a meal here simply for the atmosphere. There also are a few rooms which must be reserved well in advance. 1 Stradă Dianei (phone: 0916-18050).

Cazino Housed in one of Romania's most beautiful buildings, this ornate restaurant features huge, arched windows, an eating terrace on a promontory stretching out over the water, and good food. The building also encompasses several ballrooms and a nightclub. Open daily for dinner only. Reservations advised. On the seawall (phone: 0916-17416).

Continental An adequate downtown hotel that offers a private bath, telephone, and TV set in each of its 140 rooms and boasts its own wine cellar. The restaurant is recommended for its courteous service and good food. 20 Bulevardul Republicii (phone: 0916-15660).

Palace An excellent choice if only for the great location at the edge of the Old Town's main beach. All 262 rooms feature TV sets, private baths, and refrigerators. There's also a good restaurant, snack bar, and bar. 5-7 Remus Opreanu (phone: 0916-14696).

EFORIE NORD

Delfinul Ideally situated on the beach, this pleasant hotel offers 231 rooms (many with color TV sets). A full-service health spa is just steps away and features pampering mud baths, mineral springs, and nutritional analysis. There's a good restaurant and bar. Eforie Nord (phone: 0917-42630; fax: 917-42980).

MANGALIA

Mangalia Comfortable and modern, this 276-room hotel/spa sits on a isolated stretch of beach with indoor/outdoor pool, a 500-seat restaurant, and tennis courts. 2 Costache Negre (phone: 0917-52052; fax: 0917-53510).

Russia

Today's Russia is an amalgam of disparate elements. We see new history unfolding daily, as the effects of the fall of communism continue to be felt and a new political order emerges. There is, on one hand, the awesome beauty of Russian churches and religious icons, the music of Tchaikovsky and Rimsky-Korsakov, and the art treasures of St. Petersburg's *Hermitage* museum; on the other is the technology of space exploration, the ultra-efficiency of Moscow's metro, the frustration of long shopping lines, and the coordination of Russian industrial companies with a host of foreign firms. Russia is Stalin's purges, vodka and caviar, a *troika* ride across the snow in bitter cold, and the warmth of a family gathering around the samovar. It is the "Song of the Volga Boatman," the voices of Tolstoy and Dostoyevsky, and the chimes of the Kremlin clock ringing out across Red Square. It is borscht and ballet, balalaikas, and bureaucracy. It also is a state of intellectual, political, religious, financial, and ethnic ferment — an ever-changing economic order, with peasant women in babushkas still peddling their garden vegetables from roadside tables, while *McDonald's* is selling more *Big Moks* daily in Moscow than in most of its other franchises around the world.

For the visitor to Russia, the disintegration of the Soviet Union, the collapse of the Communist Party, and the debut of democracy have inaugurated many new options. Until recently, for example, most foreigners arriving in St. Petersburg or Moscow saw little more than these two cities. Now, thanks to an easing of travel restrictions, more and more visitors to Russia are expanding their trips to include the Black Sea coast, the Volga River and the communities along its banks, and the medieval cities of the Golden Ring.

Further helping to ease travel snags is Russia's increased receptiveness to tourism by car. Whereas only two routes were open to rental cars in the recent past, today's travelers can drive on more than 12,000 miles of main and secondary roads, and in major cities such as Moscow, cars can be rented through several international agencies including *Intourservice*. Bear in mind, however, that Russian traffic regulations are strictly enforced, and violators — particularly drunken drivers — are subject to stiff fines or jail. Note: Rental cars or cars with foreign license plates are favorite targets of the Russian traffic police, who frequently stop such cars for both legitimate and imagined violations. Remember that having a dirty license plate is a violation; going without a seat belt is frowned upon to the tune of a fistful of rubles; and (oddly enough) using headlights in cities is an infraction. (Headlights are prohibited day *and* night in urban areas; Russians just use their parking lights.) Fines are paid in rubles and are cheaper if you don't demand a receipt (meaning the officers keep the loot). It's a common practice.

Despite the many real rewards of *glasnost* and the subsequent political upheavals, some things haven't changed. You must still outline your itinerary, including all overnight stops and hotels, points of destination, and transportation reservations, when you apply for a visa (requests for changes in your original schedule, however, are no longer summarily dismissed). Allow at least 2 weeks for your visa — especially if you plan to travel on your own. Although the now privatized *Intourist* no longer has a monopoly on tourism in Russia (there are numerous new private, cooperative, or autonomous travel organizations), you still may find that you need a local travel agency — or at least a US travel agent specializing in Eastern European tours — to reliably make all the reservations you want.

So far from throwing caution to the wind and kicking up your heels, the best rule of thumb is to play it conservatively. Before arranging your itinerary, always check the US State Department's latest Russian travel advisories to find out how the current political situation may — or may not — affect your plans. In addition to its warnings about an increase in crime (mainly pocket picking and mugging), the State Department has been advising travelers in frail health not to visit Russia. Organized tours are strenuous, basic medical supplies (such as disposable hypodermic needles) are in short supply, and health care and hygiene are seldom up to the standards back home. In addition, prompted by an increase in reported cases of diphtheria at press time, travelers are advised to update their immunizations before entering Russia. For further information, call the US State Department's *Citizen's Emergency Center* at 202-647-5225.

But for those who are stout of heart and sturdy of health, adventurous in spirit and, more important, eager to become a part of living history, there's no question that stimulation and insights by the cartload await in the new Russia. The most populous and diverse of the former Soviet republics, Russia encompasses 30 autonomous ethnic regions, and its population of 150 million people includes representatives of 39 nationalities and more than 100 ethnic groups with their own cultures, traditions, and languages (Russian is the official language, but the use of local minority languages now is encouraged). Because so many of its people are not ethnic Russians, the Russian Parliament voted in 1992, after heated discussion, to give the country two names — Russia and the Russian Federation. The term "Russian Federation" is applied to the entire country, including the autonomous republics; just "Russia," however, is more commonly used.

Russia is also the largest of the old Soviet republics, covering 6.59 million square miles of the 8.65 million square miles that constituted the territory of the USSR. By far the largest country on the European continent, its vast territory sprawls over Europe and Asia. On its west, it shares borders with Norway; Finland; the Baltic states of Estonia and Latvia; and two other former Soviet Republics, Belorus and Ukraine. Its southernmost border runs along the Black Sea to Georgia and Azerbaijan, and northward again along the Caspian Sea to Kazakhstan, one of several other now-independent republics that less than 4 years ago constituted Soviet Asia. The Ural Mountains traditionally are considered the dividing line between the European and the eastern (Asian) sections of the country. The European part of Russia is the area of densest population and the area most often explored by tourists.

The tensions between West and East were important in shaping the development of this country. The evolution of the territory commonly known as Russia is a complex amalgamation of the histories of several distinct nationalities.

The Slavic tribes who lived in the areas near what are now Kiev, the capital of Ukraine, and Novgorod, Russia, from earliest times were relatively peaceful, but often they were preyed upon by Asian and Germanic tribes. In the 9th century, the Viking Varangians were invited by the Novgorod republic to come and restore order; their reign lasted until the 13th century. The Greek Orthodox religion, adopted from the Byzantine Empire, was introduced in Kievan Rus, the first East Slavic principality, and was to remain a dominant theme of East Slavic life until the Bolshevik Revolution proclaimed official atheism in this century. Note: Because Kievan Rus came to encompass all the territories inhabited by the East Slavs, including much of Ukraine's contemporary region, Ukrainians and Russians both lay claim to Kievan Rus as part of their national histories, and both Ukrainians and Russians claim to be the rightful heirs of the old Kievan legacy.

The Tatar-Mongol invasions began in the 13th century. Kievan Rus was conquered and held in bondage for about 250 years until another East Slavic principality, Muscovy, became strong enough, under Ivan IV (also known as Ivan the Terrible) to break the Mongol stranglehold. It was during the Tatar period that the institution of serfdom took hold.

In the 16th century, Russian history was dominated by Ivan the Terrible, who built a powerful united state but also imposed a reign of terror. A period of strife and upheaval followed his death. Then Michael Romanov, the first of the dynasty that would rule Russia for over 300 years, was elected czar. Peter the Great, the first powerful Romanov, came to the throne at the end of the 17th century. He introduced Western customs, culture, and technical achievements that transformed his country from a backward principality to a powerful empire. But neither he nor Catherine the Great, widow of his grandson and the next powerful Russian ruler, dealt with the system of serfdom that enslaved tens of thousands of Russian peasants. Russia's most famous serf rebellion, the Pugachev Revolt, occurred during Catherine's reign.

In the wake of the French Revolution and the Napoleonic Wars, a wave of liberalism spread over Europe, but the czars of Imperial Russia continued to run their country like a private estate. When Czar Alexander I died in 1825, there was an abortive uprising known as the Decembrist Revolt, which although crushed, became a symbol for liberals, radicals, and revolutionaries for the remainder of the century. After Russia was defeated by the French and British in the Crimean War, Czar Alexander II found it practical to issue a proclamation freeing the serfs, but most of the evils of the system continued. When the czar was killed by a terrorist's bomb in 1881, any gains that had accrued to the peasants were lost and a reactionary attitude set in that would dominate the remaining years of czarist rule.

Still, the 19th century had been an extraordinary one for the arts in Russia. Literature flourished, beginning with Alexander Pushkin, and including Nikolai Gogol, Ivan Turgenev, Dostoyevsky, and Tolstoy. In music, Russia produced Tchaikovsky, Mussorgsky, Borodin, and Rimsky-Korsakov. Toward the end of the century, there was a flowering of the dramatic arts with the plays of Anton Chekhov and the staging of Konstantin Stanislavsky. And by the early 20th century, Russia had become preeminent in ballet.

At the turn of the century, however, the plight of the peasants deteriorated further in the wake of a staggering depression and Russia's defeat in the Russo-Japanese War. When a peaceful group of workers and their families tried to petition the czar for relief, the soldiers opened fire on them. This massacre, known as Bloody Sunday, was the first act of violence in the 1905 Revolution, which led to the establishment of a more democratic form of constitutional monarchy. However, Russia's entry into World War I imposed further hardships on the country. In March 1917 (February by the new calendar), a bourgeois democratic revolution brought down the czar, and a provisional government was formed. Then, on November 7, the Bolsheviks, V. I. Lenin's Communist party, replaced the provisional government with the first Soviet state. A full-scale civil war raged until 1922, when the Red Army triumphed and the Union of Soviet Socialist Republics emerged.

After Lenin died, the Soviet leadership passed to Joseph Stalin, and the country moved into a period of rapid industrialization and collectivization of agriculture. Stalin was a ruthless leader in absolute control of the Communist Party. When he purged the party of those he considered unworthy of membership, they were not merely expelled; they were executed.

Economic development was interrupted by World War II, in which the Soviet Union was allied with Britain, France, and the United States. The people of the Soviet Union suffered extraordinary hardships during the war. Huge areas of the country were destroyed, and some 20 million soldiers and civilians were killed. Following the war, Soviet influence extended into most neighboring countries of Eastern Europe, and by 1946 the Cold War between the Soviet Union and the Western powers was a fact of life. A so-called Iron Curtain separated the West from the xenophobia of the Communist bloc.

After Stalin's death, his excesses were denounced by Nikita Khrushchev, who, as premier, preached peaceful coexistence with the West. But his tenure also saw the widening of an ideological rift between the USSR and mainland China, which reduced Soviet influence in some parts of the world. Conflicts with the US, especially over Cuba, kept the Cold War icy. Khrushchev was forced into obscurity in 1964, and ultimately was succeeded by Leonid Brezhnev, who until the Soviet invasion of Afghanistan presided over an era of détente with the West — as well as years of domestic economic and political stagnation.

Mikhail Gorbachev represented the first generation of Soviet leaders who were born after Lenin's death, and the first President of the USSR to wield real power. And until the free election of Boris Yeltsin as President of the Russian Republic in June 1991, Gorbachev's power — though challenged — was relatively intact.

Then in the summer of 1991, an abortive 72-hour coup led by the KGB and other right-wing hard-liners turned out to be the death knell for the Communist old guard and signaled the disintegration of the Soviet Union as it had existed since the 1917 Revolution. Although Gorbachev struggled to preserve the Soviet Union in some form, Yeltsin had the upper hand. He moved quickly with the leaders of the other former republics (with the exception of Georgia and the Baltic states) to found the Commonwealth of Independent States (CIS), a loose federation of 11 former republics that would both bury the Soviet Union and be a forum for the difficult issues confronting them: how to carve up the Soviet Army, what to do with nuclear weapons, and a whole slew of trade and customs arrangements.

With his power base gone, there was one final decree for Gorbachev to sign. With the dramatic timing that characterized his tenure, and with a nod to the Western world that had embraced him more readily than his own people during his 6 years in power, the architect of *glasnost* and *perestroika* and the reformer who ended the Cold War and liberated Eastern Europe resigned as President of the Soviet Union on *Christmas Day,* 1991. The Russian flag again assumed its place atop the ancient towers of the Kremlin.

The end of 74 years of Communist rule, coupled with the inroads made by *glasnost* and *perestroika,* have created a new atmosphere for intellectuals (and others) that is reflected in the theater, in the art world, on television, and in the press, and most of all, in Russian political perspectives. The effort to change to a market economy is now the country's primary priority, however, and thus far the process has been a difficult one for the Russian people, with prices skyrocketing and unemployment a looming threat. In a futile attempt to boost the economy, the Russian government in October 1992 issued currency vouchers to all citizens with the hope that this would stimulate new investments and stabilize a shaky capitalist economy. But as difficult as these growing times are for the new Russia, its citizens do not want to revert back to a Socialist regime. This was emphatically demonstrated last April, when Yeltsin's democratic referendum was overwhelmingly reaffirmed by the people. Three months later, in an effort to control Russia's money supply, the Central Bank took drastic measures and declared all pre-1993 ruble notes invalid. This move not only brought about panic in the streets, it caused Western governments to question Russia's tactics in dealing with runaway inflation.

Nonetheless, this is an exciting time to travel to Russia, an opportunity to witness history in the making. For the visitor willing to set preconceptions aside, a trip to this huge country, with its splendid cultural history and its present state of uncertainty and change, can be a fascinating adventure.

Although many people limit their tour of Russia to the major cities, traveling in the quiet countryside provides the perfect opportunity to meet and get to know the Russian people. A surprisingly high percentage of Russians speak English, German, or French. For the most part, they are proud of their country and interested in yours. You may learn more about Russia from such personal encounters than from any other aspect of your trip.

The following routes have been designed to introduce you to some of the most interesting places in the European part of Russia. The first route leads down the mighty Volga River from Kazan to Rostov-on-Don, and provides a window on the history of Russia. For rest and relaxation, we also describe a stop at Russia's largest Black Sea resort. Our last route takes us on a journey to the medieval towns of the Golden Ring, all of which are located within a few hours' driving distance of Moscow. With their villages and monasteries, these places constitute the cradle of Russian culture.

> **NOTE** In addition to our choices for hotel accommodations listed in *Best en Route* at the end of each driving tour, travelers now have the option of staying at bed and breakfast establishments in many parts of Russia. *IBV Bed & Breakfast Systems* (13113 Ideal Dr., Silver Spring, MD; phone: 301-942-3770; fax: 301-933-0024) makes arrangements for foreigners to book rooms (with baths) with local families.

The Volga

The Volga, a river the Russians call *matushka* (little mother), is the size and strength of Russia itself, a waterway that crosses a continent. Tourists who travel its route by steamer come closest to feeling the real spirit of the Russians. The timeless atmosphere of quaint rural villages is juxtaposed with the modern technology of hydroelectric installations and automobile plants. The Volga is the longest river in Europe, stretching 2,300 miles from Volgoverkhvoye northwest of Moscow to Astrakhan, a delta city on the Caspian Sea.

Since earliest times, the Volga has carried Finns, Slavs, Turks, Mongols, Tatars, Jews, Christians, and Moslems — all seeking trade and conquest. In 1552, Ivan the Terrible opened the Volga to the Russians by defeating the Kazan Tatars. The most recent conflict over the Volga came from Hitler and the German Army. During the months between August 1942 and February 1943, the Nazis ravaged Stalingrad (now Volgograd) in an unsuccessful attempt to subdue Russia and reach the oil-rich Caspian Sea.

Today, the Volga region hosts thousands of tourists from around the world each year. This river route, which is designed to be traveled by boat, goes from Kazan to Ulyanovsk, Tolyatti, Volgograd, and finally to Rostov-on-Don, 900 miles (1,440 km) to the south. You can reach Kazan, the starting point, by plane, train, or car. *Intourist* offers an 11-day Volga River cruise from Kazan to Rostov-on-Don, as well as shorter excursions. Other Russian travel companies also offer Volga cruises; in the US, consult a travel agency with experience in Eastern Europe. Cruise boats provide complete accommodations, including meals and lodging.

KAZAN This is the capital of Tatarstan, one of the most populous of Russia's autonomous republics (if the republic-wide vote in March 1992 for "sovereignty" from Russia is any indication of things to come, it may one day be the capital of an independent country). The cultural center of the Tatars (or Tartars), one of the many distinct ethnic groups living in Russia, Kazan is home to nearly 2 million people. Founded in the 15th century, it originally was the center of a typical medieval Moslem state, which struggled with both internal conflicts and invaders (in this case, the Russians). In 1552, Czar Ivan the Terrible and the Russian Army captured Kazan. Today, the city is half Russian and half Tatar.

A good place to begin a tour of the city is the Kazan Kremlin (Pervomaiskaya Ploshchad; phone: 8432-327466), which dates from the 15th and 16th centuries. The kremlin, near where the Kazanka River enters the Volga, is an architectural monument (kremlin means "fortress" in old Russian) with marvelous towers and churches. There is an impressive panoramic view of the kremlin from the Spasskaya Tower and a full view of the city from the adjacent Bashnaya Syumbeka (Syumbek Tower), which was named for a Tatar princess who was married to three khans (not all at the same time). From this point you will notice a little island in the middle of the Kazankha River, a memorial to those who died during Ivan the Terrible's siege of the city in 1522. Across the square from the Spasskaya Tower is the *Tatar State Museum* (2 Lenina Ulitsa; phone: 8432-327162), with interesting exhibits about the Volga region. The museum is open Tuesdays through Saturdays from 10 AM to 3 PM; admission charge. Near Kabanskoe Ozero (Lake Kaban) is Mardzhani, an imposing 18th-century mosque (open for services; 17 Nasiri).

During the 19th century, the University of Kazan (18 Lenina; phone: 8432-321549) was a center of liberal ideas in eastern Russia. V. I. Ulyanov — Lenin — was expelled from law school here in 1887 for taking part in student riots. (For old-times' sake, stop by 58 Ulyanov Ulitsa, where Lenin lived with his family at the end of the 19th century.) Leo Tolstoy also studied at the university.

An important processing center for sable fur, Kazan is a major rail link between Moscow and the Ural Mountains, and is one of the largest industrial centers in the Volga basin.

The main shopping street is Bauman Ulitsa. You can relax in Gorky Park on Ershova Ulitsa, or at the zoo and botanical gardens (112 Taktasha Ulitsa; phone: 8432-375032 for both). For entertainment, visit the *Musa Dzhalil Opera and Ballet Theater* (Svobodaya Ploshchad; phone: 8432-324328) or the puppet theater (21 Lukovskova; phone: 8432-389272).

En Route from Kazan By boat, the trip to Ulyanovsk takes about 12 hours. The boat passes first through the Kuybyshev Reservoir, which was created in the 1950s, making Kazan a Volga port city. Boat cruises usually run from April through October and last anywhere from 7 to 10 days. For more information, contact the local *Intourist* service desk. You may see fruit trees in bloom, wheat fields, or sunflowers in the valleys along the reservoir. Coriander is cultivated and processed in one of these valleys. Potatoes also are grown here. As you approach Ulyanovsk, the popular bathing beach on Paltsenskiy Island will come into view; it can be reached by boat from Ulyanovsk.

ULYANOVSK This small city on a high hill on the Volga-Sviyaga watershed was the hometown of one Vladimir Ilich Ulyanov, known to the world as V. I. Lenin, born here on April 22, 1870. Formerly called Sibirsk, the city was renamed Ulyanovsk in 1924, just after the death of the great Bolshevik leader.

The *Lenin Museum* (68-70 Lenina Ulitsa; phone: 8422-312222), which contains mementos of Lenin's youth, is in the house where the family lived in the 1880s before Lenin left to attend the University of Kazan. Open 10 AM to 6 PM; closed Tuesdays; admission charge. Nearby is the huge *Lenin Memorial Complex* (No. 1 Anniversary of the Birth of Lenin Square; phone: 8422-394941), which opened in 1970. It includes the house in which he was born, his grammar school, and other buildings associated with the Communist leader's life.

The main shopping street is Goncharov, named after another famous hometown boy, Ivan Goncharov, a 19th-century Russian novelist whose best-known work was *Oblomov*. Even though the writer described Ulyanovsk as rather undistinguished, the town named its main thoroughfare after him and dedicated a museum in his honor. The *Goncharov House* (20 Goncharova Ulitsa; no phone) also doubles as the *Museum of Fine Arts and Local History.* The museum is open Wednesdays through Sundays; admission charge.

En Route from Ulyanovsk The journey to Volgograd takes about 36 hours by boat and is full of fascinating sights. Shortly after leaving Ulyanovsk, you pass Vinnovskaya Grove, a popular recreation park. From here the Volga winds around the Zhiguli Mountains. Forests and small settlements of Russian vacation homes, called *dachas,* line the banks.

VOLGOGRAD Founded in the 16th century as the fortress of Tsaritsyn to guard the Volga, historically, the purpose of this city has been to protect Russia from invasions.

The city, which was called Stalingrad from 1925 to 1961, was completely rebuilt after World War II, and a memorial to the heroism of Stalingrad's people — who handed the German Army one of its most significant defeats — was soon erected. Victory Monument, on the ancient Mamaev Kurgan Hill, is one of the most moving war monuments ever built: Scenes of battle are depicted on the steps leading up from Lenin Prospekt; an eternal flame burns in the circular Hall of Military Glory; slogans of the street-fighters are carved into the walls; and the names of all the war dead are inscribed on mosaic plaques. There's also a museum dedicated to the heroic defense of the city, aptly named the *Museum of the Defense of Tsaritsyn* (10 Gogol Ulitsa). At press time, the museum was undergoing renovation and scheduled to open next year. However, the exhibits and displays are temporarily housed nearby at the *Volgograd State Museum* (38 Lenina Prospekt; phone: 8442-347272). Simply called the "Panorama" by locals, it affords visitors a spectacular 360-degree view of the city from high atop Mamaev Kurgan Hill. Artillery buffs will enjoy viewing the weapons and uniforms used in battles over the centuries. On the outer perimeter are old fighter planes, tanks, and cannons. The museum is open from 10 AM to 6 PM; closed Mondays; admission charge.

The *Volgograd Fine Arts Museum* (21 Lenina Prospekt; phone: 8442-363906) houses a fine collection of works by famous Russian artists donated by the *Hermitage* in St. Petersburg and the *Pushkin Museum* in Moscow. At press time, museum officials were hoping to open an additional exhibition hall located near the *Volgograd State Museum.* Open from 11 AM to 6:30 PM; closed Wednesdays; admission charge.

There is a planetarium (14 Yuriya Gagarina Ulitsa and Mira Prospekt; phone: 8442-363483), a gift to the city from the former East Germany as a token of reparation following the destruction of the area by Germans during World War II; a circus (on Volodarskiy; phone: 8442-363106); a musical comedy theater (on the Central Quay; phone: 8442-363105); and a puppet theater (15 Lenina Prospekt; phone: 8442-330649). Shopping is concentrated in the streets surrounding Pavshikh Bortsov Ploshchad (Fallen Fighters Square) and the Alleya Geroyev.

En Route from Volgograd The boat goes west here through the canal connecting the Volga with the Don River.

To reach the Don, tour boats must pass through a number of locks and the Tsimlyansk Reservoir, which feeds the canal and irrigates the drought-plagued Lower Don region.

ROSTOV-ON-DON (ROSTOV NA DONU) If you have come the entire way from Kazan, you may notice the difference in the appearance of this southern city, the gateway to the Caucasus. The area of Rostov-on-Don beyond the central Teatralnaya Ploshchad (Theater Square) was once the Armenian town of Nakhichevani, and the houses here are typically old, low Armenian dwellings.

Rostov-on-Don became a city in 1797, having grown up around a fortress built to defend Russia from the Turks. Its importance as a port city and trade center was enhanced by the completion in 1952 of the Volga-Don Canal. The city now has a population of 1 million.

Shops and museums are located along Bolshoi Sadovaya. Also here are 5 theaters, a racecourse (233 Malooginoy Ulitsa), a regional philharmonic orchestra, a bathing beach, a sports stadium, and several parks. The *Museum of Ethnography* (79 Bolshoi Sadovaya; phone: 8632-655213) chronicles the colorful past of the cossacks who once trod this area; the *Museum of Fine Art* (115 Pushkinskaya Ulitsa; phone: 8632-665907) houses a respectable collection of Russian works; and the *Liquor Factory* (70 Budyonovskiy Prospekt; no phone) conducts daily tours that describe the production of local potables. All three museums are open daily; admission charge for each. There are a number of cafés and gardens along Pushkinskaya, the city's premier pedestrian thoroughfare.

About 25 miles (40 km) northeast of Rostov is Novocherkassk, where cossacks made their capital in 1805. Here you will find the elaborate *Museum of Don Cossacks* (phone: 252-73470) with exhibits displaying their illustrious history.

If you are at the end of your tour, Moscow is about 2 hours away by plane (and a tortuous 28 hours by train) from Rostov-on-Don. On the other hand, this is a good starting place for a tour of the Black Sea coast (see *Russia's Black Sea Resorts* in this chapter). You also can return to Moscow by way of Kiev.

BEST EN ROUTE

Hotel prices throughout Russia will be determined more by your specific travel plans, the time of the year you choose to go (with summer the most expensive season), and the class of accommodations you pick. The dramatically fluctuating Russian economy, however, makes it difficult to provide accurate rates for hotels and restaurants; we suggest that you check costs — and the latest exchange rate — immediately prior to your departure. Be aware that at press time, the Russian government has imposed a 20% sales tax on rooms; check in advance to see whether or not the tax has been included in the price you are quoted. In addition, since the ruble exchange rate has fallen drastically in the past year, it is unknown whether a convertible currency is realistic at this point. In the meantime, payment for various goods and services, including hotels and restaurants, continues to be in hard currency.

Although *Intourist,* which is now a private company, once ran virtually all the hotels and restaurants in the Soviet Union, the ever-increasing tourism industry in Russia now is run by other private enterprises, cooperatives, and autonomous regional organizations. However, it is advisable to make your arrangements through a US travel agent specializing in Eastern European travel.

Cooperative and private restaurants in Russia usually offer better and more varied menus than hotel restaurants. Your hotel can provide the names and addresses of private or cooperative cafés and restaurants that offer local and European cuisine. You may have to make your own reservations at these places, however — that is, if you speak Russian, or have an interpreter on hand. Sometimes the easiest approach is to stop in at the restaurant earlier in the day. Restaurants generally open in late morning and close by midnight. The cuisine of the Volga region is wholesome and hearty. You might begin your meal with an array of cold appetizers called *zakuski.* Baked fish stuffed with buckwheat groats, and *solyanka* (a fish or meat stew made tart with salted cucumbers and olives) are delicious entrées.

KAZAN

Moladoni A few miles from town, this 200-room hotel-sports complex affords comfortable living quarters. Amenities include a bar, café, and restaurant. In addition, there is an Olympic-size pool, a stadium, and a fully equipped gym. 1 Deckabristov Ulitsa (phone: 8432-327954).

Navros A place frequented by locals, it serves good food and delicious desserts. Open daily for lunch and dinner. No reservations. Near the *Tatarstan Hotel,* 2 Kuybysheva Ultisa (no phone).

Tatarstan Centrally located, this hotel offers 45 comfortable rooms, a post office, a café, a bar, and a restaurant serving local dishes. Live music nightly. Open for lunch and dinner. Reservations advised. 1 Kuybysheva Ulitsa (phone: 8432-390492 or 8432-326979).

ULYANOVSK

Oktyaberskaya This pleasant hotel provides guests with a lovely view of the Volga River from many of its 54 rooms. In addition, there is a small movie theater, international direct-dial from the lobby, and a good restaurant which locals rate as the best in town. 1 Plehanova Ulitsa (phone: 8422-314697).

Rossiya This popular dining spot serves local dishes and provides live music nightly. Open daily for lunch and dinner. Reservations necessary. 23 Karl Marx Ulitsa (no phone).

Venets Run by *Intourist,* this 480-room hostelry has a restaurant, casino, café, and hard-currency shop. 19 Sovietskaya (phone: 8422-394880).

VOLGOGRAD

Dragon This newly opened Chinese-Soviet venture is the talk of the town. With a matchless view of the city, it features regional Chinese fare, including Manchurian beef, lobster Cantonese, and Szechuan blossom lamb. Open daily from 11 AM to 8 PM. No reservations. Hard currency accepted. 10 Lenina Prospekt (no phone).

Intourist A comfortable 122-room hostelry with a restaurant, hard-currency bar, and hair salon. 14 Mira Prospekt (phone: 8442-364553; fax: 8442-339175).

Myak (Lighthouse) Overlooking the Volga River, this eatery serves Russian and Uzbek food in a pleasant atmosphere. Live music accompanies your meal. Mira Prospekt (phone: 8442-363636).

Rossiya A huge complex of bars, restaurants, and fast-food stalls, this is a fun place for watching the way Russians enjoy a leisure afternoon. Open daily. No reservations. Located next to the Rechnoi Vagzal (River Station).

Volgograd More Russian fare and live music. Open daily. Reservations advised. 12 Mira Prospekt (phone: 8442-361116).

ROSTOV-ON-DON

Intourist Clean and quiet, this 200-room hostelry features 2 restaurants, a foreign-exchange desk, and a post office. An Irish pub boasts a fish tank with amazingly colorful fish and two white frogs. 115 Bolshoi Sadovaya (phone: 8632-659065).

Kafe Don Its inconspicuous red brick exterior belies the charming interior. The dining room, with a slanted high-planked ceiling, evokes the feeling of a rustic Swiss chalet. Specialties include fondue, raclette, and other Swiss fare. Open daily for lunch and dinner. No reservations. Mira Prospekt (no phone).

Petrovskiy Prichall (Peter's Landing) Actually two restaurants: The first is located inside a replica of Peter the Great's frigate; the second is on land right next door. Waiters are dressed in period uniforms, and the Russian food is prepared with care. Open daily. Advance reservations must be made in person. Located on the left bank (no phone).

Russia's Black Sea Resorts

The balmy seaside towns and holiday resorts along the sparkling blue Black Sea are ideal places to meet and mingle with the Russians who vacation here. It's easy to begin a casual conversation on the beach or in the relaxed atmosphere of an outdoor café. Actually, the people who come here are an international lot: The area is renowned for its mineral spas, and many foreigners come to take cures.

The scenery is merely spectacular. With the Caucasus Mountains as a backdrop, the landscape varies from rocky cliffs to sloping foothills lush with subtropical vegetation, and rare and unusual plants that flourish in the marvelous climate.

In fact, the climate along the Caucasian coast is so similar to that of the French Riviera, that this area has been nicknamed the "Russian Riviera." Cool water temperatures and the high salt content make swimming in the Black Sea an exhilarating experience, and though most of the beaches are composed of pebbles and small stones, many vacationers prefer Black Sea resorts to those along the Mediterranean.

Our Black Sea driving tour begins at Rostov-on-Don, the gateway to the Caucasus. From there it travels along the Sea of Azov to the port city of Novorossisk, then heads south along the coastline to Sochi, Russia's largest Black Sea resort. An alternative approach is to combine an excursion to this area with a tour of the Crimea (see the *Ukraine* route). There are car ferries and passenger boats from the Crimea to the Greater Sochi coast, and air connections between Simferopol in Crimea and the airport in Adler, near Sochi.

ROSTOV-ON-DON This city is the sieve through which Muscovites traveling to the holiday resorts on the Black Sea by car or train ordinarily pass. For more details, see the "Rostov-on-Don" entry in *The Volga* route.

En Route from Rostov-on-Don Drive south past Krasnodar to the port city of Novorossisk, about 200 miles (320 km) away. From here pick up the coastal road, which connects scores of resorts along the Black Sea on its way to the Turkish border.

As you head south, the road passes between bays and beaches to the west and the foothills of the Caucasus Mountains to the east. The first village of note is Gelendzhik, one of the oldest settlements on the Black Sea coast. Burial monuments over 4,000 years old have been found in this area. The coast road gradually climbs to about 2,625 feet, then, after cutting through the Mikhailov Pass, descends to Archipo-Ossipovka at the mouth of the Vulcan River.

Tuapse, an important port that handles and processes crude oil that is piped here from the northern side of the Caucasus, is the last good-size town before entering Lazarevskoye, the northernmost district of Greater

Sochi — an area that stretches over 90 miles (144 km) along the coast from Tuapse almost to the Georgian border.

Although war rages just a few miles south in Georgia, it is peaceful and tranquil in Sochi. At the time of this writing, UN forces were not sanctioned to land in Sochi with relief supplies; therefore, it is unlikely you will see any military equipment or personnel.

SOCHI The most important resort on Russia's Black Sea coast (about 2 million people visit Greater Sochi each year), it is sheltered by mountains which seem to descend right into the sea.

Although there was a fortress here in the mid-19th century, the town didn't begin to grow until the area's potential as a health resort (by virtue of its mineral springs) was recognized in 1893. By 1909, the first of the grand spa hotels had opened; today there are nearly 60, and most of the 250,000 people who live in Greater Sochi work in the health or holiday industry.

Spectacular panoramas of the town, the sea, and the mountains are available from an observation tower atop Mt. Bolshoi Akhun, about 14 miles (22 km) from the center of Sochi. The viewing platform stands 2,155 feet above sea level, and there is a restaurant nearby. Bus No. 39 from the Riviera section of the city goes to the mountaintop.

The 25-acre Riviera Park, with its charming outdoor cafés, scores of sports grounds, and an open-air theater, is the center of Sochi life. Kurortniy Prospekt, the main street, runs south from the park, paralleling the sea. On the roof of the main seaport building, a 114-foot spire with a star on top provides an unusual landmark for ships at sea. The public beaches are south of the center of town.

While sanatoriums once were used exclusively by Russia's elite, today the majority are frequented by tourists. One of the most beautiful of the sanatoriums that stand on Sochi's hills and cliffs is the *Ordzhonikidze Sanatoria,* which was built in Italian Renaissance style during the 1930s. The interior was decorated in traditional Russian style by local artists. A number of sanatoriums, including the *Ordzhonikidze,* have funicular railways or elevators connecting them to the beach or the town. The *Sanitoria Sochi* is another good choice. For more information, contact *Invest Services* (phone: 862-932462), a private organization that specializes in beach holidays.

In addition to the beautiful mimosas, oleanders, magnolias, and palms that grow along Sochi's streets, there are specimen trees and shrubs from all over the world in the local botanical garden, *Dendarium* (74 Kurortniy Prospekt; phone: 862-923602). The garden is open daily; no admission charge.

If you tire of the sand, sea, and sun, the Sochi area has a number of interesting sites that make for perfect day trips. Ashei, a pleasant little seaside resort just north of the village of Lazarevskoye, is known for its nearby mountains, which are popular with climbers. The Memedoo Gorge in the Ashei range near Lazarevskoye has a number of small waterfalls and grottoes. Another short excursion can be made to the Agura waterfalls near old Matsesta.

Dagomys, the northern district of Sochi, is well known as a terminus for hiking routes through the Caucasian National Preserve, and it now boasts an excellent *Intourist* holiday beach complex. From a park on the western slopes of Mt. Armyanka, there are stunning views of the Greater Sochi area, the sea, and the mountains. The yew and boxtree grove on the eastern side of Mt. Akhun in the Caucasian National Preserve is also worth a visit. Dagomys is also Russia's tea capital, and is considered the most northern area in the world where this plant is grown. *Intourist* organizes several tours which take visitors to one of the hillside plantations, where they can take part in a tea-tasting ceremony, accompanied by delicious pies and Russian entertainment. Also of interest is the unique collection of antique Russian samovars on display at the plantation.

For archaeological buffs, traces of prehistoric man have been found in caves in Vorontsovskiye and Kudepstinskiye, near Sochi. They should only be visited with an experienced guide. And for theatergoers there is the *Letniy* (Summer Theater; Frunze Park), *Zelyoniy* (Green Theater; Rivera Park), and *Zimniy* (Winter Theater; Teatralnaya Ploshchad).

Also recommended is the spectacular drive along the Myzmta River to the ancient village of Krasnaya Polyana. For details about organized tours in the Sochi area, contact your hotel service bureau or *Intourist*.

En Route from Sochi About 13 miles (21 km) south of Sochi is the town of Khosta, famous for its health treatment centers and as a hiking station. About 18 miles (29 km) from Sochi, is Adler, site of the central airport for the entire region. An extensive drainage system has helped turn Adler, once merely marshland, into a sunny, subtropical garden noted for its health spas and campgrounds.

BEST EN ROUTE

The price of your accommodations has less to do with the hotel you choose than with the travel package plan or class you select, or whether you visit the Black Sea by cruise ship. The dramatically fluctuating Russian economy makes it difficult to provide accurate rates for hotels and restaurants. Be aware that at press time the Russian government had imposed a 20% sales tax on rooms, so check in advance to see whether or not the tax has been included in the price you are quoted. In addition, since the ruble exchange rate has fallen drastically in the past year, it is unknown whether a convertible currency is realistic at this point. In the meantime, payment for various goods and services, including hotels and restaurants, continues to be in hard currency. We suggest that you check costs — and the latest exchange rate — immediately prior to your departure.

Most restaurants open late in the morning and close at 11 PM or midnight. Reservations may be advisable at the better restaurants in the most popular resort areas. Food prices were relatively low as we went to press, but it's difficult to know if they will remain so. Your hotel service bureau will supply the names and addresses of new private and cooperative cafés and restaurants in the resort areas.

Some of the best renditions of Russian, Ukrainian, Georgian, and Caucasian food are found in Black Sea restaurants. Sample the beef Stroganoff, chicken Kiev, and Caucasian *shashlik* (skewered lamb). The semitropical climate means fruit and fresh vegetables are abundant year-round. Dairy products such as the feta-like *sulguni* cheese, sour cream or *smetana,* and yogurt, called *matsoni,* are excellent.

SOCHI

Dagomys Built in 1982, this property has 1,007 rooms and a large private beach. Facilities include 7 restaurants, 7 bars, an 18-hole golf course (bring your own clubs), billiards, bowling, a sauna, a hair salon, car repair, a currency exchange office, and a helicopter pad. 7 Leningradskaya Ulitsa (phone: 862-321275 or 862-325400).

Iveria Simple Georgian meals served in the beachside setting make dining here a pleasurable experience. Live music nightly. Open Tuesdays through Saturdays for dinner. Reservations advised. Next to the *Zemchuzhina Hotel.* (phone: 862-993196).

Kamelia A seafront property with 150 rooms; a dining room that serves Georgian, Ukrainian, and Russian fare; and the Russian *Troika* tearoom on the 11th floor, which affords a great view of the city. There's also a sauna and a hair salon. A large private beach is nearby. 91 Kurortniy Prospekt (phone: 862-990201).

Kavkaz Steps away from the town's only supermarket, this hotel offers 220 rooms with TV sets. There's a hair salon, a sauna, and 24-hour room service. 72 Kurortniy Prospekt (phone: 862-923048).

Magnolia A 400-room hostelry with balconies overlooking the Black Sea, it has 3 restaurants, a bar, and a sauna. 50 Kurortniy Prospekt (phone: 862-929594).

Moskva This modern hotel has 1,000 large airy rooms all with private baths. There's a sauna and 2 restaurants; and plans call for the addition of an elegant casino. 28 Kurortniy Prospekt (phone: 862-925743).

Primorye With a spectacular view of the sea, this 77-room hotel offers private baths, a restaurant with live music nightly, 2 cafés, and an *Intourist* service bureau. 1 Sokolova Ulitsa (phone: 862-925743).

Radisson Lazurnaya Sochi Opened last year, this 25-story property overlooks the Black Sea. Its 300 rooms and suites all feature air conditioning, mini-bars, satellite phones, color TV sets, and private baths. In addition, guests get to enjoy a fitness center; a sauna; a lounge specializing in international wines and beers; and 2 restaurants, both featuring exceptional European and Russian fare. 103 Kurortniy Prospekt (phone: 862-976347; 800-333-3333 in the US; fax: 862-236259).

Restaurant 137 Good traditional cooking, with dishes not often found in other Sochi eating places, and generous servings. The three-meats special (beef, pork, and chicken) with vegetables is superb. Reservations necessary. Near the *Zemchuzhina Hotel* (phone: 862-993196).

Victoria Set in a nondescript building, this eatery offers the finest in Georgian food and a spectacular ocean view. There is music nightly, and special curtained dining booths for privacy. Try the stew served in earthenware pots or the fresh catch of the day. Open daily for dinner. Advance reservations through *Intourist.* 14 Chernamorskaya Ulitisa (no phone).

Zemchuzhina The name means "pearl," and the hotel is the city's best. The 19-story high-rise complex on the waterfront has 1,004 rooms, 7 restaurants (serving Russian and Georgian fare and seafood), 4 bars, a private beach, a heated swimming pool, tennis courts, a shop, a car rental desk, and a currency exchange. Art is sold in the salon. Helicopter service transports guests to the mountains for skiing, about 37½ miles (60 km) away. 3 Chernamorskaya Ulitsa (phone: 862-926084 or 862-927364; fax: 862-992099).

The Golden Ring

A trip to the medieval cities of the Golden Ring is a voyage back through time, to an era when principalities, with their majestic cathedrals, convents, monasteries, and kremlins, were at the center of spiritual and political life. These cities constitute the cradle of Russian culture, and with the fall of communism, they have become symbols of Russian revival, attracting thousands to once-off-limits kremlins and reconsecrated churches.

Five cities make up the Golden Ring, most of them within easy driving distance of Moscow. The scenic route goes through Sergeyev Posad, site of the Trinity Monastery of St. Sergius, one of the most important centers of Orthodoxy in the world; then on to Pereslavl Zalesskiy, birthplace of Peter the Great's navy; and Rostov-Veliky, with its 17th-century kremlin, one of Russia's best preserved and most spectacular fortresses. The route then continues on to Vladimir and Suzdal, both remarkably preserved towns of medieval churches, monasteries, and wooden isbas (log cabins).

These city-states emerged out of the turmoil that surrounded the collapse of Kievan Rus, the first Russian state, and also the religious crusades that marked the period following Grand Prince Vladimir's conversion to Christianity in the 10th century.

Later, the 13th-century Tatar-Mongol invasion destroyed many of the original buildings that marked the foundations of several principalities. Led by Genghis Khan and his successors, these nomads from Asia conquered most of Kievan Rus (except for Novgorod and Pskov) and ruled for more than 2 centuries.

Despite this, the Russian Orthodox church continued to flourish. Master of icon painting Andrei Rublev produced his best works during a stay at Sergeyev Posad and Vladimir monasteries. Sergeyev Posad was also an important center of knowledge, where chronicles were transcribed into Old Church Slavonic, the only written language in Russia; it retained its role until many centuries later when Mikhail Lomonosov (1711–65) established a modern Russian language.

Under Ivan III, Vladimir and Suzdal were incorporated into the principality of Muscovy, and with the fall of the Tatar-Mongol state, Moscow became the center of Russia until Peter the Great transferred the seat of power to St. Petersburg some 250 years later.

Soviet communism also left its mark on the Golden Ring cities. Under Joseph Stalin, churches and monasteries were closed, used as warehouses, or even demolished to make way for factories and apartment buildings. State atheism was proclaimed and authorities would only direct attention to the golden-domed churches as examples of the Orthodox church's opulent riches and exploitation of workers.

When not destroyed or put to ill use by the Soviet regime, Golden Ring destinations were turned into museum-cities and placed under the control of *Intourist,* the official state tourism agency. *Intourist* decided to tap into the potential of the cities, in part because the authorities were unable to keep Russia's faithful away. It built huge, modern "tourism complexes" that clashed with the architectural surroundings. *Intourist* hotels remain, to this day, eyesores in the landscape.

With the collapse of the Soviet Union, the Russian Orthodox church has moved to reclaim all of its former property, and most of the main churches have been reconsecrated. Monasteries and convents, once idle museums, have once again become houses of worship and spiritual centers.

At press time, a battle was underway between *Intourist* and leaders of the Orthodox church for control of revenues derived from the tens of thousands of visitors who flock to the churches and monasteries. New private firms have moved in to provide services, and plans to build new hotels are underway, but *Intourist* remains the main tourism agency in this region.

A word of advice to drivers: Russian highways and roads are not lit at night, and while most major thoroughfares are generally in good condition, secondary roads are quite another story. Travelers are well advised to avoid driving at night on these roads.

MOSCOW For a complete description of the city and its restaurants and hotels, see *Moscow* in THE CITIES.

En Route from Moscow Just 34 miles (54 km) northeast of Moscow's city limits, this route is a pleasant drive on one of the best highways in Russia (it's free of potholes). From the center of Moscow, follow Mira Prospekt, which turns into Yaroslavskoye Shosse. About 24 miles (42 km) from that point is the turnoff for Sergeyev Posad, which will take you directly into the city center and its main street, Krasnaya Armiya (Red Army). The golden domes of the monastery churches are visible from the distance.

Visitors also may take the *elektrichka* (train), which travels to Moscow suburbs and beyond to the Golden Ring, leaves from Yaroslav Railway Station (phone: 921-5914) every 20 minutes on weekdays; every 2 hours on weekends. Also, *Cox & Kings* provides an 11-day journey from Moscow on their *Bolshoi Express* steam locomotive to all Golden Ring cities. Accommodations and meals are provided. For more information contact *Cox & Kings,* 511 Lexington Ave., New York, NY 10017 (phone: 212-935-3854).

SERGEYEV POSAD Named after Sergei of Radonezh, founder of the Troitsko-Sergeyevskaya Lavra (Trinity Monastery of St. Sergius), this medieval town attracts over 1 million visitors a year who come to see one of Russia's most beautiful monasteries (see below). The city was named Zagorsk in 1930 in honor of Vladimir Zagorsky, a member of the local Communist Party, and it was only in December 1991 that authorities decided to revert to the city's original name. Photography buffs will want to go up Vokzalnaya Ulitsa on Blinnaya (Pancake Hill) for a panoramic view of the golden domes and of the blue-and-white bell tower of the monastery.

The town is also a center of the handmade toy industry and boasts two factories where *matryoshkas* are made. There are several fine arts and crafts shops with good selections of *shkatulkis* (black lacquer boxes). *Beriozka* (Birch Tree; 131 Krasnaya Armiya Prospekt; phone: 254-41001 or 254-44748) offers wooden toys and Russian chinaware. *Kolorit* (Color; 6 Vokzalnaya; phone: 254-44325) is famous for its *matryoshkas*, handmade folk clothing, painted eggs, and lacquer boxes — and its owner speaks perfect English.

Naturally, a traveler to Sergeyev Posad cannot leave the city without seeing the impressive Troitsko-Sergeyevskaya Lavra. In 1337, Sergei of Radonezh, the 23-year-old son of a pious boyar, built a small wooden church in the midst of a dense forest on a hill. Fourteen years later, news of the monk's devotion reached Constantinople and Patriarch Philotheos sent a gold pectoral cross to Sergei, calling on him to establish a monastery and to launch a religious crusade. The monastery came to prominence after Prince Dmitri Donskoy, whose army had received Sergei's blessing, defeated the Tatars in the Battle of Kulikovo (1380). Today the Troitsko-

Sergeyevskaya Lavra is a center of Russian Orthodoxy. While nothing remains of the original wood structures that were burned down by Tatars in 1408, the white-stone Troitskiy Sobor (Trinity Cathedral) was rebuilt 14 years later on the site of the original. The monastery is a complex of several churches as well as the *Museum of Art and History* (see below) and the Moscow Theological Academy. About 150 monks live in the monastery (there were over 1,000 before the 1917 Bolshevik Revolution) along with 1,000 students.

Today, thousands of Russians attend services in Troitskiy Sobor and pay their respects at the silver-plated sepulcher of Sergei, who was canonized in 1422. The cathedral's iconostatis was painted by Andrei Rublev, Russia's most famous icon painter, with the help of his student Danil Cherny. A copy of Rublev's *Old Testament Trinity,* one of Russia's most revered icons, can be seen in the lower row of the iconostatis. The original is on display in the *Tretyakov Gallery* in Moscow.

Across from Troitskiy Sobor stands the second-oldest structure in the complex, the Dukhovskaya Tserkov (Church of the Holy Spirit), built in 1476 by craftsmen from Pskov. The large Uspenskiy Sobor (Assumption Cathedral), with its five blue domes adorned with gold stars, was built under the order of Ivan the Terrible in 1559 to celebrate victories of the Moscow Army over the Tatars in the south. It was modeled after Uspenskiy Sobor in the Moscow Kremlin. The tomb of Boris Godunov, the czar who ruled during Russia's Time of Troubles at the end of the 16th century, can be seen near the main entry. Peter the Great commissioned (1686–92) the brightly painted Trapeznaya (Refectory), which explains the Western influences in its architectural style. The blue-and-white bell tower (1740–70), a monument of classical architecture, is the highest structure in the monastery. The 5-tier tower has 42 bells. The monastery is open from 6 AM to 8 PM; closed Mondays. English-speaking tours are offered by monks for about $10 per person (phone: 254-45721). Located nearby are a bookstore and souvenir shop.

The *Musey Istoricheskiy Iskutsveny* (Museum of Art and History; phone: 254-45355) houses an impressive collection of icons dating back to the 14th century and artifacts that belonged to several pre-revolutionary metropols. Open from 10 AM to 5 PM; closed Mondays; admission charge. *Intourist,* located next door to the museum, can provide English-speaking guides.

En Route from Sergeyev Posad Continue on the 4-lane Yaroslavskoye Shosse for 42 miles (67 km) to Pereslavl Zalesskiy, the birthplace of the famed Russian Prince Alexander. Pereslavl Zalesskiy literally means "The Settlement Behind the Forest." Drivers will enter the city on Sovietskaya Ulitsa, the town's main thoroughfare.

PERESLAVL ZALESSKIY Founded in 1152 by Prince Yuri Dolgoruki, the town held strategic importance as the westernmost outpost of the powerful Rostov-Suzdal principality. Russian princes from the emerging principalities of Tver and Moscow realized the military importance of Pereslavl Zalesskiy and waged a long and bloody war to control it. In 1302, it was incorporated into Moscow. During the 16th and 17th centuries, the town flourished as a key center of the Moscow-Arkhangelsk trade route linking the Far East to Western Europe. In 1688, the 19-year-old czar, Peter the Great, came here to build his *poteshnaya* (amusement flotilla) of over 100 small ships that would sail on Lake Pleshcheyevo. The town burst into a flurry of activity as woodcutters, carpenters, and blacksmiths came from all across Russia to build the country's first navy. For a better perspective, visit the *Botik Museum* (Rostovoskaya Ulitsa; no phone) with its collection of artifacts devoted to Peter the Great. Only two of his ships survived a fire in 1783; the sailboat *Fortuna* is on exhibit here while the second one is in the *St. Petersburg Naval Museum*. Open from 10 AM to 4 PM; closed Tuesdays; admission charge.

Located off Sovietskaya Ulitsa is the pride of the city on the highest hill in Pereslavl Zalesskiy. Although not much remains of the original 14th-century Goritskiy Monastery, the gate, which dates to the 17th century, is a true work of art with its façade of bas-relief sculptures. The monastery was closed by the Bolsheviks in 1919 and it became the *Musey Iskustva i Istory Pereslavla* (Pereslavl History and Art Museum), housing an impressive collection of icons and rare books. The centerpiece of the monastery is the 18th-century Uspenskiy Sobor (Assumption Cathedral). The monastery and cathedral are open daily from 10 AM to 4 PM; however, the cathedral is closed during the winter to protect the frescoes and other artwork inside from the harsh elements.

Near Krasnaya Ploshchad (Red Square) is the famous Spaso Preobrazhenskiy Sobor (Cathedral of the Transfiguration of the Savior), commissioned in 1152 by Prince Yuri Dolgoruki. The cathedral is said to be one of the oldest in Russia. Its white-stone structure is extremely plain and unpretentious, but students of Russian architecture note that its austere appearance reflects the harsh era in which it was built.

En Route from Pereslavl Zalesskiy The 41-mile (66-km) drive to Rostov-Veliky takes approximately an hour. Follow Yaroslavskoye Shosse straight into this historic town.

ROSTOV-VELIKY First mentioned as the capital of a principality in the 11th and 12th centuries, Rostov-Veliky (Rostov the Great) has retained its importance as a religious center. The Rostov Kreml (Rostov Kremlin), a complex built between 1670 and 1675, is truly among the most impressive in all of Russia. The gem of the complex is Spas-na-Senyakh Tserkov (Church of the Savior-in-the-Vestibule), with its single golden dome and an interior that has been well preserved through the centuries. Although the church has undergone renovations for the past several years, it is scheduled to reopen by the beginning of this year. Several other buildings, including the Metropolitan's House and the White Chamber, offer displays of icons and *finift* (miniature enameled icons). Centuries ago, Rostov craftspeople created these tiny icons for use on the robes of the high clergy.

Next to the kremlin is the five-onion–domed Uspenskiy Sobor (Assumption Cathedral). Ivan the Terrible ordered that it be built at a time when Rostov was a busy trading center. The cathedral doors are decorated with iron handles that date back to the 12th century. The tower has 13 bells, the largest of which weighs a hefty 32 tons. The bells can be heard daily after morning services and before evening services.

En Route from Rostov-Veliky The roads from Rostov-Veliky going directly to Vladimir are less than ideal. Therefore, we suggest an overnight rest (see *Best en Route*) before returning to Moscow on Yaroslavskoye Shosse and beginning the next leg of our journey. Located 114 miles (182 km) northeast of Moscow, Vladimir is a 2½-hour drive through small Russian villages and dense forests. Leaving Moscow, take Entusiastov Prospekt which leads directly into Vladimirskoye Shosse and the city of Vladimir.

VLADIMIR Founded in 1108 by the Kievan Prince Vladimir Monomakh, Vladimir became the capital of 12th-century Russia after Andrei Bogoliubsky (Vladimir's grandson) sacked Kiev in 1169 and moved the political center of the state northeast to what then was called Vladimir-Suzdal. Once inside the main entrance to the city, travelers immediately are struck by the Zolotaya Vorota (Golden Gate), modeled after a similar structure in Kiev. Commissioned by Andrei Bogoliubsky in 1164, today it houses a military museum open to the public. Under Bogoliubsky's rule and that of his successor, Vsevolod III, many architectural monuments were constructed, including the magnificent (Uspenskiy Sobor) Assumption Cathedral. Built in 1160, this magnificent golden-domed structure later inspired Moscow architects who used it as a model for the Kremlin's cathedral. It was built to rival Kiev's St. Sophia's Cathedral in size and elegance. All of Vladimir's and Moscow's princes were crowned here and it was considered the most important church in Russia until the 14th century. Not surprisingly, last year the cathedral was declared a UNESCO World Heritage site. Inside is a communal tomb for the 500 people who died during an attack by the Mongols; they set fire to the church, claiming the lives of the people who had taken refuge inside. One of the most famous works by master icon painter Andrei Rublev, *The Last Judgment,* can be admired under the choir loft. The remaining part of the iconostatis, painted by Rublev in 1408, is in the *Tretyakov Gallery* in Moscow. (The oldest recorded icon in Russia, *Virgin of Vladimir,* brought from Constantinople to Uspenskiy Sobor in Vladimir, can also be viewed in the *Tretyakov Gallery*.) Church services are held daily. Located on Tretyova Internationala Ulitsa.

Not too far away on Svoboda Ploshchad is Dmitrovskiy Sobor (Cathedral of St. Dmitri), a towering church built between 1194 and 1197. Once part of a huge palace complex built for Prince Vsevolod III, St. Dmitri is all that remains; it is considered a perfect example of the Vladimir-Suzdal architectural style. Solemn and richly decorated with bas-relief carvings adorning its façade, it embodies the wealth and the power of the Vladimir principality. Inside the central vault are beautiful 12th-century frescoes painted by Byzantine artists.

En Route to Suzdal From Vladimir follow Moskovsaya Ulitsa, which becomes Tretyova Internationala Ulitsa, for 22 miles (36 km). Continue to Frunzinskaya Ploshchad, straight through to Frunzinskaya Ulitsa, and north on Dobroseltskaya Ulitsa to Suzdal.

SUZDAL Situated on the banks of the Kamenka River, this town first attracted settlers in 1024 with its rich and fertile land. In the 12th century, Prince Yuri Dolgoruki, son of Vladimir Monomakh, made Suzdal the capital of the powerful Suzdal-Rostov principality, which included Vladimir and Moscow. Suzdal lost that distinction, however, after Dolgoruki's son, Andrei, transferred the capital to Vladimir. When Kiev fell to Lithuania in the 14th century, Suzdal once again came to prominence as the Orthodox capital of medieval Rus. Today, Suzdal is a small town of 12,000 people that has retained its medieval character, thanks to the absence of major urban development. Visitors agree it is the most authentic and perhaps the loveliest of all Golden Ring cities, and many of its monuments have been proclaimed UNESCO World Heritage sites. Along Lenina Ulitsa, Suzdal's main thoroughfare, is the town's oldest architectural complex. Historians estimate the Suzdal Kremlin was constructed in the early 12th century under the rule of Vladimir Monomakh. It contains Suzdal's most impressive building, which dominates the city: Rozhdestvenskiy Sobor (Cathedral of the Nativity of the Virgin). The carved lower section of the cathedral is all that remains of the original structure, the rest having been part of a major 16-century restoration, which included the five blue domes with golden stars. Under Communist rule, Rozhdestvenskiy Sobor became a museum; but it was returned to the Orthodox church in 1991 and restored as a place of worship. Next to the cathedral is the bell tower (1635), which now houses the *Suzdal Istoricheskaya Expozitsia* (Suzdal History Exhibit; no phone), an interesting collection of photographs including several magnificent cathedrals that were demolished in the 1930s on Stalin's orders. The Kremlin is open from 10 AM to 5 PM; closed Mondays.

Just across from the kremlin is the *Musey Derevniy Arckhitecturi i Jizhniy Kristianov* (Museum of Wooden Architecture and Peasant Life) with exhibits of pre-revolutionary Russia. There are several examples of intricate woodcarvings that are typical of the Russian isba (log cabin) as well as wooden windmills and churches. Tours are offered from May through October; admission charge.

Also along Lenina Ulitsa are two working monasteries, classic examples of Russian medieval architecture. Spaso-Yevfimiyevskiy Monastir

(Savior Monastery of St. Euthymius) is the town's largest monastery, built in the 14th century to protect the northern entry. Rizopolozhenskiy Monastir (Monastery of the Deposition of the Holy Robe) dates back to the 12th century, but the existing structures were rebuilt and cover various periods from the 16th to the 19th centuries. Rizopolozhenskiy's bell tower is Suzdal's tallest structure and the site of Sunday carillon concerts. Built in 1688 by Suzdal architects, the gates to this monastery, flanked by two towers with glazed tiles, are unique in Russia.

Two miles east of the city is Borisoglebskaya Tserkov (Churches of Boris and Gleb). Dating to 1152, these two churches are the oldest in the district. The white-stone structures dominate a field and are visible from the distance; however, the churches are in disrepair and not open to the public. Boris and Gleb were two sons of Prince Yuri Dolgoruki. The remains of Boris, his wife, Maria, and their son Euphrosyn have been entombed in one of the churches.

BEST EN ROUTE

This area of Russia offers several good hotels, but the dramatically fluctuating Russian economy makes it difficult to provide accurate rates for hotels and restaurants. Although the ruble exchange rate has fallen drastically in the past year, it is unknown whether a convertible currency is realistic at this point. In the meantime, payment for various goods and services, including hotels and restaurants, continues to be in hard currency. We suggest that you check costs — and the latest exchange rate — immediately prior to your departure. Be aware that at press time, the Russian government had imposed a 20% sales tax on rooms, so check in advance to see whether or not the tax has been included in the price you are quoted.

SERGEYEV POSAD

Sever (North) The best in the area, it features homemade chicken Kiev, borscht with thick sour cream, caviar, and various vegetable dishes. Open from 10 AM to midnight. Reservations advised. 140-1 Krasnaya Armiya Prospekt (phone: 254-45226 or 254-41220).

Zagorsk This 140-room *Intourist* hotel offers the only acceptable accommodations in town. Rooms are spartan but clean. There is a restaurant that offers good Russian fare, and a service bureau that is more than helpful in organizing tours to nearby sites. In the wintertime, many visitors bring their skis to enjoy the slopes at Mooco, a nearby ski facility. No credit cards accepted. 171 Krasnaya Armiya Prospekt (phone: 254-25925).

Zolotoye Kolsto (Golden Ring) The specialties here include *pelmeni* (a meat-filled dumpling served with sour cream) and other inexpensive but good meat dishes. Open from 11 AM to midnight. No reservations. No credit cards accepted. 121 Krasnaya Armiya Prospekt (phone: 254-41517).

PERESLAVL ZALESSKIY

Pereslavl A 60-room establishment that affords visitors a central location albeit with no-frills ambience. The *Frigot* restaurant serves Soviet-style fare — heavy soups and greasy meat dishes. 17 Rostovskaya Ulitsa (phone: 08535-21788 or 08535-21559).

ROSTOV-VELIKY

Mezhdunarodni Tsentr Molodezh (International Youth Center) This 26-room hotel, located inside the Rostov-Veliky Kremlin, is not exclusively a youth hostel. There is a special section of upgraded rooms for tourists which offers a bar, restaurant, sauna, and service bureau. Oktyabraskaya Ulitsa (phone: 08536-21259 or 08536-31854).

Termok This restaurant with only 20 tables serves good Russian dishes in a cozy atmosphere. The menu includes soups, meat dishes, and *pelmeni*. Open daily. No reservations. Kolkoznaya Ploshchad (phone: 08536-31348).

VLADIMIR

Kafe Dubravoshka (Café Oaktree) Russian through and through, this café lacks finesse but nevertheless provides good service. It pays to point out that you are a foreigner: It will definitely improve your chances of getting a good meal. Open daily for lunch and dinner. Reservations necessary. 11 Frunzinskaya Ulitsa (no phone).

Klyazma Not the Hilton, but this 110-room establishment, just outside the city center, offers decent accommodations. There is a restaurant serving good Russian fare. No credit cards accepted. 15 Sudogoskoye Shosse (phone: 09222-24237 or 09222-22310).

Russkaya Derevniya (Russian Village) This restaurant near the entrance to the city is considered Vladimir's best. The menu features Russian cutlets (ground meat patties) and an assortment of salads including traditional beet, potato, and cabbage varieties. Open daily. Reservations advised. Mokovskoye Shosse (phone: 09222-41624).

Vladimir Centrally located, this *Intourist* hotel has 45 clean rooms at rock-bottom rates. There is a restaurant. No credit cards accepted. Tretyova Internationala Ulitsa (phone: 09222-23042 or 09222-23074).

SUZDAL

Glavniy Turisticheskiy Kompleks (Main Tourism Complex) This 200-room establishment is not luxurious, but it offers decent accommodations at reasonable rates. Thirty-two of the rooms are located in log cabins inside nearby Pokrovskiy Monastir (Monastery of the Intercession). They feature wooden furniture in the style of ancient Kievan Rus. (Ivan the Terrible and Peter I exiled their wives to Pokrovskiy convent after having condemned them for being barren.) There is also a restaurant serving Russian dishes. Pokrovskaya Ulitsa (phone: 09321-21530 for main complex reservations; 09321-20889 or 09321-20908 for monastery reservations).

Pogrebok (Cellar) This is the place to try *medovukha* (honey wine) made only in Suzdal and served in brightly painted pitchers. The mushroom soup and beef stew served in locally made earthenware bowls are also noteworthy. Open 11 AM to 7 PM; closed Sundays and Mondays. Reservations advised. Kremlevskaya Ulitsa (no phone).

Trapeznaya (Refectory) A thoroughly unique place to eat, this former Archbishop's chamber in the kremlin features "monastic cooking" (a euphemism for Russian no-frills fare). An uninspired menu offers chicken and beef dishes, as well an assortment of vegetable salads and a cold fish platter. Open for lunch and dinner; closed Sundays. Reservations advised. Lenina Ulitsa (09321-21639).

Ukraine

Ukraine, "the borderland," has had a long and often troubled history. Born of the mighty Slavic state of Kievan Rus, the country that has been called the breadbasket of Eastern Europe has been coveted for its natural riches by a succession of invaders and overlords. With independence, Ukrainians hope, history has now come full circle.

The third-largest of the republics that once comprised the Soviet Union, Ukraine has a total area of 233,089 square miles and a population of over 51 million. Well-developed agriculturally and industrially, Ukraine slopes down from the Carpathian Mountains in the west to rolling hills with beautiful oak and beech forests, and broad plains where the soil is rich and black. The Dnieper River (Dnipro in Ukrainian) runs the length of the country from north to south. Ukraine shares a long, circuitous border with Russia, and also is bounded by Poland, Hungary, Slovakia, Romania, and Moldova (another former Soviet republic). Its northern neighbor is Belorus and to its south is the Black Sea and the Sea of Azov.

In ancient times, the region that is now Ukraine was inhabited by the Scythians, and later the Sarmatians. Ukrainians trace their roots to East Slavic tribes who settled in the area, probably in the 7th and 8th centuries, and then began to subdivide into smaller tribes. Most notable among these were the Polyani, who inhabited central Ukraine and founded Kiev. The origins of Kievan Rus, the political, commercial, and cultural entity that became one of the great European powers of its era, remain murky. What is known is that the early rulers were Varangians (Scandinavians) who were first attracted to the area because of its location along an important trade route to Constantinople.

Because Kievan Rus came to encompass all the territories inhabited by the East Slavs, including much of Ukraine's contemporary region, Ukrainians and Russians both lay claim to Kievan Rus as part of their national histories, and each group feels that it is the rightful heir to the old Kievan legacy. The issue continues to be one of bitter dispute. After centuries of being ruled from Moscow, Ukrainians especially are sensitive to what they perceive as an "imperialist Russian" attempt to usurp their history.

In AD 980, the rule of Great Prince Volodymyr (Vladimir) began, ushering in a golden era for Kievan Rus. Volodymyr was responsible for the Christianization of East Slavdom; in AD 988 he ordered his entire country to be baptized into the Byzantine faith, thus beginning the Orthodox church that has played such an important role throughout so much of Eastern Slavic history. Byzantine architecture, the style most closely identified with Ukraine and Russia, was introduced in Kiev by descendants of Prince Volodymyr, who commissioned churches in the designs of the colorful cathedrals of Constantinople.

The golden age ended soon after the reign of Yaroslav the Wise (1019–54), when most of the region split into separate principalities. Weakened by the division, these small kingdoms were conquered by a variety of invaders. In the 13th century, Kievan Rus was plundered by the Tatars (Mongols), who ruled well into the following century. Lithuania freed the Slavs from the Tatars in the mid-14th century, and under Lithuanian rule, lands that had been Kievan Rus flourished in relative safety. After the union of Lithuania and Poland in 1569, however, Kievan Rus lands came under the control of the Polish, who forced peasants into serfdom and persecuted members of the Ukrainian Orthodox church. Pressured by Polish Catholics, the Ukrainian bishops established the Uniate church, which recognized papal authority but retained the Orthodox rites.

In the 16th century, the rising principality of Moscow (Muscovy) began vying with Poland-Lithuania for control of the vast land south of their borders and the old Rus term "Ukraine," first mentioned in chronicles in 1187, came into general use.

Because of the harshness of Polish domination and religious discrimination, a number of Ukrainians fled to the area of the lower Dnieper rapids, where they formed a military order. They became known as *kozaks*, or cossacks, a Turkish name meaning "without masters." The cossacks, under leader Bohdan Khmelnytsky, launched a revolution against the Poles in the early 17th century. After a long and costly struggle, however, Khmelnytsky turned to Moscow for protection. The result was the fateful and controversial Pereiaslav Agreement of 1654, under which Ukraine agreed to some sort of Russian domination. The record is unclear as to whether Ukraine merely agreed to a form of vassalage without the czar's interference in its internal affairs or submitted to total union with Russia. Whatever the agreement, the outcome was over 300 years of Russian control in Ukraine.

Ukraine made several unsuccessful attempts to throw off the czarist yoke. An alliance with Poland in 1658 led to the Russo-Polish war, which culminated in the partitioning of Ukraine between Russia and Poland. The cossacks fought with Sweden against Russia in the Northern War (1700–21), but their defeat at the hands of Peter the Great meant the end of political autonomy for Ukraine. Throughout the 18th century, Russia acquired more Ukrainian territory from Poland, and obtained the Black Sea coast from the Ottoman Turks.

Russia colonized Ukraine throughout the 19th century, establishing its large coal and metal mining regions and industrial areas. Despite the influx of Russian colonists and the ban on the Ukrainian language, nationalist feeling survived among the people. This was demonstrated in a late 19th-century national revival movement, aimed at preserving Ukrainian culture.

Following the Revolution of 1917, Ukraine was engulfed in a civil war that saw Ukrainian nationalists fighting against invading Russian Bolsheviks. The nationalists — themselves divided into sparring factions —

managed to declare an independent Ukraine, but amid the chaos and spreading anarchy, were never able to really take control of the country. After the final Bolshevik victory, Ukraine became one of the four original republics that formed the USSR in 1922.

Ukraine eventually became the country's third-largest republic, and with its seemingly endless stretch of fertile farmland, the USSR's primary breakbasket. Ironically, from 1932 to 1933 an estimated 7 million Ukrainians died of starvation in a manmade famine brought about by Stalin's order to confiscate food and grain from the countryside. His aim was to force collectivization and to finance rapid industrialization.

Ukraine again suffered greatly during World War II; it was occupied by the Nazis from 1941 to 1944; official sources estimate that 5 million Ukrainians perished. During that time, however, the USSR united all Ukrainian lands into a single republic, adding the Carpathian region (which borders Romania) and Western Ukraine (which includes the city of Lviv). In 1954, Crimea was annexed to Ukraine, as a "gift" from Nikita Khrushchev (an act members of the Russian Parliament wanted reviewed at press time).

In the 1960s and 1970s, Ukrainian dissent against Moscow's heavy hand and continuing "Russification" started once again, most notably among writers, journalists, and other intellectuals. Though quickly crushed on Moscow's orders, nationalistic feeling in Ukraine remained strong. Ukraine's movement toward democracy began in the mid-1980s. Rukh, the republic's grassroots movement for independence and democracy, was instrumental in organizing miners' strikes, support for progressive parliamentary legislation, and calls for secession and Ukrainian independence. In 1990 their efforts bore fruit. Following the formation of a new Ukrainian Parliament, the republic declared sovereignty in July 1990. In the months that followed, Ukraine finally declared its independence after a sweeping referendum was overwhelmingly passed by Ukrainians in December 1991.

Despite many years of "Russification," Ukrainians comprise over 75% of the country's population and Russians only about 18%; there are also Poles, Belorussians, Moldavians, Hungarians, and other minorities. Russia has had a marked impact on Ukraine over the centuries, however, and in many ways this former republic remains the most similar to Russia. Both Russians and Ukrainians are descended from Slavic stock. The Ukrainian language is close to Russian, and both use the Cyrillic alphabet. (In fact, while Ukrainian is once again the national language, and the names of streets and other landmarks are being changed from Russian to Ukrainian, Russian names are still more commonly used by the residents of some areas, including the Crimea. Russian translations, therefore, appear in the Crimea section of this chapter. In the section on Western Ukraine, where Ukrainian is more widely spoken, Ukrainian names are used.)

Today Ukraine, like all the newly independent former Soviet republics, is savoring its new independence while struggling to convert to a market economy and enact democratic reforms. Progress has been slow and painful, however, in part because Ukraine's legislature and much of the industrial sector continue to be dominated by former Communists hesitant about radical reform and loath to see their old power and privileges erode.

While tourism was affected for several years after the disaster at the nuclear generating plant at Chernobyl, much of the affected area is now considered safe at least for short-term visitors. More and more travelers are discovering the beautiful, history-steeped cities, the sunny seaside resorts, and the rich, lush farmland of Ukraine.

NOTE At press time, only cars with drivers were available throughout the Ukraine. Plans for self-drive rental firms to open, however, were imminent. Therefore, it is advisable to check with your hotel service bureau for additional information. Also, travelers must be aware that due to severe fuel shortages, gasoline, while readily available in larger cities, is only in sporadic supply in rural areas. In addition, prompted by the increase in reported cases of diphtheria in Russia and Ukraine, travelers are advised to update their immunizations before entering these regions. For further information call the US State Department's *Citizen's Emergency Center* at 202-647-5225.

The Crimea

Unlike other areas in the former Soviet Union, thus far the breakup of the USSR appears to have had very little impact on this sunny peninsula in the Black Sea. Although Kiev has granted Crimea autonomy (the only region in Ukraine granted such status), Crimean legislators (virtually all Communist holdovers) have been reluctant to part with Soviet-style centralization and have resisted most political reforms. At press time, a monument to Lenin still towers over Yalta's central square. With luxury dachas outside Yalta and a relatively impressive supply of goods in the shops, the Crimea has long been home to the privileged. (Gorbachev's former dacha is 15½ miles/25 km from Yalta in Foros.) Consequently, democracy has had difficulty making inroads in the local Parliament.

But the demise of the Soviet Union has brought one important change here — a dispute has arisen as to whether Crimea belongs to Ukraine or Russia, and there is no easy solution. Inhabited for centuries by the Tatars, Crimea became a part of Russia when Catherine the Great seized the peninsula from Turkey. In 1944, Stalin expelled the Tatars to central Asia for alleged cooperation with the Germans. Then, 10 years later Soviet leader Nikita Khrushchev gave the Crimea to Ukraine as a "gift" to commemorate the 300th anniversary of the "fraternal union" of the

Ukrainian and Russian people. Russians outnumber Ukrainians in Crimea, which has a population of nearly 3 million. But Crimea is physically separated from Russia; it borders only Ukraine. More than half of Crimeans voted for Ukrainian independence in the 1991 referendum, but the peninsula doesn't have a single Ukrainian school or newspaper. The complications go on and on.

In the spring of 1992, the Crimean legislature declared the peninsula's independence, then rescinded the declaration in the face of an outraged Ukrainian Parliament. The Crimean legislature was holding out the possibility of putting the question of Crimean independence to a referendum, a move strenuously opposed by Kiev. The Russian legislature, for its part, was looking to void the 1954 grant of Crimea to Ukraine, and insisted that the issue be resolved through negotiations. Ukraine, in turn, accused Russia of reverting to its imperialist ways, and pointed to recent agreements rejecting territorial claims between the two countries and reaffirming the inviolability of their borders. At the same time, Kiev initiated a repatriation program for Tatars, who favor an autonomous Crimean republic within Ukraine. Kiev's aim was to blunt the impact of Crimea's Russian majority. At press time, some 300,000 Tatars had resettled, though many of them had returned to their ancestral homeland even before Kiev's repatriation program. Yet despite all the uncertainty, the seaside Crimean peninsula remains an enjoyable place to visit.

YALTA All passenger ships sailing to the Crimea and the Caucasus stop at Yalta, a charming Crimean resort town that lies in a natural bowl formed by mountains as high as 4,500 feet. There are also boats to Yalta from Odessa.

Yalta is best known to Westerners as the scene of the 1945 conference attended by US President Franklin D. Roosevelt, British Prime Minister Winston Churchill, and Soviet Premier Joseph Stalin during the last stages of World War II. The conference was held at Livadia, the former summer residence of the czars, just west of Yalta.

One of the special attractions in Yalta is the *Chekhov Museum* (112 Kirova Ulitsa; phone: 0654-394947) in the 2-story white house where the great writer lived during the last 6 years of his life. It was here that Chekhov wrote two of his most brilliant plays, *The Cherry Orchard* and *The Three Sisters*. The museum is open Tuesdays through Sundays from 9AM to 4 PM; admission charge.

Another favorite tourist stop is the *Wine Tasting Hall* (1 Litkensa Ulitsa) where talks on Crimean wine production are followed by free samples of the product. The wine making center of the Crimea is just northeast of the city at Massandra. Beyond Massandra, off the road to Simferopol, the Crimean capital, is the 80,000-acre Crimean Game Preserve. Guided tours can be arranged through the local *Intourist* office at your hotel. The Nikitskiy Botanical Garden (phone: 0654-335575), near the seashore east of Yalta, contains a vast rose garden, with more than 1,600 varieties (the Crimea is a major rose oil producer), and a 1,000-year-old pistachio tree.

The Crimea was first mentioned in chronicles in the early 12th century. Once a colony of Genoa, it was under Turkish domination for centuries until it became part of Russia at the end of the 18th century. Another 100 years later, it had become a popular resort. There are scores of sanatoriums along the coast, including dozens in Yalta itself. It is estimated that over a million people a year used to vacation here before economic turmoil and sharply rising prices put a dent into Yalta's tourism industry. One of the best bathing beaches in the Crimea is Zolotoy Plyazh (Golden Beach), southwest of Yalta between Livadia and Miskhor. The sunbathing season in this area runs from May to October. Alupka, a bit farther to the southwest, is one of the most beautiful resort towns in the Crimea. Its Vorontsov Palace (10 Dvortzovoye Shosse; phone: 0654-722281 or 0654-722951), surrounded by a 100-acre park, was designed by Edward Blore, one of the architects of Buckingham Palace. From Alupka, a cable car ascends Mt. Ai-Petri, for sweeping views of the coast and as far east as Giurzuf, a colorful old Tatar town of tumble-down houses perched above the sea that has attracted painters and writers, including Pushkin and Chekhov.

On the Crimean plateau north of Yalta is Bakhchisarai, the fabled capital of the Crimean Khanate built in the 17th and 18th centuries and immortalized by Pushkin in his poem *The Fountain of Bakhchisarai*. The khan's palace, harem, mosques, gardens, and mausoleums are still extant.

East of Yalta, you can visit Feodosiya, famous in the 15th century as a slave market town, and Kerch, an industrial center and fishing base on the Kerch Straits. There is a railroad from Kerch across the straits to the Caucasian coast. It's also possible to travel from the Crimea to the Russian Caucasian coast by boat. There are car ferries and passenger boats to take visitors to the Greater Sochi coast, and air connections between Simferopol in the Crimea and the airport at Adler, near Sochi.

BEST EN ROUTE

Hotel accommodations in Crimea can be booked through *Intourist* at the *Yalta* hotel (0654-350132 or 0654-352240) or through a travel agent that specializes in Eastern Europe (see *Ukraine* in FACTS IN BRIEF); hotels may be completely booked months in advance. Due to Ukraine's uncertain economic situation, it's difficult to provide accurate rates for hotels; we suggest that you check costs — and the operative exchange rate — immediately prior to your departure. At press time, most Crimean hotels accepted only hard currency from tourists, but this situation is expected to change when Ukraine introduces its own convertible currency in the near future.

Most restaurants open late in the morning and close at 11 PM or midnight. Reservations may be advisable at the better restaurants in the most popular resort areas. Food prices are relatively low by Western standards. Note that some restaurants in resort areas offer a floor show, usually starting about 9 PM, that might include partially clad dancers. Your hotel service bureau will supply the names and addresses of new private cafés and restaurants in the resort areas.

YALTA

Gurman Specialties such as assorted smoked fish, barbecued lamb, and pork fricassee in puff pastry put this centrally located restaurant high on most diners' lists. There's late evening music and dancing as well. Open daily for dinner. Reservations necessary. 11 Lenina Ulitsa (phone: 0654-320306).

Hostynnitsa Palas Recently renovated, this 1905 hotel is just 2 blocks from the seaside walk. The 32 large no-frills rooms and suites (many with balconies) all feature TV sets, refrigerators, and private baths. Guests also enjoy a restaurant and a bar. Local currency only. 8 Chekhova Ulitsa (phone: 0654-324380).

Kruiz (Cruise) Across from the sea terminal, this restaurant offers a well-chosen menu that's particularly strong on seafood. An entire meals can be fashioned from appetizers alone: Try the assorted cold fish platter, fish livers, and spicy cole slaw. The service in the spacious dining room is attentive and the seating comfortable. There's also a late-evening floor show and dancing to live music. Open daily for lunch and dinner. Reservations necessary. 8 Roosevelta Ulitsa (phone: 0654-326063).

Oreanda Yalta's best, this renovated European-style hotel overlooks the sea. Featured here are 125 large and comfortable rooms and suites (some with balconies), marble floors, a good restaurant, a café, bar, sauna, hair salon, tennis courts, and a private beach. Close to a Crimean wine tasting hall and artisans' pavilion. 35-2 Lenina Ulitsa (phone: 0654-328286).

Venetsia (Venice) Despite its name, there's no Italian food gracing the menu at this simple eatery. Instead, it serves fish — all varieties and prepared to order. Nightly floor show and dancing. Open for lunch and dinner. Reservations advised. 16 Mokovskaya Ulitsa (phone: 0654-320303).

Yalta The sheer size of this Crimean *Intourist*-run property is overwhelming — 2,500 small rooms in a 16-story building. Guests enjoy a private beach, a number of restaurants and bars, a casino, a heated swimming pool and sauna, tennis courts, and a currency exchange bureau. Massandrovkski Park, 50 Drazinskovo (phone: 0654-350150 or 0654-325594; fax: 0654-353093).

Western Ukraine: Kiev to Lviv

Stretching from conifer-covered mountains to vast golden plains of wheat, Western Ukraine offers a wealth of historic sights. For most of its convulsed history, it was ruled by an assortment of outsiders, and the legacy of centuries of Hapsburg and Polish rule is still evident in local architecture and traditions. Geographically and politically, Western Ukraine has been aligned with Vienna and Warsaw longer than it has with Kiev or Moscow. Russification is least noticeable here — much of Western Ukraine was not absorbed into the Soviet Union until World War II — and the area has been a major force in the rising Ukrainian nationalism that finally propelled the country to independence.

This route cuts through the historic towns of Rivne and Lutsk, then to Olensk, where a delightful castle and museum are set in a landscape right out of a Brueghel painting, and ends in Lviv; the most thoroughly Ukrainian of Ukraine's cities, it is treasure trove of well-preserved Gothic, Renaissance, and baroque architectural styles.

The direct road from Kiev to Lviv is 347 miles (560 km), with an additional 62 miles (100 km) to Lutsk. Although Lviv can be reached in a day, we recommend that you budget an overnight stop in Rivne or Lutsk, allowing ample time to take in the sights and beauty of the landscape.

KIEV For a complete description of the city and its restaurants and hotels, see *Kiev* in THE CITIES

En Route from Kiev The city's urban sprawl ends abruptly at the police checkpoint that marks the start of Route E40 and the 198-mile (320-km) drive to Rivne. Heading west, you pass through flat farmlands of golden wheat fields and tidy but poor roadside villages. About 87 miles (140 km) east of Kiev is Zhytomyr, one of the earliest settlements in princely Kievan Rus. During World War II, the city was heavily damaged and today holds little of interest to travelers, save perhaps the restored 17th-century Town Hall. There's a car service station (36 Myru) near the *Yalynka* hotel. Continue on Route E40 west for another 112 miles (180 km) to the city of Rivne.

RIVNE Nestled among broad swaths of parkland next to the narrow Ustia River, Rivne (pop. 270,000) has been right in the middle of repeated and bloody conflict since World War II. Most of Rivne's tourist sights are related to its turbulent history, most notably its occupation by Nazis. First mentioned in 13th-century chronicles, Rivne was fought over by Polish and Lithuanian princes, assaulted by Tatars, then became part of Russia in 1793. Starting in the mid-18th century and lasting for 150 years, Rivne was the feudal seat of the Lubomirski family, a Polish clan that ruled hundreds of nearby villages and towns from a sumptuous palace that was ravaged by fire in the 1920s.

Rivne reverted to Poland between World Wars I and II, then became the "capital" of the Nazi occupation of Ukraine. Nazi headquarters was in the building that today houses the interesting *Krayeznavchyu Muzey* (Regional Studies Museum; 19 Drahomanova Vulytsia), with its extensive exhibits relating to local history and Nazi occupation (closed Mondays; admission charge). The residence and bunker used by Erich Koch, who was in charge of the occupation, can be seen right next to the museum. Nearby is the 39-foot *Victims to Fascism Monument* (35 Bila Vulytsia), marking the site of one of three Nazi concentration camps in which 102,000 Jews, Ukrainian nationalists, and Soviet prisoners of war were killed between June 1941 and February 1944. (Jews accounted for nearly 60% of Rivne's 1940 population of 46,000.) With few exceptions, little remains of old Rivne, now a textile and electronics manufacturing town. Worth a look, however, is the beautiful 18th-century Church of the Dormition (113 Shevchenko Vulytsia), well known throughout the Ukraine for its rare mosaic floors. Also nearby is the blue-stained wooden Uspenskiy Sobor (Assumption Cathedral) and adjacent belfry, built in 1756, and the 19th-century Sviatovoskresna (Resurrection) Cathedral (Soborna Vulytsia).

En Route from Rivne From Rivne, take Route 257 northwest for 62 miles (100 km) through the vast "breadbasket" fields into Lutsk.

LUTSK At first glance, Lutsk (pop. 220,000) looks like most other small industrial towns in Western Ukraine: a bit drab and bedraggled from years of neglect. Founded in the 11th century as a frontier post of the Kievan Rus Empire, Lutsk later became part of the Volyn principality, passed to Lithuania in the 14th century, became part of Poland at the end of the 16th century, and was absorbed by Russia in 1795. Between World Wars I and II it again reverted to Poland. A major trading center in the 15th and 17th centuries, Lutsk today produces automotive equipment, electronic goods, and textiles.

But at the heart of what is one of Ukraine's oldest cities lies a wonderful medieval center, complete with the surprisingly well-preserved Lubart's Castle and a jumble of leafy side streets edged by old dwellings and historic churches. Located near the Teatralna Ploscha (Town Square), the 14th-century castle was originally the design of a Lithuanian prince. Tall Gothic towers anchor the unusually shaped triangular structure and afford visitors an impressive view of the city. Inside the courtyard are the remains of an 11th-century church around which the original fortress was built. There's also a small art museum displaying wonderful 16th- through 18th-century icons from Western Ukraine. The castle is open daily from 9:30 AM to 5 PM; admission charge. Nearby and just west of the castle is one of

Lutsk's landmarks, a towering early 17th-century Jesuit church built in baroque-rococo style; the bell tower across from the church entrance has no bells, since, according to legend, Peter the Great had them cast into cannons. Just south of the castle stands the 18th-century Monastery of the Brigittes, used as a prison under Polish and czarist rule, and later as an execution site by the Nazis.

En Route to Lviv Return to Rivne on Route 257. From this point take Route E40 southwest for 74 miles (118 km) to the village of Olensk, which leads to one of the region's great gems, *Olesky Zamok,* a meticulously restored castle that looms above the landscape. With two sturdy buildings connected by a gateway tower, the castle houses the *Lviv Picture Gallery* and its exquisite collection of 14th- to 18th-century Western Ukrainian artwork. Among the castle's treasures is a superb collection of 15th-century Galician icons, 18th-century baroque wooden sculptures, and the 15th-century painting *The Battle of Vienna* by Martino Altamonte. The castle is open from 11 AM to 5 PM; closed Mondays. The view alone is worth a stopover.

Return to Route E40 (which becomes Route M17) for 44 miles (70 km) southwest to Lviv.

LVIV The heart and soul of Western Ukraine, Lviv straddles empires and cultures. Decidedly Central European in look and atmosphere, it is the most westernized of Ukraine's major cities, largely because of its long history as part of Poland and the Austro-Hungarian Empire (Lviv did not fall under Moscow's rule until 1939). It's also one of Ukraine's most beautiful towns. Full of cobblestone streets, crooked alleyways, leafy and peaceful nooks and crannies, carefully manicured parks, and obscure little museums, Lviv is a fascinating mix of style and culture. Politically, Lviv has cast a big shadow in recent years: A hotbed of Ukrainian nationalism (Russian is rarely spoken here), the city played a key role in Ukraine's march toward independence.

Lviv was founded in the mid-13th century by Prince Danylo Romanovich of Halychyna (Galicia), a western principality of Kievan Rus. (Some historians view Halychyna as the successor state to the Kievan Empire after Kiev's fall to the Mongols in 1240.) Lviv is named after Romanovich's son Lev (Ukrainian for lion), and the lion motif seen all over town is the city's coat of arms. Located at the crossroads of major trading routes from the Baltics to the Black Sea, Lviv grew into an important trading and artisan hub, and later into a major cultural center that attracted many writers. Around 1349, after years of political and military strife, it passed to Poland and remained under its rule until 1772 when it became part of the Hapsburg Empire. Together with much of Galicia, it again reverted to Poland between World War I and World War II, was occupied by the Nazis from 1941 to 1944, then was absorbed into the Soviet Union.

Many of Lviv's major tourist sites are within a short walk from the well-preserved *rynok* (market square), lined with dozens of 3- and 4-story buildings dating back to the 16th century. Nearby is the exquisite Eastern Orthodox Uspenskiy Cathedral (Russkaya Vulytsia), which has been restored several times since its construction in the 1400s. Its design is traditional Ukrainian wooden architecture with touches of Italian Renaissance. Even more spectacular is the 200-foot bell tower built in 1572 and its 5-ton cast bell made in the Lviv area in 1783. Sculpted on the exterior façade of its Boimiv Kaplytsia (Boims Chapel) are elaborate Biblical carvings; inside is an array of 17th-century icons and a magnificent 18th-century altar. Orthodox services are held daily.

To the west of the *rynok* is Svobody Prospekt (Freedom Street), a wide boulevard lined with hotels, museums, and shops. The boulevard's grassy median is reminiscent of London's Hyde Park; here, public speeches, political demonstrations, bird watching, or even people watching are often the sport of the day. At its northernmost point is the *Lviv Opera House,* where Caruso once entertained.

Farther along is Zamkovaya Gore (Castle Hill), the site of a fortress built in the 14th century by Casimir III. Nearby is a park with a stone monument to Krivonos, the cossack colonel, who in 1648 captured and liberated the fortress.

For a complete change of pace, visit the open-air *Muzey Narodnoyi Arkhteklury ta Pobutu* (Museum of Local Architecture and Rural Life), an authentic collection of 18th-century wooden houses and churches located on 150 acres of lush green park just an hour outside of Lviv. Arrangements can be made through your hotel service bureau. Although there are few restaurants in this area, plenty of Ukrainian street vendors selling food and beverages will satisfy your needs. The museum is open daily from 11 AM to 7 PM; admission charge.

Although Lviv is today a busy, traffic-choked industrial center and major university town, there are excursions available into the unspoiled Carpathian Mountains where locals still adhere to centuries-old folk traditions. For information, contact your hotel service bureau.

BEST EN ROUTE

Hotel prices throughout Western Ukraine will be determined by your specific travel plans, the time of the year you choose to go (with summer the most expensive season), and the class of accommodations you select. The rapidly changing Ukrainian economy makes it difficult to provide accurate rates for hotels and restaurants; we suggest that you check costs — and the operative exchange rate — immediately prior to your departure. At press time, major Ukrainian hotels accepted only hard currency, but this situation is expected to change when Ukraine introduces its own fully convertible currency.

The service bureau in your hotel might be able to provide the names and addresses of restaurants. Reservations are highly recommended at all establishments. If the meal plan at your hotel includes breakfast and lunch, don't assume you will automatically be seated for dinner. Restaurants that cater to foreign visitors (still mostly in hotels) have better access to delicacies and are thus a magnet for Western Ukrainians with money to spend. At press time meals were paid for in local currency at most restaurants and prices were very low by Western standards. Restaurants open in late morning and usually close by midnight.

RIVNE

Myr Sparse but functional, this centrally located 200-room hotel is the only game in town for travelers. The 2- and 3-room suites feature color TV sets and telephones. The charming restaurant is noted for its first-rate Ukrainian fare. There's also a café and live music nightly. 332 Mitskevitchva Vulytsia (phone: 0362-20177).

LUTSK

Svytlaz Just a 5-minute walk from the Old Town, this fairly new 170-room white-brick property, is a favorite with travelers from Poland. Rooms are spartan but clean and feature TV sets and telephones. There's a restaurant, bar, nightclub, and sauna. The staff will arrange for English-speaking guides. 4 Naberezhna Vulytsia (phone: 0362-03322 or 0362-47140).

Ukraina This 1960s red brick structure won't win any architectural prizes, but its convenience to the city's main square and Old Town make it extremely popular. The 138 rooms and suites are comfortably furnished and all feature private baths. A restaurant serves decent food. Local currency only. 2 Slovatskoho (phone: 0362-03322 or 0362-26180).

LVIV

Dnister This early 1980s Soviet-style structure seems out of place in its neighborhood of elegant mansions. Still, the 7-story, 150-room hotel has long been the top choice of visitors from abroad. Amenities include an English-speaking concierge, a bar, and a gift shop. Its hilltop location, about a 15-minute walk from the city center, affords guests a spectacular view of the city. A restaurant offers adequate food, although the service is a bit indifferent, and the live music much too loud. 6 Mateyko Vulytsia (phone: 0322-720783).

Grand Truly exquisite by local standards, and for now the best Lviv has to offer, this recently opened 60-room hotel, partly owned by an American firm, occupies a beautiful renovated 1898 mansion located on the city's main thoroughfare. *The* place to eat, the sprawling 120-seat restaurant offers traditional Ukrainian fare and English-speaking waiters (a rarity!). All rooms feature color TV sets and telephones, and 24-hour room service. Car rental (with driver) is also available. Major credit cards accepted. 13

Svobody Prospekt (phone: 0322-769170; 800-822-7286 in the US and Canada).

Intourist A bit frayed at the edges, this once stylish hotel (called the *Georges*) offers sprawling Art Deco rooms, a restaurant, and a convenient location. Ask for No. 25, a 3-room suite with a piano, gas fireplace, refrigerator, and a spectacular view. 1 Ploscha Mitskevitcha (phone: 0322-726751; fax: 0322-742182).

Index